CANADIAN AND WORLD POLITICS

John Ruypers
London District Catholic School Board

Marion Austin
London District Catholic School Board

Patrick Carter
Appleby College, Oakville

Terry G. Murphy
Limestone District School Board (formerly)

2005
EMOND MONTGOMERY PUBLICATIONS LIMITED
TORONTO, CANADA

We acknowledge the financial support of the Government of Canada through the Book Publishing Industry Development Program (BPIDP) for our publishing activities.

To muses Janet and Jeanne, and sons Mark, Paul, Ben, and Josh—J.R.

To my sons, Jeremy and Noah, for their understanding and love—M.A.

To my wife, Susan—P.C.

To my wife, Katherine, and my wonderful granddaughters, Macy and Ella—T.G.M.

Library and Archives Canada Cataloguing in Publication

Canadian and world politics / John Ruypers ... [et al.].

Includes index.
ISBN 1-55239-097-7

1. International relations.   2. World politics.
3. Political science—Textbooks.   4. Canada—Politics and government—Textbooks.   5. International relations—Textbooks.   I. Ruypers, John

D863.C35 2004   320   C2004-907217-X

Publisher
Tim Johnston

Coordinating editors
Kate Hawkins   Dayne Ogilvie

Consulting editor
Ian M. Hundey
University of Toronto/OISE (formerly)

Developmental editors
Loralee Case   Francine Geraci   Kate Hawkins
Dayne Ogilvie   Jessica Pegis

Contributing writers
Francine Geraci   Dayne Ogilvie   Nora Rock

Editorial assistant
Joyce Tannassee

Production editor, copy editor, & image researcher
Francine Geraci

Image researcher & permissions editor
Lisa Brant

Interior designer and compositor
Tara Wells, WordsWorth Communications

Indexer
Paula Pike, WordsWorth Communications

Production coordinator
Jim Lyons, WordsWorth Communications

Reviewers
James Delodder
London District Catholic School Board

Emily Faries
Native Studies, Laurentian University

Roger Hutchinson
Emmanuel College, University of Toronto

Matthew Mahoney
York Region District School Board

Patrick Mason
Ottawa–Carleton District School Board

Grace Skogstad
Department of Political Science, University of Toronto

Rebekah Tsingos
Toronto District School Board

Table of Contents

Features of This Text   viii

Unit 1: The Nature of Politics

Chapter 1:
The Concept of Politics   2

The Nature of Politics   3
    Plato, Aristotle, and the *Polis*   3
    Formal and Informal Politics   4
    Divisions of Government   5
The Nature of Political Science   7
    Early Reflections on the Nature and
      Practice of Politics   7
    The Roots of Modern Political Science   8
    New Disciplines and Modern Political
      Science   10
    Political Ideals and Political Realities   11
Political Power and Authority   12
    Traditional Authority   12
    Legal Authority   13
POINT COUNTERPOINT   Debating the
  Constitutional Monarchy   14
    Autocratic Authority   17
    Political Authority in Action   17
Political Leadership and Political Change   18
    Elections   19
    Hereditary and Designated Succession   20
    Coups d'État   21
    Lobby Groups and Interest Groups   22
Politics in Daily Life   24
    Politics and Technology   25
    Politics: From Local to Global   28
    Politics: International and Global   29
Individuals in Politics Worldwide   31
    A Few Committed Individuals   31
TAKING A STAND   Daw Aung San Suu Kyi   32
    Professional Politicians   33

METHODS OF POLITICAL INQUIRY
    Asking Questions about Language   35
STUDY HALL   36

Chapter 2:
Ideologies and Values   37

Political and Social Ideologies   38
    Conservatism   39
    Liberalism   40
    Authoritarianism   41
    Anarchism and Libertarianism   43
TAKING A STAND   George Woodcock   44
Economic Theory and Political Ideologies   46
    Communism   46
    Socialism   47
    Democratic Socialism   48
    Capitalism   50
    Fascism   52
Blended Ideologies   54
Ideologies in Canadian Political Parties   57
    Progressive Conservative Party   57
    Liberal Party   59
    Rise of Third Parties   59
    Modern Third Parties   61
Ideologies Outside Political Parties: Think Tanks
  and Citizen Coalitions   64
    Council of Canadians   64
    Fraser Institute   65
Other Ideologies Affecting Politics in Canada   66
    British Influence   66
    American Influence   68
    Feminism: Ideology and Social Movement   69
    Environmentalism   71
    Nationalism   72
METHODS OF POLITICAL INQUIRY
    Assessing Point of View in Photojournalism   73
STUDY HALL   74

Chapter 3:
Religion and Politics   75

Politics and Religion in History	76
Validation of Rule	76
Social Stabilization	76
Eastern Religions and Politics	78
Hinduism: The Politics of Cosmic Order	78
Confucianism: The Politics of *Ren*	79
Buddhism: The Politics of Non-violence	80
Western Religions and Politics	81
Judaism: The Politics of Diaspora	81
Catholicism: The Politics of Papacy	83
Islam: The Politics of Empire	86
Protestantism: The Politics of Dissent	88
Secular Humanism: The Politics of Reason over Religion	90
Individuals in Politics and Religion	91
Mahatma Gandhi and Indian Nationalism	91
Dietrich Bonhoeffer and Anti-Nazism	92
Mother Teresa and the Politics of Poverty	93
The Dalai Lama and the Defence of Tibet	95
Religion in Contemporary Politics: Case Studies	96
Republic of Ireland: Religion and the Constitution	97
Northern Ireland: The Politics of Demographics	97
India, Pakistan, and Bangladesh: Religion and Partition	98
Israel: Contested Homeland	100
China: Revolution and Religion	102
Iran: Theocracy versus Democracy	103
The United States: Christian Fundamentalism and Democracy	104
TAKING A STAND Shirin Ebadi	105
Separation of Church and State	106
France	107
POINT COUNTERPOINT Debating the Ban on the *Hijab*	108
The United States	110
Canada	111
METHODS OF POLITICAL INQUIRY	
Conducting an Interview	113
STUDY HALL	114

Chapter 4:
Nationalism and Internationalism   115

The Concepts of Nationalism and Internationalism	116
POINT COUNTERPOINT Debating Aboriginal Sovereignty	118
Forces of Internationalism in History	120
Internationalism and Religion	120
Internationalism and Imperialism	122
Internationalism and Trade	123
Internationalism by Means of Agreements	123
Nationalism in History	125
Nationalism and Democratic Revolutions	126
Nationalism and *Realpolitik*	127
Nationalism and Imperialism	128
Nationalism and the Dissolution of Empires	128
TAKING A STAND Julius Nyerere	131
Nationalism in the Global Community	132
Chechnya	132
Yugoslavia (the Balkans)	133
Czechoslovakia	135
Nationalism and Immigration	136
Aboriginal Internationalism and Nationalism in Canada	138
Aboriginal Internationalism: A History, a Future	138
Aboriginal Nationalism: Confederation and After	140
Canadian Nationalism and Internationalism	142
Wars and Nationalism in Canada	143
Canadian Nationalism: Breaking Free of British Influence	143
Canadian Nationalism and the United States	145
War and Canadian Internationalism	146
Quebec Nationalism	148
The Roots of Quebec Nationalism	148
The Rise of Quebec Separatism	149
Quebec Separatism in the Mainstream	150
METHODS OF POLITICAL INQUIRY	
Interpreting Maps	152
STUDY HALL	154

Unit 2: Decision Making and Participation

Chapter 5: Forms of Government   156

Internal and External Influences on Forms of
Government   157

Democracy   158
    Indicators of Full Democracy   158
    Limitations of Full Democracy   160
    Decolonization and Democracy   161

Emerging Democracies   166
    Russia   167

Dictatorships: Left and Right   171
    The People's Republic of China   172

POINT COUNTERPOINT   Is China's One-Child
Policy Justified?   174
    Cambodia ("Democratic Kampuchea")   178
    Argentina   180
    Republic of Korea   182
    A Tale of Two States: North and
       South Korea   184
    Dictatorship: An Assessment   185

Oligarchy   186
    South Africa   186
    Guatemala   188

TAKING A STAND   Rigoberta Menchu   190

METHODS OF POLITICAL INQUIRY
Using the Internet for Political Research   191

STUDY HALL   193

Chapter 6:
Democratic Decision Making   194

Democratic Systems Compared   195
    The Importance of the Constitution   195

The Executive Branch   198
    The Executive in the Parliamentary System   198
    The Executive in the Presidential System   200
    The British Parliamentary System   203
    France's Semi-Presidential System   204

The Legislative Branch   206
    The Canadian House of Commons   207
    The American House of Representatives
       and Senate   209

The Judicial Branch   212
    The Role of the Judiciary in Political
       Decision Making   213

TAKING A STAND   Earl Warren, Chief Justice
of the United States Supreme Court   216

The Unitary and Federal Systems   218
    Unitary System   218
    Federal System   218

Electoral Systems   221
    The Single-Member Plurality System   221
    Preferential Ballot System   222
    Proportional Representation   222
    Recalls and Initiatives   223

POINT COUNTERPOINT   Should Canada
Adopt Proportional Representation?   224
    Referenda   226

METHODS OF POLITICAL INQUIRY   Debating a
Political Issue   227

STUDY HALL   228

Chapter 7:
Participation by Individuals
and Groups in Politics   229

Rights and Responsibilities of Individuals in
Democratic Countries   230
    Traditionally Recognized Responsibilities   230

The Role of Interest Groups   231
    Types of Interest Groups   232

The Role of the Media   234
    Media and Government   235
    Public and Private Ownership of Media   237

The Role of Social Movements   238
    Social Movements and Human Rights   239
    Origins of Human Rights   239
    The US Civil Rights Movement   240

TAKING A STAND   Rosa Parks   243
    The Rights of Indigenous Peoples   244
    Women's Rights   248
    Lesbian and Gay Rights   251
    Children's Rights   255

POINT COUNTERPOINT   Are Citizens Morally
Obliged to Break "Bad" Laws?   258

STUDY HALL   260

Unit 3: The Politics of Internationalism

Chapter 8:
Governments: Participation in the International Community — 262

The Birth of the United Nations — 263
   The United Nations Structure — 264

International Human Rights — 270
   The *Universal Declaration of Human Rights* — 271
   The United Nations and Children's Rights — 273

POINT COUNTERPOINT
The *Universal Declaration of Human Rights*:
Success or Failure? — 274
   The *International Bill of Human Rights* — 276

Alliances, Treaties, Covenants, and Conventions — 278
   Military Alliances and the Arms Race — 278
   The *Geneva Conventions*:
      Humanitarian Law — 285
   Nuclear-Weapons Control Initiatives — 286

Keeping the Peace — 288
   The Birth of UN Peacekeeping — 288
   Peacekeeping: From Suez to Today — 290

TAKING A STAND   Lester Bowles "Mike" Pearson — 291

METHODS OF POLITICAL INQUIRY
Writing a United Nations Resolution — 295

STUDY HALL — 296

Chapter 9:
Canada's International Roles — 297

Implementing Canada's Foreign Policy — 298
   Foreign Affairs and International Trade — 298
   The Department of National Defence
      and the Canadian Forces — 299
   The Canadian International Development
      Agency — 303

Canada's International Partners — 309
   The Commonwealth — 309
   La Francophonie — 313

POINT COUNTERPOINT   Should the
Commonwealth Be Abolished? — 314

Canada and Global Environmental Initiatives — 317
   A Closer Look at Sustainable Development — 318
   The Rio Earth Summit — 319

The Johannesburg Earth Summit — 320
Criticism of the Earth Summits — 320
The *Kyoto Protocol* — 321

Canadians Making a Difference — 324
   Matthew Coon Come: Global Activist — 324
   Maurice Strong: Custodian of the Planet — 325
   David Suzuki: International Scientist and
      Environmentalist — 325
   Louise Fréchette: UN Deputy
      Secretary-General — 326
   Stephen Lewis: AIDS Activist — 327

METHODS OF POLITICAL INQUIRY
Documenting Sources — 330

STUDY HALL — 331

Chapter 10:
Major Participants in the International Community — 333

Types of International Organizations — 334

Human Rights NGOs — 335
   Amnesty International — 335
   Human Rights Watch — 337
   Physicians for Human Rights — 338

TAKING A STAND   Jody Williams — 339

Health and Humanitarian Aid NGOs — 340
   Doctors Without Borders/Médecins Sans
      Frontières — 340
   International Committee of the Red
      Cross/Red Crescent — 341
   World Medical Association — 342
   NGOs and the World Health Organization — 343

Other Important NGOs — 344
   Greenpeace — 344
   The International Olympic Committee — 345

International Economic Organizations — 346
   The World Bank and the International
      Monetary Fund — 347
   General Agreement on Tariffs and Trade
      and the World Trade Organization — 348

Regional and Specialized Organizations — 352
   The European Union — 352
   Organization of American States — 353
   African Union — 354
   Asia–Pacific Economic Cooperation — 355
   League of Arab States — 355

G7/G8   355
Arctic Council   356

Canada and International Trade   357
Free Trade and the *Free Trade Agreement*   358
The *North American Free Trade Agreement*   359
International Trading Blocs   361
Trade Dispute Resolutions   362

POINT COUNTERPOINT   Is Free Trade Beneficial?   364

STUDY HALL   367

Unit 4: The Global Community

Chapter 11:
Conflict Resolution in the
Global Community   **370**

Global Conflict and Security   371
The Causes of Conflict   371
The Quest for Security   372

War   374
Traditional War   375
Total War   376
The Cold War   379
Virtual War   383

Terrorism   385
Defining Terrorism   385
The Evolution of Terrorism   386
Types of Terrorism   386
Terrorism and Politics   391

POINT COUNTERPOINT   Debating Civil Liberties
and the War on Terrorism   392
Waging War against Terrorism   394

The Quest for a Lasting Peace   395
Peacekeeping, Peacemaking, and
Peace-Building   395
Personal Peace Initiatives   397

TAKING A STAND   Lieutenant-General
Roméo Dallaire   399

METHODS OF POLITICAL INQUIRY
Simulation: Debating a Resolution in the
United Nations General Assembly   401

STUDY HALL   402

Chapter 12:
Globalization   **403**

A World of Inequalities   404
Developed and Developing Countries   404
Models of Economic Development   405
Causes and Consequences of Inequalities   407
Economic Disparities and Daily Life   409

TAKING A STAND   Dr. James Orbinski   410

Global Impact of Trade and Business   412
Global Financial Institutions   413
Transnational Corporations   414

POINT COUNTERPOINT   TNCs in the
Developing World: Curse or Cure?   416

Globalization and Globalism   418
Globalization Through Time   418
A Global Culture?   421
Global Crime   422

Globalization: Protest and Debate   423
Political Responses to Globalization   424
Anti-Globalization Protests   425
Effective Global Citizenship   427

The Future of Globalization   430
Another Kind of World Summit   430
Globalization and Nationalism   430
Canada and Globalization: What Kind
of Destiny?   431

METHODS OF POLITICAL INQUIRY
Writing a Political Book Review   435

STUDY HALL   437

Glossary   438
Index   448
Credits   459

Features of This Text

Politics is an inseparable part of every aspect of human activity. It helps shape who we are and helps determine what we can hope to accomplish. Our engagement in the political process is especially crucial to our personal development and the continued vitality of our society and the world community. *Canadian and World Politics* explores these dimensions of political involvement through history and across cultures, and the features embedded in the text show how politics matters to everyone, in interesting and thought-provoking ways.

Agenda	**Agenda** opens each chapter by highlighting the chapter's primary learning objectives.

SOUND BITE	**Sound Bite** presents quotations from politicians, writers, and others that complement the concepts being considered in the text, often in contradictory, challenging ways.

Press Play	**Press Play** describes domestic and international films that can broaden your perspective on political concepts and conflicts and encourage further discussion.

THE WEB	**The Web** guides you to Internet sites for further research, opening up some of the many political resources in the world of the Web.

The **Architecture**, **Art**, **Language**, and **Music and Politics** features explore how politics shapes (and is shaped by) many aspects of daily life and culture, from the ways in which we talk and what we talk about, to art that moves us, buildings that impress us, and the music we listen to.

CAREERS

Careers presents interviews with individuals working in a political world and shows the different ways in which you can pursue political interests.

Grassroots Politics and Protest

Grassroots Politics and Protest examines various methods of political organization and activism at the local level.

Law in Motion

Law in Motion reminds you that many political decisions are intimately connected with laws and legal actions.

METHODS OF POLITICAL INQUIRY

Methods of Political Inquiry enables you to develop skills in political research, interpretation and analysis, and communication.

Party Politics provides interesting background information about mainstream and other political parties.

Point Counterpoint presents two sides of a controversial political issue, and provides a clear and accessible means of structuring classroom debate.

Study Hall provides an extensive end-of-chapter assessment of your progress.

Taking a Stand

Taking a Stand highlights political activism by individuals, why they stood up for their political beliefs, and how they brought about change.

The Nature of Politics

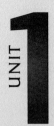

Chapter 1
The Concept of Politics

Chapter 2
Ideologies and Values

Chapter 3
Religion and Politics

Chapter 4
Nationalism and Internationalism

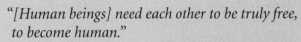

"[Human beings] need each other to be truly free, to become human."

Archbishop Desmond Tutu

1

The Concept of Politics

Agenda

In this chapter, you will consider

• how ideas of politics have changed over history
• the difference between formal and informal politics
• the field of political science as a discipline and as a potential career
• the nature of political power, political influence, and political leadership
• different means of effecting political change
• how politics influences your daily life
• actions of individuals who have influenced global events
• how to analyze the language of politicians

Figure 1.1 In 1956, this tank helped crush civil unrest in Poznan, Poland. In the summer of 1998, US artist Jerilea Zempel and Polish students crocheted a net of roses to cover the tank, which had been on display for decades as a symbol of Soviet conquest. The installation was called *Guns and Rosettes*.

As you begin this study of politics, consider the words of Nobel laureate Archbishop Desmond Tutu, of South Africa: "[Human beings] need each other to be truly free, to become human. We can be human only in fellowship, in community, in *koinonia*, in peace." As the future generation of citizens and leaders, you are already community members and, therefore, members of political society. Look around and consider how politics affects your everyday actions and interactions.

In this chapter, you will read about many societies and ideas, past and present. In the records of the past, you will find lessons about political power, leadership, and change that you can apply today and in the future. Chapter 1 is a sampler of themes designed to present a broad picture of political issues. In-depth studies of many of these issues will follow in later chapters.

The Nature of Politics

Human beings are social animals. Since earliest recorded history, humans have come together in large and small groups for many purposes. **Human societies** are groups of people who observe common rules. A group can be as simple as a family or neighbourhood. Larger and more complex societies may form on the basis of extended family or clan relationships, leadership, or commitment to a common cause. Societies may also be based on ethnic heritage, which is racial, national, religious, linguistic, or cultural, or on international cooperation.

Plato, Aristotle, and the *Polis*

The Greek philosophers of the Classical Period (490–323 BCE) were among the first thinkers to record reflections on politics and government. In *The Republic*, the Greek philosopher **Plato** described the human instinct to seek social connections to meet basic needs. He argued that people could not achieve happiness or fulfillment outside community, or the ***polis*** (in his day, the Greek city-state). The proper goal of human beings, Plato wrote, is to bring about happiness within the community. If the community is happy, then individual citizens are happy.

The word "politics" derives from the Greek word *politikos* (civic), which comes from *polites* (citizen), which comes from *polis*. This is an etymology of "politics"; a definition is a more complex matter. This textbook defines **politics** broadly, as the many connections and interactions that people have with one another to meet basic needs. Other definitions distinguish between

Figure 1.2 This 18th century engraving shows the Areopagus, or "hill of Ares," where leading citizens of the democratic city-state of Athens met to make decisions on legal and political issues.

SOUND BITE "He who is unable to live in society, or who has no need because he is sufficient for himself, must be either a beast or a god."

Aristotle, Politics, *350 BCE*

social and political interactions, or between personal and collective actions. These will be examined later in this chapter.

For **Aristotle**, who was taught by Plato, the goal of politics was the good of the community, and the role of government was to tell people what to do and what not to do. Because men and women were thought to achieve their highest potential by interacting with others for the good of all, Aristotelian political discussions referred to ideals, morality, and ethics.

Types of Government

Plato and Aristotle examined governments structurally and classified them as lawful or lawless. They were among the first thinkers to classify governments according to types of rulers, in what is known as a **typology**. Both Plato and Aristotle placed a higher priority on whether a government was lawful or lawless than on whether it reflected rule by one, by few, or by many (see Figure 1.3).

In the Greek typology, one-person rulers were categorized as either monarchs or tyrants. Monarchs ruled for the common good within the laws of the *polis.* Tyrants ruled for private interest outside any legal framework. If a small group of the nobility or the wealthy held and exercised political power under law, for the common good, the government was an **aristocracy**. If a small group ruled for its own interests alone, outside the law, the government was described as an **oligarchy**. Government in the hands of the many was categorized as **polity** if political power was exercised within a constitutional framework that prevented the oppression of minorities. Democracy, in contrast, was a type of mob rule—the rule of the many outside any legal structure. These terms are still used today, but some meanings have changed. Most notably, legal rule by the many, called "polity" in this typology, is now called "**democracy**."

Formal and Informal Politics

Formal politics involves the collective action of individuals in pursuit of common goals. It can also be defined as a process of resolving conflicts in which support is mobilized and maintained for collective action. The formal level of politics involves individual or collective action in public forums, social movements, media, citizens' groups, or political parties. The informal level of politics involves each individual in the social and personal interac-

Government Type	Lawful	Lawless
rule by one	monarch	tyranny
rule by few	aristocracy	oligarchy
rule by many	polity	democracy

Figure 1.3 Platonic–Aristotelian typology of governments.

tions of everyday life. The smaller and simpler the social grouping, the more likely it is that politics stays at the informal level, with decisions arising from discussion or consensus.

Decisions are made in all aspects of human interaction. Should you eat fish if the species is endangered? Should you buy jeans made by child labourers in a developing country? Should you eat food containing genetically modified products that may damage the environment? Should you associate only with people of your ethnic background? Each of these decisions is political; it reveals your attitude toward other members of the *polis*. Personal decisions are shaped by political factors and have political implications.

Formal politics involves **government**, the set of institutions that make and enforce collective decisions for a society. Often, people agree to be governed because they seek order in society. Governments can settle conflicts among a society's many competing interests and concerns. At what age should children be considered adults? Should education be free? Should males and females have equal rights? Should corporations pay more or less tax than individuals? Historically, the answers to these questions have reflected conflicted and changing opinions.

In order to have **legitimacy**, a government or ruler's right to make binding rules must be accepted as appropriate by the *polis*. Legitimacy may be acquired by selection through the will of the governed or by the rules of heredity. A government may also attempt to claim legitimacy through coercion—that is, by police or military force or through the judiciary.

Divisions of Government

All government leaders rely on councillors, advisers, and civil servants to manage government affairs. The larger the government, the greater is the need for this kind of government organization, or **bureaucracy**. Many early societies developed very complex systems to make and enforce laws, dispense justice, manage the economy, and maintain security.

In India, during the Gupta Dynasty (4th–6th century CE), a highly complex bureaucracy evolved. The king, who developed and enforced the laws, relied on a council of ministers. He appointed governors to the provinces, who in turn appointed district officers. To make the administrative structure cohesive, representative citizens' groups from villages or towns advised the appointed local officials (see Figure 1.5).

Modern governments are usually composed of three branches: executive, legislative, and judicial. The **executive branch** is usually composed of elected politicians—in Canada, this is the prime minister and the cabinet (senior ministers who set policy) and the unelected bureaucracy of civil servants. The executive branch makes decisions, implements policies and rules, and administers the resources of the government. In a democracy, the executive power often relies on the law-making power of the **legislature**. In an

Figure 1.4 Members of People for the Ethical Treatment of Animals demonstrate against the wearing of fur at a 1999 fashion exposition in Montreal.

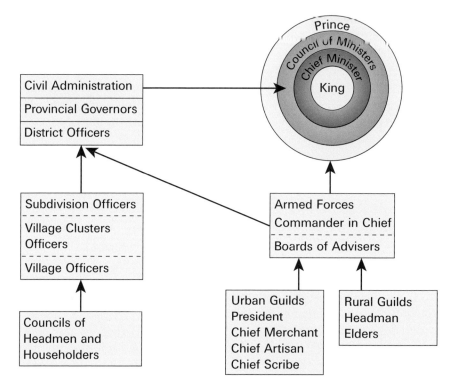

Figure 1.5 Political organization in Gupta India. The king and council of ministers were similar to the modern executive branch of government. The councils of headmen and householders were forerunners of the modern legislative branch. The civil administration served as the bureaucracy of Gupta governments.

Source: Arthur Haberman & Ian Hundey, *Civilizations: A Cultural Atlas* (Toronto: Gage Educational Publishing, 1994), p. 58.

authoritarian government, the executive may pay lip-service to a legislature, but it will not be representative of the population nor have any real power.

The **legislative branch** of government makes laws. It may be selected by the voters from a wide range of choices or from only one choice. These choices are usually presented in the form of political parties. A **political party** is an organized group that has a common set of values and goals, one of which is to form the executive branch of government. In a democratic government, voters can choose between at least two parties. In an authoritarian government, voters may or may not have the opportunity either to vote or to have different parties from which to choose.

The **judicial branch** of government is composed of the courts; members of the judiciary are usually appointed by the executive branch. The judiciary interprets laws and, in some situations, resolves disputes between governmental interests.

The bureaucracy is composed of civil and public servants who work in such government departments as transportation, foreign relations, and finance. Civil servants usually enter the bureaucracy based on the results of competitive civil service examinations. Public servants, however, can be politically appointed. For example, in Canada the prime minister appoints ambassadors and the heads of federal agencies, such as VIA Rail and the CBC.

Check YOUR UNDERSTANDING

1. Re-examine the reasons that humans form groups. Which reason do you think is most important? Why?
2. Review the typology of Plato and Aristotle. What types of government in the world today fit into these categories? Suggest one modern country for each style of government.
3. a) Describe the difference between formal and informal politics.
   b) You decide not to buy a pair of jeans made by child labourers. This action might be considered "informal politics." What steps might you take that would turn this action into "formal politics"?
4. Describe the role of each of the branches of modern governments. Which branch do you consider most important? Why?

The Nature of Political Science

Political science is defined as the systematic study of government and politics. It incorporates studies about the politics of individual countries at the local, regional, and national levels, as well as comparative studies of countries and the field of international relations. Political science examines the impact of religion, **nationalism**, and other belief systems on human actions. It also examines the impact of economic development and of major events—such as wars—on citizens and governments. Political scientists have the tools to make value judgments about the effectiveness of government actions. The study of political science prepares students to consider the implications of citizenship in Canada and the world. A background in political science can also be an entry into professions such as the civil service, the media, party politics, law, and university research and teaching.

Early Reflections on the Nature and Practice of Politics

Reflections on government, which are the beginnings of political science, are found in the records of early societies. In the Old Kingdom of Egypt (2700–2200 BCE), for example, government was concentrated in the absolute power of the pharaoh, who was perceived to be a god on Earth. The power of the pharaoh was constrained only by the god Thoth (wisdom) and the principle of Maat (truth).

The religious principles of Islam are found in the Qur'an, the Muslim holy book set down by the prophet Muhammad in the year 610. In early Muslim societies, these principles guided the rulers or *caliphs* (an Arabic word meaning "successors") and governments. The *caliphs* sought advice from religious experts in

Figure 1.6 The Muslim sage Burzuya reads his book to King Kisra Anushirwan, from *The Book of Kalila and Dimna* (ca. 1390, Persia). Burzuya's moral fables, which he brought back from India at the king's command, formed the basis for Aesop's and La Fontaine's fables.

Figure 1.7 *Piazza Granducale*, by Bernardino Gaffuri and Jacques Bylivert (1599). The main square of Florence features a statue of Cosimo I de' Medici, who at 18 became Duke of Florence after his cousin was assassinated in 1537. Cosimo consolidated his family's power by means as ruthless as those described in Machiavelli's *The Prince*.

SOUND BITE "[A] prince . . . cannot possibly exercise all those virtues for which men are called 'good.' To preserve the state, he often has to do things against his word, against charity, against humanity, against religion. Thus he has to have a mind ready to shift as the winds of fortune and the varying circumstances of life may dictate."

Niccolo Machiavelli, The Prince, *1513*

applying religious laws to daily community life. They were advised to avoid worldly pleasures and to act for the good of the people. In Islam, all believers are equals, regardless of class, race, or language. Political philosophy was disseminated in books on good government and through fables in which animals demonstrated wise and ethical behaviour.

Good behaviour and good government were also linked and encouraged by the civil service examination introduced in China's Tang Dynasty (618–907 CE). The principles of the examination—designed to create an ethical and efficient bureaucracy—dated back to the philosopher Confucius in the 6th century BCE. Success in the week-long tests translated into wealth and power. The originator of the examination, Emperor Tang Taizong, enunciated the political philosophy that virtuous rulers must set an example for their followers. The preservation of the people must be every ruler's first concern: "A king who exploits the people for his personal gains is like a man who cuts his own thighs to feed himself."

In the West, Aristotle married politics to ethics in the 4th century BCE. It was not until 1513 that Niccolo Machiavelli, a native of Renaissance Florence, became the first Western thinker to separate politics from ethics. In *The Prince*, Machiavelli approached politics from the viewpoint of what succeeds, not what is right or wrong. If rulers had political foes, Machiavelli observed, they must either make them allies or kill them. To their subjects, leaders should always appear to be religious, merciful, and honest, regardless of their true character and actions. If lying helps keep power, the prince should lie. It is better for a ruler to be feared than to be loved, yet a ruler should avoid being hated. Machiavelli was describing the practice of politics in the city-states of Renaissance Italy as he observed it. He did not necessarily approve. However, from Machiavelli onward, political science inevitably includes a study of the role that self-interest plays in individual political actions.

The Roots of Modern Political Science

European political philosophers of the 17th and 18th centuries conceived new theories of political organization and new ways to conceptualize the study of politics. Three of the most prominent—Thomas **Hobbes**, John **Locke**, and Jean-Jacques **Rousseau**—described a social contract existing between the government and the governed.

English writer Thomas Hobbes was the first modern political commentator to provide a secular (non-religious) rationale for dictatorship. Hobbes lived in a time of civil war. In his 17th century work *Leviathan*, he wrote that human beings exist in a state of constant warfare and experience life as "nasty, brutish, and short." He believed that people fear anarchy enough

Figure 1.8 *Cavalry Making a Sortie from a Fort on a Hill,* by the Dutch painter Philips Wouwermans (1646), depicts the "nasty, brutish" life during the time of Thomas Hobbes.

to surrender their freedom to an absolute ruler in exchange for peace, security, and the **rule of law.**

While Hobbes justified absolutism, countryman John Locke championed **constitutionalism.** Locke argued that human beings have certain natural rights such as life, liberty, and property. To protect these rights, the people establish an implicit (not plainly expressed) contract with government. The contract implies that the governed will act as reasonable beings and the government will maintain order. If the government breaks the contract by taking away property without consent, for example, the people have a right to rebel. Locke's ideas were used by the English Parliament to justify its removal of King James II in 1688 and by the American colonies when they revolted against King George III in 1776.

French philosopher Jean-Jacques Rousseau viewed human beings as living in a state of innocence with nature before being corrupted by society. For Rousseau, the social contract was fatally flawed by the duplicity (double-dealing) of the wealthy and powerful. It had to be reshaped to protect the rights, liberty, and equality of all. Rousseau saw the renewed contract as an agreement among the people themselves: he believed that all individuals surrendered their natural liberty to one another, and he questioned the institution of private property and the assumption that the will of the majority is always correct. Leaders of the French Revolution (in the late 18th century) were inspired by Rousseau's ideas on such diverse political themes as democracy, socialism, and dictatorship.

In the 18th century, the perspectives of Scottish writer Adam **Smith** and French observer Baron de **Montesquieu** carried political science beyond the scope of the social contract. In *The Wealth of Nations,* Smith used economic

SOUND BITE   "We are all qualified, entitled, and morally obliged to evaluate the conduct of our rulers."

John Locke,
Second Treatise on
Government, *1690*

Press Play

The Crucible, by English director Nicholas Hytner (1996), stars Daniel Day-Lewis and Winona Ryder. In this adaptation of Arthur Miller's famous play, Puritan morality, superstition, and law collide with horrifying results in the Salem witch trials in 1692 Massachusetts. (PG-13)

reasoning to argue that minimal government is the best government. Montesquieu, in *The Spirit of Laws*, called for a separation and balance of powers in government. He pointed to England—with its mixture of monarchy, aristocracy, and democracy—as a model to be emulated (imitated). Montesquieu's ideas influenced the creation of the constitution of the United States, and Smith's ideas are still often quoted in political discussions.

New Disciplines and Modern Political Science

Political writers of the 17th and 18th centuries concentrated on government and institutions. By the 20th century, emerging disciplines such as psychology and sociology had influenced the methods of political science. New studies in political science examined human behaviour. Surveys and statistical analysis revealed information about how and why people vote as they do. Today, political scientists can predict, with acceptable accuracy, how certain demographic groups, such as young people aged 18 to 25, will vote on issues and the types of leaders they will support. Moreover, the impact of pressure groups, lobbyists, and public opinion polls on government decision making is also an area of keen interest.

Modern political scientists also recognize that worldview shapes a society's outlook and must be considered when analyzing its political actions. A worldview can be detected in the answers to such questions as: What roles should women assume? What rights should minorities enjoy? Should leisure be valued? What status should religion occupy? How should the rights of individuals compare with the rights of the state? What obligations should the state assume in relation to the well-being of its citizens? What role, if any, should the armed forces play in a society?

Historically, the worldviews of communities have shaped their governments. In 17th century Massachusetts, for example, the Puritans' strict Protestant beliefs were reflected in the creation of an ideal "City on a Hill"—a fusing of religion and politics that was intended to create a community of saints. Government imposed mandatory church attendance and laws against adultery and the consumption of alcohol. Other worldviews expressed in government are associated with the Catholic and Islamic religions. France's monarchical government in the 18th century, for example, projected the Catholic worldview of the time. More recently, in 1979, Shiite cleric Ayatollah Khomeini became government leader of the revolutionary Islamic republic of Iran after the monarch was overthrown.

Secular political systems reject overt religious influences. Many Western democracies have moved toward the complete separation of government and religion. In 2004, for example, the French government banned the Islamic *hijab* (headscarf) and other conspicuous religious symbols—such as the Jewish *yarmulke* (skullcap) and large crucifixes—from public schools and government offices (see Chapter 3, pages 107–9).

The world's indigenous peoples have also had governing systems based on their spiritual worldviews, which are passed down through oral, rather than written, traditions. For **Aboriginal peoples** in Canada, worldviews are grounded in a spiritual connection to and responsibility for the land, which is referred to as "Turtle Island" (North America) by some **First Nations**. This responsibility is central to Aboriginal governing principles, which are based on natural laws under which people live in harmony with all beings and the environment.

Political Ideals and Political Realities

The contrast between the real and the ideal in politics can be dramatic. The American *Declaration of Independence* rang out an ideal in 1776: that "all men are created equal." The legal reality of slavery, however, contradicted that dream. So did the fact that female citizens could not vote.

In his 19th century work *Das Kapital*, Karl **Marx** described an ideal society that would develop once the **bourgeoisie** (the class that owns the means of production) was eliminated and the capitalist state had "withered away." After massive Marxist experiments failed in many countries over the next century, the successful classless society remains elusive.

Political language often needs to be decoded in order to differentiate appearance and reality. "All human beings are equal" is, unfortunately, an idealistic statement. A realistic assessment requires that you question the meaning of "equal." Does it mean that all human beings enjoy the same material conditions? Does it mean all human beings have the same mental conditions, rights, and opportunities? Does a child born into poverty have the same opportunities as a child born into wealth? "Equal" has many meanings. **Equality of rights** suggests that everyone is bound by the same laws. **Equality of opportunity** suggests that all people are ensured fair and equal access in education and employment. **Equality of result** implies that all citizens achieve similar economic and social success.

A dichotomy between the real and the ideal can often be found by comparing a government's election promises with its performance once in office. In the 1974 federal election, for example, Liberal Prime Minister Pierre Trudeau mocked Progressive Conservative leader Robert Stanfield's proposal to freeze wages and prices. As a result, the election centred on Stanfield's proposal rather than Trudeau's record. Once elected, Trudeau faced the reality of high inflation and instituted wage and price controls.

Some see the art of politics—or at least political campaigning—as the art of obfuscation (the use of unclear or confusing language). One of the challenges for the student of politics is to differentiate between what seems to be true and what is true.

SOUND BITE "In place of the old bourgeois society, with its classes and class antagonisms, we shall have an association, in which the free development of each is the condition for the free development of all."

Karl Marx, The Communist Manifesto, *1848*

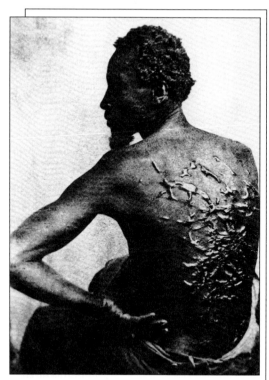

Figure 1.9 Only white male property owners were created equal under the American *Declaration of Independence* (1776). This photograph of a former American slave, whose back bears the scars of many whippings, dates from the 19th century (ca. 1861–65).

Check YOUR UNDERSTANDING

1. Choose a country and focus on a period of its history. Describe three different ways in which a political scientist might study the country during this period.
2. In the Old Kingdom of Egypt, how was the absolutism of the leader constrained by the god Thoth and the principle of Maat? What constrains leaders today?
3. Compare Hobbes's and Locke's views about human beings and the types of government that should be established. Which view do you support? Why?
4. You have examined the worldviews held by different groups at various times. How would you describe your own worldview?
5. Name three leaders in the world today that you believe would be students of Machiavelli. Defend your choices.
6. How would Plato, Hobbes, and Machiavelli describe the language of a contemporary politician of your choice?

Political Power and Authority

Political power is the ability of those in authority to induce members of the *polis* to do what they want them to do. There are three kinds of authority: traditional authority, legal authority based on the rule of law, and autocratic authority. Traditional authority is often exercised through a hereditary monarchy, while autocratic authority is usually exercised through the use of force.

It is important to note that **political influence** is different from political power. Politicians often try to influence members of the *polis* through the media and through political rewards and promises. Advertisements may persuade voters to choose one political party over another. Some voters may support a political candidate because they expect financial benefits, government payments, or tax cuts. A candidate's image and personality also influence support. Influence works both ways. Public opinion polls and focus groups influence politicians. As a result of these modern techniques, politicians must often try to decide the degree to which they will both influence and be influenced by the *polis*.

Traditional Authority

In a **hereditary monarchy**, the ruler exercises traditional authority that has been inherited from a parent or relative. For much of human history, hereditary monarchs and their advisers exerted most of the political power in human societies. Hereditary monarchs often used religion to justify their authority. As you have learned, in ancient Egyptian and Hindu societies, monarchs were perceived as gods; in medieval European societies, monarchs were believed to be divinely selected. When hereditary power passed to a child, a caretaker was usually appointed to act as regent until the child reached the age of adulthood.

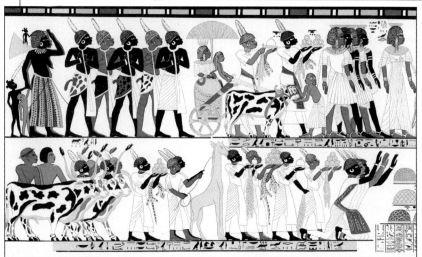

Figure 1.10 Ancient Egyptian monarchs were considered gods; medieval European monarchs were seen as divinely selected. Left: A mural from an XVIII Dynasty tomb (ca. 1380 BCE) shows Nubian nobles bringing tribute to an Egyptian pharaoh. Right: The baptism of King Clovis, from the 15th century *Great Chronicle of France*.

Monarchs still exist. With few exceptions—such as the royal family of Saudi Arabia—they wield only limited power. In keeping with Canada's tradition as a former colony of Britain, the British monarch remains Canada's official head of state. The institution of monarchy in Canada is mainly ceremonial, and political power lies in the legal authority of the Canadian constitution.

Legal Authority

Over the last 800 years, traditional authority has made a gradual transition to legal authority. The process started in England in 1215, when rebellious nobles forced King John to sign the **Magna Carta** (the Great Charter of Liberties), which limited his power and that of all subsequent English monarchs. For the first time in England, no one—not even the king—was above the law. In a society ruled by legal authority, a set of laws, usually written, creates a framework for the exercise of power. For example, a prime minister is elected for a set period of time. Today, many countries have rules describing how political power is to be exercised. Many of those rules are unwritten, or based on **convention** (a consistent practice based on long tradition). In Canada, most of the power exercised by the prime minister's cabinet, for example, is based on convention.

Many countries, including Canada, have constitutions that describe the powers and responsibilities of the branches of government. Constitutions also legally limit the state's ability to intrude into the lives of citizens by, for example, enshrining rights to privacy, property, and language. In 1982, Canada's constitution was **patriated** (brought home) from Britain and renamed the *Constitution Act, 1982*. It contained an amending formula for future changes in the document and an entrenched *Canadian Charter of Rights and Freedoms*.

THE WEB

Learn more about the Magna Carta at www.emp.ca/cwp.

Point:
Counterpoint → Debating the Constitutional Monarchy

"Yes" to Constitutional Monarchy

by Michael Valpy

Constitutional monarchy is the most brilliant form of government humanity has yet devised. The Dutch, Belgians, Swedes, Norwegians, Danes, Japanese, Spanish—especially the Spanish—all embrace it. The people vest the powers of their absolute sovereign authority over themselves in the person of the Sovereign. The Sovereign lends those powers to the elected politicians so long as they constitutionally behave. In the event that they disobey the Constitution, the Sovereign holds the emergency constitutional fire extinguishers to douse their hooligan acts. This is not some legal abstraction. Canada is no more a heavenly realm than any other nation on Earth. Power corrupts; corrupted people seize and wield power illegally. The safeguard of constitutional monarchy works, why? Because the constitutional fire extinguishers are held by

a brightly coloured personage who is strategically located . . . apart from all government structures and above all partisan and sectarian frays. . . .

The language and symbolism of the Canadian Crown permeate [appear throughout] national life. The armed forces swear allegiance to the Sovereign, personifying the people, and not to any government of the day or to the Constitution. Naval vessels are Her Majesty's Canadian Ships. New Canadians swear an oath of allegiance to the Sovereign. The Sovereign's image appears on coins and stamps. The Crown is on the coat of arms. Public lands are Crown lands. State enterprises are Crown corporations. Accused miscreants [criminals] are prosecuted in the Sovereign's name, judged by the Sovereign's justices, acquitted or convicted and imprisoned in the Sovereign's name. At the opening of Parliament and provincial legislatures, it is the Sovereign and the Sovereign's representatives, and not the politicians, who

Figure 1.11 After making controversial remarks calling for the end to the monarchy in Canada, then Deputy Prime Minister John Manley greeted Queen Elizabeth II in Ottawa in 2002.

are ceremoniously saluted. In a dozen hundred ways each day, Canadians declare that the fundamental business of their state is done in the name of the Sovereign who is the personal symbol of them all, and not by the transitory elected governors and their appointed functionaries.

The Canadian monarchy is Canadian. Not British. Not Australian. Not Jamaican or any other nation's. It has evolved over 500 years to suit our needs, rooted itself deeply in our history, our traditions, in the fundamental formations of our national society. It was there in 1497 when Cabot claimed his new found land for Henry VII, it was there in New France, there when George III issued his Royal Proclamation to protect the lands of Canada's first peoples from European exploitation, there when the language and civil law of Quebec's peoples were protected, there when loyalists fled the dodgy revolutionaries of the new Republic.

Moreover, constitutional monarchy is the concreteness of our contemporary federalism, our collective headship of state—sovereign vested in one particular individual, the reigning monarch, acting in Parliament for some purposes and in the provincial legislatures for others—which has been the key to the autonomy and identity of the Canadian provinces compared to other federations.

So the Queen lives offshore. So what? In a tiny, borderless world, Canada declares that its head of state is the descendant of a 1,000-year-old institution, an international, cosmopolitan, supremely trained-for-the-task individual enveloped with the magic of being "royal."

How wonderfully, postmodernistically imaginative of us.

Source: Excerpted from Michael Valpy, "Don't Mess With Success—And Good Luck Trying," May 1999, at http://www.irpp.org/po/archive/may99/valpy.pdf.

"No" to Constitutional Monarchy

by Rick Mercer

When you walk around the grounds of Rideau Hall, Canada's official residence for the Queen or her reasonable facsimile, the Governor General, you can't help but be impressed. This is an expensive piece of real estate. We're talking seventy-nine acres in the middle of Ottawa. And this is not the only one, either. Oh, no, the Queen of England has official residences from one end of this country to the other. And I don't know if you noticed this, but the Queen doesn't really come over here that much. Which makes me wonder, why are we paying for all this? I mean, the lights are on. She's not home.

Actually, that's the problem. She's at home in England, in another country, which raises the question, Why is a woman in England the head of the government here in Canada? As the rules are now, if the prime minister wants to call an election, he's got to get up tomorrow morning, come on over to Rideau Hall, knock on that door and ask the Queen's representative for permission. I don't think so. If I was the prime minister I'd come over, all right. I'd come over and tell the whole lot of them they had to be out of the house by the end of the month. We're not British people any more, we're Canadian. Let's act like it. Let's get the Queen off our money and turn this place into a big park.

Source: Rick Mercer, *Streeters: Rants and Raves from This Hour Has 22 Minutes* (Toronto: Doubleday Canada, 1998), p. 142.

Articulating a Personal Stand

1. After reading the "Yes" and "No" arguments regarding constitutional monarchy, reflect on the major issues and the manner in which each author presents them.
2. Using logic, relevance, accuracy, and bias as your criteria, record in a table or in point form what you believe to be each side's strongest and weakest arguments.
3. List any issues that remain unclear.
4. Find instances in both arguments where humour is used to make a point or deflect an opposing argument. Reflect on the effectiveness of humour.
5. Share your opinions with a partner to clarify issues that concern you.
6. Write a five-paragraph essay in which you take a stand on the future of the monarchy in Canada. Present reasons for your position. Acknowledge arguments that support the other side, and explain why you disagree with them. If you wish, use humour in your essay.
7. Be prepared to share parts of your essay in class.

Law in Motion

Canadian Charter of Rights and Freedoms

The Charter sets out those rights and freedoms considered essential in a free and democratic society. It protects people in Canada from unconstitutional actions at all levels of government: federal, provincial, and municipal. Canadians are entitled to seek redress (remedy) in court if they are treated unfairly as a result of the application of any law.

Since passage of the Charter, many rights cases have gone to court. In one case, 17-year-old Marc Hall took the Durham Catholic District School Board to court in 2002 after he was told he could not attend the high school prom with his 21-year-old boyfriend. The school principal believed this would violate Catholic teachings on homosexuality. The school board also rejected Hall's request. Hall then went to the Ontario Superior Court to ask for an injunction to prohibit the board from barring him and his boyfriend. Hall's lawyer argued that the school board's decision violated Hall's rights to equality, freedom of expression, and freedom of association under the Charter. The school board's lawyer argued that s. 93(1) of the constitution, which provides absolute protection for religious decisions by denominational schools, placed the board's decision beyond Charter scrutiny.

Several hours before the prom, Ontario Superior Court Justice Robert MacKinnon granted Hall's request for an injunction against the school board. The following is an excerpt from Justice MacKinnon's decision:

Figure 1.12 Student Marc Hall (right) and boyfriend Jean-Paul Dumont arrive at court in Whitby, Ontario, on May 6, 2002, to seek an injunction against the Durham Catholic School Board.

The idea of equality speaks to the conscience of all humanity—the dignity and worth that is due each human being. Mark Hall is a Roman Catholic Canadian trying to be himself. He is gay. It is not an answer to his section 15 Charter [equality] rights . . . to deny him permission to attend his school's function with his classmates in order to celebrate his high school career. It is not an answer to him . . . to suggest that he can exercise his freedom of disassociation and leave his school. He has not, in the words of the Board, "decided to make his homosexuality a public issue." Given what I have found to be a strong case for an unjustified section 15 breach, he took the only rational and reasonable recourse available to him. He sought a legal ruling. . . .

It is one of the distinguishing strengths of Canada as a nation that we value tolerance and respect for others. All of us have fundamental rights including expression, association and religion. Sometimes, as in this case, our individual rights bump into those of our neighbours and of our institutions. When that occurs we, as individuals and as institutions, must acknowledge the duties that accompany our rights. Mr. Hall has a duty to accord to others who do not share his orientation the respect that they, with their religious values and beliefs, are due. Conversely, . . . the Principal and the Board have a duty to accord to Mr. Hall the respect that he is due as he attends the Prom with his date, his classmates and their dates.

Source: Egale Canada, "Excerpts from the Judgment of MacKinnon J. in the Marc Hall Case," at www.egale.ca/index.asp?lang=F&menu=72&item =290&version=EN.

Question

Courts strive to balance individual rights and those of society. Do you believe that Justice MacKinnon's decision achieves a just balance? Support your position by referring to the Charter and citing Justice MacKinnon's ruling.

Autocratic Authority

Autocratic authority is obtained by the use of force. The governments of Vladimir Lenin in Russia and the Ayatollah Khomeini in Iran, for example, were based on autocratic authority, as are most modern dictatorships. Ideological or religious beliefs often form the basis of an autocrat's power, with further support from elite groups and a strong military. Rulers with autocratic authority may draft and adopt constitutions, but these are only a pretence of legal authority. Because such laws are imposed from above, rather than representing a contract between the governed and the governing, they are not legitimate. Even though based on force, autocratic power may receive widespread support from the governed.

Political Authority in Action

Traditional authority, legal authority, and autocratic authority rarely exist in isolation or operate in a pure form. In Canada, for example, the vestiges of traditional authority require that all bills receive final assent from the monarch's representative (federally, the governor general; provincially, the lieutenant governor) before becoming law. As you saw in this chapter's Point Counterpoint, the real power resides in the legal authority of elected representatives who act within the confines of the constitution. Even in an autocratic state, legal authority, as limited as it may be, offers citizens some protection from the government.

Figure 1.13 Shiite cleric Ayatollah Ruhollah Khomeini was Iran's political and spiritual leader from 1979 until his death in 1989. Sunni Muslims assume a direct relationship between believers and God, but Shiites (the majority in Iran) believe in the mediation of a highly trained clergy.

Check YOUR UNDERSTANDING

1. Define political power in your own words.
2. Describe the three kinds of political authority and cite examples of each.
3. Explain the differences between political power and political influence.
4. Describe how political power and political influence might work, together and separately, in each kind of political authority.

Political Leadership and Political Change

Press Play

Trudeau, by Canadian director Jerry Ciccoritti (2002), chronicles the life and times of perhaps Canada's most charismatic prime minister in a style often as unpredictable as the man himself. Broadcast originally as a CBC miniseries, the film stars Colm Feore. (NR)

At certain times, in certain places, leaders appear who inspire passion and embody the aspirations of the *polis*. During World War II, British Prime Minister Winston Churchill's speeches rallied his country in its "darkest hour." In Argentina in the 1950s, Eva (Evita) Peron, a woman from humble roots, married President Juan Peron and attracted huge crowds of admirers, especially impoverished workers—the "shirtless ones" (see Chapter 5, pages 180–81). The yearning for a new politics contributed to "Trudeaumania" in Canada in the 1960s. Ayatollah Khomeini's Islamic revolution drew millions of people into the streets of Iran's capital, Tehran, toppling the US-backed government of Shah Reza Pahlavi in 1979.

The seemingly magical power of a leader to elicit emotional commitment has been called charisma. But not all successful leaders have (or need) it. William Lyon Mackenzie King had, at best, a bland public image. Yet

Figure 1.14 Left: Prime minister or rock star? Fans in Grand Banks, Newfoundland, swarm Prime Minister Pierre Trudeau in 1971. Right: Liberal Party ads created the image of "Uncle Louis" St. Laurent, carefully posed here with children in 1953.

Canadians elected him prime minister five times. Often the *polis* wants experienced, familiar leaders, even if they seem dull. After the traumas of World War II, Canadian voters elected the uncharismatic Louis St. Laurent, who campaigned as folksy, dependable "Uncle Louis." In the United States, a post-war yearning for normalcy led to the election of Dwight D. Eisenhower, a similarly conservative elder statesman.

In Western countries such as Canada and the United States, political leaders often speak about their "vision." This suggests their particular views of their communities' potential and future direction. In the 1960s, Prime Minister Pierre Trudeau spoke of a "Just Society." In the United States, President John F. Kennedy spoke of a "New Frontier." Whether a vision is attainable is another question, but projections of the future can motivate people to act in extraordinary ways.

Figure 1.15 Voters in South Africa's second democratic election, in June 1999, formed long lines at polling stations, like this one near Johannesburg.

Elections

Elections are perhaps the most orderly means of changing political power, and usually election results are decisive. Different electoral systems translate voters' choices more or less accurately. Rules about voter eligibility also determine whether a political system is truly democratic. The 2000 presidential election in the United States, for example, was so close that the US Supreme Court had to decide the winner. Today, selection by the general populace is the usual means of acquiring and maintaining political power.

In the late 20th century, Russia, South Africa, Poland, and Hungary moved to a "one person, one vote" system to elect governments. Elections, however, can be used as camouflage to acquire and maintain political power. In Zimbabwe, former democratic revolutionary Robert Mugabe claimed a controversial fifth term as president in the 2002 election by manipulating votes and intimidating journalists and opposition politicians.

SOUND BITE "The proper role of government . . . is to represent the interest of the future to the present. . . ."

Lester C. Thurow, The Future of Capitalism, *1996*

SOUND BITE "On November 7, 2000, as black Floridians flocked to the polls in record numbers, many were met at the ballot boxes with a blunt rebuke: 'You cannot vote.' . . . Hundreds of law-abiding citizens looking to exercise their constitutional right to vote, mostly in black and Hispanic communities, were sent away—and threatened with arrest if they protested."

Michael Moore, Stupid White Men, *2001*

Figure 1.16 Kim Jong-Il stands with dignitaries shortly after his father's death in July 1994. Kim Il-Sung is still revered as god-like in North Korea.

Hereditary and Designated Succession

In monarchical systems, traditional rules ensure peaceful succession. In a hereditary monarchy, succession usually falls to the oldest son. King Edward VIII abdicated the British throne in 1936 because tradition would not allow him to marry Wallis Simpson, a twice-divorced American woman. Edward's brother George, the next in line, became King George VI. King George VI had two daughters. When he died in 1952, the elder, Elizabeth, acceded to the throne as Queen Elizabeth II.

Governments built on autocratic authority rarely have rules of succession, yet non-monarchical dictators have often tried to designate successors or to impose hereditary succession. Emperor Napoleon Bonaparte was so concerned about establishing a ruling bloodline that he divorced his first wife, Josephine, in 1810 in order to find a spouse who would bear him a son. Napoleon's second wife, Maria Louisa, did bear a son, known as Napoleon II, but military defeat dashed Napoleon's dreams of succession. In North Korea, communist dictator Kim Jong-Il succeeded his father, Kim Il-Sung, in 1994. Although the son did not assume full power until after three years of mourning, vows of loyalty from military and party leaders guaranteed his accession.

Power struggles have disrupted the hierarchies of other communist dictatorships over succession. A dying Vladimir Lenin, leader of the Soviet Union for six years, warned against succession by Joseph Stalin. In a confi-

Figure 1.17 Every picture tells a story. Top right: Stalin (left), Lenin, and Kalinin at the Eighth Bolshevik Party Congress, 1919. This photograph, a detail from the larger one at the left, was cropped to make Stalin appear to be "close" to Lenin. In a later version (middle right), Kalinin was removed; finally, a 1938 version showed Stalin, heroically, alone.

dential letter to Leon Trotsky, a potential successor, Lenin wrote that Stalin was "too rude" and advocated a leader who was more patient, loyal, and polite. Stalin, however, outmanoeuvred Trotsky and became leader of the Soviet Union after Lenin died in 1924. Trotsky was better educated and better spoken; Stalin controlled the party bureaucracy.

After Stalin died in 1953, Nikita Khrushchev won a three-cornered leadership battle. Like Stalin, Khrushchev had gained control of the Communist Party. Many members supported Khrushchev because they owed their appointments to him. In his campaign to consolidate power, Khrushchev denounced Stalin's methods. In 1956, Khrushchev launched a de-Stalinization program, stripping Stalin's images from public offices and his name from cities, streets, squares, and schools. In many communist states, strong party organization contributed to relatively smooth succession. Communist ideology also often motivated leadership groups to hold on to dictatorial rule long after all-powerful leaders, such as Lenin or Stalin, had died.

Coups d'État

A **coup d'état** ("blow against the state") overthrows an existing government to establish an autocratic government. It usually takes place within 24 hours and involves a small group supported by the military. General Augusto Pinochet staged a coup in Chile in September 1973, overthrowing the democratically elected government of President Salvador Allende. Documents later linked the administration of US President Richard Nixon to the coup and to efforts to destabilize the regime of Allende, who was initiating socialist reforms. In 1971, for example, the Allende government nationalized (took over) Chilean copper mines owned by US businesses. In protest, the United States used the World Bank and **transnational corporations** to blockade Chile economically. The US Central Intelligence Agency (CIA) also secretly organized and funded strikes, demonstrations, and media attacks against Allende. On the morning of September 11, 1973, after the army stormed the presidential palace, Allende was found dead. As military dictator, Pinochet ruled for 17 years, banning opposition parties and torturing and executing thousands.

Figure 1.18 General Augusto Pinochet strafed Chile's Presidential Place with artillery fire and bombed it from the air during the coup in September 1973. Pinochet said President Allende died of a heart attack. Others say he was assassinated.

SOUND BITE "I don't see why we need to stand by and watch a country go communist due to the irresponsibility of its people."

US Secretary of State Henry Kissinger, commenting on Allende's election in Chile, 1970

Press Play

In *Missing* (1982), directed by Constantin Costa-Gavras, with Jack Lemmon and Sissy Spacek, a conservative American father discovers horrifying facts about his government as he searches for his missing son in a South American country after a military coup. (PG)

Lobby Groups and Interest Groups

Lobby and interest groups try to influence governments and the public to support political changes that they favour. Such groups require funding for the printed material, media advertisements, and staff they use to achieve their goals. Often, private money is involved. For example, billionaire George Soros has used the fortune he amassed as a US-based entrepreneur to promote political change in the former communist states of Czechoslovakia and Poland. Born in Hungary in 1930, Soros experienced **totalitarianism** firsthand under both **fascism** and **communism**. While studying at the London School of Economics, he became influenced by the ideas of philosopher Karl Popper, who coined the term "open society" as the antithesis (opposite) of totalitarian states. Soros became committed to supporting the ideal of the open society and is credited with helping to overthrow the totalitarian regimes of Franjo Tudjman in Croatia (1999) and Slobodan Milosevic in Yugoslavia (2000).

In 1979, Soros formed the Open Society Institute, a foundation dedicated to opening up closed societies and making open societies economically stronger. Today the foundation operates in more than 50 countries. In 2003, the Open Society Institute provided three-day courses for at least 1,000 students in the former Soviet republic of Georgia, where the government of Georgian President Eduard Shevardnadze stood accused of widespread corruption. The purpose was to train Georgians to conduct peaceful street demonstrations. Open Society also funded an opposition television station that mobilized support for a peaceful revolution. In November 2003, Shevardnadze resigned.

> **SOUND BITE** "[An open society] is characterized by the rule of law; respect for human rights, minorities, and minority opinions; the division of power; and a market economy. . . . [T]he ultimate truth, the perfect design for society, is beyond our reach. We must therefore content ourselves with the next best thing—a form of social organization that falls short of perfection but holds itself open to improvement."
>
> *George Soros, "Toward a Global Open Society," 1998*

People Power

Massive street demonstrations can bring about political change, but only if the armed forces and police remain neutral or supportive. In Russia, people power helped dethrone absolute ruler Czar Nicholas II, in March 1917. Extremely heavy Russian losses on the Eastern Front during World War I and fuel and food shortages brought hundreds of thousands of protestors into

Figure 1.19 Protestors at Georgia's Parliament, in Tbilisi, demand that President Shevardnadze step down after contested elections in November 2003.

the streets of Petrograd, then Russia's capital. Among them were women who stood in line daily in the bitter cold to buy bread, only to be told none was available. Nicholas brutally dispersed demonstrations using the police and the military, but when troops refused to fire on protestors, military leaders urged the czar to abdicate. Facing strikes, riots, and troop mutinies, Nicholas II finally stepped down. Later, he and his entire family were executed.

Check Your Understanding

1. List five qualities that you believe a leader should have. Explain why you have selected these qualities.
2. Describe how both Joseph Stalin and Nikita Khrushchev were able to take and keep political power in the Soviet Union.
3. What is a coup d'état?
4. Should it be possible for an individual to use a personal fortune to bring about political change? Why or why not?
5. Evaluate the effectiveness of people power. If you felt very strongly about an issue, what form of protest would you be prepared to engage in?

Politics in Daily Life

Formal and informal politics are as close as your mailbox, television, computer, or movie theatre. Formal politics arrives in the form of election advertising, government pamphlets, and requests for party funding; it is also the core of television news, public affairs and documentary programs, newspapers, magazines, and countless Web sites. Informal politics often surfaces in casual discussions.

In conversation, people sometimes say, "I am not political" or "I am not politically involved." Yet in the broad definition of politics—the definition of Plato—that position is impossible. Practically any human action that has a beneficial or harmful influence on another person can be considered political in some way.

Today, political entities called "states" or "countries" claim most of the Earth's land and much of its water. Therefore, all people fall under some form of government authority. In Canada, government intrudes into the daily lives of citizens—for both good and ill—to an extent unknown a century ago. Governments provide social services such as health care, welfare, old age security, and employment insurance. They warn Canadians about the dangers of tobacco, and regulate who can buy it and where it can be used. Automobile drivers must pass tests, pay fees, carry insurance, and wear seatbelts—because governments own and build most roads. On public property, dog owners must obey bylaws. Workplaces, consumer products, and medical services are all monitored and regulated by governments. DNA data banks and iris scans at airports open up new possibilities for government protection—but also new invasions of personal privacy. On an international level, government agreements attempt to limit nuclear proliferation, abolish landmines, and reduce emissions of greenhouse gases. But who builds the bombs and lays the mines in the first place?

Figure 1.20 US Customs fingerprints and photographs a foreign passenger at a US airport in January 2004. The controversial program screens visitors from most countries and is meant to keep out terrorists.

Politics and Technology

The sights and sounds of politics are familiar and sometimes stirring aspects of modern life: a solitary protestor defies tanks in Tiananmen Square, a UN envoy fights AIDS in an African country, an Aboriginal MLA holds a ceremonial white feather and stops passage of Canada's Meech Lake Accord, a political prisoner emerges from 27 years of detention and becomes president of South Africa. Sometimes the images are more disturbing, as when abuses by US forces against Iraqi detainees were exposed in early 2004.

In politics, images and phrases often live on long after people have forgotten the events themselves. In communist-encircled West Berlin in 1963, US President John F. Kennedy voiced his commitment to German freedom saying, "Ich bin ein Berliner [I am a Berliner]." In 1970, when asked what he would do next in light of two political kidnappings in Quebec, Prime Minister Pierre Trudeau snapped at the reporter: "Just watch me." Key phrases become embedded in the subconscious of the *polis*, playing a powerful role in how political issues are remembered and represented. Political strategists know this, and they help leaders create sound bites that will play well in the media. Some commentators argue that exposure to mass media—such as television and the Internet—has shrunk the attention span of modern citizens. In keeping messages brief, the news media may oversimplify complex political issues.

Figure 1.21 An iconic image: Beijing resident Li Lu stares down tanks near Tiananmen Square in the early hours of June 5, 1989. Tanks later dispersed pro-democracy demonstrators, killing hundreds, perhaps thousands, of people.

Figure 1.22 The fog of war: A news program broadcasts video showing US-led bombing of unspecified targets in Baghdad in April 2003. Televised images created an abstract, bloodless version of the war for millions worldwide.

Art and Politics

Political Cartoons

THE WEB

To learn more about the history of political cartoons, go to www.emp.ca/cwp.

Political cartoons use humour to make unique commentaries. They shift perceptions, presenting people and events in new perspectives. To appreciate a cartoonist's viewpoint, you need to understand the situation being commented on.

Forerunners of today's political cartoons originated in Germany during the **Protestant Reformation**. Martin Luther, German leader of the Reformation, used woodcuts to protest abuses within the hierarchy of the Catholic Church. In his pamphlet *Passional Christi und Antichristi* (1521), he used two images by his friend, Lucas Cranach, to juxtapose the actions of Jesus and the Catholic hierarchy (Figure 1.23): Jesus drives moneychangers from the Temple; the pope sells indulgences to the wealthy. Two hundred years later, in the 1751 engraving *Gin Lane* (Figure 1.24), British artist William Hogarth used humour and exaggeration to draw attention to the misery and poverty that alcohol abuse was causing in London.

Political cartoons grew in importance and became an acceptable means of presenting serious issues. Figure 1.25 shows three examples of modern political cartooning, one from the 19th, one from the 20th, and one from the 21st centuries.

In all six cartoons, the artists have used various techniques to get their messages across.

Figure 1.23 Luther skillfully juxtaposed Jesus driving the moneychangers from the temple (top) with the pope writing indulgences as common folk pay their hard-earned money in tribute (bottom).

Figure 1.24 In Hogarth's *Gin Lane*, only the pawnbroker and the coffin maker prosper.

THIRSTY OR HUNGRY?

- Satire, the use of sarcastic wit to expose foolishness or vice, is seen in Hogarth's images of the effects of gin.
- Irony, the discrepancy between the predictable and the actual, is seen in the presence of Saddam Hussein in the Canadian House of Commons.
- Symbolism, the use of an object to represent an idea, is seen in the crown on John A. Macdonald's head.
- Caricature, the exaggeration of a physical feature or habit, is seen in the drawing of Jean Chrétien's ears.
- Juxtaposition, the association of people, situations, or ideas, is seen in the predatory American cat and the unsuspecting Canadian goldfish.

Questions

Choose one of the political cartoons shown here and analyze it using the following method.

1. What objects or people appear in the cartoon?
2. Which of these are symbols? What ideas do the symbols represent?
3. Is the cartoonist using satire or irony? Describe how. Is it effective? Why or why not?
4. Has the cartoonist used caricature? How?
5. What other techniques has the cartoonist used? Describe their effect.
6. What is the political issue presented in the cartoon?
7. What is the cartoonist's point of view?
8. Who might agree or disagree with the ideas expressed in the cartoon? Why?

ALL PROVINCIAL BUSINESS TRANSACTED AT OTTAWA

"CENTRALIZATION;"
OR, "PROVINCIAL AUTONOMY ABOLISHED."
IS THIS WHAT SIR JOHN IS AIMING AT?

Figure 1.25 Above: John Wilson Bengough's 1882 cartoon, "Centralization," was an early reflection on federal–provincial relations. Top left: In the 1970s, *Toronto Star* cartoonist Duncan Macpherson expressed Canadians' concern over US ownership of much of Canada's industry. Top right: Brian Gable's 2003 cartoon comments on Prime Minister Jean Chrétien's refusal to back the US-led invasion of Iraq.

THE WEB

Learn more about the International Criminal Tribunal for Rwanda at www.emp.ca/cwp.

In the 21st century, technology has created a global *polis*. People separated by thousands of kilometres seem to be neighbours. Famine, genocide, terrorist attacks, and warfare—as well as peace agreements, orderly changes in government, and international cooperation—are reported vividly and instantaneously. In this sense, technology plays a role in political socialization (the transfer of values and attitudes from one generation to another).

The political power of communications technology was underlined in December 2003 when the United Nations International Criminal Tribunal for Rwanda sentenced three media executives to prison terms ranging from 27 years to life. Two radio owners and a newspaper publisher were found guilty of encouraging listeners and readers to seek out and kill ethnic-minority Tutsis in 1994. The radio station had broadcasted the names, licence plate numbers, and hiding places of prospective victims. Canadian Lieutenant-General Roméo Dallaire, head of the UN peacekeeping mission in Rwanda, had begged superiors for the authority to stop the radio broadcasts, but the UN did not grant him that authority.

The Internet has had an enormous political impact. In November 1999, for example, it was used to coordinate the arrival and agendas of more than 5,000 international activists in Seattle. The World Trade Organization (WTO), a global organization that promotes freer trade and enforces existing trade agreements, was meeting in Seattle, and demonstrators were there to protest its secrecy and lack of accountability. Environmentalists, trade unionists, and anti-poverty advocates clashed with riot troops, capturing global media coverage. The protests were called "five days that shook the world" (see Chapter 12, page 426). The tactics of both the activists and the police were criticized, but the protestors proved something: the Internet can be used to confront a political structure in which individuals are not directly represented and over which they have no control.

The Internet can also be used for political satire, as the Canadian television program *This Hour Has 22 Minutes* proved in 2000. Under leader Stockwell Day, the Canadian Alliance (now part of the Conservative Party of Canada) had promised that, if elected, it would hold more frequent plebiscites (direct votes) on controversial issues if a minimum of 3 percent of voters signed a petition demanding a national **referendum**. Comedian Rick Mercer suggested it was a matter of national urgency that Stockwell Day change his first name to Doris. Within days, Mercer's petition—posted on the Internet—had received millions of signatures, far in excess of the necessary 3 percent. Mercer later pointed out that a national referendum would could cost $150 million; the 3 percent figure was "ridiculously" low.

Politics: From Local to Global

As a young person, you encounter politics at different levels. At the local level, you may be politically involved in working to create more green space in your neighbourhood or advocating change at school. Provincial political jurisdiction enters your life in laws related to tobacco, alcohol, driving, and education. You may be aware of issues involving the federal government—for example, changes to the youth criminal justice system, funding for post-secondary education, or Canada's commitment to foreign aid and development. You may also be involved in volunteer work for international organizations. (Have you ever collected money for UNICEF on Halloween?) Joining political organizations, writing letters to politicians, or organizing committees are just a few ways in which citizens of all ages influence the political process at all levels of government.

Politics: International and Global

THE WEB

Learn more about Marshall McLuhan at www.emp.ca/cwp.

Computer technology has hastened the arrival of "the global village," something communications theorist Marshall McLuhan predicted in the 1960s. Governments and **non-governmental organizations** (NGOs) have also helped foster a global sense of interconnectedness. Almost every nation on Earth (191 in 2004) is a member of the United Nations, which strives to resolve international conflicts and create cooperation on social, cultural, economic, and political issues. The proliferation of terrorist attacks in the 21st century underlines the need for people with different political outlooks to communicate with one another to reach mutual understandings.

Through other organizations, countries have reached agreements on such global matters as the use of airspace, time zones, laws of the sea, and so on. The economic powers of huge transnational corporations have induced countries to take global approaches to regulate businesses. Since the Soviet Union launched the space satellite *Sputnik* in 1957, nations have negotiated agreements on the use and exploration of outer space. Many countries cooperate in law enforcement through Interpol, an international police organization, and through extradition treaties.

Global connections can also lead to global infections. In 2003, an outbreak of severe acute respiratory syndrome (SARS) strained the resources of local and national public health organizations as well as the World Health Organization, stressing the need for greater cooperation to contain contagious diseases. Many countries have also signed agreements to limit greenhouse gas emissions, which damage the atmosphere. Other treaties limit the proliferation (rapid spread) of nuclear weapons.

The International Criminal Court has been established to bring war criminals to justice and protect people around the world from war crimes. Canada played a vital role in a recent treaty prohibiting the use and production of landmines.

Figure 1.26 US astronaut Peggy Whitson (right) and Russian cosmonaut Sergei Treschev share a meal on board the International Space Station, October 2002.

Countries also cooperate through treaties and organizations for geographic and social interests. For example, the 53 member states of the African Union are dedicated to achieving a better life for the people of Africa, defending territorial integrity, and eradicating the worst effects of colonialism. The League of Arab States seeks to strengthen ties among its 22 member states, coordinate their policies, and promote their common interests. Canada belongs to the 53-member Commonwealth, the organization of former British colonies, and to La Francophonie, whose 53 member states meet to discuss cultural and political issues of concern to French-speaking people.

Economics and Globalization

The term **globalization** suggests a trend toward freer international markets and trade in goods and services. Economic associations have grown in size and importance. One of the most important is the World Trade Organization (WTO). Two other organizations approve loans to developing countries and so have a large political influence: the World Bank and the International Monetary Fund. At a time when freer trade zones were forming into large trading blocs in other regions of the world, Canada entered into the *Free Trade Agreement* (FTA) with the United States in 1989. Five years later, Mexico joined Canada and the United States in the *North American Free Trade Agreement* (NAFTA). The purpose of the two agreements was to eliminate trade and investment barriers among the three countries.

The **European Union** is arguably the most powerful regional organization and trading bloc in the world. The member countries of the EU (25 in 2004) use two decision-making political philosophies. Under **intergovernmentalism**, member states maintain their separate, or sovereign, powers and decisions are made by unanimous agreement. Under **supranationalism**, power is held by independently appointed officials or by representatives elected by the legislatures, or peoples, of member states. The trend in the European Union appears to be toward supranationalism, as member states increasingly pool their authority.

Check Your Understanding

1. Identify three ways in which government is involved in your daily life. Are you satisfied with this degree of involvement, or would you like to change it? Explain your views.
2. How has technology made the world into a global village?
3. What role do you think the media should play in the world today?
4. Identify and explain the three levels of government in Canada.
5. Identify three ways in which international politics affects your life.

Individuals in Politics Worldwide

Whether travelling across international borders, viewing a television program originating in another country, buying a product from a transnational corporation, or surfing the Internet, you are experiencing the impact of global politics. While the world seems to be filled with ever larger and more impersonal organizations, it is important to remember that individuals can still have an enormous effect on the *polis.*

What motivates an individual to become immersed in public life? Is there a leadership gene? Does upbringing create a commitment to improve social conditions for others? Are some people motivated by specific incidents to act for the collective good? Do individuals choose public life to assuage their guilt about their own privilege, or to find advantages? Or, as Aristotle suggested, do people simply derive satisfaction from performing virtuous acts?

A Few Committed Individuals

Betty Williams and Mairead Corrigan Maguire are two individuals who acted for the common good when they founded the Peace People Organization in Northern Ireland to stop political violence and improve life in their troubled country. The two women were spurred to political action after seeing three of Corrigan Maguire's sister's children killed by a wounded IRA terrorist's automobile. Having organized huge rallies and marches to stop violence in the divided Protestant and Catholic areas, Williams and Corrigan Maguire also agitated for reconciliation through the integration of schools, residential areas, and athletic clubs. Williams and Corrigan Maguire were awarded the Nobel Peace Prize in 1976.

Bob Geldof, who achieved fame in the 1970s punk rock group the Boomtown Rats, became a political activist after being moved by pictures of starving Ethiopian children. Geldof organized Live Aid concerts in 1985 to raise funds for famine relief. Since then, he has devoted his energy to Drop the Debt, a campaign that asks developed countries to cancel debts owed them by the world's most economically challenged countries. Bono, lead singer of the rock group U2, is another individual who believes that as members of a global *polis,* we are responsible for one another's well-being. Like Geldof, Bono has focused attention on Drop the Debt. He has also drawn public attention to the AIDS crisis in Africa. Bono notes the absurdity of business's ability to supply carbonated soft drinks to the most remote corners of the world, while medicines and health information are in short supply.

Geldof, Bono, Williams, Corrigan Maguire, and Daw Aung San Suu Kyi (see Taking a Stand, page 32) are all examples of private citizens who have performed what Aristotle would call virtuous or ethical activities in the political community.

THE WEB

Learn about opportunities for community involvement and youth leadership in Canada and internationally at www.emp.ca/cwp.

Press Play

The *Live Aid: The Day Music Changed the World* DVD set captures 10 hours of performances from rock music royalty on July 13, 1985. The global event raised millions of dollars for famine relief in Ethiopia; royalties from the DVD go toward hunger relief in Africa. (NR)

Figure 1.27 Mairead Corrigan Maguire and Betty Williams pose together in 1998, 22 years after being awarded the Nobel Peace Prize.

Taking a Stand   Daw Aung San Suu Kyi

Daw Aung San Suu Kyi (pronounced Soo Chee) is an international symbol of the power of democratic ideals and of women. In 1988, Suu Kyi, daughter of assassinated independence leader General Aung San, left the comforts of life in England to return to her native Myanmar (formerly known as Burma) to nurse her dying mother. She stayed on to become leader of the National League for Democracy, a party that champions democracy and human rights in the face of the country's 26-year-old **junta** (military government).

Although Suu Kyi was under house arrest in July 1989, her party won 80 percent of the vote in the national elections of 1990. This made her head of Myanmar's government in title only. Than Shwe, leader of the military government and an expert in psychological warfare, never handed over power. Since then, Suu Kyi has been under house arrest on four occasions, once for a period of six years. At times, she lost all contact with her husband (who died in 1999) and her two children.

While in detention, Suu Kyi was awarded the 1991 Nobel Peace Prize. In an essay that her son read at the award ceremony in Oslo, she wrote: "Where there is no justice there can be no secure peace." Her essay went on to say, "It is not power that corrupts but fear. Fear of losing power corrupts those who wield it, and fear of the scourge of power corrupts those who are subject to it." Suu Kyi's political philosophy is grounded in Buddhism, and she speaks of "truth, justice, and compassion" as bulwarks against repression. By means of a smuggled video, she spoke at a 1995 women's conference in Beijing against the "war toys of grown men."

On May 30, 2003, Suu Kyi led a peaceful protest of hundreds of her supporters. They were attacked by a mob of thousands of men wielding sticks and hurling rocks. According to supporters in exile, at least 70 people were killed by the government-sponsored mob. Suu Kyi was again placed under house arrest. She remains determined to replace the authoritarian government of her homeland by peaceful means and to protect human rights for all members of Myanmarese society.

Question

Do you agree that "fear of losing power corrupts those who wield it and fear of the scourge of power corrupts those who are subject to it"? Why or why not? Present your views in a short paragraph, including an example drawn from an actual political situation: personal, local, or national.

Voter Apathy

In democratic societies, citizens have many freedoms—including those of expression, religion, and association. Most democratic states also guarantee voting, mobility, and legal rights. These rights, however, entail responsibilities. One right and responsibility that needs more exercise is the right to vote. In Canada and the United States, the participation rate in national elections has dipped below 60 percent. Studies indicate that the poor and the young are not voting in large numbers. In the 2004 federal election in Canada, only 38.7 percent of voters aged 18 to 30 cast ballots. Possible remedies include lowering the voting age to 16 to spark interest among younger citizens, or adopting the Australian practice of compulsory voting. Voting is the most basic form of political participation for citizens of a democracy. To benefit from living in the *polis*, people should be willing to participate in many more activities in concert with their fellow citizens.

THE WEB

Check out a 12-step program to overcome apathy at www.emp.ca/cwp.

Professional Politicians

Those who enter public life often pay a high price. Long hours of service and many kilometres of physical separation can harm a politician's family life. Today a politician's private life is also open to public scrutiny. Questions commonly asked by the media include: Did you ever smoke marijuana? Were you ever convicted of a criminal offence? Did you ever commit adultery? Are any of your children in trouble with the law? Did one of your parents belong to a Nazi or communist organization? The modern politician must be prepared to answer these questions publicly.

Under freedom of information laws, the inner workings of government are open to public scrutiny. For example, in 2003, Canada's privacy commissioner, George Radwanski, resigned from his appointed position after a parliamentary committee found irregularities in his office's spending. In February 2004, Auditor-General Sheila Fraser's explosive report on misuse of funds in a federal sponsorship program contributed to a collapse in popular support for the Liberal Party in the 2004 election.

A life in politics can also be deadly. Between 1963 and 1968 in the United States, President John F. Kennedy, civil rights leaders Malcolm X and Martin Luther King, and presidential candidate Robert Kennedy were all assassinated. In India, over a span of 43 years, Mahatma Gandhi, leader of the national independence move-

Figure 1.28 Reverend Martin Luther King, Jr., at the civil rights movement's March on Washington, August 28, 1963.

ment, Prime Minster Indira Gandhi, and her son, Prime Minister Rajiv Gandhi, met the same fate. In the Middle East, Egyptian President Anwar Sadat (in 1981) and Israeli Prime Minister Yitzhak Rabin (in 1995) were assassinated. The 2003 fatal stabbing of Swedish Foreign Minister Anna Lindh came 17 years after the murder of Swedish Prime Minister Olof Palme. In 2004, Chechen President Akhmad Kadyrov was killed by a terrorist's bomb. Because politicians often embody the aspirations and ideals of their constituents, an assassination is often perceived as the destruction not only of a human being but also of an entire political program.

In the world of politics, there are stories of heroism and compassion. There are also stories of intolerance and selfishness. Politics is people, and the best and the worst of the human condition is reflected in the *polis*. In this textbook, you will examine the many fascinating details that come into play as men and women interact on the local, national, and global stages.

Check YOUR UNDERSTANDING

1. What do you believe motivates an individual to become immersed in public life? Describe circumstances that might compel you to become involved with a political issue.
2. Should the media report on the private life of a politician? Explain your views.
3. How might a government improve voter turnout on election day?

METHODS OF POLITICAL INQUIRY
Asking Questions about Language

Is it cynical to question the credibility of politicians? Or is it simply necessary when political "spin" sanitizes issues for the public? For example, many politicians now use the term "collateral damage" to describe civilians who have been killed during military attacks. The term diminishes the reality.

As a student of politics, you need to be able to decipher what a politician is really saying. Politicians can bolster their own point of view and denigrate another's through the use of repetition, association, and composition. Below are some suggestions about what to listen for in a politician's words.

Repetition: Listen for repeated words, themes, images, or symbols. Assess the frequency, duration, and intensity of a politician's repetition. In this context, you might consider US President George W. Bush's phrase "weapons of mass destruction" and its effect on the public in the buildup to the war on Iraq in 2003.

Association: Politicians often use association to sway their audience. For example, they may make a speech at a historic site to connect themselves with their country's past. They may refer to a fallen hero or other celebrated person to associate themselves with favourable sentiment. Why, for example, was the 2003 Ontario Budget presented from the headquarters of auto parts manufacturer Magna International?

Composition: Analyze the composition of political speeches. What are the key words? What are the generalities and the specifics? What are the absolutes, and where are qualifiers used? Equally important are non-verbal cues, such as smiles, frowns, or tones of voice. If you have ever watched Question Period on the public affairs channel CPAC, you might ask why members of Parliament sometimes adopt a theatrical stance when defending their own party or attacking their opponents.

SOUND BITE "Political language . . . is designed to make lies sound truthful and murder respectable, to give an appearance of solidity to pure wind."
George Orwell, Politics and the English Language, 1946

Politicians also downplay the weakness of their own arguments and the strength of their opponents' through omission, diversion, and confusion.

Omission: When listening to a political speech, consider what you are *not* hearing. Are there relevant omissions about people, conflicts of interest, past errors, carelessness, neglect, or inflated costs? Has contradictory evidence been suppressed? Are euphemisms masking the impact of unpleasant facts? Consider this statement made in 2000 by Ontario's former environment minister in relation to government responsibility for deaths caused by contaminated water in Walkerton: "We are just one piece in the puzzle. We recognize that built-in redundancies or fail-safes in the notification procedures may have resulted in some confusion about reporting obligations."

Diversion: Is time, effort, or money being spent on trivial matters or side issues? To divert your attention, politicians may attack opponents personally rather than their ideas. Politicians may appeal to an audience's emotions rather than its rationality to evoke sympathy for their cause. Evasion, changing subjects, and humour are powerful diverting devices. For example, in a 2003 speech announcing his country's reluctance to **ratify** the *Kyoto Protocol*, Russian President Vladimir Putin joked that global warming would mean Russians would spend less on winter clothing.

Confusion: Speakers may try to create confusion by using unclear and unfamiliar words. Jargon, generalities, ambiguities, euphemisms (vague expressions), and statistics can all be used to conceal the truth. What exactly is "tree-density reduction"?

Source: Adapted from "Questions You Can Ask About Political Language," at www.govst.edu/users/ghrank/Political/Elections%20/questions_pol.htm.

Applying the Skill

1. Translate the following terms into plain English: axis of evil, ethnic cleansing, human intelligence, servicing the target, spin, aerial ordinance, embedded reporter, vertically deployed anti-personnel devices, shock and awe, friendly fire.
2. Find examples in a newspaper or the electronic media of repetition, association, composition, omission, diversion, and confusion.

Study Hall

Thinking/Inquiry

1. Using a blank map of the world provided by your teacher, label the following countries that have been mentioned in this chapter: South Africa, Greece, India, Egypt, China, England, Scotland, France, Iran, North Korea, Russia, Argentina, Zimbabwe, Chile, Hungary, Croatia, Georgia, Germany, Rwanda, Northern Ireland, Myanmar, Sweden, and Israel. Be prepared to link the country to a political concept discussed in Chapter 1.

2. Imagine what could have happened if colonizing Europeans had adopted the Aboriginal governing principles described on page 11. In groups of four, choose a current political controversy and use this law to achieve a resolution. Present your findings to the class.

3. Duff Conacher, head of the non-partisan group Democracy Watch, has proposed the establishment of an honesty commission to give Canadians a means of challenging politicians who lie. The commission would investigate complaints and would have power to fine or remove members of Parliament. In small groups, create a list outlining both the positive and negative aspects of this proposal.

4. Identify at least five international organizations that have been created since the end of World War II in 1945. In chart form, illustrate how each organization contributes to a global sense of interconnectedness. Be prepared to discuss in class the positive and negative aspects of global interconnectedness.

Communication

5. As a speech writer for a national leader, you are required to write a response to one of the following:
   a) supporting an unpopular issue (such as declaring war),
   b) explaining why a project has cost significantly more than originally predicted, or
   c) denying a newspaper story alleging that your boss made racist remarks about a minority group.

6. Hold a debate supporting or rebutting Hobbes's belief that people need an absolute ruler to provide peace, security, and the rule of law because life is "nasty, brutish, and short."

7. Obtain a copy of the *Canadian Charter of Rights and Freedoms*. In small groups, choose a right that you consider to be very important, and create a short drama to illustrate its importance for the class. Be prepared to defend your choice after your presentation.

8. Look back at Figure 1.1 on page 2. What idea(s) do you think the artist wished to convey? Why might she have chosen crocheting as a form of expression? To find out more about this project, visit www.emp.ca/cwp.

Application

9. Find three different political cartoons dealing with the same issue. Analyze the three cartoons, using the questions on page 27.

10. Select a current political issue about which you feel strongly. Use library or Internet resources to research it. Create a visual display to describe the issue and to elicit support for your point of view.

11. Select four prominent world leaders. Using the list of attributes of a successful leader that you were asked (on page 23) to prepare, decide how these leaders rate. Prepare a brief report outlining your findings.

12. Select a country in the world outside North America. Using library, Internet, or other resources, find information about its government structure and the country's connections to the rest of the global community. Apply the political concepts learned in this chapter to prepare a report on your selected country for the class.

Ideologies and Values

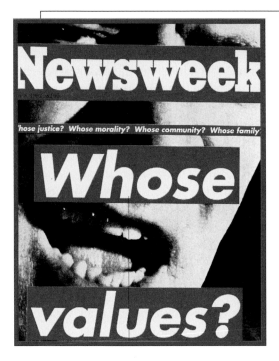

Figure 2.1 American artist Barbara Kruger raises questions about political and cultural values in a cover commissioned by *Newsweek* magazine for a June 1992 issue.

Agenda

In this chapter, you will consider

- political and social ideologies, such as conservatism, liberalism, authoritarianism, and libertarianism
- economic theories of communism, socialism, capitalism, and fascism
- ideologies of Canadian political parties
- ideologies of Canadian think tanks and citizens' coalitions
- British and American influences on ideologies within Canada
- feminist and environmentalist ideologies
- points of view in photojournalism

Have you ever examined your beliefs about society? Do you believe, for example, that education is a right for both rich and poor? Do you believe in school dress codes, same-sex marriage, or conservation of the world's forests? The sum of your beliefs about these and other subjects reflects your personal philosophy, which may change as you mature.

This chapter challenges you to examine your personal philosophy in the light of established political, social, and economic philosophies, or ideologies. It invites you to examine the ideological perspectives embedded in photojournalism and other media. It also presents the platforms of Canada's major political parties, ideologies that will be increasingly relevant as you become a voting member of Canadian society.

THE WEB

Take the "world's smallest political quiz" at www.emp.ca/cwp.

Political and Social Ideologies

A **political ideology** is an organized collection of ideas and values that describes a political system, movement, or way of thinking. When shared by many people, a political ideology can motivate individuals, parties, non-governmental organizations, and governments. Since ideologies represent broad patterns of abstract thought, individuals may agree with only certain aspects of a particular ideology. Such opinions are usually termed a personal perspective rather than an ideology.

Ideological terms such as "liberal" and "conservative" express complex political ideas in simple words. Broadly speaking, **liberalism** today is a political and social ideology that advocates government activism, civil liberties, and social reform. The political and social ideology of **conservatism**, by contrast, advocates limited government intervention and the preservation or restoration of traditions. These ideologies will be explored in greater detail later in this chapter, but some basic distinctions can be made here.

For example, do you think that possession of a small amount of marijuana should be a criminal offence? Do you support or oppose same-sex marriage? Should government spend more money to help the poor and marginalized in Canada and other countries? Your answers to these questions reflect your values, and your values reflect your political ideology. They may place you in the conservative camp on some issues and in the liberal camp on others.

The conservative–liberal division covers social and political concerns. For example, what are your thoughts on your school's dress code? If you believe that the dress code should be stricter, then on this issue, your view is conservative. If you believe that the dress code should be less strict, your view is liberal. Your opinions place you somewhere on an imaginary line called the **political spectrum**. Conservatism is on the right side and liberalism on the left. A student who favours the present dress code is at the centre of the political spectrum and is therefore termed a **centrist**.

The concept of the right–left political spectrum dates back to the French Revolution (1789). Elected conservative politicians sat to the right of the speaker's chair in the National Assembly and the elected liberals sat to the left.

The **social spectrum** provides more information about people's political attitudes. In this continuum, a belief in personal freedom is at one extreme and a belief in authority is at the other. **Libertarianism** is a belief in total personal freedom without the constraints of imposed rules. **Authoritarianism**

Figure 2.2 The left–right political spectrum.

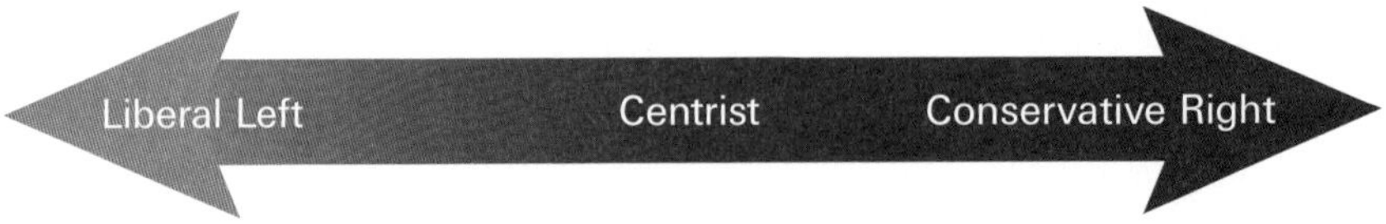

Liberal Left   Centrist   Conservative Right

is a belief in the individual's duty to follow established rules. A student who believes in personal choice and who advocates the abolition of all rules concerning school dress has a libertarian outlook. A student who believes in following any and all rules set by the school administration supports the philosophy of authoritarianism.

When ideologies are placed on a political or social spectrum, belief systems overlap to some extent. For example, someone who is on the liberal side of the political spectrum may still respect authority. Conversely, someone on the conservative side of the continuum may believe strongly in personal freedom. One reason for the overlap is that political and social ideologies do not deal with exactly the same sets of ideas.

Conservatism

A person who conserves traditional values has a conservative political ideology. The word "conservative" comes from the same Latin root as the word "conservation."

Conservatives believe that traditional values are the building blocks of society and are worth preserving because they have held society together. Conservative theory tends to oppose innovations that threaten traditional values and institutions. For example, it views the traditional family as an institution that has provided and continues to provide a workable foundation for society; it therefore opposes same-sex marriage as a threat to that institution and society as a whole.

Conservative ideology tends to favour strict rules. Conservatives believe that people are easily led into making poor decisions. Therefore, authorities (in home, school, and government) should impose guidelines to encourage

> **SOUND BITE** "A disposition to preserve, and an ability to improve, taken together, would be my standard of a statesman."
>
> *Edmund Burke,* Reflections on the Revolution in France, *1790*

Figure 2.3 A clearcut area contrasts starkly with old-growth forest at Clayoquot Sound, British Columbia. At the root of conservatism is the notion of preserving something of value from destruction. In that sense conservatism is not unlike conservation, and some conservatives are also environmentalists.

good behaviour. For example, conservative philosophy opposes the decriminalization of marijuana in the belief that this would lead more people to make bad decisions. In a school setting, conservative values are compatible with regulations regarding uniforms, modest dress and language, and bans on tattoos and body piercing.

Conservative philosophy stresses individual responsibility. The government may act as a police officer, but should never act as a babysitter. Adults must learn to make wise decisions. If they make bad decisions, they should look to themselves, not government, for help. Conservative ideology generally opposes government intervention, whether in the economy or in people's personal lives. It therefore opposes welfare payments, subsidized housing, and other financial aids. An extreme conservative view—or reactionary view—advocates a return to the perceived better conditions of the past. In Canada, such reactionary thinking may advocate reinstating the death penalty for certain crimes or restoring province-wide secondary school graduation examinations.

Liberalism

Classical liberalism developed in Europe in the 18th century. It emphasized rational analysis of traditional institutions and distrust of state power over individuals. Today, modern liberalism—what some have called "ethical liberalism"—accepts state intervention when it results in greater political, economic, and social equality. This **egalitarian** view emerged as a response to **utilitarianism**, a theory of ethics that defines as "good" any action that produces the greatest benefit for the greatest number of people. First proposed by English thinker Jeremy **Bentham** (1748–1832), the ideas of utilitarianism were further developed by John Stuart **Mill** (1806–73).

Liberal political philosophy emphasizes freedom of choice and the innate dignity and potential of the individual. In the liberal view, individuals should be free to express their uniqueness. For example, if a student wishes to dress in gothic black, display a nose piercing, or wear spiked hair, personal choice should be respected. Judgment based on appearances should be avoided. Because liberals think that people are essentially good,

Figure 2.4 Liberalism promotes the values of personal choice and the dignity of the individual, regardless of outward appearances.

strict rules are considered unnecessary. An individual who makes a bad decision will learn from it, and society will benefit from that learning. For example, liberal philosophy opposes criminalizing Canadian citizens for simple possession of a small amount of marijuana.

Modern liberal ideology supports new ideas, especially those that advocate a more egalitarian society. Liberals support same-sex marriage because it extends equality and dignity to all citizens. Laws that provide opportunities for women, minority groups, the poor, and the marginalized are generally supported. These laws and programs often require government involvement in people's lives and public funding.

Liberal thinkers believe that society is not static. They view human history as the development of progressive reforms ranging from the abolition of slavery to the constitutional recognition of equal rights for women. Liberal philosophers seek to help all members of the human family at home and abroad.

SOUND BITE "[M]ost of the great positive evils of the world are in themselves removable, and will, if human affairs continue to improve, be in the end reduced within narrow limits. Poverty, in any sense implying suffering, may be completely extinguished by the wisdom of society, combined with the good sense and providence of individuals."

John Stuart Mill,
Utilitarianism, *1861*

Conservative View	Liberal View
Values tradition	Values progress
Encourages continuity	Encourages change
Discourages government intervention	Accepts government intervention when it produces greater equality

Figure 2.5 Comparison of modern conservative and liberal views.

Authoritarianism

Authoritarianism, like conservatism, liberalism, and libertarianism, has both political and social dimensions. As a political philosophy, authoritarianism requires strong governmental power. The rights of the government take precedence over the rights and freedoms of individual citizens. Authoritarianism allows for little or no political opposition. The military and the police are used to maintain obedience to an authoritarian leader or government. The ideology of authoritarianism is found on both the right and left of the political spectrum.

The governments of the former Soviet Union, North Korea, and Cuba are examples of left-wing authoritarian governments. Most state power is vested in one **political party**, the Communist Party, and individual rights, such as freedom of religion, speech, mobility, and association, are curtailed. Citizens are encouraged to adhere to the authoritarian model because it benefits society in a more equitable distribution of wealth and greater equality in health care, housing, education, and so on.

Right-wing authoritarianism is usually based on the power of the military. Ideologically, its policies favour free enterprise, under the watchful eye of the state. Examples of right-wing authoritarianism include the governments of South Korea (1960s–80s), Chile under President Augusto Pinochet (1973–90), and Myanmar in the last half of the 20th century. Typically, such governments grab power by means of a coup d'état organized by a military faction. Often, the claim to legitimacy is that they are striving to achieve nationalistic goals. Organizations and institutions such as churches, labour unions, and business groups may be allowed to function as long as they adhere to government policies.

According to some political scientists, the most extreme form of authoritarianism is **totalitarianism**, in which the government assumes total control of all aspects of society and individual life. The Soviet Union under Joseph Stalin and Germany under Adolf Hitler are often cited as examples of totalitarian regimes on the left and right, respectively. Totalitarianism rarely existed before the 20th century because the technology needed to control large populations did not exist.

Figure 2.6 May Day celebrations in Red Square, Moscow, 1933. Displays of military might were meant to demonstrate the superiority of the authoritarian Soviet system and the unity of its people.

The term authoritarianism can also be applied to politicians in democratic governments who practise a style of leadership that rejects diversity of opinion and rule by consensus. In Canada, for example, the prime minister may ignore the advice of cabinet and the bureaucracy and make decisions based on personal beliefs. Of course, the party may also rebel against a prime minister who has an authoritarian style. Leaders of ostensibly democratic countries may use extralegal means to increase their powers. For example, Robert Mugabe, the elected leader Zimbabwe, has been accused of keeping power through intimidation and electoral fraud.

Authoritarianism may express itself in family and school settings. For example, liberal school authorities would consult with students and parents before setting a dress code. An authoritarian approach would impose a code without consultation.

SOUND BITE "However sugarcoated and ambiguous, every form of authoritarianism must start with a belief in some group's greater right to power, whether that right is justified by sex, race, class, religion, or all four. However far it may expand, the progression inevitably rests on unequal power and airtight roles within the family."

Gloria Steinem, "If Hitler Were Alive, Whose Side Would He Be On?," 1980

Anarchism and Libertarianism

Anarchism

The political ideology of **anarchism** holds that all forms of enforced control and authority are unnecessary and undesirable. Anarchism advocates a society based on voluntary cooperation and free association in which government is unnecessary. Some see the 2,000-year-old Chinese philosophy of Taoism, with its emphasis on individual freedom and non-interventionist government, as an early expression of anarchism.

The English writer William Godwin (1756–1836) expressed anarchistic views when he concluded that by its very nature government impedes the improvement of the human mind. In his conclusions, Godwin was a pioneer of anarchism. Pierre-Joseph Proudhon (1809–65) was the first thinker to call himself an anarchist. Under the influence of Proudhon's writings, Peter Kropotkin (1842–1921) codified anarchism into a set of beliefs. In Proudhon's vision, the state would be abolished, society would be organized by a federation of communes operating on democratic principles, and private property would be limited to personal possessions. All other property would be held communally and controlled democratically. Today, Godwin, Proudhon, and Kropotkin are considered to fall on the left side of the political spectrum.

SOUND BITE
"Property is theft."

Pierre-Joseph Proudhon, What Is Property?, 1840

SOUND BITE "[A]narchism is not a revolutionary [but] rather a restorative doctrine, telling us that the means by which we can create a free society are already there in the manifestations of mutual aid existing in the world around us. . . ."

George Woodcock, "The Ending Century: Prospects and Retrospect," 1990

Taking a Stand   George Woodcock

George Woodcock—writer, critic, **pacifist**, anarchist—was born in Winnipeg in 1912 to British parents. The family failed to prosper and soon returned to Britain, where George spent his first 37 years.

Although he was a brilliant scholar, Woodcock's family was too poor to send him to university, and at 18 he went to work as a railroad clerk. This experience of class discrimination fuelled his interest in communism and **radicalism**, ideas that inspired other youth in Britain during the Great Depression. The collapse in 1939 of the anti-fascist effort in the Spanish Civil War (see Art and Politics, page 53) left him disillusioned with leftist politics.

By 1940, Woodcock's political beliefs inclined toward anarchism, the mutual non-involvement of the state and the individual. Woodcock expressed his views in many publications, including *NOW*, a literary–political journal he founded in 1940. (Like many British radicals, he believed that literature and ideology were inseparable.) When World War II broke out, Woodcock registered as a **conscientious objector**, an official status that exempted him from the military but required him to work for the government's War Agriculture Committee (WAC) as a farm labourer.

The WAC was a haven for pacifists, anarchists, leftists, and gays who shunned—or were barred from—military service. Some of those who continued their political activism were charged under Britain's *Incitement to Disaffection Act*, an old law that was used to suppress "agitators." In 1944, police raided the offices of a civil liberties group that Woodcock had helped found, but he was never brought to trial. The experience, however, affected him deeply, and he applied for a Canadian passport in 1947.

Returning to the country of his birth in 1949 was exhilarating for George and his German-born wife, Inge. They settled on Vancouver Island on a small farm where they grew vegetables. George soon gained a reputation as a writer and literary critic.

In 1954, Woodcock was offered a position at the University of Washington, but the United States deemed him "inadmissible" because of his left-wing politics. The "red scare," exploited by anti-communist US Senator Joseph McCarthy, was in full swing. Woodcock wrote an eloquent letter to the US government explaining the difference between communism and the philosophical anarchism that he espoused, yet he refused to renounce his views. He was denied entry into the United States. Soon after, Woodcock accepted a teaching position at the University of British Columbia.

When he sat down in 1959 to write *Anarchism* (1962)—today considered the definitive account of the movement—Woodcock did so knowing that

> anarchism has failed. . . . But there is a . . . profound way in which the anarchist idea may retain a purpose . . . in our modern world. To acknowledge the existence

and the overbearing force of the movement toward universal centralization . . . is not to accept it. If human values are to survive, a counter-ideal must be posed to the totalitarian goal of a uniform world, and that counter-ideal exists precisely in the vision of pure liberty. . . .

Woodcock's political writings include *The Anarchist Prince: A Biographical Study of Peter Kropotkin* (1950), *The Doukhobors* (1960), *Pierre-Joseph Proudhon* (1956), and *Gandhi* (1971). His literary criticism includes studies of Aldous Huxley and George Orwell, his political and literary antagonist and ally.

George Woodcock, whom his friend and biographer Doug Fetherling dubbed "the gentle anarchist," died in Vancouver in 1995 at the age of 83.

Questions

1. How might Woodcock's phrase "the overbearing force of the movement toward universal centralization" be interpreted today?
2. Do you agree with Woodcock that literature and ideology are inseparable? Explain your answer.

Libertarianism

Like anarchism, libertarianism is an ideology that advocates maximum individual freedom and an absence of government intervention. Libertarian ideas were popularized by Russian-born US writer Ayn Rand (1905–82) in her novels *The Fountainhead* (1943) and *Atlas Shrugged* (1957).

Libertarians believe that people should be free to do what they want, as long as they do not infringe on the rights of others. Libertarianism argues for freedom of choice, both economic and social. For libertarians, there are no positive rights, such as shelter or health care, but only negative rights, such as the right to be free from violence or censorship. Whereas Godwin and Proudhon advocated the abolition of private property, libertarians believe that freedom is impossible without protection of this right. Libertarianism falls on the right side of the political spectrum.

SOUND BITE "America's abundance was not created by public sacrifices to the common good, but by the productive genius of free men who pursued their own personal interests and the making of their own private fortunes."

Ayn Rand,
The Fountainhead, *1943*

Authoritarian View	Anarchist/Libertarian View
Promotes rights of government over those of the individual	Promotes rights of the individual over those of government
Permits little/no opposition	Advocates dissent as a means to individual expression
Controls via military/police	Does not acknowledge government control as legitimate

Figure 2.7 Authoritarian and anarchist/libertarian views.

Like anarchists, libertarians wish to eliminate all government intervention in people's lives. Unlike anarchists, they believe that human nature is egoistic and competitive rather than cooperative. Libertarians oppose such liberal initiatives as pay equity and universal health care. They also favour a flat tax (one rate for all) over the system of **graduated taxation**, in which higher earners pay higher taxes. These policies are actively promoted by the Libertarian Party, which has chapters in the United States and Canada.

Check YOUR UNDERSTANDING

1. Why does conservative theory oppose innovation? Do you agree with this view? Why or why not?
2. How does conservative ideology perceive the individual? How could this view influence a conservative government's policies?
3. Explain how modern liberalism developed from utilitarianism.
4. What do you think is the most fundamental principle of liberalism? Why?
5. Distinguish between right-wing and left-wing authoritarianism. Cite examples of each type of government.
6. What did Hannah Arendt mean when she wrote "totalitarianism has discovered a means of dominating and terrorizing human beings from within"? Do you agree or disagree?
7. Assess the practicality of anarchism and libertarianism as forms of government, citing examples to explain your point of view.
8. Examine the political spectrum in Figure 2.2 (page 38). Where would you place yourself? Why?

Economic Theory and Political Ideologies

Like political ideologies, economic ideologies can be placed on a left–right spectrum. Communist economies are on the left, socialist economies toward the centre, and capitalist and fascist economies on the right.

Communism

Communism is based on the theories of Karl **Marx** (1818–83), Friedrich Engels (1820–95), Vladimir Lenin (1870–1924), and Mao Zedong (1893–1976), among others. Revolutionary communism attempts to bring about equality in society by radical means—that is, by violently seizing power from the bourgeoisie (those who control capital and property, such as landlords, factory owners, and store proprietors) and vesting it instead in the **proletariat** (wage earners who do not own property and who must sell their labour to survive). Marxist ideology envisions a temporary dictatorship by the proletariat that will eventually wither away, giving rise to a classless society. By the end of the 19th century, the Communist Party had become the mechanism

SOUND BITE "[F]or Marx himself, Communism had never meant less than the means for freeing human creativity in all persons to the fullest. . . . [T]he passion for human creativity forced Marx into the study of how Capital, by its own internal laws, had suppressed the flow of human activity and passions."

Adrienne Rich, "The Muralist," in What Is Found There: Notebooks on Poetry and Politics, *1993*

for the takeover of governments and the control of nations. Marx's cry for revolution had become a worldwide call: "Workers of the world unite: you have nothing to lose but your chains!"

Communist ideology calls for a strong, centralized government with full authority to plan economic growth. For example, a central committee decides industrial policy: the state will produce a large number of tractors and trucks but few personal hygiene products. The central committee exercises control in the name of the proletariat—but it does not actually share power with the workers.

Aside from controlling the economy, communist governments also control what citizens watch, read, and hear in an effort to curb bourgeois influences. The Communist Party traditionally controls the news media and restricts personal freedom of movement. In the interests of the common good, political opposition is not tolerated. In most communist states, the belief systems of established religions are discouraged or openly persecuted.

Communist governments have worked to achieve the Marxist goal of economic equality. They have attempted to provide housing, medical care, old age pensions, education, and employment for all citizens. Yet, these efforts have often come at a high price. In the People's Republic of China and the former Soviet Union, for example, millions of people have been killed or imprisoned for real or perceived opposition to communist ideology. In communist states, some people may be "more equal" than others. For example, leading members of the Communist Party and star athletes have received privileges not accorded others.

In the mid-20th century, centralized political and economic control led to major scientific and technological advances in the Soviet Union. With the 1957 launch of *Sputnik*, the Soviet Union created the first Earth-orbiting satellite and demonstrated superiority in space exploration. Other areas of the economy, however, suffered. By 1991, the Communist Party had lost its absolute authority and the Soviet economy was in disarray. The Soviet Union was dismantled by governmental decree. Today, Russia is making a transition to a market economy (see Chapter 5).

With their emphasis on control of the economy and the individual, communist governments—including those in China, Cuba, North Korea, and Vietnam—have proven to be finely tuned totalitarian states.

Socialism

Like communism, **socialism** is based on the Marxist ideal of public ownership of the **means of production**. Socialists favour democratic and peaceful means of achieving their goals of redistributing political and economic power ("the ballot, not the bullet"). For example, they advocate political action such as the formation of socialist and labour parties, **trade unions**, labour protests, and strikes. Once elected, socialist governments allow opposition parties.

PRESS PLAY

Reds (1981), written and directed by Warren Beatty, portrays American John Reed's first-hand account of the communist revolution in Russia as detailed in the writer's 1919 book, *Ten Days That Shook the World.* (PG)

SOUND BITE "Religion is the sigh of the oppressed creature, the heart of a heartless world, and the soul of soulless conditions. It is the opium of the people."

Karl Marx, A Contribution to the Critique of Hegel's Philosophy of Right, *1844*

SOUND BITE "All animals are equal, but some animals are more equal than others."

George Orwell, Animal Farm, *1945*

PRESS PLAY

In the 1955 animated version of George Orwell's novel *Animal Farm,* a group of animals, oppressed by the cruelty and inefficiency of their master, take over a farm but find new tyrants among themselves. (NR)

Figure 2.8 A matchmakers' strike in London, England, 1871. The socialist movement supported labour unions to address the low wages, long working hours, and poor living conditions endured by working-class people.

Rather than strive for complete economic equality, socialist philosophy seeks to lessen the income gap between rich and poor by advocating government funding for education, housing, health, employment, and pensions.

The roots of socialism go back to the 16th century, when English philosopher Thomas More (1478–1535) advocated equality as an aspect of an idealized society in his book *Utopia*. French writer Charles Fourier (1772–1837) explored the idea of a chain of communes whose citizens shared the Earth's riches. Fourier's ideas were implemented by various movements, such as the Utopian community of Brook Farm (1841–47) in the United States and the Fabian Society (1883) in England.

In Canada, a number of political parties have incorporated socialist ideals, including the Co-operative Commonwealth Federation (CCF) in its *Regina Manifesto* (1933; see Grassroots Politics and Protest, page 60) and the New Democratic Party (1961).

PRESS PLAY

Motorcycle Diaries (2004), director Walter Salles's homage to Ernesto "Che" Guevara, hero of the 1959 Cuban revolution, explores the young man's conversion to radical socialism as a result of a road trip through South America in the early 1950s. (14A)

SOUND BITE ". . .[W]hen I weigh in my mind all the other states which flourish today, . . . I can discover nothing but a conspiracy of the rich, who pursue their own aggrandizement under the name and title of the Commonwealth. They devise ways and means to keep safely what they have unjustly acquired, and to buy up the toil and labour of the poor as cheaply as possible and oppress them. When these schemes of the rich become established by the government, which is meant to protect the poor as well as the rich, then they are law. With insatiable greed these wicked men divide among themselves the goods which would have been enough for all."

Thomas More, Utopia, *1516*

Democratic Socialism

Over the years, many political and economic thinkers have re-examined socialist doctrine in relation to contemporary economic trends. Such re-evaluation has given rise to **democratic socialism** (also known as "social democracy"). Democratic socialists do not insist on total public ownership of the means of production. Instead, they prefer a **mixed economy** that permits private enterprise. For this reason, democratic socialism is placed to the right of socialism, more to the centre of the economic spectrum.

Social democrats reject the Marxist notions of violent class struggle and dictatorship of the proletariat. They emphasize a democratic approach to political and economic reform that respects human rights and freedoms. They argue that political democracy, however, must expand to include social and economic democracy. Therefore, they favour initiatives and programs to help people at the lowest economic levels—for example, a minimum wage, universal health care, old age pensions, unemployment insurance, parenting benefits, and housing subsidies. Social democrats favour a graduated income tax system to fund these programs, which lessen the gap between rich and poor. Social democrats also seek greater equality among regions. In Canada, for example, they support government programs that redistribute wealth from the richer to the poorer provinces.

SOUND BITE "We aim to replace the present capitalist system, with its inherent injustice and inhumanity, by a social order from which the domination and exploitation of one class by another will be eliminated, in which economic planning will supersede unregulated private enterprise and competition, and in which genuine democratic self-government, based upon economic equality, will be possible."

The Regina Manifesto, *1933*

The governing policies of most industrialized countries include a degree of democratic socialism. Some countries, like Sweden, provide a large portion of "cradle to grave" protection. Others, like the United States, provide a smaller portion. The gap between rich and poor is smaller in Sweden than it is in the United States because Swedes consistently have voted for more social democratic initiatives than have Americans.

THE WEB

Learn more about the gap between rich and poor in Toronto and how it is affecting students at www.emp.ca/cwp.

Figure 2.9 Anti-poverty demonstrators chained themselves in Quebec City in 2002 to protest measures that reduced their welfare payments because they receive child support from previous spouses. The women demanded "economic asylum" in Sweden, which they believe has a more progressive social welfare system than Canada.

Debt and the Welfare State

By the late 20th century, many governments were incurring large annual **deficits** in providing the benefits of social democracy. A deficit occurs when a government spends more money than it collects. An accumulation of deficits over a number of years leads to an increase in total government **debt**. In the 1980s and 1990s, governments in many countries, including Canada, decided that interest payments on the debt were consuming too much government revenue. Middle-income voters, faced with rising taxes, were also hesitant to fund more social spending. High debts and high taxes became roadblocks for social programs. In Canada, federal, provincial, and municipal governments cut back funding in health, education, and welfare programs. Plans for a federal universal daycare program were shelved indefinitely.

In recent years, democratic socialism has been criticized by both the left and the right. Many critics on the left argue that social democratic reforms are superficial, leaving the abuses of the capitalist system intact. Critics on the right argue that the high costs of administering a social democratic **welfare state** will bankrupt the country.

Capitalism

Scottish economist Adam **Smith** (1723–90) was the first to express the principles of **capitalism**. In his 1776 book, *The Wealth of Nations*, Smith praised the free marketplace and the power of competition.

According to capitalist theory, individuals who follow their own selfish economic interests benefit society as a whole. For example, your school cafeteria sells food because of the self-interest of the food business. Staff and students benefit from that self-interest by eating food that is conveniently provided at reasonable prices. For capitalism to work, no single business should control the food industry and set prices artificially high. Government must regulate and enforce fair competition; otherwise, it should intervene to a minimum.

Smith was reacting against the 18th century philosophy of **mercantilism**, which espoused strict government control over trade and commerce. For Smith, government intervention in the marketplace was a bad idea. Government projects might be well intended, but too often they wasted money. According to Smith, government should maintain the armed forces, supervise the administration of justice, and run certain public works and institutions. It should not be involved in activities that can be run by private enterprise, such as airlines, oil companies, electrical generating stations, liquor stores, and so on. In the 18th century, French economist Anne-Robert-Jacques Turgot offered this advice to government: *laissez-faire*, or "leave it alone."

According to capitalist theory, the laws of the marketplace will create a balance between supply and demand. If there is a demand for more cellular phones, for example, the market will supply them. If there is no demand for skateboards, their prices will drop and they will stop being made.

SOUND BITE "Every individual necessarily labours to render the annual revenue of the society as great as he can. He generally, indeed, neither intends to promote the publick interest, nor knows how much he is promoting it. . . . He intends only his own gain, and he is in this, as in many other cases, led by an invisible hand to promote an end which was no part of his intention."

Adam Smith, The Wealth of Nations, *1776*

Figure 2.10 Pacific Place shopping mall, Hong Kong. The city was a centre of free-market capitalism before its handover to the People's Republic of China in 1997.

According to free-enterprise capitalism, when competition produces the best quality shoes at the lowest price, all consumers benefit. Less government intervention means a corresponding decrease in the need for revenue in the form of taxes. Lower taxes allow more consumer spending and therefore greater economic activity, giving people more employment opportunities.

Capitalism embraces the belief that the individual is much better suited than a government agency to make wise choices when spending money. Believers in capitalism are believers in individual choice and individual motivation.

In the early 19th century, especially in England, Smith's beliefs were used to keep government out of the economy. During this period of intense industrialization, there were almost no regulations on child labour, female labour, work hours or conditions, and wages. Protections such as unemployment insurance, workers' compensation, and old age pensions were

SOUND BITE "If a man can write a better book, preach a better sermon, or make a better mouse-trap, than his neighbor, though he build his house in the woods, the world will make a beaten path to his door."

Ralph Waldo Emerson, American essayist, 1871

SOUND BITE "Surely there never was such fragile china-ware as that which the millers of Coketown made. . . . They were ruined, when they were required to send labouring children to school; they were ruined, when inspectors were appointed to look into their works; they were ruined when such inspectors considered it doubtful whether they were quite justified in chopping people up with their machinery; they were utterly undone, when it was hinted that perhaps they need not always make quite so much smoke."

Charles Dickens, Hard Times, *1854*

PRESS PLAY
The 1988 film *Hard Times*, directed by Joã Botelho, relocates Dickens's novel in modern-day Portugal, where a circus child is brought up in the loveless household of a man who teaches his children to respect facts over imagination. (NR)

unheard of. English novelist Charles Dickens vividly described the plight of urban workers.

Capitalism's emphasis on freedom of economic choice and its acceptance of the social and economic inequities it produces place it on the right side of the political spectrum. By the late 19th and early 20th centuries, social democratic governments had emerged to address some of capitalism's abuses. In many countries, charitable and social-welfare initiatives were wed to the individualism of capitalism. Labour unrest was also an impetus. Social programs were introduced to help workers and the "deserving" poor as they struggled in a competitive capitalist economy. In Canada, programs provided some care for the infirm, injured, unemployed, aged, and sick. Workers' compensation (initiated in 1914), employment insurance (1941), and the family allowance (1945–93) furthered social equality and helped move Canadian capitalism toward the centre of the political spectrum.

Fascism

PRESS PLAY

German director Leni Riefenstahl used dramatic cinematography to portray the strength of fascism in her classic films *Triumph of the Will* (1934) and *Olympiad* (1936). (NR)

At the far right of the economic spectrum, **fascism** blends authoritarianism, state ownership, and capitalism. Conceived in Italy after World War I and nurtured in Germany, fascism completely subordinates the individual to the state. Citizens are organized into supposedly representative associations, based on profession or vocation, which are closely controlled by the government (a system known as **corporatism**). Workers are cared for with free vacations and affordable consumer products. Free enterprise is allowed, but businesses are also controlled for the good of the state.

Fascism supports a hierarchical view of society. Certain people, such as the "Aryan race" (Caucasians of Nordic stock), are seen to be at the top of the social pyramid, and other groups, such as the Roma, Jews, Slavs, and people of colour, are seen to be at the bottom.

Fascism builds its appeal on order, nationalism, opposition to communism, and loyalty to a charismatic leader. A fascist system allows only one political party, and that party uses violence and the threat of violence to dispel any opposition to the government. During World War II, fascist regimes used paramilitary units such as the Black Shirts in Italy and the Brown Shirts in Germany to secure and maintain power. The good of the nation is constantly extolled, and the threat of war is used as a means both to promote unity and demonstrate national superiority.

The fascist regimes of Italy and Germany, under Benito Mussolini and Adolf Hitler, respectively, accommodated the Roman Catholic Church and allowed it to function. In Germany, most Protestant churches were induced to support the fascist state.

Fascism was also the political ideology of General Francisco Franco (1892–1975). In the Spanish Civil War of the 1930s, Franco led a revolt against the democratic socialists and communists who controlled the government of the Spanish Republic. In the civil war that ensued, Franco received

Art and Politics

Guernica: "A Monumental Outcry of Human Grief"

In April 1936, the Spanish-born artist Pablo Picasso was commissioned by Spain to produce a mural for its pavilion at the 1937 World's Fair. A year later, Picasso had produced nothing—until April 26, 1937. On that day, the German *Luftwaffe*'s Condor Legion, on loan to Francisco Franco from Adolf Hitler, destroyed the Spanish Basque village of Guernica in three hours. Bombers dropped 100,000 pounds of high explosive and incendiary (fire) bombs. Guernica burned for three days, and more than 1,800 people were killed. It was the first time in history that a civilian population had been attacked from the air without military reason. When news of the bombing reached Picasso in Paris, his reaction to the atrocity was to paint.

Within three months, Picasso had created a 7.5- by 3.5-metre mural. Painted entirely in black, white, and grey, *Guernica* shows a nightmarish scene of men, women, children, and animals shattered by bombardment. English art historian Herbert Read described the work as "a cry of outrage and horror amplified by a great genius."

After the World's Fair, the painting was shown throughout Europe and North America to warn of the danger of fascism. Picasso would not allow his painting to be displayed in Spain until after the death of Franco in 1975.

The United Nations building in New York displays a large copy of *Guernica* near the entrance to the Security Council. In January 2003, it was covered by a curtain while US Secretary of State Colin Powell gave a press conference in which he advocated war against Iraq.

Questions

1. *Guernica* does not depict the aggressor. What might this say about the nature of warfare?
2. When asked to interpret his painting, Picasso said, "The public who look at the picture must interpret the symbols as they understand them." Examine the painting. What symbols do you see? What might they represent?
3. Why do you think *Guernica* was covered during Powell's press conference? Who do you think ordered it to be covered? Research this issue on the Internet.

Figure 2.11 *Guernica* (1937), Pablo Picasso's denunciation of war and its horrors.

millitary aid from Hitler and Mussolini. The supporters of the republic were aided by democratic socialists from Western countries and the communist government of the Soviet Union.

Fifteen hundred Canadian volunteers fought for the republican side as part of the Mackenzie–Papineau Battalion. Other Canadians, such as Norman Bethune, worked for the republican side in medical units. Franco won the Spanish Civil War. Using support from the Catholic Church and government-controlled trade unions, he led an authoritarian government that survived until his death.

Franco was often called a fascist by his enemies, but as George Orwell argued in a 1946 essay, the word fascism, in the post-war world, had lost all meaning, except as "something not desirable."

Figure 2.12 The economic spectrum.

Check YOUR UNDERSTANDING

1. Why did Marx view religion as a conspiracy by the bourgeoisie to keep workers submissive?
2. How have communist governments tried to achieve the socialist goal of economic equality? How successful have they been?
3. How do socialist governments attempt to lessen the income gap between rich and poor?
4. How does democratic socialism differ from communism?
5. Name five manifestations of democratic socialism in Canada's federal and provincial government programs.
6. Why does capitalist theory advocate keeping government's role to a minimum?
7. According to free-enterprise capitalism, how do all people benefit from the laws of the marketplace?
8. How are people kept happy in a fascist state?

Blended Ideologies

As you have seen, when ideologies are placed on a political spectrum, some overlapping becomes obvious. For example, conservatism, on the right, may embrace some ideas from socialism on the left. Communism, on the left, may share some of the traditional moral values of conservatism on the right. One reason for overlaps is that each ideology deals with a somewhat different set of ideas.

Language and Politics

The Short Satire: "Two Cows"

Satire is a form of humour that is often used to mock established institutions. All political ideologies have been satirized at one time or another. Consider the effectiveness of the following satirical piece:

Under *communism*, you have two cows; the government seizes them and provides you with sour milk.

Under *democracy*, you have two cows; your neighbours decide who gets the milk.

Under *capitalism*, you sell one cow, buy a bull, and build a herd of cows.

Under *democratic socialism*, the government owns the cows but allows you to sell some of the milk.

Under *fascism*, the government takes one cow, sells you its milk, and gives the other cow to the army.

Questions

1. Analyze the role of brevity and repetition in this political satire.
2. Analyze the bias in this political satire.
3. Use both brevity and repetition to satirize the viewpoint of a liberal, conservative, fascist, and communist government in relation to one of the following topics: rap music, genetically altered food, the death penalty, or cloning.

"There's not a dime's worth of difference between the candidates. They're both carnivores."

Figure 2.13

Figure 2.14 Canada's major political parties are so centrist that it is hard to tell a "red Tory" (Joe Clark) from a "blue Liberal" (Paul Martin).

Many political parties, especially those near the centre of the left–right spectrum, adopt blended political and economic philosophies. In Canada, liberalism cannot be strictly equated with Liberal Party philosophy. Nor can conservatism be strictly equated with the platform of the Conservative Party. The Liberal Party in Canada has included members with a conservative political bent. For example, Paul Martin, selected as leader of the federal Liberal Party in 2003, cut funding for social programs when he was finance minister. Similarly, the Conservative Party has included members with a liberal political philosophy, who are often called "red Tories." For example, Joe Clark, the leader of the Progressive Conservative Party until 2003, emphasized the need for economic and social equality in Canada. In fact, it is ideologically possible to imagine Paul Martin as leader of the Conservative Party of Canada and Joe Clark as leader of the Liberal Party.

Political leaders outside Canada have also repositioned their parties on the political spectrum in reaction to such new realities as increased international trade and the interdependency of world economies. Starting in the late 1990s, both Tony Blair in Britain and Gerhard Schroeder in Germany followed centrist and right-of-centre policies while leading parties—Labour and the Social Democrats, respectively—that had been traditionally left of centre.

Some political scientists have suggested that traditional classifications such as "left" and "right" are no longer meaningful in today's complex world. Although these terms are still broadly useful in political discussions, a more complex spectrum attempts to combine political, economic, and social dimensions.

For example, in Figure 2.15, the authoritarianism of Joseph Stalin may be placed in the upper left quadrant and that of Augusto Pinochet in the upper right quadrant. With their emphasis on the rights of the individual over the state, Tibet's Dalai Lama and India's Mahatma Gandhi might be placed in

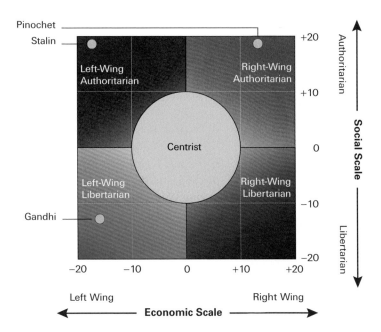

Figure 2.15 The political compass. This graph allows a more complex appreciation of the dynamics between political/economic views and social attitudes.

the lower left quadrant. Members of Canada's Libertarian Party would be placed in the lower right quadrant.

Check Your Understanding

1. Why is it possible to imagine Paul Martin as leader of the Conservative Party and Joe Clark as leader of the Liberal Party?
2. How have leaders in Canada and other countries repositioned their parties in recent years?

Ideologies in Canadian Political Parties

In Canada, a political party is an organization that seeks to control the government by being elected to power. The party's ideology keeps its organization intact and attracts voters. The following section briefly examines Canada's major political parties and their ideologies.

Progressive Conservative Party

The Conservative Party originated before Confederation and gave Canada its first prime minister, John A. Macdonald. At that time, it favoured high tariffs, assistance to big business, and a strong British presence in Canada. In the late 19th century, the Conservative Party devised a National Policy

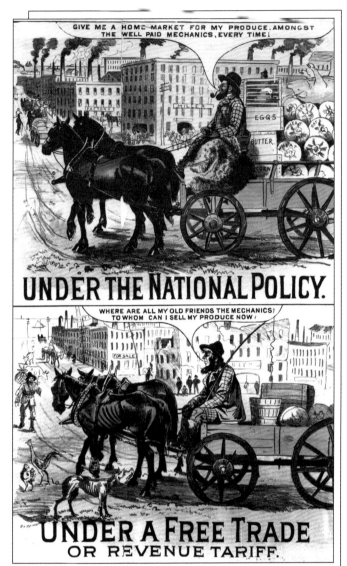

Figure 2.16 The National Policy was the rallying cry of Sir John A. Macdonald's successful 1878 election campaign.

that protected Canadian industry, supported railway construction, and increased Western settlement. It sought an east–west economic axis to defend Canada from the southern pull of American influences.

The Conservative Party's championing of British traditions hurt its fortunes in French Canada. The hanging of French-speaking Métis leader Louis Riel for treason, in 1885, and the imposition of conscription during World War I, also added to its unpopularity. In addition, its failure to find strong francophone party leaders made electing Conservative MPs in Quebec difficult. Brian Mulroney, a bilingual Quebecker, was Conservative prime minister from 1984 to 1993. The party collapsed after that time partly because it could not maintain a strong foundation in Quebec.

The Conservative Party adopted the adjective "Progressive" in 1942 in an attempt to present a reformist image. At this time, the party was probably slightly to the right of the Liberals, Canada's other major political party. For the most part, the Progressive Conservatives supported the social welfare and human rights measures introduced by the Liberals. Progressive Conservative Prime Minister John Diefenbaker introduced Canada's first *Bill of Rights* in 1960. The party's commitment to human rights was emphasized in 1988 by the apology and compensation it offered to Japanese Canadians who had been interned and whose property had been confiscated during World War II. Conservative ideology opposes large-scale government intervention in the economy. However, Conservative administrations created such large government institutions as the Canadian National Railroads, the Canadian Radio Broadcasting Commission (now the Canadian Broadcasting Corporation), and the Bank of Canada.

In December 2003, members of the Progressive Conservative Party voted to merge with the Canadian Alliance Party to create the Conservative Party of Canada. This was precipitated by the declining electoral fortunes of the Progressive Conservatives in the 1993, 1997, and 2000 federal elections and by the failure of the Canadian Alliance Party to secure votes east of Manitoba in the 2000 election (see Reform Party and Canadian Alliance Party, page 62).

Liberal Party

The Liberal Party originated with a reform tradition and a willingness to look outside the British political model. The Liberal Party has always paid special attention to the aspirations of francophone Canadians. From its earliest history, the party selected francophone leaders from Quebec: Wilfrid Laurier, Louis St. Laurent, Pierre Trudeau, and Jean Chrétien. This strategy translated into frequent election victories.

The Liberal Party's historical approach to French Canada placed it to the left of the Conservative Party. The Liberals further consolidated their position on the left by introducing federal programs to improve economic equality: baby bonuses, unemployment insurance, old age security, university student loans, and national health care. The Liberals introduced policies of bilingualism and multiculturalism. Under Liberal Prime Minister Pierre Trudeau, the *Canadian Charter of Rights and Freedoms* was entrenched in the Canadian constitution in 1982. However, sensing a public swing toward conservative economic values in the last decade of the 20th century, the party shifted to the right. It cut back government spending in an effort to eliminate deficits and shelved new social programs, such as a national daycare program.

Rise of Third Parties

When the Conservatives and the Liberals were unable to relieve the economic difficulties of the 1920s and 1930s, **third parties** came into existence. The following section examines the Progressive Party, the Co-operative Commonwealth Federation (CCF), and the Social Credit Party, Canada's major third parties from this era.

Progressive Party

In the 1921 federal election, the Progressive Party won 65 seats and formed the official opposition by appealing to farmers in the West, Ontario, and New Brunswick. The sudden rise of a third party acted as a wakeup call for the governing Liberal Party, which adjusted its platform to appeal to Progressive followers. Thomas Crerar, the Progressive leader in 1921, was eventually persuaded to become a Liberal cabinet minister.

Co-operative Commonwealth Federation (CCF)

The CCF, established in 1933, sought to replace unregulated capitalism with a socialized economy in which the principal means of production and distribution would be owned and operated by the people. The Western provinces had suffered greatly during the Depression, and the CCF was a strong voice of third-party protest.

THE WEB

Learn more about Canada's political parties at www.emp.ca/cwp.

Grassroots Politics and Protest

James Shaver Woodsworth and the CCF

James Shaver Woodsworth, son of a Methodist minister, was born in 1874 in Etobicoke, Ontario. In 1885, the family moved to Manitoba. Woodsworth was later ordained a minister and worked with the poor in Winnipeg. A socialist and pacifist, Woodsworth was fired from a government position for opposing conscription during World War I. For a short time, he worked as a longshoreman on the docks in Vancouver, but the General Strike in 1919 brought him back to Winnipeg. There he became editor of the *Western Labour News* and organized the Manitoba Independent Labour Party. In 1921, Woodsworth was elected to the House of Commons for Winnipeg North Centre. In 1925, the Liberal Party needed Woodsworth's vote to stay in power. In return for his support, the government passed Canada's first *Old Age Pension Act* in 1927.

During the Depression, Woodsworth and the Independent Labour Party united with other labour groups to form the CCF, a new socialist party. Woodsworth was chosen as its first leader. The new party published the *Regina Manifesto*, which outlined its goals: to replace the "inherent injustice and inhumanity" of capitalism with a "social order" that would eliminate class exploitation and allow for "genuine democratic self-government." The manifesto also advocated public ownership of key industries and the creation of a welfare state (universal pensions, health insurance, family allowances, unemployment insurance, and workers' compensation).

In the 1935 federal election, the CCF received 8.9 percent of the vote and sent seven members to the House of Commons. In 1939, Woodsworth opposed Canada's entry into World War II but was not supported by the members of his party. He was re-elected in 1940, but he suffered a series of strokes and died in Winnipeg in 1942.

Perhaps the best tribute to James S. Woodsworth came from Prime Minister Mackenzie King during the debate on Canada's decision to declare war: "I admire him in my heart, because time and again he has had the courage to say what lay on his conscience, regardless of what the world might think of him. A man of that calibre is an ornament to any parliament."

Questions

1. What most impresses you about Woodsworth's life? Why?
2. Read the *Regina Manifesto* Sound Bite on page 49, and rephrase it in your own words.
3. Find the *Regina Manifesto* at www.emp.ca/cwp and summarize its key points. Where would you place the document on the political spectrum? Explain your response.

Figure 2.17 J.S. Woodsworth speaks to workers preparing to strike, 1935.

Social Credit Party

Another voice of Western protest emanated from the Social Credit Party, which came to power in Alberta in 1935. Led by William Aberhart, the party advocated the granting of a monthly "social dividend or credit" of $25 to every voter. The dividend was designed to create more consumer spending and to stimulate the economy. But the provincial program was never implemented because fiscal and monetary policies are federal responsibilities. The Social Credit Party governed Alberta and British Columbia for almost four decades. Beginning in 1935, Social Credit usually elected between 10 and 20 MPs, winning a record 30 seats in 1962. The party evolved into a **grassroots** conservative party, often expressing regional discontent from the West and from Quebec. (Grassroots refers to political actions undertaken by ordinary individuals and groups, as opposed to large organizations or powerful individuals.) It disappeared from the federal scene after the 1979 election. Some followers found a home in the Reform Party of the 1990s.

Modern Third Parties

Like their early counterparts, modern third parties arose because of voter discontent with established parties. The following section examines the origin and evolution of the New Democratic Party (NDP), the Bloc Québécois, and the Reform Party.

THE WEB

Learn why Tommy Douglas topped the CBC's *Greatest Canadians* list for weeks at www.emp.ca/cwp.

New Democratic Party

In 1961, the merger of the CCF and the unions in the Canadian Labour Congress created the New Democratic Party (NDP). The NDP has formed provincial governments in British Columbia, Saskatchewan, Manitoba, and Ontario. Historically, the party is to the left of the Liberal Party on the political spectrum. However, in order to gain power in provincial politics, the NDP has shifted to the right in recent years like other parties. At the federal level, the NDP is considered a third party, with little likelihood of forming the government. From 1972 to 1974, the NDP supported the minority government of Pierre Trudeau. During this time, it persuaded the Liberals to introduce some social democratic measures, such as the establishment of the government-owned oil company Petro-Canada.

Figure 2.18 T.C. (Tommy) Douglas is carried in triumph after being chosen first leader of the NDP, 1961. Supporting him are trade unionist Claude Jodoin (left), national CCF president David Lewis (centre), and British Labour leader Hugh Gaitskell.

Bloc Québécois

The Bloc Québécois has a single focus: sovereignty for Quebec. The party was formed in 1990 by disaffected members of the Conservative and Liberal parties who came together under the leadership of former Conservative cabinet minister Lucien Bouchard. In the 1994 federal election, the Bloc won 54 seats and became the official opposition in Parliament. In the next elections, its representation dropped to 44 and then to 38 seats. The Bloc rebounded to 54 seats in the 2004 election. On many issues, the Bloc leans to the left. However, as a single-issue party promoting Quebec sovereignty, the Bloc attracts voters from both the left and the right. A declining interest in sovereignty in the early 21st century presented a challenge to a party with such a narrow ideological focus. (See Chapter 4.)

Reform Party and Canadian Alliance Party

The Reform Party of Canada arose in 1987 because of Western Canadian discontent with Liberal and Progressive Conservative policies. The founder and first leader of the Reform Party was Preston Manning. From the beginning, the party adopted a strong free-market and limited-government stance. It promised tax reduction and repayment of the national debt. It sought to have senators elected to the Canadian Senate. It criticized government extravagance. On social policies, the party tended to downplay the full-equality aspirations of such groups as French Canadians, women, and homosexuals. The party also opposed gun control. When the 1993 Canadian federal election reduced the Progressive Conservative Party's representation from 169 to 2 seats in the House of Commons, the Reform Party moved into the vacuum created on the centre-right. Reform won 54 seats, only one representing a victory east of the Ontario–Manitoba border. In 1997, the Reform Party became the official opposition in Parliament.

To attract more voters, the Reform Party evolved into the Canadian Alliance Party in 2000 and elected former Alberta cabinet minister Stockwell Day its new leader. In the 2000 federal election, the Canadian Alliance remained the official opposition, winning 66 seats. The Liberal Party adopted some Reform–Alliance principles, such as reducing government spending and eliminating deficits, in the 1990s. Many commentators believe that the Canadian Alliance was too far right to gain support from centrist voters. In December 2003, the Canadian Alliance Party merged with the Progressive Conservative Party to form the new Conservative Party of Canada. The new party's first elected leader was Stephen Harper.

Figure 2.19 Political cartoonists sharpened their pencils at the news in December 2003 that the Canadian Alliance and Progressive Conservative parties were merging.

PARTY POLITICS

The Rhinoceros Party

The Rhinoceros Party of Canada embodies political satire. It was founded in 1963 by a group of humourists, led by Jacques Ferron, to poke fun at politicians and the federal government. It participated in every election until 1993, when new electoral rules made it difficult to recruit candidates. In the 1984 federal election, it received 99,207 votes across Canada.

The party adopted the rhinoceros as its symbol because of the animal's thick skin and predisposition "to wallow around in the mud." Its most important electoral promise was to break its promises in the manner of other parties. The Rhinos also pledged that its first elected member would sell her seat to the highest bidder. As early as the 1970s, the Rhinos had a solution to Canada's growing national debt: legalize marijuana and tax its use.

The Rhinos enlivened election campaigns with promises to place an "import quota on lousy winters" and repeal the law of gravity. Their researchers scoured federal, provincial, and municipal legislation and found that no law passed since 1867 contained the word "fun." The presence of the Rhinos, however, kept the principle of fun alive in the Canadian political arena for many years.

Questions

1. In what way is the Rhinoceros Party a form of political satire?
2. What is the purpose of fringe political parties such as the Rhinoceros Party? Should they be allowed to run candidates in an election? Why or why not?

Check Your Understanding

1. Describe similarities between the Conservative and Liberal parties.
2. Some people view the New Democratic Party as the "conscience" of Parliament. Do you agree with this description? Explain your view.
3. How does the Bloc Québécois attract voters from both sides of the political spectrum?
4. Describe the ideological differences between the Canadian Alliance and the Progressive Conservative parties.

Ideologies Outside Political Parties: Think Tanks and Citizen Coalitions

The Council of Canadians and the Fraser Institute are two institutions that exist for the purpose of influencing Canadian citizens and governments. Working from different ideological positions, both organizations try to affect public awareness by such means as press releases, speeches, and online discussions.

Council of Canadians

The Council of Canadians was founded in 1985 to promote Canadian sovereignty and social democracy. It aims to safeguard social programs, promote economic justice, advance alternatives to corporate free trade, and preserve the environment. With 100,000 members and over 70 local chapters, the council sees itself as the advocate of ordinary Canadians who share its concerns. The council is a non-profit organization that operates on volunteer time, energy, and donations. To raise awareness and create change, local chapters organize demonstrations, host public events, lobby their MPs, facilitate discussion groups, share council campaign information, and write letters to the editors of local newspapers. Maud Barlow, chair of the Council of Canadians, has come to represent the ideals of the organization in the public eye.

In the 1988 federal election campaign, the council warned that the *Free Trade Agreement* (FTA) with the United States would damage Canada's econ-

Figure 2.20 Targeted advertising: The Council of Canadians erected this billboard just outside the Ottawa offices of Finance Minister Paul Martin in 1998.

omy, culture, social programs, and environment. The council also campaigned against cutbacks to the CBC and social programs, the deregulation of the energy industry, and the 1994 *North American Free Trade Agreement* (NAFTA). In 1998, the council helped defeat the Multilateral Agreement on Investment (MAI). Had the MAI been adopted, it would have greatly increased the rights of global businesses at the expense of democratic national governments.

Convinced that concentration of power harms ordinary Canadians, the council has fought against bank and media mergers. It has campaigned against genetically engineered foods and warned against introducing bovine growth hormone into the milk supply. Protecting Canada's universally accessible health care from privatization is one of its chief concerns. The council has also campaigned against the misuse of the world's water and bulk export of Canada's freshwater. It advocates that citizens hold governments responsible for establishing new strategies based on watershed management, conservation, and equity.

Fraser Institute

The Fraser Institute is an independent public policy organization, founded in 1974, that advocates the economic and social benefits of free-market competition. Known as a **think tank**, it brings together academics, economists, and policy analysts from around the world. The institute releases policy statements on topics such as **free trade**, government debt, welfare reform, **privatization**, taxation, education, poverty, deregulation, and health care. It has no links to any political party and relies on individual and corporate sponsors for support.

Economic freedom, a major theme in the institute's press releases, is perceived as the pursuit of economic activity without government interference and with security of property rights, the right to personal choice, and lower taxes. The institute advocates "market dynamics" within the public health care system. It sees the FTA and NAFTA as steps in the right direction, which raised the overall standard of living for Canadians. In 2003, it questioned the concerns of "climate alarmists" in the context of the *Kyoto Protocol*, the international agreement designed to reduce the emission of greenhouse gases. The institute publishes school ratings in various provinces and stresses the right of parents to choose the schools their children will attend. It also supports tax credits for parents who send their children to private schools. According to the institute, if education is viewed as a marketplace, with schools competing for students, the educational system and results will improve.

Figure 2.21 Canadian Alliance MP Preston Manning addresses the annual meeting of the Fraser Institute in 2001.

Check Your Understanding

1. Where would you place the Council of Canadians and the Fraser Institute on the political spectrum? Use examples to explain your decision.
2. Which political parties in Canada would support these organizations? Why?
3. Do you believe it would be preferable if Canadians paid less tax and had fewer government services? Divide into two groups: those who answer "yes" and those who answer "no." Devise a strategy consisting of 10 arguments that might be used in a formal debate on the subject.

Other Ideologies Affecting Politics in Canada

Historically, Canadian politics has been strongly influenced by ideologies coming from Britain and the United States. Feminism, environmentalism, and nationalism—ideologies with both domestic and international histories—have also influenced Canadian politics.

British Influence

Conservatism was the dominant political philosophy in the colonies of British North America. In the late 18th century, the United Empire Loyalists—people who were loyal to the British monarch—moved north from the Thirteen Colonies to escape the republican aspirations of the American Revolution (see Chapter 5). They brought with them a strong attachment to tradition and monarchy. These people sought "peace, order, and good government" in Canada, and rejected the "life, liberty, and pursuit of happiness" philosophy of the future United States.

British adherence to an established church was reflected in the predominant role the Anglican Church played in Upper Canada. In its first century as a country, Canada reflected many of the conservative elements of British society. For example, Victorian-era laws restricted the use of alcohol, and pride in British imperial history was taught in schools. Organizations such as the Monarchist League of Canada and the Imperial Order of the Daughters of the Empire (IODE) are continuing reminders of Canada's British ideological connections.

Leftist ideas also came to Canada from Britain in reformist sentiments about **responsible government** and the **separation of church and state**. The Earl of Durham (1792–1840) was known as "Radical Jack" in England because he supported democratization in British politics. When he came to investigate rebellions in Upper and Lower Canada, he recommended the same approach be adopted in governing the two Canadas. In the 20th century, immigrants initiated activism in Canada through trade unionism and socialism. British immigrant Abraham Albert Heaps was arrested eight years

Figure 2.22 British trade unionism helped unite workers across the city during the Winnipeg General Strike of 1919.

THE WEB
Learn more about the Winnipeg General Strike and labour unrest in Canada at www.emp.ca/cwp.

after he arrived on a charge of seditious conspiracy for being a leader in the Winnipeg General Strike of 1919. Heaps was acquitted and later elected to Parliament, where he served for 15 years as an advocate for labour and social reforms.

Another British ideological influence was economist John Maynard Keynes, whose theories eventually won wide acceptance in the 1930s. Keynes believed that in times of **recession**, when the economy did not grow, governments should lower interest rates and increase spending to stimulate growth. During economic upturns, when the economy grew, governments should raise interest rates and pay back the money borrowed to finance the spending from recessionary times.

The Labour government elected in Britain in 1945 was one of the most leftist in 20th century British history. It **nationalized** such industries as coal, electricity, gas, railways, and steel. It instituted a comprehensive welfare state that provided health care and aid for the unemployed, the aged, the sick, and the handicapped. Inspired at least partially by British ideas, Canadians constructed their own welfare state some 15 to 20 years after the appearance of the British model. David Lewis, a longtime CCF theorist and later an NDP leader, was influenced by British Labour Party ideas while attending Oxford University.

Keynesian economics enjoyed popular acceptance in many countries until the 1980s. Governments, including most in Canada, followed some Keynesian theories in financing deficits, but ignored others by failing to pay back deficits. Politicians sometimes courted votes by promising new programs, which were then financed with borrowed money. By the 1980s, many governments had accumulated massive debts, and Keynesian ideology was widely discredited. In Britain, Prime Minister Margaret Thatcher carried the philosophy of **neoconservatism** into government. Her administration tried to reduce the role and size of government and **privatized** many government-owned enterprises. These measures led to less emphasis on social welfare and equality. In Canada, the federal governments of Brian Mulroney and Jean Chrétien and some provincial governments adopted many of the policies advocated by neoconservatives in Britain and elsewhere.

American Influence

THE WEB

Learn more about the life and career of William Lyon Mackenzie at www.emp.ca/cwp.

American ideologies have influenced Canada's politics throughout its history. William Lyon Mackenzie, a reformer who opposed the oligarchic government of Upper Canada, was inspired by American ideas of representative democracy. His second newspaper, the *Constitution*, openly advocated republicanism. Mackenzie, who was the first mayor of Toronto, led an armed rebellion in 1837 in an attempt to overthrow the government of Upper Canada. His actions and those of other reformers induced Britain to introduce responsible government to the North American colonies. The American political system also influenced the architects of Canada's Confederation in 1867. They rejected the "states' rights" principles of the United States in favour of a strong federal government, which would hold all residual powers. To avoid the decentralizing tendencies of the US constitution, the Canadian constitution was designed to create a stronger federal government.

During the early 20th century, American reformers attempted to shift more power to the people and away from elected politicians. Two democratic innovations were introduced in this period: the referendum and the **recall**. The binding referendum allows citizens to dictate the outcome of important issues by means of a yes–no vote. The recall allows citizens to recall from office a politician who has been unresponsive to the needs of constituents. Referenda have been used in Canada at both the federal and provincial levels. For example, referenda concerning secession were held in Quebec in 1980 and 1995, and a national referendum concerning the Charlottetown constitutional amendments was held in 1992. British Columbia has a mechanism for representative recall. If enough voters in a particular riding or constituency sign a petition, a member of the legislature can be recalled in a special by-election. In 1993, the election platform of the Reform Party of Canada promised to institute both the binding referendum and the recall at the federal level.

Facing re-election during the Depression in the 1930s, Canadian Prime Minister R.B. Bennett copied the **New Deal** program of US President Franklin D. Roosevelt. The New Deal was a major shift away from a free-market economy toward an economy that relied on government intervention to create employment and wealth. Bennett's conversion, however, failed to win him re-election in 1935. In the second half of the 20th century, government involvement in economic and social welfare expanded more fully in Canada than in the United States, where emphasis on individual freedom and responsibility prevailed in economic decision making and health care.

Feminism: Ideology and Social Movement

Feminism is an ideology that evolved principally in Western societies. It is based on the belief that women and men should be treated equally in all aspects of life: legal, economic, political, cultural, and social.

English teacher and author Mary Wollstonecraft (1759–97) expressed a feminist ideology in 1792 in her book *A Vindication of the Rights of Woman*. Wollstonecraft argued that women are equal to men and therefore should have equal rights in education, the vote, property, and profession. In his 1869 essay "The Subjection of Women," English philosopher John Stuart Mill had argued that women should be freed from domestic servitude and allowed to compete equally with men. Women should possess complete legal equality, and marriage should be an equal partnership. Emmeline Pankhurst (1858–1928), who founded the Women's Franchise League in England with her daughters and supporters, used civil disobedience and broke laws to obtain voting rights for women before World War I.

Emily Stowe (1831–1903), Canada's first woman physician, founded the Canadian Women's Suffrage (right to vote) Movement in 1876. Author and activist Nellie McClung (1873–1951) fought for women's suffrage and organized *Mock Parliament*, a satirical theatrical production that reversed the roles of men and women. The 1914 production in Winnipeg depicted disenfranchised men humbly asking women law makers for the right to vote. Emily Murphy (1868–1933), another Canadian early advocate for feminism, became the first female magistrate in the British Empire in 1916. Some Canadian women obtained the right to vote in federal elections in 1918. Early expressions of feminism—such as those in the work of Stowe, McClung, and Murphy—are sometimes referred to as "first-wave feminism." These works were part of a British and North American **social movement** that focused on the abolition of slavery and voting rights for women between 1849 and 1919.

Social movements are informal networks of individuals and groups whose shared values and identity lead them to undertake collective action to expand the boundaries of the political system. Those people involved in a social movement ("activists") hope that their values and identities, which have been neglected, will be recognized and accommodated. New social movements are usually grassroots: they work outside traditional political channels and challenge the conventional attitudes and behaviours of government and society (see Chapter 7).

Second-wave feminism is sometimes called **women's liberation** or the "women's movement." It began in 1963 with the appearance of US journalist Betty Friedan's book, *The Feminine Mystique*. Friedan argued that women did not necessarily reach their fullest potential by washing the whitest

SOUND BITE   "It is time to effect a revolution in female manners—time to restore to them their lost dignity—and make them, as a part of the human species, labour by reforming themselves to reform the world."

Mary Wollstonecraft,
A Vindication of the
Rights of Woman, *1792*

THE WEB

Learn more about pay equity at www.emp.ca/cwp.

laundry or cooking the tastiest dinners. In a survey she conducted of female classmates from Smith College 15 years after graduation, Friedan found many were profoundly dissatisfied in their lives. She concluded that women must be free to realize their full potential in both private and public spheres: society and government must replace arbitrary sex-based definitions with the recognition of individual gifts, regardless of gender.

The feminist philosophy of Friedan and others eventually affected Canada in many ways. Governments introduced **pay equity** (equal pay for work of equal value) programs and pregnancy leave benefits. Federal and provincial human rights codes prohibited discrimination on the basis of sex. Family law was changed to reflect the equality of partners in marriage. Birth control and abortion became more accessible. There was also an increased emphasis on the use of gender-inclusive language; "letter carriers" replaced "postmen," for example.

Near the end of the 1960s, "equality feminism" was influenced by radical feminism. This held that women's oppression was rooted in **patriarchy**, the rule by men in all aspects of society, including government, business, and education. Radical feminists viewed sexual violence and harassment against women as a means of social control. Rape became a metaphor for the physical, economic, and spiritual treatment of women.

Some radical feminists advocated separation of the sexes, suggesting, for example, that only female journalists and photographers should cover women's issues and politics. This demand led to more women being hired in previously male-dominated areas, such as the media. Other radical feminists saw lesbianism as a political statement. From lesbian separatists came the term "women-identified women," meaning women whose main friendships and emotional support come from other women. For many radical feminists, "the personal is political" became the principal slogan of the 1970s. Areas previously considered personal, such as housework and child care, were now seen as political issues.

Third-wave feminism is a global ideology that developed around 1990. It is based on recognition of cultural and racial diversity and the importance of environmental issues. Third-wave feminists suggest that equality feminism and radical feminism ignore the experiences of non-Western women, who may find that their gender oppression is secondary to racial, cultural, or class oppression.

Feminism, in its many shades, has profoundly affected every aspect of Canadian life. Parliament has changed sexual assault laws to remove biases that favour men. It has enacted an anti-stalking law. Human rights codes now specifically target sexual harassment as a form of discrimination. In the 1992 Supreme Court decision *R v. Butler*, the court was persuaded by the feminist argument that pornography is harmful to society because it degrades women. Government support for women's shelters and rape-crisis centres, which began in the 1970s, is further evidence of the impact of feminist thinking on Canadian society. However, as Canada enters the 21st century, a national system of government-sponsored child care is not yet a reality.

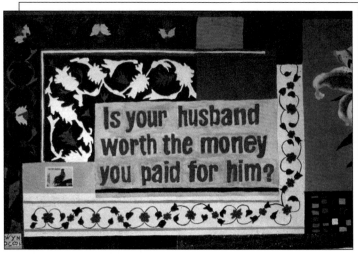

Figure 2.23 Toronto artist Sarindar Dhaliwal often uses autobiography in her work. This detail from *Indian Billboard*, a 1990 mixed-media piece, refers to a woman's dowry, the practice in many cultures that obligates a bride's family to give money, property, or both to the groom.

Environmentalism

Environmentalism has roots in Canada, but the belief system has been affected by ideological influences from outside Canada. In a broad sense, environmentalism involves preservation and care of the environment by human beings. People can express an environmentalist philosophy by, for example, driving a fuel-efficient automobile or taking action to preserve an ecological area. Greenpeace, a non-governmental organization (NGO) founded in British Columbia in 1971, was an early activist organization in the **environmental movement**. Greenpeace objectives include ending nuclear testing, suspending international commercial whaling, and preserving ancient forests. The movement is widespread in Canada, with more than 1,000 environmental organizations.

Political parties devoted to environmental issues emerged in the 1970s. The term "Green Party" was first used by the German Green Party in the national election of 1980. Green parties now exist in most countries, including

Figure 2.24 Environment Minister David Anderson poses for photographs with members of Greenpeace dressed as polar bears in Ottawa, just before the parliamentary vote on the *Kyoto Accord*, 2002.

Canada, and exchange ideas. Ecological conservation, grassroots democracy, social justice, and non-violence were the four original principles of the German Green Party. **Ecology** is a science that examines the interactions between living things and the environment. **Social justice** involves upholding human rights, and non-violence emphasizes the development of human relationships without force.

In 1993, in Clayoquot (pronounced klak-wit) Sound, British Columbia, environmentalists mounted a huge protest against forestry practices in the province. Temperature and precipitation in the area have created rainforests that are more than 1,000 years old. Over 12,000 people from Canada and elsewhere joined in demonstrations and blockades to prevent industrial logging. First Nations in the region were vigorous participants in the campaign and sought to maintain their ancient relationship with the natural environment. Environmentalists did not achieve their main objective—to halt all logging in Clayoquot Sound—but they forced logging companies and the British Columbia government to change their methods and exempt a portion of the forest from harvesting.

Today, environmentalism is part of public consciousness. Environmental threats are regularly debated publicly in Canada and other countries. International studies that deal, for example, with pesticides, the ozone layer, and global warming affect environmental philosophy and government policies in Canada. At each level of government in Canada, large-scale projects rarely proceed without an environmental impact study. The *Kyoto Protocol*, an international plan to reduce carbon dioxide emissions into the atmosphere, has created much debate in Canada and other countries (see Chapter 9).

Nationalism

Nationalism is a feeling of attachment and loyalty to a particular nation, society, or territory, and strong support for its interests. As an ideology, it has affected Canada and many other parts of the world. It will be examined in Chapter 4.

Check YOUR UNDERSTANDING

1. Cite examples of British and American influences in Canada today. Consider cultural as well as political influences.
2. What is Keynesian economic theory? Why did its popularity diminish in the 1980s?
3. Do you agree or disagree that a mechanism to remove politicians from office partway through their term is beneficial? Why or why not?
4. Outline the differences between equality feminism and radical feminism. How has each brought about change for Canadian society?

METHODS OF POLITICAL INQUIRY

Assessing Point of View in Photojournalism

Consider the Pulitzer Prize–winning photograph in Figure 2.25. In a single photo, student John Filo presented a poignant image of the human cost of protest. But do photographs always provide truthful accounts of events?

Photojournalism is not neutral: it conveys point of view. Consider the following crucial stages of photojournalism: (1) the set-up of a shot, (2) the alteration of an image, and (3) the publication of the image.

When setting up a shot, the photographer makes many decisions. What is the content? Should a photograph about war, for example, show many bodies or none? What lens should be used? A zoom lens shows details of a subject's expression, while a wide-angle lens shows an entire scene. How does the photographic angle affect the drama of the shot? What kind of lighting is appropriate for the desired mood? Is the photo posed or candid?

Once a photo has been taken, the photographer may alter the image by burning or dodging (adding light or shade) and by adjusting the colour through saturation, brightness, and contrast. News photographers have an ethical obligation not to mislead the viewer; however, they commonly seek to persuade. A photographer may also alter an image by cropping—that is, by showing only a portion of a photo to heighten the desired impact or to remove unwanted details. With digital imaging, profound alteration is possible since significant components of a photograph may be added or removed.

Once a photographer submits an image for publication, an editor makes a number of decisions. Is the photo placed on the front page or somewhere less prominent? Is it reproduced in large or small format? Does it appear in colour or in black and white? Is the picture juxtaposed with other images? Is it cropped? Does the caption describe "who, what, when, and where," or does it use charged lan-

Figure 2.25 Mary Ann Vecchio kneels over the body of slain student Jeffrey Miller at Kent State University on May 4, 1970. Ohio National Guardsmen fired into a crowd of students protesting the Vietnam war, killing four.

guage to interpret the image? Does the image suggest facts that are not included in the article it accompanies?

How can you, the viewer, judge the photograph's credibility? When you have questions about an image, consider the following:

- How reliable is the source in which it appears (is it in a tabloid or a more respected news source)?
- Does a similar photo appear in various news sources?
- What is the effect of the photo (has it an intellectual or an emotional appeal)?
- What is the point of view of the photographer and the editor?

Applying the Skill

1. Examine several photographs from the front page of your local newspaper. Using the criteria listed above, evaluate their credibility.
2. In small groups, develop a code of ethics for photojournalists. Share your recommendations as a class.
3. Scan a photograph or download one from the Internet. Using a program such as Adobe Photoshop, alter the image. Present both your original and any altered photos to your class. Explain the changes you have made and the effect you sought to create.
4. Visit www.emp.ca/cwp to link to the Poynter Institute of Journalism. Read the article and scroll to "Not Hiding Facts." There you can view various front pages showing the train bombings in Madrid in March 2004. Compare three and comment on how content and design affect the photographs' impact.

SOUND BITE "I worry more about what editors do with my work and how they abuse it than I do about misleading people with my images. [Editors] are more likely to mislead because they are sitting miles away from the events and lack any understanding of the place or situation."

Asim Rafiqui, freelance photographer, 2003

Study Hall

Thinking/Inquiry

1. Read or view one of the following political satires:
   a) the book *Animal Farm* by George Orwell;
   b) the film *Wag the Dog*; or
   c) the CBC television show *This Hour Has 22 Minutes*.
   Write a review, including a brief description of what the satire is about, and analyze its effectiveness.

2. Using a graph similar to the one in Figure 2.15 on page 57, locate each of Canada's major political parties on the grid. Explain your reasoning behind each placement.

3. There is bias subtly woven into the photographic material presented in this chapter. Analyze the point of view represented in the placement, number, and choice of photographs. How would you illustrate this chapter? Either produce original art or find material on the Internet.

4. "Anarchism is a tiny voice of corrective protest. . . . This is why . . . anarcho-feminism and eco-anarchism [have] become the most important new forms of anti-authoritarian thought in recent years, important to anarchism itself and to the larger movements of which they are a part." Respond to this statement using library, Internet, or other resources to explore the influence of anarchism on either feminism or environmentalism.

Communication

5. Look back at Figure 2.1 on page 37. Explain what you think the artist wished to express.

6. Assume that you are a member of a political party that opposes the liberal ideology of the party in power. (Your party's ideology may be conservative, libertarian, socialist, or communist.) The governing party has put forth legislation
   a) abolishing the current two-tier health care system,
   b) requiring mandatory retirement at age 65, and
   c) changing the legal driving age to 18 from 16.
   Choose one issue and write an argument outlining why your party refuses to support the government.

7. Write and illustrate pamphlets to outline the platforms of each of the major political parties in Canada. Remember to keep your language precise and suitable for your audience.

8. In groups of four, select a school issue that concerns you. Create a short drama that illustrates how students with the following political ideologies would react: liberal, conservative, communist, socialist, capitalist, and fascist.

Application

9. You and a small group of classmates have decided that Canada is in need of a new political party. Give that party a name, and design a poster or brochure outlining your party's political ideology.

10. In small groups, select one Canadian woman who has contributed significantly to the battle for equality rights, and create a "Heritage Minute." You may either videotape your segment or present it as a brief drama. Research your subject before writing your script.

11. In small groups, create a list of questions you would like to ask a representative of one of Canada's political parties. Contact a member of your chosen political party at either the federal or the provincial level and arrange to conduct an interview. Report your findings to the class.

Religion and Politics

Figure 3.1 In *Flag for a State of Perpetual Motion* (1988), Canadian artist Joanne Tod uses religious imagery to explore individual identity and the complex relationships within and among peoples.

Agenda

In this chapter, you will consider

• the relationship between politics and religion throughout history

• how people such as Mahatma Gandhi, Mother Teresa, Archbishop Desmond Tutu, and the Dalai Lama have exerted international political influence

• the role of religion in contemporary global politics

• the relationship between church and state in countries such as Iran, France, the United States, China, and Canada, among others

• how to conduct an interview

Every day, religion has an impact on what you see and read in the news. Indeed, many current events cannot be grasped unless you can recognize the role of religion within the *polis*. This chapter will help you develop that awareness by giving a perspective on religions that have shaped values, beliefs, and ideologies around the world. You will also examine the lasting political influence a few individuals have exerted through their religious convictions and actions, both in their own countries and globally. Finally, you will develop a sense of the interplay between organized religion and political institutions as you observe some countries trying to separate church and state, while others try to bring them closer together.

THE WEB

Learn more about religious empires at www.emp.ca/cwp.

Politics and Religion in History

Religion and politics have long intertwined, and the relationship has often been mutually beneficial for religion and state. Religions and their institutions have sometimes needed state protection to survive and grow. Equally, states have needed religion to guide and justify their actions and sometimes morally endorse their policies.

Validation of Rule

Historically, most rulers governed with some form of religious authority. As you learned in Chapter 1, pharaohs in ancient Egypt were believed to be gods on Earth. Rulers in the Inca and Aztec empires were also ascribed god-like powers. Roman emperors in the early centuries of the Common Era ruled through the doctrine of the emperor's divinity. All these rulers publicly practised the religions in question and usually accepted their validity and obligations.

When Emperor Constantine converted to Christianity in 312 CE, that religion gained favoured status within the Roman Empire. When the empire fell in 476 CE, Europe no longer had a dominant **secular state**, but it did have a unifying and central ecclesiastical (church) power: the Christian Church. The Church played a dominant role in medieval politics. It monopolized education and law and possessed great material wealth. The Church influenced monarchs, who ruled under the doctrine of the **divine right of kings**. This held that royal power flowed from God, not from the governed. Deposing a monarch or restricting a monarch's power was thus contrary to God's will.

A concept similar to the divine right of kings was widespread in Asia much earlier. In China, the kings of the Zhou dynasty (1027–256 BCE) and later emperors ruled under the **mandate of heaven**. However, the monarch's power was not absolute. Rulers who behaved poorly offended the mandate of heaven and could be dethroned, and successors did not have to come from the nobility. Although the founders of the Han (202 BCE–220 CE) and Ming (1368–1644) dynasties were commoners, they ruled under the mandate of heaven. In Japan, the sovereign was known at times as "heavenly emperor" and "god-king."

Social Stabilization

Religious belief systems often support social cohesiveness and order. They can create a shared worldview and respect for authority, both of which help make a society governable. Governments have looked to religion to help achieve social stability. In turn, religious institutions have supported governments across the political spectrum, from present-day social justice movements in Latin America, Africa, and the Arab world, to fascist regimes in Italy, Germany, and Spain.

SOUND BITE "Religion is excellent stuff for keeping common people quiet."

Napoleon Bonaparte, emperor of France, 1804–14

In Quebec, for example, the Roman Catholic Church was a powerful social force from the time of New France (1604). It ran the public education system, and through its parishes and associations controlled public morality. By the late 19th century, Quebec, like most of Canada, was 90 percent rural. Church, school, and family were its fundamental social institutions. But Quebec was modernizing, and with that came a rise in liberal values among many business people and politicians. Church leaders in Quebec, however, favoured **ultramontanism**. This ideology upheld the supremacy of religion over civil society and insisted on loyalty to the Church in Rome. Religious leaders in Quebec believed that the Church in France had become too liberal. In 1871, ultramontanists tried—and failed—to form a Catholic political party that would have advocated reforming laws to comply with Church teachings and giving the province's bishops power to oversee civil legislation.

The Catholic Church dominated many aspects of Quebec society until the mid-20th century. Besides running the school system, it invested in real estate and financial markets. Communities such as the Grey Nuns managed hospitals and real estate holdings. The Church's influence began to wane only when the traditionalist Union Nationale gov-

Figure 3.2 *Lazare* (1941), by Jean-Paul Lemieux. The Catholic Church was the bedrock of Quebec society for centuries. Historians still debate whether the influence slowed Quebec's development or offered a different route to modernity.

ernment of Maurice Duplessis, who was premier for almost 30 years, fell to Jean Lesage's Liberals in 1960. Lesage's reforms shifted responsibility for education and social services from the Church to the province and helped usher in the **Quiet Revolution**, which transformed Quebec society.

Check YOUR UNDERSTANDING

1. Explain the doctrines of the divine right of kings and the mandate of heaven. How were they similar and different? Which would you prefer as a governing principle if you were a ruler? Why? If you were a citizen? Why?
2. How have both government and religion benefited from their relationships in the past?
3. In what ways did the Roman Catholic Church provide social stability in Quebec in the 19th and early 20th centuries?

Eastern Religions and Politics

Many religions have been born in the East, and this section will briefly describe three: Hinduism, Confucianism, and Buddhism. Since their rise in Asia, the influence of all three religions has spread worldwide through missionaries and scholars and, in recent decades, through increased immigration.

Hinduism: The Politics of Cosmic Order

Hinduism, the oldest of major world religions, originated in India around 1500 BCE. The Persian word "Hindu" originally described people who lived in the Indus River valley of northwest India. Later, the word was used to describe a belief system. Hinduism has no founder but has many roots and branches. It has influenced and been influenced by other religions. Between 300 and 1200 CE, Hinduism introduced temples, rituals, and vernacular (commonly spoken) languages for worship.

Hindus believe in a single divinity that is present in everything, and in successive reincarnations of the soul. Ultimate reality, or *brahman*, is the life force of the universe: gods and humans, plants and animals, all share in its essence. Through reincarnation, at death a soul passes from one body to another—for example, from a human body to the body of an insect or animal. Good actions in this life lead to a better situation in the next incarnation, while bad actions lead to a worse situation or a lower incarnation.

Hinduism lays out individual rights and duties and rules governing diet, family, caste (hereditary social class), and politics. Because the cosmic order is mirrored in the smallest details of daily life, all decisions—including political ones—are considered religious decisions in some sense. For example, since *brahman* is present in all life, all living creatures are sacred and must not be harmed.

The doctrine of non-violence, or *ahimsa*, was the basis for Mahatma Gandhi's use of **civil disobedience** against British rule before India gained independence in 1947. Some Hindus opposed Gandhi, particularly his efforts to abolish the "untouchability" of the lowest caste. A nationalist organization dedicated to maintaining traditional Hindu practices emerged and evolved into the Bharatiya Janata Party (Indian People's

Figure 3.3 Indian school children dressed as a Sikh (extreme left), Hindu, and Muslim demonstrate for peace and unity in New Delhi in 2002 in the wake of religious violence. The placards at the top, from left to right, read, "India is one, religions are many, God is one, despite many names"; "Humanity is crying, our eyes are full of tears"; and "Rise and make others rise."

Party, or BJP), which governed India from 1998 and lost to the Indian National Congress Party (or Congress Party) in 2004. Although the BJP distanced itself from extremist views, members have been accused of inciting violence against non-Hindus. The secular Congress Party has dominated Indian politics since independence.

Confucianism: The Politics of *Ren*

Distressed by the upheaval and political oppression of his times, the Chinese philosopher and political theorist Confucius (551–449 BCE) evolved a system of "right living" known as *ren*, or humaneness. Confucius taught rulers in various states, advising them to act humanely toward their subjects. An inhumane ruler ran the risk of losing the mandate of heaven and thus the right to rule. As preserved by his disciples in the *Analects*, the sayings of Confucius became a guide for wise government, emphasizing ritual behaviour, family loyalty, and *ren*.

Confucianism became part of the Chinese way of life. There were no priests; instead, parents, teachers, and government officials were the guardians of this **civic religion**. For Confucius, social courtesies and etiquette were important rituals. All human relationships involved defined roles and mutual obligations. In the social hierarchy, men took precedence over women, elders over youth, and fathers over sons. Some Chinese governments gave awards based on Confucian precepts. Thus, obedient sons and wives were honoured. The Confucian emphasis on parental respect contributed to a strong family unit, a basic component of stable governments. With its emphasis on ritual and family, Confucianism preserved the status quo. During the Han dynasty (202 BCE–220 CE), Confucianism became a state ideology and contributed to the stability of this longest-reigning dynasty.

The Confucian concept of *ren*, or humaneness, required that personal conscience and character be cultivated through education and reflection. Respect and honour were expected of all members of society. *Ren* charged ritual with ethical content, giving it meaning. Confucianism encouraged followers to strive for perfection. As you learned in Chapter 1, Emperor Tang Taizong (629–649 CE) introduced a civil service examination system that was based on Confucian principles. The Chinese bureaucracy comprised the most accomplished and ethical Confucian scholars.

During the Tang Dynasty (618–907 CE), Confucianism encouraged egalitarianism

Figure 3.4 Dancers in traditional costume perform at a shrine in Seoul, Korea, during *Sokchonje*, a spring rite celebrating the birth of Confucius. Confucianism spread from China to Korea, Japan, and Vietnam.

(the promotion of equality) An underlying principle of Confucianism was that a person acquires nobility not by birth but through lifelong education and the development of *ren*.

Confucianism coexisted with other religions that entered China after the collapse of the Han dynasty (202 BCE–220 CE). Buddhism came to China from India, and its emphasis on harmonizing human desires contributed to the internal stability and peace of the Tang and Song (960–1279 CE) dynasties. Taoism, a religion that emphasizes spontaneity and individual freedom, complemented Confucian concerns about moral duties and governmental responsibilities. The three creeds combined to allow the development of a dynamic government structure that was grounded in personal responsibility and social harmony. Confucianism remained the intellectual and ethical backbone of Chinese governments for centuries, until the victory of rebel leader Mao Zedong (1893–1976) and the Communist Party in 1949, when the state outlawed all religions.

Buddhism: The Politics of Non-violence

SOUND BITE "Better than a thousand hollow words is one word that brings peace."

Siddhartha Gautama Buddha, Dhammapada

A "buddha" is someone who has awakened to the true nature of universal cause and effect, and whose awareness transcends birth, suffering, and death. In the Buddhist tradition, anyone may attain this enlightenment through Buddhist practice and teachings.

Buddhism has a single founder: Siddhartha Gautama (ca. 563–483 BCE). Siddhartha was born a prince in what is now Nepal. On a spiritual quest through India, he came to believe that enlightenment was to be found in the Middle Way, the path that lies between indulgence and asceticism (rigid self-discipline). Siddhartha adopted many Hindu teachings, such as the practice of meditation to still the mind and the doctrine of *ahimsa*, non-violence. As Gautama Buddha, the "enlightened one," he preached compassion and kindness toward all beings.

Siddhartha's initial teachings are known as Hinayana Buddhism, the "lesser vehicle," which emphasizes individual attainment. The Mahayana ("greater vehicle") school, which arose around 100 CE, practises Buddhist teachings to benefit all beings. It emphasizes forgoing one's personal enlightenment in favour of helping others attain it. In the 7th century CE, the Vajrayana ("diamond vehicle") school blended Mahayana teachings with ancient Hindu practices in which all daily activities are dedicated to universal enlightenment.

The Emperor Ashoka (ca. 273–232 BCE) united India by conquest but then accepted Buddhism and its pacifist philosophy of non-violence. Buddhism became the **state religion** and grew with government support and protection. Ashoka built monasteries and sent missionaries throughout India and to Egypt, Greece, and Syria. This raised Buddhism from a simple Indian sect to a world religion. After Ashoka's death, Buddhism declined in India but remained influential elsewhere.

In the 1st century CE, missionaries carried Buddhism to China. Mahayana Buddhism appealed to the Confucian worldview by placing new emphasis on texts that stressed family loyalty. It also taught that individual enlightenment contributed to the common good. In this way, Buddhism was recognized and adopted by several emperors. From about the 3rd century CE, Buddhism spread further beyond India and was adapted to suit local cultures.

Today, Hinayana Buddhism is found in Sri Lanka, Thailand, Myanmar, and Cambodia; Mahayana in China, Japan, Vietnam, and Korea; and Vajrayana in Tibet, Mongolia, and Japan. In 1959, persecution by the Chinese government led the leader of Tibetan Buddhism, the Dalai Lama, and thousands of his followers to flee the country (see page 95). The resulting **diaspora** (forced abandonment of a homeland by an ethnic group and its dispersal among other countries) has spread Tibetan Buddhism around the world.

As with any religion, state support can lead to dominance and corruption. Sri Lanka's 1972 constitution, for example, made Buddhism the state religion. This increased tensions between the majority Buddhists and the Hindu minority Tamils. In Thailand, the state has supported Buddhism for centuries. Thailand's military rulers even used the Buddhist faith as a cultural weapon to fight socialist and communist movements in the 1960s and 1970s. During a recent economic downturn, the Sangha Supreme Council (Thailand's highest Buddhist body) called on certain monks and sects to end widespread profiteering and commercialization. There are increasing demands that the Buddhist church become accountable to the public.

THE WEB

To learn about the Buddhist Peace Fellowship, a grassroots social-justice and human rights group, visit www.emp.ca/cwp.

Check Your Understanding

1. Explain why in Hinduism every political decision is also a religious decision.
2. In what ways was Confucianism an indispensable component of political stability in China?
3. How was Buddhism adopted and adapted by several Chinese emperors and the governments of various dynasties?

Western Religions and Politics

Of the many religions to arise in the West, Judaism, Christianity, and Islam have the greatest number of adherents and have had the greatest political impact. All three religions believe in a single, all-powerful God who created the universe and gave human beings souls. The Qur'an, the holy book of Islam, acknowledges the kinship among the three traditions by designating Jews, Christians, and Muslims *ahl ul-kitab*, or "People of the Book."

Judaism: The Politics of Diaspora

The term "Jewish" describes both followers of a religion (Judaism) and members of an ethnic group that originally lived in the area known today as

Israel. The government of the Jewish people was destroyed by Roman conquest in 70 CE, when the Romans demolished the Temple of Jerusalem. As a consequence, Jewish people dispersed throughout the world in what became known as the Diaspora. Because they had no territorial homeland for almost two centuries after the Roman conquest, Jewish communities developed their own informal political structures. Often these were rooted in religion. For example, a court of rabbis (Jewish religious leaders) settled community disputes. Religion also shaped educational and charitable institutions.

Many Jews maintained a strong sense of cultural identity despite the Diaspora. Rabbis continued to teach that Jerusalem was the centre of the world and that the Jews would someday return to their homeland. Rabbinical interpretations of the Torah, or "God's Law," helped maintain the social structure and rituals of Jewish communities. Scattered across North Africa, Europe, and Asia, Jewish people achieved success and prominence in such professions as medicine, astronomy, trade, and banking. Many host countries viewed Jewish people as transients and restricted the right of Jews to own land. As a result, the traditional Jewish connection to agriculture was weakened.

Anti-Semitism

Press Play

Fiddler on the Roof, set in 1905 czarist Russia, centres on Tevye the milkman's attempts to maintain Jewish traditions despite social isolation and persecution. The 1971 film, based on the musical stage play, was directed by Canadian Norman Jewison. (NR)

In some parts of the world, particularly Muslim countries, Jews historically enjoyed relative political and religious freedom. In most countries, however, they were viewed as outsiders and often treated with hostility. Although Jews and Arabs are both Semitic peoples, the term "anti-Semitic" has come to mean hatred of the Jewish people. The term first appeared in 1880s Germany, but such prejudice and persecution had existed for more than 2,000 years.

As early as the Greco-Roman period (332 BCE–395 CE), Jewish people were often perceived as rejecting assimilation into the dominant culture. After the Roman conquest (70 CE), Jews were unwelcome in some host countries and socially and politically isolated. Not only were Jews prohibited from owning land in many countries; work choices were also restricted. As a result, Jews entered such unpopular professions as tax collecting and money lending. Over time, the animosity directed toward these professions became focused on the Jewish people.

Sometimes people of different faiths saw Judaism as a rival religion. For a time, Christianity held the Jewish people responsible for the death of Jesus Christ. In the Middle Ages (5th–15th centuries CE), the Catholic Church condemned usury (the charging of interest on loans) as sinful; Judaism had no such prohibition. When Jewish bankers charged interest on loans, all Jewish people suffered from the resulting prejudice.

Many European Jews migrated to Poland to escape persecution during the Middle Ages. But after Russia seized control of a portion of Poland in the late 18th century, it viewed the large Jewish population as a threat to its power. The Russian government organized **pogroms** (violent attacks against

Figure 3.5 Demonstrators in Paris wear yellow stars inscribed with the French word for "Jew" to protest anti-Semitism after neo-Nazis desecrated graves at a Jewish cemetery.

a minority group), portraying the Jews as enemies and inciting nationalistic and religious fanaticism.

The worst expression of anti-Semitism occurred during the **Holocaust** (1933–45), when the German Nazi regime killed 6 million Jewish people. Adolf Hitler exploited anti-Semitism in his rise to power and later called for a "final solution to the Jewish question." Jews in Germany and in the countries that fell to the Nazis had their possessions seized by the state. They were forced to wear yellow stars, rounded up, and finally imprisoned and systematically killed in concentration and extermination camps. The Holocaust obliterated Jewish secular and religious life in Europe.

Catholicism: The Politics of Papacy

The Roman Catholic Church is led by the pope (from the Latin word for "father"), who is seen as the successor to Saint Peter as Christ's representative on Earth. This claim is accepted only by Roman Catholics. Papal authority was established in the West during the first five centuries of the Common Era. The refusal of the Eastern churches to accept the authority of the Roman pope resulted in the Great Schism of 1054 (see page 85).

The Western Church

During the Middle Ages, the authority of the Roman Catholic pope was as great as or greater than the power of secular monarchs. A dramatic confrontation

THE WEB

Learn more about the Holocaust at www.emp.ca/cwp.

in 1077 between Emperor Henry IV of Germany and Pope Gregory VII illustrates this well. As head of the Roman Church, Pope Gregory insisted that
he alone had the power to appoint bishops. When Henry appointed the
German bishops himself, Gregory excommunicated him. The power of
excommunication—excluding a person from the sacraments of the Church—
was the most powerful step a pope could take. To a believer, it meant eternal
damnation. Learning he had been excommunicated, Henry travelled to Pope
Gregory's temporary residence at Canossa and stood outside for three days
in the January snow, weeping and begging Pope Gregory to be forgiven.
Pope Gregory forgave Henry, and the phrase "going to Canossa" came to
signify the power of the Church over secular authority in spiritual matters.

In Spain and France, governments used Catholicism to their political
advantage. In the late 15th century, for example, the Spanish Inquisition rooted out heretics (dissenters), often Jewish and Muslim citizens who were found
guilty of practising their own religions after being forced by the state to convert to Catholicism. King Ferdinand's treasury was filled with the property of
condemned heretics who fled the country or who were imprisoned or executed.

In 1685, Louis XIV tried to unify France under state Catholicism by
revoking the Edict of Nantes, which 87 years earlier had established religious equality. As a result, more than 100,000 French Protestants (known
as Huguenots) sought refuge in neighbouring countries. France lost some
of its most dynamic and enterprising citizens.

As the power of absolute monarchs declined in 19th century Europe, so
did the direct political influence of the Roman Catholic Church and other

Figure 3.6 Pope John Paul II greets Solidarity leader Lech Walesa (right) in
Vatican City, 1981.

religions. No longer could a Ferdinand or a Louis impose a state religion that excluded and persecuted other faiths. The Roman Catholic Church continued to influence social and political life through its leadership and teachings. It established denominational schools and discouraged divorce and abortion. In the late 19th century during a period of deep social unrest, the Church encouraged trade unions and issued encyclicals (papal letters to bishops) directing governments to provide for working people and the poor. At the same time, it spoke out against the dangers of socialism.

A century later, in 1981, and then in 1991, Pope John Paul II criticized the inadequacies and injustices of both capitalism and communism. He spoke out against the imposition of martial law in communist Poland, his homeland, in 1981 and quietly used Church resources to support the banned pro-democracy Solidarity movement. Many historians and political analysts suggest that these acts contributed to the collapse of communism and the end of the Cold War.

SOUND BITE *"... it is within the competence of the rulers of the State that, as they benefit other groups, they also improve in particular the condition of the workers.... For the State is bound by the very law of its office to serve the common interest."*

Pope Leo XIII, Rerum Novarum (On the Condition of the Working Classes), paragraph 48, 1891

The Eastern Church

When the Christian emperor Constantine moved the capital of the Roman Empire to Constantinople in 330 CE, he created two political and religious centres. The language of the Eastern, or Byzantine, Empire was Greek; the language of the Western Empire, centred in Rome, was Latin. In each sphere the Catholic Church developed different traditions in music, art, architecture, ritual, and government. With the collapse of the Roman Empire in the 5th century, the pope gained political power in the West.

During the 7th and 8th centuries, Muslims conquered much of the Byzantine Empire, which reduced the power of the Catholic patriarchs (leaders) in the East. When the pope tried to exert power over Eastern Catholics from Rome, a schism (division) split the Catholic Church. Rejecting papal superiority, Eastern Christians saw themselves as orthodox, or carriers of the original Church's traditions. The Eastern Church maintained its own doctrines, which differed from those of the West. For example, married men could be ordained priests. In 1054, the leaders of Rome and Constantinople excommunicated each another and the Great Schism was complete. Tensions between the two sides increased to the point where the Roman pope sanctioned Crusaders (see page 88) to destroy Constantinople in 1204.

Missionaries from the Eastern Orthodox Church converted many of the Slavic people of Eastern Europe and Russia beginning as early as the 9th century. When the Byzantine Empire fell to the Ottoman Turks in 1453, some believers viewed Russia as the new base for the Eastern Orthodox religion. From 988 to 1917, the Orthodox Church was the state religion of Russia.

In recent years, Pope John Paul II travelled to Egypt, Syria, Ukraine, and Kazakhstan and received Patriarch Bartholomew I of Constantinople in Rome. These attempts at reconciliation between the Eastern and Western branches of Catholicism remain inconclusive.

Islam: The Politics of Empire

Muhammad (570–632 CE) taught that he was a messenger of Allah (God) and that he recorded the word of Allah, as conveyed to him by the angel Gabriel, in the Qur'an, the holy book of Islam. "Islam" is an Arabic word that means "submission." A follower of Islam is called a "Muslim," which means "one who submits to the will of Allah." The introduction of Islam by the prophet Muhammad in the 7th century CE had an immediate impact in the Arab world and helped unite warring tribes. Islam soon spread to other parts of the world.

In Islamic states, religion and government were inseparable. The state was expected to provide an environment for the practice of religion, and people were entitled to depose a leader who failed to do so. Historically, the Qur'an influenced government structure by advocating human dignity, righteous living, moral responsibility, and social justice. For example, while discrimination against Jews was common in medieval Christian lands, it rarely arose in Muslim regions. Muslim governments also did not discriminate on the basis of race or class. With the spread of Islam throughout the Arab world, women were given legal status and protection.

In Islam, the concept of nation was less important than religious belief; thus, by the 8th century, the Muslim Empire, united by religion, stretched from North Africa to Asia. Invaders in the 11th century brought Islam to India. In the early 16th century, the Turkic conqueror Babur created the Mughal (or Mogul) Empire in India. Many of Babur's subjects, including high-ranking officials, followed Hinduism, but the empire itself was Islamic. The Hindu population and its bureaucracy coexisted with the Muslim elements of the Mughal Empire.

Figure 3.7 Muslim invaders approach Messina, the last outpost in Sicily to resist Arab occupation, in 964. This manuscript, written in medieval Greek, was preserved by Eastern Orthodox scholars.

Law in Motion

Tribunal to Apply Islamic Law in Ontario

Through the efforts of a group of Canadian Muslims, a judicial tribunal that will implement Islamic law, or **sharia**, was created in 2003. The tribunal will operate in Ontario as a forum to resolve marital disagreements and civil disputes. Under Ontario law, as long as agreements are voluntary, negotiated through an arbitrator, and not in violation of the *Canadian Charter of Rights and Freedoms*, they will be upheld by the courts.

Muslim reaction to the tribunal has been mixed. Some Muslims in Ontario believe the tribunal will be a cheaper, quicker, and more private way to resolve disputes. Others wonder how a body of law based on religious principles will be interpreted in Ontario and whether it favours men. For example, Islamic family law decrees that males receive a greater share of an inheritance and that only husbands may begin divorce proceedings.

Tarek Fatah, a member of the Muslim Canadian Congress, supports the establishment of the tribunal in theory but has concerns about its potential to highlight divisions within the Islamic community. He wonders which interpretation of Islamic family law will be used, and is concerned that "this idea will become the whipping post for all right-wing bigots."

Syed Mumtaz Ali, a retired lawyer, believes the tribunal will serve Muslims well, observing that "Islamic law obliges Muslims to follow local law, and Islamic law where possible." He believes that Ontario's *Arbitration Act* supports the establishment of the judicial tribunal.

Brendan Crawley, a spokesperson for the Ontario Ministry of the Attorney General, agrees with this view, stating: "People can use any arbitrator they want and can use a religious framework if it is mutually acceptable." He notes, however: "If the award is not compatible with Canadian law, then the court will not enforce it. You can't agree to violate Canadian law."

Source: Adapted from Marina Jimenez, "Islamic Law in Civil Disputes Raises Questions," *The Globe and Mail*, Thursday, December 11, 2003, pages A1, A15.

SOUND BITE "Muslims . . . will do everything possible to maintain the values we came here for in the first place. Canada becoming religious or non-religious doesn't matter as long as the Charter . . . remains in place."

Letter to the editor,
The Globe and Mail,
June 7, 2004

Questions

1. In a two-column chart, list the arguments made for and against the establishment of the tribunal based on Islamic law. What arguments can you add?
2. Research *sharia* using library, Internet, or other resources. Are there any Islamic laws that you believe conflict with Canadian laws? Describe any potential conflicts.

After the Muslim conquest of Palestine, leaders in Christian Europe feared that pilgrimages to the holy sites of Jerusalem, Nazareth, and Bethlehem might be blocked. From the 11th to the 13th centuries, popes sanctioned "holy wars" to regain control of the "holy land" from Muslim governments. These military campaigns were called Crusades, and Christians who participated in them were promised eternal salvation. In the Muslim world, the Crusades were viewed as a savage attack on Islam. Historians agree that the Crusades often degenerated into economic plunder and barbaric attacks on civilian Muslim populations.

Today, many people perceive Islam to be inherently political, allowing for no separation of mosque and state. Other commentators state that militant Muslim groups that advocate political violence contradict Islam's traditional teachings and fail to carry its message of peace and harmony. For most Muslims, the *jihad* (holy war) described in the Qur'an is the ongoing inner struggle of conscience to be a better Muslim, not an outer struggle against a political or religious enemy.

Islam remains a major political force in the regions of the former Mughal Empire, from Morocco to Indonesia. After Christianity, it has the largest number of adherents of any religion in the world. Islam is also growing faster than any other religion, as high birth rates, proselytization (encouragement to convert), and immigration help spread it around the world.

Protestantism: The Politics of Dissent

In the 16th century, a number of European religious thinkers opposed the power of the Roman Catholic Church and demanded reforms. The movement they led became known as the **Protestant Reformation**, and the Protestant creeds that resulted were often supported by governments.

In Germany, Martin Luther (1483–1546) translated the Latin Bible into German, which appealed to German nationalism. It marked the first time the Bible had been printed in a vernacular language. The new technology of the Gutenberg printing press allowed Luther's reformist writings to be mass-produced, making them widely available to common people. The ruler Frederick of Saxony supported Luther's work, even after Luther was excommunicated by Pope Leo (1520). Luther had never intended to break with the Catholic Church. Later, the princes of northern Germany embraced Lutheranism. In England, under King Henry VIII, Parliament stripped the Roman Catholic pope of his authority through the *Act of Supremacy* (1534). This made the Church of England the **state church**, with the king its supreme head.

In both Germany and England, governments encouraged new religious organizations and beliefs. Often, however, this strategy had more to do with gaining political power and Roman Catholic assets—monasteries, art, and lands—than with religious faith. Civil authorities who wanted to stop the flow of taxes to Rome also found wide support in the rising middle classes.

The religious teachings of John Calvin (1509–64) appealed to the middle classes as well. Calvinism taught that an elect group of hard-working people would go to heaven and that worldly success was a sign of God's favour. German sociologist Max Weber (1864–1920) later described this philosophy as the "Protestant work ethic." Under John Knox (ca. 1514–72), Calvinism evolved into Presbyterianism and became Scotland's official religion. Calvinism established strong roots in the Netherlands and, for a time, in France. Calvinist beliefs blended well with middle-class ideals of material success, values that the governments of Scotland and the Netherlands were eager to nurture.

The Puritan sect, which evolved from Calvinism, established a **theocracy** (in which religious law is dominant over civil law) in the Massachusetts Bay Colony in the 17th century. The Puritan community elected its officials, but only white, male members of the Puritan Church could vote. It was the duty of elected officials to serve God by supervising the moral and physical improvement of the society. For example, they devised specific punishments for spousal quarrels, adultery, and eventually, witchcraft. Citizens who desired religious freedom were expelled from the colony.

Figure 3.8 The Devil plays Martin Luther's nose in this 16th century caricature. The Catholic Church excommunicated Luther for stating that salvation is based on faith alone.

As new Protestant denominations emerged, many became intertwined with political institutions. Anglicanism became the state religion in England. The Lutheran Church became the state church in Norway, Iceland, and Denmark (where it remains so to this day). For a time, the Calvinist Dutch Reformed Church was the state church of the Netherlands. State churches receive special status from government, which may or may not include state financial support and official political functions.

Some Protestant denominations acted as political voices of conscience. The Society of Friends, or Quakers, founded by George Fox in the 17th century, rejected the state power of the Church of England. Fox taught that all people posses the same "inner light," or divine presence. Quaker teachings emphasize equality between sexes and races, and oppose war. Quakers were among the early activists seeking the abolition of slavery, prison reform, female **suffrage**, and world peace.

In general, Protestantism rejected the hierarchical structure of the Roman Catholic Church and the role of priests as intermediaries to God. Protestant reformers viewed every believer as a priest who could read the scriptures and reconcile directly with God through faith. This humanist outlook made Protestantism well suited to the movement toward political democracy in the 19th and 20th centuries.

SOUND BITE "Let every man recognize what he is, and be certain that we are all equally priests, that is, we have the same power in the word and in any sacrament whatever."

Martin Luther,
The Babylonian Captivity of the Church, *1520*

Secular Humanism: The Politics of Reason over Religion

Secular humanism is a philosophy that affirms the ability of people to lead an ethical life without reference to the supernatural. This belief system is based on the works of the philosophers, scientists, and poets of Classical Greece and Rome and on the ideals of Chinese Confucian society. Its roots can also be found in the 18th century European **Age of Enlightenment**, which emphasized reason over religion. Secular humanism seeks the betterment of humanity, and is guided by reason and inspired by compassion. It holds that as knowledge and experience increase, human values can change for the better.

In the views of humanist thinkers, traditional religion had affected politics adversely: religions had approved the subjugation of colonial peoples, blessed warfare, practised sexism, and supported the exploitation of human and natural resources. Secular humanism seeks to separate religion from politics. It suggests that basic moral principles can be discovered by human reason. Shunning factionalism and divisiveness, it proposes that humanist principles share the core beliefs of all religions. Secular humanists typically describe themselves as atheists (deynying the existence of a god) or agnostics (uncertain about the existence of a god).

The secular humanist emphasis on keeping religion and government separate has attracted the attention of political scientists. Secular humanism is not opposed to religion but to the imposition of religious doctrine on society through government. It is not a universal **dogma**: secular humanists disagree on many issues. Yet, most believe in free inquiry, reason, tolerance, education, rational moral principles, skepticism toward religion, and the **separation of church and state** (as in France and the United States, below). As modern governments serve increasingly diverse populations, secular humanism has become more widespread.

Check YOUR UNDERSTANDING

1. a) How did the Jewish people maintain their cultural identity despite the Diaspora?
   b) Why were Jews often isolated socially and politically?
2. Describe the relationship between the Roman Catholic Church and Henry IV of Germany, Ferdinand of Spain, and Louis XIV of France.
3. Why did the Catholic Church split into the Western and Eastern churches?
4. What is the relationship between religion and government in Islam?
5. Why did Calvinism appeal to the middle classes?
6. How did the Protestant Reformation affect the relationship between church and state?
7. What do you believe is the appeal of secular humanism?

Individuals in Politics and Religion

Historic evidence shows that the teachings of the world's major religions can have beneficial effects on politics over time. Respect for life, human rights and dignity, and peace—as rooted in religious faith—has inspired many individuals to work for change locally and globally.

Religious leaders and thinkers have been powerful voices of conscience in the secular world of politics. Individuals such as Mahatma Gandhi, Lutheran theologian Dietrich Bonhoeffer, Mother Teresa, Desmond Tutu, and the Dalai Lama have all been guided by religious principles that reject violence and emphasize love of humanity and compassion as a means to create a better society.

Press Play

Romero, a 1989 film directed by John Duigan and starring Raul Julia, examines the transformation of a conservative El Salvadoran priest into a leading opponent of his country's oppressive government in the late 1970s. (PG-13)

Mahatma Gandhi and Indian Nationalism

Mohandas K. Gandhi (1869–1948)—born in Porbandar, India, educated in London, England—began his political life as a lawyer and civil rights activist in South Africa. In 1915, he returned to India and became the leader of the national movement for independence from Britain. The name Mahatma, a Sanskrit word meaning "great soul," was given to Gandhi by his followers.

Gandhi supported the separation of politics and religion and believed that the state should favour no one religion. Even though he was a devout Hindu, Gandhi spoke of a spiritual belief that transcended a single faith and was a permanent element in human nature: "You must watch my life, how I live, eat, sit, talk, behave in general. The sum total of all those in me is my religion."

In his struggle against the British colonizers, Gandhi perceived that elected legislatures had no power independent of the people. For him, civil disobedience was the source of power. If an entire population refused to conform to the law and was prepared to suffer the consequences of non-compliance, it could bring government to a standstill; neither the military nor the police could bend its will. Resistance to government violence would eventually defeat government violence. Gandhi taught followers that devotion to non-violence must be reflected in every thought, word, and deed. One of his strategies was to make the oppressor and the oppressed recognize their common humanity.

Figure 3.9 A signed portrait of Mahatma Gandhi, ca. 1930. Gandhi was assassinated by a Hindu extremist in 1948 for his beliefs and practice of non-violence.

SOUND BITE   "If I seem to take part in politics, it is only because politics encircles us today like the coil of a snake from which one cannot get out, no matter how much one tries. I wish therefore to wrestle with the snake."

Mahatma Gandhi, 1920

Press Play

The 1982 film, *Gandhi*, starring Ben Kingsley and directed by Richard Attenborough, depicts Mahatma Gandhi's peaceful political protests, first in South Africa and later in India. (PG)

To defeat the British presence in India, Gandhi schooled his followers in the tactics of civil disobedience and passive resistance. He called on Indians to withdraw from British institutions and to return honours conferred by Britain. In 1930, he led a resistance movement against laws that gave the British a monopoly on the production and sale of Indian salt. During the "salt march" to the sea, Gandhi and his followers picked up small lumps of natural salt in defiance of British law. More than 60,000 resisters were arrested and went peacefully to jail. A year later, Gandhi met with the British government in London and was recognized as head of India's Congress Party. The salt laws were amended.

Britain recognized India's independence in 1947, and Gandhi's non-violent political philosophy, which has influenced many other activists, was credited as the driving force behind that achievement. It would not have been possible without the religious base on which it was founded.

Dietrich Bonhoeffer and Anti-Nazism

Dietrich Bonhoeffer (1906–45) was a university professor of theology, a Lutheran pastor, and a central figure in the resistance to Nazism in Germany. Bonhoeffer believed that religion and the Bible were pertinent to public life and to state institutions. He affirmed that religion had public—and thus, political—responsibilities, and he acted on that belief. Unlike many other German religious leaders, Bonhoeffer spoke out against Hitler's rise to power in January 1933. Two days after Hitler became chancellor of Germany, Bonhoeffer warned Germans of the dangers of the Nazi regime in a radio broadcast. His microphone was disconnected just moments into his speech.

Under Hitler, the German Lutheran Church barred men who had converted from Judaism, had Jewish ancestors, or had Jewish wives from becoming ministers. In response, Bonhoeffer and others formed the Confessing Church, a group opposed to the pro-Hitler state church. After visiting England for two years, Bonhoeffer returned to Germany to train pastors for the Confessing Church. When the Gestapo (fascist police) closed the seminary, Bonhoeffer continued training students secretly.

Figure 3.10 Dietrich Bonhoeffer, ca. 1943.

SOUND BITE "No cause is left but the most ancient of all, the one, in fact, that from the beginning of our history has determined the very existence of politics, the cause of freedom versus tyranny."

Hannah Arendt,
The Origins of Totalitarianism, *1951*

In 1940, Bonhoeffer's books were banned and he was dismissed from teaching at the University of Berlin. With the help of a relative, he got a job with Nazi military intelligence. There he became involved in secret plots to remove Hitler from power or assassinate him. Bonhoeffer's roles in the plots and in helping a group of Jews escape to Switzerland were uncovered in 1943. He was imprisoned and, in April 1945, at the age of 39, was hanged at Flossenburg concentration camp. A few weeks later, Germany surrendered.

Although Bonhoeffer was a pacifist and admired Mahatma Gandhi, he could rationalize his involvement in the plot to murder Hitler: "If I see a madman driving a car into a group of innocent bystanders, then I can't, as a Christian, simply wait for the catastrophe and then comfort the wounded and bury the dead. I must try to wrestle the steering wheel out of the hands of the driver." Bonhoeffer saw limits to non-violence in certain situations. He believed that sometimes a good person must do evil to achieve a greater good. In this context, he stated, "Being evil is worse than doing evil."

THE WEB

Learn more about Bonhoeffer at www.emp.ca/cwp.

Mother Teresa and the Politics of Poverty

In 1931, at the age of 21, Agnes Bonxha Bojaxhiu (1910–97) became a Roman Catholic nun and took the name Sister Teresa. She was sent from Yugoslavia to India to work in a high school. After almost two decades of teaching in Kolkata (Calcutta), she felt compelled to devote her life to helping the poorest of the poor. With a group of nuns, she acted as a nurse and social worker for the homeless and the hungry in the slums of Kolkata. In 1950 she started her own religious organization, the Missionaries of Charity, to administer to the most rejected people in society.

Through the dedication and work of Mother Teresa, the organization grew to include priests, brothers, sisters, and lay workers and became a worldwide ministry. Its activities now include slum schools, homes for orphaned children, mobile clinics, leprosy centres, hostels for the dying, food kitchens, vocational training, and, in general, help for those whom society has abandoned.

Mother Teresa lived by her vow of poverty, but through tireless dedication and efforts she drew worldwide attention to her work. In 1979, she was awarded the Nobel Peace Prize. This recognition was, in a sense, a victory for her constituency: the hungry, the diseased, and the poor. According to Aristotle, the goal of politics is the good of the community. Mother Teresa demonstrated one way in which good in the community can be achieved. By drawing attention to the depth of suffering and need in Kolkata—and the world—Mother Teresa inspired many others to do something about this political issue.

Figure 3.11 Mother Teresa holds a newborn infant in her mission in Kolkata, India, 1976.

Grassroots Politics and Protest

Archbishop Desmond Tutu and Apartheid

Desmond Tutu (1931–) gained worldwide attention in the 1980s as a peace activist who opposed **apartheid**, the political system that instituted minority white domination and separated the races in South Africa. Under apartheid, interracial marriage was prohibited and criticism of the system was stifled. Black people were restricted in where they could live, and they could not vote, form labour unions, or enter certain professions. People of colour were required to carry passports for travel within their own country.

In his first profession as teacher, Tutu was appalled at the state's deliberately inferior education system for black students. Determined to change the system, he entered the Anglican priesthood, becoming the first black leader of the Anglican Church in South Africa and the first black general secretary of the African Council of Churches. Tutu used his position to attack the "evil and un-Christian" apartheid system. He encouraged citizens to engage in non-violent resistance and foreign governments to join international trade embargoes against South Africa. It was partly through Tutu's efforts and international prominence that apartheid was repealed in the early 1990s and that non-white South Africans gained the right to vote.

In his lecture accepting the 1984 Nobel Peace Prize, Tutu revealed how political action can spring from deep religious beliefs:

> There is no peace in Southern Africa. There is no peace because there is no justice. There can be no real peace and security until there be first justice enjoyed by all the inhabitants of that beautiful land. The Bible knows nothing about peace without justice, for that would be crying "peace, peace, where there is no peace." God's *shalom*, peace, involves inevitably righteousness, justice, wholeness, fullness of life, participation in decision making, goodness, laughter, joy, compassion, sharing and reconciliation.

Figure 3.12 Archbishop Desmond Tutu speaks after receiving an honorary degree from Simon Fraser University in Vancouver, 2004.

> We have the capacity to feed ourselves several times over, but we are daily haunted by the spectacle of the gaunt dregs of humanity shuffling along in endless queues, with bowls to collect what the charity of the world has provided, too little too late. When will we learn, when will the people of the world get up and say, "Enough is enough. God created us for fellowship. God created us so that we should form the human family, existing together because we were made for one another." We are not made for an exclusive self-sufficiency but for interdependence, and we break the law of our being at our peril.

Questions

1. Describe the impact of the policy of apartheid on the black people of South Africa.
2. How did Desmond Tutu use his position to fight apartheid?
3. Visit www.emp.ca/cwp for a link to Desmond Tutu's acceptance speech on receiving the Nobel Peace Prize. Describe what he has to say about education, justice, the arms race, or human rights. Do you agree or disagree with him? Explain your views.

The Dalai Lama and the Defence of Tibet

Born into a peasant family in northeastern Tibet, Tenzin Gyatso (1935–) was recognized at the age of two as the reincarnation of the Buddha of Compassion and the 14th Dalai Lama. In 1950, at the age of 15, he became the spiritual and political leader of Tibet, a country that has had little contact with the outside world throughout its history. In the same year, Chinese troops and settlers flooded into Tibet, claiming it as part of China. Educated as a Buddhist monk, the Dalai Lama's belief in *ahimsa* (non-violence) and compassion moulded his political response. He confronted the Chinese peacefully and attempted to negotiate a solution acceptable to both the Chinese and the Tibetans. His repeated efforts were rejected by the Chinese, who denied all claims of Tibetan **sovereignty**.

After the Chinese suppressed the Tibetan National Uprising in 1959—the largest demonstration in Tibet's history—the Dalai Lama and many of his followers escaped to northern India, where they were granted political asylum. Today the Dalai Lama's government-in-exile is still based in northern India and there are more than 120,000 Tibetan refugees.

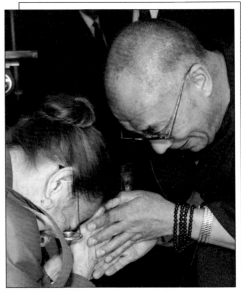

Figure 3.13 The Dalai Lama (right) greets a well-wisher after arriving in Ottawa, April 2004.

Tibetans have listened to the Dalai Lama's message and refrained from using violence against the Chinese. Drawing on Buddhist teachings, the Dalai Lama has demonstrated determination in his political leadership and has also become a spokesperson for environmentalism. As part of his political and spiritual strategy, he has travelled widely to gain support for Tibet. He has attended interfaith conferences and met with other religious and political leaders.

The Dalai Lama has asked for a stop to Chinese immigration to prevent Tibetans from becoming outnumbered in their homeland. He has asked that Tibetans be allowed to use their own language. He has asked for a halt to Chinese logging in the Himalayan Mountains in order to preserve Tibet's rich environmental heritage. He has asked China to stop producing nuclear arms in Tibet and dumping nuclear waste there. The Dalai Lama has said he is willing to concede control of defence and foreign policy to China if Tibetans are allowed full control of their internal politics. The government of China has rejected or ignored all these proposals and requests.

Press Play

The 1997 film *Kundun*, directed by Martin Scorsese and starring Tenzin Thuthob Tsarong, chronicles the life of the Dalai Lama as he braves China's takeover of Tibet in 1950 and finally escapes through the Himalayas to exile in India in 1959. (PG-13)

SOUND BITE "Up to now my involvement in the Tibetan freedom struggle has been part of my spiritual practice, because the issues of the survival of the Buddha Teaching and the freedom of Tibet are very much related. In this particular struggle, there is no problem with many monks and nuns, including myself, joining. But when it comes to democratic political parties, I prefer that monks and nuns not join them—in order to ensure proper democratic practice. The Dalai Lama should not be partisan either, should remain above."

Dalai Lama, conversation with Robert Thurman, 1997

1922 Partitioning of Ireland; north remains British

1968 Civil rights protests by minority Catholics

1969 British troops quell violence

1974 Protestants win 11 of 12 seats in British Parliament

1980s–90s Catholic–Protestant terrorism escalates

1998–99 Peace accord establishes degree of Home Rule

2001 Catholic militants agree to disarm

2002 Britain suspends Home Rule after arrest of Irish officials charged with spying for Catholic militants

2003 Extremist Catholic and Protestant parties outpoll moderates in national election

Figure 3.15 Timeline: Northern Ireland.

Figure 3.16 Security barricades like this one in Belfast have been erected since the 1960s to separate Catholic and Protestant neighbourhoods in Northern Ireland.

committed to union with Britain. Since 1968, there have been prolonged periods of violence between the two groups.

Demographics may play a key role in the outcome of the conflict in Northern Ireland. It is predicted that Catholics will become the majority by 2010. In 2003, Catholics represented 44 percent of the population of Northern Ireland, and 30,000 more Catholic than Protestant students were enrolled in Northern Ireland's schools.

Religion is not the only factor in political decision making in Northern Ireland. Not all Catholics are nationalists, and not all Protestants are unionists. Some Catholics see an economic advantage in maintaining British ties, which can lead to better employment opportunities and government funding. And Britain is committed to a peaceful and democratic resolution. If a Catholic majority should come to pass and vote for union with the Republic, Britain will honour the result.

India, Pakistan, and Bangladesh: Religion and Partition

Religion has been a political flashpoint in the Indian subcontinent for centuries. This was made terribly clear by events in 1947, when nearly 350 years of colonization ended and Britain recognized Indian independence. Many Hindus resented that Muslims had once ruled India. And many Muslims, believing that the British favoured Hindus, feared India would be Hindu-controlled. The British partitioned India, creating the separate state of Pakistan to meet Muslim demands for a homeland. Pakistan itself was a two-region country: East Pakistan and West Pakistan, separated by the land-mass of India. Gandhi strongly opposed partition, believing religions could coexist peacefully in a unified and secular India.

Pakistan became an Islamic republic, and India became a secular state with a large majority of Hindus. As 14 million Hindu and Muslim refugees crossed new borders to avoid religious persecution, violence raged out of control. More than half a million people died. To this day, debates continue about Britain's decision. India and Pakistan have been at war formally twice since partition (1965 and 1971).

People in East Pakistan who felt repressed by West Pakistan formed an independence movement that led to a violent civil war and a flood of refugees into India. When India intervened in 1971, war broke out between India and Pakistan. That year, East Pakistan became the new country of Bangladesh, partially with India's assistance. Both Pakistan (the former West Pakistan) and India now have nuclear weapons and, at times, have threatened each other with war. The two countries continue to be deadlocked over claims to the border province of Jammu and Kashmir.

As a secular democracy, India promotes tolerance among its diverse religions and communities. Nonetheless, violence has often erupted between members of the 83 percent Hindu majority and the 14 percent Muslim minority. The history of the Babri Mosque exemplifies the religious passions that have marked Indian politics. A Muslim emperor of India built the mosque in the 16th century after an ancient Hindu temple on the site was destroyed. In December 1992, a mob of Hindu nationalists destroyed the Babri Mosque. Riots broke out between Hindus and Muslims across India. In the decade that followed, some political factions supported the rebuilding of the mosque, others the building of a Hindu temple, but nothing has yet been built.

1947 India gains independence from Britain; Pakistan splits from India; both claim border province of Jammu and Kashmir (unresolved as of 2004)

1965 Border clashes lead to war between India and Pakistan

1971 Conflict between East and West Pakistan; India intervenes; war erupts between India and Pakistan; East Pakistan declares independence as Bangladesh

1974 Pakistan recognizes independence of Bangladesh

1992 Hindu–Muslim violence erupts in India over Babri Mosque

1998 BJP, the Hindu nationalist party, wins Indian national election; India and Pakistan test nuclear weapons

2004 Secular Congress Party wins Indian national election

Figure 3.18 Timeline: India, Pakistan, and Bangladesh.

 Press Play

Earth, a 1998 film directed by Deepa Mehta and featuring Aamir Khan, depicts life in Lahore, India, in 1947. The story of a love triangle is set against the background of Hindu and Muslim nationalist movements as Lahore becomes part of Pakistan after partition. (NR)

Figure 3.17 A Pakistani (right) and an Indian soldier perform the daily flag-lowering ceremony at Wagah, a border checkpoint. The ritual is a formalized display of anger and determination on both sides.

1917 British *Balfour Declaration* supports Jewish homeland

1919 Palestine made British Mandate

1920s–30s Jewish refugees fleeing Nazism admitted

1945 League of Arab States opposes Israel

1946 Holocaust survivors admitted

1947 Arabs reject UN partition of Palestine

1948–49 Israel declares statehood; wins war with Egypt, Syria, Lebanon, and Iraq

1949 UN brokers ceasefire

1964 Palestine Liberation Organization forms

1967 Egypt expels UN peacekeepers; Six-Day War fought

1973 Israel and Arab neighbours fight "Yom Kippur War"

1977 Egyptian President Sadat and Israeli Prime Minister Begin discuss peace in Jerusalem

1979 Camp David Israel–Egypt peace agreement signed

1981 Sadat assassinated

1987 Palestinian *intifada* (uprising) launched in occupied territories

1993 *Oslo Accords* grant limited Palestinian self-rule

1994 Palestinian Authority assumes limited government in Gaza and West Bank

2000 Second Palestinian *intifada*

2001 Israel begins building security fence

2004 UN declares security fence illegal

Figure 3.19 Timeline: Palestine and Israel.

Israel: Contested Homeland

The rationale for establishing a Jewish state was based on a blend of politics and religion. **Zionism** holds that the Jewish people are a nation and thus entitled to a homeland. Some religious Jews believe that the Jewish people have a permanent right to the land of Israel because God gave it to the ancient Israelites. Zionism, however, also has secular foundations. The brutal anti-Semitism of 1890–1945 convinced many Jewish people, both religious and non-religious, of the need for a Jewish homeland.

At the Paris Peace Conference of 1919, held after World War I, the British received a **mandate** to administer Palestine. Palestine had been part of the defeated Ottoman Empire. The word "Palestinian" was used then to refer to both the Jewish and overwhelmingly Muslim Arab peoples living in the area. In 1947, after World War II, the United Nations voted to partition Palestine into an Arab state and a Jewish state. Jerusalem was designated an international city. The Arab population that had lived in Palestine fought against the presence of a Jewish state and an ongoing influx of Jewish settlers.

After Israel declared statehood in 1948, a war ensued with five neighbouring Arab states (Lebanon, Syria, Iraq, Egypt, and Jordan). Israel won the conflict. Citing national security, it claimed another quarter of the original total mandate of Palestine. Still, no Arab state recognized Israel, and approximately 700,000 Palestinians fled. Eventually, some of these Palestinians became citizens of Jordan; many more became refugees in Egypt, Lebanon, and Syria. Palestinian homelessness intensified ongoing conflicts.

Jewish fundamentalism has affected attempts to reconcile warring factions within Israel. Mainstream Judaism has historically supported

Figure 3.20 A Bedouin man and an Israeli nature protection officer discuss a well in the Sinai peninsula. Water rights have been a source of conflict between Israeli settlers and Palestinians in the desert region.

human and equality rights. But Zionist fundamentalists, like fundamentalists in all religions, believe in the literal interpretation of sacred texts. Basing their beliefs on the Torah (the first five books of the Old Testament), some Jewish fundamentalists believe that God gave all of Israel to the Jewish people.

In 1967, a border skirmish escalated into the Six-Day War, a full military battle between Israel and Egypt, Syria, and Jordan. Israel won, and occupied East Jerusalem, the West Bank, the Gaza Strip, the Golan Heights, and the Sinai Peninsula, which it later returned to Egypt. Some of the "occupied territories" in Gaza and the West Bank have been settled by Israelis, including members of fundamentalist groups such as Gush Emunim. The Palestinian population, however, has demanded that the land be returned to them. Palestinian militants have used terrorist tactics, such as suicide bombers, and have targeted civilians to drive out Israelis. Israel has a vastly superior military to any of the Arab states.

In 2001, Israel began building a security fence in the West Bank to stop terrorist attacks (see Figure 5.16, page 177). Critics said it was an effort to claim more Palestinian land. In 2004, Israel's Supreme Court ordered changes to the route of the fence, ruling that it "disrupts the delicate balance between the obligation of the military commander to preserve security and his obligation to provide for the needs of the local [Palestinian] inhabitants." In the same year, a non-binding ruling of the UN International Court of Justice in the Hague stated that the entire fence was illegal. Israel dismissed the ruling, saying the fence is a political issue to be resolved between Israelis and Palestinians. Israel's plans to withdraw from settlements in Gaza, yet maintain settlements in the West Bank, have been criticized by both Jewish fundamentalists and Palestinians.

Religious tensions within Israel have contributed to other acts of violence. Both the 1994 killings of 29 Muslims at prayer in a Hebron mosque and the 1995 assassination of Prime Minister Yitzhak Rabin were carried out by Jewish fundamentalists opposed to making concessions to Palestinian demands in the peace process.

Today, the word "Palestinian" is used almost exclusively to describe Arab people with ties to the region and who view themselves as a distinct branch of the Arab peoples. Many Palestinians reject Israeli citizenship because they consider Israel an enemy. In the early 21st century, deep distrust and violence marked relations between the two peoples.

Figure 3.21 Israel's changing boundaries.

Israel's Electoral System

Israel's electoral system is based on **proportional representation** and accommodates small, religious-inspired blocs of voters. There are no individual constituencies, and a party with a minimum of just 1.5 percent of the popular

THE WEB

Read about a century of Middle Eastern conflict at www.emp.ca/cwp.

THE WEB
Learn more about the Israeli–Palestinian conflict and a youth group trying to bring peace at www.emp.ca/cwp.

vote can he represented in the Knesset (parliament). Each party has a list of candidates, and citizens vote for the party, not individuals. If a party receives 30 percent of the vote and that translates into 38 members in the 120-seat Knesset, the top 38 members on the party's list are elected.

The United Torah Judaism Party (UTJP) is based on religious principles that oppose negotiating with Palestinians and recognition of a Palestinian state. The UTJP polled 4.3 percent of the vote in the January 2003 election and has five representatives in the Knesset. The National Religious Party, which strongly favours Jewish settlements in the occupied territories and opposes any territorial concessions to the Palestinians, also elected five representatives.

China: Revolution and Religion

In its history, China experienced a number of religious uprisings, such as the Taiping Rebellion of 1850–64, in which a charismatic leader claiming to be the brother of Christ spurred a peasant revolt. Today, China's leaders seem determined to protect the communist state against any real or perceived religious threat from within. Since its revolutionary beginnings in 1949, the People's Republic of China has banned or restricted religious practices. In a sense, though, the communist government replaced Confucianism with Maoism. Like Confucianism, the teachings of Chairman Mao Zedong stress ritual and loyalty.

Certain religions and places of worship are allowed in China, under strict conditions. There is a government-controlled Catholic Church, for

1949 Mao Zedong establishes People's Republic of China; religion banned

1959 China represses Buddhists in Tibet; destroys monasteries, jails monks and nuns

1966–69 Cultural Revolution; many shrines, mosques, and churches destroyed

1970s Restrictions on religion eased; practice is permitted by Chinese constitution but still discouraged

1990s–Present Program undertaken to rebuild shrines, mosques, and churches destroyed during Cultural Revolution

1999 China bans Falun Gong

Figure 3.22 Timeline: People's Republic of China.

Figure 3.23 Falun Gong members perform their exercises in Hong Kong during an international economic conference in May 2001. The demonstration was staged to protest China's persecution of the sect. Demonstrators were detained and later released.

example, but it has no official ties to the Roman Catholic pope. There are also underground churches in China. For example, an unofficial Catholic Church has an estimated 8 million members who are loyal to the pope. The Chinese government also restricts Muslim religious practice and, since the 1959 uprising in Tibet, has enforced repressive policies against Buddhists there.

The Chinese government has banned Falun Gong, calling it a dangerous cult. Literally, Falun Gong means "the practice of the law of the Dharma" (the workings of natural law, or the spirit of the Buddha). It combines traditional Chinese exercises, meditation, and Buddhist teachings. China has harassed practitioners, destroyed Falun Gong books and tapes, and blocked the movement's Internet sites. Some adherents have been arrested, and some have disappeared. In February 2004, China sentenced five Falun Gong members to prison for posting articles on an Internet discussion board. China's treatment of the Falun Gong and other religious groups has prompted international protests that the country disregards human rights, even though it is a **signatory** to the United Nations' *Universal Declaration of Human Rights*.

Iran: Theocracy versus Democracy

As you learned in Chapter 1, Ayatollah Ruhollah Khomeini swept to power in Iran in 1979. The Ayatollah ("gift of God") had been in exile for 14 years, and millions of supporters cheered his return and the ousting of the US-backed Shah Reza Pahlavi. Khomeini established an Islamic republic strictly based on his interpretation of the teachings of Muhammad. Khomeini became both head of the government and supreme spiritual leader. Only candidates he approved could run for office.

Khomeini filled all government positions with his supporters. Thousands of opponents of the new regime were imprisoned, and many were executed. Khomeini instituted a strict interpretation of *sharia* that made few concessions to the secular, Westernized lifestyle that Iranians, especially urban Iranians, had grown accustomed to. Alcohol, dancing, and Western music were forbidden. Women were expected to wear the traditional *hijab*, or headscarf, and the *chador*, a black, loose-fitting garment that covers the body. Women were segregated from men at recreational facilities and beaches. Because a woman's ability to think was rated at half that of a man's, the testimony of any woman in a trial had to be supported by a male witness to be considered credible. From the age of nine, girls could be given away in marriage. Men could have up to four permanent wives at one time, but wives were legally required to be faithful or face public stoning for adultery. It was extremely difficult for a woman to obtain a divorce.

Iran's Islamic revolution took on international dimensions. In 1979, after the Shah found refuge in the United States, Khomeini supporters invaded the US embassy in the capital, Tehran. They took 52 Americans hostage, holding them for 444 days. Khomeini called the United States "the Great Satan" and offered a spiritual reward to anyone who executed the Shah.

1979 Shah Reza Pahlevi ousted by coup; Islamic Republic established under Ayatollah Ruhollah Khomeini

1988 Khomeini pronounces *fatwa* against British author Salman Rushdie for "blasphemy"

1989 Death of Ayatollah Khomeini

1997 Election of reformist President Muhammad Khatami; restrictions against women in public life eased

Figure 3.24 Timeline: Iran.

Figure 3.25 A campaign worker puts up posters for a female parliamentary candidate in Iran's 2004 elections.

SOUND BITE   "In Islam, the legislative power and competence to establish laws belong exclusively to God Almighty."

Ayatollah Ruhollah Khomeini, supreme leader of Iran (1979–89)

Khomeini also called for Islamic revolution in other Muslim countries. This alarmed Saddam Hussein, the US-backed secular dictator of neighbouring Iraq. Islam has two major divisions: Shiite (also known as Shi'i and Shi'a) and Sunni. Although Sunnis make up 85 percent of all Muslims, the more militant Shiite sect is the dominant religion in both Iran (89 percent) and Iraq (63 percent). Hussein wanted to keep Iran's religious fervour from spreading to Iraq's Shiite population and threatening his power. With US backing, Hussein attacked Iran in 1980. The resulting war lasted eight years.

In 1988, British author Salman Rushdie published *The Satanic Verses*, and Khomeini declared that the novel blasphemed against (was irreverent toward) Islam. He declared a *fatwa* (death sentence) on Rushdie, who was forced into hiding.

After Khomeini's death in 1989, Iran continued as an Islamic state, but some reforms softened the rigid rules of the theocracy. With the election of President Muhammad Khatami in 1997, women were allowed more participation in higher education and in local and national politics.

The United States: Christian Fundamentalism and Democracy

Christian fundamentalists—both Catholic and Protestant—have become a powerful voting bloc in the United States. Not all Christian fundamentalists hold the same views. Yet, political scientists have been able to identify a significant body of fundamentalist voters in the United States. Generally, Christian fundamentalists support the Republican Party (the centre-right US political party) in funding and votes. President George W. Bush was elected in 2000, and re-elected in 2004, with strong support from this group, which is also known as the "religious right."

Highly committed fundamentalist Christians have attempted to change US politics to suit their morality and ideological views. Many are determined to overturn the 1973 Supreme Court decision in *Roe v. Wade*, which protects women's right to abortion. Well-organized and well-funded Christian groups have also sought to amend the US constitution to define marriage exclusively as the union between one man and one woman. Many fundamentalists also advocate that the Biblical account of creation, rather than evolution, should be taught in public schools, or that evolution be taught only as theory. Upset by the exclusion of Christian prayers in US public schools, fundamentalists often support home schooling and private schooling. In general, Christian fundamentalists oppose the prevalence of secular humanism in American life on the grounds that it diminishes the presence of Christianity.

Taking a Stand   Shirin Ebadi

Shirin Ebadi has been a leading human rights advocate in Iran for many years. Working as a legal assistant, lawyer, judge, consultant, professor, and writer, she has represented and defended hundreds of dissidents, women, and children in Iran's patriarchal judicial system. In 2000, she was sentenced to 15 months in prison for an alleged political offence and served three weeks before her sentence was suspended. Ebadi has continued to call for reforms to Iranian laws, especially those that discriminate against women. In 2003, she was awarded the Nobel Peace Prize.

According to Ebadi, the role of women in Iran is changing slowly. In 2003, there were only 14 women in Iran's 270-seat parliament, but women outnumbered men in university admissions. Ebadi advocates peaceful reform. If human rights are to improve, she believes that Iran's education system must change and teach young people about human rights from an early age. She insists that Iranian law must be reformed to comply with international human rights law—particularly in family and criminal law. For example, the current age for criminal responsibility is nine for a girl and 15 for a boy. This means that a nine-year-old Iranian girl may receive the same punishment as an adult. In her Nobel acceptance speech, Ebadi blamed the "discriminatory plight" of women in Iran on the "patriarchal and male-dominated culture," not the religion of Islam.

Ebadi believes that Islam promotes human rights and stands against terrorism. She argues that people who believe that human rights, democracy, and Islam are incompatible are only attempting to impose their own beliefs and "justifying dictatorship." She is committed to her country and her religion, and believes that by persistent and peaceful work, the interplay between Islam and politics can be changed in Iran. In her Nobel lecture, Ebadi made the following comment about her country and its dominant religion:

> The people of Iran have been battling against consecutive conflicts between tradition and modernity for over 100 years. By resorting to ancient traditions, some have tried and are trying to see the world through the eyes of their predecessors and to deal with the problems and difficulties of the existing world by virtue of the values of the ancients. But, many others, while respecting their historical and cultural past and their religion and faith, seek to go forth in step with world developments and not lag behind the caravan of civilization, development and progress. The people of Iran, particularly in recent years, have shown that they deem participation in public affairs to be their right, and that they want to be masters of their own destiny.

In an Indian interview in 2004, Ebadi challenged aspects of US President George W. Bush's "war on terror": "America and the West should know that Islam does not support terror. In Bosnia when so many Muslims were killed, we did not consider it Christian terrorism." She went on to note that the

Press Play

In *The Circle* (2000), Iranian director Jafar Panahi explores the oppression of women in contemporary Iran through a series of inter-related stories. (PG)

way to eradicate terrorism is not simply to punish or kill terrorists but also to strike at the roots of terrorism: "Terrorism is the reaction, the wrong reaction, to injustice and discrimination."

Questions

1. How has Shirin Ebadi challenged patriarchal views of women in Iran?
2. How has the role of women changed in Iran?
3. Do you agree with Ebadi's vision for democracy in Iran? Why or why not?
4. Do you agree with Ebadi's analysis of terrorism? Explain your views.

Check YOUR UNDERSTANDING

1. Cite examples of the influence of the Roman Catholic Church in the politics of the Republic of Ireland.
2. Explain how demographics have influenced Northern Ireland's politics in the past and how they may do so in the future.
3. Explain how religion played a role in creating present-day India, Pakistan, and Bangladesh.
4. Explain why Israel was created in 1947, and describe the problems associated with its creation.
5. How does the government of the People's Republic of China deal with religion?
6. Present three specific examples of *sharia* as instituted by Ayatollah Khomeini in Iran after 1979.
7. Describe three Christian fundamentalist beliefs that have affected contemporary US politics.

Separation of Church and State

An important development in modern politics is the philosophy that organized religion and government should be kept separate. At the constitutional, or structural, level of government, the separation may be clear. Legislative and other governmental bodies, for example, are physically distinct from religious institutions. However, at the everyday level, religious beliefs frequently impinge on political procedures and decision making.

Should a legislative session open with a prayer? Should church property be exempt from taxation? Should religious symbols be allowed in public schools and government offices? Should religious beliefs have precedence over—or be exempted from—human rights legislation? The governments of France, the United States, and Canada—like many other governments—have struggled to find answers to questions such as these and to strike an appropriate balance in the domains of religion and politics.

France

Thinkers of the 18th century Enlightenment such as **Voltaire**, **Montesquieu**, and **Diderot** viewed the established religion of France as intolerant and divisive. During the French Revolution, the power of the Roman Catholic Church in France was virtually eliminated. Under the *Civil Constitution Law* of 1790, Church lands were confiscated and sold at public auction. Priests and bishops were elected by the people and paid by the government. No papal decree or ruling was allowed into France without government approval. In some provinces, priests were forbidden to wear vestments (robes); in others, they had to be married men. Protestants and Jews were guaranteed full religious freedom. In 1801, Napoleon Bonaparte negotiated a **concordat** with Pope Pius VII that allowed the Roman Catholic Church some influence in the elementary education system.

In 1905, France passed legislation that prohibited state funding or recognition of any one religion. This action formally separated church and state. Churches, temples, and synagogues built before 1905 with public funds could be used for religious purposes, but they became government property. Government funding of private religious schools continued, with the requirement that the schools follow state curricula.

When President Jacques Chirac called for a law to ban religious symbols in public places in France in December 2003, the phrase "separation of church and state" took on new urgency. Chirac made his remarks after a commission recommended that the Jewish *yarmulke*, Muslim *hijab*, and large Christian crucifixes be banned in public schools, hospitals, and government offices. Chirac reminded French citizens of the secular nature of the republic, and popular opinion strongly supported the ban. France's estimated 5 million Muslim citizens, however, appeared to be the group most directly affected by the proposed legislation, and Chirac's announcement ignited public controversy and protest (see Point Counterpoint, page 108).

1789 French Revolution

1790 Confiscation of church lands

1798/1809 France marches on Rome against pope

1905 Law on separation of church and state

1937 Schools instructed to eliminate religious signs

1989 Ban on religious signs ruled illegal

1994 Minister says schools can ban "ostentatious" signs

2003 President Chirac calls for legislative ban on religious symbols in schools, hospitals, and government offices

2004 Religious symbols are banned

Figure 3.26 Timeline: France.

Figure 3.27 This 1790 print depicts the confiscation of Church property under France's *Civil Constitution Law*.

Point:
Counterpoint → Debating the Ban on the *Hijab*

"Yes" to the Ban

by French President Jacques Chirac

School is a republican sanctuary that we must defend in order to preserve equality during the acquisition of values and knowledge in girls and boys; in order to protect our children; so that our youth is not exposed to the bad winds that divide, separate and bring us into conflict with one another.

It is not, of course, a question of making the school into a place of uniformity, of anonymity, where religious allegiance is forbidden. It is about allowing teachers and heads of establishments, currently in the front line and faced with genuine problems, to fulfill their mission with the assurance of a clear rule.

The debates on secularism, integration, equality of chances and the rights of women all raise the same question: what France do we want for ourselves and our children? We have inherited a country with a rich history, language and culture, a nation with strong values and ideals.

Everyone must be proud of France, our country. Everyone must feel a guardian of her heritage. Everyone must feel responsible for her future. Let us transform today's problems into tomorrow's assets by resolutely pursuing the unity of the French people. By confirming our commitment to an open and generous secularism such as we have been able to create year after year. By improving equality of opportunity, the spirit of tolerance and solidarity. By fighting resolutely for the rights of women. By uniting behind the values that have constituted and that still constitute France.

It is in this way that we will remain a confident, assured and cohesive nation. It is in this way that we can reaffirm our ambition to build for our country and our children a future of progress and justice.

Source: Jacques Chirac, "School Must Be a Secular Sanctuary," *The Independent*, December 18, 2003; http://argument.independent.co.uk/podium/story.jsp?story=474230.

Figure 3.28 Muslim students demonstrate against the headscarf ban in Paris, France, January 2004.

"No" to the Ban

by Sheema Khan

The land of *liberté, egalité et fraternité* has taken a decidedly selective definition of these ideals. The banning of all forms of visible religious symbols in state schools (except for discreet pendants) is ostensibly based on France's secular foundations. Some view it as secular orthodoxy, a mirror image of religious extremism that the nation purports to curtail.

Yet, it seems clear to me that the target of the ban is the hijab, a visible symbol of France's five-million strong Muslim community....

There is even the patronizing arrogance of Bernard Stasi, head of the commission on secularism in French society, who has equated the banning of the *hijab* as "a chance for Islam to save itself."

France—having once colonized the people of Algeria, Tunisia, Morocco, Syria and Lebanon—will now attempt the same on its own shores. The French model of colonization was to strip away the indigenous identities of its subjects, replacing language and culture with that of the motherland. It never succeeded, however, in turning people away from Islam.

The most vocal opponents of the *hijab* have been so-called feminists who have decided that the Muslim headscarf is a symbol of women's oppression and subjugation.

Apparently irrelevant is the voice of Muslim women themselves who choose to abide by the precepts of modesty of their faith. Feminism, which is about the empowerment of women to make their own choices, now falls prey to the very dictates it once battled. Within certain extreme Muslim circles, a Muslim woman's voice is never to be heard in public, while her intellect is deemed deficient. Ironically, French feminists seem to agree with these views, having decided how a woman in France must dress, without any respect for the diversity of women's own thoughts on the matter. Call it imperial feminism.

The debate also centres on the role of religion in the public sphere.

France has decided to take the path of strict separation between church and state. Germany is also grappling with the growing presence of the *hijab*, with battles under way to ban it altogether for government employees. In Italy, a local court upheld a complaint (brought by a Muslim) to forbid the display of a school crucifix, much to the horror of most Italians, including the local Muslim community. All of these policies are on a collision course with article nine of the *European Convention on Human Rights*, which guarantees the right to freedom of religion.

Given the history of religion and state in Europe, it is not surprising that issues of faith cause so much consternation. Throw in a few centuries of colonial rule and former subjects who now demand rights to their religious identity as citizens of the motherland. How then do societies balance the rights and interests of various groups? While there is no pat answer, the best policy is one that is attuned to the changing dynamics of the population. As long as there is give and take, there is hope for all to live together with mutual respect. Absolute decrees only serve to alienate.

Indeed, the rejectionists on both sides of the debate are happy with the French ruling. Those trying to improve relations between West and East, trying to convince Muslims that the West is not their enemy, will now have an uphill battle....

Source: Excerpted from Sheema Khan, "Banning *Hijab*: The New Colonialism," *The Globe and Mail*, Thursday, January 1, 2004, page A17.

Articulating a Personal Stand

1. List President Chirac's arguments for banning the hijab. With which do you agree or disagree? Why?
2. List Sheema Kahn's arguments against banning the *hijab*. With which do you agree or disagree? Why?
3. In a five-paragraph essay, state your own opinion on the subject.

1776 *Declaration of Independence* invokes "divine Providence"

1787 US constitution written

1791 First Amendment bans laws establishing or prohibiting religions

1863 Gettysburg Address refers to "this nation under God"

1954 "Under God" added to the Pledge of Allegiance

1955 "In God We Trust" stamped on all currency

1962 Supreme Court rules public school prayers unconstitutional

1983 Supreme Court authorizes nativity scene as part of secular display

1983 Supreme Court authorizes prayers to open legislative session

2003 Alabama chief justice removed for refusing to remove Ten Commandments monument

Figure 3.29 Timeline: United States.

The United States

The US experience illustrates that it is easier to separate church and state in the constitution than in actual practice. The First Amendment to the US constitution (1791) states, "Congress shall make no law respecting an establishment of religion or prohibiting the free exercise thereof." Early presidents Thomas Jefferson and James Madison did not want the government to support one religion or group of religions. They believed that both government and religion would be stronger if each remained separate. The constitution of the United States is a secular document. It makes no mention of God or religion other than in the First Amendment and article VI, which prohibits a "religious test" for public office. The writers of the constitution were not opposed to religious belief, but many were aware of the oppression and conflicts created by church–state partnerships in Europe.

Unlike some European countries, and Canada, the United States has not allowed public funding for religious schools. In the early 1960s, two US Supreme Court decisions declared mandatory Bible reading and government-sponsored religious activities—such as reciting the Lord's Prayer—to be unconstitutional in public schools. Silent, private prayer in school by any teacher or student was allowed.

In 1983, the US Supreme Court ruled in *Lynch v. Donnelly* that the city of Pawtucket, Rhode Island, could display a nativity scene at Christmas without violating the principle of separation of church and state. The court ruled that since the nativity scene was part of a larger display featuring Santa Claus, reindeer, and candy-striped poles, it was secular in nature. Subsequent court rulings have indicated that government-sponsored nativity scenes

Figure 3.30 In this 1871 cartoon by Thomas Nast, the female figure Columbia, symbolizing the United States, reinforces separation of church and state by refusing union with a number of churches.

standing alone are unconstitutional. In the same year, the US Supreme Court ruled in *Marsh v. Chambers* that it was constitutionally acceptable to open a legislative session with prayers said by a government-paid chaplain. The court decided that the prayers did not favour one religion and were part of a historical tradition dating back to the first opening of the House of Representatives and Senate in 1789.

Sometimes US judges have defied the constitution. In 2001, Alabama Chief Justice Roy Moore designed a 2,400-kg monument to the Ten Commandments and had it installed in the state courthouse rotunda. A district judge ordered the monument removed after a complaint that it promoted religion in a government place. Judge Moore appealed that decision all the way to the US Supreme Court, where he lost. Moore still refused to remove the monument. In November 2003, a state judicial panel removed Judge Moore from office on the ground that he had defied a federal order. Moore was not alone in his stand. Christian fundamentalist and other groups supported his "right to acknowledge God." Americans United for Separation of Church and State, the group that launched the complaint against Moore, applauded the removal of both the monument and the judge.

SOUND BITE "I believe in an America where the separation of church and state is absolute—where no Catholic prelate would tell the president (should he be Catholic) how to act, and no Protestant minister would tell his parishioners for whom to vote—where no church or church school is granted any public funds or political preference—and where no man is denied public office merely because his religion differs from the president who might appoint him or the people who might elect him."

John F. Kennedy, US president, 1961–63; address to the Greater Houston Ministerial Association, 1960

Canada

In some ways, Canada has been less committed to the separation of church and state than France or the United States. Canada has permitted government support of religious schools (mostly Roman Catholic) in Alberta, Ontario, Quebec, and Newfoundland. Section 93 of the *Constitution Act, 1867* protects any rights that were held by "denominational schools" at the time a province entered Confederation. Catholic schools, for example, were publicly funded in Canada West (Ontario) before Confederation, and were constitutionally entitled to funding after 1867.

Public funding of Catholic schools was a major issue in the federal election of 1896. In 1890, Manitoba had eliminated the separate-school system that the Catholic Métis had been given 20 years earlier. In the federal election, the Conservatives promised to pass legislation to force Manitoba to reinstitute publicly funded Catholic schools. The Liberals, who won the election, promised a compromise with the provincial premier. Federal Liberal leader Wilfrid Laurier fashioned an agreement that allowed public schools to provide a half-hour of religious instruction after school on request. A century later, in 1997, the people of Newfoundland voted in a referendum to abolish government funding for religious schools. The wording of the referendum stated that the new single-school system would still provide "opportunities for religious education and observances."

Questions around religious freedom—and the relationship between religion and government—were contested more often in Canada after 1982,

1774 *Quebec Act* recognizes rights of Roman Catholics in Quebec

1841 Catholic schools funded in Canada West (Ontario)

1867 Rights of "denominational schools" protected in *Constitution Act, 1867*

1890 Manitoba abolishes provincial Catholic schools

1982 Preamble to *Constitution Act, 1982* recognizes "the supremacy of God"

1982 Charter guarantees "freedom of conscience and religion"

1985 Supreme Court strikes down law forbidding Sunday commerce

1988 Ontario Court of Appeal prohibits religious opening exercises in public schools

1997 Newfoundland referendum abolishes government funding for religious schools

2003 Ontario Court of Appeal legalizes same-sex marriages

Figure 3.31 Timeline: Canada.

when the *Canadian Charter of Rights and Freedoms* was embedded in the constitution. The preamble to the *Constitution Act, 1982* declares that "Canada is founded upon principles that recognize the supremacy of God and the rule of law." However, a number of court decisions based on the Charter have widened the separation between government and religion.

In *R v. Big M Drug Mart Ltd.*, the Supreme Court of Canada ruled in 1985 that a provision in the *Lord's Day Act* prohibiting the sale of goods on Sunday violated section 2(a) of the Charter, which guarantees freedom of conscience and religion. The court concluded that the *Lord's Day Act*, with its compulsory observance of the Christian Sabbath, created a hostile environment for non-Christians and was therefore unconstitutional.

In 1988, the Ontario Court of Appeal ruled that religious exercises used to open the school day and the provincial regulations that authorized them were unconstitutional. In the case of *Zylberberg v. Sudbury Board of Education*, Jewish and Muslim parents claimed that the daily reciting of the Lord's Prayer violated their children's freedom of religion, guaranteed under section 2(a) of the Charter. Although the students were exempted from saying the Christian prayer, the court agreed with the parents that there was subtle coercion to conform to classroom practices.

Although government support for Christianity diminished as a result of judicial interpretations of the Charter, religion remains a part of Canadian political life. The Parliament of Canada has always incorporated prayer. Since 1994, it has used a **non-sectarian** prayer that addresses "God."

In 2003, citing the Charter, the Ontario Court of Appeal ruled same-sex marriage to be legal. The Vatican's Congregation for the Doctrine of the Faith quickly issued a statement telling Catholic politicians they had a "moral duty" to oppose any legalization of same-sex marriage. Roman Catholic Bishop Fred Henry of Calgary told the press that then Prime Minister Jean Chrétien was making a "morally grave error" and jeopardizing his eternal salvation by not appealing the court's decision. Leaders of Ottawa's Muslim and Hindu communities urged Chrétien not to allow "political expediency [to] redefine marriage." Chrétien and his successor Paul Martin are both Catholics, but both prime ministers stated that they were elected to serve the public. When it came to a conflict between Charter protection of minorities and the teachings of their religion, they must uphold the Charter. In other words, there must be a separation between church and state.

Check Your Understanding

1. Describe the historical separation of church and state in France.
2. Provide examples of how the United States has separated politics and religion yet allowed them to intermingle.
3. Do you agree or disagree that Canada has been less committed to the separation of church and state than France or the United States? Why?
4. How has the *Canadian Charter of Rights and Freedoms* affected the relationship between politics and religion? Give reasons for your answer.

METHODS OF POLITICAL INQUIRY
Conducting an Interview

For political scientists, interviews are an important means of obtaining in-depth information. How better to understand a government policy than to talk with the person who designed it?

Good interviews do not just happen. They require preparation and a specific set of skills. Here is a list of suggestions to help you when you conduct an interview.

Before the Interview

- Set up the appointment. Don't just show up expecting the person to talk to you.
- Become familiar with the person's background.
- Write your questions down before the interview. You don't have to ask them exactly as written, but writing them beforehand will help you focus on what is most important. Questions should be brief and require more than a "yes" or "no" answer.

During the Interview

- Arrive on time with all the equipment you need to conduct the interview, i.e., paper or pen, tape recorder.
- Ask one question at a time and begin with questions that are not controversial.
- Do not interrupt when the person is speaking, and allow him or her time to think when answering a question.
- Take good notes. If you miss an important point, ask the person to repeat what he or she said. You might wish to review your notes with the interviewee at the end of your conversation.
- End the interview in a reasonable amount time—an hour is good.
- Thank the interviewee for taking the time to talk with you.

After the Interview

- Write up your notes immediately after the interview. They should include a summary and possibly any personal reflections you may have.
- Send a handwritten thank-you note.

Source: Adapted from San Diego City Schools, *Process Student Guides*, "Interviewing Techniques"; http://projects.edtech.sandi.net/staffdev/tpss99/ processguides/interviewing.html.

Applying the Skill

In this chapter, you have looked at the role that religion has played in politics. To help you gain a better appreciation of these religions, your task will be to interview a member from a religion that is different from your own. This might be a religious leader in your community, a family friend, or a neighbour. Ask your interviewee how religious beliefs and practices have influenced his or her political views and activities. Once you have finished your interview, write a report and present it to the class.

Study Hall

Thinking and Inquiry

1. Create an organizer using the following headings: "influence of religion on political thought" and "impact of religion on political activity." Use it to compare and contrast Hinduism, Confucianism, Buddhism, Judaism, Roman Catholicism, Islam, and Protestantism.

2. Examine various causes for the development of anti-Semitism. Which do you believe has most affected discrimination against Jewish people? Explain your answer.

3. Controversy has recently arisen over the question of marriage rights for same-sex couples. How have leaders of the different religions reacted? What steps do you believe the Canadian federal government should follow? Why?

4. Could a person who is an atheist be an effective political leader in the world today? Why or why not?

5. Examine the Nobel lectures of either Martin Luther King, Jr. or Desmond Tutu through the links at www.emp.ca/cwp. To whom were they directing their words? Why do you think they chose to use religious language?

6. Define the voting method through which the Irish people have expressed their opinions on the questions of abortion and divorce. Cite some of the results of this type of voting in Ireland and elsewhere.

Communication

7. Look back at Figure 3.1 on page 75. Identify some of the religious imagery and cultural symbolism used by the artist. What message do you think she may have wished to convey?

8. "In many ways, religious fundamentalism is a modern phenomenon, characterized by a sense of embattled alienation in the midst of the surrounding culture, even where the culture may be nominally influenced by the adherents' religion." Do you agree or disagree with this statement? Explain your views in a brief formal essay.

9. Write an editorial for a major national Canadian newspaper either supporting or rejecting one of the following: formal prayer in school, religious holidays, or government support of religious schools.

10. Create a visual display illustrating the life and beliefs of a religious spokesperson. You may select a person mentioned in the chapter or another individual. Confirm your selection with your teacher before beginning your research.

11. Conduct a formal debate on the question of whether or not religion and politics should be separate.

12. What is your impression of the status of church and state in the United States currently? Write a paragraph outlining your views.

Application

13. The *Oslo Accords* of 1993 have not resolved the conflicts of Israel and the Middle East. Using the library and the Internet, research the present situation. Compile a report of current problems and progress, if any. Offer what you believe are some workable solutions.

14. Shirin Ebadi believes that in order for human rights to improve in Iran, the education system needs to change. Using the school library and the Internet, research human rights education. Develop a proposal describing how you would educate young people about rights. Create one lesson on human rights education and present it to a grade 10 Civics class or an elementary school class.

Nationalism and Internationalism

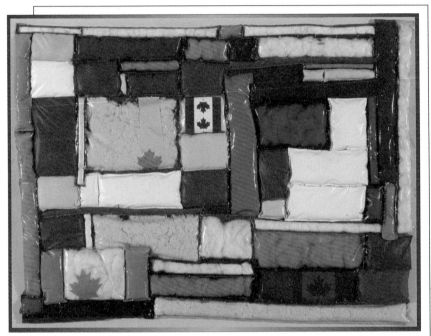

Figure 4.1 Internationally acclaimed Canadian artist Joyce Wieland (1931–98) created the collage *Confedspread* for Expo '67, the Universal Exposition held in Montreal to celebrate Canada's centennial in 1967.

Agenda

In this chapter, you will consider

- the concepts of nationalism and internationalism
- internationalism across time, cultures, and continents
- nationalism and the rise of nation-states
- imperialism and the decline of empires
- challenges and conflicts caused by nationalism globally
- Aboriginal nationalism and internationalism
- nationalism and internationalism in Canada
- Quebec nationalism
- how to interpret maps

Have you ever felt the excitement when Canada wins Olympic gold and the Maple Leaf flag is hoisted high to "O Canada"? When Team Canada wins the World Cup of hockey, hundreds of thousands, perhaps millions, of people take to Canada's streets to celebrate. Those same streets may once have been filled with people demanding that Canada join a war, oppose a war, support an empire, or break free from an empire—or rallying for national unity or for separation from Canada.

In all these examples, patriotism—love of one's country—is at work. So too are **nationalism** and **internationalism**, the themes of this chapter. In the following pages you will trace these ideologies back through time and place. You will study their political and human consequences. In the process, you will be challenged to examine assumptions you may hold about identity and belonging.

The Concepts of Nationalism and Internationalism

Like religion, nationalism shapes worldview and can inspire and unite communities. As an extreme ideology—for example, Hitler's appeals to ultranationalism in Nazi Germany—it can also tear communities apart. To understand nationalism, you need to understand related political concepts.

Although the terms "nation" and "state" are often used interchangeably, in political science they mean different things. A **nation** can be defined as a political community (or a people) that shares a collective identity that is based on ethnicity (race, language, culture, history, and possibly religion). A **state**, or country, can be defined as a geographical territory containing a population that is ruled by a government that exercises sovereignty. In turn, **sovereignty** can be defined as the exclusive right to the exercise of force within a given territory and the sole right to raise taxes, pass laws, and represent the territory internationally.

A people can be a nation, even without a state. Palestinians, Québécois, and Aboriginal peoples are all examples. A people (or nation) may inhabit several states; for example, the Kurdish people live in border areas of Turkey, Iraq, Iran, and Syria. Sometimes a state that is home to a people, or nation, can be divided—for example, North and South Korea or the former East and West Germany—through political events (see Chapter 5). Such situations create political instability and can lead to demands for an autonomous state or **self-government** within an existing state.

Many political commentators use the term **nation-state** to describe countries that are seen as something more than an organized system of government over a certain territory. Nation-states were usually built on ethnic foundations and are often seen as "homelands." For example, most citizens in Italy or Japan speak the same language and share a common religion, history, and customs. The same might be said of citizens of Poland, Germany, Ireland, and so on. Ethnic commonality creates strong bonds and a common identity, which contribute to feelings of nationalism.

Many modern states are home to people from all over the world, and cannot be based on ethnicity. In such countries, common identity is based on political values and institutions. In Canada, for example, multiethnicity—or multiculturalism—has become a source of shared identity and patriotic pride.

In *Blood and Belonging*, Canadian writer Michael Ignatieff describes two kinds of nationalism that reflect two kinds of states. **Civic nationalism** is an outgrowth

Figure 4.2 A Multicultural Festival in Kitchener, Ontario, June 2001. Professor Peter H. Russell of the University of Toronto has observed that Canadians are, or are becoming, a "people of peoples." What does he mean?

of the European Enlightenment (17th and 18th centuries). It is based on a belief that the state is home to all people who subscribe to its political values and ideals. **Ethnic nationalism** can be traced to Romantic German philosopher Johann Gottfried von Herder, in the late 18th century. Herder theorized that language was the primary source of culture: to be legitimate, the state must be built around a culturally distinct *Volk* (folk), or people.

SOUND BITE "Patriotism is when love of your own people comes first; nationalism, when hate for people other than your own comes first."

French President Charles de Gaulle,
Life *Magazine, May 9, 1969*

Like human beings, states cannot exist in complete isolation. As a political philosophy, internationalism promotes economic and political cooperation. This view holds that cooperation among states, rather than nationalistic self-interest, will advance the common good. It is related to **cosmopolitanism**, the understanding of diverse cultures that are different from one's own. **Geopolitics** is concerned with the way in which physical location on the globe affects political power relationships. *Realpolitik*, a political philosophy that emerged in 19th century Germany and Italy, is based on **realism**. A realist perspective sees international politics as a largely anarchic (without order or regulation) arena in which each state pursues its self-interest regardless of the interests of others. Both geopolitics and *realpolitik* shape a state's foreign relations and international decisions about national borders, spheres of political influence, conflict resolution, military alliances, trade, environmental issues, and so on. (See pages 127–28 on Bismarck in Germany and Cavour in Italy.)

SOUND BITE ". . . it is impossible for one to be internationalist without being a nationalist. . . . It is not nationalism that is evil, it is the narrowness, selfishness, exclusiveness which is the bane of modern nations which is evil."

Mahatma Gandhi, 1925

Nationalism and internationalism run throughout the world of politics. Internationalism has connected people from the time of the Holy Roman Empire and the Muslim Empire to the age of the United Nations. It is a reaching out, an effort at resolving and accepting differences. Internationalism seems to run in cycles, alternating with periods of nationalistic self-interest. The student of politics must learn to study the strengths and limits of both ideologies. In the Point Counterpoint that follows, you will see how debates around these political concepts go to the very heart of what it means to be a Canadian and an Aboriginal person living in Canada today.

Point:
Counterpoint → Debating Aboriginal Sovereignty

"Yes" to Aboriginal Sovereignty

by John A. Olthuis and Roger Townshend

The non-aboriginal Canadian takes as self-evident the legitimacy of the Canadian state and its **jurisdiction** over Canadian territory. The average aboriginal person, on the other hand, views much of the power exercised by the Canadian state as illegitimate, oppressive, and as infringing on the powers of the First Nations. . . .

There is no question that prior to European contact native nations in North America had stable cultures, economies, and political systems. They unmistakably exercised full sovereignty over their lands, although in somewhat different ways than European nations. It would be arrogant and **ethnocentric** to recognize only a European model of political organization as a sovereign state. . . . International law then and now recognized changes in sovereignty based on **conquest, discovery and settlement**, or **treaty**.

There is nothing in Canadian history that could qualify as a conquest in an international law sense. . . . There are . . . treaties that read as land transactions, which by their silence concerning matters of jurisdiction would seem to provide little help in rooting a claim that they are a source of Canadian sovereignty. Furthermore, there are vast areas of Canada where there are no treaties

whatsoever. Thus, the invocation of treaties is wholly unsatisfactory as a foundation for Canadian sovereignty. What is left is the doctrine of discovery and settlement. The difficulty with this is that it was intended to apply only to lands that were vacant. Its initial application to a claim of European jurisdiction required the step of considering the aboriginal people as legal non-persons. In fact, the "discovery" of the Americas sparked lengthy theological and judicial debates in Europe about whether indigenous people indeed were or should be treated as humans. . . .

Aboriginal people firmly believe that the political key to a better future is the recognition of jurisdiction of First Nations . . . that would allow and encourage the development of new types of structures that would reflect the distinct cultural, political, economic, and spiritual aspects of aboriginal society. This must be a jurisdiction that is provided with sufficient resources to be viable. It would indeed mean a fundamental restructuring of the institutions of the Canadian state, or perhaps more accurately, a rolling back of the Canadian state to allow for a just and peaceful coexistence of First Nations and the Canadian state. . . .

It is puzzling that the idea of native sovereignty should be so threatening to nonaboriginal people. The very nature of the Canadian political system involves a

Figure 4.3 Nisga'a leaders stand below portraits of King George V and Queen Mary in Ottawa following passage of the *Nisga'a Treaty,* April 2000. The Nisga'a now exercise self-government over some matters.

division of powers between federal and provincial governments. It is but an easy step in theory to implement another order of government and provide for an appropriate division of powers. . . . Demands for the recognition of aboriginal jurisdiction are not going to go away. If "legitimate" avenues for advancing these demands are shut down, other means may be sought. The continued peace and security of Canada may well depend on accommodating aboriginal jurisdiction.

Excerpted from Mark Charlton and Paul Barker, eds., *Crosscurrents: Contemporary Political Issues* (2nd ed.) (Toronto: Nelson, 1994), pp. 5–8.

"No" to Aboriginal Sovereignty

by Thomas Flanagan

It makes no sense to speak of sovereignty unless there is, as in the classical definition of the state, an organized structure of government ruling over a population within defined territorial boundaries. Native societies in what is now Canada did not possess sovereignty before the coming of the Europeans; neither the concept nor the underlying institutions were part of the culture of their hunting–gathering societies.

As a way of increasing their political leverage in contemporary Canada, native political leaders have adopted the classical language of statehood to describe their communities. What used to be called bands or tribes are now called "nations," and these nations are said to have possessed sovereignty from the beginning and to possess it still. This strategic use of language has served native leaders well in their struggle for greater power within the Canadian polity, but politically effective assertions should not be confused with intellectually persuasive analysis. . . .

In the ten provinces, Canada has over 600 Indian bands living on more than 2,200 reserves, plus hundreds of thousands of Métis and nonstatus Indians who do not possess reserves. These scattered pieces of land and disparate peoples are not going to be recognized as independent sovereign states, now or ever. They are simply not viable as sovereign states paying their own way and defending their interests in the international community. Nor is there any practical way to weld them into a single sovereign state. Native peoples are deeply divided by language, religion, customs, and history and in no way constitute a single people. . . .

Status Indians in Canada have suffered terribly under the regime of the *Indian Act* and the Department of Indian Affairs. . . . As quickly as possible, Indian bands should receive full ownership of their reserves, with the right to subdivide, mortgage, sell and otherwise dispose of their assets, including buildings, lands, and all natural resources. As much as possible, they should assume the self-government responsibilities of small towns or rural municipalities. . . .

However, a large and ever-increasing majority of native people do not live on reserves and never will, except for occasional visits. For this majority, neither self-government nor sovereignty can have any meaning except to the extent that they, as Canadian citizens, participate in the government of Canada. For them, the political illusion of self-government is a cruel deception, leading them out of, rather than into, the mainstream of Canadian life. Their future depends on fuller participation in the Canadian society, economy, and polity. They are, to all intents and purposes, internal immigrants, and for purposes of public policy their problems are fundamentally the same as those of other recent immigrants.

In the last analysis, the most harmful thing about the quest for sovereignty is the opportunity cost. The "brightest and best"—the leaders of native communities—are led to devote their talents to a cause that produces nothing except ever-growing levels of discontent and disappointment.

Excerpted from Mark Charlton and Paul Barker, eds., *Crosscurrents: Contemporary Political Issues* (2nd ed.) (Toronto: Nelson, 1994), pp. 9–15.

Articulating a Personal Stand

1. Why do you think groups of Aboriginal peoples call themselves "nations"?
2. Create a chart outlining the arguments presented in both articles on the question of Aboriginal sovereignty.
3. Which arguments do you feel are the strongest? the weakest? Give your reasons.
4. Write a one-page opinion response either supporting or opposing Aboriginal sovereignty. Refute arguments that support the other side, and explain why you disagree.
5. Return to your responses to these questions when you have finished studying this chapter and make any changes that you feel are politically relevant.

Check Your Understanding

1. Describe a situation in which you have felt strong feelings of nationalism. Why do you think you experienced these feelings?
2. Using examples, explain the differences between the concepts of "state" and "nation."
3. Describe two kinds of nationalism.
4. How can nationalism be both a beneficial and a harmful social force? Give specific examples that show both aspects of nationalism.
5. Define internationalism, cosmopolitanism, and *realpolitik* in your own words.

Forces of Internationalism in History

Internationalism has been driven by many forces throughout history. Four of these will be examined in the following pages. Religion, as you learned in Chapter 3, weaves throughout politics. Empire building and imperialism are a second force. Economic need drives trade, which brings nations and states into contact and is a third force of internationalism. A fourth force expresses itself through diplomacy and negotiation, in agreements, alliances, ententes, and treaties.

Internationalism and Religion

In Chapter 3, you learned that Arab armies spread Islam around the Mediterranean and into Asia and Africa after the death of the Prophet Muhammad in 632. The strength of the Muslim Empire, an enormous international organization, was the unifying influence of religious belief. The political head of the Muslim state, or *caliph* (an Arabic word meaning "successor"), ruled in accordance with the Qur'an and was believed to be the successor to the Prophet.

The Muslim Empire was marked by diversity and a flowering of cultural, social, and political institutions. It endured even after the Crusades (11th–13th centuries). By 1400, Muslim Turks from central Asia established the Ottoman Empire, which stretched from the Middle East into the Balkan region of Europe. At the height of its power in the 17th century, the conquests of the Ottoman Empire threatened Christian Europe. Increasing nationalism, however, sent the empire into a decline that ended with its dissolution after World War I (1914–18).

In the Middle Ages (ca. 400–1400), Christianity was the dominant religion of what is now Western Europe. Charlemagne (742–814), King of the Franks, used Christianity to convert "pagans" (non-believers) and unify what is now France and part of Germany. For this he was crowned Emperor of the **Holy Roman Empire** by the pope in 800. After Charlemagne's death, a series of monarchs centred in Germany took the title. From roughly 900–1800 CE, the Holy Roman Empire covered a large section of Europe.

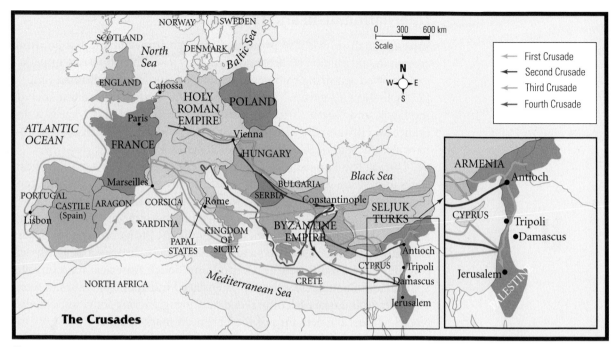

Figure 4.4 The Crusades, 1096–1212. Christian Crusaders tried, and failed, to drive Muslims from the Holy Land for more than a century.

At various times, the empire was composed of about 360 political entities (kingdoms, principalities, and so on) differing in size and power. Although most rulers and subjects were German, the empire included French, Czech, Polish, and other Slavic peoples. The emperor was elected from Roman Catholic candidates by fellow monarchs, who possessed local autonomies. Once elected, the emperor travelled to Rome to be crowned by the pope.

In the *Reichstag*, the empire's legislative body, both secular and ecclesiastical leaders could check the power of the emperor. Politically, the universal authority of the Church often conflicted with the limited power of the secular rulers. (Recall the phrase "going to Canossa" from Chapter 3, page 84.) Rulers needed Church support to ensure loyalty from their subjects, who were mostly peasants. Of course, the Church also needed state support to maintain its authority.

In the Middle Ages, the Roman Catholic bureaucracy reached into each European country, and Latin was the main language of communication. After the Protestant Reformation changed this in the early 16th century, members of the Holy Roman Empire became more autonomous by breaking away from the Church. Even with the weakening of the Church's unifying influence, the empire remained cohesive, displaying some characteristics of a modern international association of states, such as the European Union.

Figure 4.5 The Holy Roman Emperor and the pope, in a woodcut ca. 1493.

Internationalism and Imperialism

Internationalism was also promoted through **imperialism**, the political, economic, and military control of one country over other countries. Imperialism involved acquiring colonies and building empires. The Roman Empire (27 BCE–476 CE) covered the area around the Mediterranean Sea, including Egypt and North Africa, and stretched northward into what is today France and Britain. It endured as a political model in Western Europe. You have already read of the Muslim and Ottoman Empires.

During the Renaissance (ca. 1400–1600), several Western European states undertook sea explorations to find new trade routes. By the 18th century, they had become dominant world powers with colonies in the "new" worlds they "discovered." Internationalism in this stage of imperialism was achieved through force and superior technology. **Indigenous peoples** were exploited and their languages and religions were displaced as European colonies were established. In Central and South America, for example, Spanish and Portuguese conquerors enslaved indigenous peoples to work on plantations. Local agricultural and hunting–gathering activities were displaced to meet the demands of the European marketplace.

By the late 19th century, European imperial powers had divided up much of Africa, Asia, and the Pacific Islands. Again, this stage of imperialism was often ruthless. In the Congo, for example, historians suggest that up to 15 million Africans died harvesting rubber and other resources for King Leopold II (1835–1909) of Belgium, who ran the central African country as a private business. In China, the British forced opium imports to create favourable trade balances.

	Classical Antiquity 400 BCE–400 CE	Medieval Age 400–1400	Modern Age 1400–
government form	*polis* to empire	feudal fiefdom to nation-state (absolute monarchy)	constitutional monarchy to representative government to liberal democracy
central moral-political concepts	virtue; citizenship	natural law; divine right of kings	popular sovereignty; individual rights
economic forms	slavery; military; agriculture	agrarian; military–industrial; commercial	commercial
religion	pagan	Roman Catholicism	Christian pluralism to secularism
intellectual approach	philosophical	scholastic (Church-centred)	scientific

Source: Joy Esberey and Larry Johnston, *Democracy and the State: An Introduction to Politics* (Peterborough, ON: Broadview Press, 1994), p. 54.

Figure 4.6 Western European political history.

At its peak in the late 19th century and before World War I, the British Empire stretched from America to India and from Africa to New Zealand. It was the empire "on which the sun never sets." Britain ruled a quarter of the Earth's people. Even in India, an ancient civilization, English became the language of politics and commerce. Subject peoples often resisted political domination and economic exploitation. Yet sometimes imperialism recognized human aspirations. The British, for example, introduced systems of laws, education, and government that continue to have influence—much of it beneficial—on former colonies, including Canada. During the imperialism of the 19th and early 20th centuries, colonizers were most often white and the colonized were people of colour. The inherent racism and use of political power eventually led to nationalism and independence movements that continue to the present day.

Internationalism and Trade

Trade is a historic force of internationalism. In 12th century Northern Europe, for example, almost 100 trading cities—including Nijmegen in the Netherlands, Hamburg in Germany, Danzig in Poland, and Riga in Latvia—joined the Hanseatic League, an economic association that promoted trade. Members acquired monopolies and privileges, including military protection along trade routes. The Protestant Reformation and the rise of nationalism led to the League's collapse in the 16th century.

In 1834, 38 independent German states, led by Prussia, created the *Zollverein* (customs union) to remove trade tariffs. This proved to be a major step in the eventual formation of the nation-state of Germany in 1871.

The Hanseatic League and the *Zollverein* were forerunners of the European Coal and Steel Community, founded by the Netherlands, Belgium, Luxembourg, France, West Germany, and Italy in 1951. This organization of economic cooperation evolved into the European Economic Community, which became the European Union in 1993. At each stage, member states sacrificed some sovereignty for closer economic and political integration.

Internationalism by Means of Agreements

Internationalism has also been achieved through diplomacy and agreements between states. These can be called by many names, including "agreements," "conventions," "covenants," and "protocols." All are binding under international law and each signatory accepts a moral obligation to respect the terms. (You will study recent international agreements and their implementation in later chapters.)

Very often, international agreements have resulted from conflicts. In 1814–15 after the Napoleonic wars, for example, the victorious major European states redrew the map of Europe at the Congress of Vienna. Delegates from Britain, Prussia, Russia, and Austria wanted to restore the authority of dynasties that had been threatened by Napoleon and to expand

SOUND BITE "The greatest gift of any statesman rests not in knowing what concessions to make, but recognizing when to make them."

Prince Metternich (1773–1859), Austrian negotiator at the Congress of Vienna, in *Concessionen und Nichtconcessionen, 1852*

Figure 4.7 This engraving (ca. 1814–15) shows political leaders attending the Congress of Vienna to draft a peace settlement.

their territory and power. Using secret diplomacy and treaties, they did just that. They also suppressed the aspirations of groups that wished to further liberal nationalistic goals.

For the next century, as Western Europe dominated the globe, the most striking examples of agreements were the alliances, ententes, and secret treaties that marked international diplomacy. International conflicts and tensions resulted, making World War I (1914–18) inevitable. In this climate, in 1864, 16 European states signed the first *Geneva Convention* to establish rules for the humane treatment of battlefield casualties (see Chapters 8 and 11). In 1899 and 1907, peace conferences at The Hague, in the Netherlands, promoted compromise and arbitration as alternatives to war. They had little success.

One example in which arbitration did work peacefully was a boundary dispute between Canada and the United States in 1903. Canada lost its claim to sovereignty over some territory of the Alaska Panhandle when the British commissioner abandoned his Canadian fellow commissioners. As a result, Canadian delegates refused to sign the agreement. The settlement revealed that Britain was more interested in keeping the United States as an ally than in supporting Canada. A wave of anti-British public opinion swept over Canada.

In 1919, another effort at cooperation was the founding of the **League of Nations**. The League grew out of the *Treaty of Versailles*, 1919, which ended World War I. US President Woodrow Wilson proposed the League. He was convinced an international organization dedicated to preventing armed conflict could preserve world peace. Based in Geneva, Switzerland, the League grew to 63 member states. Powerful states like Russia and Germany quit at times, however. The League's strongest promoter never joined: the US Senate rejected President Wilson's idea of international cooperation (see Chapter 8).

THE WEB
To learn more about the League of Nations, visit www.emp.ca/cwp.

Check YOUR UNDERSTANDING

1. Identify four historical forces of internationalism.
2. Describe two "religious" empires that nourished internationalism.
3. How did the British Empire serve as an agency of internationalism?
4. List the benefits and drawbacks of imperialism. In your opinion, which was more significant? Why?
5. Identify two European trade associations that existed before the 20th century. How did they encourage internationalism?
6. Describe three international agreements that displayed internationalism in the period prior to 1920.
7. Describe some of the efforts made by independent states at internationalism. Assess how effective they have been.

Nationalism in History

The modern concept of the state dates back to 15th century Europe. Prior to this, if people in Europe saw themselves as belonging to any *polis* larger than the local village or feudal estate, it was to "Christendom," a vast collective unified by Catholicism and ruled from Rome. Very few people could read at the time, and travel was very limited. Over time, powerful monarchies in England, France, and Spain worked to suppress regionalism. They tried to make subjects conscious of a common identity, which would help unite them to fight common enemies.

As you learned in Chapter 3, the Protestant Reformation in the 16th century also contributed to nationalism. The Spanish Inquisition, a state–church agency, rooted out and punished non-Catholics. In a region of what is now Germany, however, Frederick III of Saxony supported Martin Luther—even after the pope excommunicated Luther in 1520. Lutheranism fed German nationalism. In England, King Henry VIII broke with Rome in 1534, creating a separate Church of England and making himself its head. People such as adviser and minister Thomas More, who remained loyal to Rome, paid with their lives.

The decline of Latin as the universal language and the increased importance of the written vernacular (the native language of a country or region) also boosted nationalistic sentiments. The difference between an English person and a French person became much more pronounced when neither could communicate in Latin. The wars between England and France and between England and Spain became as much wars of nationalism as wars of religion.

Nationalism grew with the *Treaty of Westphalia* (1648), which ended the Thirty Years' War in Europe. The Netherlands, for example, broke from Spanish rule and became an independent nation-state. Because the Holy Roman Emperor lost much of his authority, German princes and rulers could declare the religion of their lands. With the loss of authority of the emperor, various nation-states emerged, gaining in prominence and power.

Press Play

Luther (2003; directed by Eric Till), starring Joseph Fiennes (as the title character) and Peter Ustinov (as Frederick of Saxony), explores the religious and nationalistic basis of Luther's fight against the international power of the Roman Catholic Church. (PG-13)

Figure 4.8 This 18th century print depicts Captain Rouget de Lisle singing his new composition, "*La Marseillaise*," before the Mayor of Strasbourg in 1792.

SOUND BITE "The cause of America is in a great measure the cause of all mankind. Many circumstances hath, and will arise, which are not local, but universal, and through which the principles of all Lovers of Mankind are affected, and in the Event of which, their Affections are interested."

Thomas Paine, Introduction to Common Sense, *1776*

Nationalism and Democratic Revolutions

When leaders of the United States' war of independence (1775–83; see Chapter 5) proclaimed the *Declaration of Independence* in 1776, they voiced a new kind of nationalism. In the words of Thomas Paine, "an island [Great Britain] should no longer rule a continent." An identifiable group of people in the colonies united to oppose the imperialist policies of Britain and used military force to free themselves. About a third of people in the Thirteen Colonies, however, were loyal to Britain. As war wore on, laws were passed against them. Eventually up to 100,000 "Loyalists" fled, mainly to Canada.

The new country of the United States saw itself as a beacon of liberty and democracy. This core belief fed American nationalism and was supported by the creation of national symbols and myths. The French Revolution (beginning in 1789) was also fuelled by nationalism and democratic ideals. French revolutionaries were loyal to the "nation," not the monarchy. They abolished the *Estates Général* (a legislative body called at the whim of the monarch) and replaced it with the *Assemblée Nationale* (National Assembly), composed of delegates answerable to "the people."

"*La Marseillaise*," a revolutionary war song, became France's national anthem. It is imbued with nationalistic sentiments: "Come, children of the nation, the Day of Glory has arrived." People were encouraged to sacrifice and fight for France. The entire hierarchy of social classes—including the aristocracy and clergy—was reduced to a single status: that of *citizen*. Military conscription created citizen-armies, which defeated the aristocratic and mercenary forces of the Revolution's enemies. The French Revolution inspired the spread of nationalism.

Napoleon's Empire Building

As leader of France (1799–1815), Napoleon pursued a France-first policy, using his army to dominate Europe. Napoleon moved the Italian silk industry to the south of France and introduced French into the schools of Flemish Belgium, arousing nationalistic reactions in both countries. Eventually, expressions of Spanish and Russian nationalism opposed to French domination contributed to Napoleon's final defeat.

At the beginning of the 19th century, very few nation-states existed. This changed by mid-century. Just as America had created and used nationalism to fight its war of independence, so would ethnic groups in Europe. Nationalist aspirations at this time were often allied with liberal ideology, including demands for equality, representative government, freedom of expression, and freedom of religion. Greece fought a war (1814–21) for its sovereignty and declared independence from the Ottoman Empire after four centuries of subjugation. It continued to fight to repatriate Greek-speaking portions of the empire. The Irish people struggled for freedom from Great Britain. The Polish people yearned for a nation separate from Russia.

Nationalism and *Realpolitik*

In the second half of the 19th century, two leaders used nationalism to create the new nation-states of Italy and Germany. Although a desire for unification had been present for many years, the Italian peninsula was a patchwork of small states. These were controlled by outside powers, such as Austria and Spain, as well as individual Italian rulers and the pope in Rome. Camillo Cavour (1810–61), a statesman from Piedmont–Sardinia, used *realpolitik* to unite Italy. Through strategic military alliances, secret diplomacy, and force of arms, Cavour achieved his goals: the United Kingdom of Italy was proclaimed in 1861. Cavour became prime minister but died the same year. By 1870, Italian unification was complete.

The nationalism sweeping across Italy was also a form of internationalism: it brought together states that had distinct cultures, customs, dialects, and languages. This was true further north, where Otto von Bismarck (1815–98) used *realpolitik* and authoritarianism to unify 39 separate states into one Germany.

Figure 4.9 Unification of Italy, 1860–70.

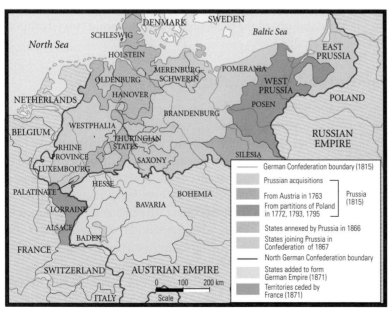

Figure 4.10 Unification of Germany, 1740–1871.

As the Prussian leader, Bismarck fought wars against Denmark, Austria, and France to unify German states and annex or intimidate other states into joining a united Germany under Prussia's monarch. After German unification in 1871, which created the German Empire, the **militant nationalism** of *realpolitik* spread across Europe to become the backdrop to World War I.

Nationalism and Imperialism

In the late 19th century, nationalism and imperialism merged. Whether practised by France, Germany, Britain, Spain, and others, imperialism was built upon an assumption of cultural superiority. Imperial powers saw themselves as bringing civilization to inferior cultures. Christian missionaries helped carry the message. Charles Darwin's (1809–82) *Origins of Species* also had an enormous impact when it was published in 1859. Darwin's theories of evolution and of natural selection (commonly known as "survival of the fittest") were applied to human societies as **social Darwinism**. European leaders could view their conquests as inevitable and justifiable on scientific and moral grounds.

By the outbreak of World War I, competing European powers had portioned off all of Africa (see the map in Figure 4.28 on page 152). In Asia, the French took Vietnam and Laos, the Dutch held Indonesia, and the English controlled India, Burma (Myanmar), and Singapore. The United States took part of Mexico and annexed Puerto Rico, Hawaii, and the Philippines. In Asia, Japan avoided the imperialist tide from the West. After first meeting American visitors in 1853, Japan reformed its government to incorporate Western ideas. This strengthened Japanese nationalism. In the late 19th and early 20th centuries, Japan became an imperial power in the Pacific. It fought wars with Russia and China, annexing territories including Taiwan and Korea. Japan's military became one of the most powerful in the world (see Grassroots Politics and Protest, page 129).

Nationalism and the Dissolution of Empires

A number of new nation-states resulted from the dissolution of the 600-year-old Ottoman Empire, which collapsed after being defeated in World War I. Between 1915 and 1917, Turkey had mass-deported all Armenians. An estimated 1.5 million Armenians died in what has been called the "Armenian Genocide." (In 2004, Canada became one of the few countries to recognize and condemn this genocide. Turkey denies it ever happened.) The treaties ending World War I established an independent Armenia and an autonomous Kurdish area. Turkey rejected both, and invaded and reclaimed the Kurdish lands. It fought the Soviet Union for control of Armenia. In 1920, Armenia became a Soviet Republic.

The treaties also enlarged Greece at the expense of Turkey. In the Turkish war of independence with Greece (1919–22), Turkey regained its territory. When the Republic of Turkey was declared in 1923, war hero Mustafa Kemal

THE WEB

For more on social Darwinism, go to www.emp.ca/cwp.

PRESS PLAY

In *Ararat* (2002), Armenian-Canadian director Atom Egoyan examines the Armenian Genocide through the eyes of an 18-year-old driver who is working on the film set of a historical epic about the collapsing Ottoman Empire and the Armenian massacres. (14A)

Grassroots Politics and Protest

Ho Chi Minh

Among 20th century revolutionaries, Ho Chi Minh (1890–1969) led the longest and—in terms of human lives—one of the costliest fights against a colonial power. Ho cultivated the public image of a kindly "Uncle Ho." In reality, he was a nationalist revolutionary obsessed with a single goal: independence for Vietnam. In his quest, he led his **guerrilla** fighters to victory over the Japanese, the French, and the Americans.

As early as 1918, Ho advocated Vietnamese independence. At the Paris Peace Conference in 1919, he tried and failed to win US support for a Vietnam free of French colonial rule. A year later, Ho, a Confucian scholar, helped found the French Communist Party. He travelled to China and the Soviet Union. Later, he said "It was patriotism, not communism, that inspired me." Still in exile, in 1930 he helped found the Indochinese Communist Party to overthrow the French and create an independent Vietnam governed by the people.

Ho returned to Vietnam for the first time in 30 years in 1941 at the height of World War II, when the French presence was weak. He established the League for the Independence of Vietnam and led commandos against Japanese invaders. By 1945, he had captured Hanoi, Vietnam's capital. He read to the people of Hanoi the Vietnamese *Declaration of Independence*, quoting the US *Declaration of Independence*. But his hopes for US support were again dashed. After World War II, Vietnam was divided: non-communist Chinese controlled the North, and the South was returned to France. When Ho returned to power in the North in 1946, he warned the French the Vietnamese people would "fight to the bitter end any attempt by the French colonialists to reconquer their country." The French nonetheless invaded North Vietnam. When the Indochinese War ended in 1954, France withdrew and Vietnam remained divided into North and South Vietnam.

With France gone, the United States supported a series of governments in South Vietnam. As president of the North, Ho fought the Vietnam War (1961–75) against the South and the United States to reunite the country. Vietnam was unified and Ho's dream of independence was achieved in 1975, six years after he died. An estimated three million North and South Vietnamese people had paid with their lives.

Ho fought until his death to free his country from foreign control. In his final testament, "Democratic Republic of Vietnam Independent Freedom Happiness, May 10, 1969," he wrote: "Our mountains will always be, our rivers will always be, and our people will always be." Against his wishes for a simple cremation, the body of Ho Chi Minh was embalmed and put on display in a granite mausoleum.

Questions

1. What evidence in Ho Chi Minh's life indicates he was a nationalist above all else?
2. Why do you think the United States would not work with Ho Chi Minh for Vietnam's freedom?
3. Why do you suppose Ho was able to defeat three countries that were far more powerful than his?

Figure 4.11 Ho Chi Minh is surrounded by children at a youth rally in Hanoi, 1955.

(Ataturk) (1881–1938) became its first president. Ataturk, a militant nationalist, worked to make Turkey a modern secular state, and in 1924 it ceased to be an Islamic state. Ataturk remained president until his death.

The collapse of the Austro-Hungarian Empire after World War I also led to a series of new nation-states. During peace conferences, US President Woodrow Wilson advocated for national **self-determination**. He believed that repressed nationalism in Austria–Hungary had been a major cause of World War I. The new states of Hungary, Czechoslovakia, Yugoslavia, and Austria were created. Poland was carved out of Russian and German territory. Russia's early withdrawal from the war led to the creation of independent states in Finland, Estonia, Latvia, and Lithuania. As much as possible, the map of Europe was redrawn along nationalistic lines. With German-speaking people living in Czechoslovakia and Poland, boundaries would not be stable.

Figure 4.12 While the Kurdish people are spread throughout the Middle East, the central portion of this map shows the "Kurdistan" envisioned by many Kurds. What sovereign states does it touch upon?

The Kurds: A Nation Without a State

Even with the dissolution of the Ottoman Empire, the Kurds did not create a nation-state. Then, as now, most Kurds lived in the mountainous territory straddling the borders of Turkey, Iraq, Iran, and Syria. Today, a majority (12 million) of Kurds reside in southeastern Turkey. Many Kurds view this region as the country of Kurdistan. Kurds have their own language and culture, and the majority are Sunni Muslims.

Ethnically and linguistically, Kurds are non-Arabic and are closest to Iranians. Kurds can be seen as a people, but there are several reasons why Kurdistan has not become a state or gained sovereignty:

- The Kurds are nomadic and tribal.
- Turkey, Iraq, and Iran would lose territory to a separate Kurdistan.
- Turkey, Iraq, and Iran have taken steps to suppress Kurdish nationalism and block statehood.
- The Kurds are vulnerable to attack in the border territories they inhabit.

Figure 4.13 Kurdish women visit a gallery memorializing the gassing of 5,000 Kurds in the Iraqi town of Halabja by Saddam Hussein's regime in 1988.

Taking a Stand   Julius Nyerere

Julius Nyerere was born in 1922 to a tribal chief in Tanganyika. He started school at age 12 and eventually graduated from the University of Edinburgh on a government scholarship. Returning to teach, Nyerere immersed himself in the movement to gain independence for Tanganyika, a former German colony that had been ruled by the British since 1922. Nyerere's skill at working with many factions helped Tanganyika achieve independence peacefully in 1961. Three years later, Tanganyika united with Zanzibar to form the Republic of Tanzania. Nyerere became prime minister and held that position until retiring in 1985.

Nyerere worked to build a just society in one of Africa's poorest countries. Emphasizing harmony, equality, and self-sacrifice, he helped unify far-flung tribes. He blended European socialism with African **communalism** in a rural-based cooperative movement called *ujamaa* (Swahili for "familyhood"). Nyerere stressed personal development above material gain. Under his leadership, Tanzania maintained peace when violence engulfed neighbouring countries such as Rwanda and Uganda.

Also known as *Mwalimu* ("teacher"), Nyerere rejected the colonial education system's primary focus on examinations and paper qualifications. Instead, the new system stressed self-reliance and lifelong learning. Nyerere connected urban students to the importance of manual labour by leading them on marches through rural villages. His dedication to equality led to high literacy rates and good health care.

Nyerere's nationalism was not defined by European-imposed borders. Instead, he supported "African nationalism." He helped found the Organization of African Unity (today the African Union) in 1963, an association of African states that works for African solidarity and **decolonization**. Tanzania was a base for groups that worked to liberate Mozambique from Portuguese rule and Rhodesia (now Zimbabwe) and South Africa from white-minority regimes.

Tanzania's one-party system was criticized, but Nyerere said it offered stability and broad new freedoms. In creating an independent, self-reliant country, Nyerere had limited resources and foreign aid. His *ujamaa* movement faced setbacks. He refused a German offer to build a sugar factory, for example, because the price was a German naval station in Zanzibar. Although a member of the British Commonwealth, Tanzania was a **non-aligned country** during the **Cold War** (1947–89). This means that it was not associated militarily or politically with the West or the Soviet Union, although at times it tilted toward Communist China.

The life of Julius Nyerere encompassed the triumphs and challenges in Africa's decolonization. When he died in 1999, he was widely revered in Africa and around the world.

Questions

1. How did Julius Nyerere use both colonial and African ideas as a leader?
2. a) Research decolonization in the African states of Burundi, Rwanda, Uganda, Zimbabwe, Zaire, and Angola.
   b) Draw a sketch map illustrating the position of these states in relation to Tanzania.
3. In an essay, analyze the major problems associated with nationalism and decolonization in Africa.

Check Your Understanding

1. How did the decline of Latin as a universal language boost nationalist sentiments?
2. How has religion contributed to the rise of nationalism?
3. Why do you think nationalism merged with liberal ideology in the early 19th century?
4. Describe how pragmatic politics was used to create Italy and Germany. What German word describes this political philosophy?
5. Using Figures 4.9 and 4.10 on page 127, identify the two states that were the centres of Italian and German unification under Cavour and von Bismarck, respectively. Speculate about why the other individual states came together to form the nations of Italy and Germany.
6. How were Darwin's theories of the struggle for survival used to justify the policies of imperialism?
7. Describe how the political situation of the Kurds exemplifies a "nation" without a state.

Nationalism in the Global Community

The complexity of nationalism is reflected in the many ways states come into being. Sometimes war imposes borders. Sometimes borders are imposed by a military conquest. For example, England militarily conquered Ireland, and Scotland was joined to England to create Great Britain—yet Irish and Scottish nationalism remain very much alive. Sometimes states are created by imperial powers. Britain partitioned India and Pakistan, and Northern Ireland and the Republic of Ireland, to deal with nationalism. Sometimes international organizations are involved, as with the United Nations' partition of Palestine in 1947 (see Chapter 3). Yet borders alone cannot resolve nationalist tensions or fulfill the aspirations of various peoples for their own states.

As you learned earlier, the dissolution of empires led to decolonization. At the end of the Cold War rivalry between the United States and the Soviet Union, pockets of ethnic nationalism that had been suppressed by **superpower** political alliances were unleashed (see Chapter 5). The following pages provide overviews of situations involving ethnic nationalism today: Chechnya, the former Yugoslavia, and the former Czechoslovakia.

Chechnya

THE WEB

To find out more about the political situation in Chechnya and its ethnic and religious roots, go to www.emp.ca/cwp.

When Premier Mikhail Gorbachev reformed communism in 1989, he reduced the power of the central authority (see Chapter 5). The Soviet Union began unravelling. Nationalist groups established nation-states in Lithuania, Estonia, and Latvia. In 1991, 11 more states—including Belarus, Ukraine, Kazakhstan, Georgia, and Uzbekistan—declared independence. These states and Russia then formed the Commonwealth of Independent States to coordinate trade, lawmaking, and security. The collapse of the Soviet Union in

1991 was, in a sense, a triumph of ethnic nationalism over a once unified sovereign state.

States such as Estonia and Georgia had already been "union republics." Chechnya had not, and Russia would not recognize it as independent. Chechens are the indigenous people of the North Caucasus mountains, on the northern border with Georgia. Chechnya is predominantly Sunni Muslim. Its conflicts with Russia go back centuries, including deadly mass deportations under Stalin. A powerful Chechen separatist movement involving guerrilla warfare emerged in the 1990s and led to two separate wars with Russia. Much of Chechnya, especially the capital Grozny, was devastated by the Russian military. Tens of thousands of civilians were killed.

After the terrorist attacks of September 11, 2001, Russian President Vladimir Putin compared Russia's war in Chechnya with the US war on terrorism. Putin alleged Chechen rebels had links to Osama bin Laden's al-Qaida network. Critics suggested that Putin was inventing the connection to justify Russian actions. Chechnya is extremely important to Moscow. It has rich oil reserves and is prime pipeline territory. Russia has also justified its military response to the Chechen insurgency by saying it must prevent ethnic and religious tensions from spreading within the North Caucasus region of the Russian Federation.

Chechen rebel attacks have led to many hundreds of deaths. In October 2002, about 50 Chechen terrorists—both male and female—seized a Moscow theatre. They threatened to kill the 700 audience members unless Russian troops withdrew from Chechnya. Some hostages were released, but after three days Russian forces piped in an anesthetic gas and stormed the theatre. Many terrorists were shot as they lay unconscious. Some 100 hostages died as well from the effects of the gas. Russian authorities said they had no choice— the terrorists had bombs strapped to their bodies. Chechen terrorists have continued to use suicide bombers, kidnappings, and sieges. In 2004, hundreds of children and teachers were killed when terrorists took an entire school hostage in Beslan, North Ossetia, a predominantly Christian republic in the North Caucasus. Political analysts feared that ethnic and religious tensions would spread throughout the region.

Yugoslavia (the Balkans)

Under communism in 1945, Yugoslavia expanded into a confederation of six republics: Bosnia, Croatia, Macedonia, Montenegro, Slovenia, and Serbia, including Serbia's two semi-autonomous provinces, Kosovo and Vojvodina. As the communist system collapsed in the 1980s, violent nationalism splintered Yugoslavia. After several years of unrest, Slovenia and Croatia declared independence in 1991. The next year, so did Macedonia and Bosnia–Herzegovina. Violent nationalism and religious intolerance spread.

The roots of nationalist tensions in the Balkans go back hundreds of years. In 1389, in the Field of the Blackbirds in Kosovo, Ottoman Turks

1785 Sheik Mansur defeats Russian forces, becomes Chechen hero

1858 Czar annexes Chechnya

1917 Communists crush Chechen uprising

1939–44 Chechens welcome German forces

1944 Stalin deports Chechens, exterminates half the population

1950 Chechens allowed to return

1950–91 Muslim faith repressed

1994–97 Russians and Chechens clash in Chechnya

1997 Chechnya becomes autonomous

1999 Islamic law established; Russian occupation condemned

2000 Russia appoints Chechen leader; resistance erupts

2002 Chechen rebels seize Moscow theatre

2004 Russian-appointed leader killed; Beslan school attacked

Figure 4.14 Timeline: Chechnya and Russia.

Figure 4.15 Yugoslavia in 1945 and the Balkans in 2004.

1389 "Field of the Blackbirds" battle fought in Kosovo

1914 Serbian nationalist assassinates Austrian archduke; World War I breaks out

1945 Communist leader Marshall Tito (1892–1980) creates Yugoslavia

1989 Yugoslavian President Milosevic incites Serbian nationalism at Blackbirds anniversary

1991–92 Communism collapses; nationalism fractures Yugoslavia in civil war

1992 Canadian Major-General Lewis Mackenzie commands UN peacekeepers

1995 NATO forces impose peace; 200,000 Serbs flee Croatian attacks

1999 NATO bombs Serbian targets; Milosevic indicted for war crimes in Bosnia, Croatia, Kosovo

2000 Democratic elections and protests oust Milosevic

2003 Yugoslavia ceases to exist

Figure 4.16 Timeline: The Balkans.

defeated Serbian forces under Prince Lazar. Rather than pay tribute to the Muslim Turkish conquerors and live, Prince Lazar and his Christian soldiers fought to the death. The prince became an iconic national hero: Serbian pilgrims still come to Kosovo to honour him.

During 600th anniversary celebrations of the Field of the Blackbirds in 1989, Slobodan Milosevic, the Serbian president of Yugoslavia, reminded Serbs that Muslim invaders had settled in Kosovo. "No one will ever beat you again," he promised. Milosevic used hostilities to advance his policy of expanding Serbia. He encouraged the Serbian minority in Kosovo to rebel against the province's Albanian leadership. Eventually, Serbs controlled Kosovo's government, courts, businesses, schools, and police—even though the population was 90 percent ethnic Albanian and Muslim. Some Serbs used the Field of Blackbirds to take revenge on the Muslim population of Kosovo in the 1990s.

NATO forces were drawn into the conflict, and the term "**ethnic cleansing**" was used for the first time to describe what they found: entire ethnic populations were being systematically killed or forced to escape a geographical area to make way for another ethnic group. The term described the actions of Serbian, Croatian, and Albanian forces in the Balkans—the geographic region of the former Yugoslavia plus Albania.

Milosevic sent a Serbian-dominated army into Serb-populated territories in Croatia and Bosnia, vowing to protect Serbian minorities from what he called "Islamic fundamentalism" and "Croatian genocide." Between 1991 and 1995, almost 300,000 people died. Many Bosnian Muslims and Croats were killed under a policy of ethnic cleansing, which included massacres, rape, and concentration camps. Extreme nationalism, however, affected all groups in the Balkans. For example, Croatian President Franjo Tudjman publicly dismissed the mass killings of Serbs in Croatia and Bosnia–Herzegovina during World War II.

Some analysts see religion as the root of the Balkan conflicts. They point out that all groups share Slavic ethnic origins. One exception is the Albanians in Kosovo, who are descendants of Illyrian tribes from the south and who are mainly Muslim. The Serbs in the Balkans are almost entirely followers of the Serbian Orthodox Church, while most Slovenes and Croats are Roman Catholic.

During the civil war in Yugoslavia, Milosevic drew on ancient hatreds to forge a nationalism that saw Serbia fight different groups in Bosnia, Croatia, and Kosovo. Leaders of Muslim and Croatian groups drew on similar hatreds to fight Serbs. Horrific mass murders in the Balkans, of neighbours by neighbours, revealed to the world how ethnic and religious belief systems can grip the human psyche. Unchecked, they can play a deadly role in how people relate to one another in a community.

Czechoslovakia

While ethnic conflicts shattered Yugoslavia, two other ethnic groups in central Europe negotiated separation peacefully. On January 1, 1993, the country of Czechoslovakia ceased to exist. In its place were two nation-states: the Czech Republic and Slovakia. Czechoslovakia had been created out of the old Austro-Hungarian Empire after World War I. Ethnic tensions had troubled the new democratic country in the years before World War II, when German and Slovak minorities were often unhappy with Czech dominance. Adolf Hitler took over Czechoslovakia by 1939, before the outbreak of World War II.

After World War II, Czechoslovakia's communist government made it a **client** (dependent) **state** of the Soviet Union. In 1968, Soviet troops crushed the "Prague Spring," a popular social movement led by intellectuals and students for democratic reforms. Two decades later, in 1989, the **Velvet Revolution** peacefully overthrew the repressive communist government. Pro-democracy demonstrations in Prague spread to other cities—and neighbouring Soviet **satellite states**—and Czechoslovakia's communist government resigned to allow free elections in which Vaclav Havel became president

Figure 4.17 The state of Czechoslovakia, formed in 1918, became two separate republics in 1993.

1918 Republic of Czechoslovakia proclaimed

1939 Germany takes over Czechoslovakia

1945 Soviet troops expel German forces

1946 Communist Party shares power

1968 Soviet forces crush liberal reforms of "Prague Spring"

1989 Velvet Revolution ends communist rule

1993 Czech Republic and Slovakia declared

Figure 4.18 Timeline: Czechoslovakia.

of Czechoslovakia. This was a political turning point, as Havel later pointed out in a speech in Philadelphia, Pennsylvania on July 4, 1994:

> The two most important political events in the second half of the twentieth century [are] the collapse of colonial **hegemony** [effective political control, whether formal or informal] and the fall of communism. . . . The central political task of the final years of this century, then, is the creation of a new model of coexistence among the various cultures, peoples, races and religious spheres within a single interconnected civilization.

A strong secessionist movement in Slovakia led to the decision to split the country peacefully in 1993. From a Slovak perspective, Czechoslovakia had come to stand for Czech hegemony over its affairs.

Early in the 20th century, Slavic nationalists (including Czechs and Slovaks) had agitated for the state of Czechoslovakia as protection against German hegemony in central Europe. Early in the 19th century, German Romantic nationalists had opposed the hegemony of French Enlightenment culture and pushed for German unification. Secessionist and nationalist movements are always anti-hegemonic. Once a nationalist movement achieves its objective, however, it too becomes hegemonic—the dominant power in its territory. In independent Slovakia, for example, the Hungarian minority has complained of mistreatment.

Nationalism and Immigration

Nationalism can be a force that unifies a country and welcomes people from other countries to become citizens. It could be argued that without a spirit of nationalism, Canada could become the next US state. If citizens have little pride or attachment to their country, how will it remain independent? Might Canada, for example, not enjoy economic benefits by politically joining the United States, a larger economic entity? Nationalism can also be used to promote non-inclusion. Political parties in many countries cite nationalistic concerns to support anti-immigration policies. Usually these parties are on the right of the political spectrum.

In Australia, the One Nation party attracted 8 percent of the popular vote when it ran in its first election in 1998. One Nation demanded that all Asian immigration stop until Australia's unemployment rate fell to zero. It spoke out against Aboriginals living on welfare. For One Nation, the "nation" of Australia had its roots in white European settlers and their descendants, although it denies its policies are racially based.

In 2001, Australia made headlines when Prime Minister John Howard's Liberal government sent navy ships to stop 434 mainly Afghan asylum seekers from landing on Australian territory. The Norwegian freighter *Tampa* had rescued the Afghans after their ship sank in the Pacific. Norway and Amnesty International accused Australia of violating the 1951 *UN Convention*

Press Play

Welcome to Canada (NFB, 1989), by Canadian director John N. Smith, dramatizes an actual event in which Newfoundland fishers rescued a boatload of Tamil refugees and took them home to their village. (NR)

Relating to the Status of Refugees, to which it is a signatory. Australia said it had to stop a flood of "boat people." Commercial ships may now hesitate to rescue such disabled ships and their passengers at sea. Many of the *Tampa*'s refugees went to New Zealand. A year later, Australia accepted some dozens of the asylum seekers. Many commentators believe the government was catering to a wave of anti-immigration sentiments in Australia.

In the first round of France's presidential election in 2002, Jean-Marie Le Pen, leader of the far-right National Front party, garnered almost 18 percent of the vote, finishing a close second to leader Jacques Chirac's 20 percent. Le Pen lost decisively to Chirac in the final round, but his support shocked Europeans. Le Pen's platform emphasized law and order, and opposed immigration and France's participation in the European Union. In his 50-year political career, Le Pen has often described immigrants from France's former North African colonies as an "invasion," linking them to crime and calling them a threat to French culture. In 1987, he called Nazi gas chambers "a detail of history." Ten years later he was banned from holding public office for a year after being found guilty of punching a female Socialist Party deputy.

In Austria, Joerg Haider pulled the nationalist Freedom Party to the right in the 1990s as its new leader. Haider opposed immigration as well as Austria's entry into the European Union and adoption of its common currency, the euro. In controversial comments, he referred to Nazi concentration camps as "punishment camps" and said Nazi SS veterans deserved respect as army officers. He supported a nationalist movement for a "greater Germany," suggesting an alliance of German-speaking Austria with Germany.

Figure 4.19 French high school students protest right-wing National Front leader Jean-Marie Le Pen on May 1, 2002.

Haider's policies were described as racist and intolerant, but the Freedom Party won 28 percent of the vote in 1999 elections and Haider joined Austria's right-of-centre coalition government. After a few weeks of intense criticism, Haider resigned as leader. Although the party lost much support in the 2002 Austrian elections, it remained in the government.

Check YOUR UNDERSTANDING

1. Briefly describe events that led the Chechen people to declare independence in 1991.
2. How has the Russian government reacted to the Chechen declaration of independence? Why has it reacted in this way?
3. What do you believe the future holds for Chechnya? Should the international community become involved? Why or why not?
4. Why did ethnic violence break out after the collapse of the state of Yugoslavia?
5. Why do some people believe the Balkans conflict is more a religious than an ethnic conflict? What do you think?
6. Compare how nationalist conflicts were resolved in Czechoslovakia and Yugoslavia.
7. How can nationalism be used to preach a message of non-inclusion?
8. What does history teach about the consequences of targeting groups of people in a country?

Aboriginal Internationalism and Nationalism in Canada

The concepts of nationalism and internationalism are not timeless. They are fluid intellectual constructions. As you learned at the beginning of this chapter, Aboriginal peoples in Canada had distinct social, economic, and political systems long before European contact. The conflicts and political dialogues that resulted from that contact have a long history and are also changing.

Aboriginal Internationalism: A History, a Future

Aboriginal peoples in Canada are composed of North American Indians, Inuit, and Métis. The designation "Indian" was applied by early Europeans who believed they had landed in India. The term "First Nations" refers to Indian groups that first met the Europeans; it does not include the Inuit and Métis. As you learned earlier in this chapter, the concept of private property was almost unknown to Aboriginal peoples in Canada at the time of European contact. The European concept of nation—a population within geographic borders—did not reflect Aboriginal concepts of political organization. However, Aboriginal nationalism predated contact and remains strong.

Aboriginal relations with the natural and spiritual worlds were and are regulated and maintained through rituals, ceremonies, and taboos. Hunting–gathering activities, for example, were governed by spiritual rules that were intended to respect the universal order and maintain the balance of nature (ecosystems). Aboriginal groups (Figure 4.20) were also guided by these principles in their relations with one another.

Aboriginal groups related to one another through internationalism, through many oral treaties and reciprocal trade agreements. Gift-giving was central to economic and social relations. Gifts sealed agreements and alliances and established prestige. In some cases, tribes could be so intent on establishing good relationships that gift-giving led to poverty. On the Pacific coast, the **potlatch** ceremony was a means of distributing wealth among groups and of acquiring social status. The Law of Hospitality furthered relations among groups, and to violate that law was considered a crime. Chiefs and leaders commonly spoke several languages—including sign language—to advance trade and diplomacy. Warfare and violence broke out among Aboriginal groups, and international diplomacy was applied.

Many tribes worked on developing and maintaining good relations and alliances with neighbouring tribes. For example, the Siksika (Blackfoot) entered into a confederacy (union) with four other nations. At the height of its power, the Blackfoot (or "Plains People") Confederacy covered the great plains from the Saskatchewan River in the north to the Missouri River in the south and from the Rocky Mountains in the west to what is now the Alberta–Saskatchewan border.

Term	A group of:
clan	related families
band	several clans
tribe (Nation)	bands with shared customs, beliefs, and language
confederacy	several tribes, or nations; e.g., Blackfoot, Huron, Iroquois

Figure 4.20 Aboriginal social groupings.

THE WEB

To learn more about the potlatch, visit www.emp.ca/cwp.

The Iroquois Confederacy

The First Nations union that best exemplified the internationalism of Aboriginal cultures was the Iroquois Confederacy. Located in the eastern half of North America, the Confederacy dates back to the early 15th century and first consisted of five tribes. The Tuscarora joined in the 1720s, and it became the Six Nations Confederacy. The Confederacy was founded by Dekanawida, an advocate of League of Nations–style diplomacy 500 years before the League came into existence. Dekanawida, born in what is now southeastern Ontario, travelled lands bordering lakes Erie and Ontario carrying a message of peace to warring tribes. He was joined by a Mohawk chief named Hiawatha (not the fictional Hiawatha), who was a gifted orator.

Together, Dekanawida and Hiawatha succeeded in persuading the leaders of the five tribes, or Nations—Mohawk, Oneida, Onondaga, Cayuga, and Seneca, all with different languages—to meet. Fifty chiefs met at Onondaga, the geographical centre of the Five Nations. At the Grand Council, as the assembly was known, diplomacy and negotiation replaced violence with reason. Leaders met under a giant white pine, called the Great Tree of Peace, and buried their weapons. Leaders of the Iroquois Confederacy declared their nations to be *Haudenosaunee*, "the people of the longhouse."

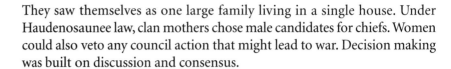

1982 UN Working Group on Indigenous Populations established

1993 UN draft *Declaration on the Rights of Indigenous Peoples* produced

1994 UN proclaims International Decade of the World's Indigenous People

2004 Few of the draft Declaration's 45 articles approved

Figure 4.21 Timeline: Indigenous rights at the UN.

They saw themselves as one large family living in a single house. Under Haudenosaunee law, clan mothers chose male candidates for chiefs. Women could also veto any council action that might lead to war. Decision making was built on discussion and consensus.

How the Iroquois Grand Council Worked

At the Grand Council, the Onondaga introduced a topic, which the Mohawk took under consideration. When these two groups reached a decision, it was passed to the Seneca, who in turn passed it to the two tribes on the other side of the council fire, the Oneida and the Cayuga. If these two groups agreed, the decision was unanimously carried. If not, negotiations began again. If unanimity could not be reached, the matter was set aside and the fire extinguished. The rules of negotiation emphasized that the chiefs should use reason and oratory to convince the council to act. The Iroquois Confederacy used the same diplomatic skills in their dealings with the French, Dutch, and English and later with the colonial and post-colonial governments of Canada and the United States.

In the 20th and 21st centuries, the Iroquois Confederacy broadened its international efforts. In 1923, Deskaheh, as president of the Iroquois Six Nations Council, petitioned the League of Nations in Geneva, Switzerland. The government of the Netherlands supported Deskaheh's presentation, but he failed to win League recognition of Haudenosaunee sovereignty. In his last public speech in 1925, which was broadcast from Rochester, New York, Deskaheh made these observations:

> The governments at Washington and Ottawa have a silent partnership of policy. It is aimed to break up every tribe of Redmen so as to dominate every acre of their territory. Your high officials are the nomads today—not the Red People. Your officials won't stay home. Over in Ottawa, they call that policy "Indian Advancement." Over in Washington, they call it "Assimilation." We who would be the helpless victims say it is tyranny.

Since these first international efforts, indigenous peoples around the world have continued to press for international recognition of Aboriginal rights (see Chapter 7).

Aboriginal Nationalism: Confederation and After

When the British Parliament created the self-governing Dominion of Canada in 1867, it was hailed as a model of peaceful decolonization. But not all groups felt comfortable in the new Canadian state. For Aboriginal peoples, it meant treaties would now be negotiated with the Canadian government.

Figure 4.22 Deskaheh, photographed in Geneva, 1923. He died two years later.

With the *Indian Act, 1876*, the Canadian government took control of almost every aspect of First Nations life. The Act stipulated that new elected band councils, not traditional Aboriginal political institutions, would negotiate with the Department of Indian Affairs. Band councils had very limited powers, and the federal minister controlled all financing.

The list of abuses under the Act is long. Aboriginal infants were sometimes taken to be adopted by non-Aboriginal parents. First Nations children were forcibly removed from their families and communities to attend distant residential schools, where they were deprived of their language, names, and culture. Government policy "promoted" assimilation into mainstream Canadian society. Aboriginal children suffered physical, psychological, and sexual abuse at the schools. Between 1927 and 1951, it was an offence under the *Indian Act* for an Aboriginal person to hire legal counsel to bring a claim against the federal government—without its consent. Aboriginal leaders and political analysts have since described the policy of assimilation as cultural genocide (see Chapter 7).

Rights, Land Claims, and Aboriginal Sovereignty

In much of Canada, Aboriginal peoples signed treaties in which they surrendered land for reserve rights. In newer parts of Canada—such as British Columbia and the Northwest Territories—few treaties were ever signed. After 1970, as Aboriginal groups organized, the federal government began negotiating land claims based on occupancy and use rather than treaty. As a result of one land-claim negotiation, a new territory was created in 1999: Nunavut, which was carved out of the Northwest Territories. Nunavut is populated by a large majority of Inuit, and thus functions as a form of Aboriginal self-government.

The federal and British Columbian governments also recognized a degree of Aboriginal sovereignty earlier. In the late 1990s the Nisga'a of northwest British Columbia negotiated an agreement that included a $190 million payment to the Nisga'a, establishment of a Nisga'a municipal-style government, and ownership and self-government of 1,900 square kilometres of land. The final agreement took effect in 2000 (see Figure 4.3 on page 118).

THE WEB

For more on Aboriginal land claims and landmark decisions, visit www.emp.ca/cwp.

Land claims have also led to violence. At Oka, Quebec, in 1990, the mayor's decision to expand a golf course onto Mohawk burial grounds led to a standoff with the Canadian army after a Quebec police officer was killed. At Ipperwash, Ontario, in 1995, Dudley George, one of 30 unarmed Aboriginal protestors, was killed by a police officer during a peaceful land-claims demonstration. After nine years of demands, a public inquiry into Ipperwash started hearing testimony in July 2004. (See also Chapter 5.)

Supreme Court of Canada decisions have also supported Aboriginal rights. In both *R v. Sparrow* (1990) and *R v. Marshall* (1999), the court recognized Aboriginal fishing rights. In the case of *R v. Powley*, two members of the Métis Nation of Ontario shot a moose near Sault Ste. Marie and were

THE WEB

Learn more about the *Powley* case at www.emp.ca/cwp.

charged with hunting out of season and without a licence. (The Métis people originated from mixed marriages between Aboriginal women and Scottish or French fur traders in west-central North America. As a people, they identify themselves as the Métis Nation.)

At trial, the Powleys asserted their Aboriginal hunting rights and were acquitted. The Ontario government appealed the case all the way to the Supreme Court of Canada. In September 2003, the Supreme Court ruled that Métis hunting rights are protected by the *Constitution Act, 1982*. It also stated that Métis communities have a collective identity, which must be examined historically. At the time of the ruling, the Métis numbered approximately 300,000 of a total of 1.3 million people of Aboriginal origin living in Canada (2001 Census).

Métis leaders argue that the *Powley* ruling means that governments in Canada must now recognize the Aboriginal rights of Métis and can no longer refuse to negotiate with them. This argument reflects the goals of other Aboriginal leaders, who are working for Aboriginal peoples to be recognized not as one of many ethnic minorities, but as a "nation," with greater powers of self-government, autonomy, and sovereignty.

Check YOUR UNDERSTANDING

1. How did the European and Aboriginal ideas of a nation differ?
2. Explain the differences between a clan, a band, a tribe, and a confederacy.
3. Why was gift-giving important to Aboriginal internationalism?
4. Explain the role of women in the Iroquois Confederacy. Is it a powerful role? Why or why not?
5. Using an example, describe how members of the Iroquois Confederacy arrived at decisions.
6. How do Aboriginal peoples in Canada exhibit the characteristics of a nation?
7. How successful have Aboriginal groups been in negotiating land claims in the 1990s? Give examples.
8. What impact do you believe the case of *R v. Powley* will have on Métis rights in Canada?

Canadian Nationalism and Internationalism

Canada was created as late–19th century imperialism was reaching its peak. This was reflected in how Canada dealt with Aboriginal peoples and in the tensions between Canadians with British and French backgrounds. Nationalism in Canada was not unified, but split. At the root of the schisms was the reality that two European empires had colonized and dominated history after contact. In Canada's early history, outside wars often exposed that rift.

Wars and Nationalism in Canada

As the 19th century ended, Britain went to war against the Boers in South Africa (see Chapter 5). Most English-speaking Canadians identified with Britain and wanted Canada to send troops. Their response was a trans-Atlantic version of British nationalism. In Quebec, most French Canadians adamantly opposed supporting Britain and wanted Canada to act in its own interests. In fact, many French Canadians sympathized with the Boers, Dutch settlers who were fighting British imperialism.

Faced with a political firestorm, Prime Minister Wilfrid Laurier (1841–1919) did a very Canadian thing: he compromised. Ottawa would organize volunteers to go to South Africa, where they would be funded by Britain. The solution satisfied neither side. In English Montreal, the Imperial Order of the Daughters of the Empire (IODE) promoted solidarity with the British Empire. In Ottawa, Quebec Liberal MP Henri Bourassa (1868–1952) resigned in 1899 to protest the war. In 1900, Bourassa returned as an independent MP and championed French Canadian nationalism.

The Boer War (1899–1902) had exposed the English–French split in Canadian nationalism. World War I (1914–18) again revealed Canada's fractured nationalism. Many French Canadians saw it as "England's war." Laurier—now opposition leader—and Bourassa both applauded voluntary enlistment, yet vigorously opposed compulsory conscription unless Canada were under direct attack.

As the war wore on, differences deepened. In 1917, Prime Minister Robert Borden's Union government held an election on the issue of conscription. Pro-conscription Borden won the election and 74 of 82 seats in Ontario. In Quebec, anti-conscription Laurier won 62 of 65 seats. Although there were pockets of opposition to conscription in English-speaking Canada, its nationalism was largely defined as loyalty to the British Empire. In an open letter published in August 1916, Henri Bourassa analyzed the complex situation around enlistment:

> English-speaking Canadians enlist in much smaller numbers than newcomers from England, because they are more Canadian; French Canadians enlist less than English Canadians because they are totally and exclusively Canadian. To claim their abstention is due to the "baneful" influence of the Nationalists is pure nonsense.

Canadian Nationalism: Breaking Free of British Influence

As a British colony, Canada was automatically at war when Britain declared war in 1914. However, Canada's Minister of Militia, Sam Hughes, insisted that Canadian troops fight in Canadian divisions under Canadian command. Canada made tremendous sacrifices during World War I, and the Canadian divisions distinguished themselves especially at Ypres (1915) and Vimy Ridge

THE WEB

Learn more about Canada and the Boer War at www.emp.ca/cwp.

Figure 4.23 In this 1919 German cartoon depicting the signing of the *Treaty of Versailles*, the "big four" signatory powers—Britain, the United States, France, and Italy—are depicted as Greed, Revenge, and other devils seeking to punish Germany.

THE WEB

Find out more about the Persons Case at www.emp.ca/cwp.

(1917) Canada also assumed new political responsibilities, becoming a member of the British war cabinet.

At the end of World War I, Canada sent two delegates to the Paris Peace Conference to sign the *Treaty of Versailles* in 1919. However, the British prime minister, David Lloyd George, signed for the entire British Empire. Still, Versailles was the first time Canada was a signatory to a **multilateral treaty**. Canada also became an autonomous member of the League of Nations (1920–46). Until this time, Canada's voice in international forums had been the British voice "with a slightly different accent." Now Canada was speaking independently.

After World War I, Canada moved toward becoming more of a North American state. This intent was revealed in the Chanak Crisis of 1922, when an uprising of Turkish nationalist troops under Ataturk threatened British troops near Chanak, Turkey. Britain appealed to the colonies for military support. Opposition leader Arthur Meighen insisted on supporting Britain. Prime Minister Mackenzie King (1874–1950) said Canada's foreign policy would not be dictated from London but by Canada's Parliament, which was not in session. Before Parliament reconvened, the crisis had passed. King kept working for Canadian autonomy at imperial conferences in the 1920s. The *Statute of Westminster*, passed by the British Parliament in 1931, formally recognized Canada's independence in domestic and foreign affairs. Canada was now a self-governing state in the British Commonwealth rather than a colony of the British Empire.

Judicial and constitutional developments also heightened Canada's independence. Under the *British North America* (BNA) *Act* of 1867, Canada's highest court of appeal was the Judicial Committee of the Privy Council in London, England. It was to that body, for example, that five Alberta women, including Emily Murphy and Nellie McClung (see Chapter 2), took the famous Persons Case. The Supreme Court of Canada had ruled that, for the purposes of Senate appointments, the word "person" in the BNA Act meant only male persons. In 1929, the Judicial Committee overturned that decision, ruling that women were persons and eligible for Senate appointment. In 1949, the Supreme Court of Canada became the final court of appeal for constitutional cases.

Until 1982, amendments to the Canadian constitution (the BNA Act) had to be approved by the British Parliament. In 1982, the constitution was patriated (brought home) to Canada and enshrined in the *Constitution Act, 1982.* This Act contained the constitution, an amending formula, and the *Canadian Charter of Rights and Freedoms.* Constitutional amendments no longer required the involvement of the British Parliament.

Canada took other important steps in expressing a separate identity. Canadians were "British subjects" until after World War II, when growing nationalism led to the enactment of the *Canadian Citizenship Act, 1947*. Canada was now a country with citizens. Five years later, the British monarch appointed a Canadian (Vincent Massey) governor general of Canada for the first time. Britain's flag, the Union Jack, was still officially Canada's flag. After months of heated debate over many proposed new flag designs, Liberal Prime Minister Lester Pearson proclaimed the red maple leaf Canada's new flag in 1965. It was free of any references to the British or French colonial past. In 1967, Canada's centennial year, Parliament recognized "O Canada" as Canada's national anthem. It was officially proclaimed so on July 1, 1980.

Canadian Nationalism and the United States

In becoming more North American, Canada had to deal with the "giant to the south," the United States. Canadian nationalists had long fretted over US influence on Canada's identity. Would Canadians be able to resist American hegemony? Many Canadian nationalists feared

Figure 4.24 Prime Minister Lester Pearson thanks an unsuccessful would-be designer of the new Canadian flag, 1965.

absorption into the United States. This fear expressed itself in free-trade elections in 1911 and 1988. Nationalists who opposed free trade argued that once there was free movement of goods, services, and capital between the two countries, it would be only a matter of time before Canada was economically and politically integrated into the United States.

Similar concerns led to legislated protection of Canada's cultural industries—in book, magazine, and newspaper publishing and in radio, television, recording, and films. The question was: if Canada's cultural industries are controlled by US interests, what happens to the Canadian identity?

Some commentators say fears of US dominance are unnecessary. In his 2003 book *Fire and Ice*, pollster Michael Adams, president of the Environics Research Group, concluded that the Canadian and American psyches have historically been very different. Canada was formed as a conservative country. It valued peace, order, and good government, and rejected revolution and innovation. Canadians deferred to the authority of political institutions, trusting them to improve the well-being of their country. Americans mistrusted government, encouraged private interests, and admired individuals who fought for truth and justice.

Drawing on decades of research, Adams compared changes in the outlooks of Americans and Canadians in the last quarter of the 20th century. He concluded that Canadians became more liberal, independent, and worldly, distancing themselves from traditional authority such as the patriarchal family and organized religion. In the same period, Americans became more conservative, looking for safe havens in the very social institutions Canadians were rejecting.

To demonstrate the differences, Adams used some specific examples. When asked in 2002 if they agreed that "the father of the family must be master in his own house," only 18 percent of Canadians agreed, compared to 49 percent of Americans. Adams also noted that SUVs outsell minivans two to one in the United States. In Canada, minivans outsell SUVs two to one. Does this prove that Canadians are more environmentally sensitive than Americans, as Adams suggests? Or does it prove that Canadians have less money to spend on automobiles? Not everyone approved of Adams's research methods, but he articulated a perception held by many: Canadians and Americans have different values.

Public opinion surveys indicate that Canada's universal health care system is a source of nationalism. It is also a source of political debate as costs escalate: can private, for-profit (American-style) health care be allowed into a public (Canadian) health care system? How that debate is resolved will reflect the Canadian identity in the years ahead.

War and Canadian Internationalism

When Canada attended the signing of the *Treaty of Versailles* and joined the League of Nations, the country was demonstrating growing nationalism and internationalism. This growth continued. In 1923, Canada signed the *Convention for the Preservation of the Halibut Fishery of the Northern Pacific Ocean* with the United States. It was the first time Canada had signed a **bilateral treaty** without Britain's co-signing. Britain was reluctant to surrender control; Canada insisted its fishery was a domestic matter.

During the 1930s, the League of Nations could not stop the aggressive acts of such countries as Japan, Germany, and Italy. The Canadian government was silent when Japan invaded Manchuria in 1931, when Italy invaded Ethiopia in 1935, and when Germany took over part of Czechoslovakia in 1938. Prime Minister R.B. Bennett lamented that Canada could do little on the international stage. His successor in 1935, Mackenzie King, was determined to do nothing that might provoke another world war. He also wanted to avoid a conscription crisis like that in World War I. King rejected sanctions against fascist dictator Benito Mussolini after Italy invaded Ethiopia. Although he disagreed with some of his policies, King at first admired Adolf Hitler. He believed Hitler could be dealt with through a policy of appeasement, which soon meant agreeing to the German dictator's demands.

Canada's response to Mussolini's aggression was especially weak. In the fall of 1935, the Department of External Affairs told Dr. Walter Riddell, head of the Canadian delegation at the League of Nations in Geneva, that newly elected Prime Minister Mackenzie King favoured economic sanctions against Italy. Riddell drew up a resolution that petroleum, iron, steel, and coal would not be traded to Italy. The "Canadian resolution" passed quickly through committee. When King learned Quebec was uneasy with Riddell's proposal, he joined other League members and backed away from sanctions. Like most League members, Canada would take no diplomatic risks to stop international aggression.

On September 10, 1939, Canada declared war on Germany. It entered World War II independently, seven days after Britain. In the early war years, Canadian nationalism focused on creating a massive war economy and mourning dreadful losses in battles in Hong Kong and Dieppe. Later, Canadian forces played important roles in invasions of Italy in 1943 and Normandy in 1944.

War also tightened Canada–US bonds. In 1940, Canada and the United States signed the *Ogdensburg Agreement* to integrate defence. In 1941, the *Hyde Park Declaration* laid the foundation for cooperation on defence production.

Canada's commitment to internationalism expanded in the post-war years. Canadian borders had been closed to Jewish refugees in the early years of World War II. However, immigration policy became more open after the war—particularly to refugees from war-torn Europe. Through roles in international organizations such as the United Nations and the North Atlantic Treaty Organization (NATO), Canada became an important **middle power**. (You will learn more about these developments in Unit 3.)

Figure 4.25 In Ottawa in 1999, two Canadian peacekeepers regard a large poster commemorating a "Century of Valour" in which Canadian troops have served in international conflicts.

Check YOUR UNDERSTANDING

1. Why did Canadians of British and French backgrounds disagree on the Boer War? Why did Laurier's compromise fail?
2. Why did most French Canadians oppose conscription in World War I?
3. Why was Canada's international voice no longer that of Britain after World War I?
4. How was the *Statute of Westminster* important to Canadian nationalism?
5. What do you believe was the most important step that Canada has taken in gaining an identity separate from British influence? Explain your choice.
6. What evidence does author Michael Adams offer to support the belief that Canadian and American values are different? Do you agree or disagree with his views? Explain.
7. Assess Canada's international role in the years up to 1945. How did it change?

THE WEB

For an update on the Acadian Expulsion, go to www.emp.ca/cwp.

Quebec Nationalism

The French presence in Canada dates back to 1534, when Jacques Cartier was the first European to claim areas around the Saint Lawrence River and explore the interior of what is now Canada. France engaged in fur trading with the Aboriginal peoples, and in the early 17th century established settlements in Acadia (now Nova Scotia and New Brunswick) and Quebec. As trade and colonization expanded, British and French forces fought over territory. In 1759, New France fell to the British at the Battle of the Plains of Abraham. In Acadia, the British stepped up the expulsion of the Acadians (1755–62), a mass deportation that began when Acadians refused to swear allegiance to the British monarch. Some modern analysts have described it as ethnic cleansing.

The Roots of Quebec Nationalism

The British could not apply the Acadian solution in Quebec, where francophones formed an overwhelming majority. British policies of assimilation quickly failed. Quebec francophones were determined that their culture and language would survive. The *Quebec Act* of 1774 guaranteed them language, religious, and legal rights. The Roman Catholic Church supported the "revenge of the cradle," a high birth rate that would guarantee the survival of the French Canadian identity.

SOUND BITE "I expected to find a contest between a government and a people: I found two nations warring in the bosom of a single state: I found a struggle, not of principles, but of races. . . ."

Lord Durham's report, 1838, describing "the hostile divisions of French and English" in Lower Canada (now Quebec)

When Confederation was negotiated in 1867, it too recognized French language rights in Canada East (Quebec). Many francophone Quebeckers saw Quebec and themselves as an ethnic nation—with a shared historical experience, language, territory, and culture. Indeed, in one view of Confederation, Quebec was seen as one of two founding nations, the other being English Canada. In another view, Quebec was simply a province, no more and no less than any other. Regardless, Quebec nationalism survived. Until 1960, it was quite inward-looking and conservative. It sought expression in traditionalism and the practices of the Roman Catholic Church. Yet, there were different views of Confederation.

With the election of Jean Lesage as premier (1960–66), Quebec underwent a Quiet Revolution (see Chapter 3). Under Lesage, who was a Quebec nationalist, the provincial Liberal government used its legal, economic, and political powers to pursue policies in the collective interests of the Quebec people. It reformed areas of education, culture, and labour laws. It nationalized electrical production, turning Hydro-Quebec into an enormous corporation. It created a Quebec pension plan and challenged federal–provincial relations. Quebec's economy shifted from its agricultural base, and the influence of the Catholic Church withered. Many Quebeckers looked at the world and their role in it with new confidence and values.

The Rise of Quebec Separatism

During the Quiet Revolution, Quebec's separatist movement grew—and became much less quiet. In the 1960s, journalists René Lévesque and Pierre Bourgault became outspoken leaders for independence. They pointed to nationalist struggles in Algeria and Northern Ireland. In 1963, the Front de Libération du Québec (FLQ), a small underground Marxist group, formed to fight for independence. It used terrorist tactics—bombings, robberies, kidnappings, killings—against federal and British targets. In 1968, a new provincial party—the Parti Québécois—was founded to achieve Quebec sovereignty.

Prime Minister Pierre Trudeau fought Quebec nationalism by trying to make francophone Canadians feel at home everywhere in Canada. An official policy of bilingualism was one way to do so. In 1969, the *Official Languages Act* made French and English Canada's two official languages and the federal public service and judicial systems bilingual. As a result, many provinces improved the educational and language rights of francophone minorities. In 1969, New Brunswick became the only officially bilingual province. While francophones across Canada generally welcomed bilingualism, many inside Quebec saw it as an empty gesture that ignored their nationalist aspirations.

When the FLQ kidnapped Quebec cabinet minister Pierre Laporte and British Trade Commissioner James Cross in October 1970, the October Crisis erupted (see Chapter 11). After the Quebec government asked for federal help, Prime Minister Trudeau invoked the *War Measures Act*, declaring a state of "apprehended insurrection." Tanks rolled on Montreal streets

Figure 4.26 Revellers celebrate St. Jean Baptiste Day in Quebec City, June 24, 2002.

Press Play

The CBC documentary *Black October*, by director Terence McKenna, blends archival footage with dramatic re-enactments and interviews to shed light on how the October Crisis changed Canada's political landscape forever. (NR).

and civil liberties were suspended as hundreds of people were arrested. By the time the crisis was over, the FLQ had murdered the Quebec cabinet minister and violent Quebec nationalism had been discredited.

Quebec Separatism in the Mainstream

In the 1970s, census information showed that francophones in Quebec were declining as a percentage of the population. The francophone birthrate in Quebec, once the highest in Canada, had become the lowest. And the vast majority of immigrants to Quebec were electing to speak English. In this atmosphere, the Parti Québécois (PQ) won its first election in 1976 under founder René Lévesque. The PQ immediately promised a provincial referendum on Quebec sovereignty. In 1977, Quebec nationalism expressed itself in Bill 101. After passage of this bill, French became the province's official language. The use of any other language in the workplace and on outdoor signs was strictly regulated. Today, only children with at least one parent educated in an English school in Quebec can be educated in English. Immigrants must send their children to French-language schools.

The PQ was unsure of support during the referendum campaign of 1980. Polls showed that the non-francophone 20 percent of Quebec would not support separation, while 20 percent of the population was strongly committed to separatism. The remaining 60 percent were "soft separatists," or undecided. The phrasing of the referendum question became a hot political issue. Finally, voters were asked to vote "Yes" or "No" to giving the PQ permission to negotiate **sovereignty-association** with the government of Canada. The question asked only for permission to negotiate. Sovereignty was not complete, but would maintain economic association with Canada, including a common currency. Even with these qualifiers, the referendum attracted a "Yes" vote of only approximately 40 percent. Lévesque and his followers were devastated.

When the Canadian constitution was patriated in 1982, Quebec was not a signatory. Premier Lévesque rejected what had been masterminded by Prime Minister Trudeau, a passionate Quebec federalist. In 1987, Progressive Conservative Prime Minister Brian Mulroney—another Quebec federalist—tried to get Quebec to sign the constitution. At a conference centre at Meech Lake, Mulroney got all provincial leaders to agree on a constitutional accord that recognized Quebec as a "distinct society" and also gave the provinces more power in the federation. Quebec nationalists were open to this because it recognized Quebec's difference from other provinces. Critics feared that future judicial interpretations of the term "distinct society" could give Quebec greater power than other provinces.

Trudeau attacked the Meech Lake Accord, saying Quebec's extra powers were unnecessary and that provincial demands for extra powers would destroy federalism. Aboriginal leaders, excluded from discussions, attacked the accord for failing to recognize their collective rights. To be enacted, the accord had to be ratified by the legislatures of all 10 provinces within three

SOUND BITE "In Latvia we have a language that had lost its place in society after 50 years of russification. The [new] language law simply reinstates the rights of the Latvian language as the state language. . . . It is analogous to [Quebec's] Bill 101. . . . It sets up certain requirements for people to use it who otherwise would not. It's not a hardship to learn a language . . . it's an enrichment."

Latvian President Vaira Vike-Freiberga, in a BBC interview, March 2000

THE WEB

For links to sound and TV clips of René Lévesque and Pierre Trudeau facing off about Quebec separatism, visit www.emp.ca/cwp.

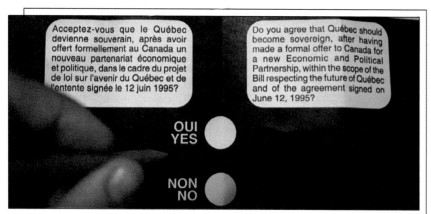

Figure 4.27 The wording and results of the 1995 Quebec referendum led the federal government to pass the *Clarity Act* (see Chapter 6).

THE WEB

To learn more about the conflict between Quebec and Canadian nationalism during the 1995 referendum, go to www.emp.ca/cwp.

years. In 1990, Cree MLA Elijah Harper refused to approve the Meech Lake Accord in Manitoba's Legislative Assembly. Nor had the Newfoundland legislature ratified. The Meech Lake Accord was dead.

Cabinet minister Lucien Bouchard had resigned from the Mulroney government in the spring of 1990, before the Meech Lake Accord died. With several other Quebec MPs, he formed the Bloc Québécois, a federal party dedicated to Quebec sovereignty (see Chapter 2). Nationalist sentiment soared in Quebec. Under Bouchard, the Bloc won 54 of Quebec's 75 seats to become the official opposition in Ottawa in 1993. In 1994, the provincial Parti Québécois returned to power and, under Premier Jacques Parizeau, held another referendum. The 1995 referendum once more proposed sovereignty-association, but this time Quebec nationalism almost triumphed: 49.4 percent of Quebeckers voted "Yes." Parizeau blamed the loss on "money and the ethnic vote," and resigned as premier. Quebec nationalism had come within 53,498 votes of forever ending Canada as Canadians have known it.

Bouchard resigned from the Bloc and replaced Parizeau as leader of the Parti Québécois. Quebec nationalism seemed to decline for the rest of the 1990s. In the federal election of November 2000, the Bloc Québécois won only 38 seats. In 2003, the provincial Liberal party won a huge majority, ending almost a decade of PQ governments. Quebec nationalism, however, has deep roots. In 2004, the Bloc again won 54 seats in the federal election, as popular support for the federalist provincial Liberal government plummeted.

Check YOUR UNDERSTANDING

1. Why was Bill 101 important to francophone culture in Quebec?
2. Why did the Meech Lake Accord fail?
3. Why is it ironic that the Bloc Québécois became the official opposition in 1993?
4. Why do you think that until about 1960, Quebec nationalism was conservative and inward-looking? Why did it change?

METHODS OF POLITICAL INQUIRY

Interpreting Maps

Maps are important resources for students of political science. In a small amount of space, it is possible to extract a great deal of information about what has happened in national and international politics over time. For example, if you examine political maps of Europe before 1914 and after 1919, you will immediately see how boundaries shifted after World War I. Some countries grew while others shrank, some merged into new entities, and others vanished.

People often view maps as factual representations, but as a student of politics you must look critically. In the

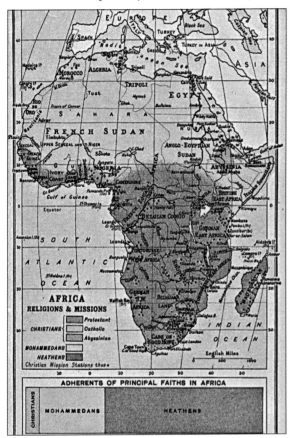

Source: University of Texas Libraries, Perry–Castañeda Library Map Collection, at http://www.lib.utexas.edu/maps/historical/africa_religion_1913.jpg.

Figure 4.28 "Africa Religions and Missions," from *Literary and Historical Atlas of Africa and Australasia*, by J.G. Bartholomew, 1913.

words of Australian geographer Noel Richards, "Maps, as with other forms of human communication, inevitably represent the interests of the people that create them and therefore need to be interpreted with care." As you examine any map, ask questions such as these:

- Who made the map? When and why?
- Was the map made by someone living inside or outside the geographical area?
- What choices did the mapmaker make? (What details were included and considered important? What details were omitted and considered unimportant? Why?)

For example, when English mapmaker and explorer James Cook "discovered" the east coast of Australia in 1770, the British claimed the territory citing the doctrine of *terra nullius* (empty land). They believed this gave them the authority to occupy this "unused" land. The Aboriginal presence was ignored.

- How do you read beyond the borders of the map?

Any map is influenced by the culture and scientific knowledge of its time. And maps are often used by all sides in territorial and political disputes. For example, both official Indian and Pakistani government maps show the disputed regions of Kashmir as part of their national territory.

Applying the Skill

1. Examine the map of Africa from 1913 in Figure 4.28 and write down your answers to the questions listed above. What does the map tell you about the time period in which it was made and the worldview of the mapmaker?
2. Using the Internet or the library, find two maps of a country or region that has changed significantly (for example, Africa at the beginning of the 20th and 21st centuries; Eastern Europe before and after the fall of communism). Your task is to interpret the maps, analyzing changes that have occurred and predicting future political developments. (An excellent Web site for maps can be found at www.emp.ca/cwp.)

CAREERS

Bob Lopinski, Political Adviser

Bob Lopinski, Director of Issues Management and Legislative Affairs for Ontario Premier Dalton McGuinty, believes that whether or not you want a political career, you have a responsibility to be politically informed. Do you agree?

Q: Please describe your position.

A: There are two quite separate segments in the province's administration. There's the civil service—a pool of workers who do the day-to-day work of administering the business of government. Civil servants are non-partisan: their job duties continue even when there is a change in government.

Then there's the elected government's political staff—a smaller group of individuals who are affiliated with the particular party that's in power. I'm a member of this political staff; I report directly to the premier.

Q: What are your job duties?

A: I monitor political issues as they arise for the purpose of advising the premier and of supporting an appropriate political response. If something is going to be in the newspaper tomorrow, I am expected to know about it today. I research the issue, communicate with the affected ministries, and consult with the premier about the government's position.

Where more than one ministry is involved, I work to coordinate ministry responses, and I give policy, political, and communications advice. In some ways, the most important aspect of this work is that, in supporting an appropriate response to political issues, I help keep these issues from becoming a distraction to the government in its efforts to carry out its policy agenda.

Q: What skills are important to someone in your position?

A: To do this work, it's essential to be able to quickly develop a working understanding of a wide range of complicated subjects and to be able to convert that knowledge into simple terms—plain English—that the average person can understand. You need to be able to distill an issue so that the government is in a position to react effectively.

Q: What did you do to prepare for this job?

A: I've always been interested in politics; I majored in political science in university, I was involved in student government, and I was a member of the Young Liberals.

I think that one of the best things a student interested in politics can do is simply to read the paper every day. All Canadians, not only those with political aspirations, have a responsibility to inform themselves about government policy and political issues, because these issues have an impact on their daily lives. If you do have political aspirations, it's important to get involved even if a party or candidate's policies are not perfectly in line with your own values, because the best way to effect change is from within.

Questions

1. Is Bob Lopinski a civil servant or political staff? Explain the difference.
2. Does Lopinski's position make him only a "spin doctor," or can his advice affect government policy? Explain.
3. List the key aspects and requirements of Lopinski's job.
4. Using the Internet and library, research intern opportunities with various political parties.

Study Hall

Thinking/Inquiry

1. You have read that the United States enhances the loyalty of its citizens by the use of national symbols and myths. Select one American symbol or myth and assess how effective it has been in promoting American nationalism.

2. Create a timeline highlighting key steps taken by Canada to find its identity as an independent nation.

3. You have learned of Deskaheh's presentation to the League of Nations and of the 1993 United Nations draft *Declaration on the Rights of Indigenous Peoples*. Conduct research to find out what is in the present declaration and what actions have been taken.

4. Ho Chi Minh and Julius Nyerere both had strong beliefs and ideas about decolonization and nationalism. In a brief essay, compare their ideologies and evaluate the pragmatism of their ideas.

Communication

5. Look back at Figure 4.1 on page 115. What does this work say to you about Canada and how the artist viewed it? What other symbols might Wieland have used to represent Canada today?

6. The federal government has decided that Canada needs to develop a new national symbol that reflects the country's multicultural makeup. You and three of your classmates have decided to submit your new national symbol. You will need to produce both a visual presentation of the symbol and a one-page explanation of why you believe your symbol is appropriate.

7. A radical group in Canada has targeted an ethnic group and has advocated its expulsion. You, as the editor of a major newspaper, are strongly opposed to this. Write an editorial outlining the reasons for your opposition.

8. Using a series of maps to tell the story, create a visual display of how one of the empires listed below gained or lost territory, or both.
   a) the Holy Roman Empire
   b) the British Empire
   c) the Ottoman Empire
   d) the Austro-Hungarian Empire

9. Conduct a classroom debate based on the following resolution: "Countries that have not been damaged by war have a moral obligation to accept immigrants from war-torn countries."

Application

10. You and a classmate are asked to role-play René Lévesque and Pierre Trudeau. Present Lévesque's view of Quebec nationalism in a debate during which your classmate presents Trudeau's view of Canadian nationalism.

11. Conduct a mock symposium at which spokespersons for various groups present their rationales for sovereignty. Organize your classmates to represent the following groups: Kurds, Chechens, Quebec separatists, and Aboriginal peoples in Canada. After conducting adequate research, classmates role-play spokespersons for the respective groups. Decide which groups have the best arguments for sovereignty.

12. You have read in this chapter how many peoples in the world are fighting to gain their independence. What role should international agencies such as the United Nations play in such situations? Conduct research to find out what actions have been taken. Assess how effective these steps have been in a one-page report.

Decision Making and Participation

Chapter 5
Forms of Government

Chapter 6
Democratic Decision Making

Chapter 7
Participation by Individuals and Groups in Politics

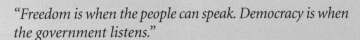

"Freedom is when the people can speak. Democracy is when the government listens."

Alastair Farrugia, Canadian mathematician
and human rights activist

Dear Mr. President,
Before you veto the Civil Rights Bill, please think about the number of Black African-Americans you have sent to the Persian Gulf willing to die for someone else's human rights.

155

Forms of Government

Agenda

In this chapter, you will consider

• factors that influence a state's form of government
• direct democracy and representative democracy
• the relationship between decolonization and democracy
• the problems of emerging, or partial, democracies
• the nature of dictatorships
• how dictatorships are established, maintained, and overthrown
• the nature of oligarchies
• how to use the Internet for political research

Figure 5.1 *Esclarecimiento* ("Clarification"; 1998), by Guatemalan artist Daniel Hernandez-Salazar, is one of a series of works remembering those who died fighting for democratic reforms during his country's 36-year civil war.

The trend toward democratic governments in recent decades has led some political scientists to call this the "age of democracy." Few would dispute that there has been a movement away from dictatorship to democracy. But how "democratic" is a democracy? And how does democracy work in cultures with vastly different values?

This chapter raises these and other questions as it examines two other forms of government: dictatorships and oligarchies (rule by the few). You will study **decolonization** and compare the ideologies behind dictatorships—whether left or right—that continue to affect world politics. You will see how oligarchy gripped Central American countries, such as Guatemala, and South Africa during the apartheid era (1948–91). As different cultures embrace democracy—a form of government that originated in the West—how will it and they be changed?

Internal and External Influences on Forms of Government

Tradition plays a major role in a country's form of government. Most European countries have traditions of democratic government that reach back centuries. When Portugal and Spain abandoned dictatorship in favour of democracy in the 1970s, their nearness to other European democracies influenced those decisions. Many of Britain's former colonies—such as Canada, India, Australia, and New Zealand—inherited democratic traditions. Other former British colonies—such as Myanmar and Nigeria—did not.

A democratic legacy was not the case in most other colonial empires. Spain, for example, was an **absolute monarchy** in the 16th century and administered its colonies on the absolutist model. As a result, many of Spain's South American colonies, such as Argentina, established authoritarian governments when they became independent in the 19th century.

France's tradition of democracy goes back to the French Revolution of 1789. When France's empire collapsed in the mid-20th century, however, many former colonies, such as Algeria and Benin, developed authoritarian governments. Some political scientists argue that France, by ruling its empire on an authoritarian model, did not prepare its colonial territories for democracy.

The internal dynamics of a country can lead to an oligarchy. In South Africa, a well-organized and educated European minority ruled over a non-European majority for most of the 20th century. In Guatemala, a small group of wealthy landowners ruled the predominantly Mayan indigenous majority throughout much of the country's history.

Outside forces also shape a country's form of government. Japan's democracy resulted from US occupation after World War II. In the same period, the military of the Union of Soviet Socialist Republics (USSR) occupied most of eastern Europe and imposed authoritarian communist governments. This transformed East Germany, Poland, Hungary, and Czechoslovakia into Soviet satellite states (countries that are controlled by, or dependent on, another state). These governments became democracies only after the Berlin Wall fell in 1989 (see Architecture and Politics, page 176) and the USSR was dissolved in 1991.

Figure 5.2 East and West Germans celebrate the destruction of the Berlin Wall, November 1989.

Check YOUR UNDERSTANDING

1. Describe three basic forms of government.
2. Explain the factors that influence a state's form of government.

Democracy

The democracy of 5th century BCE Athens was **direct democracy**, in which citizens—native-born free men over the age of 18—were directly involved in making decisions. Public issues were discussed in a large forum composed of all concerned citizens; these could number several thousand in a city-state such as Athens. In such a venue, issues could be obscured by emotional rhetoric, and demagogues could overpower rational speakers. Once debate subsided, the question under consideration was determined by simple majority vote.

In a **representative democracy**, decisions affecting the community are made by elected representatives of the people. Representative democracy allows large numbers of people to participate in the political process without having to be physically present. The system is structured by rules, one of which stipulates regularly scheduled elections.

Two forms of representative democracy are the constitutional monarchy and the **republic**. Constitutional monarchies have a hereditary monarch as the largely ceremonial head of state. Elected officials actually exercise power and run the government, receiving their authority from a constitution. Britain, Canada, and the Netherlands are all modern examples of constitutional monarchies. In republics, the people elect the head of state. The head of state and the head of government may be the same person (as the president is in the United States) or two separate persons (as in France, where the head of state is the president and the head of government is the prime minister).

Democracies can be classified according to degree. **Partial democracies** have only some of the characteristics of full democracies. **Emerging democracies** are partial democracies that are attempting to become **full democracies**, which are described in detail below.

Indicators of Full Democracy

A full democracy usually has a constitution (a set of laws) that guarantees individual rights and freedoms. Elected rulers and representatives agree to govern according to the constitution.

Full democracies ensure **majority rule**, and most also protect **minority rights**. For example, the language rights of French Canadians are protected under the *Canadian Charter of Rights and Freedoms*. In the later half of the 20th century, the rights of African Americans were increasingly enshrined in law: the *Civil Rights Act* of 1964 protected all citizens from discrimination and segregation in such areas of public life as education and employment, and the *Voting Rights Act* of 1965 guaranteed the right to vote.

Full democracies recognize the **rule of law**, which is the principle that the law applies equally to all and that no one, not even those who govern, is above the law.

A full democracy permits voters a choice of parties, recognizes free and fair elections, and responds to the wishes of the electorate. Citizens may join and work to elect political parties, or start their own. They may work for candidates of their choice during an election, or become candidates themselves. They can try to influence public policy by writing letters, attending protests, and joining **interest groups**.

A full democracy has a judiciary that is independent from the political policies of the government. An independent judiciary acts as a check on the power of the executive branch and the legislative branch of government and can settle constitutional issues between them (see Chapter 6). For example, the judiciary can test a law passed by a legislature and declare it unconstitutional and therefore null and void. The Canadian Supreme Court did this in 1988 in *R v. Morgentaler*, when it struck down a law prohibiting women's right to abortion. An independent judiciary may also grant rights that the

Figure 5.3 Constable Baltej Singh Dhillon, shown here with his classmates, was the first RCMP graduate to win the right to wear the traditional Sikh turban and beard. Minority rights are enshrined in the Charter.

executive and legislature have not. For example, in 1954, the US Supreme Court granted African Americans equal access to public schools in *Brown v. Board of Education*. In 2003 in Canada, the Ontario Court of Appeal recognized the constitutional right of lesbian and gay people to full marriage in *Halpern et al. v. Attorney General of Canada et al.*

A full democracy maintains civilian control over its armed forces and police. Elected officials determine the use of the military at home and abroad. In 1951, for example, US President Harry Truman relieved General Douglas MacArthur of his duties as Allied Command of United Nations forces in Korea when MacArthur threatened to attack communist China—defying the elected president's policy. In 1995, an Ontario Provincial Police officer shot and killed Dudley George, one of approximately 30 unarmed Aboriginal demonstrators in a protest at Ipperwash Provincial Park (see Chapter 10). The police officer was tried and found guilty of criminal negligence causing death. In 2004, a new Liberal Ontario government called a public inquiry into George's death.

Full democracies extend economic, political, and social rights to all citizens. In the United States and Europe, these rights have often been enshrined as the result of lobbying by labour unions and other citizens' groups.

A full democracy remains open to philosophies and ideas proposed by its citizens. In the last quarter of the 20th century, democratic governments made major legal changes (considered progressive by some and regressive by others) in such areas as divorce, abortion, and lesbian and gay rights. In 2003, the United States passed the *Partial-Birth Abortion Ban Act*, which prohibited late-term abortions; the Canadian government drafted the *Act Respecting Certain Aspects of Legal Capacity for Marriage*, which grants same-sex couples the right to marry.

THE WEB

Learn more about the Ipperwash Inquiry at www.emp.ca/cwp.

THE WEB

For an update on the status of the government's same-sex legislation, go to www.emp.ca/cwp.

Full democracies allow for freedom of information, the press, expression, and religion. Many have laws guaranteeing citizens access to government documents (although some, such as Cabinet documents, may be subject to a stated period of non-disclosure). Freedom of the press allows media to question government without fear of reprisal. Freedom of expression allows public airing of diverse viewpoints: governments can be criticized in editorial cartoons, television programs, Internet sites, and so on. Freedom of expression also applies to political parties, whose ideologies can range from neo-fascist and ultranationalist to communist.

Limitations of Full Democracy

Modern full democracies have flaws. Elections may be open to all, but the rich and the educated are much more likely to vote—and to be elected—than the poor and the uneducated. In some democracies, such as the United States, campaign costs also create an advantage for wealthy candidates. (In 2004, Canada placed a limit of $1,000 per year on corporate and union donations to individual candidates.)

The demands and influence of lobby and interest groups that speak for powerful institutions, such as multinational corporations, can override concern for the common good. Critics argue that the $80 million in donations that US President George W. Bush received during the 2000 presidential campaign from corporations and wealthy individuals affected his political agenda. For example, while in office, Bush eased environmental protection laws, protected the patents of pharmaceutical companies, and legislated tax cuts for the wealthy.

Democratic electoral systems are less than perfect. Whether a country uses the "first past the post" system, proportional representation, the preferential ballot, or a hybrid system (see Chapter 6), some voters will argue that the results do not accurately reflect public will.

Some observers believe that the modern democratic state cannot cope with the challenges posed by globalization and international free trade. Democracies give up a degree of sovereignty when economic decisions are made by such organizations as the World Trade Organization and the International Monetary Fund, which make decisions with limited representation from those most likely to be affected.

Democracies have often failed to protect identifiable groups and have sometimes discriminated against them. In Canada, for example, 22,000 Japanese Canadians were interned in 1942 as security risks during World War II. In the United States, the civil rights of suspected communists were infringed in the 1920s and 1950s, when many lost their jobs because of a "red scare."

In the 21st century, the freedoms of belief and expression have been limited by legislation intended to increase national security. In Canada, the *Anti-Terrorism Act* (2001) and the *Public Safety Act* (2004) have been criticized as increasing police powers at the expense of civil liberties. In 2003,

PRESS PLAY

Fahrenheit 9/11 (2004), directed by Michael Moore, examines irregularities in the election of US President George W. Bush and his base of support with the rich and powerful. It also investigates ties to "oil money" in the United States and Saudi Arabia that may have determined Bush's political responses to the terrorist attacks of 9/11.

the US government spent $8.5 million of its "war on terror" budget to police a Free Trade Area of the Americas conference in Miami. When they confronted protestors, Miami police invited selected journalists to accompany them and film the proceedings (a controversial practice known as "embedding," initiated during the US invasion of Iraq in 2003).

Democratic states can act arbitrarily (without justification). In 2002, US officials detained Canadian Maher Arar in New York at an airport during a stopover from a vacation in Tunisia. Believing Arar had links to **al-Qaida** (the Islamist terrorist group behind 9/11), US officials deported Arar to Syria, a country in which he held dual citizenship. Arar was released a year later and returned to Canada, where he reported being imprisoned and tortured in Syria. In 2004, the Canadian government held a public inquiry into the case.

Figure 5.4 Syrian-born Canadian Maher Arar (right) and his wife Monia Mazigh hold a news conference in Ottawa, January 2004. Arar alleges the US sent him to Syria knowing he would be tortured.

Modern democracy has been described as an "oligarchy of the wealthy." That is because it has often failed the homeless, unemployed, illiterate, and other disadvantaged groups that lack the political power to effect change. In both Canada and the United States, the gap between rich (the upper 20 percent) and poor (the lower 20 percent) widened as deficit-conscious governments reduced funding for social programs in the late 20th century.

Western-style democracies have also been criticized for their focus on individual rights at the expense of the common good. For example, the US constitution guarantees individuals the "right to bear arms" despite evidence that widespread ownership of firearms contributes to injury and death among innocent civilians.

THE WEB

For background on the Arar case, go to www.emp.ca/cwp.

Decolonization and Democracy

Decolonization occurs when a colonial power recognizes the right of a colony to self-government and independence. This section examines the progress toward democracy of three former colonies: the United States after achieving independence from Britain, and Algeria and Benin after achieving independence from France.

The United States

In the mid-18th century, leaders of the revolt of the Thirteen Colonies against Britain were determined to establish a system of government that was responsible to the people. After years of paying heavy British taxes and duties

Figure 5.5 Timeline: United States.

(largely to finance the Seven Years' War, which ended in 1763), colonists protested: they boycotted British goods, intimidated tax collectors, demonstrated against "taxation without representation," and committed acts of vandalism, such as dumping East India Company tea into the waters of Boston Harbour.

Inspired by such thinkers from the European **Age of Enlightenment** as John **Locke**, Baron de **Montesquieu**, and Jean-Jacques **Rousseau**, colonial leaders framed their efforts as a revolutionary struggle between a people seeking democracy and Britain, an autocratic colonizing power. In the *Declaration of Independence*, America's founders articulated their belief that democracy is concerned with rights, including those of "life, liberty, and the pursuit of happiness."

In 1775, the long war of independence began. Using guerrilla tactics and relying on military aid from France, the Americans finally obtained British recognition of their sovereignty in the 1783 *Treaty of Paris*.

Many citizens of the new country were experienced with democracy. Elected representative bodies in the individual colonies, such as the Virginia House of Burgesses, had often challenged the authority of governors appointed by Britain. In many colonies, assemblies elected by landholders had made decisions involving local matters.

The original American constitution (the *Articles of Confederation*) specified a loose union of 13 independent republics and made no provision for a strong central authority or executive. When that weakness became appar-

Figure 5.6 The Boston Massacre, 1770 (engraving by Paul Revere). When Americans protesting the British military presence harassed a sentry, troops responded by firing into the crowd, killing five people and wounding six.

ent, 55 delegates met in Philadelphia in 1787 to draft a new document. The new constitution was accepted by all states and officially implemented in 1789. It remains the present constitution and, aside from the Magna Carta, is the world's oldest written instrument of government still in operation.

Although many of the ideas behind the American revolution were found in the European Enlightenment, US democracy evolved in a manner consistent with its physical realities. The frontier conditions that settlers faced in America stressed individual self-reliance, which broke down class distinctions and prejudices to some degree. The democratic political structure that developed was marked by individualism, civil liberties, and a government limited by law. As US democracy evolved, emphasis shifted to giving more citizens the right to vote and improving government responsiveness to the will of the people. For example, the Fifteenth Amendment to the constitution, adopted in 1870, forbade denying the vote on the basis of race, colour, or previous condition of slavery, while the Seventeenth Amendment of 1913 provided that senators be elected by direct popular vote rather than by state legislatures.

Algeria

Algeria came under Ottoman rule in the 16th century. But in 1671, the dey of Algiers (chosen by local civilian and military leaders) became lifetime ruler of the country, with a degree of autonomy from the Ottoman Empire. The deys ruled until 1830, when France invaded. Despite strong resistance, colonization continued, and France declared Algeria a territory in 1848.

By 1900 Algeria had gained administrative autonomy under a European governor general. Colonists had developed Algeria's agriculture, industry, and infrastructure (such as roads, schools, and hospitals), but these benefited the Europeans rather than the indigenous population. Most Algerians lived in poverty and had few political or legal rights. Officially, Algerians were encouraged to adopt European ways to prepare for full French citizenship. In reality, that policy was never implemented.

Algerian resistance increased in the 1920s, and two factions emerged: one demanding full independence, the other seeking assimilation with France and full equality between Algerians and Europeans. Ferhat Abbas (1899–1985) was the assimilationist leader, but in the early 1950s, after decades of France's indifference, Abbas joined the independence movement.

When the violent struggle for national self-determination broke out in 1954, approximately 1 million European settlers lived in Algeria. The National Liberation Front (FLN) led the war of independence, using rural and urban guerrilla tactics against French military and civilian targets. France was forced to recognize Algerian independence in 1962.

The leaders of newly independent Algeria—former terrorists who had fought the French—took a left-wing, militaristic approach to government. The new constitution provided for a one-party system (the FLN) with a

1671 Algeria achieves autonomy within Ottoman Empire

1830 France invades Algeria

1848 France declares Algeria a territory

1920s Algerians organize protests

1954–61 FLN attacks French offices, civilians

1962 Algeria gains independence

1971 Foreign oil companies nationalized

1989 Opposition parties and strikes permitted

1991 Civil unrest; election cancelled

1992 Military takes command, outlaws FIS

1999 Abdelaziz Bouteflika elected president; grants amnesty to Islamists

2002 Opposition parties boycott parliamentary elections

2004 Bouteflika re-elected

Figure 5.7 Timeline: Algeria.

PRESS PLAY

The Battle of Algiers, Italian director Gillo Pontecorvo's suspenseful 1965 film, is set in the mid-1950s and recreates, with documentary-like realism, Algeria's escalating struggle for independence. The film portrays the organization of a guerrilla movement and the steps taken by the colonial power to destroy it. (NR)

strong head of state. Elections were held, but all candidates belonged to the same party.

Algeria described itself as a republic, but was a military dictatorship. Its leaders wanted to build a socialist society in which government owned the means of production. Key industries—iron and steel production, mining, construction—were quickly nationalized (placed under government ownership and control). By 1971, Algeria had also nationalized all foreign oil and gas companies.

During the 1960s and 1970s, Algeria hosted conferences for African states, developing countries, and oil-producing countries. It also trained anti-colonial fighters from other African states in guerrilla warfare. On the domestic front, the state-directed economy ran into problems with agriculture, unemployment, and distribution of consumer goods.

By the 1980s, riots and protests were challenging the FLN's grip on power. Many Algerians began to turn to Islamist political groups. In response to the unrest, the FLN's monopoly on power ended—other parties were allowed. In 1990, the Islamic Salvation Front (FIS) finished ahead of the FLN in local elections. Tensions increased between the FIS and the secular rulers after the FIS won the first round of national legislative elections in 1991. When it seemed certain the FIS would win control of the National Assembly—and thus the government—the army seized power in 1992, cancelling previous election results. The military dictatorship outlawed the FIS. Over the next six years, Islamic groups took up arms against the government. Both sides resorted to brutality in the resulting civil war.

In 1996, the government passed a constitutional amendment banning political parties that were based solely on religion or ethnicity, in an attempt to eliminate the weakened FIS. At the same time, provisions were made for

Figure 5.8 An Algerian soldier patrols a street in the capital, Algiers, during the political crisis after elections were cancelled, February 1992. Campaign posters for the banned FIS appear behind him.

a multiparty system. Power remained in the hands of a president elected to a five-year term.

By the end of the 20th century, Algeria had taken some steps toward democracy. It offered amnesty to the armed wing of the FIS and held elections. Algeria's military leaders, however, were not prepared to allow the election of a party based on Islamic principles, even if it won a majority. The 2002 parliamentary elections were boycotted by opposition groups and many voters, and the FLN consequently won more than half the seats.

In 2003, a strong earthquake devastated many towns east of Algiers, killing more than 2,200 people. The government's ineffective response to the disaster led to public outrage and widespread criticism. Late in 2003, tensions between President Abdelaziz Bouteflika and the FLN party leader, Ali Benflis, led to a split in the government and within the party. Bouteflika was returned to power in the presidential election of 2004, which outside observers found to be free of fraud and reflective of the wishes of the Algerian people.

Also in 2004, an Algerian appeals court upheld the conviction of journalist Mohamed Benchicou, ostensibly for violation of a currency law. But as Benchicou had recently published a book critical of the Algerian president, the judgment was widely viewed as an attempt to curtail freedom of the press.

Benin

The West African republic of Benin, originally called Dahomey, became a colony of France in the mid-19th century. In 1946, France granted Dahomey representation in its National Assembly as an overseas territory. Dahomey became an autonomous state within the French Community in 1958 and gained full independence in 1960. Three years of economic and social unrest led to a coup d'état that established a military dictatorship. In its first 12 years, Benin experienced no fewer than six coups, 10 changes in government, and five different constitutions.

In 1989, the 17-year rule of Marxist dictator Mathieu Kerekou was threatened by a nationwide strike precipitated by a crippled economy. Faced with daily demonstrations, Kerekou agreed to hold a National Conference, with participation from a wide cross-section of Beninois society. Reluctantly, Kerekou empowered the conference to make decisions for the country.

In February 1990, 520 delegates—including students, workers, business people, and military leaders—attended the nine-day conference. Faced with the possibility of another coup, the delegates voted for sovereignty and a new democratic constitution. They also voted to abolish Marxist ideology as the state philosophy, allow multiparty elections, release political prisoners, and establish a declaration of human rights. Kerekou and the military accepted these decisions.

One year later, Benin completed a non-violent transition to democratic government when Nicephore Soglo became president in a free election. Kerekou was returned to power in the 1996 and 2001 elections. The transition

1863 French Protectorate established

1946 Dahomey represented in French National Assembly

1958 Autonomy recognized within French Community

1960 Dahomey achieves independence

1963 Military coup establishes dictatorship

1972 Kerekou seizes power

1975 Dahomey becomes People's Republic of Benin

1989 Kerekou calls National Conference

1990 National Conference chooses democracy

1991 Soglo wins first free elections

1996 Kerekou re-elected

1999 Opposition party wins majority in legislature

2001 Soglo withdraws from election; Kerekou re-elected

Figure 5.9 Timeline: Benin.

THE WEB

Find out more about Benin's transition to democracy at www.emp.ca/cwp. You will also find five other African case studies here.

Figure 5.10 Jubilant Beninois celebrate hosting *La Francophonie* summit in Cotonou, Benin, in 1995.

to democracy was not free of controversy: in 2001, Soglo alleged electoral fraud, withdrew as a candidate, and thus allowed Kerekou to win easily.

Although Benin and Algeria are both African states that became independent from France, their transitions from colony to democracy were different. For example, while Benin attained increasing autonomy from France between 1946 and 1960, Algeria's early demands for autonomy went unheeded.

Check YOUR UNDERSTANDING

1. How do direct democracy and representative democracy differ?
2. Describe five indicators of a full democracy. Which do you consider to be the most important? Why?
3. Describe two flaws in modern democracy and suggest ways in which they might be rectified.
4. Describe the role the military played in the government of Algeria since independence. Why might the military have taken this role?
5. Compare and contrast Benin's transition to democracy with that of Algeria. Why might the French government have taken different approaches to decolonization with the two countries?

Emerging Democracies

Today, most political systems describe themselves as democracies. But many have not encouraged competing political parties or emphasized individual rights and other elements of Western-style democracy. With the collapse of one-party communist rule in Eastern Europe, the fall of authoritarian dictatorships in Latin America, and the end of some one-party states in sub-Saharan Africa, the number of multiparty democracies has increased in recent decades. However, a 2002 United Nations report stated that more than half of the world's states still limit the rights and freedoms of their citizens.

An emerging democracy is a partial democracy in transition. Its government may hold elections, for example, but restrict press freedoms. It may have a weak judiciary, or suffer from widespread government corruption. Some analysts believe that to achieve full democracy, a state requires political stability, a degree of economic development, and a sizable middle class. Emerging democracies are usually found in developing economies with a small middle class and a history of political instability.

The next section examines one of the largest emerging democracies: Russia.

Russia

When the Communist Party selected Mikhail Gorbachev as its general secretary in 1985, the USSR began a slow transition from totalitarian dictatorship. Faced with a stagnant economy, Gorbachev introduced a comprehensive program of reforms to liberalize political, economic, and social institutions under the slogans *glasnost* (openness) and *perestroika* (restructuring). *Glasnost* allowed more open exchange of ideas and greater freedom of expression. *Perestroika* called for re-evaluation of the Soviet economy, the arms race, and the Soviet military presence in Eastern Europe and Afghanistan. In the late 1980s, the Soviet government released political prisoners, allowed increased emigration, attacked corruption, and encouraged critical re-examination of Soviet history.

In 1989, a Congress of People's Deputies convened by Gorbachev voted to end the Communist Party's control over government and to recognize the independence of Soviet satellite states in Eastern Europe. This effectively ended the Cold War. For his contribution to reducing East–West tensions, Gorbachev was awarded the 1990 Nobel Peace Prize.

The drive toward openness and democratization moved quickly. Gorbachev could not control Soviet forces that suffered from the diminished power of the Communist Party— forces such as the military and state security. In 1991, Gorbachev was placed under house arrest in an attempted army coup. By now, support had shifted to his rival, Boris Yeltsin, who opposed the coup attempt and became the *de facto* (in reality) leader of Russia. Before leaving office, Gorbachev recognized the independence of the Baltic states of Latvia, Lithuania, and Estonia, and proposed a much looser, chiefly economic, federation among the remaining republics.

In December 1991, 11 of the former Soviet republics founded the Commonwealth of Independent States (CIS), and the Soviet Union was no more. Russia, shorn of its satellite republics and under Yeltsin, embarked on the road to democracy.

1917 Russian Revolution

1918–20 Civil war

1922 USSR established

1924 Death of Lenin

1953 Death of Stalin

1985 Gorbachev initiates reforms

1989 Communist Party's control over government abolished

1991 Attempted coup; Gorbachev resigns; formal dissolution of USSR; Yeltsin assumes presidency

1993 Unsuccessful coup; new constitution drafted

1996 Yeltsin re-elected

1997–98 Economic crisis

1999 Yeltsin resigns; appoints Putin acting president

2000 Putin elected president; re-elected, 2004

Figure 5.11 Timeline: Russia.

Figure 5.12 In 1991, Russia and 11 former republics of the USSR formed the Commonwealth of Independent States to coordinate the economic and foreign policies of member nations. The former Soviet republics of Estonia, Latvia, and Lithuania joined the European Union in 2004.

Many Russians welcomed the new freedoms associated with democracy. But the country faced problems in transforming a **command economy** into a free-market system. In the former USSR, a central authority decided what goods to produce and how to produce them. It also controlled rents, prices, and pensions. Free-market capitalism arrived in the early 1990s and was accompanied by extreme **inflation**. In some years, prices rose more than 1,000 percent. People's life savings and pensions became worthless.

At the same time, privatization of industry and loosening of government controls led to worker unrest as wages were paid late or not at all. While some citizens experienced a poverty that had been unknown in recent times, others exploited the new capitalism and became enormously wealthy. Yeltsin invited some of Russia's first entrepreneurs (now known as "oligarchs") to back the government financially in return for shares controlling major industries, including natural resources and communications. This offer resulted in government favouritism and corruption, which have characterized the new economy. To function, democracy needs public support. Given their country's economic upheavals, however, Russians developed an uneasy attitude toward democracy.

Beset by a default on Russia's international debt payments in the late 1990s and personal health problems, Yeltsin resigned a few months before the 2000 election, in which Vladimir Putin was elected president.

Russia's 1993 constitution gives significant powers to the president, who is elected to a four-year term and rules with the cooperation of the Duma, or elected lower house. The president chooses the prime minister and cabinet, and has the power to veto laws passed by the Duma.

Of the Duma's 450 seats, half are contested by proportional representation. Therefore, in 2003, for example, the Communist Party received 13 percent of the 225 seats that were available for the party list vote. The other 225 Duma seats are contested by individual candidates running in districts (ridings).

SOUND BITE "When people saw what democracy looked like, they changed their minds about it."

Grigory Yavlinsky, leader of Russia's Yabloko Party, December 2003

SOUND BITE "Whoever does not miss the Soviet Union has no heart. Whoever wants it back has no brain."

President Vladimir Putin, 2000

Figure 5.13 Women sell homemade preserves and pickles in downtown Moscow, 1999. As Russia's economy unravelled in the late 1990s, many people, especially pensioners, became street vendors, selling produce grown in their gardens.

Russia's uneasy transition from dictatorship is reflected in the government's term "managed democracy," which describes its attempts to balance new freedoms with political, economic, and social stability. In his first term, President Putin, a former member of the secret police, closed or nationalized six independent television stations. He encouraged the business community to pursue free-market activities but to stay out of politics. In 2003, Russia's richest oligarch, Mikhail Khodorkovsky, was arrested on charges of fraud and tax evasion after he funded liberal parties opposed to Putin. In the 2004 presidential election, Putin won 70 percent of the vote, but his rivals were denied media broadcast time. To ensure the required 50 percent voter turnout, people in some regions were offered such incentives as movie tickets and vouchers for haircuts.

Putin's election victory in 2004 was seen as a vote for stability. Many citizens were willing to accept his authoritarian style of leadership if it would lead to economic progress.

PRESS PLAY

In *Anna* (1993), Russian director Nikita Mikhalkov juxtaposes news reports and propaganda films charting the collapse of the Soviet Union with footage of his daughter Anna that he filmed over 13 years, beginning in 1980—showing how personal and political life are intertwined. (NR)

PARTY POLITICS Russia's Fledgling Political Parties

When Russia abandoned its one-party system in the early 1990s, new political parties began springing up like the country's beloved wild mushrooms. In the 1995 parliamentary elections, 43 parties fielded candidates for the Duma's 450 seats; in 2003—after electoral laws were changed to require that a party receive a minimum 5 percent of the popular vote to gain a seat in parliament—23 parties ran candidates. It's no wonder some Russians felt bewildered: in 2003, 4.8 percent of voters marked their ballot "Against All Candidates."

On the surface, Russian democracy offers voters a broad choice. In the 2003 Duma elections, the main parties were the centrist coalition United Russia, which backed President Putin and took nearly half the seats, and the Communist Party, which still speaks for Russia's left wing and took 13 percent. Other contenders included the People's Party, which split from United Russia; two ultranationalist parties, Motherland and the Liberal Democrats; the social democratic Yabloko; and the pro-business Union of Right Forces. Less successful were a glut of smaller, weaker parties, such as Unity; Party for Peace and Unity; For Holy Rus; True Patriots of Russia; Russian Pensioners' Party; and the Party of Life.

Aside from this confusing proliferation, Russians had little chance to evaluate (or even hear about) the parties' platforms. United Russia, for example, refused to participate in the candidates' televised debates: its party slogan was simply, "Together with the President!" Voters also complained of vague campaign advertising (the slogan of the Union of Right Forces was "Vote for Your Future"; the Party of Life, "Vote for the Russia That We Love and Are Proud Of"). The campaign saw no discussion of such issues as health care and education, which in other democracies receive intense analysis.

After the presidential election of March 2004—which Putin appeared to win on the strength of personal popularity rather than on any platform—one of his opponents, Irina Khakamada, commented on Russia's weak party system:

> No political party has made a serious attempt to reach voters. . . . More than 45 percent of voters stayed away from the polls in December 2003, a clear protest against . . . the major political parties' indifference to the real problems facing society.

To strengthen the system, Khakamada recommended

- amending election laws to require that all candidates (including the president) take part in debates;
- enforcing the law that TV networks must provide airtime to all candidates;
- decreasing the number of signatures (2 million) required to register candidates;
- running all 450 state Duma deputies in direct district elections.

The last point, Khakamada argues, would bring the Duma closer to voters, enlarge the parties, strengthen their role in the political process, and encourage new leadership from the grassroots.

"Champions of democracy have one main untapped source of support: **civil society** [non-governmental institutions such as human rights and environmentalist groups, labour unions, and charitable and religious organizations]," Khakamada wrote. "To get these people to turn out on election day, politicians will have to roll up their sleeves and get to work at the grassroots. Only then will we see political parties emerge from civil society rather than being created by Kremlin fiat [decree] or the oligarchs' money."

Sources: Michele A. Berdy, "How Not to Communicate Your Message," *The Moscow Times*, December 5, 2003, p. 8; "Putin's Way," *The Economist*, December 13, 2003, pp. 24–28; Irina Khakamada, "A Grassroots Approach to Building Democracy," *The Moscow Times*, April 13, 2004, p. 10.

THE WEB

For more on building civil society in Russia, go to www.emp.ca/cwp.

Questions

1. Why is Russia's political party system weak?
2. Which of Irina Khakamada's recommendations do you think is most important? Explain.
3. Why is civil society seen to be a requisite for democracy?

Check YOUR UNDERSTANDING

1. What problems has the emerging Russian democracy experienced?
2. Can the Russian concept of "managed democracy" be considered true democracy? Explain.
3. Why have the Russian people accepted President Putin's actions?
4. What factors in a country seem to promote the development of democracy?

Dictatorships: Left and Right

As you learned in Chapter 1, dictatorship is a form of government in which one person or a small group holds absolute power and is not subject to the consent of the governed. The word "dictator" derives from the Latin term for the Roman magistrate appointed to govern for a six-month period following a state of emergency. In 44 BCE, however, Julius Caesar abolished the constitutional limits to this power.

Dictatorship is the most common non-democratic form of government in the world, and may fall on the left or the right of the political spectrum.

In the 20th century, left-wing dictatorships arose in the Soviet Union, the People's Republic of China, Cuba, Vietnam, Cambodia, and many Eastern European and African states. China and Cambodia (or Kampuchea) are studied in the pages that follow.

In the same period, right-wing dictatorships sprang up in Italy, Germany, Spain, and in countries in Asia and Central and South America. Two such dictatorships—Argentina and South Korea—are examined in the following pages. Beginning in the early 1990s, both countries began instituting democratic reforms.

SOUND BITE   "Power is not a means, it is an end. One does not establish a dictatorship in order to safeguard a revolution; one makes the revolution in order to establish the dictatorship."

George Orwell, Nineteen Eighty-Four, *1949*

1911 Manchu dynasty falls; Sun Yat-Sen elected

1921 Communist Party of China is founded

1927–37 Civil war

1937 Japanese invade

1949 Communist Party takes control

1953–57 First 5-Year Plan

1958–60 Great Leap Forward

1966–76 Cultural Revolution

1976 Death of Mao

1979 One-child policy implemented

1989 Tiananmen Massacre

1993 "Socialist market economy" introduced

1997 Hong Kong reverts to Chinese rule

2001 China joins WTO

Figure 5.14 Timeline: China.

The People's Republic of China

From the time of the Zhou Dynasty (1122–256 BCE), the politics of most Chinese empires showed strong centralizing tendencies. Today, the People's Republic of China is ruled by a single political party that claims ideological allegiance to communist principles. It asserts leadership in all spheres of society and silences all dissent. China is a unitary state whose regions are subordinate in all important matters to the central government.

The traditional imperial system of government practised by the Manchu dynasty collapsed in 1911, and the Republic of China was established under the leadership of its first president, Sun Yat-Sen. In 1927, a power struggle developed between the US-backed Nationalist (or Kuomintang) Party led by Chiang Kai-Shek (1887–1975) and the Chinese Communist Party under Mao Zedong (1893–1976). The civil war abated in 1937, when Japan invaded China, but it resumed at the end of World War II.

By 1949, famine, inflation, and police repression weakened public confidence in the Nationalist government, and the communists seized control. Chiang Kai-Shek and his party retreated to the island of Taiwan, 120 kilometres offshore, claiming to be the true rulers of China. The United States supported the claim and refused to recognize the communist government of China.

Under Mao, the government redistributed land to the least-advantaged peasant class and eradicated social problems such as prostitution and opium addiction. Following communist philosophy, agricultural and industrial production were nationalized. Communist ideology in China differed from Soviet communism in one key way: Chinese communism—which became known as Maoism—focused more on peasant farmers than on the industrial working class. Mao was convinced his vision was correct and eventually developed an adversarial relationship with Russian communism.

Mao implemented ambitious national schemes. The first Five-Year Plan (1953–57) nationalized industry and **collectivized** agriculture. The Great Leap Forward (1958–60) reorganized the countryside into gigantic communes, or cooperatives, composed of as many as 20,000 families. To boost steel production, people were encouraged to build backyard steel furnaces. The Great Leap Forward failed—both agricultural and industrial production declined.

In the 1950s, Mao urged citizens to engage in political discussions to "let a hundred flowers [opinions] bloom." When dialogue evolved into criticism challenging his authority, Mao repressed all dissent. Opponents were jailed, banished to labour camps, or executed.

Mao was called the Great Helmsman and attained cult-like popularity. Portraits and records of his accomplishments were exhibited everywhere. Copies of Quotations from Chairman Mao ("the little red book") were distributed in the millions. By 1966, Mao inaugurated a Great Proletarian Cultural Revolution designed to stop "revisionists" who favoured straying from pure Maoism. He recruited millions of students, known as the Red Guards, to seek out enemies of the peasants and working class. The country descended into chaos. Many political leaders were beaten, jailed, or executed.

After Mao's death in 1976, Communist Party leadership took a more moderate direction. Some of the radical members behind the Cultural Revolution, such as Mao's widow Jiang Qing, were arrested and tried. Deng Xiaoping became *de facto* leader in the 1980s and concentrated on modernizing China's economy. Individual farmers were given more authority. The government allowed a market economy to develop alongside communist central planning and encouraged small-scale industrial development in the countryside.

China's economy improved through Deng's reforms, but not personal and political freedoms. In 1979, the government introduced a "one family, one child" policy to limit population growth. Compliance brought better housing and salaries; defiance brought job loss and reduced benefits. Because boy babies have long been favoured in China, the one-child policy has contributed to female infanticide (baby killing) and the abandonment of female babies.

Figure 5.15 This propaganda poster dating from China's Cultural Revolution (ca. 1965) proclaims, "Hold high the great red banner of Mao Zedong to wage the Great Proletarian Cultural Revolution to the end—Revolution is no crime; to rebel is justified."

Political dissent was tolerated, briefly, but in 1989 the government crushed a student-led and popular pro-democracy movement. The killing of hundreds, perhaps thousands, of young demonstrators in Beijing's Tiananmen Square outraged people around the world (see Chapter 1, page 25).

In the 1990s, Deng increased China's economic power by introducing a "socialist market economy" that permitted more free enterprise and more foreign trade and investment. Hong Kong, long a hub of free-market capitalism, was returned to China in 1997, after its 99-year lease to Britain expired. Beijing subsequently abolished Hong Kong's British-style government and established a provisional legislature; a chief executive was also appointed. When elections were held in 2004, pro-democracy parties took 25 of the 60 seats on the Legislative Council, but they were outnumbered by the 34 seats chosen by pro-Beijing business and professional constituencies (one independent member was also elected).

In 2001, after years of diplomatic efforts, China was admitted to the World Trade Organization. The country had lobbied for WTO membership on the strength of its commitment to economic reform, which in recent decades resulted in an explosion of foreign investment and increased prosperity for China's new middle class.

Today, political power remains with the Communist Party, whose membership represents approximately 6 percent of the population. No factory manager, school principal, town mayor, or commune leader can make an important decision without consulting the party.

SOUND BITE "Politics is war without bloodshed, while war is politics with bloodshed."

Mao Zedong, "On Protracted War," 1938

Point:
Counterpoint → Is China's One-Child Policy Justified?

"Yes" to the One-Child Policy

by Christopher A. Reed

Although China today is larger than the continental United States, it sustains a population nearly five times greater on the 11 percent of its land area that is arable [suitable for agriculture]. Population pressure on the small proportion of China's land mass that is arable has increased steadily since the 18th century, when traditional China's standard of living peaked along with its population. In the modern period, official efforts to reclaim wilderness areas, reminiscent of the Soviet Union's Virgin Lands campaigns of the 1950s, have often failed. Urbanization since the late 1970s, by which time China's population was at least one-fifth urban, has also depleted farmland. For these reasons, population control has often seemed a necessary, if not always a politically viable, complement to the increased economic (both agricultural and industrial) productivity, national wealth, and international respect that China has sought throughout the modern period. . . .

In the 1950s, the leadership dismissed advice by leading sociologist Ma Yinchu and others regarding the Malthusian cul-de-sac into which China was heading. . . . From 1961 to 1980, each new year added about 17 million people, the rough equivalent of adding the population of Holland each year for 19 years. . . .

With population growth of this magnitude and no special efforts to rein it in, to achieve a standard of living comparable with those in the [industrialized countries], China would have had to undertake, in a matter of decades, industrial and green revolutions the likes of which Europe, America, and Japan did not experience in the past two centuries. And it would have had to do so without the vast migrations and social dislocations experienced by those other regions of the world. Clearly, something had to be done to stifle this population growth if China were to achieve wealth, power, and domestic security in modern terms.

In 1980, Premier Hua Guofeng announced in the National People's Congress, China's national assembly, that henceforth all couples would be limited to one child each; those who had three or more would be punished. The policy, which rapidly became known as the "one-child policy," had already been tested for about two years, and was intended to bring the annual rate of increase down to zero per thousand by the year 2000. . . .

Within a couple of years, more realistic goals emerged. In policies implemented from the top down, different provinces were allotted varying targets, all with the overall goal of restricting China's population to 1.2 billion by the year 2000. . . .

Although rarely as uniformly restrictive as it has sometimes been portrayed in the Western press (by 1984, for instance, several exempted groups already existed, including minorities, remarried persons, parents of handicapped children, the very poor, and parents of one daughter), the one-child policy has also not been as successful as its original enforcers hoped it would be. This patchy record of accomplishment has been partly due to coercive measures pursued by overzealous local officials. Coercion, officially outlawed from the start, was eventually more firmly discouraged, and abortion and sterilization drives of the early years were abandoned in favor of contraception. Further, severe economic penalties for noncompliance were discontinued in the 1980s. . . .

It is striking that Chinese human rights activists, with rare exceptions, do not raise their voices in opposition to the one-child policy. Such activists, themselves mostly relatively educated urbanites, share the government's desire to raise living standards by, among other means, reducing population. Urbanites and wealthier rural dwellers with access to reliable state-run or enterprise-run pension systems now acknowledge they will no longer have to rely on their children for support in their old age. . . .

Source: Adapted from Christopher A. Reed, "Malthusian Survivalism: The One-Child Policy and Its Importance in Limiting China's Population." National Institute for Research Advancement, *NIRA Review*, Autumn 1998, at http://www.nira.go.jp/publ/review/98autumn/reed.html.

"No" to the One-Child Policy

by Scott Weinberg

Late in the summer of 1999, many Western newspapers carried the welcome news that the Chinese government was no longer rigidly enforcing the quota that had allowed only one child for each married couple. But Steven Mosher of the Population Research Institute has raised serious questions about the accuracy of those reports.

Mosher—whose 1984 book *Broken Earth* provided a detailed account of the Chinese policies, which routinely led to forced abortion and sterilization—believes that the reports of an easing in Beijing's stance were the product of an international campaign to encourage American support for population control. . . .

On October 13, Chinese Premier Zhu Rongji thought it necessary to correct the record. "China will continue to enforce its effective family planning policy in the new century," said Premier Zhu, stressing that China would continue to make "family planning" a fundamental state policy.

In reality, Mosher insisted, there is no evidence that China is likely to ease up on enforcement of its family-planning campaign. On the contrary, he said: "The Chinese government has made it clear that the one-child policy will be continued into the foreseeable future."

What does China mean, then, when it claims that its one-child policy is voluntary? Mosher explained:

> There are cases in China where brute force is used to perform abortion and sterilization. But more commonly, the Chinese government abides by its own Orwellian definition of voluntary, which is to say that you can fine the woman; you can lock her up; you can subject her to morning-to-night brainwashing sessions; you can cut off the electricity to her house; you can fire her from her job; you can fire her husband from his job; and you can fire her parents from their jobs. All of this psychological mauling, sleep deprivation, arrest, and grueling mistreatment is inflicted upon these women in order to break their will to resist. But as long as the pregnant women walk the last few steps to the local medical clinic under their own power, then the abortions that follow are said by the government to be "voluntary."

Mosher said that the Chinese government has failed to consider the social consequences of its policy:

> In enforcing a one-child policy, the Chinese government has put the Chinese people in a position of having to reject their daughters in their desire to have sons. It has put parents in the position of having to choose between a son, who will support them

in old age, or having a daughter who will go to live with her husband's family upon marriage. The result is that little girls have to run a gauntlet from conception through birth. Many of them do not survive that gauntlet.

The first part of that gauntlet is sex-selective abortion. The second part is female infanticide. Mosher revealed: "Reports throughout the length and breadth of China reveal that little girls are dying shortly after birth in mysterious circumstances." After twenty years of discouraging births, he added, the country is now observing a serious demographic imbalance between the sexes, so that "now there is a shortage of 30 million brides in China."

China's population-control policies are enforced with special vigor for members of ethnic minorities, Mosher reported, "in accord with China's 1987 eugenics law which reflects a desire to 'breed a better Chinese man, and a better Chinese woman.'" He argued that the Beijing regime is targeting minorities such as the Uyghur people in order to depress their birthrates below replacement. "In a few generations," he concluded, "a declining Uyghur people will cease to be a threat to China's 'territorial integrity.'"

Source: Scott Weinberg, "An End to the One-Child Quota?" *Catholic World Report*, February 2000, at http://www.catholic.net/rcc/Periodicals/cwr/Feb2000/Dossier3.html.

Articulating a Personal Stand

1. The adjective "Malthusian" is derived from the economist Thomas Malthus. In *An Essay on the Principle of Population*, published in 1798, Malthus predicted population would outrun food supply, leading to economic decline. Malthus based his theory on the idea that population, if unchecked, increases at a geometric rate, whereas food supply grows at an arithmetic rate. List the arguments presented in Christopher Reed's article that support China's one-child policy. With which arguments do you agree or disagree? Why?

2. Follow the same steps for the article by Scott Weinberg, listing his arguments in opposition to the one-child policy.

3. Which side do you find more convincing—"Yes" or "No"? Why?

Architecture and Politics

Walls

"Something there is that doesn't love a wall,
That wants it down"

Robert Frost, from the poem "Mending Wall"

Throughout history, walls have been built to define political and social boundaries. The Great Wall of China, the largest fabricated structure on Earth, was designed to keep out the Huns, Mongols, and other nomadic tribes. The Great Wall, eventually 6,400 kilometres in length, was begun in the 3rd century BCE and completed during the Ming dynasty (14th–17th centuries CE). Some historians and political analysts maintain that the wall reinforced a Chinese "fortress mentality" that contributed to Chinese isolation and a slow pace of development in modern times.

Another wall, Hadrian's Wall, runs 117 kilometres across northern Britain. It was built in 120–123 CE by the Roman Emperor Hadrian to defend occupying Roman forces from local tribes. Roman soldiers built the wall of local stone, with turrets as lookout points and a ditch and communications road running parallel with it. Forts built along the wall housed soldiers and supervised north–south traffic. After Hadrian's Wall was completed, military conflict in the region declined. The structure fell into disuse by the 4th century CE with the decline of the Roman Empire.

The Demilitarized Zone (DMZ) that splits North from South Korea is the world's most heavily fortified border or "fence." It is 4 kilometres wide and runs 240 kilometres across the Korean Peninsula. The DMZ is pockmarked with landmines and bunkers, criss-crossed by barbed wire, and guarded by nearly 1 million North Korean soldiers on one side and 600,000 South Korean troops on the other. The United States maintains 37,000 military personnel in South Korea (though in 2004, the Bush administration announced its intention to reduce that number) to ensure that North Korea's army does not cross over. Since the DMZ was created in 1953 at the end of the Korean War, there have been a number of clashes. In 1976, North Korean soldiers shot and killed two US officers who were pruning a tree in the DMZ to improve their view of the North. Soldiers in the South have detected attempts by Northern sappers (demolitions experts) to tunnel under the DMZ into Southern territory. One tunnel was large enough to drive a jeep through.

The 155-kilometre Berlin Wall (Figure 5.2, page 157) was constructed by the East German government in 1961, at the height of the Cold War.

Unlike most walls, the Berlin Wall was designed to keep people in. After World War II, Germany was partitioned, with communists controlling the East and capitalists the West. The capital, Berlin, in East Germany, was also divided into East–West sectors. Between 1952 and 1961, about 2.6 million East Germans fled to West Germany via Berlin in search of a freer life. Faced with this loss of skilled and professional workers, the East German government built the wall to stop the flood. The wall was a complex system of fences, watchtowers, trenches, and barriers. Over the years, at least 100 people were killed and more than 200 injured attempting to cross it. In November 1989, after hundreds of thousands of East Germans fled westward via Hungary and Czechoslovakia, the beleaguered East German government lifted travel restrictions. Days later, the dismantling of the wall began. East and West Germany were unified one year later.

In 2002, the Israeli government began building a security fence to keep out suicide bombers from the West Bank (see Chapter 3). Palestinians objected that the fence wound through their territory, separating farmers from their land, children from schools, and workers from employment. The wall did not follow the 1948 border established for Israel and placed disputed land under Israeli jurisdiction. As originally planned, the fence would mean Israel absorbed as much as 18 percent of the West Bank. The projected length of the structure was about 700 kilometres. Israelis called the wall an "anti-terror fence"; Palestinians called it an "apartheid wall." In 2004, the International Court of Justice ruled the fence illegal, but Israel continued its construction.

Questions

1. Identify a common reason why these walls were constructed.
2. Evaluate the success of physical walls constructed for political reasons.
3. The United States is concerned about national security. Might a wall ever be built between Canada and the United States? Between the United States and Mexico? Explain your reasoning.

Figure 5.16 Palestinians walk past the Israeli security wall in the West Bank village of Abu Dis, which has been divided by the barrier.

1854 Cambodia requests
French aid

1863 French protectorate
established

1947 First constitution drafted

1950 First elections held

1953 Cambodia achieves
independence

1954 Second Indochina War
begins

1955 Sihanouk abdicates,
becomes premier

1961 US enters Vietnam War

1965 Cambodia severs US
diplomatic ties

1970 Sihanouk overthrown;
civil war; Lon Nol declares
Khmer Republic

1973 US withdraws from
Vietnam

1975 Khmer Rouge overthrows
Lon Nol

1991 Peace treaty signed;
Sihanouk heads state

1993 First democratic
elections; new constitution;
Sihanouk reinstated as king

1998 Death of Pol Pot

2003 Election results disputed;
liberals and royalists seek
coalition with left-wing
government

2004 Sihanouk abdicates,
chooses exile in China;
succession falls to son, Prince
Sihamoni

Figure 5.17 Timeline:
Cambodia.

Cambodia ("Democratic Kampuchea")

The golden age of Khmer civilization lasted from the 9th to the 13th centuries. During this time, the kingdom of Kambuja—which gave Kampuchea, or Cambodia, its name—ruled large territories from its capital in the Angkor region of present-day western Cambodia. The Angkor kings were absolute monarchs, and later Cambodian leaders adopted this manner of rule. From the 15th century, however, Cambodia's powerful neighbours Siam (Thailand) and Annam (Vietnam) attacked Cambodia, annexing some of its richest land.

In 1854, the Cambodian monarchy asked France to help quell fighting in the region, and the country came under French control that lasted almost a century. After a brief interlude of Japanese occupation during World War II, the French returned and installed King Norodom Sihanouk (1922–) as head of state. Sihanouk began a "royal crusade for independence" that won French recognition by 1953.

Although an authoritarian ruler, Sihanouk drafted a constitution that made Cambodia a limited monarchy and allowed democratic elections. In 1955, he abdicated the throne, entered politics, founded the Popular Socialist Party, and ruled as premier. He was popular with Cambodia's Buddhist and rural populations. In foreign relations, Sihanouk tried to remain neutral during the Cold War. He accepted US economic and military aid while keeping close ties with China and trying to maintain friendly relations with the Democratic Republic of Vietnam (North Vietnam). To avoid war, he allowed Vietnamese communists (Viet Cong) to use Cambodian territory during the Second Indochina War (1954–75).

After the United States entered the war in 1961, Sihanouk's balancing act became impossible. It ended in 1965 when he severed diplomatic relations with the United States after Cambodians were killed in US and South Vietnamese raids into Cambodia. He was overthrown in a bloodless military coup in 1970. Under the US-backed government of General Lon Nol, US and South Vietnamese troops could pursue Viet Cong forces from Vietnam into Cambodia, something Sihanouk had blocked. Lon Nol abolished the monarchy and established the Khmer Republic.

Shortly after Lon Nol took power, US and South Vietnamese troops entered Cambodia to attack communist bases. Their actions, combined with heavy US air bombings, destroyed villages and killed civilians, creating sympathy among Cambodians for the communists.

The Cambodian communists—the Khmer Rouge—were led by Saloth Sar (ca. 1926–98), a Paris-educated radio engineer and Marxist who later became known as Pol Pot. With support from the deposed Sihanouk and the People's Republic of China, the Khmer Rouge seized the capital, Phnom Penh, in 1975. Over the next four years, Pol Pot and the Khmer Rouge presided over one of the most devastating reigns of terror in political history. At least 1 million people—in a country of 7.3 million—died of disease or starvation, or were executed. Pol Pot oversaw the genocide of his own people.

Like communist dictators Stalin and Mao, Pol Pot was an ideologue (a zealous adherent to an ideology). After renaming Cambodia "Democratic Kampuchea," the government began to implement "pure communism." The Khmer Rouge demanded strict adherence to the principle of self-reliance based on an idealized rural agricultural life. Intellectuals were punished with death; schools were closed. Religion was banned. The Khmer Rouge drove Phnom Penh's 2 million residents, as well as the residents of other cities and towns, into the countryside to work as farm labourers or at handicrafts.

Pol Pot and the Khmer Rouge tried to engineer a rural utopia based on total equality. The 1976 constitution declared that workers and peasants were the masters of their factories and fields and that there was no unemployment in Democratic Kampuchea. Even though he exercised totalitarian control, Pol Pot maintained the trappings of democracy. In Kampuchea, the People's Representative Assembly was composed of 250 members representing workers, peasants, and the Kampuchean Revolutionary Army. Beginning in 1976, the legislature was popularly elected every five years.

While the communist governments of China and the Soviet Union allowed some private property, the Khmer Rouge government owned all land through cooperatives. The Khmer Rouge believed that Kampuchea should be a classless society of "perfect harmony." It also believed Kampuchea should be cashless, so it confiscated all currency. With no money in circulation, shops closed, and workers received their pay in the form of food rations.

Pol Pot's dictatorship ended when Vietnamese forces invaded in 1979 and he was driven into the jungles bordering Kampuchea and Thailand. He remained there until his death in 1998. The Vietnamese stayed in Cambodia for 10 years, and the Khmer Rouge continued to receive support from other Asian nations and the United States for fighting Vietnam. After the Vietnamese withdrew from Cambodia in 1989, UN-sponsored elections brought into power a government free of Khmer Rouge influence.

Like other dictators, Pol Pot undertook purges (periodic crackdowns on dissenters) to wipe out real or perceived opponents. He especially targeted people of Vietnamese descent or those sympathetic to the Vietnamese. Unlike Mao Zedong, Pol Pot did not encourage a personality cult; he seemed to submerge his personality in his ideology. His authoritarian rule was in part motivated by a desire to develop a nationalistic Kampuchea separate from its long-time adversary, Vietnam.

Figure 5.18 Foreign tourists stare at the skulls of victims of the 1975–79 Khmer Rouge regime in a memorial in Cheung Ek, Cambodia, 2000.

SOUND BITE "Why should we flagellate ourselves for what the Cambodians did to each other?"

Henry Kissinger, Assistant for National Security Affairs under US President Richard Nixon, commenting in 1998 on the 1973 US bombings of Cambodia

SOUND BITE "We evacuated the people from the cities, which is our class struggle."

Pol Pot, article in Tung Padevat (Revolutionary Flags), *1976*

1516 Spanish colonizers arrive

1810 Spanish viceroy ousted

1816 Argentina declares independence

1816–52 Civil wars lead to dictatorships

1853 Constitution adopted

1870s Territorial expansion leads to slaughter of indigenous peoples

1930 Coup d'état imposes conservative government

1943–44 Juan Peron leads coup

1946 Peron elected president

1948 Factories, utilities, railroads nationalized

1955 Military coup overthrows Peron

1973 Peron returns to power

1974 Death of Peron

1976 Military stages coup

1976–82 Dirty War kills dissidents

1982 War with Britain over Malvinas (Falklands); military leader resigns

1983 Civilian rule re-established

1994 Constitutional amendments limit presidential power

2001 Economic crisis leads to riots

2003 Nestor Kirchner elected president

Figure 5.19 Timeline: Argentina.

Argentina

Argentina's name comes from the Latin word *argentum*, which means silver, the precious metal that attracted Europeans to the region. The largest groups of indigenous peoples in Argentina were the Quechua of the northwest and the Mapuche of Patagonia in the south. With the arrival of Spanish colonizers in the 16th century, the indigenous peoples began a long resistance campaign and were devastated by European diseases against which they had no immunity.

A **junta** (a group that seizes government control) ousted the Spanish viceroy in 1810 and ruled until Argentina declared its independence from Spain in 1816. Throughout the 19th century, Argentina's politics were defined by the rivalry between Federalists and Unitarists. The Federalists, conservative landowners from the interior, advocated provincial autonomy and were supported by the rural working class. The Unitarists were city dwellers and recent immigrants who upheld the central authority of the capital, Buenos Aires. The Unitarists prevailed. Although a constitution was adopted in 1853, ongoing civil unrest brought a succession of authoritarian governments.

In the 1870s, Argentina began an aggressive territorial expansion. Hundreds of thousands of indigenous people were slaughtered as their lands were confiscated. Immigrants flooded in from Spain, Italy, England, Ireland, and Germany to claim the newly acquired lands. Today, in a country of 33 million, the indigenous population is approximately 500,000.

Modernization, rapid economic expansion, and immigration continued. By the early 20th century, socialist and anarchist movements radically reshaped Argentina's politics. But in 1930, a coup d'état, supported by an elite of landowners, business people, and the middle class, seized control and imposed a conservative government that held power until well into World War II.

Wartime industrialization brought rapid economic expansion—and political instability. After a military coup in 1943 overthrew the government, Colonel Juan Peron (1895–1974) became secretary of labour and welfare in the new regime. Peron married the actress Eva Duarte (1919–52). During the 1946 presidential campaign, Eva—or Evita, as she became known—delivered passionate speeches portraying Peron as the champion of the poor on her immensely popular radio show. Juan Peron won the election and became a dictator.

Because of her impoverished background, Evita saw herself as a leader of the *descamisados* or "shirtless ones." She worked with labour unions and created the Eva Peron Foundation to help the poor, but later reports hinted at financial irregularities within the organization.

Juan Peron's economic program—which he called a "third position" between capitalism and communism—stressed domestic industrialization and self-determination, and he tried to appeal to both conservative nationalists and working-class Argentinians. Some analysts view him as a fascist because his government supported the fascist and Nazi regimes of Italy and Germany during World War II. Peron was overthrown in a military coup in 1955 and fled to Spain.

Over the next 30 years, Argentina experienced more military dictatorships, with brief periods of civilian rule. Peron returned to rule Argentina in 1973 and died a year later. He bestowed power on his second wife, Isabel. The country was beset by political kidnappings, guerrilla warfare, strikes, and economic problems. Isabel Peron's regime ended in 1976, when the military once more seized control.

The new military dictatorship struggled with Argentina's economic and internal security problems. Between 1976 and 1982, it launched a "Dirty War," using paramilitary (unofficial yet militarized) squads to silence opposition. An estimated 10,000 to 30,000 citizens were made to "disappear." Some dissidents were dropped from helicopters into the Atlantic Ocean; others spent years anonymously imprisoned.

In 1982, the military junta declared war on Britain over possession of the Malvinas (Falkland) Islands off Argentina's coast. The war—which Britain easily won—was designed to draw public attention away from political corruption, economic mismanagement, and human rights abuses. However, after a preliminary outburst of nationalism, the country turned against the government. The leader, General Leopoldo Galtieri, resigned, and an era of military rule in Argentina ended. A civilian, Raul Alfonsin, was elected president and came to power in 1983. In 1994, the government of President Carlos Menem amended the constitution to limit presidential power and strengthen opposition parties.

In spite of its promises, Argentina's military dictatorship failed to create economic stability or to manage inflation and unemployment. Although

SOUND BITE *"Charity separates the rich from the poor; aid raises the needy and sets them on the same level with the rich."*

Eva Peron, addressing the American Congress of Industrial Medicine, 1949

Figure 5.20 Demonstrators hold banners that say "Thank you, Raul [Alfonsin]" to celebrate the 20th anniversary of return to civilian rule in Argentina, Buenos Aires, 2003.

democracy returned to Argentina in the 1990s, financial progress did not. In December 2001, the country defaulted on repayment of its $132 billion loan, the largest default in history. The resulting civil unrest—food riots, a run on the banks—led to a succession of interim governments that struggled to resolve the economic and social chaos. In the 2003 election, many of Argentina's traditionally conservative, right-wing voters shifted to the left and elected Nestor Kirchner (1950–) president.

Republic of Korea

Invasions have been frequent in the history of the Korean Peninsula. Both China and Japan mounted periodic raids from the 13th to the 17th centuries, and in 1637 the Manchu dynasty conquered the Korean population. Japan invaded the peninsula during the Russo–Japanese War (1904–5). Japan annexed and occupied Korea until after World War II, when the US took over South Korea and the USSR the North. In 1950, North Korea attacked the South. The ensuing Korean War lasted until 1953, when a negotiated settlement established the same border (the 38th parallel) as had existed before the war.

Syngman Rhee (1875–1965), who was educated in the United States, ruled South Korea from 1948 until 1960. His government received US support because of Korea's geopolitical significance in the Cold War. Rhee was considered a Korean patriot because he had fought against the Japanese invasion of 1904 and the postwar communist threat. Although his government had some democratic frills, it functioned as a dictatorship. Elections were rigged to ensure Rhee would win. In the 1960 election, corruption and manipulation were so blatant that riots broke out. After police killed 142 student protestors, Rhee was forced to resign. During his time in office, Rhee was accused of imprisoning and eliminating his political opponents and suppressing all dissent.

After a brief period of democracy, anti-communist General Park Chung Hee staged a coup in 1961 and dissolved the elected National Assembly. His US-backed military government pledged to eliminate corruption and to introduce a "fresh and clean morality." Park created the Korean Central Intelligence Agency (KCIA) to prevent countercoups and eliminate his enemies. He imposed restrictions on the press, intellectuals, and opposition politicians, but tolerated mild criticism of his government. New measures in the constitution of 1971–72 gave the president power to appoint the premier and cabinet members without legislative consent and to order emergency economic measures. Later, Park received the right to appoint one-third of the legislature and the right to dissolve it.

Park regularly used the threat of a North Korean invasion to maintain authoritarian control. He turned economic affairs over to a panel of experts. Capitalism and entrepreneurship were nurtured, exports multiplied, and South Korea's economy grew dramatically. Wealth, however, accumulated in

1231–1637 Invasions by Mongolia (1231), Japan (1592), and China (1392, 1637)

1904–5 Russo–Japanese War; Japan invades Korea

1910 Korean monarchy falls; Japan annexes Korea

1948 Two Koreas established; Rhee elected president of South

1950–53 Korean War

1960 Rhee is re-elected; resigns due to civil unrest

1961 Military coup

1963 Park elected president; re-elected 1967, '71, '72

1979 Park assassinated, succeeded by military dictatorship

1987 New constitution drafted

1992 First civilian president since Korean War elected

2000 North and South Korean leaders discuss reconciliation

Figure 5.21 Timeline: Republic of Korea.

fewer and fewer hands. After a series of large student protests were brutally put down in 1979, the director of the KCIA assassinated Park. The military once again imposed a repressive dictatorship, but widespread protests in 1987 forced the government to lift restrictions and grant greater freedom of the press and assembly.

Dictatorships dominated South Korea for almost 40 years for many reasons. For one, centralized authority was prominent in Korea's history. Perhaps the key factor was the tacit and financial support of the United States, which used South Korea as an Asian base to fight the communist threat from North Korea.

In 1992, Kim Young Sam became the first civilian to be elected president since the Korean War. In 2004, President Ryo Moo Hyun, a former democracy activist, was impeached (charged with official misconduct) for breaking a campaign rule before a general election—he publicly endorsed the candidates of a particular party, against the rules of South Korea's constitution. He was reinstated by the Constitutional Court, and apologized in a televised speech. With the end of the Cold War in Europe and the spread of democracy in the late 20th century, South Korea has evolved into an emerging democracy.

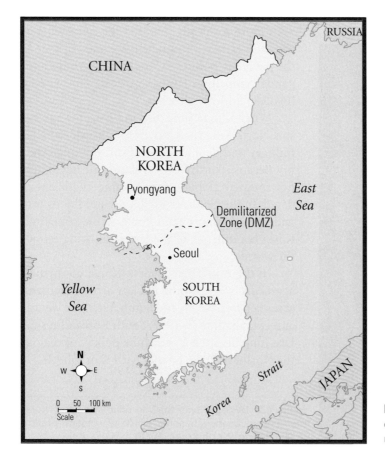

Figure 5.22 North and South Korea. A demilitarized zone (DMZ) has separated the two countries since 1953.

A Tale of Two States: North and South Korea

While Syngman Rhee was constructing his right-wing dictatorship with US support in South Korea, Kim Il-Sung (1912–94) was building a communist dictatorship in North Korea with Soviet and Chinese support. As South Korea moved toward a thriving, export-driven capitalist economy, North Korea concentrated on an official ideology of *juche*, based on the principles of self-reliance and independence. In the 1960s and '70s, the South subsidized industry and concentrated on world trade. In the North, Kim developed a Korea-first consciousness that shunned capitalism and the world economy. In North Korea (the "Hermit Kingdom"), government discouraged all foreign influences, limiting the number and personal use of telephones, radios, and televisions.

Kim presented himself as a father figure to North Koreans, an image that fit traditional views of the family and the patriarchy. Slogans and pamphlets reinforced the message that Kim was the "Great Leader" and that he and the nation were one. As an author and the originator of *juche*, Kim was seen as the national saviour. His birthday became a public holiday, and his eldest son, Kim Jong-Il, was proclaimed his successor (see Chapter 1, page 20).

Kim, and later his son, used the cult of personality to rally citizens to sacrifice individual goals for the state and the leader. Kim suppressed dissent even more ruthlessly than did the right-wing dictators of South Korea. But unlike Rhee and Park, he involved the people in politics through study groups and propaganda campaigns. His government supervised all such involvement very closely.

When Kim Il-Sung died in 1994, power passed to his son. North Korea had moved toward self-sufficiency, but military and defence expenditures drained the economy. Because North Korea's manufacturing industries did not compete globally, they became inefficient and outdated. In the 1990s, crop failures and floods resulted in widespread hunger and famine. At the same time, South Korea became one of the fastest-growing economies in the world.

In the mid-1990s, North Korea confirmed it was aggressively developing nuclear arms, heightening tensions between North and South. Yet, there were attempts at reconciliation. In 1997, South Korean President Kim Dae Jung initiated a "sunshine policy" of dialogue with the North. In 2000, he met with Kim Jong-Il. However,

Figure 5.23 During a brief thaw in relations, South Korean tourists pass banners bearing "words of wisdom" of Kim Il-Sung in Pyongyang, North Korea, 2000.

	North Korea	South Korea
Daily newspapers, 2004	3	60
Televisions, 1999	53*	520*
Radios, 1997	147*	1,033*
Telephone lines, 2001	49*	500*
Cellphones, 2002	n.a.	667*
Personal computers, 2001	n.a.	132*
Internet users, 2002	n.a.	556*
GDP/capita, 2003	US$1,000	US$17,700

*Per 1,000 population; n.a. = data not available.

Source: *CIA World Fact Book, 2004; Encyclopedia Britannica Almanac 2004.*

Figure 5.24 Communication in the two Koreas.

North Korea soon reverted to policies of isolation and self-reliance, punctuated with nuclear threats. In 2003, the government announced its decision to withdraw from the 1970 *Nuclear Non-Proliferation Treaty.*

Dictatorship: An Assessment

Dictatorships are capable of inspiring popular support. Eva Peron did so for her husband in Argentina; Mao did so in China. Dictatorships can also impose totalitarian rule that ignores the wishes of the people, as exemplified by the regimes of Pol Pot in Kampuchea and Kim Il-Sung in North Korea.

As you learned in Chapter 1, Aristotle argued that people achieve their greatest potential and happiness by being politically involved in their society. One of the many drawbacks to dictatorship is that it blocks voluntary participation in the *polis.* Because dictatorships, unlike democracies, cannot rely on the voluntary support of their citizens, they must use other means to secure popular compliance, such as force. Official intimidation—through disappearances, as in Argentina, or genocide, as in Kampuchea—is employed to suppress political dissent.

The need for social order and economic control is also a common rationale for the creation of a dictatorship. Economically speaking, statistics indicate that dictatorships perform no better and no worse than democracies.

Dictatorships typically rely on propaganda to manipulate the masses. They may also use ideology to distract people from the absence of basic human rights. In Mao's China, there was the "little red book"; in North Korea, the doctrine of *juche*; in Peron's Argentina, the myth of "Saint" Evita.

Some dictatorships have evolved into democracies in a process that is rarely smooth. In both Argentina and South Korea, former military leaders were ready to reclaim control as their countries took the first steps toward democracy.

Check YOUR UNDERSTANDING

1. Give some reasons why most Chinese empires have exhibited strong centralizing tendencies.
2. Why did the Chinese people support the government of Mao Zedong?
3. Describe the balancing act that Norodom Sihanouk followed in foreign relations.
4. How did Pol Pot's ideology of "pure communism" affect Cambodia?
5. Why do you think many dictators undertake purges to eliminate real or perceived opponents?
6. Why do some commentators view Juan Peron's regime as fascist?
7. Why did the United States support Syngman Rhee? How has US support influenced political life in South Korea?
8. How have the dictatorships of North and South Korea taken different directions?
9. What factors in a country seem to predispose it to dictatorship?
10. How does the process of succession differ between democracies and non-democracies?

Oligarchy

As you learned in Chapter 1, in their typology of governments Plato and Aristotle classified "rule by the few" into two systems: aristocracy and oligarchy. Aristocracy was defined as a system in which power is held by a small group that rules under law for the common good. In an oligarchy, by contrast, power is used by a wealthy minority to exploit an impoverished majority.

Some theorists argue that all political systems are oligarchies—that dictatorships and democracies alike serve the interests of only a privileged few. For them, the major distinction between an oligarchy and a democracy is that in a democracy elites must compete with one another for public support.

In the pages that follow, Plato and Aristotle's definition of oligarchy forms the basis of an analysis of the National Party's rule of South Africa and the landlord-dominated governments of Guatemala in the 20th century.

PRESS PLAY

In *Cry, the Beloved Country* (1995), an adaptation of Alan Paton's novel, a white South African farmer (Richard Harris) and a black preacher (James Earl Jones) find friendship through linked family tragedies. (PG-13)

South Africa

Various indigenous peoples inhabited southern Africa when Dutch settlers arrived in 1652. Great Britain also colonized the area, clashing with the Dutch over land, mining rights, and the status of non-whites, and eventually defeating them in the Boer War (1899–1902). Gold and diamond mining in the 19th century led to the development of a capitalist economy in which Europeans exploited the indigenous population as labourers, denying them civil rights. In 1910, the Union of South Africa was created.

Afrikaners (Dutch-descended South Africans) continued their resistance to British imperialism. In 1948, the Afrikaner-led government implemented apartheid (apartness)—a government policy that segregated the country. South Africa became an oligarchy in which the white minority ruled over the non-white majority (85 percent of the nation). Aside from the white and black populations, apartheid laws also regulated the lives of people of mixed race, who were known as "coloured," and people of Asian descent. Under apartheid, the mobility, occupations, and social lives of blacks were tightly restricted. Sexual relations and marriage between whites and non-whites were outlawed.

The South African government also curtailed freedom of expression. It banned communist organizations and publications in 1950. In 1960, the African National Congress (ANC), the oldest black political and civil rights organization in Africa, was banned after a peaceful demonstration in the township (residential development restricted to one race) of Sharpeville turned violent. On March 21, 1960, demonstrators gathered to protest the passbook that blacks were required to carry at all times. Police opened fire, killing 68 people and wounding 180. Sharpeville exposed the brutality of apartheid to the world and eventually led to international sanctions against South Africa's government.

After Sharpeville, civil rights leader Nelson Mandela (1918–), who had been an active member of the ANC throughout the 1950s, abandoned non-violence. After years of frustrated peaceful struggle, he and his followers became convinced that force could be met only with force. In 1963, Mandela was sentenced to life in prison for sabotage against military and government property.

1652 Dutch settlers arrive
1789–1887 Wars fought over land with indigenous Xhosa
1814 Britain gains control
1828–33 British extend rights to non-whites and abolish slavery; Afrikaners angered
1899–1902 Boer War
1910 Union of South Africa created
1912 ANC founded
1930s Non-white vote curtailed; black "homelands" created
1948 Apartheid becomes law
1960 Sharpeville Massacre; ANC banned
1961 South Africa leaves Commonwealth
1963 Nelson Mandela jailed
1976 Soweto riots
1985 State of emergency declared
1986 Archbishop Tutu seeks sanctions at UN
1989 President de Klerk eases apartheid
1990 Nelson Mandela freed
1991 New constitution drafted
1994 Mandela wins democratic elections
1996 Truth and Reconciliation Committee convened

Figure 5.25 Timeline: South Africa.

Figure 5.26 The first witness before the Truth and Reconciliation Commission is sworn in, April 15, 1996, in East London, South Africa.

THE WEB

In 1966 the UN declared March 21 the International Day for the Elimination of Racial Discrimination in memory of the Sharpeville Massacre. To learn more about this day, and for links to human rights resources, visit www.emp.ca/cwp.

PRESS PLAY

In *Cry Freedom* (1987), directed by Richard Attenborough, a South African journalist (Kevin Kline) is forced to flee the country after he investigates the suspicious death in custody of black activist Steve Biko. (PG)

SOUND BITE "If you want to make peace with your enemy, you have to work with your enemy. Then he becomes your partner."

Nelson Mandela, The Long Walk to Freedom, *2000*

South Africa's isolation increased in the 1970s after Portuguese colonial rule ended in neighbouring Angola and Mozambique, and the former British colony of Rhodesia became the independent state of Zimbabwe. By now, South Africa was perceived in much of the world as an outlaw regime, and many countries refused to trade with it (although Britain and the United States continued to do so). The United Nations condemned apartheid; armed guerrilla groups attacked South Africa from the neighbouring states of Tanzania, Zambia, and later, Angola.

In 1976, a riot in the Soweto township over mandatory use of Afrikaans (the Dutch-based language of the Afrikaners) in schools spread to surrounding areas. South African forces killed 600 people before the revolt ended. In 1984, constitutional amendments granted legislative representation to "coloureds" and Asians, but not blacks, provoking greater unrest. In 1985, the government declared a state of emergency. Archbishop Desmond Tutu (see Chapter 3) addressed the United Nations in 1986, calling for further sanctions against his own country.

By the late 1980s, the ruling Afrikaner National Party began to splinter, and the Dutch Reformed Church of South Africa wavered in its support for apartheid. In 1989, acting president F.W. de Klerk (1936–) called for a new constitution based on the principle of one person, one vote—regardless of skin colour. The government released Nelson Mandela from prison in 1990 and legalized the African National Congress.

In late 1991, a multiracial Convention for a Democratic South Africa, set up by de Klerk and Mandela, began negotiating a new constitution and planning a transition to democracy under majority rule. The first democratic elections were held in 1994, and Mandela became president of a government representing all South Africans.

In 1996, Mandela's government convened a Truth and Reconciliation Commission to investigate human rights abuses during apartheid, and to grant reparations and amnesties in appropriate cases. Chaired by Archbishop Tutu, the commission listened to testimony from white and non-white citizens, providing a forum for victim-impact statements, apologies, and condemnations. In this way, the commission aided South Africa's transition from oligarchy to democracy.

Guatemala

From the 4th to the 11th centuries, the territory now called Guatemala was the centre of Mayan civilization (the region's indigenous population). In the 16th century, Spain colonized the area, granting land ownership to a small European minority and forcing the Mayans to become a dependent labouring class.

Guatemala gained independence in 1821, but the existing social structure did not change—the oligarchy of rich landowners still controlled the country. British and American interests eventually replaced Spanish economic dominance, and coffee became the major export. The American

United Fruit Company monopolized the production of sugar and bananas, allying itself with the local oligarchy. The army was used to control the Mayan labouring class, and profits of the United Fruit Company flowed back to the United States and to a small group of landowners in Guatemala.

In 1944, the colonial power structure was shattered when working-class groups overthrew the dictatorship. Guatemala's new democratic government introduced social welfare and human rights measures and abolished forced labour. In 1951, under reformer Jacobo Arbenz (1913–71), the government redistributed land to over 100,000 peasant families. When the Arbenz government expropriated land claimed by the United Fruit Company, the United States declared that Guatemala had fallen to the communists. The US Central Intelligence Agency orchestrated the overthrow of the Arbenz government, and a military dictatorship sympathetic to US interests was installed in 1954. The new government reversed Arbenz's democratic measures and land reforms and repressed all opposition.

With the loss of land and political power, the majority of Guatemalans sank into extreme poverty. From 1954, Guatemala was primarily ruled by a series of military dictatorships. Even during short interludes of civilian rule, the army controlled politics behind the scenes. Beginning in 1960, guerrilla forces began a campaign of armed insurgency against the military regime that continued for 36 years. Many Mayans from the highland regions joined this rebellion. The army, with US support, fought the guerrillas using a "scorched earth" policy that destroyed villages and uprooted residents. Tens of thousands of civilians were killed. Death squads controlled by the government murdered opposition leaders.

In 1994, the United Nations mediated peace talks between the government and guerrilla forces, and two years later the two sides signed a peace agreement that facilitated democratic elections. However, violence plagued the elections of 1999 and 2003, and conservative governments that promised stability were installed. As Guatemala entered the 21st century, the indigenous majority was still ruled by an oligarchy of the wealthy.

1523–24 Spanish colonize Mayan territories

1821 Guatemala gains independence

1931 Jorge Ubico becomes president

1944 Ubico overthrown; democratic rule established

1951 Land and labour reforms anger ruling class

1954 CIA-backed military coup overthrows government

1960–96 Peasants fight guerrilla war

1996 UN brokers peace agreement

1999, 2003 Conservative oligarchs elected

Figure 5.27 Timeline: Guatemala.

THE WEB

To learn more about the United Fruit Company's role in the history of Guatemala and Latin America, visit www.emp.ca/cwp.

Figure 5.28 Peasants demand land reform outside Guatemala's government palace on Columbus Day, October 12, 1999. The holiday marks first contact between Europeans and the indigenous peoples of the Americas.

Taking a Stand   Rigoberta Menchu

Rigoberta Menchu, a member of the Quiche branch of the Mayan people, was born in 1959 to an impoverished family in the Guatemala mountains. As a child, she had to work on cotton and coffee plantations. As a teenager, she witnessed the expulsion of Mayans from their land. When she was a young woman, government forces killed her brother and parents. Menchu participated in strikes and demonstrations supporting her people and was forced into exile in Mexico. There she organized resistance to the oppression in Guatemala and worked to further Mayan rights.

In 1983, Menchu told her life story in the book *I, Rigoberta Menchu*. Four years later, she narrated *When the Mountains Tremble*, a film about the suffering of the Mayan people. In 1999, she was the subject of controversy when American anthropologist David Stoll challenged some of her biographical details. She responded that her book was a "testament" to the Mayan people and, as such, told their collective story as much as her own.

In 1992, Menchu was awarded the Nobel Peace Prize. This is an excerpt from her acceptance speech:

> Who can predict what . . . great scientific conquests and developments [the Mayan] people could have achieved, if they had not been conquered by blood and fire, and subjected to an ethnocide that affected nearly 50 million people in the course of 500 years. . . .
>
> The . . . vision of the Indian people [is] expressed according to the way in which they are related. . . . First, between human beings, through communication. Second, with the Earth, as with our mother, because she gives us our lives and is not mere merchandise. Third, with nature, because we are an integral part of it, and not its owners.
>
> To us Mother Earth is not only a source of economic riches that gives us the maize, which is our life, but she also . . . is the root and the source of our culture. She keeps our memories, she receives our ancestors and she, therefore, demands that we honor her and return to her, with tenderness and respect, those goods that she gives us. We have to take care of her so that our children and grandchildren may continue to benefit from her. . . .
>
> I think . . . the indigenous peoples . . . should contribute their science and knowledge to human development, because we have enormous potential and we could combine our very ancient heritage with the achievements of European civilization as well as with civilizations in other parts of the world. . . .
>
> We the indigenous are willing to combine tradition with modernism, but not at any cost. We will not tolerate or permit that our future be planned as possible guardians of ethno-touristic projects on a continental level.

In January 2004, Menchu joined the new Guatemalan government of President Oscar Berger to help oversee compliance with the UN-brokered peace accord that ended the 36-year civil war.

Source: Nobel e-Museum, "Rigoberta Menchu Tum—Acceptance and Nobel Lecture," December 10, 1992, at http://www.nobel.se/peace/laureates/1992/tum-lecture.html.

Question

Using the Internet or library resources, compare Rigoberta Menchu's view of indigenous people with the views presented by two Aboriginal spokespersons in Canada, such as Chief Dan George, Ovide Mercredi, Marilyn Buffalo, Matthew Coon Come, Phil Fontaine, or Roberta Jamieson. What similarities do you notice?

THE WEB

See photographs documenting the Mayans' experiences of civil war at www.emp.ca/cwp.

Check Your Understanding

1. What is the difference between an oligarchy and a democracy?
2. Outline the main features of apartheid as it was practised in South Africa from 1948 to 1990.
3. In the 1970s how did the world react to South Africa's policy of apartheid? Why do you think the situation began to change in the late 1980s?
4. Describe the role of the United States in the government of Guatemala.
5. Explain the link between oligarchy and colonization in the examples of South Africa and Guatemala.
6. Assess the roles played by Nelson Mandela and Rigoberta Menchu in attacking the oligarchies in their respective countries.

Methods of Political Inquiry

Using the Internet for Political Research

Because the world of politics is constantly in flux, your skill in using the World Wide Web will greatly enhance your ability to find and analyze political information and data. The Internet gives you speedy access to comprehensive information on governments, demographics, political parties, interest groups, and non-governmental agencies.

General Principles

Because the Internet is uncensored, not all the information you find there will be accurate or reliable. As a result, you must carefully evaluate the Web sites that you visit to determine whether you should use the information presented.

Here are some guidelines for evaluating Web sites.

- *Accuracy.* Does the page list the author and institution that published the page? Can you contact the author?
- *Authority.* What are the author's credentials? Also, check the domain in the URL (.edu, .gov, .org, or .net); university and government sources are generally more reliable than an individual's Web log.
- *Objectivity.* What is the author's purpose in presenting this information? Is he or she advocating a position and therefore biased? If the author expresses personal opinions, are they supported by facts? Does the page contain advertising related to the content?
- *Currency.* When was the page produced? When was it last updated? Does the page contain dead links?

- *Coverage.* Do you require special software to view the information properly? If so, must you pay a fee? Does the page contain options (e.g., text only, frames, an alternative browser)?

If you can answer these questions about the Web site to your satisfaction, it probably meets the criteria for accuracy, currency, and objectivity and will be of value in your research. Even so, cross-checking all dates and other facts will provide greater reliability than using just one source.

Source: Adapted from Jim Kapoun, "Teaching Undergrads Web Evaluation: A Guide for Library Instruction." *C&RL News* (July/August 1998), pp. 522–23, at http://www.library.cornell.edu/olinuris/ref/webcrit.html.

Applying the Skill

1. Find Web sites for the following organizations. Write up a general evaluation of the materials available from each site using the five criteria listed above.
   a) Federal government of Canada
   b) La Francophonie
   c) Amnesty International
   d) World Trade Organization
   e) Your local government
2. As a student of politics, what other kinds of Web sites would you find useful? Find two other Web sites (not mentioned above or in the box), evaluate them, and explain why they would be helpful in this course.

Useful Internet Sites for Political Research

Political Resources on the Net
http://www.politicalresources.net/

Listings of political sites available on the Internet sorted by country, with links to parties, governments, media, etc., from all around the world.

Daryl Cagle's Professional Cartoonist Index
http://cagle.slate.msn.com/politicalcartoons/

Daily cartoons by editorial cartoonists from around the world.

Canadian Politics: A Net Station
http://www.library.ubc.ca/poli/cpweb.html

University of British Columbia Library site contains a wealth of information about Canada and the federal government.

Government Information
http://www.nlc-bnc.ca/8/4/index-e.html

Library and Archives Canada maintains a selective collection of links to Canadian government sites and key federal documents. It includes a page of links to the news release pages of individual federal government departments.

The WWW Virtual Library: International Affairs Resources
http://www.etown.edu/vl/

This site presents over 2,600 annotated links on a wide range of international affairs, international studies, and international relations topics.

WCSU List: Political Science Internet Resources
http://www.wcsu.edu/socialsci/polscres.html

This site offers numerous links to a variety of topics including American government and politics, international governments and politics, political thought, etc.

Study Hall

Thinking/Inquiry

1. Democracy in the United States was born while the country was fighting against the imperialism of Britain. Research and analyze subsequent incidents in which the United States acted in the role of imperialist power and hampered the democratic development of another country.
2. Some commentators view the emerging democracy of Russia in the 21st century as an oligarchy. What evidence can you find to support this point of view?
3. Working with a partner, choose any two countries discussed in this chapter and, using Internet or other resources, research their current situation. Present your update to the class.
4. Choose two countries—one a democracy, one a dictatorship—that were not discussed in this chapter. Using Internet or other resources, research and compare their styles of government with those of the countries you have studied here. Include a timeline for each country you choose.
5. Assume that a new government has been elected and has restricted one of the freedoms you consider to be very important. Outline the steps you might take to have this situation reversed.
6. Identify the steps a government could undertake to ensure that the line between lawful protest and terrorist activity does not become blurred.

Communication

7. Read one of the books mentioned in this chapter—George Orwell's *1984*, Alan Paton's *Cry, the Beloved Country*, Nelson Mandela's *The Long Walk to Freedom*, or *I, Rigoberta Menchu*. Prepare a book report for presentation to the class.
8. As the host of a popular political interview show, you have had the opportunity to interview many of the world's leaders. With a partner, select one of the political leaders discussed in this chapter. Create a dramatic scenario. This is your opportunity to ask tough questions about this leader's policies. Present your interview before the class.
9. Look back at Figure 5.1 on page 156. What do you think the artist was trying to convey in this series of images? (Consider the title.) Do you think this work is effective? Explain your views.
10. Using Internet or other resources, find portraits of historical and contemporary heads of state and analyze how art may be used to create a leader's image or identity. Create a visual display of your findings.

Application

11. This chapter has examined in detail one present-day emerging democracy, Russia. Conduct research on another emerging democracy. Compile a report with a timeline showing the sequence of changes that have occurred, and assess how successful this country has been in its steps toward democracy.
12. Obtain the music and lyrics for the stage play *Evita*, written by Andrew Lloyd Webber and Tim Rice. Select some of the music with political overtones and play these selections for the class. Analyze how the music describes the politics of Juan Peron's Argentina, and assess the accuracy of the description.
13. Dictatorships and democracies both use propaganda to demonstrate to their people and the world that they rule in a fair and just manner. Research how propaganda has been used by both forms of government, and create a poster that might have been produced by one or more governments you have studied in this chapter. Alternatively, prepare a visual display of propaganda posters from governments around the world.

Democratic Decision Making

Agenda

In this chapter, you will consider

• how different types of democracies make decisions
• the role of the executive, legislative, and judicial branches of government in democratic decision making
• how a balance of power is maintained among different branches of government
• how a bill is introduced, debated, and passed into law
• the role of the Senate in Canada and the United States
• the difference between judicial restraint and judicial activism
• the nature of federalism
• different electoral systems
• how to plan for and hold a debate on a topic

Figure 6.1 This detail from *Clayoquot Protest* (1995), one of nine large panels by Canadian artist Ian Wallace, uses photographs, acrylics, and oils to portray the actions of some 12,000 demonstrators who protested the widespread logging of old-growth rainforest on Vancouver Island in 1993.

Democratic governments are not all the same. As you read in Chapter 1, the 18th century political theorist Baron de **Montesquieu** thought that there should be three branches of government (executive, legislative, and judicial), each with distinct powers. The different branches would check and balance the power of the others.

While most democracies use this structure, the actual balance of power differs from system to system. In some countries, the executive is pre-eminent. In others, the legislative body can act as a strong counterbalance to the executive. And in some countries, such as Canada and the United States, the judiciary plays an important role in determining the validity of a law.

In this chapter, you will examine how different democratic systems work within their constitutional framework to make political decisions.

Democratic Systems Compared

Beginning in the 18th century, with the creation of the US constitution, systems of democratic decision making have followed two different paths—the British parliamentary system or the American presidential system. In the British parliamentary system, the executive and legislative branches are fused together. The prime minister is the chief member of the House of Commons and leads the government that introduces, debates, and votes on legislation. By contrast, in the American presidential system, the executive and legislative branches are deliberately separated. The US president does not interfere with the activities of **Congress** (the legislative branch of the US government). He or she cannot introduce bills or take part in congressional debate. This separation of powers is one of the principles upon which the US constitution is founded.

The Importance of the Constitution

Every democracy requires a constitution to set the rules and guide its operations. A constitution is a set of rules and principles that govern the political institutions of the state. It also defines the relationship between the state and its citizens. In effect, a constitution describes the mechanics of political decision making.

Some constitutions are written down. The United States constitution, created in 1787, is an example of a written constitution. A constitution that is not organized into one document is usually called "unwritten." The British constitution is a good example. Parts of the British constitution are written down but it is not organized into one document. A good deal of it is made up of parliamentary statutes such as the *Magna Carta* (see Chapter 1) and customary laws—conventions or customs that have been followed consistently by the state. (An example of a convention would be the leader of the majority party in Parliament becoming prime minister and forming the government.)

Canada's constitution has a strong written core, but it also contains an unwritten portion. The written constitution is composed of two acts: the *British North America Act*, now called the *Constitution Act, 1867*, and the *Constitution Act, 1982*. The first Act describes the structure of Canada's government and the respective powers of the federal and provincial governments. The second Act includes written statutes, references to Aboriginal rights, the *Canadian Charter of Rights and Freedoms*, and an **amending formula** (see Chapter 4). The unwritten portion of Canada's constitution consists of conventions and customs, many of them adopted from the British parliamentary system. For example, Canadian party and cabinet procedures are based on the conventions of the British parliamentary tradition.

While constitutions can be changed, it is more difficult to change a written constitution. To amend the US constitution, for example, requires a two-thirds majority in both congressional houses along with the approval of three-quarters of the states. In Canada, under the amending formulae

SOUND BITE "We must never forget that it is a constitution we are expounding . . . intended to endure for ages to come, and consequently, to be adapted to the various crises of human nature."

US Chief Justice John Marshall, McCulloch v. Maryland, *1819*

adopted in 1982, some amendments require the approval of two-thirds of the provinces representing 50 percent of Canada's population, and the consent of the House of Commons and Senate. Others require the unanimous consent of Parliament and all 10 provincial legislatures.

Britain's unwritten constitution is more flexible than the American and Canadian documents. It is based on statutes, or acts of Parliament, and can be changed by an act of Parliament.

— Law in Motion

The *Clarity Act,* 2000

For more than two decades, Canadians—both those inside and outside Quebec—have been debating the status of Quebec within Canada. During two referenda (1980 and 1995), Canada watched as Quebeckers cast their vote to remain in Canada or leave Confederation. During the 1980 referendum, Quebeckers were asked the following question:

> The Government of Quebec has made public its proposal to negotiate a new agreement with the rest of Canada, based on the equality of nations; this agreement would enable Quebec to acquire the exclusive power to make its laws, levy its taxes and establish relations abroad—in other words, sovereignty—and at the same time to maintain with Canada an economic association including a common currency; no change in political status resulting from these negotiations will be effected without approval by the people through another referendum; on these terms, do you give the Government of Quebec the mandate to negotiate the proposed agreement between Quebec and Canada?

Sixty percent of Quebeckers voted "No" to that question, and 40 percent voted "Yes."

Fifteen years later, during the 1995 referendum, Quebeckers voted on this question (see Chapter 4, page 151):

> Do you agree that Quebec should become sovereign after having made a formal offer to Canada for a new economic and political partnership within the scope of the bill respecting the future of Quebec and of the agreement signed on June 12, 1995?

Figure 6.2 An angry Quebec Premier Lucien Bouchard attends a strategy session on the day the federal Liberals tabled Bill C-20.

This time, the vote was much closer, with 50.6 percent voting "No" and 49.4 voting "Yes." Although the text of the June 12 agreement had been sent to every household in Quebec a week before the referendum, many federalists said the referendum question was unclear.

In 1996, under the leadership of Jean Chrétien, the federal government sent a series of questions to the Supreme Court of Canada asking whether

Quebec had the legal authority to secede from Canada unilaterally. Two years later, on August 20, the Supreme Court ruled that Quebec (or any other province) could not leave the Canadian Confederation without consulting the rest of Canada. The court's ruling also stated that Ottawa would have to negotiate with Quebec if a "clear majority" voted in favour of secession in response to a "clear question." However, the court did not clearly define what a "clear majority" would be.

In response to the Supreme Court's ruling, Jean Chrétien's Liberal government tabled Bill C-20 (the *Clarity Act*) on December 13, 1999. At the time, Chrétien told the Commons that

> [t]he legislation . . . is a reflection of the request by the Supreme Court of Canada to make sure that the political partners state clearly their positions. The question has to be clear and the result has to be clear. The question has to be on the idea that Quebec will not be a province of Canada. We just want to clarify that so that the people know exactly what they do and what they will achieve when they are voting.

Under the proposed legislation, the House of Commons would decide whether or not the referendum question was clear and "whether the question would result in a clear expression of the will of the population of a province on whether the province should cease to be part of Canada and become an independent state." The only legitimate question would be one that clearly asked the people of the province whether or not they wished to remain a part of Canada. If the Government of Canada determined that the question was not clear, it would not enter into any negotiations with the province wishing to secede. The House of Commons would also determine whether or not there has been "a clear expression of a will by a clear majority of the population of the province" by taking into account

- the size of the majority of valid votes cast in favour of the secessionist option
- the percentage of eligible voters voting in the referendum
- any other matters or circumstances it considered relevant.

Finally, under the constitution of Canada, an amendment would have to be made to allow a province to secede, and this would require negotiations with all the other provinces and the Government of Canada.

The *Clarity Act* became law on June 29, 2000.

Questions

1. Consider the two questions from the 1980 and 1995 referenda. After reading the two questions, do you think the federal government was right in asking that future questions be clear? Explain your answer, using specific examples from the questions.
2. Create a referendum question that you believe will meet the requirements of the *Clarity Act*.

THE WEB

For more information on the *Clarity Act*, go to www.emp.ca/cwp.

Check YOUR UNDERSTANDING

1. What did Baron de Montesquieu mean by a system of "checks and balances"?
2. What two paths have systems of democratic decision making taken, and how do they differ?
3. Identify the different parts of the unwritten British constitution.
4. Why are written constitutions not easily amended? Do you consider this an advantage or a disadvantage? Explain.

The Executive Branch

The executive branch of government makes decisions and implements them. It proposes policies and administers the resources of the government. In democracies, the executive can be divided into two parts: the elected politicians and the non-elected civil servants. Civil servants advise elected politicians on making policy and carry out the administrative details of the government's policies. For example, if an executive decided to help rebuild a war-torn country, the civil servants in various government departments would help implement that policy. These functions underscore the idea that the executive is at the centre of leadership in the political process.

The Executive in the Parliamentary System

In the parliamentary system there are really two executives—the formal and the political. The formal executive comprises a monarchical element, such as the queen or the governor general. While the formal executive function is primarily ceremonial, the political executive holds true political power. This branch of government is made up of the prime minister, cabinet, and bureaucracy.

Figure 6.3 Senators and guests listen to Governor General Adrienne Clarkson read the speech from the throne in the Senate Chamber in Ottawa, October 5, 2004, marking the opening of a new session of Parliament.

The Formal Executive

In Canada, the formal executive consists of the monarch and the monarch's representative, the governor general. Originally, the governor general was selected in Britain. However, since 1926, the Canadian government has recommended the candidate for the office and, since 1952, only Canadians have been appointed.

The governor general is appointed for a term of five years, and as Canada's official head of state, performs mainly ceremonial duties such as attending state dinners and receiving ambassadors. The formal executive does have duties of political significance, but these are performed on behalf of the political executive. For example, the governor general reads the Speech from the Throne, which outlines the government's plans for the upcoming parliamentary session. Yet that speech is written by the political executive, and the governor general cannot alter it. As the representative of the monarchy, the formal executive also signs all bills passed by Parliament; no bill becomes law without this **royal assent**. In practice, no federal bill has ever been refused by a governor general. In almost every case, the formal executive does whatever the elected government recommends.

One of the few areas in which the governor general is able to act with some autonomy is the dissolution of Parliament and the appointment of the prime minister. In fact, the governor general has an obligation to ensure that the office of the prime minister is never vacant. In most cases, there is no controversy involved, as the governor general appoints the leader of the party with the most seats in the House of Commons. Controversy may arise when no party possesses a majority of seats in the House.

This was the situation in 1926 when Prime Minister Mackenzie King and his Liberals were governing with the support of the Progressive Party. When King faced the loss of the Progressive Party's support, he asked Governor General Viscount Byng to dissolve Parliament and call an election. Byng refused King's request, insisting that the Conservatives (who actually had more seats than the Liberals) should be given an opportunity to form the government. Arthur Meighen and the Conservatives did go on to form the next government, but within days, they were defeated by the Liberals and Progressives. Byng dissolved Parliament and, in the ensuing election, King attacked the British-appointed governor general for interfering in Canadian affairs. King's political tactic worked. Although his government was mired in a customs scandal at the time of the dissolution request, the scandal was forgotten by the voters and King won a majority government. The King–Byng affair, as it came to be known, established the convention that the governor general normally acts on the advice of the prime minister and cabinet, and intervenes only to the minimum extent required by Parliament to function.

Figure 6.4 William Lyon Mackenzie King campaigns in the 1926 election.

THE WEB

Learn more about the role of the governor general and the King–Byng affair at www.emp.ca/cwp.

The Political Executive

In the parliamentary system, the political executive is created by the party with the most seats in the legislature (in Canada, the House of Commons). The leader of the majority party is asked by the formal executive to create a government. In Canada, if one party elects a majority of members of Parliament (MPs) in an election, the governor general will ask the leader of that party to form a government.

The leader of the party in power selects a group of cabinet ministers who act as the executive team. This cabinet operates on the principle of **cabinet solidarity**, or collective responsibility. All members of the cabinet must publicly support all cabinet policies or else resign from the cabinet. The cabinet operates with the support of the legislature and must resign if it loses the support of the elected branch of the government. Cabinet ministers answer to the legislature for the conduct of their respective departments. They must justify department policies to Parliament and to the public. They are ultimately

Figure 6.5 Liberal MP Sheila Copps waves good-bye as she leaves Parliament Hill in Ottawa, May 14, 2004, after announcing she would not run in the next federal election. She lost her bid for the Liberal leadership to Paul Martin.

responsible for any wrongdoing that occurs in their departments. In some extreme situations, a cabinet minister may be asked to resign as a result of improprieties committed in the department under his or her jurisdiction.

One of the most difficult tasks for an incoming prime minister in the Canadian parliamentary system is to select a cabinet. By tradition, Canadian cabinets are built with regional representation. If possible, one cabinet minister is selected from each province. At certain times when a province has not elected anyone to the governing party, the prime minister has appointed a senator from that province to the cabinet. Although senators are not elected representatives, they are nonetheless a part of the legislative branch in a parliamentary system, and thus are eligible for appointment to the cabinet.

Regional divisions within the larger provinces are also sometimes recognized. For example, there is often a cabinet post for Northern Ontario and another one for Southwestern Ontario. Once appointed to the cabinet, ministers are also expected to be spokespersons for their region or province. Aside from considering regionalism, the prime minister also needs to pay attention to such factors as race and gender. Ideally, each federal government strives for a fair representation of francophones and women in the cabinet.

A Canadian prime minister "shuffles" the cabinet to renew the political executive. During a four- or five-year term, the fortunes of a political party may suffer reverses, and a cabinet shuffle may inject new life into a weary leadership. The prime minister may reward deserving party members by moving a junior cabinet minister into a higher-profile portfolio or by promoting a **backbencher** (rank and file member) into the cabinet. Under-performing ministers may be demoted within the cabinet or moved out of the cabinet completely. In 2003, after the change in the Liberal leadership from Jean Chrétien to Paul Martin, high-profile cabinet ministers such as Sheila Copps, John Manley, and Allan Rock lost their cabinet posts. In this situation, the changes were motivated by a new prime minister wishing to replace Chrétien loyalists with his own followers. The combination of control over the party and over the cabinet affords the prime minister significant power in the parliamentary system.

The Executive in the Presidential System

In the presidential system, the executive office blends the formal and political roles of the parliamentary system. The elected president is both the head of state and the political leader of the country. Unlike the parliamentary system, the presidential system separates the executive office from the legislature.

In the presidential system, the executive is chosen by the voters. The vote may be a direct vote, as exercised in France, or an indirect vote, through

Figure 6.6 Comedian and activist Dick Gregory demonstrates outside the White House, October 1990. President George Bush (Sr.) vetoed the 1990 *Civil Rights Bill* because it would impose race quotas on employers. A bill that many African Americans and civil libertarians thought had less bite was passed in 1991.

an electoral college system, as used in the United States (see Figure 6.7). The selection of the executive in the presidential system is not dependent on the majority party in the legislature. In the United States, for example, voters may select a Republican president and a Democratic legislature, and the two must learn to live with each other.

In the presidential system, the terms of office for the executive and the legislature may be different. In the United States, the president is chosen for a four-year term, whereas members of the House of Representative are selected for two-year terms, and members of the Senate for six-year terms.

As the nation's head of state, the American president carries out the duties of the formal executive. This formal responsibility includes greeting foreign leaders and attending ceremonial occasions. The president is also the chief political executive. Although not having the power to sign bills into law, he or she has the constitutional power to refuse a bill or to veto a piece of legislation. The president must accept or reject a bill in its totality. In the American system, Congress can override a presidential veto with a subsequent vote of two-thirds in both the House of Representatives and the Senate.

Despite the separation of powers in the American system, the president can propose legislation to be passed by Congress. Congress, especially if it is controlled by the president's party, may agree with the executive, and draft and pass the legislation. On the other hand, the House of Representatives, the Senate, or both may flatly refuse to pass the president's proposals. In the parliamentary system, once a prime minister obtains a majority government, the executive, with its control of Parliament, has a free hand to pass legislation.

The American Electoral College System

What is it?
A group of ordinary people called *electors* who directly elect the US president and vice-president. There are 538 electors. (California, for example, has 54, Montana has 3. Aside from each of the 50 states, the District of Columbia has 3 electoral votes.)

Who are the electors?
Ordinary citizens chosen by each state. Popular vote determines which electors will represent each state.

What do they do?
Electors cast their votes in mid-December following the presidential election in early November (the winning slate assumes office in late January of the following year). The electors must vote for the slate that won the popular vote in their state.

How does the electoral college make or break the US election?
The presidential slate that wins the majority of electoral votes (270 votes or more) becomes the next president and vice-president.

What's the bottom line?
Even with a razor-thin majority, the winning slate wins all that state's electoral vote. (Maine and Nebraska use a different system.)

What's the point?
To give states extra power in the US federal system.

Figure 6.7

THE WEB

Learn more about the US electoral college system at www.emp.ca/cwp.

PRESS PLAY

In Michael Ritchie's 1972 film, *The Candidate*, a young California lawyer (Robert Redford) is persuaded to run for the Senate, but finds the demands of politics force him to compromise his ideals. (PG)

The American president is also commander-in-chief of the military and a major force in foreign policy. In the 1960s, President Lyndon Johnson committed over a half million soldiers to fight in Vietnam without a congressional declaration of war. In the 1970s, President Richard Nixon and his advisers decided to recognize the People's Republic of China for the first time. The 1991 Persian Gulf War and the 2003 war against Iraq were both fought without declarations of war. These examples illustrate the power of the executive to mould foreign policy and to commit US military forces to war.

The American executive is limited in the conduct of non-military foreign policy. The president needs Senate approval for the appointment of ambassadors and the ratification of treaties. At the conclusion of World War I, President Woodrow Wilson presented the proposal of a world organization to preserve peace. The organization, the League of Nations, was rejected by the Senate in Wilson's own country (see Chapters 4 and 8). Hence the United States was never a member of an organization proposed by an American president. By contrast, in the parliamentary system, a prime minister with a majority in Parliament is rarely hindered in the conduct of foreign policy.

Advisers in the Executive Branch

An important function of the executive is to make public policy. In both the parliamentary and presidential systems, the executive relies heavily on personal advisers. In Canada, the Prime Minister's Office (PMO) is composed of a group of influential advisers who have been selected by the prime minister from outside the legislature. These advisers may have more power than the prime minister's cabinet or the senior members of the government bureaucracy. In the United States, the president also relies heavily on an inner circle of advisers.

Figure 6.8 Colin Powell (right), shown here in 1990, was a four-star general with 35 years of experience in the military before being chosen George W. Bush's secretary of state in 2001.

While Canada's prime minister must select a cabinet from the legislative branch of government (House of Commons and Senate), a US president must choose a cabinet from outside the legislative branch. This is seen as maintaining a separation of powers between the executive and the legislature. In choosing a cabinet, an American president is able to select experts from many walks of life. Because an American president has more latitude in choosing a cabinet than a Canadian prime minister, the former is more likely to select persons who are in tune with the executive's manner of thinking and acting. For example, Henry Kissinger, a Harvard University professor, became a trusted adviser of President Richard Nixon and held the cabinet position of secretary of state. When President Jimmy Carter asked Maine Senator Edmund Muskie to be his secretary of state in 1980, Muskie had to resign as a member of the Senate before joining the Carter cabinet. Colin Powell, George W. Bush's secretary of state, spent 35 years in the military before accepting a cabinet post.

One position that has no equivalent in the parliamentary executive is the American post of vice-president. The US president and vice-president are elected as a "ticket," or team, and the latter may balance the former politically. For example, if a presidential candidate is from the north, the vice-presidential candidate is often from the south, or vice versa. John F. Kennedy, from Massachusetts, chose Lyndon Johnson, from Texas, as his vice-president. Later, Johnson as president chose Hubert Humphrey, from Minnesota, as his vice-president. The most important part of the vice-president's political role is to assume the office of the presidency in the event of the incumbent's death, disability, or resignation. The vice-president also serves as the president of the Senate, a largely ceremonial task.

PRESS PLAY

Bush's Brain (2004), a documentary by Joseph Mealey and Michael Paradies Shoob, examines political manipulation as seen through the career of George Bush's adviser, Karl Rove. (NR)

The British Parliamentary System

The British parliamentary executive operates in a manner similar to its Canadian offspring. However, there are some differences in the practices of the two systems.

The formal executive is a hereditary position that traces its origins back 10 centuries. Thus, the monarch carries more prestige than the governor general in Canada. The monarchy also has a history of political power. As recently as 1957, Queen Elizabeth II was asked by a Conservative party deadlocked over party leadership to select a new leader and prime minister. As a result, she asked Harold Macmillan to become prime minister as the successor to Anthony Eden. In modern politics, however, the formal executive in Britain rarely acts without the advice of the political executive.

As with the Canadian system, the true power of the executive branch resides in the office of the prime minister. Unlike the Canadian prime minister, however, the British prime minister does not have to share power with provincial premiers. In this sense, the political executive in Britain wields more power than its Canadian counterpart. And because the British cabinet has no tradition of regional representation, the British prime minister has more latitude to select cabinet members. In recent history, British prime ministers Margaret Thatcher and Tony Blair have wielded an impressive amount of power over the cabinet, party, and country. Blair, for example, committed his country as an ally to the United

Figure 6.9 Tony Blair committed British troops to the 2003 war in Iraq even though polls showed fewer than one in 10 Britons supported such a war without a United Nations resolution.

Figure 6.10 The poll tax riot of April 1990 showed how unpopular some of Margaret Thatcher's Conservative fiscal policies had become with the British public.

States in the 2003 war against Iraq. He did so in the face of anti-war public opinion polls and despite opposition to his stand within his cabinet and his Labour Party.

After being elected in 1979 as Britain's first female prime minister, Margaret Thatcher placed her imprint on British politics. She followed a policy of free markets, reducing government expenditures, and privatizing industries. She won popular backing for Britain's war against Argentina over the Malvinas (Falkland) Islands in 1982. Thatcher personally set the tone of government policy, and her policies were summarized as "Thatcherism." She lost her 11-year grip on the nation when she faced a cabinet rebellion and a public riot over a proposed poll tax (an equal tax imposed on all adults) and her opposition to strengthening Britain's ties with the European Union. After her own foreign secretary resigned in November 1990, Thatcher's leadership of the Conservative party was challenged. She withdrew her candidacy on the second ballot, making way for her successor, John Major.

France's Semi-Presidential System

The governmental system of France is called a semi-presidential system, since it includes both a president and a prime minister who are active participants in the political process.

In the current French system, the power of the executive overshadows that of the legislature. This is largely the legacy of former French President Charles de Gaulle. In 1958, a crisis unfolding in the French colony of Algeria (see Chapter 5), as well as inflation and instability at home, caused the French government to fall. De Gaulle, a former general and World War II hero, came out of retirement to lead France and draft the constitution for the Fifth Republic (1958–). The new constitution, approved by almost 80 percent of French voters in a referendum, included provisions for a much stronger presidency than had been in effect during the Fourth Republic.

SOUND BITE "In order to become the master, the politician poses as the servant."

Charles de Gaulle, French general and statesman, 1890–1970

Today, the French president

- can be elected for a term of five years (reduced from seven, in de Gaulle's constitution)
- names the prime minister, who commands the support of the majority in the National Assembly (France's elected legislature)
- presides over the cabinet
- commands the armed forces
- concludes treaties
- holds the power to dissolve the legislature.

The French president also handles foreign affairs, while the prime minister presides over domestic matters. When the majority of the National Assembly backs the president, the executive is more powerful than most others in Europe. Difficulties arise if the president's political party differs from the majority party in the legislature. The president is then forced to select a prime minister from a party other than his own, which usually weakens the executive.

France's Fifth Republic was specifically designed to enable a political leader such as Charles de Gaulle to exercise great executive power. De Gaulle was president from 1958 to 1969. The current president of France, Jacques Chirac, has also been criticized for being "Gaullist" in his approach to government. When re-elected president in 2002, Chirac not only appointed the new prime minister, he also hand-picked the cabinet. Observers remarked on how key portfolios were filled by close associates of Chirac. And it was all perfectly constitutional.

THE WEB

Learn more about France's electoral system at www.emp.ca/cwp.

Check YOUR UNDERSTANDING

1. What are the roles of the elected politicians and the non-elected civil servants in the executive? Which do you believe has a greater impact on government policy? Why?
2. List the duties performed by the governor general. Which do you consider the most important? Why?
3. Why is the principle of cabinet solidarity important in the parliamentary system?
4. Why would the selection of a cabinet be a difficult task for the incoming prime minister in Canada?
5. What is the purpose of a "cabinet shuffle"?
6. How is the executive office in the presidential system different from the prime minister's office in the parliamentary system?
7. What limitations are placed on the power of the American president?
8. Should Canada have a position similar to the American post of vice-president? Why or why not?
9. How is the British parliamentary executive different from the Canadian?
10. Describe the roles of the president and the prime minister in the French semi-presidential system. What problems or benefits do you see in a system such as this?

THE WEB

Learn more about the French Revolution at www.emp.ca/cwp.

The Legislative Branch

Both democratic and non-democratic systems of government have executive branches. The legislative branch is critically important because it represents the voting public in the political process. In the Western world, legislatures developed as the representatives of the people in the struggle against the absolute power of the monarch. The legislative branch, as the name suggests, eventually usurped the lawmaking role of the monarch and claimed that right for itself alone. In England, during the 18th and 19th centuries, the elected Parliament steadily chipped away at the monarch's lawmaking powers. In France in 1789 (at the beginning of the French Revolution), the elected National Assembly declared that it alone represented the nation and had the power to make laws for the people.

In Canada, the legislative branch of the federal government is Parliament, which is made up the elected House of Commons, the appointed Senate, and the governor general. In the United States, the legislative branch of the government is known as Congress, and is divided into two chambers—the Senate and the House of Representatives. The people elect each member of Congress, including senators. Members of the House of Representatives are elected for two-year terms, and senators are elected for six-year terms.

Although legislatures originated as political institutions to represent the people, not all legislatures are popularly elected. The first legislatures were usually bicameral (two-chambered) in composition rather than unicameral. The bicameral legislatures were made up of a lower house that was popularly elected and an upper house that was usually appointed. The **franchise** for the lower house was also at times restricted—for example, to males who owned property. The upper house was created as a check on the actions of the democratically inclined lower house. Today, the British upper house is still called the House of Lords and includes hereditary nobility (who have no votes, however).

Australia is one democracy that elects its upper house. Members of the 150-seat House of Representatives are elected from **single-member constituencies**. Members of the 76-seat Senate, in which each state is represented, are also elected. All bills must be passed by both houses to become law. The Senate may not amend money bills (bills intended to use the public treasury to raise revenue); it can only pass or reject them. In the event of a deadlock between the two houses, the Australian constitution provides for a simultaneous dissolution of both houses and new elections.

Figure 6.11 This 19th century painting depicts Louis XVI and Marie Antoinette, king and queen of France, at Versailles in 1789. Although Louis made some concessions to reformers, it was too little, too late. Both monarchs were beheaded by radicals in 1793.

The Canadian House of Commons

Voters from Canada's 308 ridings choose the members of the House of Commons (MPs). The vast majority of the winning candidates are associated with a political party. In the parliamentary system, the business at hand revolves around political parties. The majority party forms the government and the leader of the majority party becomes prime minister. If the government is defeated in the House of Commons, it must resign, based on the principle that it has lost the confidence of the electorate. After a governmental defeat, the governor general may invite the opposition to form a government or agree to a new general election. Each Canadian government relies on party discipline to ensure that the members of Parliament vote as directed by the prime minister. If the members of the governing party did not vote as directed, there would be a never-ending series of new governments and new elections. (If a member feels that he or she must vote against policy, that person can quit the party and run as an independent.)

Party discipline is maintained in a number of ways. In each party's regularly scheduled caucus meeting of ministers and senators, political strategy is clarified and party unity is emphasized. Each party appoints a party whip to keep members informed about issues and to ensure that sufficient members are present in the House of Commons to vote. Presence in the House and party loyalty are especially important for the ruling party. As noted earlier, if the government loses an important vote it is obliged to step down.

In December 1979, recently elected Prime Minister Joe Clark presented his first budget to Parliament. Six seats short of a majority, Clark and his Progressive Conservative Party did not make certain that they would have enough votes to pass the budget. Support could have been obtained from the Social Credit Party with its six seats or the New Democratic Party with its 26 seats. The government lost a vote of non-confidence, was forced to resign, and then lost the ensuing election in early 1980. Although the Conservatives in this episode maintained party discipline, they failed to take the steps to ensure their legislation would pass.

Members of a party who break with party discipline may be reprimanded in a number of ways. If they are members of the party in power, they may be denied promotions or they may be demoted. In some cases, they may be ejected from the party. Party discipline is a pervasive part of life in parliamentary democracy. Many party members never vote against their party. The practice, although necessary to maintain stability in parliamentary politics, has led to criticism.

SOUND BITE

John Duncan, MP:
"Why does the minister not save everyone's time and just admit that he does not give a damn?"

Speaker:
"Perhaps Rhett Butler could say it, but not in this House."

Exchange during Question Period, November 1998

Figure 6.12 Conservative MP Peter MacKay (right) addresses a question to the government in the House of Commons, May 2004. Question Period takes place each day the House is in session. For about an hour, the opposition members can grill the prime minister and the cabinet on almost any issue. Because the most dramatic segments of Question Period often appear on the evening news, it can help to shape political imagery and political careers.

Some observers describe backbench members as trained seals who mindlessly follow the dictates of their political trainers, rather than representing their constituents.

Passing a Bill in the Canadian Parliamentary System

When the Canadian government wants to propose a new law, it introduces a bill in the House of Commons. Bills are usually introduced by cabinet ministers—the only exception is a **private member's bill**. Bills move through a series of steps, including two readings followed by a detailed examination of the bill's contents, a third reading, consideration by the Senate, and royal assent by the governor general. The purpose of the first reading is to present the bill; the purpose of the second reading is to debate the bill in the House. At this stage, a bill cannot be amended but must be "approved in principle" or rejected. After the bill passes second reading it moves to a standing (parliamentary) committee. The committee reviews each clause of the legislation in detail. It may also suggest amendments before the bill moves back to the House for third reading and a final vote.

After passage in the House of Commons, the bill moves to the Senate, where it follows a similar series of steps. Senate committees examine the bills arriving from the House. In most cases, they approve the bills without further amendments. If a Senate committee does make an amendment, the revised bill must be returned to the lower house for its approval. If all parties in the House agree on a bill, it can become law in matter of days. Most pieces of legislation are complex, however, and can take months or years to pass. Time allocation rules can shorten the debate at different stages of the bill, that is, first reading, second reading, and so on. Alternatively, the government can impose closure. **Closure** cuts off further debate on an individual clause of a bill. However, closure is inefficient if a bill has many clauses. It can also backfire if the government is seen as stifling legitimate opposition by shutting down debate.

Sometimes a bill is introduced through the Senate rather than the House of Commons. In this case, the steps to passage are similar, with the Commons reviewing the bill after it is passed by the Senate. Government bills introduced in the Senate are identified with the prefix S; those introduced in the Commons are identified with a C.

The Canadian Senate

The Canadian Senate is an appointed body, and many of its appointments are based on **patronage**, or the granting of political favours. Individuals who have worked hard for the party and have demonstrated loyalty are rewarded in this fashion. At times, a prime minister will appoint a member from the opposition, an independent, or a distinguished Canadian to the Senate. Since a 1965 constitutional amendment, senators have been allowed to serve only to age 75. Previously, they could serve for life. As an appointed body, the Senate has less clout than the democratically elected House of Commons. Nonetheless, all legislation requires its approval. For example, in 1988, the Senate successfully stalled Prime Minister Brian Mulroney's proposed free-trade agreement with the United States. The Senate's refusal to pass the legislation resulted in an election. (Free trade became a major campaign issue, and Mulroney won that election.) Senators also perform valuable committee work. At times, they suggest changes to bills that are presented to them. The Senate almost always approves bills passed by the House of Commons.

A proposal to overhaul the Senate was originally presented by the Reform Party and is currently endorsed by the Conservative Party of Canada. The proposed "Triple-E" Senate would be an elected upper house; equal, in the sense that all provinces would have the same number of senators; and effective, because it would be able to block legislation passed by the House of Commons and to safeguard regional interests.

The American House of Representatives and Senate

Since 1911, the American House of Representatives has included 435 members. The number of members per state is based on the state's population. Therefore, California, the most populous state, has 52 representatives, and North Dakota and Delaware, among the less populous states, have one representative each. Each state, no matter how small its population, is guaranteed one member in the House of Representatives. Every 10 years, the seats are reapportioned based on the most recent population census.

Unlike most upper houses in the 20th century, the US Senate has maintained its importance in the legislative process. Since its members are elected, the Senate has as much, if not more, authority as the House of Representatives. To reflect the equality of all states, the upper chamber is composed of two elected senators from each of the 50 states. Both chambers have the power to pass bills and can oppose each other over pending legislation. The Senate also has the right to approve or reject certain presidential appointments and international treaties negotiated by the executive branch. Unlike the House, senators have the right to **filibuster**, or "talk a bill to death." By continuing debate on a bill indefinitely, a group of senators can effectively prevent its passage. The filibuster can be ended by the use of **cloture** (a closing of debate).

The American executive has limited control over the legislative parties in Congress. The president can request that certain legislation be enacted, but cannot guarantee its success in the way a prime minister with a majority of members can. Although members of Congress do not adhere to party discipline in the same manner as members of Parliament, they do vote with their party most of the time.

Figure 6.13 US Senate leader Everett Dirksen organizes his reading material for a 1965 filibuster against a bill that would have nullified states' right-to-work laws. Dirksen's filibuster succeeded, and the bill died on February 10, 1966.

The power of the legislative branch in the American presidential system can be illustrated by examining two events in the presidency of Bill Clinton (1993–2001). In the 1994 mid-term elections, the Republicans won control of the House of Representatives for the first time in 40 years. Because the House has the exclusive power to introduce money bills, the president needs the cooperation of the House to fund the operation of the government. In November 1995, budget negotiations between the House and the president broke down. When the House refused to approve any appropriations, many departments of the federal government, including museums, national parks, and government offices, closed down or operated with skeleton staffs until January 1996, when the president and the House compromised on a budget.

Congress is also authorized by the US constitution to **impeach** (charge with misconduct) high officials, including the president. The House of Representatives has the exclusive power to initiate impeachment proceedings, and the Senate has the exclusive power to conduct the trial and convict the person. A two-thirds majority of senators is required to impeach a president, who is then removed from office.

In December 1998, the House of Representatives voted to impeach President Bill Clinton on charges of perjury and obstruction of justice. The charges stemmed primarily from Clinton's under-oath testimony before a grand jury about matters related to a sexual affair with political intern Monica Lewinsky. However, in February 1999, the Senate failed to convict the president. Its vote was well short of the two-thirds majority required by the US constitution. Aside from Clinton, one other president, Andrew Johnson in 1868, was impeached. Johnson was acquitted by a single vote in the Senate. In 1974, President Richard Nixon resigned after impeachment hearings against him had begun.

American Standing Committees

In the United States, standing committees exercise more power than they do in the Canadian system. In Canada, standing committee leaders are obedient to the executive of a majority government. In the United States, however, standing committee leaders enjoy a great deal of independence, even though they derive their authority from the House of Representatives and the Senate. As in Canada, the committees perform a clause-by-clause analysis of legislation. However, the American committees can also delay or defeat a bill. Members may remain on the same committee for many years (as long as they are re-elected), thereby developing expertise and seniority. Committee chairs are usually selected because they have served on a committee for several years.

One politician who exercised considerable influence as a committee chair was Republican Senator Joseph McCarthy. As chair of the Senate Permanent Subcommittee on Investigations in 1953, McCarthy was able to pursue accusations of communist influence within the government. (During this period of the Cold War, communist infiltration was considered a huge security

PRESS PLAY

Point of Order (1964), directed by Emile de Antonio, is a documentary that uses TV footage from the McCarthy hearings in the 1950s to explore the US "red scare." (NR)

threat in the United States.) President Dwight Eisenhower belonged to the same Republican Party as McCarthy, but even the president would not, or could not, publicly control him. It would take a full Senate vote of condemnation in December 1954 to erode McCarthy's power, but not before he had done a great deal of damage to the lives and careers of many.

THE WEB

Learn more about Senator McCarthy and McCarthyism at www.emp.ca/cwp.

Passing a Bill in the US System

In the American presidential system, bills are introduced simultaneously in the House and Senate. However, bills dealing with budget matters must first be introduced in the House. Any member may introduce a bill. As soon as a bill is introduced, it is sent to the appropriate standing committee, at which point

- the bill may be reviewed
- public hearings may be held on the bill
- expert testimony may be heard about the bill
- the bill may be "killed" by the committee if it refuses to consider it.

If the proposed legislation moves out of the committee, it goes to discussion and debate by the full House and Senate. If the bill passes in both chambers, it may go to another committee to ascertain that the House and Senate versions of the bill are identical. If the two versions require adjustments to make them identical, the amended bill goes back to the two chambers for final approval before it is ready for a possible presidential signature.

Figure 6.14 In the American congressional system, the opposing parties in the House of Representatives and Senate do not face each other in an adversarial way but are arranged in a semicircle around their respective presiding officers. What does this seating arrangement suggest about the US congressional system?

Check Your Understanding

1. Why were the first legislatures usually bicameral?
2. How is the Australian legislature different from the Canadian one? What problems may develop in a system such as this?
3. Describe how party discipline is maintained.
4. Create a graphic illustration of how a bill is passed in the Canadian parliamentary system.
5. Why has the US Senate been able to maintain its importance in the legislative process?
6. Why are American standing committees more powerful than their counterparts in the Canadian system?
7. Create a list describing at least five differences between the legislatures of Canada and the United States.

The Judicial Branch

In Montesquieu's 18th century conception of the three branches of government, the judiciary is the third entity to balance the power of the executive and legislative branches. Since the time of Montesquieu's proposal, the power of the judiciary has grown in importance, especially in the United States and Canada. The apex of the judicial branch contains appointed representatives or justices. In a democratic system, these appointed officials can play a large role in decision making. In both the United States and Canada, the Supreme Court, over time, has assumed the role of interpreter of the constitution.

The court system is often perceived as a check on possible abuses in the executive and legislative branches. It functions independently of the executive, the legislature, the different political parties, and interest groups.

Figure 6.15 In 2004, Taiwan President Chen Shui-bian (shown behind a bullet-proof shield) was re-elected by a narrow margin following an attempt on his life. His opponent charged that the assassination attempt unfairly influenced the election result. Taiwan's highest court ultimately confirmed Chen's victory.

The Role of the Judiciary in Political Decision Making

The judiciary can take two different approaches in exercising its power. Under the philosophy of **judicial restraint**, judges take a low-key view of their own powers. They tend to interpret the law literally and are hesitant to apply new interpretations. If changes in the law are needed, they defer to the executive and the legislature. Under the philosophy of **judicial activism**, judges take a flexible view of their powers, along with a broad view of any powers outlined in the constitution. They are willing to interpret the law in such a way that it can be adapted to changing circumstances.

However judges interpret their own powers, all judges have the right of **judicial review**. This is the power of the courts to overturn legislation that contravenes the constitution. Until the passing of Canada's *Constitution Act, 1982*, judicial review consisted of ruling on whether the provinces and the federal government were acting within their powers (*intra vires*) or whether they were acting outside their legal authority (*ultra vires*). Since 1982, judicial review also allows the courts to **strike down** legislation that contravenes the *Canadian Charter of Rights and Freedoms*.

SOUND BITE "The line is crossed, I believe, when the judge identifies himself closely with a particular faction in the legislature or executive, or when he lobbies consistently and forcefully for a specific political goal—in short, when his activities become partisan in nature."

The Hon. John Sopinka, speech accepting his appointment to the Supreme Court, 1988

The Canadian Judiciary

The Canadian Supreme Court was created in 1875, eight years after Confederation. Section 101 of the *British North America Act* authorized Parliament to provide a "General Court of Appeal" for Canada. The Supreme Court consists of nine justices appointed by the prime minister. By law, the court must contain three judges from Quebec. By tradition, three judges come from Ontario, two from Western Canada, and one from Atlantic Canada. The justices serve until age 75 or until retirement. Until 1949, the highest court of appeal in the Canadian legal system was a committee of British justices known as the Judicial Committee of the Privy Council (JCPC) in London, England (see Chapter 4). In fact, appeals from a court in a province could bypass the Canadian Supreme Court and go directly to the JCPC.

For much of its history, the Canadian Supreme Court has tended to use the philosophy of judicial restraint as opposed to that of judicial activism. This attitude changed with the arrival of the *Canadian Charter of Rights and Freedoms* in 1982. The court was now expected to give its interpretations of what was meant by such crucial Charter phrases as "freedom of religion,"

THE WEB

Learn about two important recent appointments to the Supreme Court of Canada at www.emp.ca/cwp.

"security of the person," and "equality rights" when they were applied to everyday situations. In the 1985 case *R v. Big M Drug Mart Ltd.*, the court overturned the *Lord's Day Act* because it violated the Charter's guarantee of freedom of religion. As a result of this decision, businesses were allowed to operate on Sundays. The court's interpretation of section 15 of the Charter— the section dealing with equality rights—has been particularly beneficial to the gay and lesbian communities. Although "sexual orientation" is not one of the enumerated (listed) grounds of discrimination listed in section 15(1) of the Charter, the court has decided that it is an analogous (similar) situation and has extended equality protection to gay men and lesbians in a number of court decisions.

The Supreme Court is also called upon to settle jurisdictional disputes between the federal and provincial governments. It might be called, for example, to intervene in a dispute involving the development of offshore oil and natural gas resources. Many provinces have suspected a federalist bias in Supreme Court decisions. As a result, provinces often prefer to settle differences with the federal government by means of negotiations rather than through a Supreme Court adjudication.

In Canada, the Supreme Court can also be asked to rule on the principles of a bill before it is actually legislated. This is called an advisory or reference decision. At the request of the cabinet or prime minister, the Supreme Court will present a legal opinion on the constitutionality of a proposed piece of legislation. In 1981, the Liberal government under Pierre Trudeau asked for a Supreme Court advisory on patriating the constitution. In 2003, the government of Jean Chrétien asked for a Supreme Court decision on changing the definition of marriage to include same-sex unions. A decision on this matter was expected in 2005.

The American Judiciary

In Canada, the Supreme Court did not become an active interpreter of the constitution until the mid-20th century. In the United States, Chief Justice John Marshall asserted that judicial power as early as 1803 in the case of *Marbury v. Madison*. As a result, the US Supreme Court has played an important part in political decision making from the earliest years.

In the 1857 decision in *Dred Scott v. Sandford*, the court ruled that Scott, an African American slave, had no rights as a citizen and, despite his residence for a time in the free territory of Illinois, was not a free man. In the 1896 ruling in *Plessy v. Ferguson*, the Supreme Court ruled in favour of racial segregation in public facilities. The court upheld a Louisiana law that required separate railway cars for African American and white citizens. That particular decision helped establish the doctrine of "separate but equal," which legitimized the separation of the races. However, almost 60 years later, the US Supreme Court ruled against the spirit of *Plessy v. Ferguson* in the case of *Brown v. Board of Education of Topeka, Kansas.* In that 1954 decision, the court ruled that the doctrine of "separate but equal" could not truly provide African Americans with the same educational standards as whites. The court explicitly outlawed segregated school facilities and ordered the integration of schools "with all deliberate speed." The decision had a huge impact on the US civil rights movement, which would gain momentum during the 1960s.

Another case that reverberated across the United States was the Supreme Court's 1973 decision in *Roe v. Wade.* In this case, the court recognized abortion as a constitutional right and overturned any state laws that prevented a woman from obtaining an abortion. Although the *Dred Scott* and *Plessy* rulings confirmed political practices already in existence, the *Brown* and *Roe* rulings broke significant new ground. The court, in effect, went where the executive and legislature dared not go, resulting in major changes in American politics.

Figure 6.16 One of the plaintiffs in *Brown v. Board of Education of Topeka, Kansas* reads about the Supreme Court decision in the newspaper on May 18, 1954. The court ruled that racial segregation in public schools is unconstitutional.

In the United States, the nine justices of the Supreme Court are appointed by the president, subject to approval by the Senate. The justices serve for life or until retirement. By 2004, 148 persons had been officially nominated to the US Supreme Court, and the Senate had rejected 12 outright, although some others had withdrawn their names or the president had withdrawn their nomination.

The power of the Supreme Court was well demonstrated during the Watergate affair. In 1974, Congress was trying to determine President Richard Nixon's involvement in a break-in at the Democratic National Committee headquarters (at the Watergate Hotel) two years earlier. After it was revealed that the president had audiotapes of conversations in the Oval Office of the White House, the special prosecutor in the case asked that he hand over the tapes as evidence. Nixon refused and invoked the doctrine of **executive privilege**. This doctrine asserts that under the philosophy of separation of powers, the president and other members of the executive branch are justified in withholding documents and information from the other branches of the government. The Supreme Court then ruled 8–0, with one abstention, that Nixon was required to hand over the tapes. Nixon complied with the court's ruling. The tapes contained some damaging revelations that the president had lied about his knowledge of the break-in and its coverup. Soon after the release of the tapes, Richard Nixon resigned as president.

Taking a Stand   Earl Warren, Chief Justice of the United States Supreme Court

The tenure of Earl Warren as Chief Justice of the US Supreme Court (1953–69) exemplifies that institution's important role in political decision making. Still, it is ironic that Warren, a life-long Republican, should have been the one to lead the way. The son of Norwegian immigrants, Warren served as California's attorney general from 1939 to 1943 and then as its governor from 1943 to 1953. He entered national politics when he became Republican Thomas Dewey's vice-presidential running mate in 1948. Warren wanted the presidential nomination in 1952 but it went to Dwight D. Eisenhower, who promised Warren the first vacancy on the Supreme Court in return for delivering the California vote for him. The first vacancy turned out to be that of chief justice. Warren took on the role of the country's top judge with no previous experience on the bench at any level.

The year after he became chief justice, Warren wrote the unanimous decision for the landmark case of *Brown v. Board of Education of Topeka, Kansas*. In delivering the court's opinion, Warren stated: "We conclude that in the field of public education the doctrine of 'separate but equal' has no place. Separate educational facilities are inherently unequal. Therefore, we hold that the plaintiffs and other similarly situated . . . are . . . deprived of the equal protection of the laws guaranteed by the Fourteenth Amendment." The decision was the first major victory in the struggle for civil rights. It was also the first in a string of judgments that would see the Supreme Court take a more active role. No other court before had taken on the defence of individual rights as Warren's court did.

SOUND BITE "Warren was not anti-government, but he believed that the Constitution prohibited the government from acting unfairly against the individual. In taking this position, he carved out a powerful position for the Court as a protector of civil rights and civil liberties."

Ed Cray, biographer of Earl Warren, Chief Justice, *1997*

Protection of civil rights and civil liberties seemed to be significant in yet another landmark decision rendered by Warren's Supreme Court. Today, even in Canada, we know that anyone arrested by the police must be mirandized (informed of his or her rights). The question of an individual's rights upon arrest was raised in the case *Miranda v. Arizona* (1966). In delivering the opinion of the Court, Chief Justice Warren stated:

Prior to any questioning, the person must be warned that he has the right to remain silent, that any statement he does make may be used as evidence against him, and that he has the right to the presence of an attorney, either retained or appointed. The defendant may waive effectuation of these rights provided the waiver is made voluntarily, knowingly and intelligently.

This decision had a dramatic impact on the way police arrest and question suspects.

As a result of decisions rendered by his court, Chief Justice Warren became a target of the right wing. "Impeach Earl Warren" bumper stickers appeared on cars, and at one anti-communist rally in California a speaker noted that impeachment was too good for Warren—he should be hanged. Alabama Governor George Wallace stated that Warren "doesn't have enough brains to try a chicken thief in my home county."

Warren retired from the bench in 1969 and died in 1974 at age 83.

Questions

1. Should the Supreme Court be a protector of civil rights and civil liberties? Why or why not?
2. If the Supreme Court does not protect civil rights and liberties, who do you believe should?
3. Former US President Richard Nixon stated in his memoirs that "some Supreme Court justices were too often using their own interpretations of the law to remake American society according to their own social, political and ideological precepts." Should Supreme Court justices be able to remake society through their interpretations of the law? Why or why not?

The British Judiciary

Unlike the American and Canadian judiciaries, the British judiciary does not use the practice of judicial review. In Britain, Parliament is supreme; its powers are not limited by federalism or by a charter of rights and freedoms. If someone wishes to change a law, that person must appeal to the legislature for change.

The British judiciary can intervene if the executive or legislature acts outside its scope of power. However, in a general sense, the British judiciary plays a more modest role in politics than the judiciaries in the United States and Canada.

Check Your Understanding

1. How are judicial restraint and judicial activism different? Which approach do you favour? Why?
2. What impact has the *Canadian Charter of Rights and Freedoms* had on the philosophy of judicial restraint?

3. Through its legal decisions in *Brown* and *Roe*, how did the US Supreme Court make major changes in American politics?
4. How is the role of the British judiciary different from the roles played by the Canadian and American judiciaries?

The Unitary and Federal Systems

You have seen that democratic systems operate in a number of different ways. Democratic systems also differ in the degree to which they are centralized. A system in which one central authority makes decisions for all regions of the country is called a **unitary system**. A system in which decision making is shared between a national government and local or regional governments is called a **federal system**.

Unitary System

A unitary state is governed as a single unit. It may create local governmental units with certain powers, but these are under the authority of the central parliament and may be abolished at any time. Britain, France, Japan, and Sweden are examples of unitary states. Most unitary states are relatively small in size and are usually composed of a homogeneous population.

When a unitary state creates regional parliaments that are not constituted, the process is known as **devolution**. In 1920, the British government granted local governmental powers to the province of Northern Ireland. The elected Parliament in Northern Ireland was dominated by the province's Protestant majority. Protests by the Roman Catholic minority prompted the British Parliament to end the local government's power in 1972 and to rule the province directly from London. The British government also experimented with devolution in Scotland and Wales. Following several referenda, Scotland and Wales received representative assemblies with limited powers in 1998. Health, education, and local government, for example, are powers that were devolved to the Scottish Parliament. The citizens of these regions still elect members to the British Parliament, which retains the supreme authority to amend or abolish the devolutionary arrangements.

Federal System

A federal state has two levels of government—a federal, or national, government and a second order of government made up of local units such as provinces or territories, states, or cantons. Both levels of government are recognized in the country's constitution, and both levels have their respective powers and responsibilities. The exact division of powers between national and local governments is often a source of conflict. As you read earlier in this chapter, the judiciary may be called upon to make rulings on jurisdictional authority.

Federal states are often geographically large. When powers are constitutionally granted to local regions, the people in those regions feel closer to their elected government than if all decisions were made in a far-off capital city. For example, in Canada, many people in Alberta feel closer to their provincial government than to the government in Ottawa.

One important reason for Canada's federal system is that it is the only system acceptable to Quebec. This province exercises control over matters directly related to its culture, language, and way of life. Federal systems are ideal when geographically concentrated groups sharing a common language, ethnicity, or culture wish to govern themselves within their territory. The central, or national, government is then free to deal with issues that the different parts of the federation have in common.

Federal–Provincial/Territorial Relations in Canada

Under Canada's constitution, powers are divided among the federal, provincial, and territorial governments, and different powers are granted each order of government (see Figure 6.17). The provinces and territories also control their own municipal, or local, governments. Most municipal governments provide local services and collect some taxes, but some local governments, especially Aboriginal band governments, have more latitude than most.

Supporters of a strong central government believe that Canada has an overriding national interest to equalize a standard of service, even in areas of provincial jurisdiction such as secondary education and health care. Supporters of strong provincial and territorial powers reject the right of the central government to impose national programs that impinge on provincial jurisdiction. They believe that the provinces are in the best position to evaluate the needs of their populations.

Canada's first prime minister, John A. Macdonald, worked hard to keep the balance of power in Ottawa's favour. But when Wilfrid Laurier was elected in 1896, he helped reverse that centralism. Decades later, two world wars

Federal	Provincial/Territorial	Municipal
"Peace, order, and good government"	Education	Public transit
National defence	Health services	Waste collection and disposal
Foreign diplomacy	Some natural resources	Water and sewers
International trade	Environmental issues	Snow removal
Aboriginal affairs	Solemnization of marriage	Fire protection services
Postal service	Licences	Zoning land
Banking system	Highways	Local police services
Marriage and divorce	Provincial court systems, police, and prisons	Property taxes, some licence fees
Criminal law		

Figure 6.17 Division of government powers in Canada.

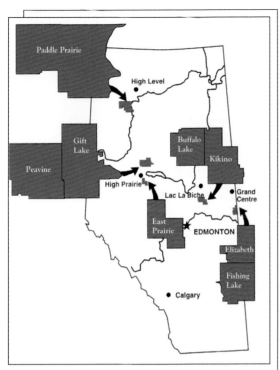

Source: Métis Settlements of Alberta, http://www.msat.gov.ab.ca/.

Figure 6.18 The Métis Settlements of Alberta, established in 1938, became local governments in 1989. Together, the eight settlements have a 40-member council that enacts laws equal in status to provincial laws and is responsible for such wide-ranging issues as hunting rights and oil and gas development.

THE WEB

Read Pierre Elliot Trudeau's essay on the failure of the Meech Lake Accord at www.emp.ca/cwp.

and the Great Depression of the 1930s caused the pendulum to swing back in favour of a strong central government. In 1940, a constitutional amendment allowed Ottawa to establish a national unemployment insurance program. During the first two decades after World War II, the federal government initiated and funded a number of social democratic programs to be administered by the provinces (see Chapter 2). Cooperation between the two levels of government is called **cooperative federalism**.

One province that did not participate in cooperative federalism is Quebec. It strongly objected to the expansion of federal influence through the use of spending powers. When the Canada Pension Plan was established in 1965, Quebec launched a separate Quebec Pension Plan and the right to "opt out" of a number of shared-cost programs in return for a greater slice of the tax pie. Its demands also resulted in Canada's other provinces receiving a greater share of tax revenue.

When Pierre Trudeau was prime minister (1968–79 and 1980–84), he was strongly committed to federalism and to the equality of the provinces. He also opposed any special recognition of Quebec as a culturally distinct society. His government was frequently in conflict with provincial governments over the ownership of natural resources—oil in Alberta, offshore oil in Newfoundland, and potash in Saskatchewan. For the Trudeau government, the issue was that benefits flowing from these natural resources ought to be available to all Canadians, not just those who were residents of the resource-rich provinces.

When Trudeau announced that he intended to patriate Canada's constitution whether or not the provinces agreed, many provinces including Quebec saw this as just one more move to weaken provincial rights. Eventually, all the premiers, with the exception of Quebec's Premier René Lévesque, supported the constitutional reforms that became the *Constitution Act, 1982*. The Supreme Court of Canada concluded that Quebec did not have a veto over constitutional change. Despite not having signed the *Constitution Act, 1982*, Quebec is nonetheless bound by it.

Brian Mulroney's Conservatives, elected in 1984, were more sympathetic to the provinces' demand for more power. When Mulroney and the 10 premiers drafted the Meech Lake Accord in 1987, they recognized Quebec as a "distinct society" and restored its veto over constitutional change. Before the Meech Lake Accord could be ratified, however, Manitoba MLA Elijah Harper withheld his consent for the Manitoba legislature to vote on ratification (see Chapter 4).

Another attempt to reconfigure federal–provincial powers—the Charlottetown Accord—was defeated in a 1992 referendum. Approval of the Accord would have led to an elected Senate, the recognition of Quebec as a "distinct society," and greater powers to the provinces in such areas as tourism, housing, forestry, and culture. Charlottetown would have been the highwater mark of provincial powers, but it was not to be.

Despite some ups and downs, federal–provincial relations have resulted in a number of positive accomplishments in Canadian politics. Some see the division of power between the federal government and the provinces and territories as a prototype for world government, in which individual states would play the role of the provinces. The World Federalist Movement is one group that advocates such a structure in which the citizens of the world elect global institutions that operate on the principles of federalism. Although no such world government has ever existed, advances in travel and communications may make the idea more feasible in the future.

THE WEB

To learn more about the World Federalist Movement, visit www.emp.ca/cwp.

Check YOUR UNDERSTANDING

1. Explain what devolution is and how it is used.
2. Why is a unitary system not possible in Canada?
3. Briefly describe what federal–provincial relations have been like since 1867.

Electoral Systems

Elections are perhaps the most visible institution of the democratic decision-making process. Regularly scheduled and free elections allow the citizens of a country to select their rulers and lawmakers. In an election, voters can judge the performance of a government by re-electing it or removing it from power. In modern democracies, elections are organized under one of the following systems:

- single-member plurality system
- preferential ballot
- proportional representation
- some adaptation of one or more of these systems.

Some states also provide for the recall, the initiative, and the referendum.

The Single-Member Plurality System

In the **single-member plurality** system, only one member is elected, no matter how many individuals are running for office in that geographical area or constituency. The winning candidate is the one who receives the most votes (a plurality), even although it may not be a majority of votes. For example, if six candidates are running in one constituency, one candidate may win by receiving 30 percent of the votes cast, while the other five candidates split the remaining 70 percent of the votes. This system, also known as "first past the post," is used in Britain, the United States, and Canada.

The single-member system seems to penalize small parties that are not regionally based. For example, during the 2004 Canadian federal election, the Green Party (an environmental party) won nearly 600,000 votes, or 4.3 percent of the popular vote. However, the Green Party still did not elect a single member to Parliament. On the other hand, the Bloc Québécois, a regionally based party, received 12.4 percent of the total vote in the 2004 federal election and won 54 seats—all within the province of Quebec.

Minority representation in the elected legislature may be minimized by the tactic of **gerrymandering**, which is the manipulation of constituency boundaries to maximize political support for one party. For example, when Northern Ireland possessed its own Parliament, the Protestant majority carved out electoral districts inhabited by a majority of Protestants and a minority of Catholics. Therefore, although Catholics constituted one-third of the population, they never received one-third of the seats in the legislature. Shifts in populations may require the redistribution of electoral boundaries. In many democracies today, independent commissions perform this task.

Preferential Ballot System

The **preferential ballot** system is a modification of the single-member plurality system. Voters list the candidates on the ballot paper by numbering them from most preferred to least preferred. If a member in a constituency does not have a clear majority, the second and third preferences on the ballots come into play until one candidate obtains a majority.

Australia uses the preferential ballot in all its elections. In recent years, voters in Australia who favour the right-wing side of the political spectrum have been able to vote for two right-of-centre parties, the Liberal and National parties. By ranking them first or second on their ballots (in either order), they can almost be assured that their votes will be counted toward one of the right-wing candidates. While left-wing voters could technically have the same advantage, in Australia, there is only one major left-of-centre party— the Labour Party.

Proportional Representation

Under a proportional representation system, the percentage of popular votes received by a party is reflected in the number of seats won in the legislature. Thus, if a party wins 15 percent of the popular vote in a national election, that party should receive 15 percent of the seats in the national legislature. Under most systems, the representatives are selected from a list held by the party, which ranks candidates on a priority basis.

As you read in Chapter 3, Israel uses proportional representation with a list system. The entire country can be viewed as one constituency that elects 120 members. If Party A receives 30 percent of the votes, Party A

THE WEB

Learn more about proportional representation at www.emp.ca/cwp.

receives 30 percent of the seats in the Knesset (parliament). That percentage translates into 38 seats, and thus the top 38 names on Party A's list are elected into the Knesset. In the Israeli system, any party receiving a minimum of 1.5 percent of the vote receives representation in parliament. Most European countries use proportional representation with the list system.

Proportional representation can foster the growth of small parties, as well as coalition governments based on alliances between like-minded parties. Majority governments are rare under systems of proportional representation. A perceived weakness of the list system is that it cannot guarantee that an individual will represent a geographically defined constituency. If Canada were to adopt proportional representation with a list system, each political party would have a "list" of candidates elected, but a local representative for Cape Breton Island, northern Ontario, or Nunavut would not be elected and the MP would no longer be seen as the voice for voters in a defined constituency.

To address this weakness of proportional representation, some countries, such as Germany and New Zealand, have adopted a combination of the single-member plurality system and proportional representation. In this combined system, on election day, voters cast two ballots, one for a candidate in the local constituency and one for a national list of candidates offered by a political party. The elected assembly is therefore composed of two types of members: those elected in constituencies and those elected from the party lists.

Recalls and Initiatives

Some jurisdictions use the **recall** to increase the accountability of politicians. Eighteen states and the Canadian province of British Columbia have provisions for recalling elected state or provincial politicians. In each case, a certain number of signatures are required on a petition to trigger the recall and re-election. In October 2003, the voters of California recalled Governor Gray Davis from office only one year after electing him. Voters charged that Davis had misled them about the true size of the state's budget deficit and about his intentions to raise taxes. Davis was the first state official to be successfully removed from office.

During the recall, voters were faced with two questions. The first question asked whether Davis should be recalled as governor. A majority "No" vote would save Davis, and a majority "Yes" vote would remove him from office. The second question asked voters to select his possible replacement from 135 choices. Citizens who voted against recalling Gray Davis could still vote for a candidate to replace him in case the recall vote succeeded.

California and some other states can also use a mechanism known as the initiative. An **initiative** is a petition submitted by citizens to force a vote on a particular issue. For example, Proposition 13 was a 1978 California initiative that passed, limiting real estate taxes.

SOUND BITE "No wonder voter apathy is on the rise when the yawn-inducing electoral system fails to excite voters. The 19th century model we're using no longer represents the 21st century world we live in. Proportional representation is far more reflective of our current political climate."

Jim Harris, leader, Green Party of Canada, 2004

Point:
Counterpoint → Should Canada Adopt Proportional Representation?

"Yes" to Proportional Representation

by Bruce Campion-Smith

For the NDP—and many others—the results of the [2004] election offer fresh evidence of the need for Canada to adopt proportional representation, a voting system that awards seats according to the percentage of votes received in an election.

It would replace the first-past-the-post system now used, a system that typically produces majority governments with a minority of the votes, while denying smaller parties a place in the Commons. . . .

The Green Party garnered 4 per cent of the votes nationwide, but no seats. In Quebec, the 300,000 people who voted Conservative—9 per cent of the vote—have nothing to show for their vote.

At the other end of the scale, the Liberals got 45 per cent of the vote in Ontario, yet collected 70 per cent of the seats—75 seats in all. . . .

It's no surprise that NDP Leader Jack Layton is an ardent proponent of overhauling the election system. Like all small parties, his has been hurt by the vagaries of the current system. In this election, the NDP garnered 15.7 per cent of the popular vote but only 6 per cent of the seats, with just 19 MPs elected. . . .

To its boosters, proportional representation is a cure for much of what ails Canada's democracy, a way to bring more minorities and women into politics, to boost the country's flagging voter turnout and give smaller parties a toehold in the Commons. . . .

The current voting system—inherited from Britain more than 200 years ago, at a time when women, aboriginals and minorities were disenfranchised—is out of date, concluded the Law Commission of Canada, which advises Parliament on legal matters.

"Canada's political, cultural and economic reality has vastly changed; the current electoral system no longer responds to 21st century Canadian democratic values," it said. . . .

The report cited declining voter turnout, increasing cynicism towards politicians and declining political participation of young people as proof that Canada is in the "grip of a democratic malaise." . . .

The commission recommended that two-thirds of the 308 Commons seats be elected in constituency races using the first-past-the-post method. The remaining one-third would be elected from a list of candidates submitted by the parties within each province and territory to reflect their share of the popular vote. . . .

Henry Milner, an expert on the topic, says the claim that proportional representation produces unstable minority governments doesn't hold water.

"I don't think the arguments are very convincing, because minority governments in Canada haven't been that bad and in the majority of Western democracies, they've worked well," said Milner, author of *Steps Towards Making Every Vote Count*, a look at proportional representation in Canada and other countries. . . .

"People look back on the (Prime Minister Lester) Pearson period very positively even though he never had a majority," said Milner, who is also a fellow at the Institute for Research on Public Policy.

That's backed up by the law commission report, which cites the examples of Scandinavia, New Zealand and Scotland. All use proportional representation and "have exhibited quite satisfactory levels of political stability."

Source: Excerpted from Bruce Campion-Smith, "Making It Count." *Toronto Star*, July 10, 2004, pp. H1, H4.

"The inherent problem with proportional representation is that no one's willing to admit they don't know what it is."

Figure 6.19 _____

"No" to Proportional Representation

by Dennis Richards

I have identified five strengths of our present first-past-the-post system. Research shows that first-past-the-post electoral systems more likely result in a single-party government, often a majority government. Voters know that when they vote for a candidate or party they are choosing a government.

Second, the first-past-the-post system results in a more stable government. Coalitions of various parties—groups forming governments—are much less likely. This form of government is not subject to defeat if the votes of non-confidence occur. This enables government freedom to complete its full legislative mandate. Government is better able to effectively carry out its legislative agenda on which they campaigned.

Third, there is a relative simplicity to the election process. The voting process is not complicated, rather it is straightforward. Simply put, the candidate who gets the most votes wins.

Fourth, the first-past-the-post electoral system supports the development of a strong party system with a strong sense of loyalty among its members. This results in government working as a team. The voter both votes for an individual to represent them and an individual who is a member of a party with a defined legislative agenda. This is critical, because parties develop positions and policies which voters can identify and choose to support or reject.

Fifth, the first-past-the-post system together with a single member being elected from a constituency ensures a direct link in connection between the elected representatives and the electors.

I will now point out what I consider to be some of the weaknesses of proportional representation. A proportional representational system does not necessarily achieve the goal it claims to achieve. A 1991 study of electoral systems in 25 countries showed that it is possible for the first-past-the-post system to produce a more proportional result than a proportional representation system. There are many other factors involved, such as the number of parties involved in the election, which may influence the personality of electoral outcomes. There is a potential in the proportional representation system to foster fringe voices and more extreme views within society because it has the potential to give such opinions a legislative platform from which to champion their cause. This can result in unduly magnifying the concern.

Since proportional representation generally produces a coalition government, it would be rare for a party to get a majority. This completely changes and undermines the basis of our system of cabinet government. Our form of democratic government depends on the party in power having enough people elected to enable it to carry out its legislative program. A party without a majority would be forced to battle every proposal or enter into a coalition with some other party or parties. This results in less stable government. With a proportional representation system, voters do not actually elect a government. The basis of the proportional representation system requires that more than one person be elected from a constituency. The electorate therefore has no say in voting for whom actually will fill and form the government.

In addition, responsible connection between the elected officials and the electorate is muddied and unclear. And finally, in a country as large and as relatively sparsely populated as Canada, which already has very strong regional feelings and interests, a proportional representation system could easily foster a greater number of regional parties at the federal level. This would only compound the problem of regional versus national interests. This is also true within certain provinces as many have strong regional tendencies within their jurisdictions.

Source: Dennis Richards, "Round Table on Proportional Representation." *Canadian Parliamentary Review*, vol. 20, no. 1, 1997.

Articulating a Personal Stand

1. a) Rank Campion-Smith's arguments in favour of proportional representation from most effective to least effective. (Refer to the criteria for effective arguments in Methods of Political Inquiry, page 227.)
   b) Follow the steps described above to rank the arguments made by Richards in favour of retaining the first-past-the-post system.
2. Write a short paper outlining which side you find more convincing, referring to specific arguments. Alternatively, you may hold a debate on this topic, following the steps outlined in Methods of Political Inquiry.

Referenda

Many countries use referenda to decide important issues. A referendum is a yes–no question presented to voters by the authority of the legislature. Canada has held referenda on such issues as prohibition of alcohol (1898) and conscription (1942). As you read earlier in this chapter, the province of Quebec has conducted two referenda on the issue of separation from Canada. Referenda have been held in European countries on the issue of adopting the euro as a common currency. In 2000, Denmark rejected the euro by 53 percent to 47 percent; Sweden rejected the euro in 2003 by 56 percent to 42 percent. The initiative and the referendum are both forms of democracy in which voters are able to make a direct impact on government.

The referendum may be binding or non-binding. If it is binding, legislators are compelled to honour the results. If it is non-binding, legislators take the results of the vote in an advisory capacity. The term *plebiscite* is at times used to describe a non-binding referendum. For the most part, the two terms referendum and plebiscite are used interchangeably.

Although the referendum or plebiscite is used occasionally by many democratic governments to decide an important issue, some commentators believe that they should not be a regular part of the democratic process. Voters in a referendum or plebiscite may not vote in the best interest of society. They may be persuaded to vote in favour of personal interest or racial bias. Some issues, such as abortion rights, may be too volatile to be debated in a national referendum campaign.

In a speech to electors in 1774, British politician Edmund Burke presented the rationale for the independence of mind of an elected representative: "Your representative owes you not only his industry, but his judgment, and he betrays, instead of serving you, if he sacrifices it to your opinion." Burke, in effect, was arguing for a well-informed politician who would lead, rather than blindly follow, the dictates of his constituents.

Democratic systems are still evolving, and even their staunchest defenders admit they are not perfect. In the future, issues such as proportional representation, the value of referenda, and whether the Senate should be elected will continue to be debated. By expressing different viewpoints on these issues, Canadians are participating in their own democracy and seeking to improve it as well.

Check Your Understanding

1. How does the single-member plurality system penalize small parties? Give an example.
2. Describe how proportional representation works.
3. Do you agree or disagree with Burke's belief that a well-informed politician should lead rather than blindly follow the dictates of constituents? Present your views in a well-written paragraph.
4. What are the differences between an initiative and a referendum?

METHODS OF POLITICAL INQUIRY
Debating a Political Issue

Half the work of debating—and half the satisfaction—lies in the preparation. If you invest time planning your debate, you will find the experience more rewarding. The goal of a debate is to persuade an audience that you stand on an issue is the sound one. To do that, you must present effective arguments to support your views, with evidence drawn from reliable sources.

Preparing for a debate has three phases:

1. Decide which issue to debate. This chapter provides some ideas. You can also glean issues from national newspapers, your local paper, or the Web sites of news organizations and broadcasters like the CBC.
2. State your position. You don't have to agree with the position you take during the debate; in fact, it can be more interesting to defend a position with which you don't personally agree. But if you are working with a team, you should all agree that this is the position you will take on the resolution.
3. Research the issue to determine the strongest arguments in support of your position. To strengthen your understanding, first gather as much background information as possible. Who are the key players, and what do they say they want? (There will probably be several key players with divergent views.) What key events have occurred to date?

Record and analyze the arguments on both sides of the issue. Knowing how the other side thinks will allow you to anticipate and deflate its arguments. As you analyze the viewpoints, ask the following questions:

- What is the evidence for the argument's claim? Is the argument based on fact or opinion?
- Is the argument logical or does it contain fallacies? (A fallacy is an error in argument that renders the argument invalid.)
- Is there exaggeration or rhetorical grandstanding? If so, take note.
- If statistics are used, are they current and reliable?
- If other sources of information are quoted, are they reliable?

Lastly, order the arguments that support your position from weakest to strongest. The strongest argument is the one that is logically sound and is backed up by reli-

able evidence. If you are on a team, assign one member one argument. Leave your strongest argument for the closing statement. The opposing team will follow the same format, so listen carefully to its closing statement.

Holding the Debate

When debating the resolution (for example, "Canada's Senate should be elected"), the affirmative side should go first. The opposition can be allowed slightly more time for its arguments because the affirmative will have the opportunity to rebut the opposition's remarks. If you wish to follow the Canadian parliamentary debate style, your two teams should comprise two members each: the government team, made up of the Prime Minister and the Minister of the Crown, and the Opposition, made up of the Leader of the Opposition and the Member Opposite. The total time for debate is 34 minutes, and the arguments are presented as follows:

- Affirmative (Prime Minister presents up to four arguments): 7 minutes
- Opposition (Member Opposite rebuts the PM's arguments and makes one new point): 7 minutes
- Affirmative (Minister of the Crown rebuts the MO's speech and reaffirms and expands on the PM's arguments): 7 minutes
- Opposition (Leader of the Opposition summarizes the government's position, rebuts it, and introduces some new points): 10 minutes
- The PM has the final say in the debate. In this short speech, only rebuttal is allowed and no new information may be introduced. The time is spent attacking every point made by the opposition and summing up the government's position: 3 minutes.

Applying the Skill

Choose a political issue to debate in class and follow the steps outlined above to prepare your team. Following the debate, debrief:

1. a) Which aspects of your preparation were successful?
   b) Which aspects were less successful?
2. What would you do differently next time?

Study Hall

Thinking/Inquiry

1. Canada's formal executive is the link to historical connections with Britain. However, the ethnic makeup of Canada has changed dramatically since Confederation. Should those historical ties be maintained in Canada's government? Working with a partner, develop a list of arguments either supporting or rejecting the formal executive. Present your list to the class. (You may wish to review the Point Counterpoint in Chapter 1, pages 14–15.)

2. Create an organizer like the one in Figure 6.20 comparing and contrasting the Canadian parliamentary system with the American presidential system.

3. Should judges be elected to their positions, as most are in the United States? In a paragraph, select a position and present arguments supporting your view.

4. Using the Internet or the school library, find out who the current members of the federal cabinet are. Has the prime minister done a good job in selecting a cabinet that represents various regions and groups from across Canada? For example, what is the representation from each of the provinces and territories? How many women, Aboriginal people, and ethnic groups are represented? Write a short report outlining your findings and your assessment on how representative the current cabinet is.

Communication

5. Write a newspaper editorial arguing for either the abolishment or the retention of the Canadian Senate.

6. You and a partner are to create and role-play a scenario in which the prime minister must discipline a member who has broken party discipline. Present your scenario to the class.

7. Look back at Figure 6.1 on page 194. Using Internet or library resources, research the circumstances of this protest. What point do you think the artist was trying to make? Do you find this an effective work of art? Explain your views.

Application

8. The grade 5 teacher in your neighbourhood elementary school has asked your class to provide visuals that will be used to teach the Social Studies curriculum on Canadian government. The teacher needs visuals for the following areas:

   - structure of the federal government
   - components of the federal government (i.e., House of Commons, Senate)
   - how governments are elected
   - services provided by the federal government
   - current political leaders at all levels
   - points of comparison between Canada and other systems of government

   In groups of three to four students, and with your teacher's approval, create your visual. (Remember that most of the students in your audience will be about 10 years of age.)

9. Your classroom is to be the location of the next First Ministers' Conference. The members of your class will role-play representatives from the federal government, the provinces, and the territories. The issue on the table is the future of health care in Canada. You will need to conduct research in order to present the views of your particular level of government.

10. This chapter has focused primarily on the Canadian, American, and British systems of government. Select a country with a different system of government and research how this government operates. Create a chart comparing the Canadian system with that of your chosen country.

Figure 6.20

Country	Executive	Legislative	Judicial	Elections
Canada				

Participation by Individuals and Groups in Politics

Figure 7.1 Canadian artist Paraskeva Clark painted *Petroushka* after Chicago police killed five striking steelworkers during the 1937 Republic Steel Corporation strike.

How do citizens in a democracy come together to reform and remake their society when needs are in conflict? The majority rules, but what happens when it discriminates against a minority? How can minorities claim and protect their rights? Does the majority have the right to maintain—and impose—its beliefs and values? This chapter investigates how difficult issues such as these are dealt with. It provides information about interest groups, and how they evolve and function. It looks at grassroots organizing, social movements, and the media's role in publicizing human rights struggles.

As you work through this chapter, think about how you have—or have not—participated in local, provincial, national, and global politics. Is there an issue that you feel strongly about? Have you worked with others to influence government? What about global issues? Are there groups you would like to work with, or against? Consider these questions as you read, and note sections that you would like to return to or use as a basis for further research and action.

Agenda

In this chapter, you will consider

• how different kinds of interest groups form
• the impact interest groups have nationally and internationally on government policies
• citizen participation in the democratic process
• different kinds of protest
• the impact of technological innovation on democratic participation
• how media can influence politics and vice versa
• human rights, their evolution, and the agencies that uphold them
• collective rights versus individual rights and liberties
• investigative journalism as a career

229

Rights and Responsibilities of Individuals in Democratic Countries

As a form of government, democracy involves much more than voting, elections, and the passing of bills into law. In a full democracy (see Chapter 5), citizens have many opportunities to participate in decision making, and there are laws to protect individual rights and freedoms, such as freedom of mobility, expression, and religion.

Democracy recognizes both majority rule and minority rights. In many Western democracies, groups representing African Americans, indigenous peoples, and gay men and lesbians have been able to secure these rights by working within the legal framework of their societies.

Traditionally Recognized Responsibilities

Citizens in a democracy have responsibilities as well as rights. In much the same way that responsible participation by staff and students contributes to a school's vitality, participation by citizens helps foster the health of a democracy. Some countries, such as Canada, actually spell out citizens' responsibilities. These can include voting (also considered a right), respecting a country's laws, respecting human rights, and preserving a country's heritage and environment.

One important responsibility citizens have in a democracy is to be informed about issues and decisions facing their governments. For example, when a government allocates resources, citizens need to know how it is making those decisions. How will funding be divided between health care and secondary education, or between the armed forces and humanitarian aid? Governments also pass laws with which some citizens and groups may disagree. Informed citizens can provide feedback to their elected representatives on all these issues. The opinions can be conveyed through opinion polling, letter writing, e-mail messaging, and public protests.

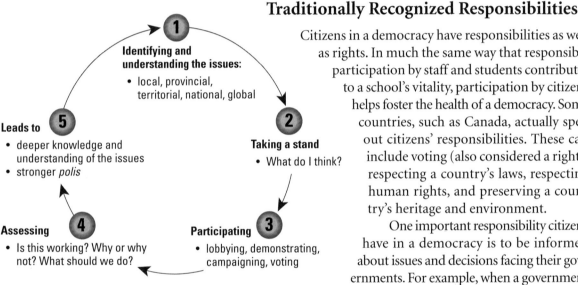

Figure 7.2 Informed citizens can become active citizens, and active citizenship leads to a deeper understanding of political issues. Any time that citizens take part in the activities of the *polis*, the *polis* is strengthened.

Check YOUR UNDERSTANDING

1. How informed do you feel about your government? Where do you obtain information? What could you do to become better informed?
2. Describe how you are an active citizen.

The Role of Interest Groups

Joining with other people and using the democratic process to change society has been a long tradition in many democracies. In the United States, anti-slavery societies worked to change American laws in the period prior to the Civil War (1861–65). In the early 20th century, suffragists in Canada and other nations pressured legislators to give women the right to vote. Since the 1950s, the number of groups seeking to advance their interests by using the democratic process has grown. Access to television has heightened people's interest in political issues, and new technologies such as fax machines, computers, and the Internet have made it easier for groups to be active in organizing and fundraising.

Interest group, **lobby group**, or **pressure group** are terms that can be used interchangeably to denote a group of people that works to promote the interests of a particular constituency. (The term *interest group* will be used primarily in this textbook.) Such groups can have a local, national, or international base. They can promote virtually any type of interest, including business, cultural, educational, or environmental interests. The Sierra Club, for example, is an international organization concerned with environmental issues; the National Citizens' Coalition, a Canadian group, is committed to a free-enterprise business climate.

Interest groups pursue a range of activities during and between election campaigns. During an election, they might provide funding or other support to a party or a candidate. Between elections, they may lobby individual ministers or members of cabinet through a letter-writing campaign or by arranging a meeting between its representative and a key political figure. Some interest groups hire a paid lobbyist—often a former bureaucrat or politician—to communicate with government officials. Interest groups also conduct opinion polls and publish the results. Some interest groups nurture contacts with newspaper columnists, speakers, journalists, and other media representatives to spread their message. Others organize rallies or demonstrations in order to have their messages heard by voters and politicians.

Interest groups are formed for a variety of reasons, but political scientists agree that one main reason is *need*. In other words, people form interest groups when government does something they disapprove of, or fails to do something they believe it should do. People who are personally affected by the government's action or inaction may be especially motivated to form an interest group.

Figure 7.3 Oscar-winning US actor Angelina Jolie is a Goodwill Ambassador for the United Nations High Commissioner for Refugees. What makes celebrities attractive spokespeople for interest groups?

Types of Interest Groups

The conditions leading to interest groups can vary widely. Labour unions and business associations are interest groups that lobby on behalf of their members by working for their social and economic good. Other groups claim to work for a much larger segment of society. Greenpeace is a **public-interest group** that lobbies to save the environment for all members of society. A pressure group that focuses exclusively on one question—such as abortion or peace—is called a **single-issue interest group**. Since its founding in 1980, Mothers Against Drunk Driving (MADD) has been highly successful in pressuring governments to change laws related to drinking and driving. MADD is an example of a single-issue interest group.

Some interest groups try to influence the government in its foreign relations decisions. Peace organizations, for example, pressure the Canadian government to avoid war. During the 1988 federal election campaign, interest groups spent millions of dollars promoting platforms that either supported or opposed the impending *Canada–US Free Trade Agreement* (FTA). (The agreement was enacted in 1989; see Chapter 10.) In the 1990s, environmental groups pressured the Liberal government to approve the *Kyoto Protocol*, which commits participating nations to reduce the emission of greenhouse gases that contribute to global warming (see Chapter 9).

The Arab–Israeli conflict in the Middle East has also contributed to pressure-group activity within Canada. Groups such as Solidarity for Palestinian Human Rights try to influence the government's agenda in one direction, while pro-Israel organizations, such as B'nai Brith, work to move government in the opposite direction. B'nai Brith is an interest group that also works to combat anti-Semitism, bigotry, and racism in Canada.

Sometimes, an interest group is sufficiently representative of the public for government to actively seek its opinions. Governments need to hear these groups' opinions on policy options. For example, the Canadian government often asks the Consumers' Association of Canada (CAC) for its opinion on what consumers want. On the other hand, the CAC's research is often funded by the government, which means that the relationship between the two entities—government and interest group—is symbiotic (mutually advantageous) rather than independent.

The Canadian government also funds certain interest groups, especially if they represent groups whose rights the government wants to safeguard or promote, such as women, Aboriginal peoples, and ethnic minorities. To counter charges of government favouritism in dealing with interest groups, democracies usually try to regulate their activities and make them as transparent as possible. Nonetheless,

Figure 7.4 These MADD buttons display a variety of slogans and messages used by this single-issue interest group.

critics contend that while activities in elections and legislatures are visible to the public, interest groups often work behind closed doors.

The federal government has become somewhat wary of the way interest groups operate during elections. In 2000, the *Canada Elections Act* was updated to reflect these concerns. Currently, the Act limits advertising and other campaign spending by lobby groups to $150,000 nationally and $3,000 in any single riding. Further updates in 2004 forbid unions and corporations from contributing to political parties and leadership contests, although they may contribute up to $1,000 per year to individual candidates. The goal of the legislation was to prevent local members of Parliament with limited resources from being overwhelmed by an aggressive campaign from a powerful national interest group. The federal government argued that there were ceilings on the campaign spending of political parties, and that lobby groups should also be restricted in their expenditures.

Grassroots Politics and Protest

Stephen Fletcher, MP

On June 28, 2004, Steven Fletcher, aged 32, became the Conservative member of Parliament for Charleswood–St. James, a suburban Winnipeg riding. He not only defeated the man expected to win—star Liberal candidate Glen Murray—he also became Canada's first quadriplegic member of Parliament.

Eight years earlier, Fletcher had been enjoying his career as an engineer working in a gold mine northeast of Winnipeg. His job also suited his passion for the wilderness, since the mine was situated near lakes and rivers that he loved to canoe on. All that changed after a car accident in January 1996, when Fletcher collided with a moose. As a result of a serious spinal injury, he was paralyzed from the neck down.

After a long recovery, Fletcher began looking for a new career. Two things helped. He rejected the prospect of living in an institution, despite being told it was his only option. He successfully fought the province of Manitoba and its public insurance system to live in his own apartment. He also entered an MBA program at the University of Manitoba.

Figure 7.5 Supporters cheer Steven Fletcher and his 2004 federal election win at campaign headquarters in Winnipeg.

The challenges, such as not being able to take notes, built Fletcher's confidence and mental acuity.

Not surprisingly, Fletcher campaigned on the issue of **community living** and says he'll keep fighting for it. Since he was elected to Parliament, he is aware that the disabled community is looking to him as their champion. "When you're a first, people look to that person to break down barriers," he says. One barrier he is still trying to break down is the lack of accessibility in Parliament. When he campaigned, he had trouble getting his wheelchair into the building's elevator and restaurant. Since his election, the House has promised to accommodate him in whatever way he wishes.

Some people have expressed surprise that Fletcher joined the right-wing Conservative Party of Canada. He is pro-business, believing in what he calls a healthier business climate in communities, with the elimination of "prohibitive business taxes." On the campaign trail, Fletcher noted that university students in particular were often surprised by his party affiliation. But he thinks his right-wing platform makes perfect sense. "I'm all about empowering the individual, and that is completely consistent with conservative ideology," he says.

Fletcher says his "in-depth and personal knowledge" of the Canadian health care system gave him great insight into the needs of patients and families and the challenges faced by physicians and nurses. He also describes himself as a "wise and wary consumer advocate and a determined political activist" based on his dealings with government and insurance companies following his accident.

Most of all, Fletcher is happy to get on with the job at hand. Raymond Cohen, editor-in-chief of

Abilities magazine, says Fletcher shows that people with disabilities are as capable as anyone else. "People tend to lower their expectations of people with disabilities as being people who can assume leadership roles. The fact that Fletcher has risen to office flies in the face of that misconception," Cohen says.

Fletcher is also fighting to live a good life. If he can help it, it won't be all about politics. "I hope my life will be all about representing my constituents and making their lives better. That's what I'd like to do."

Questions

1. What is Steven Fletcher's rationale for his political ideology?
2. Some people have expressed surprise that Fletcher is a member of a right-wing party. Using your knowledge of the political spectrum (see Chapter 2), explain why someone with Fletcher's condition might be attracted to the ideology of a left-wing party.
3. Research other Canadians with disabilities (such as Terry Fox, Rick Hansen, and Chantal Peticlerc) who have assumed leadership roles.
4. Interview a person with a disability in your school or community. Find out how the disability has affected his or her participation in the *polis*.

The Role of the Media

SOUND BITE "Were it left to me to decide whether we should have a government without newspapers, or newspapers without a government, I should not hesitate a moment to prefer the latter."

Thomas Jefferson, US President, 1801–1809; letter, 1787

In 18th century France, newspaper journalism was dubbed the **fourth estate**. The term emerged in the context of the "three estates" of pre-revolutionary France—church, nobles, and commoners. Newspapers have traditionally been viewed as an important pillar of democracy because they are independent and free. They provide news and commentary that the public is free to question.

In the latter half of the 20th century, television news became the **fifth estate**. Today, the term *media* is used to describe many varieties of mass communication, including newspapers, magazines, radio, television, and the Internet. Bloggers, for example, are commentators or journalists who compose online Internet journals, or Web logs. In 2004, for the first time, bloggers were given press passes at the American Democratic and Republican conventions. All these media play an important role in connecting political leaders to the people they represent in a democracy. Citizens rely on the media to receive information about events that are outside their range of experience, and politicians use the media to gather information about the citizenry. Modern technological developments have provided almost instant news of political events, no matter where the events may be occurring.

Media and Government

The media do not just report on events—they also influence them, or can be used to influence them. Newspaper coverage played a role when the United States declared war against Spain in 1898. Before war was declared, the US newspaper chains owned by rivals William Randolph Hearst and Joseph Pulitzer vied for readership by sensationalizing stories of Spanish atrocities committed against the people of Cuba. The not-so-subtle message was that the United States should invade Cuba and put an end to Spain's misdeeds. Newspaper coverage that places a premium on exaggeration and sensational details at the expense of factual accuracy has been called "yellow journalism." The term may have originated from Hearst's and Pulitzer's use of newsprint that quickly turned yellow.

Another news medium, television, contributed to America's withdrawal from another war in 1973. During the war in Vietnam, television camera crews "worked the war" in a way that had never before been possible, beaming horrifying images of combat into American living rooms. Television also captured scenes of anti-war protestors in the United States. It created a strong perception that the war in Vietnam could not be won, and that it had divided the country irrevocably.

Because of television's impact, the US military has tried to control the independence of journalists. During the 1983 US invasion of Grenada, for

Figure 7.6 A US marine pulls a wounded comrade to safety during fighting in Hue, South Vietnam, 1968.

PRESS PLAY

Control Room (2004), a documentary by Jehane Noujam, explores the differences in how Western and Arab news agencies (especially Al-Jazeera) covered the 2003 invasion of Iraq. (14A)

example, press passes were approved by the American government, thereby controlling journalists' movements. During the 1991 Gulf War, journalists' movements were restricted; they received most of their information from briefings organized by the military. During the invasion of Iraq in 2003, journalists were "embedded" with military units, thereby encouraging them to observe the war from the perspective of American and British soldiers. Many critics believed war coverage became uncritically pro-American as a result. Al-Jazeera, the Arabic television station based in Qatar, provided counterpoint to the views expressed by many of the United States channels. Founded in 1996, and claiming to be the only politically independent station in the Middle East, Al-Jazeera aired footage of civilian casualties and interviews with participants that could not be obtained on US networks. The World Wide Web also provided coverage of the 2003 war against Iraq. Those with access to the Internet—about a half-billion people around the world—could obtain different versions of events in Iraq.

Independent news media can also uncover criminal activity or corruption in government. Newspaper reporters in particular played a key role in exposing the Watergate affair in the United States (see Chapter 6). After five men were arrested for breaking into the headquarters of the Democratic National Committee at Washington's Watergate Hotel in June 1972, two *Washington Post* journalists began investigating. Bob Woodward and Carl Bernstein uncovered a connection between the break-in and members of a committee to re-elect President Richard Nixon. Woodward and Bernstein's reporting made the Watergate burglary a major international news story and eventually uncovered a trail that led close to the office of the US president. After being implicated in a coverup of the break-in, Nixon resigned in August 1974. Woodward and Bernstein made the public aware of how important investigative reporting can be in keeping government open and accountable.

The Watergate affair inspired journalists around the world to be more aggressive and critical in covering the conduct of public officials and in dealing with official government versions of events. Canada has had a long history of investigative reporting. With television programs such as *This Hour Has Seven Days*—originally produced in the 1960s—as well as programs such as *fifth estate, W5,* and *Disclosure,* Canadian journalists have investigated corruption in business and

Figure 7.7 An Arab American citizen in Brooklyn, New York, watches news reports from Al-Jazeera during the invasion of Afghanistan in 2001. US news coverage rarely showed images of civilian casualties during that conflict.

government circles and the plight of citizens who have been victims of government and judicial injustice.

The media can also be used to communicate government messages. Governments use press conferences and public appearances by elected representatives to get their message to the electorate. They also use the media for public service announcements. The political party in power uses the media to advertise its accomplishments. And during an election campaign, different political parties use the media to capitalize on their own strengths and highlight the weaknesses of opposition parties.

Public and Private Ownership of Media

It is difficult to have a truly democratic society without freedom of expression and freedom of the press. For the most part, both Canada and the United States enjoy this freedom. In Canada, the electronic media are characterized by a mixture of public and private ownership. The Canadian Broadcasting Corporation (CBC) is a Crown corporation created in 1936 to mitigate American cultural influence in radio—the only live medium at the time. Other radio and television networks in Canada are privately owned.

Although government ownership of media poses possible dangers, Canadian journalists have been able to criticize government policies and act as "watchdogs" for the common good, whether employed at the CBC or at privately owned networks. In 1998, the Prime Minister's Office filed a complaint with the CBC's **ombudsman** about the work of CBC reporter Terry Milewski. At issue was Milewski's reporting of the inquiry into the RCMP's treatment of protestors at the Asia–Pacific Economic Cooperation (APEC) summit in 1997. Milewski was accused of siding with the APEC complainants, advising a student on legal strategies, and generally being biased against the government. Although the CBC removed Milewski from the story, he was vindicated in his work by the CBC ombudsman.

Media Convergence

A trend toward media convergence has seen print media and broadcasting networks merge into a few huge media conglomerates. In Canada, it appears that concentrated ownership may be restricting freedom of the press. For example, one of Canada's largest media groups, with 14 major daily newspapers and a television network, is CanWest Global Communications, created by Israel Asper and run by his family after his death. In 2001, the Aspers insisted that CanWest newspapers—the largest newspaper chain in Canada—run centrally prepared editorials up to three times a week. Traditionally, the editorial staffs of local newspapers create their own. A number of editors quit. Some commentators maintained that CanWest was simply trying to save money. Others suggested the decision was ideologically driven—and that the company's central office was imposing its politics on all its subsidiary newspapers.

PRESS PLAY

All the President's Men (1976), directed by Alan Pakula, features Dustin Hoffman and Robert Redford as the two *Washington Post* reporters who helped unravel the mystery of the Watergate break-in that destroyed the presidency of Richard Nixon. (PG)

THE WEB

Learn more about media convergence in Canada at www.emp.ca/cwp.

In the last two decades, technological innovations have enhanced the transmission of political news. All-news television stations such as CNN and CBC Newsworld bring viewers a constant stream of news and images about events as they unfold. This contrasts starkly with news broadcasts in the early decades of television. Newspapers and television stations also provide instant news coverage with their own Internet sites. Governments, political parties, and interest groups maintain their own Web sites in order to provide information and also, in many cases, to encourage two-way communication.

Check Your Understanding

1. Why did the number of interest groups grow in the second half of the 20th century? In your opinion, is this a beneficial or non-beneficial development? Explain.
2. What controls has the federal government placed on lobbyists?
3. How might an interest group influence a political party?
4. Using examples, explain the difference between public-interest groups and single-issue groups.
5. Using specific examples, describe how the media may influence events.
6. Look at the two Sound Bites by Thomas Jefferson on pages 234 and 235. How might you account for the different views of newspapers expressed in each?
7. What are some possible dangers of concentrating media ownership in a few hands?
8. How do the media act as "watchdogs"? Should they?

The Role of Social Movements

You have read that interest groups promote the interests of a particular constituency. Usually, these organizations influence government policy by formally communicating with government. Interest groups can be focused on

- a single issue
- issues that affect only their members, e.g., in a union
- issues that affect the general public.

Interest groups sometimes have a paid lobbyist. They often use the media to publicize their initiatives.

Another way to participate in the democratic process is by joining a social movement. Social movements differ from organized interest groups in several respects. As you learned in Chapter 2, social movements are informal networks of groups and individuals with shared values and identity. In their own view, *who they are* is as important as *what they wish to accomplish* in society. This sense of shared identity and values leads them to undertake collective action that expands the boundaries of the political system, forcing it to accommodate values and identities previously neglected or maligned.

Social Movements and Human Rights

Participants in parallel social movements often see themselves as interconnected. Many believe that all governments, whether democratic or non-democratic, must adhere to the basic principles of human rights. In this way, human rights can be a uniting force for social movements. However, not all social movements see their struggles as universal. For example, Nelson Mandela worked tirelessly to end apartheid in South Africa. However, because he believed in violence as a legitimate tool against oppression, he was rejected by other pro-democracy, pro-peace advocates.

THE WEB

For more about Nelson Mandela and the African National Congress, go to www.emp.ca/cwp.

SOUND BITE "We can use human rights to form a national social justice coalition."

Urvashi Vaid, activist for gay and lesbian rights

SOUND BITE "A human rights framework allows us to effectively unite with people within the same movement who have different ideas."

National Center for Human Rights Education Web site, 2004

Origins of Human Rights

The concept of human rights is found in the culture of every world region. As you learned in Chapter 3, in the 3rd century BCE, the Indian emperor Ashoka became a convert to Buddhism and promoted tolerance and individual freedoms, both in government policy and in interpersonal relationships. Human standards such as respect and tolerance are found in the Christian Bible and the Muslim Qur'an, the works of Confucius, and the Japanese code of behaviour known as *bushido* (the way of the warrior). The Great Law of Peace of the Iroquois Confederacy also acknowledged human rights and many other democratic principles; portions of the Great Law found their way into the US constitution when it was drafted in 1787.

Figure 7.8 This structure in Sarnath, India, is one of many *stupas* (places of worship) built by the Emperor Ashoka (273–236 BCE) following his conversion to Buddhism.

While world literature speaks, often poetically, about human behaviour and human values, the language of individual human rights originated in the 18th century. The American *Declaration of Independence* in 1776 proposed that "all men are created equal" and are endowed with "certain unalienable rights." The 1789 *Declaration of the Rights of Man and the Citizen* in France claimed that "men are born and remain free and equal in rights." These documents, however, did not recognize universal human rights; they recognized neither women nor people of non-European heritage.

That recognition would come in 1948, when the General Assembly of the United Nations proclaimed the *Universal Declaration of Human Rights*. As you will read in Chapter 8, a Canadian, John Humphrey, helped draft this important document, which talks about the kind of communities all governments should aspire to create. Aside from the more familiar rights of freedom of expression, religion, and mobility, the document speaks of the rights to be educated, to be protected from unemployment, and to have a standard of living adequate for health and well-being. By modern definitions, human rights are universal, meaning that they apply to everyone, at all times, in all places.

The US Civil Rights Movement

The US civil rights movement is an example of an early social movement. After slavery was abolished in the United States, African Americans were still denied equal status in society. In most parts of the country, they lived as a nation apart—separated from their fellow citizens by laws and conventions. Although African Americans had won the right to vote in 1870, the southern states erected legal barriers such as literacy tests and poll taxes, which prevented them from exercising this right. (African Americans were denied access to education and so could not pass a literacy test; they were also too poor to pay a poll tax.)

In the late 19th century, the southern states instituted a system of racial segregation known as the **Jim Crow laws**. These laws required blacks and whites to be segregated on the basis of race in all venues of daily life—at school, at drinking fountains, in restaurants, restrooms, taxis, telephone booths, movie theatres, hotels, ambulances, and in cemeteries. Although Jim Crow laws were entrenched in the US South, pro-segregation attitudes were not limited to any region of the country. The 1896 Supreme Court ruling in *Plessy v. Ferguson* addressed segregation on railway cars and concluded that "separate but equal" facilities were constitutional. Although facilities for African Americans were usually substandard, the Supreme Court's decision was widely interpreted as sanctioning segregation of the races.

By the mid-1950s, large numbers of African Americans had migrated to northern American cities and were enjoying many of the benefits of urbanization, including better social and communications networks. By this time, the National Association for the Advancement of Colored People (NAACP) was working to end segregation on buses and trains.

In 1954, the NAACP gained its greatest victory when the Supreme Court overturned *Plessy v. Ferguson* with its ruling in *Brown v. Board of Education.* The *Brown* ruling declared that a separate public school system based on race was unconstitutional and that it should be ended with "all deliberate speed." (See Chapter 6.)

The US civil rights movement used various tactics to achieve its political ends. By 1955, Martin Luther King, Jr., a Baptist preacher, had emerged as a civil rights leader in Alabama; King helped organize a year-long boycott of segregated buses in the state capital, Montgomery. In 1960, African American students started sit-ins at lunch counters in Greensboro, North Carolina. The students, trained in the techniques of non-violent protest, were usually arrested, which only helped draw sympathy to their cause, especially outside the South. Highly publicized marches also attracted national and international attention to the movement.

The historic 1963 March on Washington is today remembered in the oratory of King's "I have a dream" speech, and the 1965 protest march from Selma, Alabama to Montgomery attracted media attention and public sympathy when police brutally attacked the marchers.

THE WEB

To hear Martin Luther King's speech of August 28, 1963 in its entirety, go to www. emp.ca/cwp.

The media played a major role in the success of the American civil rights movement. In a number of highly publicized confrontations, the white segregationists seemed brutish and inhuman compared to the dignified African American protestors. In his campaign to desegregate Birmingham, Alabama, in 1963, King rallied school children and led them in song; the opposition used fire hoses and police dogs. The more the segregationists protested, the more public support for the civil rights movement grew.

Around this time, there emerged some differences over the ideal forms of protest within the black community. Some leaders, such as Stokely Carmichael (1941–98) of the Student Nonviolent Coordinating Committee (SNCC), advocated a more aggressive approach toward the government and introduced the slogan "Black Power." Others, such as Malcolm X (1925–65), displayed a distrust of white support and even preached, for a time, separation of the races.

Figure 7.9 Dr. Carrie Best (right), seen here with Ontario Lieutenant Governor Lincoln Alexander in 1988, was a Canadian civil rights activist who founded her own newspaper, *The Clarion*, in 1946 to protest the poor treatment of black Canadians in Nova Scotia. Ten years before the Montgomery bus boycott, Best publicized the story of Viola Desmond, who had been arrested in a Nova Scotia theatre for sitting in the white section. Best's editorials are credited with moving the whole country toward intolerance of racism. She received the Order of Canada in 1979.

Despite such fissures in the drive for equal rights, the weight of public opinion finally forced the US federal government to act. Congress passed the *Civil Rights Act* in 1964, which prohibited discrimination in public facilities, government, and employment. Segregation became illegal in schools, housing, or hiring. The *Voting Rights Act* of the following year suspended the use of literacy tests and provided federal assistance to African Americans who encountered difficulties when registering to vote.

The civil rights movement did not end discrimination. Nor did it translate into equal opportunities for African Americans in the social and economic spheres. By the end of the 20th century, a disproportionate number of blacks still suffered from unemployment and poverty. Infant mortality rates and imprisonment rates were significantly higher for African Americans than for the population as a whole. Although a large black middle class had developed, many members of the black community remained trapped in poverty.

However, the US civil rights movement did show that non-violent protest and direct political action could bring about significant reforms. The movement made social protest respectable and inspired other oppressed groups—women, Aboriginal peoples, the physically challenged, cultural and linguistic minorities, and gay men and lesbians—both in the United States and abroad to begin their quests for equity.

Educational Attainment by Race (percent of population ages 25 older, by years)

Year	White Achievement			African American Achievement		
------	Fewer than 5 years of elementary school	High school completion or higher	4 or more years of college	Fewer than 5 years of elementary school	High school completion or higher	4 or more years of college
1940	10.9	26.1	4.9	41.8	7.7	1.3
1950	8.9	36.4	6.6	32.6	13.7	2.2
1960	6.7	43.2	8.1	23.5	21.7	3.5
1970	4.2	57.4	11.6	14.7	36.1	6.1
1980	1.9	71.9	18.4	9.1	51.4	7.9
1990	1.1	81.4	23.1	5.1	66.2	11.3
2000	0.5	88.4	28.1	1.6	78.9	16.6
2001	0.5	88.7	28.6	1.3	79.5	16.1

Source: US Department of Commerce, Bureau of the Census, US Census of population, 1960, Vol. 1, part 1; *Current Population Reports*, Series P-20 and unpublished data; and *1960 Census Monograph*, "Education of the American Population," by John K. Folger and Charles B. Nam. From US Department of Education, National Center for Education Statistics, *Digest of Education Statistics 2002*.

Figure 7.10 Closing the education gap: By 2001, 79.5 percent of African Americans had completed high school compared to 88.7 percent of whites. Twenty years earlier, barely half the African American population had completed high school. In 1940, a staggering 41.8 percent of African Americans had fewer than five years of elementary education.

Taking a Stand   Rosa Parks

In examining the lives of political activists, we often find that one person can make a tremendous difference. Such was the case with Rosa Parks (1913–).

On December 1, 1955, Rosa Parks worked as a seamstress for the Montgomery Fair department store. That night after work, she boarded the Cleveland Avenue bus and took a seat in the fifth row—the first row of the "colored section." At the time, buses in Montgomery had two sections—white and "colored." African Americans could sit only in the colored section, and could be ordered to give up a seat to a white person.

When the bus driver ordered Parks to give her seat to a white man, she said no. She said that it wasn't because she was physically tired, rather she was tired of the mistreatment that African Americans endured daily. In her book, *Quiet Strength*, Parks wrote:

> I kept thinking about my mother and my grandparents and how strong they were. I knew there was a possibility of being mistreated, but an opportunity was being given to me to do what I had asked of others.

She was arrested when the bus driver called the police and filed charges against her. Rosa was fingerprinted and held in custody until she was bailed out. That evening at a midnight meeting of the Women's Political Council, 35,000 handbills were printed. The message was simple:

> We . . . are asking every Negro to stay off the buses Monday in protest of the arrest and trial. . . . You can afford to stay out for school for one day. If you work, take a cab, or walk. But please, children, and grown-ups, don't ride the bus at all on Monday. Please stay off the buses Monday.

On that Monday, Parks was found guilty of disorderly conduct and fined. That evening, at a meeting held at the Holt Street Baptist Church, protestors decided to continue the bus boycott. A new committee was struck—the Montgomery Improvement Association—and Dr. Martin Luther King, Jr. was selected as its leader.

The bus boycott was a great success. Almost every African American who had used the bus service found another form of transportation. The bus company lost revenue but the laws did not change. The boycott lasted 381 days and attracted international attention for Parks, King, and their cause. On November 13, 1956, the Supreme Court ruled against the Montgomery ordinance that caused Parks's arrest. As a result of the ruling, racial segregation on public transportation in the city and throughout the US South was outlawed. It was a major victory for the civil rights movement.

Rosa Parks's simple refusal to give up her seat had an enormous impact. Her own lawyer, Fred Gray, said her decision "created an ever widening ripple of change throughout the world. The quiet exemplification of courage, dignity and determination mobilized people of various philosophies." Historian Gwendolyn Patton viewed Rosa Parks's refusal as "the straw that broke the camel's back. And the movement that ensued, the Montgomery bus boycott movement and the people, were the straws that finally broke the back of Jim Crow."

As a result of her decision on that day in December, Rosa Parks lost her job as a seamstress and her family was threatened and harassed. Her husband suffered a nervous breakdown. Finally, after 11 years, the Parkses left Montgomery and moved to Detroit, Michigan, where they continued to fight for civil rights. At the time this textbook was written, Rosa Parks lived there still.

Questions

1. Why is Rosa Parks a good example of the power one individual may have to bring about change?
2. What issues might force you, as an individual, to become an activist?
3. Research the lives of other activists who used the "power of one" to change society. Write a brief essay about the contributions of one individual of your choice.

The Rights of Indigenous Peoples

Indigenous peoples are those who originally occupied land settled at a later date by other occupants, often European colonizers, who fanned out across the globe beginning in the 15th century. There are indigenous peoples in virtually all parts of the world, including the Americas, Australia and New Zealand, northern Europe, and Japan. Most indigenous peoples claim a distinct identity and have preserved social, cultural, and political characteristics that distinguish them from the later occupants of the region.

Social movements led by indigenous peoples began in the 1960s and 1970s as part of a global movement to secure social justice and human rights for oppressed groups, including African Americans, women, and gay men and lesbians. Although indigenous peoples do not subscribe to the same human rights model as other contemporary social movements (see Chapter 4 for a discussion of Aboriginal nationalism), they have organized and promoted their interests in recognizable ways.

Aboriginal Peoples in Canada

Aboriginal peoples in Canada could not organize to protest their loss of land, culture, and identity until the latter half of the 20th century. Before then, the federal government had banned them from forming political organizations.

In 1968, the National Indian Brotherhood was formed from the ashes of an earlier group and immediately claimed the spotlight by clashing with the

Trudeau government over its White Paper (discussion paper) on the ***Indian Act, 1876***. Trudeau, a firm supporter of individual rights and freedoms, proposed to make all First Nations, Inuit, and Métis people equal in law to every other Canadian citizen, but with no special rights and privileges. Sensing an attack on their **collective rights**, Aboriginal opposition to the White Paper was almost unanimous. Aboriginal leaders such as Cree leader Harold Cardinal (1945–) began to articulate Aboriginal rights to self-determination and self-government to an increasingly sympathetic public.

As a result of Aboriginal political perseverance, existing Aboriginal and treaty rights were finally recognized in the *Canadian Charter of Rights and Freedoms* in 1982 and the *Constitution Act, 1982*. Section 25 of the Charter observes that other rights in the Charter cannot interfere with the rights of Aboriginal peoples. These rights include hunting, fishing, and taxation rights that are not possessed by other groups. Section 35 of the *Constitution Act, 1982* recognizes existing Aboriginal and treaty rights. Of critical importance is the issue of **Aboriginal title** to the land, which has resulted in the negotiation of many land claims. In 1999, Nunavut Territory became the largest land claim in Canadian history, based on Inuit title to land in the Northwest Territories (see Chapter 4).

In the last two decades of the 20th century, some Aboriginal leaders focused on the past injustices committed against their communities, especially the issue of residential schools. Since the 1880s, the Canadian government had promoted a policy of assimilating Aboriginal peoples into Canadian society. The campaign focused on the young, uprooting children as young as six years of age from their families and homes for 10 months of the year. Children were sent to often-distant residential schools, where they were taught British culture and the Christian faith. They were forbidden to speak their own languages, and their traditions were rigorously suppressed. Many children were abused at the hands of school staff.

By the early 1990s, thousands of former students had sued the federal government for abuses at residential school facilities. The Anglican, Roman Catholic, United, and Presbyterian churches were also sued. The vast majority of cases claimed cultural and language loss, and many also involved

Figure 7.11 Jeannette Corbière Lavell (left), shown with her husband David, challenged a section of the *Indian Act* that revoked the Indian status of Aboriginal women who married non-Indians. (This provision did not apply to men.) The Act was amended in 1985 to end this discrimination.

THE WEB

For more about the residential school system, go to www.emp.ca/cwp.

SOUND BITE "Indigenous children have the right to all levels and forms of education of the State. All indigenous peoples also have this right and the right to establish and control their educational systems and institutions providing education in their own languages, in a manner appropriate to their cultural methods of teaching and learning."

Draft United Nations Declaration on the Rights of Indigenous Peoples, Part IV, Article 15

allegations of physical and sexual abuse. In 1998, the federal government initiated a policy called "Gathering Strength." Among other goals, it outlined a strategy to address the legacy of residential schools through such mechanisms as public apology, community healing initiatives, and dispute resolution. The government also offered a system for reaching out-of-court settlements with more than 12,000 former students whose human rights had been violated in the church-run schools. The federal government's plan was to resolve most of the cases in a seven-year period. Ottawa pledged to cover 70 percent of the cost of damages, while the churches agreed to pay the remaining 30 percent.

American Indian Movement (AIM)

During the tumult of the US civil rights movement, the American Indian Movement (AIM) was created in 1968. Aware of the benefits of publicity, AIM occupied the former prison of Alcatraz Island, off the coast of San Francisco, that same year. The group claimed the island on which the prison stood under a treaty that recognized the Aboriginal right to use federal territory that the US government was not using. The 19-month occupation gave AIM a high profile and a public forum in which to air grievances about treaty rights and the generally poor living conditions on reservations (called reserves in Canada). AIM also initiated the first American Indian radio broadcast—Radio Free Alcatraz—which could be heard in the San Francisco Bay area.

In 1973, AIM selected Wounded Knee, South Dakota—where the United States Cavalry had massacred over 300 men, women, and children in 1890—as its next protest site. It occupied the nearby Pine Ridge Reservation and began a 71-day standoff with federal authorities. This time, AIM protestors demonstrated against what they saw as collusion between some tribal leaders and the US government. AIM supporters wanted the US government to acknowledge an 1868 treaty with the Sioux Indians and immediately stop development of the region. At the time, extensive strip mining was already under way, and the Black Hills—sacred land to the Sioux—were about to be sold to the government.

Figure 7.12 AIM often protests the use of Native American names in sport. It has worked to banish stereotypical images and names such as Cleveland's Indians, Washington's Redskins, Kansas City's Chiefs, and Atlanta's Braves. Here, film legend Bob Hope is shown wearing an Indians shirt in 1937.

During the protests, two people were killed and several wounded. In a later shootout at Pine Ridge in 1975, one AIM member and two US Federal Bureau of Investigations (FBI) agents were killed. One Native American activist, Leonard Peltier, fled to Canada after his friends were tried for the killings of the FBI agents. Peltier was extradited back to the United States to stand trial. His two associates were acquitted, but in 1976 Peltier was found guilty of murder and sentenced to two life terms in prison. Many argue that Peltier is not guilty and was the victim of an unfair trial. He has become the centre of an international crusade to gain his freedom.

In the decades since its founding, AIM has monitored police activities and coordinated employment programs in cities and in rural reservation communities across the United States. It has worked to disseminate information about indigenous peoples' human rights issues and concerns inside and outside the country. AIM has also sought international recognition for treaties and agreements between indigenous peoples and nation-states.

THE WEB

To learn more about AIM, Leonard Peltier, and other Wounded Knee activists, visit www.emp.ca/cwp.

Indigenous People in Australia

The story of Australia's indigenous people mirrors the treatment of Aboriginal peoples in other parts of the world. The ancestors of Australia's indigenous people probably arrived in Australia 30,000 years ago. At the time of first contact with the European colonists in the late 18th century, most Australian Aboriginals (singular, **Aborigine**) were hunter–gatherers with a complex oral culture and spirituality based upon reverence for the land and a belief in the "Dreamtime." The Dreamtime is a spiritual realm that explains the creation and the sacredness of the Earth. The Australian Aboriginal population was decimated by British colonization. Disease and loss of land reduced their numbers by an estimated 90 percent during the 18th and 19th centuries.

Australian Aboriginals endured centuries of assaults on their human rights. On large sheep and cattle ranches in the outback, some suffered conditions akin to slavery. Often wages were less than half of those paid to European workers. In the first 75 years of the 20th century, the Australian government and churches also removed Aboriginal children from their families. These children are known as the "stolen generation." At least 30,000 young children were taken from parents—often through intimidation or deception—in order to assimilate them into Australian society. Mixed-race children were

Figure 7.13 Australian Aboriginals protest the bicentennial of Australia in 1988. The history of the "stolen generation" prevented many from taking part in or celebrating the event.

Figure 7.14 Cathy Freeman waves the Aboriginal and Australian flags after winning the 400-metre event at Sydney's 2000 Olympic Games. In interviews broadcast worldwide, she spoke movingly of her grandmother, a member of the "stolen generation."

PRESS PLAY

The 2002 film *Rabbit-Proof Fence*, directed by Phillip Noyce and featuring Kenneth Branagh, explores the treatment of Aboriginal people in Australia. The movie tells the story of three half-caste Aboriginal girls who run away from a training centre where they were placed as part of a government program to give them a "better life." (PG)

also targeted. A 1997 inquiry into the treatment of Australian Aboriginal children called for a government apology. The newly elected conservative government of John Howard rejected the recommendation but later bowed to public pressure and expressed "sincere regret" over this violation of human rights.

Civil rights protest movements in the 1970s led the Australian government in 1976 and 1993 to enact land-rights legislation that has returned a degree of autonomy to its Aboriginal people. Court decisions in 1990s further recognized Aboriginal property rights. Aboriginal groups also brought attention to the issue of discrimination by establishing a large tent city near the site of the Sydney 2000 Summer Olympics.

Women's Rights

As you read in Chapter 2, feminism is the political ideology that advocates social, legal, and political equality for women. The feminist movement to end discrimination against women began in the early 20th century. By the time the century was over, many barriers to women's equality had been lifted, but there was still much to be achieved. Women are still under-represented in all of the world's legislative bodies. In the United States, for example, only 11 percent of elected representatives are women. Women also comprise most of the world's poor and illiterate. Worldwide, women earn 30 to 40 percent less than men for doing equal work.

However, women are much more a part of the system they are trying to change than they were 50 years ago. Like other enduring social movements, the women's movement has become a powerful lobby group. Today, it works with governments and the United Nations to address human rights abuses affecting women nationally and internationally.

Ranking	Country	Proportion of women in the lower house (%)
1	Rwanda	48.8
2	Sweden	45.3
3	Denmark	38.0
4	Finland	37.5
5	Netherlands	36.7
6	Norway	36.4
7	Cuba	36.0
7	Spain	36.0
8	Belgium	35.3
9	Costa Rica	35.1
10	Argentina	34.0

Source: Inter-Parliamentary Union, http://www.ipu.org/wmn-e/classif.htm.

Figure 7.15 Top democracies ranking highest for women's representation in national parliaments, lower house, August 2004. Canada ranked 33, the United Kingdom 48, and the United States 54.

Some of these human rights violations include trafficking in persons, sexual assault during armed conflict, female infanticide, genital mutilation, and "honour" killing (murder of a woman by her family because of a perceived indiscretion). As a result of intervention by groups such as the National Organization for Women and the Women's Human Rights Network, the United Nations has asked governments to address many of these abuses, even though they are difficult to curtail because of ingrained cultural beliefs.

As a result of women's lobbying efforts, the United Nations has adopted many resolutions and conventions related to the human rights of women. In support of the 1948 *Universal Declaration of Human Rights*, the 1993 World Conference on Human Rights in Vienna adopted the slogan, "Women's Rights are Human Rights." The international body has stressed that equality means more than treating all persons in the same way. Equal treatment of persons in unequal situations perpetuates rather than eradicates injustice. True equality can result only from efforts directed toward correcting the situational imbalances in which women find themselves. The 1995 United Nations Fourth World Conference on Women held in Beijing, China affirmed the right of all women to control all aspects of their health, in particular their fertility.

Women's Rights in Canada

In 1967, Prime Minister Lester Pearson created the Royal Commission on the Status of Women. Its mandate was to inquire into the status of women

THE WEB

For more about the Royal Commission on the Status of Women, visit www.emp.ca/cwp.

Figure 7.16 Judy LaMarsh (1924–80), lawyer, broadcaster, and Liberal cabinet member under Lester Pearson. As Pearson's Secretary of State, she established the Royal Commission on the Status of Women. Here she autographs copies of her 1978 novel, *A Very Political Lady*.

SOUND BITE "Nothing was so hard to accomplish during all the time I was in Cabinet as the appointment of a Royal Commission into the Status of Women. . . . When I mentioned [it], there was an immediate and scathing reaction from some of the responsible press of the country. Pearson backed off as if stung by a nettle."

Judy LaMarsh, Memoirs of a Bird in a Gilded Cage, *1968*

in Canada and to recommend the steps that might be taken by the federal government to guarantee women equal opportunities with men in all aspects of Canadian society. The Commission listened to women's voices across the country and concluded that there should be equality in practice as well as in principle, and equality of opportunity for all. Among the more specific principles addressed were

• child care, to be shared between mothers, fathers, and society
• respect for mothers and the period of maternity
• initiatives to help women overcome some discriminatory practices in employment.

At the time of the Commission's work, women lived in a very different world from today's. Many still called themselves by their husband's names, including some members of the Commission, such as "Mrs. John Bird" and "Mrs. Otto Lang." Some provinces had a minimum wage for women and another for men, based on the notion that a woman's income was only a supplement to that of the main breadwinner. Many newspapers ran separate Help Wanted columns for men and women. In the event of a marriage breakup, a homemaker wife was not entitled to an equal portion of assets acquired during the marriage. Birth control and therapeutic abortions were difficult to obtain. In full-time work, a woman earned 58 cents for every dollar earned by a man. Working women did not receive unemployment benefits for maternity absences and had no guarantees of employment after the birth of a child. Improvements in women's rights and conditions have taken place since 1967, but much work remains, particularly in the areas of female poverty and the under-representation of women in political decision making.

The National Action Committee on the Status of Women (NAC) was founded in 1973, partially as a response to the Royal Commission on the Status of Women. The NAC began life as a national organization with a grant of $15,000 from the Liberal government of Pierre Trudeau. Among other issues, the NAC helped to agitate for the rights of Aboriginal women, the decriminalization of abortion, and state-supported child care. The NAC has worked with feminists across Canada to deal with issues related to violence against women. It argued for the inclusion of sexual equality guarantees in the *Canadian Charter of Rights and Freedoms* in 1982, and later worked to have sexual orientation **read into** the Charter as a prohibited ground for discrimination. The organization has supported sexual assault centres and shelters for battered women. After the slaying of 14 young women in Montreal on December 6, 1989, the NAC campaigned with other groups to have the date commemorated as Women's Remembrance Day in memory of the victims of violence against women.

In the last decade of the 20th century, the NAC suffered from severe cutbacks in government funding. As a result, many of the organization's goals were placed on hold. Canadian women still earn, on average, only 73 cents for every dollar earned by men. Poverty often afflicts women aged 65 and older, and violence against women continues.

Lesbian and Gay Rights

The contemporary social movement to end discrimination against gay men and lesbians began with decriminalizing homosexual sex. In 1957, in Britain, the *Report of the Departmental Committee on Homosexual Offences and Prostitution* recommended that gay sex between consenting adults (males) be legalized. Up to that time, homosexual acts were punishable in Britain by a lengthy prison sentence. The Wolfenden Report, as it came to be known, eventually paved the way for the British *Sexual Offences Act*, passed in 1967. It legalized sex between two consenting males, provided both were over the age of 21. This legislation is considered a turning point for the legalization of homosexuality in Western nations. In 1967, then Justice Minister Pierre Trudeau moved to decriminalize homosexual acts in Canada as part of his omnibus bill (one containing several proposed laws) that also liberalized laws on abortion and divorce. The omnibus bill became law in 1969.

The gay rights movement was also a grassroots phenomenon. Small demonstrations were held in Canada and the United States as early as the late 1950s and early 1960s. Then, on June 27, 1969, New York police raided a gay bar, the Stonewall Inn, on the pretext of rounding up the "disorderly" patrons. Such raids were routine for the period, and Stonewall patrons had been harassed many times. This time, they fought back, throwing pennies, bricks, and bottles at police officers. The struggle turned into a riot, and for three days other members of the gay community of Greenwich Village joined in the demonstration against the police. It was the first time that gay men and lesbians had organized a formal protest against police action in New York City on such a scale—and it made headlines around the world. "Stonewall" marked the beginning of the gay rights movement in the United States and other countries.

One immediate consequence of the Stonewall riots was the growth of gay rights organizations and demonstrations. The first large gay rights march in the United States—modelled on the 1963 civil rights March on Washington—took place on October 14, 1979, in Washington, DC, and included about 100,000 participants. Today, in major cities around the world, Gay Pride days are held in June to commemorate the Stonewall riots.

In the United States, several gay rights groups predated Stonewall. Some groups had formed in response to President Eisenhower's banning of homosexuals from all federal jobs. Following Stonewall, the gay rights movement

SOUND BITE "There's no place for the state in the bedrooms of the nation. . . . What's done in private between adults doesn't concern the *Criminal Code.*"

Justice Minister Pierre Trudeau, CBC interview, December 21, 1967

THE WEB

To hear more about the passage of Trudeau's omnibus bill, visit www.emp.ca/cwp.

PRESS PLAY

In *Victim*, a British film made in 1961, directed by Basil Deardon and starring Dirk Bogarde and Sylvia Simms, a gay lawyer is blackmailed and his career ruined, but he successfully exposes his blackmailers and brings them to justice. Reputed to be the first film to use the word *homosexual*. (NR)

in North America became much more visible. US groups pushed for decriminalization of homosexual acts at the federal and state levels, while Canadian groups focused on liberation politics and human rights in employment, housing, and so on. Several groups launched publications and small presses, most prominently Toronto's Pink Triangle Press, which published the often-controversial gay liberation periodical, *The Body Politic*, from 1971 to 1987. Police raided Pink Triangle's offices several times in the 1980s. The Press now publishes *Xtra!* tabloids in Toronto, Ottawa, and Vancouver.

Lesbian and Gay Rights and AIDS

THE WEB

Learn more about the treatment of homosexuals in Nazi Germany at www.emp.ca/cwp.

By the late 1980s, the AIDS epidemic was inflicting terrible human losses and major setbacks in the struggle for lesbian and gay equality. AIDS, or acquired immune deficiency syndrome, is caused by the human immunodeficiency virus (HIV), which attacks the body's immune system. AIDS is the final stage of the HIV disease, which is transmitted in body fluids such as blood, semen, vaginal secretions, and breast milk. When AIDS was first identified, the media labelled it a "gay disease" because a disproportionate number of gay men were first diagnosed with it. Some extremists called AIDS God's punishment. Many gay men and lesbians felt attacked not only by the AIDS virus, but by homophobic (anti-gay) public responses, and by governments that remained silent on AIDS. The silence itself became a political issue. AIDS marches, demonstrations, and actions gained wide public and media attention.

During the AIDS epidemic in the late 1980s, six gay activists in New York created a "Silence = Death" poster (Figure 7.17) employing the pink triangle. In Nazi Germany, homosexuals were rounded up as "socially aberrant" and sent to concentration camps, where they were forced to wear inverted pink triangles as identification.

In the United States, activists succeeded in gaining federal civil rights protection for people with HIV/AIDS under the *Americans with Disabilities Act*, and funding for HIV/AIDS treatment through the *Ryan White CARE Act*, a federal program designed to improve the quality and availability of care for people with HIV/AIDS and their families. Ryan White was a heterosexual white teenager in Indiana who became infected with HIV from blood transfusions, which were part of his treatment for hemophilia. White was expelled from school on the ground that he was a health risk to other students—a claim that had no scientific basis. The case became a media flashpoint in the United States. Before he died at age 19, White worked to inform people about the nature of HIV.

Figure 7.17 The slogan "Silence = Death" protested the taboo against providing information about safe sex and the oppression through silence of homosexuals in the age of AIDS.

In the last decades of the 20th century, the North American gay rights movement continued to fight for equality by seeking legal recognition of gay relationships. By 1992, the Canadian government removed the ban prohibiting gay men and lesbians from serving in the military—knowing the policy of exclusion violated the *Canadian Charter of Rights and Freedoms*. A year later, the administration of US President Bill Clinton had to compromise on the issue. The US military adopted a "Don't Ask, Don't Tell" policy. This allows homosexuals to serve in the military as long as they do not disclose their sexual orientation.

In Canada, a series of Supreme Court rulings has recognized Charter equality rights for gay men and lesbians. In *Egan v. Canada* (1995), the court declared sexual orientation an illegal ground for discrimination under section 15(1) of the Charter. In the case of *M v. H* (1999), the court ruled that under Ontario's *Family Law Act*, same-sex couples should have the same rights as heterosexual couples who qualify for support payments when common-law relationships dissolve. The court signalled that other provincial statutes that discriminate against lesbians and gay men—in such areas as pensions and employment benefits, for example—should also be changed. By November 2004, six Canadian provinces and a territory joined jurisdictions in Belgium and the Netherlands in extending to gay couples the right to full civil marriage.

— Law in Motion

Legalization of Same-Sex Marriage in Canada

On June 10, 2003, just hours after the Ontario Court of Appeal rewrote the definition of marriage to include same-sex couples, Crown attorney Michael Leshner and his long-time partner Michael Stark were married by Mr. Justice John Hamilton. After the ceremony, Leshner told reporters that he viewed the court's decision as "Day One for millions of gays and lesbians around the world." It was also the culmination of a personal 20-year fight to end what Leshner called "legally sanctioned homophobia."

The Ontario Court of Appeal affirmed a lower court ruling and ordered the Province of Ontario to register the two marriage certificates issued to Elaine and Anne Vautour and to Kevin Bourassa and Joe Varnell. These couples were the plaintiffs (the parties suing) in the case. They had been married in January 2001 in a double ceremony at Toronto's Metropolitan Community Church.

In their unanimous decision, Chief Justice Roy McMurtry and justices James MacPherson and Eileen Gillese wrote the following:

A person's sense of dignity and self worth can only be enhanced by the recognition that society gives to marriage and denying people in same-sex relationships access to that most basic of institution violates their dignity.

The ability to marry, and to thereby participate in this fundamental societal institution, is something that most Canadians take for granted. Same-sex couples do not; they are denied access to this institution simply on the basis of their sexual orientation.

Preventing same-sex couples from marrying perpetuates the view that they are not capable of forming loving and lasting relationships and not worthy of the same respect and recognition as heterosexual couples.

In 2003 and 2004, courts in British Columbia and Quebec made similar decisions. Canada's three largest provinces now recognized same-sex marriage. Because it filed no appeals, the federal government drafted legislation to change the definition of marriage. In July 2003, however, it referred the issue to the Supreme Court of Canada for an opinion as to (1) whether Parliament has the authority to pass such legislation, (2) whether a new form of civil union—conferring the same benefits, protections, and responsibilities as marriage, but without the title—would meet Charter requirements, and (3) whether the Charter would protect churches if they refused to perform same-sex marriages on religious grounds.

In 2004, the government asked the court to consider a fourth question: whether current common law and civil law opposite-sex requirements for marriage are constitutional and, if not, why not. By November 2004, Manitoba, Nova Scotia, Saskatchewan, and Yukon courts had also ruled that same-sex marriage is legal. In December 2004, the Supreme Court answered the first three questions in the affirmative, and declined to answer the fourth. On the fourth question, the court said an answer would "serve no purpose" in light of the government's announced intention to introduce legislation to legalize same-sex marriage.

Questions

1. What did Michael Leshner mean by the phrase "legally sanctioned homophobia"?
2. Why is the issue of gay marriages such an emotional one?
3. What do you believe the law should say about same-sex marriages? Explain your position.

Figure 7.18 Michael Leshner (left) and Michael Stark (centre) sign their marriage licence after being married by Superior Court Justice John Hamilton (right) in Toronto on June 10, 2003.

Children's Rights

Can children's rights be considered a "social movement"? Historically, children's rights have been promoted by other groups. During the 19th century Industrial Revolution, when children were used as cheap labour in mines, mills, and factories, social reformers urged for child-protection legislation. In Canada, in the early 20th century, women's rights groups often focused on the needs of both women and children.

The 1959 Declaration on the Rights of the Child was the first United Nations statement devoted exclusively to the rights of children, but it was more a statement of morality than a legally binding convention. Nonetheless, the *United Nations Convention on the Rights of the Child*, adopted by the General Assembly in 1989, has become the most widely ratified treaty in the world. By 2004, only two nations had not yet ratified it—the United States and Somalia. The *Convention on the Rights of the Child* defines as children all people under the age of 18, unless the relevant national laws recognize an earlier age of majority. Its 54 articles are based on a "universally agreed set of non-negotiable standards and obligations" to which signatories are accountable. The individual articles spell out the human rights of children around the world. (See Chapter 8 for details on the *Convention on the Rights of the Child*.)

THE WEB

For more on the *Convention on the Rights of the Child* and UNICEF, go to www.emp.ca/cwp.

The Convention is important for a number of reasons. First, it is a legally binding document. Second, children are seldom able to speak for themselves, and are less likely than adults to form their own organizations to protect their rights. Nevertheless, because they have not yet developed intellectually or physically, children are vulnerable to human rights violations in many parts of the world. They are used as soldiers, coerced into prostitution, and forced into jobs when they should be attending school. They are often mistreated by employers and by the staff of correctional institutions and orphanages. Even in Canada, children suffer human rights abuses. They make up a disproportionately large number of the poor, and are affected by poverty at critical stages in their development. Despite being a wealthy country, Canada has not met all the standards of the *United Nations Convention on the Rights of the Child*.

In recent years, children's rights has become more of a genuine social movement—one directed by children for children. Children are now regularly invited to address the United Nations General Assembly and the Security Council directly about children's issues. The UN also holds special sessions on children attended by hundreds of child delegates from around the world. At these sessions, children make formal presentations and confer with heads of state

Figure 7.19 Gabriela Azurduy Arrieta, 13, a delegate to the Children's Forum of the UN Special Session on Children, addresses the UN General Assembly in 2002.

or other representatives of governments on such issues as child labour, child poverty, domestic violence, children with disabilities, and the sex trade. The UNICEF (United Nations Children's Fund) Web site for children declares unequivocally: "More adults are beginning to listen to young people rather than just deciding what's good for them." How far will children be able to go in shaping their own social movement? Children are typically considered powerless, but these developments in children's rights suggest that even the very young can hold governments accountable to agreed-on principles.

Both interest groups and social movements undertake some kind of political action to advance their cause. While interest groups work within the political system to promote their agenda and influence government policy, social movements—consisting of informal networks of people with shared identity and values—call attention to the ways in which government has ignored or oppressed them. Both play a key role in maintaining the vitality of contemporary democracies, and sometimes in moving non-democratic states toward a more democratic, rights-oriented model.

Check YOUR UNDERSTANDING

1. Why has there been increased emphasis on the concept of human rights in democratic societies?
2. Identify the tactics used by the American civil rights movement that you believe were the most effective in overthrowing the Jim Crow laws.
3. How effective has the American Indian Movement (AIM) been in furthering the human rights of Aboriginal peoples?
4. Why did the federal government initiate an Aboriginal policy called Gathering Strength?
5. How has the Charter ensured the protection of Aboriginal rights and freedoms in Canada?
6. From an international perspective, assess the status of women.
7. How were the 1957 Wolfenden Report and the Stonewall riots turning points in the struggle for homosexual equality?
8. How have children's rights been abused internationally? What steps have been taken by the international community to address the violation of children's rights?

CAREERS

Harvey Cashore, Television Journalist

Harvey Cashore is a broadcast journalist with CBC television. His recent credits include Senior Editor of *Disclosure*, an investigative news program that ran until April 2004. Cashore has produced dozens of documentaries including "The Scandal of the Century" (for CBC's *the fifth estate*) about false accusations of sexual abuse in Saskatchewan. In May 2004, he was honoured with the prestigious Canadian Association of Journalists (CAJ) award for best overall investigative journalism.

Q: When did you first become a "political animal"?

A: At about age two! My Dad was very active in provincial NDP politics. In our house, politics were always important; ideas were important. We were raised with the belief that individuals could make a difference.

Q: What early experiences helped steer you in the direction of journalism?

A: Well, I started a student paper in grade seven, and went from there. In high school, my brother was the prime minister of the student association and I was the editor of the school paper. That paper—*The Catalyst*—won some awards in my grade 12 year. Our faculty advisor, Frank Shepherd, was very influential—a number of students who worked with me at that time went on to become successful journalists. That work taught me that you can be active politically not only by working for a specific political party, but alternatively, by monitoring the political process as an observer. I learned that there are a lot of things going on in politics that policy makers don't want us to know about. I began to understand my responsibility, as a journalist, to understand politics from that perspective; because the public has a right to know what's going on.

Q: What makes your work rewarding?

A: Without a doubt, effecting change. Not that journalists should have a particular goal in mind when exposing a story; but when you uncover an injustice and someone is forced to remedy it, that's extremely rewarding.

Q: What's your greatest challenge?

A: Making sure that the facts I have are facts. Journalists have tremendous power to affect public opinion. Their work can do great good, but there is also the power to do harm to innocent people if you don't have your facts straight.

Q: What would you tell a student aspiring to a career in investigative journalism?

A: That it's hard work! If you have an unanswered question, you're on the right track. You have to work to uncover the information you need without losing sight of your right to know, and your responsibility to the public. For an investigative journalist, dead ends are the *beginning* of the road.

Questions

1. How does Harvey Cashore see his work as benefiting (a) himself, (b) the public, and (c) the political process?
2. Cashore never trusts his hunches. He uses them to ask more and better questions. Learn more about how investigative journalists work by visiting www.emp.ca/cwp or by conducting research at the library. From your research, list at least five techniques of investigative journalism that you can apply in analyzing political issues.
3. Do you agree that a journalist should not have "a particular goal" when writing a story? Explain.

Point:
Counterpoint → Are Citizens Morally Obliged to Break "Bad" Laws?

What would you do if your government passed a law that you strongly believed was wrong? Would you have the right to break the law? What should be the consequences of your actions? The opinions below are separated by time as well as by ideology—they were written 2,000 years apart.

"No" to Breaking a Bad Law

Plato, *Crito* (translated by Benjamin Jowett)

Plato's Crito *is a dialogue between Plato's teacher Socrates and his friend Crito. Socrates has been convicted of encouraging his students to challenge the government and has been sentenced to die. In Plato's dialogue, Crito tries to convince Socrates to leave before his death sentence is carried out. Socrates offers his reasons why he refuses to leave.*

Socrates: Then will they [the laws] not say: "You, Socrates, are breaking the covenants and agreements which you made with us at your leisure, not in any haste or under any compulsion or deception, but having had seventy years to think of them, during which time you were at liberty to leave the city, if we were not to your mind, or if our covenants appeared to you to be unfair. You had your choice, and might have gone either to Lacedaemon or Crete, which you often praise for their good government, or to some other Hellenic or foreign State. Whereas you, above all other Athenians, seemed to be so fond of the State, or, in other words, of us her laws (for who would like a State that has no laws), that you never stirred out of her: the halt, the blind, the maimed, were not more stationary in her than you were. And now you run away and forsake your agreements. Not so, Socrates, if you will take our advice; do not make yourself ridiculous by escaping out of the city. . . .

"For he who is a corrupter of the laws is more than likely to be corrupter of the young and foolish portion of mankind. Will you then flee from well-ordered cities and virtuous men? and is existence worth having on these terms? Or will you go to them without shame, and talk to them, Socrates? And what will you say to them? What you say here about virtue and justice and institutions and laws being the best things among men? Would that be decent of you? Surely not. . . .

"Listen, then, Socrates, to us who have brought you up. Think not of life and children first, and of justice afterwards, but of justice first, that you may be justified before the princes of the world below. For neither will you nor any that belong to you be happier or holier or juster in this life, or happier in another, if you do as Crito bids. Now you depart in innocence, a sufferer and not a doer of evil; a victim, not of the laws, but of men. But if you go forth, returning evil for evil, and injury for injury, breaking the covenants and agreements which you have made with us, and wronging those whom you ought least to wrong, that is to say, yourself, your friends, your country, and us, we shall be angry with you while you live, and our brethren, the laws in the world below, will receive you as an enemy; for they will know that you have done your best to destroy us. Listen, then, to us and not to Crito."

This is the voice which I seem to hear murmuring in my ears, like the sound of the flute in the ears of the mystic; that voice, I say, is humming in my ears, and prevents me from hearing any other. And I know that anything more which you may say will be in vain. Yet speak, if you have anything to say.

Crito: I have nothing to say, Socrates.

Socrates: Then let me follow the intimations of the will of God.

Source: Houghton Mifflin Social Studies, *A Message of Ancient Days*, "Understanding Primary Sources: Plato's *Crito*," http://www.eduplace.com/ss/hmss/6/unit/act5.1.html.

"Yes" to Breaking a Bad Law

by Martin Luther King, Jr.

Martin Luther King, the leader of the American civil rights movement, had been in Birmingham, Alabama to protest against segregation in that city. He led a series of non-violent actions that included a lunch counter sit-in, a march on City Hall, and a boycott of downtown merchants. On April 10, 1963, the city government obtained a court injunction directing an end to all protests. King decided that he could not obey the law and continued his protest. Two days later he was arrested and placed in solitary confinement. While in jail, he wrote this letter on the margins of the Birmingham News:

. . . You express a great deal of anxiety over our willingness to break laws. This is certainly a legitimate concern. Since we so diligently urge people to obey the Supreme Court's decision of 1954 outlawing segregation in the public schools, at first glance it may seem rather paradoxical for us consciously to break laws. One may well ask: "How can you advocate breaking some laws and obeying others?" The answer lies in the fact that there are two types of laws: just and unjust. I would be the first to advocate obeying just laws. One has not only a legal but a moral responsibility to obey just laws. Conversely, one has a moral responsibility to disobey unjust laws. I would agree with St. Augustine that "an unjust law is no law at all."

Now, what is the difference between the two? How does one determine whether a law is just or unjust? A just law is a man-made code that squares with the moral law or the law of God. An unjust law is a code that is out of harmony with the moral law. To put it in the terms of St. Thomas Aquinas: An unjust law is a human law that is not rooted in eternal law and natural law. Any law that uplifts human personality is just. Any law that degrades human personality is unjust. All segregation statutes are unjust because segregation distort the soul and damages the personality. It gives the segregator a false sense of superiority and the segregated a false sense of inferiority. Segregation, to use the terminology of the Jewish philosopher Martin Buber, substitutes an "I–it" relationship for an "I–thou" relationship and ends up relegating persons to the status of things.

Hence segregation is not only politically, economically and sociologically unsound, it is morally wrong and awful. Paul Tillich said that sin is separation. Is not segregation an existential expression of man's tragic separation, his awful estrangement, his terrible sinfulness? Thus it is that I can urge men to obey the 1954 decision of the Supreme Court, for it is morally right; and I can urge them to disobey segregation ordinances, for they are morally wrong.

Let us consider a more concrete example of just and unjust laws. An unjust law is a code that a numerical or power majority group compels a minority group to obey but does not make binding on itself. This is *difference* made legal. By the same token, a just law is a code that a majority compels a minority to follow and that it is willing to follow itself. This is *sameness* made legal.

Let me give another explanation. A law is unjust if it is inflicted on a minority that, as a result of being denied the right to vote, had no part in enacting or devising the law. Who can say that the legislature of Alabama which set up that state's segregation laws was democratically elected? Throughout Alabama all sorts of devious methods are used to prevent Negroes from becoming registered voters, and there are some counties in which, even though Negroes constitute a majority of the population, not a single Negro is registered. Can any law enacted under such circumstances be considered democratically structured?

Source: The Martin Luther King, Jr. Papers Project at Stanford University, http://www.stanford.edu/group/King/about_king/major_kingFrame.htm.

Questions

1. List Plato's arguments for obeying the law. Which do you agree or disagree with? Why?
2. Follow the same steps with the arguments presented by Martin Luther King.
3. Are there any situations in which you believe that you would break the law? Describe those situations.
4. Select one situation in which you would feel strongly that you must break the law, and write a defence of your position.
5. Take the opposite view, and develop an argument expressing the opinion that a person must never break the law.

Study Hall

Thinking/Inquiry

1. Internationally, many women's human rights are violated or denied. What do you consider to be the three most serious violations? Explain why, and offer solutions that you believe may help solve the violations.

2. Examine the standards of the *United Nations Convention on the Rights of the Child* (see the link at www.emp.ca/cwp). How has Canada failed to meet these standards? What do you believe needs to be done?

3. Many people believe that the media have too great an influence on political events. Should the government impose limits on what the media report? Why or why not?

Communication

4. While this chapter focuses on democratic decision making by various government systems, it would be a mistake to label that process the only face of democracy. Look back at Figure 7.1. What face of democracy is shown here? Which visuals in the chapter show the same face of democracy? Which do not?

5. You have just learned that the Canadian government is planning to maintain personal files on its citizens. The Privacy Commissioner is an officer of Parliament who investigates complaints related to personal information held by the Government of Canada. Write a letter to the Privacy Commissioner outlining your objections to the government plan.

6. Working with a partner, select a current news issue. Find a newspaper article on the topic from two sources and watch two different news broadcasts about it. Examine your research. How has the story been reported?

Are there differences? Offer some explanations as to why these differences exist. Present your findings in a brief oral report to the class.

7. Working with a partner, create a public service announcement about the exploitation of children. Play your announcement for the class. The class will vote on the five best announcements, which could be played over the school's public address system.

Application

8. Conduct research using the school library and the Internet on the development of human rights of mentally and physically challenged people in Canada. Prepare a visual display illustrating significant dates, events, people, and struggles of this group.

9. Your class has decided to present an Active Citizenship Day to the school. In small groups, conduct research into one of the groups mentioned in this chapter. Some examples would be the Sierra Club, Greenpeace, the Consumers' Association of Canada, the National Citizen's Coalition, and the National Action Committee on the Status of Women. Your task will be to create a display that outlines key information about your chosen group. Set up your displays and invite classes to visit them. Be prepared to answer any questions about your group.

10. Look ahead 50 years and predict what the status of Canada's Aboriginal peoples will be. Write a position paper outlining and justifying your view.

11. Working with two or three other students, discuss the possibility of forming a new public-interest or single-issue group. Formulate a rationale for your new interest group and present it to the class.

The Politics of Internationalism

Chapter 8
Governments: Participation in the International Community

Chapter 9
Canada's International Roles

Chapter 10
Major Participants in the International Community

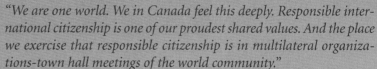

"We are one world. We in Canada feel this deeply. Responsible international citizenship is one of our proudest shared values. And the place we exercise that responsible citizenship is in multilateral organizations-town hall meetings of the world community."

Prime Minister Jean Chrétien, addressing a Commonwealth meeting in New Zealand, November 10, 1995

Governments: Participation in the International Community

Agenda

In this chapter, you will consider

• the founding of the United Nations and other organizations that promote international peace and cooperation
• how and why human rights were created to be "universal"
• international military alliances and treaties that limit war and define humane conduct
• Canada's international contributions, foreign policy, and power in the world
• the impact of the Cold War and decolonization on international relations
• the birth and evolution of UN peacekeeping
• how UN resolutions are drafted

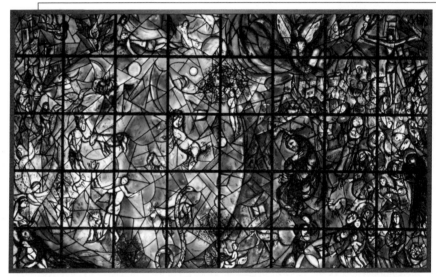

Figure 8.1 This stained-glass window in the public lobby of the United Nations was designed by French artist Marc Chagall as a memorial to Dag Hammarskjold, the second secretary-general of the UN who—along with 15 aides—died in a plane crash in 1961 while on a peacemaking mission.

In previous chapters, you have examined the nature of politics and fundamental political concepts. You have looked at forms of government and decision making. You have considered values, ideologies, movements, and "isms" as they clash and fuse and create community, be it local, regional, national, or—the focus of this and the next two chapters—international.

The time frame is the world as it emerges from the ruins of World War II to the aftermath of the Cold War. The question: how can governments learn to live and work together? What kind of international institutions, organizations, and efforts are needed to balance power, defuse rivalries, and avoid the apocalypse of another world war? You will find some answers to these questions as this chapter traces Canada's growing involvement and stature in the international community. From the founding of the United Nations to the invention and re-invention of UN peacekeeping, Canada and Canadians become key participants in the international community.

The Birth of the United Nations

The League of Nations was founded after World War I in the hope that an international organization could preserve peace and prevent another world war. The League had some success. It respected and helped establish the generally accepted protocol for international diplomacy. States maintained international diplomatic representation and, when conflicts emerged between states, an escalating scale of diplomatic responses was followed (Figure 8.2). The League successfully defused some international conflicts in the 1920s, but they were minor. Ultimately, diplomacy and the League failed, and World War II broke out in 1939 (see Chapter 4, page 124).

Why did the League fail? Among other reasons, the most important are that the League

- had no collective military force (neither would the UN)
- lacked the political will to impose military or economic **sanctions** against offending states when **moral suasion** did not work
- rarely achieved the unanimity required for decisions because of the self-interest of member states
- lacked the support of several big powers.

Although US President Wilson was a driving force behind the League of Nations, he could not convince the US Senate to **ratify** the treaty, which would have allowed the United States to join. This eroded the League's influence and ability to arbitrate disputes. Germany was admitted to the League in 1926 but withdrew in 1933 when the League would not lift arms limits imposed on the country after World War I. Germany's military buildup under Hitler alarmed the Soviet Union, which joined the League in 1934. In 1939, however, the USSR attacked Finland and was expelled from the League. Both Japan and Italy withdrew in the 1930s. In short, the League lacked the power to enforce its decisions and uphold its high ideals. It was undermined by unrealistic expectations and weak commitments from its members.

With the massive destruction wrought by World War II, many countries again came together to promote peace. In 1944, leaders of Britain, the United States, the Soviet Union, and China met at Dumbarton Oaks, an estate in Washington, DC, to discuss creating a new international organization to advance peace. Even as World War II was ending, representatives from 50 countries met at the San Francisco Conference. Prominent among them was Canada and its representative, Lester Pearson, Canadian Ambassador to the United States. The document they drafted became the *Charter of the United Nations* and was signed on June 26, 1945 (see Chapter 11, page 381). The United Nations was officially born on October 24, 1945, when the Charter was ratified by a majority of the original member states. Canada was a founding member.

The UN Charter states that the organization's main objective is "to save succeeding generations from the scourge of war" and "to reaffirm faith in fundamental human rights." Because the Charter is a treaty, it is a legally

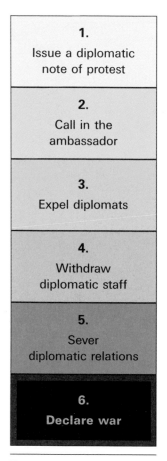

Figure 8.2 Escalating scale of diplomatic responses in a conflict between states. How might the UN (or the League of Nations) alter this traditional scale of diplomatic responses?

Figure 8.3 This sculpture, "Let Us Beat Our Swords into Ploughshares," stands in the gardens of UN headquarters in New York. It was donated by the Soviet Union in 1959. What does it symbolize about war and peace?

binding document. Charter articles have the force of international law.

The United Nations Structure

Even though the League of Nations failed to keep the peace, it paved the way for the United Nations. On April 18, 1946, the League officially dissolved itself, transferring its missions and ideals to the UN. The basic UN aims were to provide a forum where member states could work toward

- keeping world peace
- developing friendly relations among nations
- working to eliminate poverty, disease, and illiteracy
- encouraging respect for human rights and freedoms
- stopping environmental destruction.

As with the League, ideals of peace and social and economic progress were the UN's basic principles. However, these ideals were developed further to fit the complex postwar world. As you will learn in this chapter, and in Chapters 9 and 10, the UN system evolved to create and interconnect organs and agencies that work toward all its basic aims (Figure 8.4). Its philosophy was clear: world peace would be impossible to maintain unless the UN took action to promote and protect human rights, the environment, and the easing of massive social and economic inequalities—as well as dealing with international conflicts.

The United Nations is an association of governments of sovereign states, not a world government. It does not make laws. It provides an international forum for diplomacy and the development of laws. These usually find acceptance and help resolve international conflicts. Each member state—rich or poor, large or small, regardless of political views and social systems—has a voice and a single vote.

The UN has six principal organs. The General Assembly, the Security Council, the Secretariat, the Economic and Social Council, and the Trusteeship Council are based at UN headquarters in New York. The sixth organ, the International Court of Justice, is in The Hague, the Netherlands. Figure 8.4 illustrates the broad range of activities that fall under the UN umbrella.

THE WEB

Learn more about the main UN bodies at www.emp.ca/cwp.

SOUND BITE "The UN is not an entirely useless organization. Some of its agencies do some good work, possibly almost enough to offset the corruption of all the other agencies. It creates employment for the less employable relatives of presidents-for-life. It gives smaller countries a feeling their views count."

Canadian David Frum and American Richard Perle, authors, An End to Evil: How to Win the War on Terror, 2003

Figure 8.4 The United Nations system.

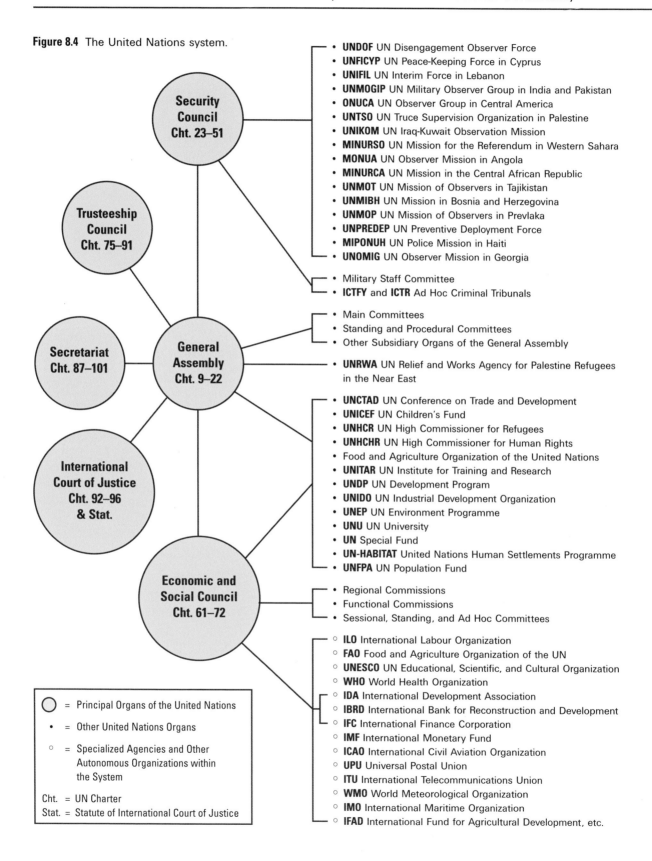

Security Council Cht. 23–51

- **UNDOF** UN Disengagement Observer Force
- **UNFICYP** UN Peace-Keeping Force in Cyprus
- **UNIFIL** UN Interim Force in Lebanon
- **UNMOGIP** UN Military Observer Group in India and Pakistan
- **ONUCA** UN Observer Group in Central America
- **UNTSO** UN Truce Supervision Organization in Palestine
- **UNIKOM** UN Iraq-Kuwait Observation Mission
- **MINURSO** UN Mission for the Referendum in Western Sahara
- **MONUA** UN Observer Mission in Angola
- **MINURCA** UN Mission in the Central African Republic
- **UNMOT** UN Mission of Observers in Tajikistan
- **UNMIBH** UN Mission in Bosnia and Herzegovina
- **UNMOP** UN Mission of Observers in Prevlaka
- **UNPREDEP** UN Preventive Deployment Force
- **MIPONUH** UN Police Mission in Haiti
- **UNOMIG** UN Observer Mission in Georgia

- Military Staff Committee
- **ICTFY** and **ICTR** Ad Hoc Criminal Tribunals

Trusteeship Council Cht. 75–91

Secretariat Cht. 87–101

General Assembly Cht. 9–22

- Main Committees
- Standing and Procedural Committees
- Other Subsidiary Organs of the General Assembly

- **UNRWA** UN Relief and Works Agency for Palestine Refugees in the Near East

- **UNCTAD** UN Conference on Trade and Development
- **UNICEF** UN Children's Fund
- **UNHCR** UN High Commissioner for Refugees
- **UNHCHR** UN High Commissioner for Human Rights
- Food and Agriculture Organization of the United Nations
- **UNITAR** UN Institute for Training and Research
- **UNDP** UN Development Program
- **UNIDO** UN Industrial Development Organization
- **UNEP** UN Environment Programme
- **UNU** UN University
- **UN** Special Fund
- **UN-HABITAT** United Nations Human Settlements Programme
- **UNFPA** UN Population Fund

International Court of Justice Cht. 92–96 & Stat.

Economic and Social Council Cht. 61–72

- Regional Commissions
- Functional Commissions
- Sessional, Standing, and Ad Hoc Committees

- ○ **ILO** International Labour Organization
- ○ **FAO** Food and Agriculture Organization of the UN
- ○ **UNESCO** UN Educational, Scientific, and Cultural Organization
- ○ **WHO** World Health Organization
- ○ **IDA** International Development Association
- ○ **IBRD** International Bank for Reconstruction and Development
- ○ **IFC** International Finance Corporation
- ○ **IMF** International Monetary Fund
- ○ **ICAO** International Civil Aviation Organization
- ○ **UPU** Universal Postal Union
- ○ **ITU** International Telecommunications Union
- ○ **WMO** World Meteorological Organization
- ○ **IMO** International Maritime Organization
- ○ **IFAD** International Fund for Agricultural Development, etc.

○ = Principal Organs of the United Nations

• = Other United Nations Organs

○ = Specialized Agencies and Other Autonomous Organizations within the System

Cht. = UN Charter
Stat. = Statute of International Court of Justice

The General Assembly

The General Assembly, the UN's central body, comprises all member states (191 in 2004). Using a "one member, one vote" formula, the Assembly debates issues of global concern and promotes consensus. The Assembly's decisions are not legally binding, but they do carry moral weight. Important issues, such as peace, security, and admission of new members, require a two-thirds majority vote. Other issues require a simple majority. The General Assembly has often been called the "town-hall meeting of the world."

The Security Council

SOUND BITE   "[T]he Security Council . . . may take such action by air, sea, or land forces as may be necessary to maintain or restore international peace and security. Such action may include demonstrations, blockade, and other operations by air, sea, or land forces of Members of the United Nations."

Article 42, Charter of the United Nations

The 15-member Security Council, the most powerful UN organ, is charged with maintaining international peace and security. While other UN bodies only make recommendations, the UN Charter empowers the Security Council to make decisions that are legally binding on members. Compliance with Council decisions is enforced by a system of sanctions.

The structure of the Security Council reflects the period in which it was created. The five major victors of World War II—China, France, the Soviet Union (now the Russian Federation), the United Kingdom, and the United States—were made permanent members, and six non-permanent seats were created. In 1965, non-permanent seats were increased to 10. Non-permanent members are elected for two-year, non-renewable terms by the General Assembly. Because a seat on the Security Council brings international prestige and opportunities to express opinions on world issues, states often lobby for years to win one. Canada has served a term in every decade since the UN was founded (last serving from 1999 to 2001).

Since 1945, the balance of world power has shifted. More than 100 (mainly non-Western) states have joined the UN. Security Council reforms continue to be considered. One proposal suggests increasing permanent membership from five to 10 states, including Japan and Germany (the second and third largest funders of the UN after the United States) and one important state from each of Africa, Asia, and Latin America. Any change to the composition of the Security Council requires unanimous approval of the five permanent members.

SOUND BITE   "Much of the world sees Security Council membership as unrepresentative because it excludes populous countries such as Brazil and India from permanent member status; some say this robs the council of legitimacy."

David Malone, Canadian Ambassador to the UN (1992–94), September 20, 2004

The Security Council meets as needed, and the decision-making process is designed for consensus. For the UN to take action on substantive matters—such as using force to resolve conflicts—requires nine affirmative Security Council votes. Voting must include the five permanent members, each of which can **veto** the adoption of any resolution. The right to veto ensured that these five countries would join the UN: each can defeat any proposal it deems to be against its interests. Permanent members can also abstain from a vote, which is not regarded as a veto. In the past, veto power limited the actions the Council has been able to take (see The Suez Crisis, page 289).

Figure 8.5 President George W. Bush watches the broadcast of Secretary of State Colin Powell making the United States' case for war against Iraq before the Security Council, February 5, 2003.

SOUND BITE

"[T]he Council's moral authority is underpinned by its willingness to respond effectively and promptly to threats of international peace and security, and it must demonstrate greater resolve in addressing sensitive and politically challenging situations."

Allan Rock, Canadian Ambassador to the UN, in a statement to the Security Council on the protection of civilians in armed conflict, June 14, 2004

The Security Council has approved the use of military force in the 1950 Korean War, the 1991 Persian Gulf War, 1993–94 operations in Rwanda, and in Haiti from 1993–96. The Security Council did not support US President George W. Bush when the United States, claiming Iraq had hidden **weapons of mass destruction**, declared war on Iraq in 2003. As of late 2004, no such weapons had been found.

Security Council resolutions established the International Criminal Tribunals for Yugoslavia (1993) and Rwanda (1994) to deal with genocide, war crimes, and human rights violations during civil strife in those countries (see Chapter 11). These were the first such courts established by the UN (also see Chapter 9, Law in Motion, page 328). The Council also supervises ongoing UN peacekeeping missions.

PRESS PLAY

In *Hotel Rwanda* (2004), Irish director Terry George tells the true story of a hotel manager at a four-star Kigali hotel in 1994 who saved over a thousand Tutsi refugees from death at the hands of Hutu militias. (PG-13)

The Secretariat

The Secretariat is the UN bureaucracy. Comprising more than 8,900 international civil servants from 170 countries, the Secretariat keeps the system running. It is headed by the secretary-general, who is appointed by the General Assembly on the recommendation of the Security Council for a five-year, renewable term. Secretary-General Kofi Annan, of Ghana, was appointed in 1997. His term was renewed in 2002. In 2001, Annan and the United Nations were awarded the Nobel Peace Prize "for their work for a better and more peaceful world."

THE WEB

To learn more about Kofi Annan and his Nobel Peace Prize, visit www.emp.ca/cwp.

The Economic and Social Council

SOUND BITE "[M]ore than 70 percent of the UN's work is social or economic. But the media, for some reason, are only interested in Iraq and the Middle East. . . . But when you see what the UN is doing in the economic and social field, it really helps the lives of thousands and thousands of people."

ECOSOC President Marjatta Rasi, quoted in UN Wire, March 8, 2004

Under the authority of the General Assembly, the Economic and Social Council (ECOSOC) does what its name implies: coordinates the economic and social work of the UN system. ECOSOC has become increasingly important as the UN's focus shifts to poverty, development, human rights, and social issues. ECOSOC's overview extends to UN commissions, committees, and affiliated organizations such as the UN Children's Fund (UNICEF); the UN Educational, Scientific, and Cultural Organization (UNESCO), which promotes collaboration among nations through education, science, culture, and communication; and the World Health Organization (WHO), the authority for coordinating and setting standards for international public health efforts.

ECOSOC has grown from 18 members in 1945 to 54 members in 2004. Member states are elected for three-year terms. The Council also consults with academics, representatives of business, and more than 2,000 NGOs on many issues. It also provides access to UN conferences and the UN system to these individuals and groups. ECOSOC makes policy recommendations to the UN, and its decisions are often controversial. Some ECOSOC efforts are not. In 2004, for example, it coordinated the mass vaccination of 2.3 million children in the Sudan against measles and the financing of refugee camps in Pakistan.

The Trusteeship Council

The Trusteeship Council, composed of the five permanent Security Council members, was established in 1945. At the time, almost a third of the world's people lived in non–self-governing territories that were dependent on colonial powers. The Trusteeship Council was established to administer colonial territories of the Axis Powers (Germany, Italy, Japan, Hungary, Romania, and Bulgaria) that had been League of Nations mandates. Its purpose was to prepare these territories for independence and self-government. For example, Italian Somaliland joined British Somaliland, becoming Somalia in 1960. In 1962, the independent states Rwanda and Burundi were created from the trust territory of Ruanda–Urundi, formerly administered by Belgium.

The Trusteeship Council suspended operations in 1994 after the last UN trust territory became independent. This was Paulu, an island group southeast of the Philippines, which joined the UN as an independent state in December 1994.

Is there a future for the Trusteeship Council? In 1997, as part of proposed UN reforms (see Chapter 9, Maurice Strong, page 325), UN Secretary-General Annan recommended that the Council focus on the atmosphere, outer space, and the oceans. No action has been taken. Some observers have suggested that the Trusteeship Council could supervise the reconstruction of war-torn states such as Afghanistan and Iraq. These countries need direct help on a scale that only an international organization can provide.

The International Court of Justice

The International Court of Justice (ICJ), also known as the World Court, was established under Articles 92 to 96 of the UN Charter. It evolved from an earlier effort at a world court system linked to the League of Nations. The purpose of the ICJ is to provide a judicial alternative to diplomacy and war in settling international disputes. In other words, it is a method to replace war with international law. To succeed, it requires states to relinquish a degree of sovereignty to the ICJ. The ICJ is the main judicial organ of the United Nations and is located at The Hague, the Netherlands.

The ICJ has two main functions: (1) to hear cases brought before it by member states that recognize its jurisdiction and (2) to give advisory legal opinions on questions referred to it by international bodies. States that consent to the ICJ's jurisdiction in a case are bound by its judgments, which are final. Individuals, NGOs, and businesses cannot bring cases before the ICJ. The court's authority is limited: UN members cannot be compelled to use it.

The ICJ has 15 judges. Each must come from a different state and act independently of that state's foreign policy. Judges are elected to nine-year terms by the General Assembly on the recommendation of the Security Council. Elections are held every three years for one-third of the seats. The ICJ hears often-technical cases ranging from territorial and sovereignty disputes to the establishment of maritime boundaries. It has also given advisory opinions on the status of human rights, the legality of the threat or use of nuclear weapons, and UN membership.

Typically, cases take years to resolve. For example, the *Oil Platforms Case (Iran v. United States)* commenced in 1992, after US military forces in the Persian Gulf attacked three oil-drilling platforms owned by the National Iranian Oil Company in 1987 and 1988. Public hearings concluded in March 2003. A decision was unlikely before 2005.

THE WEB

Learn how the ICJ dealt with Spain's complaint against Canada in an incident involving the Spanish fishing trawler *Estai* at www.emp.ca/cwp.

Check YOUR UNDERSTANDING

1. Outline four reasons why the League of Nations failed.
2. What relationship existed between the League of Nations and the United Nations?
3. Describe the UN's six main organs and identify an important feature of each.
4. Why is the Security Council the most powerful organ of the UN? Should it be? Why or why not?
5. Why is the Economic and Social Council increasing in its importance and influence?
6. What is the International Court of Justice, and what are its two main functions? Why do you think it has decided so few cases since being founded?

International Human Rights

As World War II ended, revelations of unimaginable atrocities forced the international community to reconsider the relationship between the state and the individual. Nazi ideology had classified groups of human beings—such as Jews, the Romani people (Gypsies), gay men and lesbians, the mentally disabled, and so on—as "life unworthy of life." The Nazi regime not only denied rights to these people; it used the resources of the state to gather them up systematically and murder them in the millions. Nazi Germany did this to create what it considered a better—a superior—nation. The liberation in 1945 of skeletal survivors from the wide network of Nazi concentration camps stunned the world.

For the first time in history, the international community agreed that gross violations of human rights could not be tolerated. But what were human rights? The phrase rarely appeared in textbooks or the media 60 years ago, yet the concept pre-dated the UN. More than 40 NGOs lobbied delegates to the San Francisco Conference to include human rights in the UN Charter. The media and public watched closely. The preamble to the Charter went on to state:

> We the peoples of the United Nations [are] determined to save succeeding generations from the scourge of war, which twice in our lifetime has brought untold sorrow to mankind, and to reaffirm faith in fundamental human rights, in the dignity and worth of the human person, in the equal rights of men and women and of nations large and small. . . .

Figure 8.6 Prisoners at Dachau concentration camp cheer at the arrival of the US Seventh Army, May 3, 1945.

Several UN Charter provisions specifically address human rights. Article 68 led ECOSOC to create the Human Rights Commission (HRC) "for the promotion of human rights" in June 1946. Eleanor Roosevelt, former US first lady, was elected the HRC's first chairperson, a position she held until 1951. The HRC's first task was to draft a declaration both to codify and to guarantee human rights. Drafters had to avoid specific ideological language and be sensitive to vast cultural, political, and religious differences. The challenge was enormous, and the process of drafting and acceptance consumed two years of legal and diplomatic efforts.

The *Universal Declaration of Human Rights*

Proclaimed by the UN General Assembly on December 10, 1948, the *Universal Declaration of Human Rights* (UDHR) was a defining moment in international politics. The word "universal" sent a message: the rights described would apply to all people, everywhere, at all times. The UDHR quickly became the international standard of the **inalienable** rights of all people and a banner for the human rights movement.

The preamble describes why the UDHR was created, and its 30 articles divide human rights into six categories: civil, economic, political, cultural, social, and equality. Key individual rights listed include the rights to life, liberty, and security of the person; to an education; and to participate in cultural life. Key freedoms include freedom of thought, conscience, and religion, and freedom from torture or cruel, inhumane treatment or punishment.

Because the UDHR is not a treaty, it is not legally binding. Yet its universality applies moral and diplomatic pressure on states to respect its principles. It sets aspirational standards for all nations. Since being proclaimed, the UDHR has made protection of human rights an essential part of international law. According to the *Guinness Book of World Records*, it is the world's most translated document. It has been translated into 321 languages and dialects, from Abkhaz to Zulu.

John Humphrey and the UDHR

Canada and Canadians have played a pioneering role in enshrining human rights in international law. John Peters Humphrey (1905–95), a law professor at McGill University, became the first director of the Human Rights Division, UN Secretariat, in 1946. In that position, which he held until 1961, Humphrey wrote the first draft of what would become the *Universal Declaration of Human Rights* in approximately six weeks. The 400-page document was handed to French diplomat René Cassin in 1947. Some 20 years later, Cassin was awarded the 1968 Nobel Peace Prize as the "Father of the UDHR." Twenty years later still, in 1988, researchers uncovered the original draft with its handwritten notations, and Humphrey was awarded the UN Human Rights Award. In accepting the award, Humphrey was modest: "To say I did

Figure 8.7 Canada Post commemorated John Humphrey in 1998, the 50th anniversary of the *Universal Declaration of Human Rights*. How does the artwork show the UDHR's international impact?

the draft alone would be nonsense. . . . The final Declaration was the work of hundreds."

Humphrey remained active in human rights. He was the first president of Amnesty International Canada, a founder of the Canadian Human Rights Foundation in 1967, a member of the Royal Commission on the Status of Women (1967–70), and a vice-president of the International Council of Jurists. In 1974, he was made an Officer of the Order of Canada "in recognition of his contributions to legal scholarship and his worldwide reputation in the field of human rights."

Humphrey continued to assess the effectiveness of the UDHR. In his 1984 book, *Human Rights and the United Nations: A Great Adventure*, he observed:

> Some measure of the impact of the Declaration has had on the expectations of individual men and women can be found in the thousands of communications received by the United Nations every year from people everywhere, alleging that their rights have been violated and invoking the Declaration in their appeals for help.

The Universal Declaration of Human Rights: *Into the 21st Century*

How and why has the UDHR remained significant? Perhaps its universality is the chief reason. It has provided a basic reference for NGOs such as Doctors Without Borders, Amnesty International, and Human Rights Watch as they advocate for those whose rights are abused in both developed and developing countries. It has also been a keystone for other international human rights documents (Figure 8.8).

The UDHR became a driving force for constitutional recognition of human rights, including the *Canadian Charter of Rights and Freedoms* (1982) and the *Constitution of the Republic of South Africa, 1996*. The pro-apartheid government of South Africa was one of 28 countries that abstained from voting when the General Assembly proclaimed the UDHR in 1948. In the years ahead, the UDHR on its own could not prevent massive human rights abuses, from Soviet **pogroms** (organized killings) after World War II to more recent atrocities in Cambodia, the former Yugoslavia, Rwanda, and Darfur. Eleanor Roosevelt regarded the UDHR as her greatest single achievement. She called it the "international *Magna Carta* of all of mankind." Many observers today would agree with her. Many others would not (see Point Counterpoint, pages 274–75).

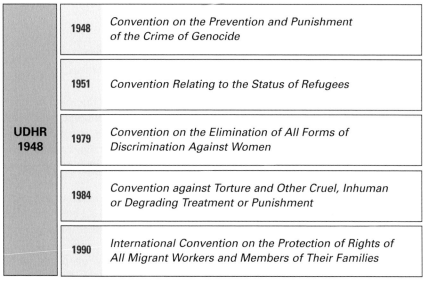

Figure 8.8 The *Universal Declaration of Human Rights* is not legally binding, but it has inspired many human rights conventions and agreements that do have the force of international law, including those in this diagram. Why might the drafters of the UDHR have used this as a strategy?

The United Nations and Children's Rights

As you learned in Chapter 7, the UN General Assembly adopted the *Declaration on the Rights of the Child* (DRC) in 1959. The DRC urges all states to protect the human rights and freedoms of all children, free from discrimination based on gender, colour, ethnic origin, social descent and status, language, religion, or political affiliation. Like the UDHR, the DRC is not legally binding. Rather, it affirms basic standards that states should aspire to, including the provision of health care, housing, at least the elementary level of education, and protection from neglect, cruelty, and exploitation.

Canada took an active lead in the UN working group that transformed the DRC into the UN *Convention on the Rights of the Child* (CRC), which was unanimously adopted in 1989 and came into force in September 1990. Canada was among the first states to ratify the CRC in 1991. It is the most widely and rapidly accepted human rights treaty in history, having been ratified by 191 countries and the Holy See (the Vatican) as of November 2004.

The CRC is the first legally binding international human rights treaty about and for children under the age of 18. Its 54 articles spell out basic human rights for children. In ratifying the CRC, states agree to submit regular reports to the UN Committee on the Rights of the Child.

As with all UN human rights treaties, the committee monitors compliance and implementation. To ensure that states meet their obligations, the committee checks state reports against data it gathers from NGOs, the media, and other sources.

Point: Counterpoint → The Universal Declaration of Human Rights: Success or Failure?

An Inspiring Standard

by Hillary Rodham Clinton, former US first lady

Forty-nine winters ago, the world acknowledged . . . the *Universal Declaration of Human Rights*, the first international agreement on the rights of humankind. . . .

In the half century since [then], . . . individuals and nations alike have a standard by which to measure fundamental rights. Many of the countries that have emerged in the last 50 years have drawn inspiration from the Declaration in their constitutions. . . .

Figure 8.9   Former US first lady Eleanor Roosevelt holds up a copy of the original UDHR, 1948.

It is telling that even in the drafting of the Declaration there was a debate about women's voices. The initial version of the first article stated, "All men are created equal." It took women members of the commission to point out that "all men" might be interpreted to exclude women. Only after long debate was the language changed to say, "All human beings are created free and equal."

Today, we still choose not to hear the voices of many women. . . . Two-thirds of the 130 million children out of school are girls. . . . Rights on paper that are not protected and implemented are not really rights at all. . . . The full enfranchisement of women's rights is unfinished business. . . .

Some critics . . . say that human rights are a Western luxury—not inalienable, but alien. But I believe . . . that human rights are as essential to life as air or water, and that they are felt, beyond culture and tradition, as innate. . . . For if they are not innate, how have people throughout history known to fight for them so valiantly?

Paradoxically, the proof of universality lies with the perpetrators of human rights violations themselves. Why have those who have dishonoured humanity run to cover their tracks were it not for the knowledge that wrong has been done? The Nazis tried to hide their concentration camps. Communism kept its terrors in the shadow of the **Iron Curtain** [the boundary between Western Europe and Soviet-controlled Eastern Europe]. Scores of bodies are hidden in the hard ground of Bosnia and in the deep forests of Rwanda. . . .

Why go to the trouble?

Because human rights transcend individual regimes and customs. The beliefs inscribed in the UDHR were not invented 50 years ago. . . . They have been with us forever, from civilization's first light. Sophocles wrote about them 2,500 years ago. . . . Confucius articulated them in ancient China. This belief that we must respect our neighbours as we would respect ourselves resides at the core of the teachings of all the major faiths of the world. . . .

It must be with realistic eyes that we look toward human rights. And it must be with clean hands and open hearts that in this—the 50th anniversary of the UDHR—we rededicate ourselves to their fulfillment.

Source: Excerpted from "On the *Universal Declaration of Human Rights*," December 10, 1997, speech during a UN ceremony marking the UDHR's 50th anniversary; http://usinfo.state.gov/journals/itdhr/1098/ijde/hillary.htm.

Destroyer of Individual Rights

by Glenn Woiceshyn

On December 10th, 1998, the United Nations celebrated the 50th anniversary of its *Universal Declaration of Human Rights*, a five-page, 30-article document specifying everyone's *alleged* rights. Rather than celebrate it, we should condemn it as a destroyer of rights and a charter of tyranny. . . .

Throughout history, governments formed to protect people from domestic criminals and foreign invaders, but people also needed protection from their own government. The greatest crimes in history were committed by governments against their own people, specifically governments that were above the law. In the 20th century alone, scores of millions were slaughtered by communist and fascist governments (both **collectivist** [marked by central state control]) which regarded their citizens as means to their ends. . . .

Individual rights are precisely what the UN's declaration is designed to destroy. No, it doesn't openly attack individual rights; that would be rejected outright by freer countries. It destroys rights by internal corruption—by perverting the meaning of rights into its exact opposite.

The declaration first covers what appears to be legitimate [individual] rights, such as "the right to life, liberty and security of the person," "the right to own property," and freedom of "thought" and "opinion." It then introduces a series of "economic rights," such as a person's "right" to work, paid holidays, protection against unemployment, social security, free education, and a standard of living adequate for the health and well-being of himself and of his family. . . .

If people are entitled to these, who will be forced to provide them? Whose property will be seized to pay for them?

Such "economic rights" obviously contradict the right to liberty and property. There can be no such thing as a right to violate the rights of others. "Economic rights" merely hand government the power to violate individual rights, thereby rendering the individual a slave to the needs and desires of others. They effectively make communism the social ideal. . . . A tyrannical country such as China or North Korea can claim that it upholds "economic rights," and thereby derive moral sanction [approval]. . . .

When rights get perverted, so does justice—and vice versa. . . .

The declaration deserves moral condemnation and rejection. The only human rights are individual rights—which have made possible the freedom and prosperity that we currently enjoy, but risk losing. Rather than allow political power-lusters to destroy the remnants of individual rights that still protect us, we should be eternally vigilant in protecting and restoring our inalienable rights.

As for those countries which blatantly violate individual rights, we should morally condemn them and boycott them—not treat them as civilized members of the "world community." That's what should have been done fifty years ago.

Source: Glenn Woiceshyn, "In Defense of Human Rights," *Capitalism Magazine*, http://www.capmag.com/article.asp?ID=210.

Articulating a Personal Stand

1. List each side's strongest and weakest arguments. With which do you agree? Explain.
2. Do you agree that human rights are a "Western luxury"? Discuss this question in small groups and try to reach a consensus, citing contrary evidence in Clinton's article.
3. Defend or refute Clinton's statement: "The full enfranchisement of women's rights is unfinished business." Use concrete examples.
4. What rights does Woiceshyn say the UDHR violates? Explain why you agree or disagree.
5. Write a five-paragraph essay in which you take a position on the UDHR's failure or success. Present reasons for your position, acknowledging arguments for the other side.

THE WEB
Learn more about child soldiers at www.emp.ca/cwp.

Figure 8.10 A child soldier guards a former brewery turned clinic for rebel fighters during civil unrest in Liberia, 2003. The *Convention on the Rights of the Child* seeks to protect children from such exploitation.

SOUND BITE "A century [the 20th] that began with children having virtually no rights is ending with children having the most powerful legal instrument that not only recognizes but protects their human rights."

Carol Bellamy, UNICEF Executive Director, 1998

The CRC states that all children everywhere, at all times, have the right to

- life, survival, and development
- free self-expression on all matters affecting them
- protection from discrimination of any kind
- participation in family, cultural, and social life.

The UN also adopted two optional protocols to strengthen the CRC's protection of children in two key areas: the sale and use of children in child prostitution and child pornography, and the use of children in armed conflict. Both protocols came into force in 2002.

As of 2004, Somalia and the United States were the only **signatories** that had not ratified the CRC. Somalia had no recognized government; the United States, like other countries, carefully evaluates the degree to which its existing laws comply with any treaty it has signed before ratification. The process can take years. For example, the United States has yet to ratify the *Convention on the Elimination of All Forms of Discrimination Against Women*, which was passed in 1979 and signed by the United States in 1987. Some critics believe the fact that youths can be executed for committing certain criminal offences while under the age of 18 in more than 20 US states is blocking US ratification of the *Convention on the Rights of the Child*.

The *International Bill of Human Rights*

Throughout the 1950s and 1960s, the UN Human Rights Commission worked to negotiate an *International Covenant on Civil and Political Rights* and an

International Covenant on Economic, Social, and Cultural Rights. Both were adopted in December 1966 and came into force in early 1976. The covenants have made many provisions of the *Universal Declaration of Human Rights* legally binding on the member states that ratified them. Together with the UDHR, these documents form the *International Bill of Human Rights.*

The covenants reflect ideological debates of the period. Generally speaking, Western countries stressed civil rights and political freedoms, while Eastern countries focused on economic and social rights. Consensus among UN members led to the two covenants being adopted simultaneously. The almost-identical preambles recall the obligation of UN members to promote human rights and to legally enforce the General Assembly's resolution, which states: "The enjoyment of civil and political rights and economic, social and cultural rights are interconnected and interdependent."

Among the many rights and freedoms that the *International Covenant on Civil and Political Rights* guarantees are the rights to life, liberty, and security of the person; freedom of thought, expression, conscience, and religion; equal protection of the law; a fair trial; freedom from slavery and torture; and humane treatment of detained persons. The *Canadian Charter of Rights and Freedoms* is largely based on the guarantees outlined in the *International Covenant on Civil and Political Rights.*

As its name suggests, the *International Covenant on Economic, Social, and Cultural Rights* deals with the economic, social, and cultural rights of the UDHR, but in greater detail. This covenant promotes the well-being of citizens and includes the rights to work, to just and favourable work conditions, to the formation of and membership in trade unions, to family life, to an adequate standard of living, to the highest attainable standard of health, to education, and to participation in cultural life. It prohibits all forms of discrimination in the enjoyment of these rights, including that based on sex, and requires that countries ensure the equal rights of women and men.

The work of the UN Human Rights Commission expanded enormously after 1946, growing from 18 member states to the present 53 members. The commission meets annually in Geneva, Switzerland. It not only monitors human rights abuses, but holds international meetings on human rights concerns and handles complaints about human rights violations. It reports to the UN Economic and Social Council.

THE WEB

Read and compare the *International Covenant on Economic, Social, and Cultural Rights* and the *International Covenant on Civil and Political Rights* at www.emp.ca/cwp.

Check YOUR UNDERSTANDING

1. Outline the six categories of human rights in the *Universal Declaration of Human Rights.*
2. Why did Eleanor Roosevelt call the UDHR "the international *Magna Carta* of all of mankind"?
3. Who was John Humphrey, and how did he contribute to international human rights?
4. List four reasons why the *Universal Declaration of Human Rights* is still significant.

5. Why do you think that the *Convention on the Rights of the Child* was the most widely and rapidly ratified human rights treaty in history?
6. Why has the United States been reluctant to ratify the *Convention on the Rights of the Child*?
7. Identify the three components of the *International Bill of Human Rights*.
8. Explain the relationship between the *Canadian Charter of Rights and Freedoms* and the *International Covenant on Civil and Political Rights*.

Alliances, Treaties, Covenants, and Conventions

As you learned in Chapter 4, diplomacy and agreements between states have helped promote internationalism. After World War II, Canada played a much more active role internationally. It formed alliances and signed and ratified treaties, covenants, and conventions. An **alliance** can be defined as a formal union or agreement to cooperate with other nations for a specific purpose or goal. The North Atlantic Treaty Organization (NATO) and the North American Air Defense Agreement (NORAD), both based on defence, are two of the most important alliances Canada joined.

A treaty is an agreement between states, international organizations, or both. Treaties take the form of conventions, covenants, and protocols. Once signed by the states, all treaties have the force of law among the signatories. Signatories also have a moral obligation to respect treaty terms. Treaties must be ratified by each state's parliament or equivalent legislative body before becoming law. This is the main distinction between a declaration and a treaty.

Treaties can be either bilateral or multinational. Bilateral treaties are negotiated between a limited number of states, usually only two, establishing legal obligations and rights between those states only; for example, the *Treaty on Extradition* (1976) and the 1996 *Softwood Lumber Agreement* between Canada and the United States. As you read earlier, multilateral treaties include several nations and establish rights and obligations between each nation and every other nation in the treaty—for example, the *Non-Proliferation of Nuclear Weapons Treaty* (1968) and the *Comprehensive Test Ban Treaty* (1996). Canada has ratified hundreds of treaties on a wide range of issues, including child abduction, culture, terrorism, trade, and human rights. Many of the most important treaties have been described in earlier chapters; others will be discussed in this chapter and those following.

Military Alliances and the Arms Race

After World War II, the Soviet Union began installing pro-Soviet governments in eastern European countries that fell within its orbit. The United States also increased its military presence to stabilize post-war Europe and contain the "communist threat." Western European countries feared that the so-called Soviet satellite states were part of a plan to spread revolutionary communism and expand Soviet power in Europe. The Cold War, the superpower rivalry between the United States and the Soviet Union, had begun (see also Chapter 11).

Canada was not a superpower or a major power, such as France or England, but a **middle power**. It was too important to be ignored, and its influence was on the rise. In 1947, Escott Reid, a public servant in Canada's Department of External Affairs, proposed an international organization to provide **collective security** in Western Europe. The United States supported Reid's initiative as a way to counter the "communist threat," and NATO resulted. Canada–US military relations became even closer than they had been during World War II. If peace was to be preserved—and the alternative was unthinkable—careful alliances would be required.

When the Soviet Union conducted its first test of an atomic bomb in 1949, it set off a competition for superior military power and nuclear weaponry with the United States that became known as the **arms race** (see also Chapter 11). In the darkest days of this period, from 1950–68, Canada experienced a "golden age" of foreign policy. Canadian leaders and diplomats had greater influence than ever before and helped resolve many world conflicts through compromise and diplomacy. Canada had found its niche as a middle power—that of mediator and peacemaker.

Figure 8.11 In 1951, spectators watch an atomic test explosion at the Nevada Testing Ground, 110 kilometres from Las Vegas. Tests stopped in 1992. In 1993, the US government started compensating nearby residents suffering from radiation-related cancers. How could the US government justify the tests at the time?

North Atlantic Treaty Organization

On April 4, 1949, Canada, the United States, and 10 European countries founded the **North Atlantic Treaty Organization** (NATO) under the framework of Article 51 of the UN Charter. It was Canada's first peacetime military alliance, and it provoked controversy. Canada, once reliant on Britain for security, was gaining stature in international affairs and also becoming more aligned with the United States. Many Canadians believed Canadian interests would be better served in the UN. They rightly suspected that NATO would be US-dominated, and opposed Canadian membership.

NATO established a unified military command for the collective protection of North America and Western Europe from possible Soviet attack and promised to reduce the cost of maintaining separate military forces. Claiming democratic principles, human rights, and the rule of law as its founding values, NATO's primary goal was to establish lasting peace in Europe. It was established under the *North Atlantic Treaty* and remains head-

PRESS PLAY

The Oscar-winning short documentary, *If You Love This Planet* (1982), directed by Terre Nash for the National Film Board of Canada, records a lecture given by outspoken nuclear critic Dr. Helen Caldicott to students, stressing the urgency of nuclear disarmament. (NR)

Figure 8.12 Russian displays of military weaponry, like this 1966 anti-missile missile, were a regular feature of Moscow's annual May Day parade during the arms race.

quartered in Brussels, Belgium. Under NATO, an armed attack against one or more of the founding states would be seen as an attack against all: all member states would be expected to come to the defence.

Structurally, the UN was ill equipped to deal with Cold War conflicts. Each superpower—the United States on one side, the Soviet Union on the other—was a permanent member of the Security Council. Each had the veto. Because the Security Council had to approve any resolution to enforce collective security, the UN was powerless whenever either determined its state interests were threatened. In this way, NATO was seen as essential for the collective security of its non-communist member states. In the same way, the Warsaw Pact (see below) was seen as essential by the Soviet Union for communist states.

After the Cold War ended in 1991, newly independent states of the former Soviet Union began the process of joining NATO. Some critics, especially Russian observers, called for NATO to be dissolved. After all, with the collapse of the Soviet Union, what military threat remained? Was NATO simply another forum for US dominance? In ongoing summits and conferences, NATO redefined itself, reducing its arms and establishing cooperative relations with Russia.

When the civil war in the Balkans spread after 1991, NATO partnered UN and international peacekeeping efforts to contain the conflict. At the request of the UN, NATO forces monitored and enforced compliance with UN resolutions. NATO militarily enforced no-fly zones and even launched air strikes to prevent humanitarian disasters in Bosnia and Serbia (see also Chapters 4, 9, and 11).

NATO Founding States*	New Members	Joined
Belgium	Greece	1952
Canada	Turkey	1952
Denmark	West Germany	1955
France	Spain	1982
Iceland	Czech Republic	1999
Italy	Hungary	1999
Luxembourg	Poland	1999
Netherlands	Bulgaria	2004
Norway	Estonia	2004
Portugal	Latvia	2004
United Kingdom	Lithuania	2004
United States	Romania	2004
	Slovakia	2004
	Slovenia	2004

* NATO founded in 1949

Figure 8.13 NATO members as of 2004. In 2002, the Russian Federation established cooperative relations with NATO through the NATO–Russia Council.

After the September 11, 2001 terrorist attacks on the United States, NATO expanded its focus to include the sharing of **intelligence** to defend against chemical, biological, and nuclear attacks. On September 12, NATO declared the terrorist attacks on the United States to be an attack on all NATO countries under Article 5 of the *North Atlantic Treaty*. This landmark decision was followed by measures to help the United States in its campaign against terrorism. In August 2003, NATO assumed command of international peacekeeping forces in the Kabul area of Afghanistan. It was NATO's first action outside Europe.

THE WEB

To learn about NATO in Afghanistan, and the Warsaw Pact, visit www.emp.ca/cwp.

The Warsaw Pact

After West Germany was allowed to remilitarize and join NATO in 1955, the Soviet Union established the **Warsaw Pact** to counter the enormous military power of the NATO alliance. The Pact was created by the *Warsaw Treaty of Friendship, Cooperation, and Mutual Assistance*, which was drafted by Soviet leader Nikita Khrushchev and signed in Warsaw, Poland, on May 14, 1955. The Soviet Union and all the communist states of Eastern Europe (Albania, Bulgaria, Czechoslovakia, East Germany, Hungary, Poland, and Romania), except Yugoslavia, were signatories.

THE WEB

Read Winston Churchill's famous 1946 "Iron Curtain" speech at www.emp.ca/cwp.

The Pact, which described itself as a unified military command, gave the (Soviet) Red Army bases in all member states. Membership was not voluntary. When Hungary tried to withdraw from the Warsaw Pact in October 1956, the Red Army invaded. The Hungarian Revolution, a student-led popular uprising demanding democratic reform and an end to Soviet domination, was crushed within two weeks. The Soviets had established an Iron Curtain, and Hungary would remain behind it. The Warsaw Pact ended formally in 1991 with the collapse of the Soviet Union and the political transformation of Eastern Europe.

The Cold War Classification of States

During the Cold War, states were categorized in several ways. The East–West classification posited the East as the Soviet Union and the Warsaw Pact countries (also known as the Soviet bloc) of Eastern and Central Europe. Opposing the East was the West, which included the United States, its NATO allies, and rich, industrialized democracies including Australia, South Africa, and later Japan and other westernized countries. The globe was also divided into three "worlds." The First World was the West, the Second World was the East (including China), and the Third World comprised the less-developed countries—in Africa, Asia, and Latin America—that were not politically aligned with either the capitalist West or the communist East.

Since the end of the Cold War, world politics has changed and these categories have fallen out of use. Today, the world is often divided instead into developed and developing countries, and sometimes North (usually developed) and South (usually developing) countries (see also Chapter 12).

North American Aerospace Defense Command

As nuclear and missile technology advanced in the 1950s, the Canadian and US governments cooperated to defend North America from possible Soviet attack. The *North American Air Defense Agreement* (NORAD) was created in 1958 and renamed the *North American Aerospace Defense Command* in 1981. Initially, NORAD focused on outside threats to North American aerospace. After the September 11 attacks, it broadened its focus to include threats from within North American aerospace. NORAD headquarters are near Colorado Springs, Colorado.

Canada's geographical position between the two superpowers made Canada's North critical to NORAD defence systems. With the approval of the Canadian government, the United States built early warning radar installations across the high Arctic. The Conservative government of Prime Minister John Diefenbaker (1895–1979; prime minister, 1957–63) also allowed US bombers and fighter planes to fly through Canadian airspace and to use Canadian bases as potential staging areas for bombing runs against the Soviets. Many Canadians were concerned that Canada was sacrificing

SOUND BITE   "We shall be Canadians first, foremost and always, and our policies will be decided in Canada and not dictated by any other country."

Prime Minster John Diefenbaker, in a speech in Rimouski, Quebec in 1962

Figure 8.14 This cartoon showing former Prime Minister John Diefenbaker "blowing his own horn" appeared in 1971, when the last US Bomarc missiles were removed from Canada.

its sovereignty and independent foreign policy to be protected under the US defence umbrella.

In 1958, under NORAD, the Diefenbaker government had agreed to US Bomarc anti-bomber missile installations at two sites in Canada. These were intended to defend the United States, and Canada, from possible nuclear attack from Soviet bombers. By 1960, however, it was learned that the Bomarcs would carry nuclear warheads. A debate about nuclear weapons on Canadian territory swept through the House of Commons and across Canada. Later, in 1962, Diefenbaker refused to put the Canadian military on high alert during the Cuban Missile Crisis (see Chapter 11). This infuriated US President John F. Kennedy. In Parliament, Diefenbaker's defence minister resigned, and the Conservative minority government fell. In the federal election that year, the Conservatives were reduced to a minority government again.

As Canada–US relations continued under strain in 1963, Liberal leader Lester Pearson came out in support of the nuclear warheads and accused Diefenbaker of being indecisive and anti-American. Diefenbaker's government fell once more, but Pearson won a minority government in the election of 1963. Not until 1969 did the Liberal government, under Prime Minister Pierre Trudeau, make Canada's armed forces officially non-nuclear. The last Bomarc missile was removed from Canada in 1971. By this time, the anti–nuclear-weapon movement had become a major force in Canadian political life. Yet Canadian forces had control over nuclear weapons, based in Europe, until 1984.

THE WEB

Learn how Canadian leaders responded to the Cuban Missile Crisis at www.emp.ca/cwp.

Music and Politics

Freedom and Protest Songs of the 1960s

People have expressed their political hopes and fears through song for hundreds of years. Before and after the US Civil War (1861–65), African Americans sang spirituals (gospel songs) about freedom. In the 19th and 20th centuries, people used songs to denounce slavery, promote temperance and women's rights, and organize workers. In the decades after World War II, there seemed to be a political silence in popular music. Then came rock and roll and the 1960s, a time of unprecedented social unrest.

In demonstrations around the world, young people protested for women's and sexual liberation, civil rights, environmental protection, and an end to the nuclear arms race. In the United States, assassins gunned down President John F. Kennedy (1963), his brother Robert (1968), and black civil rights leaders Malcolm X (1965) and Martin Luther King, Jr. (1968). Racial and political tensions flared into riots. In the same period, many young American men fled to Canada to escape compulsory military service to fight the US war in Vietnam. They were known as "draft dodgers" and became symbols of the anti-authority counterculture.

Popular music—folk, spiritual, rock—was the counterculture's lifeblood. American singers Pete Seeger and Joan Baez (who refused to pay income tax to protest US military spending) recorded "We Shall Overcome," the US civil rights anthem with deep roots in slavery times. Records by folk groups like Peter, Paul, and Mary ("If I Had a Hammer") and singer-songwriters like Phil Ochs ("I Ain't Marching Anymore") and Bob Dylan ("The Times They Are A-Changin'") topped music charts with pacifist and civil rights messages. The lyrics of "Eve of Destruction," written by 16-year-old P.F. Sloane and recorded by Barry McGuire in 1965, warned of nuclear disaster, capturing the deep anxieties of the times.

Canadian voices also sang out with political messages and insights, from Buffy Sainte-Marie's "Universal Soldier" to Bonnie Dobson's "Morning Dew" (about nuclear devastation), Gordon Lightfoot's "Black Day in July" (about 1967 race riots in Detroit), and Neil Young's "Ohio" (about four student protestors killed by the Ohio National Guard; see Figure 2.25 on page 73). Protest even landed on Broadway. In 1967, *Hair: The American Tribal Love–Rock Musical*, with music by Canadian Galt McDermott, opened and was battered by critics for vulgarity, nudity, and its love-and-peace-not-war message. It was a huge hit and ran for five years. *Hair* pushed for new priorities and the dawning of "The Age of Aquarius."

Figure 8.15 *Hair* is still packing them in with its anti-war melodies and dance numbers. This photograph is from the 2004 Paris production. Why might the musical's messages be as relevant today as they were in the 1960s?

Questions

1. Outline at least four reasons why many youths were protesting in the 1960s.
2. Use an Internet search engine to find the lyrics of one of the protest songs mentioned in the text. Then write a short report on the event or issue being protested.
3. What songs, music, plays, and TV shows might be considered controversial or offensive today? Explore why, or why not, something is offensive, controversial, or both.
4. Popular music and films have often focused on periods of political discontent. What songs or films in recent years have focused on protest movements? What controversies do these popular songs and films explore?

The *Geneva Conventions*: Humanitarian Law

As you read earlier, 16 European countries ratified the first *Geneva Convention* (the *Geneva Convention for the Amelioration of the Condition of the Wounded in Armies in the Field*) in 1864 to ensure the humane treatment of battlefield casualties. It was the first example of international humanitarian law. It was also the founding of the International Committee of the Red Cross, which was vital to the drafting and enforcement of later *Geneva Conventions* (Figure 8.16).

The *Geneva Conventions* and several protocols evolved to deal with the changing technologies and styles of war and to define the humane treatment

1864 I: Combatants wounded in the field
1906 II: Combatants wounded at sea
1929 III: Prisoners of war
1949 IV: Civilians

Figure 8.16 Timeline: The four *Geneva Conventions* and the groups covered.

THE WEB

Learn more about the *Geneva Conventions* and enforcement by the ICC at www.emp.ca/cwp.

of different groups during wartime. The 1925 *Geneva Protocol*, for example, prohibited the use of poison gas and bacteriological weapons (see Chapter 11). In 1949, the current four *Geneva Conventions* were amended and adopted. Two additional protocols, added in 1977, contain the ultimate rules limiting the impact of war.

The *Geneva Conventions* and protocols attempt to limit the barbarity of war both for combatants and for vulnerable non-combatants, such as civilians, medical and volunteer workers, and journalists. At the end of 2003, 191 states were signatories. Those who violate the *Geneva Conventions*, especially in cases of atrocities involving genocide, can be tried as war criminals by the International Criminal Court (ICC). Regardless of the crime, the ICC cannot impose the death penalty. Hoping to strengthen the Conventions, the Red Cross was a prime proponent of the ICC, which held its first session at The Hague in 2003.

Nuclear-Weapons Control Initiatives

As the US–Soviet arms race intensified, so did fears of nuclear world war. Canada, with vast natural deposits of uranium, had been one of the first countries involved in nuclear research during World War II and had worked closely with the United States. After the War, Canadian government policy renounced any interest in developing nuclear weapons—at least officially. Indian Prime Minister Jawaharlal Nehru (1889–1964) spearheaded international concerns. In 1954, two years after Britain tested its first nuclear bomb and joined the "nuclear club," he proposed a worldwide ban on nuclear test explosions. After years of negotiations, the United States, United Kingdom, and Soviet Union signed the *Partial Test Ban Treaty* in 1963. It banned nuclear tests in the atmosphere, underwater, and in space, but France and China were not signatories.

The Treaty on the Non-Proliferation of Nuclear Weapons

International fears over nuclear weapons led to the signing of the *Treaty on the Non-Proliferation of Nuclear Weapons* in 1968. It came into force in 1970 with three core objectives:

- prevention of the spread of nuclear weapons and weapons technology
- cooperation among nations in the peaceful uses of nuclear energy
- achievement of complete nuclear disarmament.

The five nuclear-weapons states could keep existing nuclear weapons but agreed to move toward nuclear disarmament and not to transfer nuclear-weapons technology. Non–nuclear-weapons states agreed not to develop or acquire nuclear weapons. By 2004, the treaty had been ratified by 189 countries. India, Israel, and Pakistan are the states that have not yet signed.

1945 United States
1949 USSR/Russia
1952 United Kingdom
1960 France
1964 China
1974 India*
1998 Pakistan*

*As of 2004, India and Pakistan had no formal delivery systems.

Figure 8.17 Timeline: Nuclear-weapons states with dates of first declared test. Iran, Israel, North Korea, and Ukraine are suspected of possessing, or having possessed, nuclear arms or nuclear arms technology.

The International Atomic Energy Agency (IAEA) is the UN body that inspects nuclear generation facilities in non–nuclear-weapons states to enforce compliance with non-proliferation. Nuclear reactors must not be used to acquire nuclear-weapons technology nor weapons-grade nuclear fuel. North Korea signed the non-proliferation treaty in 1985 but withdrew in April 2003 over IAEA inspections. It was the first such withdrawal and was officially condemned by many states.

Comprehensive Nuclear Test Ban Treaty, 1996

With full support from the General Assembly, negotiations started in 1993 to expand the 1968 non-proliferation treaty to ban all nuclear weapons tests. The *Comprehensive Nuclear Test Ban Treaty* that resulted prohibits all nuclear test explosions and was opened for signatures in New York in September 1996. Canada had advocated the ban since the 1960s and was one of the first states to sign and ratify the treaty. The treaty has become the legal cornerstone of nuclear non-proliferation and the bedrock of the global nuclear disarmament movement.

The complete ban on nuclear tests was designed also to restrict research and development of nuclear weaponry. As of late 2004, the treaty had 172 signatories and had been ratified by 117 states. To be implemented fully, however, it must be ratified by the 44 countries known or believed to have nuclear-weapons capacity (Canada is included). Thirty-two of these nuclear-weapons states—including the United Kingdom, France, and Russia—have ratified the treaty. India, Pakistan, and North Korea have not signed. China and the United States are signatories but have not ratified. US security policy—on terrorism and the positioning of nuclear testing as central to the US policy of nuclear deterrence—suggests US ratification is unlikely.

SOUND BITE "This measure will heighten regional tensions and further isolate Pyongyang from the international community. We strongly urge the Democratic People's Republic of Korea to reverse its decision and to comply fully with all its nuclear non-proliferation obligations, including its safeguards agreement with the International Atomic Energy Agency."

Bill Graham, Canada's Minister of Foreign Affairs, January 10, 2003

THE WEB

Learn more about nuclear disarmament and explosion monitoring at www.emp.ca/cwp.

Check YOUR UNDERSTANDING

1. What is the main distinction between a declaration and a treaty?
2. What is a "middle power," and why is Canada considered one?
3. What is the Warsaw Pact, and what is its current status?
4. Why was Canada's involvement in NATO and NORAD criticized by many Canadians?
5. Describe the impact of the Cold War on the UN's effectiveness.
6. How have NATO and NORAD objectives changed since September 11, 2001?
7. Describe the *Geneva Conventions* and their international significance.
8. In spite of the *Treaty on the Non-Proliferation of Nuclear Weapons* and the *Comprehensive Nuclear Test Ban Treaty*, why does the threat of nuclear war remain?
9. Why is the *Comprehensive Nuclear Test Ban Treaty* not yet in force?

Keeping the Peace

PRESS PLAY

On the Beach (1959), directed by Stanley Kramer and starring Gregory Peck, explores Cold War fears of worldwide devastation following a nuclear war. Based on the novel by Nevil Shute. (PG)

How successful has the UN been at maintaining peace? There is no easy answer to this question. Few would dispute that the UN has provided an international forum where decades of Cold War tensions and decolonization struggles could be dealt with through diplomatic channels. A string of Cold War flashpoints—such as the Hungarian Revolution (1956), the building of the Berlin Wall (1961), and the Cuban Missile Crisis (1962)—threatened world peace. Yet each crisis was contained or defused. This came at a cost. Although no direct or "hot" war broke out between the superpowers, the economic, ideological, and political rivalry fuelled deadly regional wars around the world.

Among the causes of the Cold War were

- Soviet fear of US nuclear attack after Hiroshima (1945)
- US refusal to share nuclear technology
- US President Truman's dislike of Soviet dictator Joseph Stalin
- US fear of Soviet nuclear attack (after 1949)
- Soviet rejection of Western capitalism and colonialism
- Soviet military dominance of Eastern European satellite states
- Soviet support of revolutionary communism around the world.

The Birth of UN Peacekeeping

Peacekeeping was not outlined in the UN Charter, yet nothing has distinguished the UN more in the public eye. Instead, peacekeeping developed from early UN observer missions that were sent to trouble spots to observe, monitor, and report findings. Canadian troops participated in the earliest UN observer missions and supervised truces in the Arab–Israeli conflict in 1948, and later along the India–Pakistan ceasefire line in Kashmir in 1949 (see Chapter 3, pages 100–1 and 98–99). These were small-scale, non-force, observer groups only, and not substantial military forces.

Peacekeeping involves the use of substantial military forces. Military personnel—peacekeepers from the UN or a multinational group of neutral nations—are literally positioned between warring factions. Peacekeeping soldiers do not negotiate peace agreements; they simply keep the sides apart physically and maintain order. This is the procedure followed when UN troops are invited to help maintain peace or ceasefire agreements. UN peacekeeping did not exist until 1956, when the Suez Crisis threatened world peace.

The Suez Crisis and the UN Emergency Force

The year 1956 saw a violent realignment in the balance of power in the Middle East and a flareup in the Cold War. Newly elected Egyptian President

Gamal Abdel Nasser (1918–70), who had introduced a one-party system and socialist reforms, strongly asserted Egypt's independence. His charisma had also made him a leader of Arab nationalism and the **non-aligned movement** ("Third World" countries not allied with either the West or the East during the Cold War). In 1956, the United States, with British support, withdrew the financial support it had promised Egypt for the construction of the Aswan High Dam. In response, Nasser nationalized the Suez Canal, which was owned by the Franco–British Suez Canal Company. Henceforward, ships using the canal would pay a toll to Egypt. Revenues would help finance the Aswan Dam, which was central to Egypt's massive hydro-electricity and irrigation projects.

The Suez Canal links the Mediterranean to the Red Sea and is a vital shipping route between the Middle East and Europe. When the British and French made threats, Nasser did not back down. He spoke out in support of the Palestinians and threatened Israel. In what many saw as an act of Western arrogance, France, Britain, and Israel secretly plotted and then attacked Egypt to regain control of the canal on October 29, 1956.

The attack on Egypt fractured NATO relations. The United States condemned Britain and France. In Britain, Prime Minister Anthony Eden was forced to resign. In France, the public strongly supported the attack on Egypt. Canada officially would not support either Britain or France. The attack on Egypt was also condemned by the UN—and the Soviet Union. The Soviet Union was too preoccupied quashing the Hungarian Revolution to be directly involved, but threatened to bomb London and Paris. It provided Egypt (and Iraq and Syria) with military and economic support. Fears mounted: would war break out between the world's two military superpowers as they vied for influence in the region? US foreign policy was clear: it would use force, if necessary, to stop the "communist threat" in the Middle East from spreading.

Canadian diplomats at the UN tried to negotiate a solution. When Britain and France vetoed ceasefire resolutions in the Security Council, the General Assembly convened an emergency special session, in which a ceasefire won overwhelming support. After the passage of the General Assembly resolution, Britain, France, and Israel complied. Canada's Secretary of State for External Affairs, Lester Pearson, proposed that a large, multinational UN force be created and positioned between the Egyptian and Israeli forces to supervise ceasefire compliance. The so-called "Canadian initiative" was adopted by the General Assembly on November 3, 1956. Tensions remained high until mid-November, when the UN Emergency Force (UNEF) arrived in Egypt, with soldiers from more than 20 countries. The United States pressured Britain and France to allow the UN action.

By late December, Britain and France had withdrawn from Egypt. Israel followed in early 1957. The Suez Canal was cleared of wreckage and returned

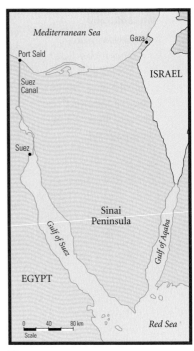

Figure 8.18 The Suez Canal.

1952 Col. Nasser and Egyptian officers overthrow monarchy

1955 World Bank offers Egypt $1 billion loan for Aswan Dam

1956 April Egypt forms military alliance with Syria, Saudi Arabia, and Yemen

1956 May Egypt recognizes communist China

1956 June Nasser is elected, signs arms deal with USSR

1956 July Loan cancelled

1956 July 26 Suez Canal is nationalized

1956 October Israel attacks Sinai, seizes Gaza Strip

1956 October/November Britain and France bomb canal

1956 November UN ceasefire adopted

1957 March Canal reopens under UN supervision

Figure 8.19 Timeline: The Suez Crisis.

THE WEB

Learn more about the Suez Crisis and Pearson's role in it, his life, and his Nobel lecture ("The Four Faces of Peace") at www.emp.ca/cwp.

to Egypt in March 1957 under the supervision of a UN police force. The UN force remained in Egypt's Sinai Peninsula until May 1967, when Nasser ordered it to leave. Weeks later, the Six-Day War erupted in the Middle East (see Chapter 3). The UN Emergency Force had kept the peace, but it hadn't resolved the conflict.

For his extraordinary diplomatic achievement, Pearson was awarded the 1957 Nobel Peace Prize. The honour reflected well on Canada in the world. In Ottawa, however, opposition leader Diefenbaker accused the Liberal government of stabbing Britain in the back. Diefenbaker was livid when Liberal Prime Minister St. Laurent described Britain and France as "supermen of Europe whose days are about over." In the 1957 election, the Liberals' Suez position contributed to their loss at the polls: a minority Conservative government under Diefenbaker was elected. St. Laurent retired the next year. In 1958, Diefenbaker called an election—and the Conservatives won 208 of 265 seats in the House of Commons.

The Suez mission established the characteristics for UN peacekeeping and conflict resolution:

- a ceasefire in place
- consent from the disputing parties to deployment of a UNEF
- an impartial, lightly armed force, permitted to shoot only in self-defence.

Peacekeeping: From Suez to Today

UN peacekeepers, including thousands of Canadian soldiers, faced another complex challenge in 1960 when the Congo (now Zaire) collapsed into anarchy days after becoming independent. Thousands of UN peacekeepers were rushed to Africa to ensure that Belgian troops withdrew and that civil war did not break out. At the height of the four-year Congo mission, nearly 20,000 peacekeepers were on duty. Canada's longest UN peacekeeping involvement started as an observer mission in 1959 to Cyprus, just before the Mediterranean island gained its independence from Britain in 1960. By 1963, ethnic conflicts were breaking out between Greek and Turkish Cypriots. When Greece and Turkey threatened to intervene, a regional conflict became an international crisis. Britain hoped to maintain peace through UN intervention, and UN peacekeepers, including a large Canadian contingent, were dispatched. As you may recall, Canadian troops had been distrusted as being essentially British during the Suez Crisis. In Cyprus, this was no longer so. Canada was perceived as neutral. Eventually, Cyprus was partitioned into Turkish and Greek republics. Canada kept an infantry battalion in Cyprus until the mid-1990s and still maintains a small group of observers there.

THE WEB

Learn more about Canada's roles in both UN and non-UN peacekeeping missions at www.emp.ca/cwp.

Taking a Stand   Lester Bowles "Mike" Pearson

Lester B. Pearson (1897–1972) believed in internationalism and practised it throughout a long and distinguished career. As Undersecretary of State for External Affairs (1946–47), he guided Canada's response to the Cold War. His principles were clear: strong opposition to totalitarian Soviet communism, support for multilateral organizations, and expansion of Canada's role in international affairs. During debates leading to the founding of NATO, Pearson's input was far-sighted and daring. He argued for a broad alliance whose concerns would extend beyond security to include socio-economic issues. After serving as Secretary of State from 1948 to 1958, Pearson became Liberal Party leader in 1958, president of the UN General Assembly in 1962, and Canada's 14th prime minister from 1963 to 1968.

Pearson's greatest achievement was the creation of the United Nations Emergency Force during the Suez Crisis. It was a defining moment in Canadian international politics. With support from UN Secretary-General Dag Hammarskjold, Pearson crafted a General Assembly motion that called for the creation of a peacekeeping force and the withdrawal of the invading forces. The British were irritated, even though Pearson argued he was saving them from catastrophe. His solution also allowed Britain and France to save face and stay in favour with the United States. Pearson's initiative was attacked by the conservative anglophone media in Canada. The Egyptians objected to the presence of Canadian soldiers because the flags on their uniforms reminded Egyptians of the British colonizers and invaders. Nonetheless, with Canadian General E.L.M. Burns as its first commander, UN peacekeeping was born.

In his 1957 Nobel Peace Prize lecture, Pearson described the "greatest enemy of peace":

> I believe myself that the Russian people—to cite one example—wish for peace. I believe also that many of them think that the Americans are threatening them with war, that they are in danger of attack. So might I, if I had as little chance to get objective and balanced information about what is going on in the United States. Similarly, our Western fears of the Soviet Union have been partly based on a lack of understanding or of information about the people of that country. Misunderstanding of this kind arising from ignorance breeds fear, and fear remains the greatest enemy of peace.

Pearson never won a majority government. Yet, his two minority governments, guided by his Canadian nationalism and skills in the art of compromise, helped create the Canada we know today. During his time as prime minister, the Canadian flag was adopted, and universal health care, the Canada Pension Plan, and the principles of bilingualism and biculturalism were introduced.

When "Mike" Pearson died on December 27, 1972, Canadians and people around the world mourned his passing. The obituary in the *New York Times* expressed not only a profound respect for Pearson, but keen political insight and appreciation:

> His skill as negotiator and mediator during and after World War II enabled Canada to play a world role out of proportion to its size and power. His contributions to the launching of the UN and the Atlantic Alliance [NATO] were creative and enduring . . . [and] climaxed by his heroic part in defusing the Suez crisis of 1956 that might have exploded in World War III. He richly deserved the Nobel Peace Prize.

Questions

1. Why was Pearson's peacekeeping plan a defining moment for Canada in international politics?
2. What opposition did Pearson experience to his peacekeeping force? Was it justified? Explain.
3. Of the many lasting achievements of Pearson's minority governments, which is the most important to you, and why?
4. Interpret Pearson's analysis of the impact of ignorance and fear on peace in your own words. Use examples from today's world conflicts to illustrate your interpretation.

Peacekeeping After the Cold War

The end of the Cold War marked the beginning of the most intense period UN peacekeeping has ever faced. Canada became involved in many missions in the 1990s. Several of these exposed deep problems within both UN peacekeeping and the Canadian military. Missions in Bosnia, Croatia, Somalia, Rwanda, Central Africa, and East Timor strained Canadian and UN resources to the breaking point. UN peacekeeping clearly had to change. The United Nations expanded the mandate and focus of peacekeeping to include **peacemaking** and **peace-building**. A 1992 UN Security Council policy statement, "An Agenda for Peace: Preventive Diplomacy, Peacemaking and Peace-keeping" outlined a new, multi-level approach:

> 15. With the end of the cold war . . . demands on the United Nations have surged. Its security arm . . . has emerged as a central instrument for the prevention and resolution of conflicts and for the preservation of peace. Our aims must be:
>
> - To seek to identify at the earliest possible stage situations that could produce conflict, and to try through diplomacy to remove the sources of danger before violence results;

Where conflict erupts, to engage in peacemaking aimed at resolving the issues that have led to conflict;

- Through peacekeeping, to work to preserve peace, however fragile, where fighting has been halted and to assist in implementing agreements achieved by the peacemakers;
- To stand ready to assist in peace-building in its differing contexts: rebuilding the institutions and infrastructures of nations torn by civil war and strife; and building bonds of peaceful mutual benefit among nations formerly at war; . . .

You will learn more about these and other new directions in conflict prevention and resolution in Chapters 9 and 11, but a brief review and overview will conclude this chapter. These terms, like the processes they describe, are still in transition. Different groups may use them slightly differently.

Peacekeeping is defined as the use of an invited multinational group of soldiers to help maintain peace or ceasefire agreements. Peacekeepers do not conduct peace negotiations. In *peacemaking*, leaders and diplomats try to negotiate a peaceful settlement to conflict. While peacemaking may involve only the parties in conflict, third-party mediators, such as UN diplomats, are often used to help parties draft a workable peace. UN peacemaking may, under certain circumstances, use military force to enforce peace and prevent human suffering or human rights abuses. This is detailed in Chapter VII of the UN Charter and Articles 42 and 43 in particular. *Peace-building* takes action on the root causes of conflict to create the conditions for long-term

SOUND BITE
"[Peace-building is] action to identify and support structures which will tend to strengthen and solidify peace in order to avoid a relapse into conflict— rebuilding the institutions and infrastructures of nations torn by civil war and strife [and tackling the] deepest causes of conflict: economic despair, social injustice and political oppression."

Secretary-General Boutros Boutros-Ghali, "An Agenda for Peace," 1992

Figure 8.20 A US soldier helps a survivor after a suicide bomber destroyed UN headquarters in Baghdad on August 19, 2003. Twenty-three people were killed, including the UN's special envoy to Iraq and one of Canada's most promising young diplomats. What long-term consequences could such attacks have on peace-building efforts?

SOUND BITE "The United Nations will not be reckless. Nor, however, will it be intimidated. The service of the UN is not simply a job. It is a calling, and those who have attacked us will not deflect us from it. We shall find a way to continue our work. . . ."

UN Secretary-General Kofi Annan, August 20, 2003, in New York, after UN staff were killed in Iraq

peace and to prevent conflict. It includes a wide spectrum of efforts in the political, developmental, humanitarian, and human rights spheres.

A Canadian diplomat and future prime minister invented UN peace-keeping. Since then, Canada has played a leading role in creating and implementing new UN peace-building principles that extend beyond the traditional UN peacekeeping criteria. In missions in Afghanistan and Haiti, Canadian peacekeepers and peace-builders have taken on such responsibilities as supervising elections, monitoring human rights, distributing relief supplies, repatriating refugees, and training police. Conditions in Afghanistan have been dangerous and unstable. Rebels have attacked humanitarian NGOs. The mission structure in Afghanistan is awkward: the UN has determined the force's mandate, but military command is in NATO's hands. Because the NATO force relies on volunteer forces—even from non-NATO countries—the alliance has had to consult different governments on key decisions. Yet elections in Afghanistan were held in October 2004. UN peacekeeping in the 21st century is a work in progress.

Check YOUR UNDERSTANDING

1. What were some of the main causes of the Cold War?
2. What were four objectives of early UN observer missions?
3. Why might the Suez Crisis have led to World War III?
4. What situation did UN peacekeeping face after the Cold War?
5. Distinguish among peacekeeping, peacemaking, and peace-building.
6. How has Canada's traditional peacekeeping role changed in recent years?
7. Why is Canada's peacekeeping mission in Afghanistan a problem?

METHODS OF POLITICAL INQUIRY

Writing a United Nations Resolution

One way to hone your political science skills is to take part in a UN General Assembly simulation (see Chapter 11, page 401). For now, you will role-play the ambassador or delegate of a UN member state and write a resolution to be debated, and voted on, by the General Assembly. Your teacher will name your country.

In order to role-play the ambassador accurately, you need to research extensively the history, culture, geography, economics, and politics of your designated country. You also need to brief yourself on current world issues and the role of the UN.

Before drafting your resolution, formulate questions about your country's international role. Decide whether the resolution will be an opinion or a recommendation for UN action.

The Elements of a UN Resolution

A UN resolution is one long sentence punctuated with commas and semicolons and ending with a period. UN resolutions follow a common format. Each resolution has three parts: the *heading*, the *preamble*, and the *operative clauses*.

The heading includes the resolution topic, the UN body being addressed (e.g., the General Assembly), and the states sponsoring the resolution.

The preamble describes a problem that needs to be solved and often refers to the UN and its work. Phrases used in the preamble include: alarmed, aware, bearing in mind, concerned, conscious, deeply disturbed, endorsing, mindful of, observing, reaffirming, stressing, and so on. Each clause in the preamble should end with a comma.

Operative clauses express the country's main policy goals on the topic. Verbs frequently used include: affirms, appeals, calls upon, congratulates, directs, endorses, reminds, recommends, recognizes, and reiterates. The first word in each operative clause should be underlined or italicized. All operative clauses end with a semicolon except the final clause, which ends with a period.

A Sample UN Resolution

Heading:

Topic: Status of *Geneva Convention Relative to the Treatment of Prisoners of War*

Submitted to: The General Assembly

Sponsored by: Canada, France, Spain, and the Netherlands

Preamble: The General Assembly,

Acknowledging the benefits of the *Geneva Convention Relative to the Treatment of Prisoners of War* (Convention III) of 1949,

Reminding all the member states that the *Geneva Conventions* are a most vital part of the United Nations,

Reiterating the inviolable right to national sovereignty as enshrined in the UN Charter,

Recognizing the urgency of addressing acts of international terrorism,

Understanding that formal declarations of war are not common in today's world,

Operative Clauses:

1. *Urges* that all member states adhere to the principles of the *Geneva Convention Relative to the Treatment of Prisoners of War*;
2. *Recommends* the formation of a conference to discuss the application of *Geneva Convention III* in a global community that deals with undeclared wars and international terrorist groups.

Applying the Skill

1. Examine the sample UN resolution above. Research *Geneva Convention III*, and prepare arguments for and against the resolution. You will find a useful link at www.emp.ca/cwp.
2. Using the Internet and library, research your country's attitudes to human rights, peace and security, and international economic development. Determine your country's relationship with the world's superpower, the United States. Establish the identity of your country's allies and find out why they are allies. Then write a UN resolution that accurately reflects your country's political interests.
3. Go to www.emp.ca/cwp to listen as Lester B. Pearson presents a UN resolution to deal with the "grave and dangerous" Suez Crisis on November 3, 1956. Describe how he treats an earlier resolution to bring about and supervise compliance with a ceasefire.

Study Hall

Thinking/Inquiry

1. Demands for major reform of the UN Security Council have been increasing. In groups no larger than four, review the existing structure and reasons for some current criticisms. Then, brainstorm proposals for reforming the Council and share your recommendations with the class. As a class, select the best or most effective proposal and defend your selection.

2. Research and write a two-page report explaining the reasons for the significant increase in the number of multilateral treaties and conventions created since 1945. In your report, indicate if all these documents are necessary, and why or why not.

3. Create a chart to compare and contrast the minority government of John Diefenbaker in 1957 with that of Lester Pearson in 1963. Include the following headings: time period in office, number of seats held by the parties, major foreign policy issues, and an assessment of the overall contribution of the achievements to Canadian political history.

4. What is the most pressing issue facing the United Nations today? Choose from the following issues or define your own: spread of weapons of mass destruction, environmental degradation, ethnic conflicts, or weak commitments from important members. Prepare a dossier explaining your choice for either a group seminar or class presentation.

Communication

5. Look back at Figure 8.1 on page 262. The artist used a variety of symbols in this work. Some are personal; for example, Chagall included musical symbols when told of Dag Hammarskjold's love of Beethoven's Ninth Symphony. Other symbols are more general. Identify some, and explain what they convey to you.

6. Many Nobel Peace prizes have had links to the UN. In small groups, research how many there have been and the background on such recipients, including the reasons for their awards. Present your findings to the class as a multimedia presentation. As a class, prepare a "Top Five" list and justify your selections.

7. The *Universal Declaration of Human Rights* has been the foundation for many subsequent conventions. Research and prepare a report on a UN convention that deals with one of the following: children's rights, genocide, refugees, discrimination against women, torture and other degrading treatment, or migrant workers.

8. In small groups, review the Music and Politics feature on page 284 and the songs mentioned. Write a protest song, poem, or short story that reflects a current concern. Share your compositions as a class.

9. Find a print or Internet article that discusses an existing or potential violation of international law. Research the issue further, and determine how international law applies. Prepare a report outlining your findings.

Application

10. Create a visual report on a current international human rights concern. Use the Internet, magazines, and newspapers to gather visuals to illustrate the human impact locally, nationally, and internationally. Prepare an oral report to explain your visuals.

11. Locate three editorial cartoons that highlight an international organization or human rights issue. Outline the cartoonist's perspective and then analyze the cartoons, using the questions in Chapter 1, page 27.

12. Use the Internet to compile a list of Canada's peacekeeping missions since the 1956 Suez Crisis. Outline the details of the conflicts involved, including the objectives and outcome, and the length of time of each mission. Summarize your findings, using maps, tables, and graphs.

13. In Chapter 7 you examined the rights and responsibilities of citizens in democratic national communities. You observed, for example, that citizens have the right to equality before the law, and the responsibility to become informed about political issues. Using a two-column table, outline the parallel rights and responsibilities that states have in the international community. In your comparison of citizens and states, use specific examples.

Canada's International Roles

CHAPTER 9

Agenda

In this chapter, you will consider

• the nature of Canada's foreign policy
• the key federal agencies that develop and implement foreign policy
• Canadian peacekeeping missions
• Canada's role in Afghanistan
• Canada's membership in the Commonwealth and La Francophonie
• Canada's participation in global environmental initiatives
• some prominent Canadians who practise global citizenship
• how to document sources in formal writing

Figure 9.1 Canadian student Ashley Akins's multimedia artwork, *Seeds of Life*, portrays a role that she feels Canada must play internationally. It was a 2004 winner in CIDA's *butterfly 208* contest (see below).

Since the end of World War II, Canada has worked to establish itself internationally through a network of multilateral organizations and associations. Most of Canada's international relations take place through memberships in political organizations such as the United Nations, NATO, and NORAD, and economic organizations such as the International Monetary Fund, the North American Free Trade Agreement, and the World Bank.

This chapter will help you understand how federal departments and agencies shape and administer Canada's foreign policy. You will examine the ways in which Canada uses its influence in multilateral organizations to promote democracy, human rights, and international development. You will also examine Canada's support for UN and global initiatives to prevent environmental degradation and ensure a sustainable future. Finally, you will learn about a few Canadians who are practising responsible citizenship and making a difference in the global community.

Implementing Canada's Foreign Policy

As a middle power, Canada takes a multilateral approach to establishing its international influence. Canada's foreign policy embraces the need for co-operation and compromise and respects internationally accepted codes of conduct. By participating in international organizations, Canada is able to influence and support developing countries and moderate the activities of larger and more powerful allies. It achieves these goals through various foreign policy tools, from "soft" diplomatic measures such as trade, human rights discussions, and humanitarian and technical aid, to "hard" diplomacy such as peacemaking (involving military action), economic sanctions, international monitoring missions, and support for UN resolutions condemning the conduct of states.

The official principles of Canadian foreign policy—internationalism, multiculturalism, mediation, compromise, and peaceful change—reflect domestic political values. The blend of these characteristics creates a unique place for Canada in the global community, helping to preserve and foster Canada's national identity at home and abroad.

Foreign Affairs and International Trade

Foreign Affairs and International Trade are two of Canada's most powerful federal departments. For much of the 20th century, there was one department, known as External Affairs. In 1993, it became the Department of Foreign Affairs and International Trade. Then, in 2003, the department was divided into two ministries: Foreign Affairs Canada and International Trade Canada.

Foreign Affairs Canada manages Canada's day-to-day international relations in order to promote stability, prosperity, and Canadian values in other countries. It works to achieve these goals multilaterally through its wide range of relationships in international organizations as well as bilaterally through direct relations with other countries. Foreign Affairs Canada coordinates Canada's responses to international security, including protecting Canadians and Canadian government facilities abroad, handling international terrorist acts involving Canadians, and managing relations with foreign diplomats in Canada.

One main foreign policy objective is to promote human rights and democratic values. Canadian initiatives have included a leading role in establishing the Office of the High Commissioner for Human Rights and the International Criminal Court. Canada has signed all principal UN human rights treaties and regularly submits its own human rights record to UN monitoring bodies.

The role of International Trade Canada is to promote the country as a business leader and to negotiate trade agreements that will help Canadian businesses compete in the international marketplace. International Trade Canada is also responsible for regulating Canada's imports and exports.

SOUND BITE "Human rights are increasingly seen as inseparable from questions of international peace and security, international trade, and development assistance. In effect, human rights cannot be seen as an afterthought to other considerations in international relations, but must be seen as a 'threshold issue,' integral to our other foreign policy concerns."

Lloyd Axworthy, Canadian Minister of Foreign Affairs, Gordon Henderson Distinguished Lecture, University of Ottawa, November 1997

Sometimes the federal government faces difficult foreign policy choices when it comes to trade. For example, in the 1980s, Progressive Conservative Prime Minister Brian Mulroney led the Commonwealth campaign to impose economic sanctions on South Africa during the era of apartheid. Two of Canada's closest allies, the United States and Britain, opposed sanctions. In this case, the government placed the need to enforce democratic principles in South Africa above the need to expand trading opportunities. Canada's position on South Africa earned it respect among African countries. Different governments take different approaches to these issues at different times. In the 1990s, the Liberal government under Jean Chrétien believed the best way to promote democracy—and human rights—was through trade. Chrétien led trade delegations to countries such as China, which has a history of human rights abuses. Chrétien's policy was criticized by many human rights organizations, but many in the business community welcomed the emphasis on building new trade relationships.

The Department of National Defence and the Canadian Forces

In Canada, the federal government has sole authority in matters involving defence and protection of Canadian sovereignty. The Department of National Defence has three major objectives:

- to protect Canada
- to contribute to world peace and international security
- to protect Canadian interests abroad.

Domestically, the Canadian Forces protect Canadian territory and national interests and help during national emergencies. For example, Canadian Forces troops helped people threatened by severe flooding in Quebec and Manitoba in 1997 and by crippling ice storms in Ontario, Quebec, and the Maritimes in 1998. In partnership with the United States, the Canadian Forces defend North America by protecting Canada's borders, promoting the security of the Arctic, and participating in joint defence operations.

These objectives became critically important after the September 2001 terrorist attacks in the United States. Since then, agreeing on ways to protect North America from terrorist attacks has been a prominent issue in Canada–US relations.

The Canadian Forces as Peacekeepers in the 1990s

The Canadian Forces contribute to global security, peace, and stability through their participation in multilateral organizations such as the UN and NATO as well as in regional organizations. They also support humanitarian relief efforts to maintain peace in areas of conflict around the world. Canada's involvement in international peacekeeping is something many Canadians identify as the most important aspect of foreign policy. Although its contributions have sometimes been small, Canada has participated in every peacekeeping mission since the UN was created. Canadian troops also participated in the US-led Gulf War in 1991 and the UN-mandated security force in Afghanistan starting in late 2001. Since 1990, Canada has contributed to multinational peacekeeping and humanitarian relief efforts in many countries, including Bosnia, Rwanda, Somalia, Haiti, and Sudan, and continues to participate in 16 UN peacekeeping missions (see Chapters 1, 4, 8, and 11).

Chapter 4 described how, in 1991, the Balkans region collapsed in intense fighting among Bosnian Muslims, Croats, and Serbs. The world was shocked by reports of ethnic cleansing and the discovery of mass graves containing the remains of thousands of men, women, and children. As chief of staff for the UN Protection Force in the former Yugoslavia (UNPROFOR) in 1992, Canadian Major-General Lewis MacKenzie oversaw a coalition of 14,000 troops. The UN Protection Force took control of the airport at Sarajevo to ensure delivery of civilian relief supplies, but chaos reigned elsewhere. MacKenzie negotiated ceasefires with military leaders on all sides, but they were soon broken. Peacekeepers themselves became frequent targets of sniper gunfire. Ultimately, the UN mission did not bring peace. Because of the problems he encountered, MacKenzie became an outspoken critic of both the UN and Canada for providing inadequate funding, troops, and supplies. He continues to speak out, demanding reform of peacekeeping operations.

In the spring of 1993, Canadian peacekeeping faced a crisis in Somalia, a country in East Africa that was being ravaged by anarchy, civil war, drought, and famine. The proud image of Canada's peacekeepers was tarnished after it was learned that a 16-year-old Somali boy, Shidane Arone, had been killed by members of the elite Airborne Regiment. Investigators uncovered videotapes showing renegade Canadian soldiers performing sadistic acts of torture.

The Airborne Regiment was disbanded in 1995, but Canadians were not satisfied. Bowing to public pressure, the federal government convened a public inquiry. After two years of contentious hearings, and over the objections of the commissioners, the government ordered the inquiry to wrap up. In its final report, *Dishonoured Legacy*, the inquiry charged that military

SOUND BITE "We had thought of our peacekeepers as our ambassadors to the world, carrying Canadian values of toleration and moderation to less fortunate nations. Now we had to cope with the incredible suggestion that they were carrying our values when they ran amok in Somalia."

Peter Desbarats,
Somalia Cover-Up:
A Commissioner's
Journal, *1997*

Figure 9.2 In 2001, the Canadian Forces joined the multinational security force sent to Afghanistan. In April 2004, Prime Minister Paul Martin announced Canada's role would be expanded to serve as an example of the "3D approach" to international crises: diplomacy, defence, and development.

leaders had failed to prepare the troops for conditions in Somalia. It also condemned military high command for blaming subordinates for the incident and for failing to accept responsibility for the collapse of military discipline. Still, with the inquiry cut short, the report was incomplete. Questions remained about how Canada's peacekeeping forces had fallen into such disgrace and how far up in the military hierarchy coverups had gone.

The Role of Politics in the Military

Military spending is one of the most contentious areas of political decision making. In 1963, the federal government unified the army, navy, and air force into the Canadian Forces to improve efficiency and to cut costs. The decision launched a debate that lingers to this day. Critics charged unification would destroy morale in the Canadian military. Subsequently, Liberal governments under Pierre Trudeau reduced military spending; their foreign policy objectives focused more on peacekeeping than on defence. In the 1990s, further budget cuts led to major reductions in military personnel and equipment.

One of the most controversial defence decisions was made in 1992, when Prime Minster Brian Mulroney's Conservative government awarded a $5.8 billion contract to a European consortium and its Canadian partner to build 50 EH-101 helicopters to replace Canada's aging Sea Kings. During the 1993 federal election, the Liberals attacked the plan as a waste of taxpayers' money. Liberal leader Jean Chrétien campaigned promising to cancel the deal. As prime minister, Chrétien kept his word, scuttling the deal at a cost of approximately $500 million. The issue remained a low priority for more than a decade. Then, in July 2004, the newly elected minority Liberal government

Figure 9.3 This cartoon comments on the federal government's announcement in July 2004 to buy Sikorsky helicopters from US makers. What messages does it convey to you?

THE WEB

Learn more about the Canadian Forces and HMCS *Chicoutimi* at www.emp.ca/cwp.

of Prime Minister Paul Martin faced political pressure from the military and the opposition to replace the helicopters. The Department of National Defence announced a more modest plan to buy 28 Sikorsky S-92 helicopters for $3.2 billion. That decision was still controversial; critics argued that the original EH-101 helicopters were better. In October 2004, the federal government had to delay signing the Sikorsky contract—the original EH-101 consortium had issued a court challenge.

In October 2004, tragedy struck when electrical fires broke out onboard the submarine HMCS *Chicoutimi* during its first voyage for the Canadian Forces. Later, Lieutenant Chris Saunders died as a result of smoke inhalation. The *Chicoutimi* was part of a controversial 1998 deal to replace Canada's aging submarines with four refurbished British submarines. After the incident, all four submarines were docked and a military board of inquiry was called to examine the causes of the fire. In Parliament, the Liberal government was accused of buying inferior submarines and risking Canadian lives. For the first time in more than 40 years, Canada had no active submarines in service. There were widespread demands for a full public inquiry.

Debates over Defence Spending

Canadian opinion has long been divided over military spending. Many Canadians question the need for a full-scale military defence force. They argue that Canada is the sixth-highest military spender among NATO countries and that, at $13.6 billion (in 2004), military spending is too high. They believe money could be put to better use in health and social programs. Others insist that military spending must be increased to ensure that members of the Canadian Forces can safely fulfill their roles as peacekeepers and defenders of Canada, especially with heightened fears of terrorism.

The Canadian International Development Agency

Aid is a vital part of Canada's foreign policy. By supporting social and economic development around the world, foreign aid contributes to global security and prosperity. It also gives Canada an important voice on the world stage, promotes Canadian values and institutions, and strengthens the cultural links between Canada and other countries. Each year, Canada distributes billions of dollars in international development assistance in the form of goods and services, human knowledge and skills, and financial contributions to developing countries. Some of this is short-term humanitarian assistance to provide emergency relief during natural disasters such as earthquakes, floods, and droughts. Most of it is committed to improving the quality of life for people in developing countries through **sustainable development** programs (see page 318).

The Canadian International Development Agency (CIDA) was created in 1968 to plan and implement Canada's foreign aid programs. CIDA distributes 80 percent of Canadian aid; the Department of Finance, Foreign Affairs Canada, and International Trade Canada administer the other 20 percent through contributions to the World Bank and other organizations.

SOUND BITE "In the past few decades, successive Canadian governments have habitually referred to Canada as a 'peacekeeping nation'. . . . The more our leaders emphasize this secondary duty for the military (secondary to protecting the country), the easier it is to justify spending less money on essential equipment, training, and personnel—based on the erroneous . . . premise that peacekeeping units can get by with cheaper versions (and much less) of just about everything."

Lewis MacKenzie,
The Washington Post,
January 14, 2001

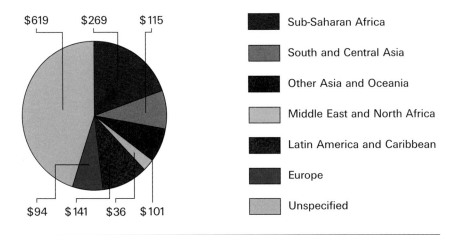

$619 $269 $115

■ Sub-Saharan Africa

■ South and Central Asia

■ Other Asia and Oceania

□ Middle East and North Africa

■ Latin America and Caribbean

■ Europe

□ Unspecified

$94 $141 $36 $101

Source: Organisation for Economic Co-operation and Development, http://www.oecd.org/dataoecd/42/21/1860310.gif.

Figure 9.4 Canada's official development aid by region (in millions of US$) for 2001–2.

CIDA supports projects in more than 150 countries that represent almost 80 percent of the world's people. The largest share of Canada's aid budget goes to the poorest countries of Africa, Asia, Latin America, and the Caribbean.

CIDA distributes aid in three ways. Multilateral aid provides funds to international agencies operating through the UN and other organizations. Bilateral aid is negotiated between Canada and individual countries according to their needs and level of development. Often, aid is tied to certain conditions, requiring recipients to use the funds to buy Canadian goods and services. Critics charge that such **tied aid** is self-serving, placing the interests of the donor country above those of the recipient. CIDA also donates aid to non-governmental organizations (NGOs). These agencies raise money through private fundraising. Then CIDA matches, doubles, or triples the amount of money raised.

CIDA's objective is to help developing countries generate the tools that will enable them to meet their own needs. Canada's official long-term aid strategy concentrates on six priorities:

- to meet basic human needs by providing primary health care, basic education, family planning, nutrition, water and sanitation, and shelter
- to promote gender equality by supporting programs that foster the equality of women in the sustainable development of their societies

	1999–2000 Base Year	2000–1 Year 1	2001–2 Year 2	2002–3 Year 3	2003–4 Year 4	2004–5 Year 5	Total 5-Year Investment
Basic health and nutrition	$152	$182	$203	$248	$275	$305	$1,213
Basic education	$41	$49	$82	$110	$150	$164	$555
HIV/AIDS	$20	$22	$36	$62	$70	$80	$270
Child protection	$9	$10	$18	$27	$31	$36	$122
Integrated basic human needs[1]	$94	$90	$101	$101	$101	$101	$494
UN social development priority funding[2]	$26	$26	$26	$32	$35	$38	$157
Total social development priorities	$342	$379	$466	$580	$662	$724	$2,811

[1] "Integrated basic human needs" covers programs that cannot be disaggregated by sub-area of activity or that are designed to strengthen the community to address basis human needs.

[2] The UN "social development priority" category includes CIDA contributions to the following UN agencies: UNICEF, UNIFEM, UNFPA, and WHO.

Source: "CIDA's Social Development Priorities: A Framework for Action," p. 15, at http://www.acdi-cida.gc.ca/INET/IMAGES.NSF/vLUImages/Social_Development3/$file/SDPFramework.pdf.

Figure 9.5 Funding for CIDA's social development priorities, 1999–2000 to 2004–5 (in millions of dollars).

Figure 9.6 This family plants cash crops on less than a hectare of land in Zimbabwe. Small family-run businesses are better able to utilize local resources and meet local needs than large, automated factories—because profits stay in the community, rather than going to foreign corporations.

- to help developing countries and **countries in transition** (former communist states making the transition from socialism to capitalism) build environmentally sound infrastructures
- to promote democratic values, good governance, and respect for human rights
- to promote economic development by supporting private-sector initiatives
- to help developing countries protect their environments and address regional environmental concerns.

Linking Aid to Human Rights and Environmental Protection

In 1990, Canada was one of the first countries to link foreign aid and human rights. As part of this policy, Canada has sometimes reduced or withdrawn financial aid to countries that have committed human rights violations. In other cases, aid has been redirected to organizations that promote democratic and human rights within a country. Still, the policy has not been universally applied. Canada continues to provide aid to China, for example, in spite of its human rights violations. Yet China is also one of the world's fastest-growing economies and a vast potential market for Canadian goods and services. Some human rights groups suggest that Canada is placing its trading interests ahead of its commitment to human rights.

THE WEB

Learn more about the Millennium Summit and its goals at www.emp.ca/cwp.

As the agency responsible for Canada's foreign aid, CIDA also supports the UN's primary commitment to prevent environmental destruction. CIDA supports the Millennium Development Goals, which were established at the Millennium Summit in September 2000 (see chapter 12, page 413. With a 2015 deadline, all 191 UN member states pledged they would set targets and meet goals to

- eradicate extreme poverty and hunger
- achieve universal primary education
- promote gender equality and the empowerment of women
- reduce child mortality
- improve maternal health
- combat HIV/AIDS, malaria, and other diseases
- ensure environmental sustainability
- develop a global partnership for development.

CIDA's Commitment in Afghanistan

Following the terrorist attacks of September 11, 2001, a US-led military coalition bombed Afghanistan and sent in troops to hunt down al-Qaida terrorists and end the rule of the Taliban, an Islamist movement that had rigidly ruled the country since 1996 and had harboured terrorists. Since then, aid organizations such as CIDA have worked to help Afghanistan recover from decades of civil war, drought, and famine. As the country begins its transi-

Press Play

In *Osama* (2003), a 12-year-old Afghan girl and her mother lose their jobs when the Taliban closes the hospital where they work. Feeling that she has no other choice, the mother disguises her daughter as a boy. (NR)

Figure 9.7 Afghanistan's new constitution, adopted in January 2004, formally recognizes women's rights. CIDA supports organizations that promote these rights, which were crushed under the Taliban. Here, Afghani women leave a polling booth in Kandahar during the October 2004 election.

Figure 9.8 A minesweeper works carefully near Kabul, Afghanistan, in 2001. The *Convention on the Prohibition of the Use, Stockpiling, Production and Transfer of Anti-Personnel Mines and on Their Destruction* (Mine-Ban Convention) was signed by 122 countries in Ottawa in 1997. Canada continues to contribute to global mine-ban efforts (see Chapter 10).

tion to democracy, reforms have included a new constitution, democratic elections, and school enrollment of more than 1 million girls.

Although reforms are under way, Afghanistan remains one of the world's poorest countries. The per capita (per person) annual income for its 24 million people is less than US$150. The country lacks a skilled and educated work force. Its infrastructure is crumbling. Life expectancy, at 46 years of age, is one of the lowest in the world. The infant mortality rate is the world's second highest: 25 percent of children die before the age of five.

Before 2001, Canada provided about $10 million a year to Afghanistan to help meet basic human needs. In January 2002, CIDA greatly expanded its role, including programs specifically dedicated to reconstruction and peace-building initiatives. By March 2004, CIDA had contributed $266.5 million to reconstruction programs, pledging an additional $250 million through 2009. Some of the programs have included

- development of a new-voter registration program
- funding of literacy programs
- funding of a women's centre to promote gender equality and provide leadership training
- rebuilding of the country's irrigation network and agricultural system
- removal of landmines
- funding a "micro-financing" program that provides credit and loans to individuals to start up small businesses.

These types of foreign aid initiatives by Canada and other countries are vital to creating lasting security for the people of Afghanistan.

Art and Politics

The Art of Involvement and *butterfly 208*

As minister of international cooperation in 2003, Susan Whelan had a clear idea of what *butterfly 208* can set in motion. By participating in *butterfly 208*, she said, "Canadian youth have taken a first step in getting involved in the fight against poverty and inequality around the world." An outrageous claim?

Butterfly 208 is an initiative of CIDA, in partnership with Canadian schools. Created in 2000, it is an annual art, writing, and multimedia contest for Canadian youth between the ages of 14 and 18. The name derives from the "butterfly effect," a theory that says if a butterfly flaps its wings in one part of the world it may set off a chain of events that eventually triggers a storm somewhere else in the world. The "208" represents the total number of countries of the world. Therefore, the contest's name represents an inter-connected world in which even small actions can have big consequences.

How can a contest engage Canadian young people in global issues? *Butterfly 208* identifies five overwhelming challenges that young people in developing countries face: HIV/AIDS; child protection; basic education; environmental degradation; and health and nutrition. Students who enter the contest must express their opinion about one of these global issues and offer their ideas for ways to initiate positive change. The program helps students develop the knowledge and skills they need to become responsible global citizens. It challenges students to think about how their actions may affect the rest of the world—just like a butterfly flapping its wings. It also provides the opportunity for students to make connections with young people in developing countries: contest winners travel to CIDA projects to observe and take part in development work firsthand.

THE WEB

Check out more winning *butterfly 208* entries at www.emp.ca/cwp.

Figure 9.9 Eighteen-year-old Keeley Haftner of Saskatoon won first prize, art, in 2004 for her pencil–crayon artwork, *Meet Beautiful Africa*. The face is beautiful; the reality is not. Haftner's intent is deadly serious: "She is my new ad campaign for hunger."

Questions

1. Explain the meaning of *butterfly 208*.
2. Working in small groups, debate the significance of the "butterfly effect" and try to reach a consensus about its validity.
3. How does *Meet Beautiful Africa* differ from many of the traditional images you see of hunger in Africa? Is the message effective? Give reasons for your answer.

Check YOUR UNDERSTANDING

1. What values does Canada promote in its foreign policy?
2. Why does Canada favour a multilateral approach in its foreign policy?
3. What challenges do Canadian peacekeepers face?
4. In what ways does politics play a role in the military?
5. Which side of the debate over defence spending do you support? Explain your views.
6. What is the purpose of the Canadian International Development Agency?
7. What is tied aid? Do you think criticism of tied aid is justified? Explain.
8. Do you think aid should be tied to a country's human rights record? Why or why not?
9. Why has CIDA made such a strong commitment to Afghanistan?

Canada's International Partners

Although the United Nations is the primary international organization, many other agencies influence relationships among countries. Through membership in these organizations, Canada can promote its principles and values internationally. Canada also uses these memberships to counterbalance its close relationship with the United States. Membership in organizations such as the Commonwealth and La Francophonie has helped Canada strengthen its economic and political ties with many countries.

The Commonwealth

The Commonwealth is a multicultural association of 53 independent states. It includes some of the world's richest countries, such as Canada and Australia, and some of the poorest, such as Bangladesh and Swaziland. Membership ranges from the small country of Tuvalu, an island in the South Pacific with a population of 11,500, to India, with a population of 1.1 billion. On the other hand, half of all Commonwealth members have populations of less than 1 million. In total, the Commonwealth represents 1.7 billion people—almost 30 percent of the world's population.

Founded in 1931, membership in the Commonwealth was based on the colonial ties of the British Empire. It was an association of countries that shared a common language, a belief in the rule of law, and an allegiance to the British monarchy. After World War II, as British colonies demanded and gained independence, the focus of the Commonwealth changed. Most of the newly independent states chose to remain in the Commonwealth and to recognize the British monarch as its symbolic head. Although the United States was once a British colony, it has never been a member of the Commonwealth. Many member countries value the Commonwealth because it is the largest and most important international organization not dominated by the United States.

SOUND BITE "We are all committed to the rule of law, and democratic principles. Many of us speak other languages as well in our home countries and practise different religions. We are of different cultures. The colour of our skin is not the same. Yet . . . by choosing to be enriched by differences, we have made the organization work."

Jean Chrétien, Seventh Commonwealth Lecture, March 30, 2004

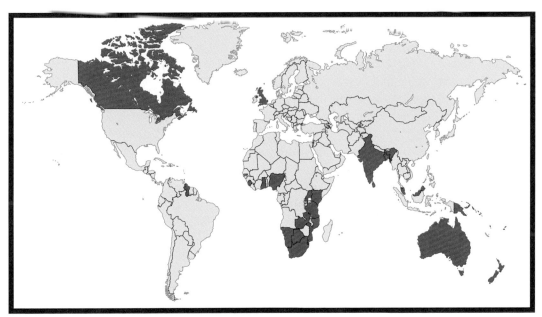

Figure 9.10 The Commonwealth, with member states and date joined.

Antigua and Barbuda **1981**	Dominica **1978**	Malawi **1964**	Papua New Guinea **1975**	Sri Lanka **1948**
Australia **1931**	Fiji Islands **1970**	Malaysia **1957**	St. Kitts and Nevis **1983**	Swaziland **1968**
The Bahamas **1973**	Gambia **1965**	Maldives **1982**	St. Lucia **1979**	Tonga **1970**
Bangladesh **1972**	Ghana **1957**	Malta **1964**	St. Vincent and the	Trinidad and Tobago **1962**
Barbados **1966**	Grenada **1974**	Mauritius **1968**	Grenadines **1979**	Tuvalu **1978**
Belize **1981**	Guyana **1966**	Mozambique **1995**	Samoa **1970**	Uganda **1962**
Botswana **1966**	India **1947**	Namibia **1990**	Seychelles **1976**	United Kingdom
Brunei Darussalam **1984**	Jamaica **1962**	Nauru **1968**	Sierra Leone **1961**	United Republic of
Cameroon **1995**	Kenya **1963**	New Zealand **1931**	Singapore **1965**	Tanzania **1961**
Canada **1931**	Kiribati **1979**	Nigeria **1960**	Solomon Islands **1978**	Vanuatu **1980**
Cyprus **1961**	Lesotho **1966**	Pakistan **1947**	South Africa **1931**	Zambia **1964**

In recent years, membership in the Commonwealth has expanded to include states with no colonial ties to Britain. In 1995, Mozambique was the first such country to join. Its admission followed a formal request by then South African president Nelson Mandela to offer the country membership in recognition of its role in ending apartheid in South Africa.

Every two years, prime ministers and presidents gather for the Commonwealth Heads of Government Meeting to discuss political, economic, and social issues. Their broad objectives are to promote racial harmony and understanding, human rights, gender equality, and economic and social development. Although the Commonwealth has no formal constitution, membership is based on respecting key principles:

- pursuit of international peace and order in support of the UN
- recognition of racial equality and the need to combat racial discrimination and oppression

- promotion of representative institutions and guarantees for personal freedoms under the law
- lessening the disparities of wealth among nations.

Failure to respect and practise these principles can result in suspension or expulsion. Member states also sometimes voluntarily withdraw. This was the case in 1961 when South Africa withdrew from the Commonwealth because the organization opposed the country's policy of apartheid. In 1961, Canadian Prime Minister John Diefenbaker sided with black African leaders not to readmit South Africa. Only in 1994, when apartheid ended and government rule passed to the black majority under President Nelson Mandela, did South Africa rejoin the Commonwealth.

In 1972, Pakistan withdrew when the Commonwealth recognized the new state of Bangladesh, formerly known as East Pakistan (see Chapter 3). Pakistan returned to the Commonwealth in 1989 but was suspended in 1999 after a military coup in which General Pervez Musharraf seized control of the government. In 2004, Pakistan was allowed to rejoin the Commonwealth in recognition of its role in supporting the war against terrorism. President Musharraf promised to leave the army by the end of the year.

In 2002, the Commonwealth voted to suspend the African country of Zimbabwe for a year after voting irregularities marred the presidential election campaign. After 22 years, President Robert Mugabe was determined to keep his grip on power (see Chapter 1). Mugabe reduced the number of polling stations in areas where he faced strongest opposition and launched campaigns to stuff ballot boxes in his favour. Voters were also intimidated with violence. Some Commonwealth members, led by Britain, Australia, and New Zealand, voted to extend Zimbabwe's suspension, but the debate split the Commonwealth. Many African members saw Mugabe as a liberator who, in the 1970s, had freed the black peoples of Zimbabwe from white minority rule. They wanted Zimbabwe reinstated. Canadian Prime Minister Jean Chrétien presented a compromise that broke the deadlock: no further action would be taken until international observers ruled on whether Zimbabwe's election had been fair. Although Commonwealth members accepted Chrétien's proposal, Mugabe withdrew Zimbabwe from the organization in December 2003.

Canada's Role in the Commonwealth

As one of the developed countries in the Commonwealth, Canada plays an important role in North–South relations. Canada was at the forefront of Commonwealth efforts to end apartheid in South Africa when it chaired the Commonwealth Committee of Foreign Ministers on Southern Africa, established at the Commonwealth Conference in Vancouver in 1987. The committee coordinated Commonwealth support for a peaceful transition to full democracy. Following the election of a multiracial, democratic government

SOUND BITE "I have an intense hatred for discrimination based on colour."

Canadian Prime Minister John Diefenbaker, Maclean's *magazine, March 29, 1959*

SOUND BITE

"John Diefenbaker is going to be troublesome about South Africa. He is taking a 'holier than thou' attitude, which may cause us infinite trouble."

British Prime Minister Harold Macmillan, in Memoirs: Pointing the Way, 1959–1961

in South Africa in 1994, many observers credited the Commonwealth with having been a more effective force against apartheid than the United Nations.

Since 2001, Canada has also played a leading role in developing the Commonwealth's Plan of Action on Terrorism, adopted in March 2002. In it, Canada stressed the importance of dealing with underlying causes of terrorism, such as poverty and economic disparity. The plan stipulates that any Commonwealth member that aids, supports, instigates, finances, or harbours terrorists will be expelled.

Canada contributes approximately $28 million annually to Commonwealth programs and institutions. This aid is distributed through NGOs and businesses operating in various Commonwealth countries. The funds assist developing countries with programs including the defence of human rights, the establishment of democratic elections, and the promotion of sustainable development and equality for women.

Although the Commonwealth advocates democratic values, some critics question its actual commitment to them. They argue that if the Commonwealth cannot agree to suspend a country such as Zimbabwe, then it has failed to enforce its own democratic principles. They suggest that NGOs such as Amnesty International are more effective in achieving some of the Commonwealth's goals. Others charge that the Commonwealth has not taken a leading role in addressing urgent issues such as the spread of HIV/AIDS in Africa and Asia. They argue that since these issues affect many member states, developed countries of the Commonwealth should provide support to combat them.

Figure 9.11 Canadian Kyle Shewfelt wears the gold medal for men's floor gymnastics, standing between Shu Wai Ng of Malaysia (silver) and Philippe Rizzo of Australia (bronze) during the 2002 Commonwealth Games in Manchester, England. The games, held every four years, began in Hamilton, Ontario, in 1930 and now include an arts festival.

La Francophonie

La Francophonie is a social, cultural, and educational organization of French-speaking peoples on five continents. It includes countries as large as Canada and as small as Monaco. Some members, such as Switzerland and Canada, are among the wealthiest countries in the world, while others, such as Burundi and the Democratic Republic of Congo, are among the poorest. With 53 member countries and 10 observer states having a total population of almost 600 million people, La Francophonie represents 25 percent of the membership of the United Nations and 10 percent of the world's population.

As with Britain in the Commonwealth, France's colonial past served as the foundation for the creation of La Francophonie. Officially, the organization was created at a conference of French-speaking states held in Niamey, the

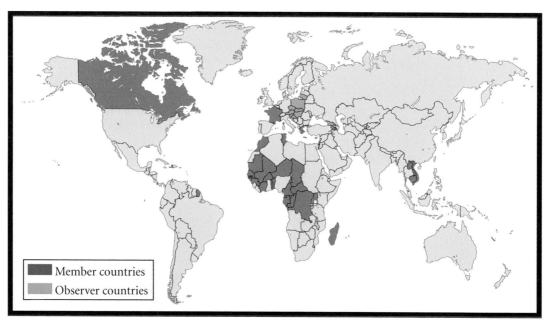

Member Countries:

Albania	Central African Republic	Haiti	Romania	**Observer Countries:**
Andorra	Chad	Ivory Coast	Rwanda	Armenia
Belgium	Comoros	Laos	Saint Lucia	Austria
Benin	Congo	Lebanon	Saō Tomé and Principe	Croatia
Bulgaria	Congo, Democratic Republic	Luxembourg	Senegal	Czech Republic
Burkina Faso	Djibouti	Macedonia	Seychelles	Georgia
Burundi	Dominica	Madagascar	Switzerland	Hungary
Cambodia	Egypt	Mali	Togo	Lithuania
Cameroon	Equatorial Guinea	Mauritania	Tunisia	Poland
Canada	France	Mauritius	Vanuatu	Slovakia
Canada, New Brunswick	Gabon	Moldova	Vietnam	Slovenia
Canada, Quebec	Greece	Monaco		
Cape Verde	Guinea	Morocco		
	Guinea-Bissau	Niger		

Figure 9.12 La Francophonie gives Canada the opportunity to promote its values to a diverse range of countries around the world.

Point:
Counterpoint → Should the Commonwealth Be Abolished?

"Yes" to Abolishing the Commonwealth

by Rachel Marsden

[President] Robert Mugabe used Zimbabwe's recent election to once again run around his country dousing the flames of democracy. . . . Mugabe has always fought opposition with violence, and even leading up to the election it seemed extremely unlikely that he would choose this opportunity to stop.

At a meeting of Commonwealth members held shortly before the election, Britain, Australia, and New Zealand pressed for other Commonwealth states to adopt sanctions against Mugabe, but were met with immediate resistance from most African Commonwealth countries. Viewing themselves as guardians of their collective sovereignty, they simply weren't prepared to join forces with former colonialists to overpower a neighbouring state.

Where did that leave Canada? Firmly planted on the fence, with Jean Chrétien successfully proposing that any sanctions against Zimbabwe be postponed until after the election. . . .

By adopting such a middling, wishy-washy stance . . . Commonwealth leaders . . . undermined the fundamen-tal principles which their organization supposedly stands for—namely, those of democracy and respect for human rights. . . .

[A]ny action that the Commonwealth takes against Mugabe will risk alienating a large number of its own member countries—namely, those that resent interference from white-dominated states. And since it's the member states who direct the Commonwealth, it really cannot be said to have any relevant purpose unless its members are capable of forming a consensus. Without cooperation amongst all members, the organization is a lame duck. . . .

By its very nature, [the Commonwealth] has an innate problem of credibility and optics because it is in and of itself a symbol of colonialism and white domination rather than cooperation. And for that reason, it should hand this issue off to the United Nations before it fumbles it even worse than it already has.

The UN Charter deals with issues involving human rights and democracy, and represents the highest form of international law. More importantly, the [UN] . . . has long supported decolonization. And in terms of gaining cooperation, it seems reasonable to assume that Zimbabwe and other African Commonwealth countries would feel more comfortable answering to an organization headed

Figure 9.13 Queen Elizabeth II's opening address to the 2003 Commonwealth Summit in Abuja, Nigeria, is broadcast over a huge monitor. Critics like Rachael Marsden have described the Commonwealth as dysfunctional and outdated. Do you agree?

by Kofi Annan, who hails from Ghana, than one that is still technically represented by the Queen of England. . . .

[W]hat [the Commonwealth] truly needs is a make-over—a new focus outside the realm of political babysitting. With most meaningful action on global governance taking place elsewhere regardless, Canada and other member countries would be better off channelling the energy and resources that they devote to current Commonwealth activities into more useful ventures.

From ensuring safe drinking water to fighting infectious diseases to providing micro-enterprise loans to promote business growth, there are plenty of ways in which Commonwealth funds could be redirected so that they would actually reduce the burden on those living in developing states, and create the circumstances needed for democracies to flourish. . . .

Source: Rachel Marsden, "The Commonwealth Needs a Makeover," *PunditMag*, March 15, 2002; http://www.rachelmarsden.com (a similar article appears under Archived Opinion Pieces).

"No" to Abolishing the Commonwealth

by Alastair Endersby

The Commonwealth does not deny the injustices of history, but instead transforms them positively by building upon the common links between the member nations, almost all of which have English as a major language and political and legal systems modelled upon the British precedent. Today all the countries of the Commonwealth have equal status and Britain is no longer dominant in the way it was in the immediate post-colonial era. Many of the members have entered through deliberate choice, not just through an accident of history. . . .

Aside from the UN, the Commonwealth is the only major international organisation to unite a diverse range of developed and developing countries, covering nearly 30 percent of the world's population. This makes it valuable in fostering dialogue on democracy and development, as well as a great deal of cultural and academic exchange. . . . [T]he Commonwealth has provided practical and moral support for states in transition from dictatorship or colonial rule. Nor is there a conflict between membership of the Commonwealth and of other major global organisations. Smaller, developing nations perhaps gain the most from the Commonwealth, which gives their voice greater prominence than it could achieve in the much larger, more polarised United Nations. They gain technical assistance on a range of development issues, a forum in which bilateral trade and investment deals can be negotiated in an atmosphere of goodwill, and practical help in maintaining permanent missions to the UN. . . .

It may be true that the developed nations in the Commonwealth, such as Britain, are able to ignore other members from time to time. Nonetheless, it acts as a forum for them to seriously commit attention and resources to the problems of the developing world and this in turn affects their actions in global bodies, such as the UN and the World Trade Organisation. The real winners from the Commonwealth are the smallest and least developed nations, who can use its formal and informal channels to win bilateral trade deals, development assistance, and support in international negotiations.

Proceeding by consensus and through moral suasion are [means] always open to accusations of weakness, but the Commonwealth has never pretended to be a powerful organisation for enforcing international norms—and many of its members would never have joined it in the first place if it did. Instead the Commonwealth works through constructive engagement, encouraging its members to aspire to high standards of human rights and democratic accountability and running programmes which educate their citizens in these concepts. Action has been taken in the past against the worst transgressors and is all the more effective for being rare.

Source: Alastair Endersby, Debatabase: The Online Debate Topic Database, June 24, 2001; http://www.debatabase.org/details.asp?topicID=128.

Articulating a Personal Stand

1. In an organizer, list Marsden's and Endersby's arguments. With which do you agree and disagree? Explain.
2. Do you think the UN is better suited than the Commonwealth to deal with issues involving human rights and democratic principles? Discuss in small groups and try to reach a consensus.
3. Write a five-paragraph essay in which you take a position on the Commonwealth's effectiveness. Your essay should present the reasons for your position and acknowledge opposing arguments.

Figure 9.14 Team Canada's Jeff Adams takes first place in the 1,500 metre handisport event at La Francophonie Games held in Ottawa/Hull in 2001. More than 3,000 athletes representing 51 countries participated. The games also include cultural exhibits and activities.

capital of Niger, in March 1970. The initiative was the work of the leaders of Niger, Senegal, and Tunisia, who wanted a multilateral, collaborative organization for French-speaking nations. Canada's membership promotes the country's bilingual heritage and francophone community. In recognition of their large French-speaking populations, Quebec and New Brunswick have official status as "participating governments." They may vote on issues of global economic development and cooperation, but only the federal government of Canada may vote on political issues.

As with the Commonwealth, national leaders of La Francophonie meet every two years. Through educational, agricultural, scientific, health, and social programs, developed countries work with developing states to build a better quality of life. La Francophonie identifies three sets of objectives —political, economic, and cooperative—to meet its goals. At times, La Francophonie and the Commonwealth work together. For example, they were invited by the government of the Seychelle Islands to jointly observe presidential and national assembly elections in 1998.

La Francophonie holds athletic games every four years. Morocco hosted the first games in 1989, with 1,800 athletes representing 30 countries. Medals are awarded both to athletes in sporting events and to artists in cultural activities. La Francophonie also uses media outlets such as TV5 to promote francophone culture. TV5 is the world's foremost francophone television network and one of the three largest cable networks in the world. TV5 began broadcasting in 1984 and reaches 164 million homes in over 203 countries (2004). In 1988, the network launched TV5 Quebec Canada, which reaches 6.2 million homes via cable. TV5 provides Canada's French language audio-visual industry with an international audience, and francophone Canadians are connected with French-speaking peoples in Europe, Asia, Africa, and the Americas.

Canada's Role in La Francophonie

Membership in La Francophonie is an important part of Canada's foreign policy. As one of the wealthiest members, Canada exercises considerable political and financial leadership within the organization. In particular, Canada works to develop democratic institutions, human rights, the rule of law, and international peace and security in poor and politically unstable countries such as Haiti. La Francophonie provides Canada with a means to promote its democratic, economic, and cultural values as well as cultural diversity in the global community. In conjunction with other members, Canada works to support sustainable development, reduce poverty, and create a more equitable global economy.

La Francophonie also has its critics. Some argue that Canadian membership costs taxpayers millions of dollars annually and is not an effective investment. Other critics believe that La Francophonie no longer serves its original purpose of uniting French-speaking countries. They cite the fact that some members and observer states—Bulgaria, Cape Verde, the Czech Republic, Lithuania, Macedonia, Moldova, Poland, Romania, Saint Lucia, São Tomé and Principe, Slovakia, and Slovenia—do not identify French as an official language. Others believe that La Francophonie has evolved into a predominantly African and non-francophone organization and question whether a common bond still exists among its members.

THE WEB

Learn more about La Francophonie in Canada at www.emp.ca/cwp.

Check YOUR UNDERSTANDING

1. How important do you think the Commonwealth is among international organizations?
2. Traditionally, what countries became Commonwealth members, and what was their relationship to Britain?
3. What led to the expulsion of Zimbabwe from the Commonwealth? Why did this expulsion become a source of controversy?
4. Identify some criticisms of the Commonwealth. Do you agree with them? Explain your views.
5. How important do you think La Francophonie is among international organizations?
6. Why do Quebec and New Brunswick have membership in La Francophonie? How is their role in the organization different from Canada's role?
7. Identify some criticisms of La Francophonie. Do you agree with them? Explain.
8. In a graphic organizer, list the pros and cons of Canada's participation in the Commonwealth and La Francophonie.

Canada and Global Environmental Initiatives

Environmental protection moved to the forefront of Canada's international agenda in the 1960s amid growing concerns over the state of the environment. In 1972, Canada co-sponsored the historic Conference on the Human Environment in Stockholm, Sweden. Political leaders, environmentalists, and activists from around the world gathered at this first **Earth Summit**. The meeting established 26 basic principles to deal with issues confronting the environment and outlined global responsibilities of countries and their citizens. It marked the beginning of the official global environmental movement, as participants pledged to hold Earth Summits every 10 years to reassess the environmental health of the planet.

The second summit took place in Nairobi, Kenya, in 1982, during a period of heightened Cold War tensions. The conference failed to attract widespread attention from world leaders, however, and fell short of expectations established in Stockholm. As a result, the Nairobi meeting was not recognized as an official Earth Summit.

Following the failure of the Nairobi conference, the UN appointed a commission to investigate critical areas of global environmental degradation. Gro Harlem Brundtland, prime minister of Norway, chaired the commission. In 1987, the commission's findings were published as *Our Common Future*, also widely known as the Brundtland Report. *Our Common Future* was a startling wakeup call to the dangerous state of the world's environment. It formally recognized and defined sustainable development as "development that meets the needs of the present without compromising the ability of future generations to meet their own needs." It established the benchmark for measuring global environmental issues.

Our Common Future identified the need to improve quality of life for all the world's people—but without consuming more resources than the environment can regenerate. Following the publication of *Our Common Future*, Canadian Prime Minister Brian Mulroney and Norwegian Prime Minister Gro Harlem Brundtland co-hosted an international environmental conference in Toronto in June 1988. The conference described the impact of global climate change as being "second only to global war" and called for a 20 percent reduction in greenhouse gas emissions by 2005.

THE WEB

Learn about the United Nations Environment Programme (UNEP) at www.emp.ca/cwp.

A Closer Look at Sustainable Development

What exactly does *sustainable development* mean in political terms? It means that meeting the needs of future generations depends on how well society balances its social, economic, and environmental needs today. It means that the economic decisions made at all levels—globally, nationally, and locally—have environmental consequences for the future. For example, what happens if the world's developed countries continue to consume massive amounts of non-renewable natural resources? What happens when a country's hydro-electric power production pollutes the lakes and rivers of a neighbouring country, or when a company attempts to reduce costs by cutting workers' wages? What happens when pollution threatens the quality of the air you breathe? What are you willing to do to help sustain your own environment? For example, are you willing to help preserve the quality of the air by taking public transportation to school or work, instead of driving a car?

Who decides how to create a sustainable environment? Should it be the United Nations, or individual countries? Should it be businesses? local governments? environmental groups? Clearly, sustainable development is everyone's responsibility. Because inaction threatens dire consequences, all levels of government are under pressure to find new ways to change traditional practices and structures and to influence the behaviour of businesses and individuals to ensure the future health of the planet.

The Rio Earth Summit

Canada played an influential role at the second Earth Summit in Rio de Janeiro, Brazil, in June 1992. Attended by 108 heads of state and representatives from 172 governments, it was the largest gathering of world leaders ever held. Hundreds of thousands of people around the world urged their governments to participate and make the difficult political decisions needed to ensure a healthy planet for present and future generations. Environmentalists, scientists, indigenous peoples, celebrities, and young people went to Rio, too, to express their views about the need to preserve and protect the environment.

The Rio Earth Summit resulted in several agreements, including *Agenda 21*, a comprehensive global action plan for local, national, and international sustainable development. *Agenda 21* provided a blueprint for action on such issues as

- eliminating poverty by enabling the poor to achieve sustainable livelihoods
- reducing wasteful use of natural resources by changing consumption patterns
- protecting the atmosphere, oceans, and animal and plant life through sustainable development programs
- promoting sustainable agricultural practices to feed the world's growing population.

SOUND BITE   "Canada believes the establishment of an international financial and economic system that is conducive to sustainable development must be a cornerstone of efforts to implement *Agenda 21*. Canada strongly supports efforts to reform international organizations to ensure effectiveness and efficiency in the promotion of global sustainable development."

Government of Canada, Report of Canada to the UN Commission on Sustainable Development, *1996*

Figure 9.15 UN Earth Summit Secretary-General Maurice Strong, from Canada, greets Brazilian Indian Chief Kanhok Caiaopo in Rio de Janeiro in 1992 at the opening of the International Indigenous Peoples Conference held during the summit.

The Rio Summit created unprecedented public awareness of global environmental issues and focused international attention on the importance of protecting the environment to ensure the health and well-being of future generations. It underscored the fact that population, human rights, social development, the role of women, and human settlements are all interrelated, a concept that laid the foundations for a variety of UN conferences that followed. One of the most important achievements was an agreement to hold a Convention on Climate Change to discuss greenhouse gas emissions and their effects on global warming. At the conclusion of the summit, the United Nations formed the Commission on Sustainable Development to follow up on *Agenda 21* and to act as a catalyst for action at the national and international levels.

The Johannesburg Earth Summit

SOUND BITE "Poverty is really unsustainable and . . . is one of the greatest environmental threats and sources of environmental degradation."

Desiree McGraw, royal youth ambassador to the 1992 Earth Summit

The third Earth Summit was held in Johannesburg, South Africa, in August and September 2002. Nicknamed "Rio Plus 10," over 100 heads of state and 40,000 delegates attended. While water, energy, health, agriculture, and **biodiversity** were on the conference agenda, the most compelling issue was poverty and achieving economic equity among the world's countries.

At the summit, participants agreed to work toward the following objectives:

- to cut the number of people living on less than $1 a day by half by 2015
- to cut the number of people living in hunger by half by 2015
- to improve living standards for at least 100 million people dwelling in slums by 2020
- to establish programs for energy efficiency in developing states
- to place greater emphasis on development opportunities in the countries of Africa
- to increase corporate, environmental, and social responsibility and accountability.

In Johannesburg, Canada reinforced its earlier commitment to spend $6 billion in aid to Africa. Canadian delegates focused on access to health care and medical services as fundamental human rights and critical elements to creating social stability and economic development.

Criticism of the Earth Summits

Despite some accomplishments, many environmentalists and other analysts believe the overall results of the Earth Summits have been disappointing. Countries have failed to implement many of the agreements. Critics charge that many business leaders have "greenwashed" their corporate images to create the false impression that their business practices comply with summit guidelines and recommendations. They fault the world's richest countries, which have the financial means to implement change, for failing to do enough to clean up the environment or to improve the quality of life of the billions of people who live in poverty.

THE WEB

Learn more about the 1992 and 2002 Earth Summits at www.emp.ca/cwp.

The *Kyoto Protocol*

At the Rio Summit, many countries recognized the urgent need to reduce greenhouse gases to reduce the threat of global warming and climate change. As a result, the *Rio Convention* called on the world to stabilize greenhouse gas emissions at 1990 levels by the year 2000. The agreement was signed by 154 countries, including Canada. By 1997, however, a review of the goals of the *Rio Convention* concluded that they were inadequate and ineffective. Therefore, in December 1997, Canada joined 160 other countries in Kyoto, Japan, to establish new goals for reducing greenhouse gas emissions. The result was the *Kyoto Protocol*. It established several objectives, including

- targets for the reduction of greenhouse gas emissions on a country-by-country basis
- a greenhouse gas emissions trading program
- additional meetings to establish penalties for failing to meet targets and implement procedures.

The *Kyoto Protocol* called for industrialized states to reduce their total greenhouse gas emissions by 5 percent below 1990 levels between 2008 and 2012. Each country received a specific target based on its level of emissions. Canada is to cut its greenhouse gas emissions by 6 percent, the United States by 7 percent, and the countries of the European Union by 8 percent. Each country can develop its own means of reaching its target. During this first phase, developing countries, including the world's two most populated states, China and India, are not required to reduce greenhouse gas emissions before 2012. This is because on a per capita basis their emissions are much lower than those of developed industrial countries and their economies are less able to absorb the initial costs of changing to cleaner fuels.

SOUND BITE "Canada has the sad global reputation of being the largest per capita consumer of energy in the world and the second largest emitter of greenhouse gases in the world."

Jim Fulton, executive director of the David Suzuki Foundation, August 2002

Implementing the Kyoto Protocol

The *Kyoto Protocol* was to come into force 90 days after its ratification by at least 55 countries that collectively produce 55 percent of the world's total carbon dioxide emissions, based on 1990 levels. By September 2004, 125 states had ratified or accepted the agreement, thereby surpassing the first condition for implementation. However, these countries represented slightly more than 44 percent of all greenhouse gas emissions, far short of the 55 percent required in the second condition.

Press Play

In *The Day After Tomorrow* (2004), directed by Roland Emmerich, a climatologist tries to save Earth from global warming. The film imagines a world in which the greenhouse effect continues unchecked, resulting in devastating weather phenomena such as massive hurricanes, tornadoes, tidal waves, floods, and even a new Ice Age. (PG-13)

LEGEND:

Kyoto Protocol Status

- Not signatory
- Signed, not ratified
- Ratified
- No data

Figure 9.16 As of November 4, 2004, 84 parties had signed and 126 parties had ratified or accepted the *Kyoto Protocol*.

Opposition to the Kyoto Protocol

One reason for the difficulty in achieving the second condition of the Protocol was the United States's refusal to ratify the agreement. The United States signed the *Kyoto Protocol* during the administration of President Bill Clinton. However, in March 2001, President George W. Bush announced that the United States, which produces 35 percent of all greenhouse gas emissions, would not ratify the deal. Bush argued there was not enough sound scientific evidence on global warming and climate change to warrant the *Kyoto Protocol*, and that to implement the agreement would have a detrimental impact on the US economy.

Without US participation, several other industrial countries, including Australia, questioned the relevance of the Protocol and also refused to ratify. Russia initially hesitated, but on November 4, 2004, President Putin signed a bill confirming Russia's ratification of the Protocol. Many Russian officials still opposed the treaty, stating it would stifle economic growth. The deciding factor may have been that ratification of the Protocol would increase European Union support for Russia's entry into the World Trade Organization.

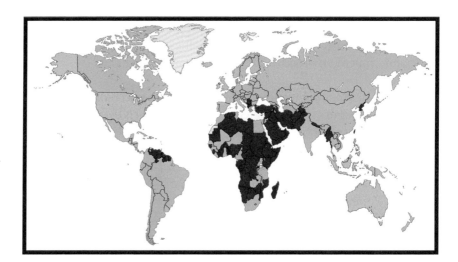

Canada's Implementation Plan

Since 1997, the federal and provincial governments have worked to develop a Canadian strategy for meeting emission reduction targets. Recommendations include

- establishing mandatory reductions in greenhouse gas emissions
- upgrading standards for more energy-efficient buildings, homes, appliances, and vehicles
- providing financial incentives for smaller businesses to cut their emissions
- offering tax incentives for using public transit.

Implementation of the *Kyoto Protocol* has sparked debate across Canada. With its energy-based economy, Alberta is the largest source of greenhouse gas emissions; Ontario ranks second. Together, the two provinces account for more than 60 percent of the proposed cuts to meet the Kyoto target. Many people argue that, since these two provinces have the largest stake in the outcome, the federal government should collaborate with them, as well as with the other provinces and territories, to reach the Kyoto target. Others claim that although Quebec, Manitoba, the Northwest Territories, and Nunavut support the *Kyoto Protocol*, the provinces that oppose the deal want to delay the process. Therefore, the federal government should act unilaterally.

In 2002, several leading organizations representing Canadian industries formed the Canadian Coalition for Responsible Environmental Solutions (CCRES). Its goal is to draw public attention to and discussion of the issues surrounding the *Kyoto Protocol* and to motivate citizens to urge the federal government to move cautiously in implementing the agreement. The members of CCRES believe that fulfilling Canada's Kyoto commitment on schedule would be too costly for businesses and, in the long term, could cost the economy billions of dollars and lead to a drop in **gross domestic product** (the total market value of all goods and services produced in the country over a given period). As a result, Canadians' quality of life would decline.

Other groups, such as the Sierra Club and the World Wildlife Fund, want the government to move quickly to meet the emissions target. They want Canada to shift its reliance on highly polluting energy sources, such as fossil fuels and nuclear power, to renewable forms of energy. According to the Sierra Club, for Canada to reach its target by 2010, the federal government must declare a long-term goal to reduce total greenhouse gas emissions by 50 percent by 2030.

SOUND BITE "Canadians deserve a [full] debate on the merits of the Protocol. Canada's target under Kyoto amounts to a 30 percent reduction in energy use for every Canadian, with important implications for how we live and work."

Thomas d'Aquino, President and Chief Executive, Canadian Council of Chief Executives, September 2002

THE WEB

Learn more about the *Kyoto Protocol* at www.emp.ca/cwp.

Check Your Understanding

1. Why was the 1972 Earth Summit in Stockholm significant?
2. What is sustainable development, and what does the global community need to do to achieve it?
3. Why was the 1992 Rio Summit a landmark event?
4. Identify the criticisms of the Earth Summits. Do you think these criticisms are valid? Give reasons for your answer.
5. What does the *Kyoto Protocol* hope to achieve? How important do you think this goal is? Explain your views.
6. Why has the United States not yet ratified the *Kyoto Protocol*? Do you agree with this decision? Explain.
7. Should developing countries be exempt from the first phase of the *Kyoto Protocol*? Why or why not?
8. Why is the *Kyoto Protocol* the subject of debate in Canada? Create a graphic organizer listing the arguments on both sides. Which side do you support, and why?

Canadians Making a Difference

While Canada exerts its influence in the global community through its participation in multilateral organizations and conferences, many individual Canadians have established high-profile roles as global citizens. Here are just a few of the many Canadians who are working to make a difference.

Matthew Coon Come: Global Activist

Matthew Coon Come was born in a trapper's hut near Mistissini, Quebec, in 1956. He attended residential schools in Moose Factory and Hull before attending Trent and McGill universities. Following his post-secondary education, Coon Come returned home to spend two years learning the traditional ways of the Cree. He served as chief of the Mistissini Cree from 1981 to 1986 and as grand chief of the Northern Quebec Cree from 1987 to 2000. From 2000 until 2003, Coon Come was the national chief for the Assembly of First Nations.

Coon Come gained international attention in the late 1980s when he led a fight against the massive $13 billion Great Whale hydro-electric power project that threatened to flood much of the Cree's traditional territory in northern Quebec, destroying their way of life. With a keen understanding of politics and a knack for publicity, in August 1991 Coon Come organized a trip by Cree elders to draw attention to the plight of the James Bay Cree. They travelled by canoe from James Bay to the Hudson River and into New York City harbour. Coon Come hoped to appeal directly to the people of New York, whose state electricity authority planned to buy the hydro-electricity the project generated. Many New Yorkers sympathized with the Cree and opposed purchasing power from a project that would have such devastating consequences on the environment and the Cree people. As a result, New York State cancelled its billion-dollar contract to buy the power in 1992. The Quebec government was forced to cancel the project and to negotiate the terms of future hydro-electric power projects with the Cree Nation.

Coon Come has effectively used the international courts, the United Nations, and the international media to defend the rights of Aboriginal peoples. He has played a key role in many international initiatives to advance Aboriginal rights.

Figure 9.17 Robert Kennedy, Jr. (centre) helps Cree Grand Chief Matthew Coon Come (right) portage in Toronto, 1996. In 1991, Coon Come and Cree elders paddled the canoe *Odeyak* from James Bay to New York City to protest Hydro-Quebec's plans to flood Cree territory around James Bay.

At the Earth Summit in Rio, he formed a coalition with other indigenous peoples and environmental organizations to defend the rights of Aboriginal peoples to use the land for traditional purposes. His knowledgeable advocacy for the rights of all the indigenous peoples of the world has earned him international recognition.

Maurice Strong: Custodian of the Planet

Born in Oak Lake, Manitoba, in April 1929, Maurice Strong is one of Canada's most powerful and influential figures. As an industrialist and a public servant, he has had a varied career as a business leader, environmentalist, and diplomat. He was president of the Montreal-based Power Corporation until 1966, when he left to become the head of what would later become the Canadian International Development Agency. In 1972, he was secretary-general of the UN Conference on the Human Environment held in Stockholm, Sweden. The following year, he became the first executive director of the UN Environment Programme (UNEP). Strong served as secretary-general again at the Earth Summit in Rio de Janeiro in 1992, a landmark event he called a "historic moment for humanity." At the Rio meeting, Strong introduced one of Canada's most far-reaching initiatives, the creation of the Earth Council, headquartered in Costa Rica. He is widely credited with introducing the *Kyoto Protocol* in 1997.

While Maurice Strong is one of the world's most influential citizens, he is also one of its most controversial. In 1997, he was appointed special senior adviser to UN Secretary-General Kofi Annan and was given wide-ranging responsibility for reforming the United Nations. Strong has long advocated the need to place global cooperation ahead of national sovereignty in order to protect the world's environment. Many people support his view that the most effective way to do this is through a powerful, centralized United Nations. Others disagree, and see a stronger UN as a threat to the sovereignty of the world's countries.

David Suzuki: International Scientist and Environmentalist

Born in Vancouver in 1936, David Suzuki is a third-generation Japanese Canadian. As a child during World War II, he and his family were forced into an internment camp in British Columbia. The Canadian government had invoked the *War Measures Act* to round up Japanese Canadians living within kilometres of the Pacific as threats to "national security."

After the war, Suzuki and his family relocated to Ontario. After graduating from high school there, Suzuki attended college in Massachusetts and earned a doctorate degree in zoology from the University of Chicago in 1961. He returned to Canada to teach at the University of British Columbia, where his work earned him the recognition of scientists around the world. Suzuki remained at the university until his retirement in 2001.

THE WEB

Learn more about Matthew Coon Come and the Cree at www.emp.ca/cwp.

SOUND BITE "The concept of national sovereignty has been an immutable, indeed sacred, principle of international relations. It is a principle which will yield only slowly and reluctantly to the new imperatives of global environmental cooperation. It is simply not feasible for sovereignty to be exercised unilaterally by individual nation states, however powerful. The global community must be assured of environmental security."

Maurice Strong, the Earth Summit, Rio de Janeiro, Brazil, 1992

Suzuki gained an international reputation for his dedication to the preservation of the environment through the popular television series *The Nature of Things*, which began broadcasting on the CBC in 1960. The program, aired in 50 countries, has helped raise public awareness of the concept of sustainability. Suzuki's 1985 series *A Planet for the Taking* captured a television audience of 1.8 million viewers per episode and earned him a United Nations Environment Programme medal in 1988. In addition to his broadcasting accomplishments, Suzuki has written more than 30 books on the environment.

Suzuki warns Canadians not to believe in the popular misconception that Canada has a leading environmental record in the global community. He cautions that Canada's record is, in fact, quite poor and is growing worse according to most environmental indicators, such as water and energy consumption, the disposal of hazardous wastes, and greenhouse gas emissions. Suzuki continues to work to reverse this trend and to create a sustainable future through the David Suzuki Foundation. The Foundation provides timely information on environmental issues and encourages people and governments to find and implement solutions to the planet's most urgent environmental problems.

Louise Fréchette: UN Deputy Secretary-General

As deputy-general of the United Nations, Louise Fréchette is the highest-ranking woman in UN history and one of the most powerful women in the world. Born in Montreal in July 1946, she graduated from the University of Montreal before beginning her career in public service in the Department of External Affairs in 1971. In 1972, Fréchette became a member of the Canadian delegation to the UN General Assembly and served in the Canadian embassy in Greece before returning to Canada in 1975. Over the next decade, she held many diplomatic positions abroad before becoming ambassador to Argentina in 1985.

In 1988, Fréchette became assistant deputy minister for Latin America and the Caribbean. In this capacity, she directed a review of Canada's relations with Latin America, which led to Canada's entry into the Organization of American States (OAS) in 1990. In 1992, Fréchette became Canadian ambassador to the UN before returning to Ottawa to serve as deputy minister of national defence from 1995 to 1998.

In 1997, the position of deputy secretary-general was created as part of the reforms introduced by Maurice Strong at the United Nations. Fréchette assumed the newly created position in March 1998. As second in command, she shares the responsibilities of the secretary-general and runs the day-to-day administration of the UN. Fréchette speaks about a wide variety of global issues as she promotes the UN's agenda to achieve sustainable development, reduce poverty, eliminate global conflicts, and promote human rights. In so doing, she helps extend Canadian values and principles within the global community.

Stephen Lewis: AIDS Activist

Born in Ottawa in 1937, Stephen Lewis has had a varied career in public service, as a politician and diplomat, and as an international envoy for humanitarian aid. In 2003, he was *Maclean's* magazine's inaugural choice for Canadian of the Year in honour of his leadership and work on behalf of people living with HIV/AIDS in Africa.

After studying at the universities of Toronto and British Columbia, Lewis spent two years teaching and travelling in Ghana, Kenya, Nigeria, and Uganda. He was elected to the Ontario legislature in 1963, where he served for 15 years, including eight years as the leader of the New Democratic Party (NDP). In 1984, Lewis became Canada's ambassador to the United Nations, a position he held until 1988. In 1990, he became a special representative to UNICEF (the United Nations Children's Fund), assuming the role of deputy executive director of the agency in 1995. Through his work at UNICEF, Lewis established himself as a passionate advocate for the needs and rights of children, especially those in developing countries.

In June 2001, UN Secretary-General Kofi Annan appointed Lewis special envoy for HIV/AIDS in Africa. Lewis has travelled extensively in countries across the African continent, working with prominent activists and leaders such as former US President Bill Clinton to focus the world's attention on the HIV/AIDS crisis that has killed over 25 million people in sub-Saharan and southern Africa and has orphaned over 12 million children. Lewis has been an outspoken critic of the lack of funding committed to AIDS by international financial institutions and the reluctance of some governments and transnational pharmaceutical corporations to provide low-cost drugs to combat the disease.

SOUND BITE "Finally the world seems to understand that [in Africa] this is a gender-based pandemic. Unless there is recognition that women are most vulnerable . . . and you do something about social and cultural equality for women, you're never going to defeat this pandemic."

Stephen Lewis, interview, June 2001

Figure 9.18 Stephen Lewis visits the Umoyo Training Centre for Girls in Lusaka, Zambia. In Africa, 8.6 million people between the ages of 15 and 29 are living with HIV/AIDS; 67 percent of them are girls and women.

THE WEB

To learn more about the Stephen Lewis Foundation, go to www.emp.ca/cwp.

In 2003, Lewis created the Stephen Lewis Foundation to further efforts to combat HIV/AIDS. The foundation's goals are to sponsor grassroots projects to provide care to women dying of AIDS, to help children orphaned by AIDS or infected with HIV/AIDS, and to support associations of people living with HIV/AIDS.

Law in Motion

Louise Arbour: Changing International Law

As UN High Commissioner for Human Rights, Louise Arbour is charged with protecting the human rights of people around the world. She replaced Brazilian Sergio Vieira de Mello, who had been in office only a few months when he was one of 22 people killed in the bombing of UN headquarters in Baghdad in 2003. Since assuming this position in July 2004, Arbour has been undaunted as an outspoken advocate for establishing human rights law as an enforceable branch of international law and for trying violations of these laws at the International Criminal Court (ICC). In her role, Arbour is particularly concerned with the impact the war against terrorism is having on human rights and the rule of law. She acknowledges that all countries have the right to defend citizens and the state from terrorist acts. However, she disagrees that they have the right to do so by denying suspected terrorists their civil rights and the due process of law, as many human rights advocates charge is happening at the US military base at Guantanamo Bay, Cuba, where suspected terrorists are being held (see Chapter 11, page 394). She has stated:

> Insisting on a human rights–based approach and a rule of law approach to countering terrorism is imperative. It is particularly critical, in time of crisis, when clarity of vision may be lacking and when institutions may appear to be failing, that all branches of governance be called upon to play their proper role and that none abdicate to the superior claim of another. . . .
>
> For even though it may be painted as an obstacle to efficient law enforcement, support for human rights and the rule of law actually works to improve human security. Societies that respect the rule of law do not provide the executive a blanket authority even in dealing with exceptional situations. . . . Ultimately, respect for the rule of law lessens the likelihood of social upheaval, creating greater stability both for a given society and its neighbours.

Her role as human rights commissioner is not Arbour's first high-profile role in international law. In 1996, she was appointed chief prosecutor of war crimes at the International Criminal Tribunal in The Hague in the Netherlands. The tribunal was the first international forum for trying war crimes since the Nuremberg trials after World War II. Arbour prosecuted

SOUND BITE "It is incumbent on all of us to ensure that the prevention of terrorism is not pursued with a single-minded zeal that leads us to give up our freedom in exchange for our security."

Louise Arbour, UN High Commissioner for Human Rights, August 2004

THE WEB

Learn more about Louise Arbour at www.emp.ca/cwp.

the people responsible for committing genocide in Rwanda in 1994 at the International Criminal Tribunal for Rwanda (see Chapter 11, page 399). In 1999, she issued an international arrest warrant for former Yugoslav President Slobodan Milosevic for crimes against humanity, including murder, committed during the civil war in the former Yugoslavia in the 1990s (see Chapter 4, pages 134–35). Milosevic was arrested in April 2001 and held for trial at the International Tribunal for the Former Yugoslavia in The Hague.

In Canada, Arbour had a distinguished career as an advocate for human rights and civil liberties. Between 1974 and 1987 she served in many capacities, including vice-president of the Canadian Civil Liberties Association and associate professor and associate dean at Osgoode Hall Law School, York University. In 1987, Arbour was appointed to the Supreme Court of Ontario, followed by a move to the Ontario Court of Appeal in 1990. In 1995, she headed a landmark inquiry charged with investigating the abuse of inmates in Canada's prisons. The inquiry's report led to wide-ranging reforms in the treatment of inmates in the federal prison system. Following her term at the International Criminal Tribunal, Arbour was appointed to the Supreme Court of Canada in 1999, where her rulings worked to ensure that Canada maintains its traditions of tolerance, equality, and accountability.

Questions

1. Why is Arbour concerned about the impact of the war against terrorism on human rights?
2. Do you agree that civil rights and the due process of law should apply to all people who are under arrest, regardless of the nature of their crime? Give reasons for your answer.
3. How significant do you think it is for Canada's international reputation that people such as Louise Arbour occupy prominent and influential positions? Explain.

Check YOUR UNDERSTANDING

1. How has Matthew Coon Come made an impact as an activist for indigenous peoples?
2. Why does Maurice Strong support a strong United Nations, and why is this position controversial?
3. What is David Suzuki's concern over Canada's environmental record?
4. How does her role as deputy secretary-general of the United Nations make Louise Fréchette one of the world's most powerful women?
5. How does the Stephen Lewis Foundation plan to provide aid to people with HIV/AIDS in Africa?

METHODS OF POLITICAL INQUIRY

Documenting Sources

When writing a formal political essay or book review, you must document for readers where you found your information. Sources should be cited each time you use a statistic, a direct quotation, a paraphrase, an author's opinion, or a controversial piece of information. Documentation and citation styles—such as footnote, endnote, or parentheses—vary, and teachers and schools have their own preferences. Check with your teacher to see which style is used in your classroom.

Parenthetical Documentation

In parenthetical documentation, the author's last name and the page number of the book are placed in parentheses after the reference in the body of the paper. For example: (Klein 62).

Footnotes/Endnotes for Books

In the footnote/endnote style, you refer readers to citations by using an Arabic number at the end of the sentence or phrase containing the language or idea being cited. The number appears in superscript (at the same level as apostrophes). For example: [12]

Footnotes or endnotes should be numbered consecutively throughout the paper. Citations for footnotes are placed at the foot of each page, and citations for endnotes appear at the end of the report. Footnote and endnote citations are presented with their corresponding superscript number in the following fashion:

[12]   Naomi Klein, *No Logo: Taking Aim at the Brand Bullies* (Toronto: Knopf Canada, 2000), p. 62.

The first time a work is cited in a footnote or endnote, give complete bibliographical information. As in the example above, present information in this order: author's name (surname last), a comma, book title (underlined or italicized), volume number (if any), place of publication, publisher, date of publication (the last three items are placed in parentheses), comma, and the page number on which the information is found.

Collection of articles with an editor:

In the case of a collection of articles with an editor, the designation is as follows:

[13]   Michael Whittington and Glen Williams, eds., *Canadian Politics in the 21st Century* (Toronto: Nelson Thomson Learning, 2000), p. 90.

Newspaper, magazine, or journal article:

[14]   Linda McQuaig, "Stephen Harper: PM?," *The Toronto Star*, June 27, 2004, p. A11.
[15]   Stuart Hickox, "Listening to the Locals," *Maclean's*, September 6, 2004, p. 36.

Internet source:

[16]   "Hong Kong: Elections Marred by Intimidation." Online: Human Rights Watch, http://www.hrw.org/english/docs/2004/09/09/china9325.htm (date accessed: September 11, 2004).

Once a complete citation has been used in an earlier footnote or endnote, use the shortened form. It includes only the author's surname and the page reference. For example:

[17]   Klein, p. 77.

If the work being cited is the same as that immediately above it, you may use *Ibid.* (an abbreviation of the Latin, *ibidem*, "in the same place"). For example:

[18]   *Ibid.*, p. 88.

Bibliography/Works Cited Page

A bibliography page (for footnotes or endnotes) or a "works cited" page (for parenthetical documentation) is required at the end of the paper. List all sources. All but the first line of each reference should be indented. Authors are cited alphabetically, surname first. For example:

Hickox, Stuart. "Listening to the Locals," *Maclean's*, September 6, 2004.
Klein, Naomi. *No Logo: Taking Aim at the Brand Bullies.* Toronto: Knopf Canada, 2000.

Applying the Skill

1. Using a topic given by your teacher, write two paragraphs in which you use at least three different citations correctly.
2. List the three different citations correctly in a Bibliography or Works Cited page.

Study Hall

Thinking and Inquiry

1. Promoting and protecting human rights is a key element of Canada's foreign policy. Research the ways in which Canada supports human rights in the global community and prepare a report of your findings.

2. Michael Ignatieff suggests that the focus of Canada's foreign policy should be to promote the Canadian values of "peace, order, and good government." Do you agree? Give reasons for your answer.

3. Many of the issues discussed in this chapter are ongoing. Working with a partner, research recent developments in one of the following areas and present an oral report of your findings to the class:
   • reconstruction in Afghanistan
   • the Commonwealth
   • La Francophonie
   • the *Kyoto Protocol*
   • humanitarian aid to fight HIV/AIDS in Africa

4. Create a graphic organizer of one of the following interest groups and report to the class on its composition and mandate and the ways in which it uses its position to influence Canada's foreign policy:
   • the World Wildlife Fund
   • Greenpeace
   • Sierra Club
   • Canadian Manufacturers and Exporters
   • Canadian Association of Petroleum Producers
   • Canadian Chamber of Commerce

5. Find a newspaper article about a current controversial issue in Canadian foreign policy. Research the issue to learn more about Canada's position and the reasons behind it. Prepare a short report explaining your findings.

Communication

6. Look back at Figure 9.1 on page 297.
   a) What imagery has the artist incorporated into this work? Do you find these images effective? Why or why not?
   b) What does the image of the butterfly carrying an AIDS ribbon from Canada to Africa symbolize to you?

7. Using the Internet, newspapers, and magazines, create a photo essay showing how Canada is actively involved in a current global crisis. Photographs should show the nature of the problem, the impact it has on the local people, and the actions being taken to resolve the issue.

8. Divide the class into five groups. Each group is to research one of the following five topics and prepare an oral and visual report on the HIV/AIDS crisis in Africa. When each group has completed its report, organize an HIV/AIDS awareness presentation for your school.
   • the history of HIV/AIDS in Africa
   • the economics of HIV/AIDS
   • the religious and cultural issues surrounding HIV/AIDS
   • the effect of HIV/AIDS on families and communities
   • the international response to HIV/AIDS in Africa

Application

9. Find an editorial cartoon that comments on a current aspect of Canadian foreign policy. (You will find a good online source for Canadian cartoons at www.emp.ca/cwp.) Explain the cartoon's message and point of view. Do you agree with this viewpoint? Give reasons for your answer.

10. As a class, brainstorm a list of local community issues, such as road construction, zoning bylaws, or garbage collection. Record your list on the chalkboard. Then form groups of three or four students to examine one of these issues in detail. Go to the CBC archives on the James Bay Project at www.emp.ca/cwp to read about the ways in which Matthew Coon Come and the Cree were able to lobby the Quebec government and stop its hydro-electric power project. Then, develop an action plan to resolve the issue. Present the plan to the class and, if appropriate, to members of the local government. Groups must be able to defend their points of view and support their action plans.

11. In small groups, brainstorm a list of 10 life-style changes that you and your family could make to create a more sustainable environment in your home and your community. Rank these changes from the easiest to the most difficult to implement. Then do research on the Internet to find out what governments and agencies are doing to help families develop a more sustainable lifestyle. Using this information, review your list of priorities and reorder your rankings, if necessary. Distribute your list to members of your family and apply these lifestyle changes to do your part to make the environment more sustainable.

Major Participants in the International Community

CHAPTER 10

Agenda

In this chapter, you will consider

- the role of non-governmental organizations (NGOs) and intergovernmental organizations
- the concepts of neutrality and impartiality
- politics of NGOs
- international economic organizations
- regional organizations
- pros and cons of free trade
- trade disputes and their resolution
- NGO project management as a career

Figure 10.1 An AIDS quilt on display in Kampala, Uganda, 1998. Since 1987, when the NAMES Project began in San Francisco, California, as a way to commemorate individuals who had died of AIDS and to raise awareness about HIV, 40 countries around the world have joined the project.

In Chapter 9, you examined Canada's role in international politics. In this chapter you will have the opportunity to learn more about the international community itself, especially the organizations, forums, and trading blocs within it. The term "international community" is often used by politicians, state leaders, and activists to mean "everyone in the world."

As you read this chapter, consider whether this community is truly all-inclusive. Can international organizations represent and serve everyone? How are states' interests served through participation in international blocs or alliances? What is free trade? Does it benefit everyone? How are free-trade disputes resolved? How does the country in which you live affect your participation in an increasingly global community?

Types of International Organizations

There are two main types of international organizations. **Intergovernmental organizations** (IGOs) are made up of sovereign states working cooperatively for some purpose. Some of these organizations are open to all world states—for example, the United Nations (UN) and its specialized agencies, or the World Trade Organization (WTO). Canada has links to many of these groups. Others may be organized according to region, such as the Organization of American States. Still others may be united on a particular issue, often with a humanitarian focus. The European Union (EU) is an intergovernmental body that defies categorization in some respects. It is an alliance of member states, a trading bloc, a political union, and a common market. You will read more about the EU in this chapter.

Non-governmental organizations (NGOs), as their name implies, are organizations that are not controlled by governments and are thus a feature of civil society. The World Bank defines NGOs as "private organizations that pursue activities that relieve suffering, promote the interests of the poor, protect the environment, provide basic social services, or undertake community development." The term "non-governmental organization" came into use in 1945 when the UN recognized the need to consult with international organizations that were neither national governments nor political parties. In the early years of the UN, NGOs played a major role in urging the incorporation of human rights provisions into the UN Charter.

Many NGOs maintain a high profile. You or someone you know may belong to at least one of these groups. They depend on private membership fees and charitable donations to pursue their activities free of government interference. Some examples of well-known NGOs include Amnesty International, the International Olympic Committee, and Greenpeace.

Of the more than 25,000 NGOs operating in the world today, some are global organizations, often headquartered in **developed countries** such as Canada, the United States, or Great Britain. Others are national organizations operating in **developing countries**. With recent improvements in electronic communication, more locally based groups, referred to as grassroots or **community-based organizations** (CBOs), have become active at the national or even global level. The growth of community-based groups also reflects new ways of thinking about development in general. In the past, developed countries and international organizations have tried to steer the development of poorer countries in a top-down fashion by imposing programs that sometimes made no sense to the local people. Today, the focus has shifted to partnerships—working with local residents on community projects that help them achieve economic self-sufficiency and a better standard of living.

While governments do not control NGOs, they do consult with them. The United Nations, for example, grants some NGOs associate status through its Economic and Social Council (ECOSOC; see Chapter 8, page 268). NGOs often have an impact on the social, economic, and political activity of a state or region. They can also be effective advocates for ordinary citizens who are the victims of local unrest or government policies that run counter to the principles of human rights.

In the next few pages, you will examine several NGOs operating in four main areas—human rights, health and humanitarian aid, the environment, and sport. Later in this chapter, you will also examine various intergovernmental organizations, including an economic and political union (the EU), specialized and regional groups, and trading blocs, some of which include Canada as a partner.

THE WEB

For more about global NGOs and an NGO research guide, visit www.emp.ca/cwp.

Human Rights NGOs

Human rights NGOs monitor human rights violations in specific regions, investigate them, and act to curtail them through various means. Some human rights NGOs are grassroots organizations; others are driven by experts in certain fields, such as law or journalism.

Amnesty International

> Open your newspaper—any day of the week—and you will find a report from somewhere in the world of someone being imprisoned, tortured or executed because his opinions or religion are unacceptable to his government. The newspaper reader feels a sickening sense of impotence. Yet if these feelings of disgust all over the world could be united into common action, something effective could be done.

Those sentences, written in 1961 by British lawyer Peter Benenson, marked the founding of Amnesty International (AI). Amnesty International is one of the most effective human rights NGOs ever created. Back in 1961, Benenson had pleaded for an international campaign to alert authorities and citizens around the world to the plight of "forgotten prisoners." Within months, his call for action resulted in a permanent international movement, recognized by its candle and barbed-wire logo.

Today, AI is composed of a network of more than 1.8 million members in approximately 160 countries. It operates independently of any government, political ideology, religion, or economic interest, and is concerned solely with promoting and safeguarding human rights. It is perhaps best known for its campaigns against the death penalty and against the torture and abuse of prisoners.

AI thoroughly investigates all claims of human rights abuses that come to its attention. If a claim of abuse is found to be true, Amnesty urges its members to write letters of protest to

Figure 10.2 Amnesty International's "Globalize Human Rights" poster was created to target its Youth+Student Program, which in 2004 had 400 groups across Canada.

the appropriate government leaders or to protest the abuse through publicity campaigns or demonstrations. AI is well known for its **shaming tactics**, which have been successfully adopted by other NGOs. These tactics include human rights "report cards," in which countries are assigned a grade on their human rights record, and intense, often embarrassing, publicity campaigns about individual human rights violations.

For its efforts in defending human rights around the world, AI was awarded the Nobel Peace Prize in 1977. But Amnesty has not entirely escaped criticism. Although AI adopted Nelson Mandela as a forgotten prisoner during his 27-year incarceration in Cape Town, South Africa, its membership was split over support for him. Mandela's refusal to renounce violence as a legitimate tool in the fight against South African apartheid (see Chapter 5, page 187) eventually caused him to be dropped from the AI list of forgotten prisoners. Some observers criticized this move as short-sighted. Others, however, believed that AI had no choice but to refuse to defend Mandela, who openly admitted using violence and terror to dismantle an unjust regime.

Although Canada has a fairly good human rights record, it has not always escaped the scrutiny of Amnesty International. On September 4, 2003, AI released a report about the shooting of Dudley George by an Ontario Provincial Police (OPP) officer. George was killed on September 6, 1995, when he and other members of the Stoney Point Band were in Ipperwash Provincial Park, on the shores of Lake Huron. The unarmed members said that they were in the park because of its Aboriginal burial grounds. Technically,

Figure 10.3 Demonstrators march in Sarnia, Ontario, in 2000, calling for a public inquiry into the shooting death of Aboriginal activist Dudley George during a confrontation with police at Ipperwash Provincial Park.

however, the land belonged to the federal government, which had expropriated it in 1942. When the OPP were called in to remove the protestors, they believed they were armed.

Amnesty's report, *Canada: Why There Must Be a Public Inquiry into the Police Killing of Dudley George*, helped renew the call for an impartial public inquiry into the incident. Although the officer responsible for the shooting had been convicted of criminal negligence causing death, the province of Ontario delayed an inquiry into the shooting for nine years. The effect of the AI report, combined with the lobbying efforts of the George family, culminated in the Ipperwash Inquiry, which began on July 13, 2004.

THE WEB

Learn more about Amnesty International at www.emp.ca/cwp.

Human Rights Watch

Human Rights Watch (HRW) is an international NGO based in New York City dedicated to protecting human rights around the world. It started out in 1978 to monitor the compliance of the then Soviet bloc countries with the **Helsinki Accords**. Unlike AI, HRW has a much smaller grassroots base. It is an agency made up largely of experts, including trained researchers, lawyers, investigative journalists, and ex-diplomats with specialized knowledge about a country or region. However, AI and HRW are closely allied, as they are the only two international human rights organizations operating worldwide in situations of severe abuse or repression.

Like Amnesty International, HRW carries out fact-finding missions in regions where human rights abuses have been reported. Its researchers can spend years in an area or region, gathering and carefully documenting information. The process culminates in a HRW report and often widespread media attention. HRW may also enlist the support of influential parties such as the UN, the European Union, the US government, and international organizations, and campaign for the withdrawal of economic and military support if the abuses are especially severe.

One area in which HRW has been a major contributor is the area of children's rights. In 1996, HRW released *Death by Default*, an indictment of the orphanage system of the People's Republic of China, which charged that "most orphaned or abandoned children in China die within one year of their admittance to state-run orphanages." The report resulted in worldwide press coverage and sparked a discussion about the fate of abandoned children in several other countries, including Russia and Kenya. However, some observers stated that HRW had embarrassed the Chinese government to such an extent that its international adoption program was jeopardized. China shut down its international adoption program for several months as a result of the HRW investigation.

HRW is also one of several NGOs that helped create an international coalition banning the use of child soldiers under the age of 18. It has documented the use of child soldiers in more than 15 countries, including Afghanistan, Angola, India, Nepal, Sierra Leone, and Uganda. Currently,

SOUND BITE   "The best NGOs are loyal to their causes, not to countries, and they aren't afraid to blow the whistle on their own governments."

Naomi Klein, "Bush to NGOs: Watch Your Mouths," 2003

more than 300,000 children are serving as army combatants in rebel forces worldwide (see also Chapter 8, page 276). Human Rights Watch is also well known for speaking out against human rights abuses occurring in the United States, including the treatment of young offenders, police abuse of prisoners, and the death penalty, which, like most human rights groups, HRW opposes.

Physicians for Human Rights

Since its founding in 1986, the US-based Physicians for Human Rights (PHR) has worked "to promote health by protecting human rights." Like Human Rights Watch, PHR sends its professionals into the field to investigate allegations of human rights abuses and then publishes their documented findings. Over the years, PHR members have worked to

- stop torture and mass killings
- protect the rights of women in Afghanistan
- increase spending on AIDS treatment and prevention in Africa and around the world.

PHR is another human rights group that focuses on the US justice system. It openly criticizes the incarceration rate of youth in the United States, estimating that 80 percent of young convicts commit non-violent offences. PHR also charges that young prisoners receive little education or health care inside prison. Its Health and Justice for Youth Project confirms that "health professionals have a central role to play in public dialogue and decision-making on youth justice issues" in five major areas:

- racial disparities
- unhealthy facilities
- mental health needs
- transfer into the adult system
- juvenile death penalty.

From 1990 to 2004, only six countries executed prisoners under 18 years old: Iran, Nigeria, Pakistan, Saudi Arabia, Yemen, and the United States. The United States executed the greatest number of young offenders: 13.

> **SOUND BITE** "Awareness of young people as 'works in progress,' whose ongoing development, mental health and physical well-being are crucial to their own and society's future, has been overtaken by the political expedience of retribution."
>
> *Physicians for Human Rights Web site,*
> *on the US criminal justice system*

Taking a Stand

Jody Williams

The International Campaign to Ban Landmines

One of the greatest myths of modern times is that when wars end, the killing stops. Reality, however, is far more grim. Landmines, the silent sentinels planted in the ground by opposing armies in every war since World War I, continue to kill and maim long after peace treaties are signed. Jody Williams, long-time activist and 1997 Nobel Peace Prize winner, has spent more than a decade fighting this invisible scourge that no longer kills well-trained soldiers, but rather innocent and unarmed civilians.

In 1981, Williams was a temporary office worker in Washington, DC, when a leaflet handed to her as she left a subway sparked a career in global activism. She began working on human rights campaigns in Central America, seeking to change US policy in the region. She soon met activists in the veterans' community who were trying to do more than simply fit landmine victims with prosthetic limbs. Acting upon the old proverb, "an ounce of prevention is worth a pound of cure," these veterans were trying to convince the world's leaders that removing landmines before they harm innocent people was the most effective solution to this deadly problem.

In the early 1990s, Williams began the International Campaign to Ban Landmines (ICBL). Within seven years, the ICBL had grown from two offices in as many countries to several hundred in over 50 states around the world. The ICBL generated international headlines when the late Princess Diana began championing the drive to ban landmines.

Canada has played a large role in the ICBL. In 1996, Canada's Foreign Affairs Minister, Lloyd Axworthy, hosted a conference during which 50 governments and the ICBL joined to create the *Ottawa Declaration*. It challenged governments to return to Canada in 1997 to sign an international treaty banning landmines. Many states worked closely with the ICBL to negotiate a strong treaty that was free of the influence wielded by the large military powers. In December 1997, 121 states led by Canada signed the *1997 Convention on the Prohibition of the Use, Stockpiling, Production and Transfer of Anti-Personnel Mines and on Their Destruction* (Mine Ban Treaty) and pledged $500 million to implement it. As of August 2004, 152 states had signed the treaty and 143 had ratified it. One of the treaty's holdouts has been Williams's own country: the United States claims that landmines remain an integral part of US military strategy.

The October 1997 announcement that Williams and ICBL would share the Nobel Peace Prize firmly established her as a political force to be reckoned with. Nonetheless, the fight to rid the world of landmines is far from over. Every 20 minutes a landmine claims another victim somewhere in the world. One hundred million mines currently lie in the ground in areas where farmers harvest their crops and children play. The hope that these "silent soldiers" will not continue to claim life and limb is being made a reality by the tireless work of activists like Jody Williams.

Source: Adapted from Jeff Trussel, "Lifesaver Heroes: Jody Williams," http://myhero.com/myhero/hero.asp?hero=JodyWilliams.

Questions

1. How do NGOs such as ICBL have both advantages and disadvantages over governments in creating an international treaty?
2. What is the difference between signing and ratifying a treaty? (Hint: Check the Glossary.) Why do you think there is this two-stage process?
3. Find out more about one country that opposes the landmine treaty, and state its reasons for opposition.

Check YOUR UNDERSTANDING

1. Why have NGOs become so influential in world affairs? What features do these influential NGOs have in common?
2. Distinguish among IGOs, NGOs, and CBOs.
3. Was Amnesty International's refusal to keep Nelson Mandela on its list of "forgotten prisoners" the right thing to do? Why or why not?
4. Why did the killing of Dudley George at Ipperwash become a political issue?
5. How is the work of Amnesty International and Human Rights Watch similar, yet different? Why is it important that they remain independent organizations?
6. Why is Physicians for Human Rights concerned about the fact that the United States has not yet signed the Mine Ban Treaty?
7. Why was Canadian Lloyd Axworthy a significant player in the International Campaign to Ban Landmines?

Health and Humanitarian Aid NGOs

Although there are hundreds of international humanitarian NGOs, this section will focus on three significant ones that provide medical and humanitarian relief: Doctors Without Borders, the Red Cross/Red Crescent, and the World Medical Association. A fourth agency—the World Health Organization—is a specialized UN agency and the world's coordinating authority on international public health.

Doctors Without Borders/Médecins Sans Frontières

Since its founding by a small group of French doctors in 1971, Doctors Without Borders/Médecins Sans Frontières (MSF) has become the world's largest independent medical relief NGO. Its mission is to deliver health care to people who need it, no matter where they live. The organization's membership includes physicians, nurses, and other medical professionals. A Canadian chapter of MSF was founded in 1991 by Dr. James Orbinski (see Taking a Stand, Chapter 12, page 410).

MSF has brought medical relief to people living in more than 80 countries. Many of these patients have been victims of

- wars and armed conflicts
- natural or human-made disasters
- epidemics, such as cholera, malaria, and HIV/AIDS.

Figure 10.4 A doctor from MSF treats a child at a refugee camp in northern Burundi in central Africa. Worldwide, the number of refugees and displaced persons has increased from 2 million in the early 1970s to more than 39 million people today.

MSF epitomizes the challenges that face humanitarian aid NGOs operating in a politically charged environment. For 25 years, the agency delivered health care in Afghanistan, operating medical clinics that provided a wide range of medical services from treatment for tuberculosis to obstetrical care. MSF persisted in Afghanistan throughout the civil wars of the 1980s and even during the **Taliban** regime (1994–2002). Then, on June 2, 2004, five of its members were ambushed in their clearly marked MSF vehicle and killed. The following month, MSF withdrew from Afghanistan, citing deteriorating security, the unresolved deaths of the aid workers, and its frustration with the US and NATO forces, who tell locals they must produce information about Taliban and **al-Qaida** operatives to qualify for humanitarian aid.

In a July 28, 2004, press release, MSF stated:

> The violence directed against humanitarian aid workers has come in a context in which the United States–backed coalition has consistently sought to use humanitarian aid to build support for its military and political ambitions. MSF denounces the coalition's attempts to co-opt humanitarian aid and use it to "win hearts and minds." By doing so, providing aid is no longer seen as an impartial and neutral act, endangering the lives of humanitarian volunteers and jeopardizing the aid to people in need.

In November 2004, MSF withdrew from Iraq.

International Committee of the Red Cross/Red Crescent

The International Committee of the Red Cross/Red Crescent is probably the world's largest humanitarian NGO. The idea of the Red Cross was born in 1859 when Swiss businessman Jean Henri Dunant came upon the aftermath

SOUND BITE "We simply cannot sacrifice the security of our volunteers while warring parties seek to target and kill humanitarian workers. Ultimately, it is the sick and destitute that suffer."

Marine Buissonnire, MSF Secretary-General, 2004

Figure 10.5 The Red Cross also works to reunite people who have been separated by war or natural disasters. Here, a Canadian Red Cross worker escorts a young refugee as he prepares to board an aircraft to return home to Kosovo.

THE WEB

Learn more about the Red Cross and its mandate at www.emp.ca/cwp.

of a battle scene in Northern Italy. About 40,000 soldiers lay wounded, with no one to tend to their injuries. Dunant appealed to the local residents to comfort the soldiers and bandage their feet.

Convinced that humanity could make a difference to the suffering of people wounded in war, Dunant went on to found the International Committee of the Red Cross in October 1863. Sixteen countries attended the first planning conference. By 1864, 12 countries had ratified a document that paved the way for the first **Geneva Convention** (see Chapter 8, page 285). This international treaty protects individuals who do not fight but who may be wounded in war (medics, civilians, aid workers), as well as combatants who can no longer fight (the wounded and sick, and prisoners of war). The *Geneva Convention* was the beginning of international humanitarian law (see also Chapter 11, page 380). In 1909, Canada's federal government passed the *Canadian Red Cross Society Act*, which legally established the Red Cross as the corporate body responsible for providing volunteer aid in Canada in accordance with the *Geneva Convention*.

Today, there are national Red Cross societies in 178 countries working with more than 115 million volunteers. The principles of the Red Cross movement are humanity, impartiality, neutrality, independence, voluntary service, unity, and universality. Throughout the 20th century, the Red Cross has offered medical assistance during some of the world's most tragic events, including World War II (1939–45), the Korean War (1950–53), the Hungarian Revolution (1956), clan warfare and drought in Somalia (1991–92), the Rwanda genocide (1994), and recent crises in Iraq, Afghanistan, and Darfur, Sudan. Because the Red Cross remains politically neutral, it was in a unique position to assist during the 1990 Oka Crisis at Kanesatake and Kahnawake, Quebec. The Red Cross provided food and medical supplies to Mohawk protestors behind the barricades.

World Medical Association

In the aftermath of the Holocaust (see Chapters 3 and 8) and the discovery that Nazi physicians had participated in medical experiments on Jewish civilians, including children, a group of physicians gathered in Paris, France, for the first general assembly of a new kind of medical organization. The new group would work to ensure that medical ethics remained centre-stage in medicine. The World Medical Association (WMA), as it came to be known, is currently recognized for its commitment to ethical standards in medical treatment, research on human subjects, and patient rights. The *Declaration of Helsinki* is the WMA's best-known policy statement, first adopted in 1964 and since amended several times. It is a primer for physicians and researchers on ethical medical research on human subjects, and includes guidelines on such issues as

THE WEB

Learn more about the World Medical Association and its mandate at www.emp.ca/cwp.

- when medical research should and should not be conducted
- the well-being of the human subject versus the well-being of society
- rights of human subjects
- vulnerable research populations that require special protection (such as prisoners).

Canada was a founding member of the WMA, and the Canadian Medical Association is one of 80 national medical associations that belong to the organization.

NGOs and the World Health Organization

In 1948, the UN established the World Health Organization (WHO) to coordinate the development of standards for international public health. Although WHO is an intergovernmental organization, it works closely with health and humanitarian-aid NGOs, forging relationships based on mutual understanding and interests. WHO also tries to harness NGOs' particular expertise. Some NGOs, for example, have been instrumental in helping WHO draft guidelines for the use of infant formula.

WHO also works to control and eliminate disease and to improve the health and quality of life of the world's citizens. To this end, WHO sometimes issues **advisories** when there is an outbreak of illness, warning people to limit travel to affected areas. In 2003, 44 people in Toronto died of Severe Acute Respiratory Syndrome (SARS), caused by a virus that also struck other cities of the world. After the WHO issued a travel advisory warning people not to visit Toronto, the city's entertainment and tourism industries were dealt a severe blow and economic recovery was slow.

Figure 10.6 This benefit concert by the Rolling Stones on July 30, 2003, helped put Toronto back on the tourism map after the SARS crisis.

Check YOUR UNDERSTANDING

1. Why is it important that Doctors Without Borders and the Red Cross be impartial, independent, and neutral?
2. Since the UN has many agencies that supply services similar to Doctors Without Borders and the Red Cross, why are these two organizations still needed?
3. In what way does the World Medical Association differ from Doctors Without Borders?
4. Why is the World Health Organization actively participating with NGOs?
5. Given the devastating impact of SARS on Toronto's economy, do you think that the WHO's travel advisory was warranted? Explain.

Other Important NGOs

Other NGOs are active in such areas as the environment and sport.

Greenpeace

Can you imagine a world in which the words "environment" or "ecology" are virtually unknown, except to a few scientists? This was the case back in 1971, when a small group of Canadian activists and US draft-dodgers decided to sail from Vancouver to Amchitka Island, Alaska, to halt US nuclear testing. The island was home to many species of endangered wildlife. When the US military ordered protestors to leave, the group refused. The tense standoff captured the attention of people around the world, and Greenpeace was born. It was eventually successful in pressuring the United States to abandon nuclear testing at Amchitka.

Today, Greenpeace is an international environmental NGO with headquarters in Amsterdam, the Netherlands, 2.8 million supporters worldwide, and offices in 41 countries. As its mission statement emphasizes, Greenpeace continues to engage in "high-profile non-violent, creative confrontation to expose global environmental problems and to force solutions for a green and peaceful future."

Greenpeace works to

- halt climatic change, e.g., global warming
- encourage sustainable development
- help consumers eliminate the use of toxic chemicals such as aerosols, pesticides, and detergents
- save the ocean and preserve the forests
- stop whaling, nuclear proliferation, and genetic engineering.

Although Greenpeace opposes the commercial whaling industry, it does not oppose the right of the Inuit or other Aboriginal groups to pursue sub-

SOUND BITE "Life is not an industrial commodity. When we force life forms and our world's food supply to conform to human economic models rather than their natural ones, we do so at our own peril."

Greenpeace Web site, 2004

Figure 10.7 An anti-nuclear demonstration in London, England, 1995, commemorating the 10th anniversary of the sinking of Greenpeace's ship, the *Rainbow Warrior*. In July 1985, the *Rainbow Warrior* was docked in New Zealand to protest French nuclear testing in the Pacific. French agents set off explosives, and the ship sank. The French government eventually admitted responsibility and paid $8 million in compensation to Greenpeace.

Press Play

In *The Rainbow Warrior* (1992), directed by Michael Tuchner, starring Jon Voight and Sam Neill, New Zealand police investigate the deadly 1985 sinking of Greenpeace's flagship in Auckland Harbour. The crime was terrorism, and the subsequent investigation by the police revealed French responsibility. (PG)

sistence whaling. Most of its anti-whaling campaigns are directed at Asian, European, and South American commercial whalers. It is also opposed to any resumption of international trade in whale blubber. Under the *Convention on the International Trade in Endangered Species* (CITES), it is illegal to export or import whale products.

The International Olympic Committee

The International Olympic Committee (IOC) is the umbrella organization of the Olympic Movement. This NGO, founded in 1894,

- promotes sport for all, as well as sport for gifted amateurs
- ensures that the Olympic Games are held every four years
- supports policies of inclusiveness and non-discrimination in sport
- promotes ethics in sport and sports competitions, and the protection of athletes.

The IOC is an extremely wealthy NGO. It owns the rights to market and broadcast the Olympic Games, as well as the rights to all Olympic trademarks and symbols, such as the interlocking rings. It makes the most of its assets through the sale of broadcast rights to the major television networks every four years, when the games are held. Much of the credit for this brilliant

Figure 10.8 Human chains form the interlocking Olympic rings at the closing ceremonies for the Athens Games, August 29, 2004.

THE WEB

Learn more about the IOC, WADA, and the 2004 Athens Games at www.emp.ca/cwp.

marketing strategy must be given to Canadian Dick Pound, a former Olympic swimmer and president of the Canadian Olympic Committee. During the 1980s, Pound turned the Olympics into a multibillion dollar industry by marketing the Olympic rings for the first time, and by negotiating worldwide TV rights for phenomenal sums. He also led the campaign to initiate drug testing of Olympic athletes, which led to the creation of the World Anti-Doping Agency (WADA) in 1999. In 2001, WADA moved its headquarters from Switzerland to Montreal, with Dick Pound as its head.

The IOC is controlled by delegates from each country. It is these members who determine where the games will be held. Countries wishing to host the Olympics must submit bids to the IOC, which makes the final selection. This often is a political process, and a few IOC members have been caught in scandals, taking advantage of the bidding cities to extort financial and other rewards. Six dismissals from the 113-member International Olympic Committee ensued after it was revealed that some delegates accepted such "influence" as travel, free medical care, and other lavish gifts in order to vote for the Sydney location in 2000 and the Salt Lake City venue in 2002.

The site chosen for the Olympics can also have political reverberations. Some credit the IOC's awarding of the 1988 Summer Games to Seoul, South Korea, with helping to usher out a repressive right-wing regime (see Chapter 5). The selection of Beijing, China, as the site of the 2008 Summer Games was also welcomed by some human rights activists as a way to keep the spotlight on human rights abuses in China.

Check Your Understanding

1. Where does Greenpeace get its political power?
2. Why might some people and groups consider Greenpeace too influential?
3. Why is the selection of the Olympic host city such a political decision?
4. Debate the following resolution: "The Olympic Games have become too commercialized and too politically corrupt, and should therefore be abolished."

International Economic Organizations

International economic organizations can be specialized UN agencies or they can be made up only of member states. These organizations have several goals in common. They all work to achieve global economic growth through trade; they encourage development of poorer countries; and they try to keep the economies of individual countries stable.

The World Bank and the International Monetary Fund

The World Bank and the International Monetary Fund (IMF) were founded together in 1944, in the small New Hampshire village of Bretton Woods. On this occasion, the leaders of 44 countries had gathered to find ways to promote a more stable world economy and avoid economic crises such as the Great Depression of the 1930s. Also on the agenda was how to rebuild Europe after the devastation of World War II. Today, many people assume that both organizations are remote from the lives of ordinary people. Indeed, the IMF itself acknowledges that "most people have only the vaguest idea of what these institutions do."

The World Bank

The Bretton Woods group created the World Bank primarily as an engine of economic development. The Bank's first loans went to European countries to assist in reconstruction following World War II. After Europe was rebuilt, the World Bank began lending money to poorer countries in the developing world.

Although the World Bank lends and manages money like a regular chartered bank, it differs in many important ways. It is owned by its 184 member states who are jointly responsible for how the institution is financed and how its money is spent. Unlike other banks, the World Bank often makes interest-free or low-interest loans to states in need that are unable to borrow money in international markets. Countries borrowing from the Bank have a long period—between 35 to 40 years—in which to repay their loans, with a 10-year grace period.

The International Monetary Fund

The IMF was created primarily to regulate the global monetary system. When a country joins the IMF, it agrees to have its exchange rate policies and exchange arrangements overseen by the organization. In this way, member states hope to avoid the sudden and large fluctuations in currency values that occurred during the Great Depression. The 1990s brought some new challenges to the IMF. There were economic challenges associated with **globalization** and with integrating the markets and economies of several states. There was also a great deal of turbulence in emerging financial markets, notably in Asia and Latin America (see Chapter 12, page 409).

Following the September 11, 2001, terrorist attacks in the United States, the IMF expanded its efforts to combat money laundering and the financing of terrorism. In 2003, a joint IMF–World Bank project was launched to monitor policies and actions needed to achieve the UN's Millennium Development Goals (including poverty reduction, universal primary education, lower child mortality, and access to clean water) by 2015, and its first annual Global Monitoring Report was issued in July 2004.

Critics of the IMF and World Bank believe that there are too many economic and political conditions attached to loans to developing countries. For example, countries must show that they have cut their public spending before obtaining World Bank funding. These cuts can severely limit a country's ability to supply health care and education to its people. Sometimes countries must spend more on debt repayments than they do on health or education. Other critics say that sizable loans to former military dictatorships and military juntas have been used to enrich only a small part of the population, while the loans are repaid by the entire population once it is free from political oppression.

Some believe that these organizations have little effect on the democratization of sovereign states, as economic chaos is not a good starting point for a stable democracy (see Chapter 5, page 167). They have been blamed for financing infrastructure projects such as roads and dams instead of addressing people's basic needs. Too often these large-scale projects have been unsuitable and damaging to the environment. Finally, others claim that these organizations are generally apathetic about human rights, democracy, and labour rights. These criticisms helped spark the anti-globalization movement discussed in Chapter 12.

General Agreement on Tariffs and Trade and the World Trade Organization

When the IMF and World Bank were established in 1945, a third organization to promote world trade was also contemplated. Two years later, the *General Agreement on Tariffs and Trade* (GATT) was signed in Geneva by 23 countries. GATT was not an international organization, but a multilateral treaty on the rules of world trade. Countries that signed the 1947 GATT held subsequent rounds of negotiations until they agreed on substantial reductions in trade barriers, especially reductions in **tariffs**. They also agreed to other rules of international trade, including non-discriminatory treatment of other GATT members.

GATT was incorporated into the newly created World Trade Organization (WTO) on January 1, 1995, when new agreements on trading services, trade-related **intellectual property**, and foreign investment were added. The 1995 agreement also effectively limited countries' ability to subsidize their agricultural sectors for the first time.

Whereas GATT regulated trade in merchandise goods, WTO also covers trade in services, such as banking and telecommunications. Currently, it governs about 97 percent of all world trade, and is closely associated with globalization (see Chapter 12). WTO decisions are reached by consensus

Economic Body	Date Formed	Purpose and Function	Members
Organisation for Economic Co-operation and Development (OECD)	1961	Counterpart to NATO Develops and improves economic and social policy Maintains an extensive statistical base that is widely used	30 member countries in Europe, Asia, North America, and Australia Relationships with 70 other countries and NGOs
Organization of Petroleum Exporting Countries (OPEC)	1960	Coordinates policies to manage the oil supply in an effort to set and control oil prices on the world market Supplies about 40 percent of the world's crude oil and possesses about 75 percent of the world's oil reserves	Iran, Iraq, Kuwait, Saudi Arabia, Venezuela, Algeria, Indonesia, Libya, Nigeria, Qatar, and the United Arab Emirates

Figure 10.9 Other economic organizations.

and are binding on its members. So, for example, if the United States and Canada are locked in a trade dispute over beef, wheat, or softwood lumber, the WTO would rule on the dispute through its Dispute Settlement Body, if either country asked it to do so. The WTO has the authority to issue sanctions against a member country that refuses to comply with its rulings, but it tries to resolve conflicts through negotiation. Trade dispute resolutions are discussed in the last section of this chapter.

Two other notable economic organizations are listed in Figure 10.9.

Protests Against the WTO

The WTO is criticized by many people who are opposed to its policies of **free trade** and to economic globalization in general. Opponents charge that they are not totally opposed to free trade *per se*—they are opposed to the WTO's vision of free trade. Among the charges:

Figure 10.10 Police use tear gas to push back demonstrators at the WTO's meeting in Seattle, Washington, in November 1999. The first of many organized protests against the WTO, the Seattle event attracted more than 30,000 protestors from around the world.

- Business interests have too much influence over the policies of free trade. Large corporations that benefit from free trade push the WTO to implement rules and policies that benefit them. These institutions are not democratically elected.
- A country's national safety standards and environmental regulations are often viewed by the WTO as trade barriers. Should the WTO have the power to compel sovereign states to change their laws by declaring them to be in violation of free trade?
- Many developing countries believe that WTO negotiations are settled in favour of developed countries—the true beneficiaries of free trade.

Law in Motion

Bill C-9 and Generic Drugs

In August 2003, the WTO brokered a deal that began allowing the international sale of generic (non–brand-name) drugs to developing countries to treat HIV/AIDS, tuberculosis, malaria, and other diseases. For years, the United States had opposed such an agreement in order to protect the patent rights of its brand-name pharmaceutical firms. Under the old WTO rules, developing countries could produce their own generics but could not import them. The new deal allows developing countries to buy generics produced in other countries.

Immediately following the WTO's decision, Canada drafted legislation allowing the export of low-cost generic drugs to countries in need. Then Prime Minister Jean Chrétien, supported by Stephen Lewis and a coalition of NGOs, called it "the right thing to do, the moral thing to do."

Bill C-9, *An Act to Amend the Patent Act and the Food and Drugs Act*, received royal assent on May 14, 2004—but not without a great deal of debate over some of its clauses. The bill was amended many times as legislators listened to arguments from pharmaceutical companies on the one hand and numerous NGOs, such as the Canadian Labour Congress, Doctors Without Borders, and Oxfam, on the other.

One of the most contentious clauses was the "right of first refusal" clause. This clause granted the patent-holding drug companies the right to assume the contracts of the generic companies at the price negotiated by the generics in the developing country. This provision was favourable to the brand-name pharmaceuticals but provided zero incentive to the generic companies to develop contracts abroad. The clause was eliminated from the bill.

The original bill also specified which countries could import the generics (only WTO member countries) and which medicines would be allowed. Critics found these lists too restrictive, so the government partially aban-

Figure 10.11 A Tanzanian woman carries her 30-year-old son, who suffers from AIDS, to sit in the shade.

doned them. Similarly, an earlier requirement for an NGO in the disease-stricken country to notify that country's government before contacting a Canadian generic firm was ultimately dismissed as needless red tape. However, some people still think that Bill C-9 makes it too difficult for non-WTO member countries to receive help.

Finally, Bill C-9 in its original form opened the door for brand-name pharmaceuticals to sue the generic companies. In the past, brand-name companies had sued Nelson Mandela's government for shipping generics to South Africa. Although the Canadian government also amended these clauses, fears remain that the courts could be used to intimidate producers of generic drugs. A parliamentary review of the legislation is scheduled to occur in 2006, at which time amendments may be offered.

THE WEB

Learn more about the WTO, the generic drug deal, and other WTO initiatives at www.emp.ca/cwp.

Questions

1. a) According to the critics of Bill C-9, what provisions in the bill are considered objectionable?
   b) Speculate why those provisions were included in Bill C-9.
2. Although the WTO and many member states are excited about this deal, many aid agencies are much more skeptical. Research this drug deal and, with a partner, try to reach consensus on whether or not it is a good one.

Check YOUR UNDERSTANDING

1. What is the difference between the International Monetary Fund and the World Bank?
2. Outline three criticisms of the IMF and the World Bank.
3. How is the OECD an economic counterpart to NATO?
4. Why is OPEC such a powerful economic organization?
5. What is the relationship between the GATT and the WTO?
6. How do WTO decisions differ from those of most other international organizations?
7. Outline three criticisms of the WTO. Which do you think is the most serious, and why?
8. What is the significance of the Canadian government's Bill C-9?

Regional and Specialized Organizations

Some international organizations are created among groups of sovereign states in a particular region. They may act as a "regional UN" by defining and promoting their local and political interests. Other organizations are created to advance a special interest, such as economic cooperation and development among groups of states, stewardship of the Arctic, and culture. Specialized international organizations often cross regions and have a specific focus and objectives.

The European Union

1952–58 Belgium, France, Germany, Italy, Luxembourg, the Netherlands
1973 Britain, Ireland, Denmark
1981 Greece
1986 Spain, Portugal
1995 Austria, Finland, Sweden
2004 Cyprus, Czech Republic, Estonia, Hungary, Latvia, Lithuania, Malta, Poland, Slovakia, Slovenia

Figure 10.12 Timeline: Membership in the European Union, showing year joined.

Although listed here as a regional organization, the **European Union** (EU) represents a unique alliance of countries. It is a regional organization, a political union, and a common market. What later became the EU began in 1957, when six European countries signed the *Treaty of Rome* to form a customs union by 1970. Known then as the European Economic Community (EEC), it was as much a pact designed to prevent war among member countries as it was an economic and trade organization. Other countries joined over time, and new treaties were signed to create a single market by December 31, 1992. On that day, 12 European countries dissolved their economic borders and agreed to the free exchange of goods, services, capital, and people among their member states. Most members of the renamed European Union adopted a single currency—the euro—in 1999. Since 1993, the EU has grown to 25 members (Figure 10.12).

The EU is unique as an international organization in that its member states have established common institutions, including a European Parliament and a Court of Justice. The power of these institutions is impressive and growing. However, there are still many matters over which member countries alone have sovereignty, such as military forces and marriage laws.

Citizens of member states of the European Union also have unprecedented mobility. They are not only permitted to cross borders without car-

Figure 10.13 A British man protests in favour of keeping the pound as the country's currency, 2003. Britain—along with Denmark and Sweden—refused to adopt the euro. Britain's pound sterling has an unbroken history of more than 900 years.

rying a passport or being subjected to a border check, but they can also live and work in another EU country without legal restriction. Once they take up residence in a new country, EU citizens have the right to vote for candidates or run for political office in that country. Citizenship in the EU is considered to exist along with national citizenship and does not replace it.

Canada formally established relations with the EU in 1976. It is Canada's largest trading partner after the United States, with the EU importing $33.6 billion worth of goods and services from Canada in 2003.

THE WEB

Learn more about the European Union, the euro, and Canada–EU relations at www.emp.ca/cwp.

Organization of American States

The Washington-based Organization of American States (OAS) is the world's oldest regional organization. It was established in 1948 to promote military, economic, and cultural cooperation among countries of North, Central, and South America. The OAS commits its member states to the promotion and consolidation of representative democracy while respecting the principle of **non-intervention** enshrined in its charter. Currently, 35 independent member states have ratified the OAS Charter.

Canada did not join the OAS until 1990 because of the agency's close ties with the United States. Critics believe that the OAS frequently caters to American interests, citing, for example, the hasty suspension of Cuba from the OAS following the Cuban revolution and the 1962 **Cuban Missile Crisis**. The official reason for suspending Cuba was concern for human rights and democracy in the country, yet the OAS has failed to suspend other Latin

American governments for severe human rights violations. Canada had no wish to oppose the United States on such issues as Cuba, nor did it wish to risk becoming an American puppet. However, when major economic reforms created new opportunities in the region, and issues such as drug trafficking in the Americas became more pressing, Canada decided to join this international organization.

African Union

As individual African states emerged from **colonialism** in the 1960s, some African leaders argued that Africa could survive only as a single organization. Others believed that the newly independent countries must first build strong national states. The Organization for African Unity (OAU) was originally established in 1963 to promote unity, solidarity, and cooperation among the newly independent African states. As the 20th century wore on, however, African leaders recognized the effectiveness of well-integrated organizations such as the European Union. In 2002, they formed the African Union (AU), with 53 member states. Its general goals are the promotion of development, the eradication of poverty, and the integration of African countries into the global economy.

The AU faces many challenges. Its member states do not share a common standard of living—there is a wide divergence in living standards among members, as well as civil war in Liberia, Sierra Leone, Guinea–Bissau, and Sudan. In July 2004, the AU sent troops to Sudan's Darfur region, where more than 1 million black Africans had fled attacks by Arab militias. These were the first foreign troops to intervene in a situation described as the world's "worst humanitarian crisis," yet one in which the UN avoided intervention.

THE WEB

Learn about the Canada Fund for Africa at www.emp.ca/cwp.

Figure 10.14 The UN's ineffectual response to the genocide in Sudan is the subject of this 2004 editorial cartoon.

Asia–Pacific Economic Cooperation

The Asia–Pacific Economic Cooperation (APEC) was formed in 1989 in recognition of the growing interdependence of the Asian and Pacific economies. APEC started as an informal discussion group and now includes 21 member countries. It represents three of the most important economies of the world—China, Japan, and the United States—as well as the most dynamic region of the globe. In the last 10 years, the Asia–Pacific economies have generated about 70 percent of world economic growth. Unlike other multilateral trade organizations, APEC has no treaty obligations, and decisions are reached by consensus. Historically, APEC has also been viewed as a way to counterbalance the emerging trading blocs of Europe and North America.

Canada was a founding member of APEC. Today, Canadian government representatives are involved with many of APEC's working groups, including fisheries, telecommunications, energy, sustainable development, human resources, and economic analysis.

League of Arab States

The Arab League was founded in 1945 by seven Middle Eastern states. It now includes 22 member states that use Arabic as a common language. Its mandate is to promote closer ties among members and coordinate their policies and economic, security, and cultural programs. Egypt's membership was suspended in 1979 after it signed a peace treaty with Israel, but in 1987 Arab leaders renewed diplomatic ties, leading to Egypt's return to the League in 1989. Canada has strong economic and people-to-people ties with the Arab states.

G7/G8

In 1975, the leaders of the world's six largest industrial states (Britain, France, Germany, Italy, Japan, and the United States) met in France to deal with emerging economic and political issues. At that time, large increases in oil prices had destabilized the global monetary system. Canada joined in 1976 to make it the G7 ("group of seven"). Russia began meeting informally with the G7 in 1994, and became the eighth official member at the 1998 G8 summit in Birmingham, England.

Although the G8 began as an economic forum, other world issues—such as crime and drugs, terrorism, and human rights—have gained importance in its discussions. The G8 is not a formal international organization like the UN or the World Trade Organization (WTO), and its decisions are not binding. It has no permanent staff, headquarters, or budget, and relies on a host country each year to provide facilities and security for summit meetings. The G8 is also not universal; it comprises the world's largest political and industrial democracies. G8 countries have enormous influence on

Figure 10.15 Prime Minister Jean Chrétien tastes a local vegetable as he visits Nigeria in 2002 to discuss issues of debt, aid, development, and commitment to NEPAD. In that year, Canada committed $6 billion over five years to assist in Africa's development in such areas as government, trade, education, health, and agricultural research, and lobbied G8 leaders to follow its lead.

THE WEB

Learn more about the G7/G8 and the 2002 summit in Kananaskis Valley, Alberta, at www.emp.ca/cwp.

SOUND BITE "While many in the South characterize climate change as an environmental and/or economic issue, to us it raises questions of culture and survival."

Inuit Circumpolar Conference Canada Web site, 2003

the UN Security Council and the WTO. In fact, it is through these formal international institutions that many of the G8's decisions become reality.

The G8's most powerful players are Japan, Germany, and the United States. The United States in particular does not hesitate to use its financial, economic, and military power to pressure other countries to follow its lead. However, Canada is also an active player in the G8. Recently, former Prime Minister Jean Chrétien placed the issue of development in Africa before the summit, and obtained a commitment from leaders to support the New Plan for African Development (NEPAD). Since the 1998 summit, these annual meetings have become an opportunity for anti-globalization demonstrations. The 2001 summit in Genoa, Italy, resulted in a protester's death (see Figure 12.13, page 425).

Arctic Council

The Arctic Council (AC) was inaugurated in Ottawa on September 19, 1996. The mandate of this intergovernmental forum is to protect the arctic environment and promote the economic, social, and cultural well-being of northern peoples. Its eight members are Canada, Denmark, Finland, Iceland, Norway, Russia, Sweden, and the United States. (Greenland is a member as a province of Denmark.) All member countries have, or administer, territories that border the Arctic Ocean.

A unique feature of the Arctic Council is the involvement of six international indigenous peoples' organizations as permanent parties. These groups possess detailed knowledge of the arctic environment, including the impact of recent climatic changes and increased ultra-violet radiation on the region. The AC addressed the issue of climate variability in the arctic in a November 2004 scientific symposium, and acknowledged the contribution of "traditional knowledge" to its understanding of these environmental changes.

THE WEB

Learn more about the Arctic Council and Canada's circumpolar involvement at www.emp.ca/cwp.

Check YOUR UNDERSTANDING

1. Why did Canada delay becoming a member of the Organization of American States?
2. In what way is the European Union a unique international organization?
3. What concerns exist for the success and survival of the African Union?
4. In what way is the Asia–Pacific Economic Cooperation a unique international organization?
5. Why is Canada, as part of North America, a partner in both APEC and ASEAN?
6. How does the G8 differ from regional international organizations?
7. Why do you think G8 summits provoke anti-globalization demonstrations?
8. What is the purpose of the Arctic Council, and what link binds its members?

Canada and International Trade

In the 19th century, trade was the engine of economic growth. Canada's first trade agreement with the United States was signed in 1854. The US Congress cancelled it in 1866, hoping to force the Canadian colonies to join the United States. However, this threat only propelled Canada toward Confederation in 1867 and the election of Sir John A. Macdonald as Canada's first prime minister. Macdonald's 1879 National Policy advocated protective tariffs for Canadian industry from foreign imports, especially from the United States, to boost economic growth (see Figure 2.16, page 58). Macdonald also believed that a transcontinental railway would stimulate east–west trade and that high tariffs would encourage Canadians to shop at home. Over the next century, a recurring theme in Canadian elections was the battle between free trade and removal of tariffs versus a policy of **protectionism**.

After passage of the *Statute of Westminster* by the British Parliament in 1931, Canada was totally free to shape its own foreign policy. Canada immediately sought to take advantage of the power and economic strength of the United States. In 1935, Liberal Prime Minister Mackenzie King and President Franklin Roosevelt signed a trade treaty that lowered the American tariff on many Canadian exports to the United States; in return, Canada granted the United States **most-favoured-nation** status. In 1938, this agreement was further expanded to lower tariffs on about 80 percent of Canadian exports to the United States. But when *Time* magazine called Canada "the 49th state,"

Mackenzie King, worried about voter reaction in Canada, abandoned free-trade negotiations.

In 1965, the *Canada–US Automotive Agreement*, the **Auto Pact**, was signed. It permitted the duty-free movement of new vehicles and their parts across the border, which benefited large American auto makers. Before this agreement, a 15 percent tariff had been imposed on all American automobiles and parts imported into Canada. The Auto Pact allowed US branch plants in Canada to operate without having to pay tariffs when their products crossed the border. In return, jobs were guaranteed for Canadian workers, and North American automobile production became more competitive, efficient, and profitable. (Automotives is Canada's primary export industry.) The Auto Pact's success encouraged other free-trade negotiations between Canada and the United States, leading to the *Free Trade Agreement*.

Free Trade and the *Free Trade Agreement*

The decision to pursue free trade was made in 1985 by the government of Prime Minister Brian Mulroney (1984–93) following a recommendation to do so by the Royal Commission on the Economic Union and Development Prospects for Canada (nicknamed the Macdonald Royal Commission). The decision was motivated by the desire to secure access to the large US market.

Figure 10.16 Prime Minister Brian Mulroney and his wife Mila joined US President Ronald Reagan and first lady Nancy in singing "When Irish Eyes Are Smiling," March 1985. The so-called Shamrock Summit paved the way for free-trade negotiations, but was criticized by those who felt Canada would be at a disadvantage in closer trade with the United States.

Canada depended on this market, but some exports (softwood lumber and agricultural products) were shut out by US protectionist policies. Large Canadian businesses were major supporters of this initiative.

Since Canada's economy is relatively small, it seemed reasonable that Canadian businesses could benefit by reaching outside domestic markets. The goal of free trade—the free exchange of goods and services without any tariffs or other barriers—was to promote full employment and greater productivity, and to strengthen the competitiveness of Canadian firms in global markets. This belief was strengthened when a serious recession hit the country, and many Canadians thought that prosperity would be found in free trade, not protectionism.

By 1980, Canada and the United States were each other's largest trading partners, and the Canada–US bilateral trading relationship was the world's largest. In May 1986, the two governments began negotiating a free-trade agreement that was finalized in 1987.

The Free-Trade Controversies

The *Free Trade Agreement* (FTA) greatly liberalized trade between the two countries, removing most remaining tariffs and establishing a schedule for the elimination of all trade tariffs by January 1, 1998; it also included rules governing trade in services, resulting in a rapid increase in cross-border trade and more integrated economies for both countries. But the FTA also sparked vigorous debate and controversy in Canada. Business supported improved access to US markets, which could lead to higher employment, economic growth, and prosperity. Consumers also believed that free trade would result in greater product choice and lower prices.

Many Canadians—and the federal Liberal and NDP parties—accused the Progressive Conservative government of "selling out" to the United States and undermining Canada's sovereignty. Would Canada eventually be forced to join the United States? Others felt that the agreement would threaten Canadian institutions such as health care and education, and cultural industries such as magazines, newspapers, and television. Women's organizations and labour groups were skeptical of free trade, believing that it would force issues such as pay equity and working conditions onto the back burner. Unions feared a loss of jobs.

After the majority Conservative government was re-elected in 1988 (with 43 percent of the popular vote), it re-introduced the FTA in Parliament. The FTA was ratified in 1988 and implemented on January 1, 1989.

The *North American Free Trade Agreement*

In the 1993 federal election, voters threw the Conservatives from power, reducing their seats in the House of Commons from 155 to two. The free-trade agreements that had formed the core of the Conservative economic policy were one reason for this stunning electoral defeat. However, new Liberal Prime Minister Jean Chrétien let the FTA stand and continued negotiation of the *North American Free Trade Agreement* (NAFTA). This angered Canadians who had supported the Liberals' opposition to the FTA during the election. On January 1, 1994, NAFTA was proclaimed exactly as negotiated by Brian Mulroney and former US President George Bush, Sr.

NAFTA is a trilateral agreement among Canada, the United States, and Mexico. It created the world's largest free-trade area, which then included some 360 million people. The agreement applies to trade and investment as well as environmental and labour issues. It immediately eliminated tariffs on most goods, with remaining tariffs scheduled to be phased out within five to 15 years. Under NAFTA, bilateral schedules were negotiated by Canada and the United States with Mexico for tariff elimination. Following a final tariff reduction between Canada and Mexico, effective January 1, 2003, virtually all trade in the NAFTA region has been tariff-free. NAFTA, as an international agreement, is similar to a treaty. Pressure from environmental NGOs, particularly in the United States, ensured that trade and environmental issues were linked for the first time in NAFTA.

NAFTA: Ten Years Later

More than 10 years later, NAFTA still incites controversy (see Point Counterpoint, page 364). Critics in organized labour and public advocacy groups have often dismissed NAFTA as a total failure. Labour unions in North America have opposed NAFTA, fearing that jobs would move to Mexico because of lower wage costs. After the passing of NAFTA, the Canadian Labour Congress (CLC) estimated that total Canadian manufacturing employment was 10 percent below pre-NAFTA levels, while wages had remained the same or declined; the Canadian Auto Workers Union also noted that thousands of jobs had moved from Canada to Mexico. As time has gone on, however, some of these views have moderated. In the fall of 2004, then-president of the CLC Ken Georgetti acknowledged that free trade was not only a reality, but also a benefit. In a speech he noted that

> [t]he reality today is that much of our domestic economy is part and parcel of a North American economy. And to a much greater extent than was the case before the FTA and NAFTA. Nor are we immune to the pressures on North American manufacturing posed by the rapid rise of China and developing Asia to world dominance in the production of consumer goods.

Georgetti also acknowledged that the thousands of jobs lost during the "brutal restructuring" of the 1990s were slowly returning.

A 2003 Ipsos–Reid poll of more than 1,000 Canadians showed that 70 percent supported NAFTA. Supporters continue to believe NAFTA has benefited all three countries. The Canadian government says Canada's economy has grown by an average of 3.8 percent annually and generated 2.1 million jobs since NAFTA. Transnational corporations suggest that tariff elimination has increased their profits, while major business groups in all three countries jointly declared NAFTA an "extraordinary success for all three countries." Since NAFTA, Mexico has surpassed Japan and become the United States' second largest trading partner after Canada; about 87 percent of Canada's exports head to the United States, while Canada gets 77 percent of its imports from there. Trilateral trade among the three countries has doubled over the decade to US$620 billion annually.

Those who continue to oppose NAFTA note that increased trade has led to further environmental degradation in Mexico, where companies can transfer their operations and avoid tough environmental standards. Since NAFTA, however, Mexico has begun a serious effort to enforce its environmental laws for new companies, thereby diminishing any incentive for firms to relocate there to avoid environmental enforcement. In addition, the Mexican government has begun a process to enforce more effectively its

Figure 10.17 A refinery of Petroleos Mexicanos, the state-owned oil company, spews fumes perilously close to people's houses in Salamanca, Mexico.

environmental laws by imposing sanctions against the more visible polluters. It has also developed a program of voluntary environmental audits.

Despite NAFTA, trade disputes still occur between Canada and the United States. For example, NAFTA has failed to improve trade in such areas as softwood lumber. Canada claims that the United States continues to violate the agreement by imposing protectionist policies. Two NAFTA panels have ruled that US softwood lumber producers are not threatened by Canadian imports, but the United States continues to challenge Canadian laws. The United States can legally raise trade challenges indefinitely in the hopes of making Canada capitulate and negotiate a settlement that will appease Americans. So far, however, despite the millions of dollars it costs to fight these challenges in court, Canada has resisted capitulation.

THE WEB

Learn more about NAFTA at www.emp.ca/cwp.

International Trading Blocs

Around the world, countries are forming new trading blocs or signing bilateral trade agreements. A trading bloc is a large free, or nearly free, trade zone; in 1994, NAFTA was then the world's largest with 360 million people. As the old world empires ended, a number of regionally based economic blocs formed to promote trade among member states. The European Union, for example, expanded eastward with 10 new members in 2004, making it the world's most powerful trading bloc, with 454 million people.

Since NAFTA, Canada has continued to expand free trade by signing further agreements. The proposed Free Trade Agreement of the Americas (FTAA) is intended as a successor to NAFTA and would unite all countries in the Western Hemisphere (except Cuba) into a single free-trade area.

THE WEB

Learn more about the FTAA at www.emp.ca/cwp.

However, because of ongoing protests against globalization, the FTAA has not been signed, and some of the more controversial issues are being referred to the WTO.

Other bilateral trade agreements that Canada has recently signed include

- the *Canada–Chile Free Trade Agreement*, implemented in 1997
- the *Canada–Israel Free Trade Agreement*, implemented in 1997, with further concessions in 2003
- the *Canada–Costa Rica Free Trade Agreement*, implemented in 2002.

Trade Dispute Resolutions

SOUND BITE "Giving subsidies to farmers was a brilliant idea that transformed the food shortages after the second world war into a surplus. But it has grown into an institutionalized nightmare preventing developing countries from fulfilling their potential in one of the few areas where they enjoy a natural advantage—agriculture."

The Guardian,
August 18, 2003

Trade liberalization and expansion has naturally resulted in more trade disputes. In many cases, these conflicts can be settled through successful negotiations, **arbitration**, or international cooperation. Countries also have an obligation to refer disputes to the WTO and its Dispute Settlement Body (DSB), rather than act unilaterally to settle their trade disputes. NAFTA also has a trade dispute resolution mechanism for its three member states.

Once a dispute has been heard by the WTO and a decision issued, the DSB may direct the appropriate member to bring its laws or policies into line with the WTO. The DSB will give the member a reasonable time (usually three months) to conform. About 300 disputes have been brought to the WTO since it was set up in 1995. Recent WTO decisions include a ruling that duties imposed by the United States on imported steel are illegal, and a March 2004 ruling that Mexico was unfairly limiting competition in its domestic telephone market.

Figure 10.18 Oxfam aid workers wearing fibreglass heads of the G8 world leaders gather outside the World Trade Organization meeting in Cancun, Mexico, in September 2003. The "Big Head" leaders sat down for a symbolic breakfast of "dumped" cereal, sugar, and milk to demonstrate the waste of European and US agricultural subsidies.

On July 31, 2004, the 147 WTO member states agreed on a framework for negotiating a reduction of US and EU agricultural subsidies in return for opening developing states' markets to manufactured goods. This agreement had a long history. For years, developing countries had accused developed countries of protecting their farmers through subsidies, then dumping their produce on poorer countries at low prices, undermining local farmers. Developed countries, such as Canada, EU member states, Japan, and the United States, would agree to eliminate export subsidies, to limit other subsidies, and to lower tariff barriers. Developing countries would win the right to protect "special" products crucial to the well-being of their economies, while developed countries would have better access to markets in developing countries for their industrial goods. Agricultural subsidies, sometimes known as "the last free lunch in economics," have been heavily criticized in recent years. Observers are anxious to see how far the trend toward eliminating them will go.

Check YOUR UNDERSTANDING

1. Why has a battle between free trade and protectionism been a recurring Canadian election theme?
2. Outline the main arguments for and against the *Free Trade Agreement.* Which do you think is the stronger position, and why?
3. What conclusions can be drawn about Canadian voters' attitudes in the 1988 election toward free trade?
4. What similarities and differences exist between the FTA and NAFTA?
5. Why were NAFTA critics concerned about environmental damage? Were these concerns valid? Explain.
6. To what extent is the EU much more than a simple trading bloc and regional organization?
7. Why do you think Canada continues to negotiate and sign free-trade agreements?
8. Why was the July 31, 2004, WTO agreement a historic event?

Point:
Counterpoint ⤷ Is Free Trade Beneficial?

"Yes" to Free Trade

by James K. Glassman

In the din over trade—NAFTA, WTO, fast track, and the rest—the true and best arguments for trade have not been heard. I believe there are two of those arguments—one is extremely powerful and has been made cogently by economists for more than 200 years; the other is a briefer argument from principle. Neither of these arguments has a thing to do with jobs, jobs, jobs—or exports, exports, exports.

The argument for exports has only one thing going for it: it seems to carry political punch at the local level. Or it did. But no longer. Americans can now see through it. And the results of NAFTA belie it.

"Free trade does not create jobs," writes Melvyn Krauss of the Hoover Institution in *How Nations Grow Rich*, his excellent book on trade. Instead, "it creates income for the community by reallocating jobs and capital from lower-productivity to higher-productivity sectors of the economy." In other words, trade allows us to concentrate on what we do best. It may kill jobs in the textile industry, which is labor intensive, but breed jobs in electronics, where ingenious Americans have a "comparative advantage," in the famous phrase used by David Ricardo in 1817.

Say, for example, that a country is full of brilliant electronics engineers but won't allow textile imports across its borders. The engineers would have to sew their own shirts. They'd have less time for electronics, and the country would be poorer for it. That would be true even if the engineers were great at both electronics and sewing. What counts is their comparative advantage: what do they do better (meaning more profitably) than other people?

Another example is the lawyer who is an excellent typist. In fact, he may be a better typist than his secretary. Yet what makes the most sense for a sound economy: for the lawyer to split his time between lawyering and typing or for the lawyer to lawyer and the typist (who's not good at lawyering) to type? Obviously, the latter. Thus, comparative advantage.

It's not necessary to go into fancy economic discussions to understand why we trade. We trade for imports.

This is the first of two thoughts I want to leave you with today: not exports, imports.

No one said it better than Adam Smith more than 200 years ago: "It is the maxim of every prudent master of a family never to make at home what it will cost him more to make than to buy. . . . If a foreign country can supply us with a commodity cheaper than we ourselves can make it, better buy it of them."

That is why electronics engineers do not sew their own shirts. It's also why most American families do not grow their own wheat, grind their own flour, and bake their own bread. They have better things to do with their time. It is the same with foreign as with domestic trade.

Milton and Rose Friedman wrote years ago: A "fallacy seldom contradicted is that exports are good, imports are bad. The truth is very different. We cannot eat, wear or enjoy the goods we send abroad. We eat bananas from Central America, wear Italian shoes, drive German automobiles, and enjoy programs we see on our Japanese TV sets. Our gain from foreign trade is what we import. Exports are the price we pay to get imports."

In exchange for imports, we offer other countries the things we produce cheaper or better: computers, chickens, movies, power generators. Or we just offer dollars. . . .

Taking down barriers has brought competition that's made our auto industry better, our communications industry the best in the world. The demonstration effect will be powerful. Other nations will see the success of what we've done and will rush to do it themselves.

Source: Excerpted from James K. Glassman, "The Blessings of Free Trade" (Washington, DC: The Cato Institute, Trade Briefing Paper No. 1, May 1, 1998); http://www.freetrade.org/pubs/briefs/tpb-001.html.

"No" to Free Trade

by Noam Chomsky

The free market is socialism for the rich: the public pays the costs and the rich get the benefit—markets for the poor and plenty of state protection for the rich. . . .

Furthermore, what's called trade isn't trade in any serious sense of the term. Much of what's called trade is just internal transactions, inside a big corporation. More than half of US exports to Mexico don't even enter the Mexican market. They're just transferred by one branch of General Motors to another branch, because you can get much cheaper labour if you happen to cross a border, and you don't have to worry about pollution. But that's not trade in any sensible sense of the term, any more than if you move a can of beans from one shelf to another of a grocery store. It just happens to cross an international border, but it's not trade. In fact, by now it's estimated that about 40% of what's called world trade is internal to corporations. That means centrally managed transactions run by a very visible hand with major market distortions of all kinds, sometimes called a system of corporate mercantilism, which is fairly accurate. . . .

Consider the matter of democracy. Power is shifting into the hands of huge transnational corporations. That means away from parliamentary institutions. Furthermore, there's a structure of governance that's coalescing around these transnational corporations. This is not unlike the developments of the last couple of hundred years, when national states more or less coalesced around growing national economies. Now you've got a transnational economy, you're getting a transnational state, not surprisingly. The *Financial Times* described this as a de facto world government, including the World Bank and the IMF, and GATT, now the World Trade Organization, the G7 Executive, and so on. Transnational bodies remove power from parliamentary institutions. . . .

These misnamed free-trade agreements, GATT and NAFTA, carry that process forwards. They are not free-trade agreements but investor-rights agreements and they are designed to carry forward the attack on democracy. If you look at them closely, you realize they are a complicated mixture of liberalization and protectionism carefully crafted in the interests of the transnational corporations. So, for example, GATT excludes subsidies except for one kind: military expenditures.

Military expenditures are a huge welfare system for the rich and an enormous form of government subsidy that distort markets and trade. Military expenditures are staying very high. . . . That is a system of market interference and benefits for the wealthy.

Another central part of the GATT agreement, and NAFTA, is what are called intellectual property rights which is protectionism: protection for ownership of knowledge and technology. They want to make sure that the technology of the future is monopolized by huge and generally government-subsidized private corporations. GATT includes an important extension of patents to include product patents; this means that if someone designs a new technique for producing a drug, they can't do it because they violate the patent. The product patents reduce economic efficiency and cut back technical innovation. France, for example, had product patents about a century ago and that was a reason why it lost a large part of its chemical industry to Switzerland which didn't, and therefore could innovate.

Source: Excerpted from Noam Chomsky, "How Free Is the Free Market?" *LiP* magazine, May 15, 1997; http://www.lipmagazine.org/articles/featchomsky_63_p3.htm.

Articulating a Personal Stand

1. James Glassman and Noam Chomsky view free trade from two different perspectives. In your own words, summarize their viewpoints.
2. Glassman refers to "comparative advantage." Explain comparative advantage using your own example. Conduct research to find the definition of the economic concept of "absolute advantage."
3. Chomsky argues that "transnational bodies remove power from parliamentary institutions." Conduct research on the gasoline additive MMT produced by Ethyl Corporation and sold in Canada. Find out what occurred when the Canadian government attempted to ban this product in 1997.
4. Apply the arguments of James Glassman and Noam Chomsky to the *North American Free Trade Agreement* (NAFTA). Conduct a classroom debate on the resolution: "NAFTA has been beneficial to Canada."

CAREERS

Mary Beshai, NGO Program Manager

Mary Beshai is the program manager for Dignity in Motion Inc. (DIMI), a not-for-profit organization started by members of the Hawkesbury, Ontario, district Rotary Club. In the following interview, she describes the agency's mission and methods and what she hopes it can achieve.

Q: What is Dignity in Motion Inc.?

A: It's a non-governmental agency created to promote the design and distribution of prosthetics and orthotics, or "P&O" systems. These include artificial limbs and other assistive technologies such as leg braces. Our particular focus is on post-conflict settings and the developing world—for example, countries such as El Salvador, Cambodia, and Afghanistan. We're working on models of P&O systems that combine high performance and controlled cost.

An important goal of the organization is to create a supportive infrastructure in the countries to which we distribute, so that we can, with our partner organizations, provide followup and maintenance. We also try to address accessibility issues, by providing technologies specifically designed to accommodate the diverse daily activities of those in need, and to provide environmentally responsible solutions.

Currently, the provision of prosthetics to developing countries often amounts simply to the donation of quite poor-quality prosthethics, with little or no followup support. We hope to provide a more responsible alternative.

Q: What is your role within the organization?

A: At the moment, I'm the only employee! My responsibilities will evolve with the organization; my focus is on strategic and operations planning: bringing the various parties—designers, fundraisers, manufacturers—together for the purpose of moving into the production phase, and handling startup issues such as obtaining grant funding. In the near future, I will work closely with partner agencies in other countries to establish a sustainable distribution and support system.

Q: What kind of training did you need for this job? How does politics fit in?

A: I'm an engineer with a special interest in biomedical design. As we moved toward production, we realized we had a wealth of technical expertise but little knowledge of how to manage a not-for-profit organization with an international focus. So I pursued a master's degree in public administration, with a sub-specialty in innovation, science, and environment.

A knowledge of politics and public administration has proven useful as new issues emerge. An important challenge, as we move forward, will be finding ways to be true to our own business principles overseas while respecting the political and social culture of other countries.

Q: What goal would you like to accomplish in the next five to 10 years?

A: I believe that Canada is well placed, both politically and technologically, to play a key role at the forefront of prosthetics research and production. I'd like to see Canada emerge as a leader in the provision of high-performance, economically accessible P&Os to people in need both internationally and here at home, and I'd like to see our organization play an important role in that achievement.

Question

Besides her professional training, how might a knowledge of politics help Mary Beshai in her work? Give specific examples.

Study Hall

Thinking/Inquiry

1. Working with a partner or in small groups, select one international organization discussed in this chapter and, using the Internet and other resources, research some of its current issues and initiatives and their likelihood of success. In a brief presentation to the class,
   a) outline one issue or problem faced by the group
   b) summarize its initiatives on this issue or problem
   c) forecast the likelihood of success.

2. In a chart, outline the strengths and weaknesses of NGOs. Consider such variables as financial support, adaptability, effectiveness, and so on.

3. Review the information on the passage of a bill in Chapter 6, page 208, and the information on interest groups in Chapter 7, pages 231–33.
   a) Imagine that you are a lobbyist for a generic pharmaceutical company. What strategies and arguments would you use to gain a favourable draft of Bill C-9?
   b) Imagine that you are a lobbyist for a brand-name pharmaceutical company. What strategies and arguments would you use to gain a favourable draft of Bill C-9?

4. Is giving developing countries a voice on matters affecting them in international organizations, such as the IMF and the WTO, reasonable and practical? If so, can you imagine any problems in giving them a say? How would you deal with these problems?

5. Since its signing in 1994, NAFTA has sparked controversy among various interest groups over issues related to agriculture, economics, the environment, and labour. In groups, research these four areas to determine whether NAFTA is beneficial or harmful for Canada, and in what ways. Present your findings to the class, giving both sides of the issues and providing possible alternatives. Use visuals, if possible, to clarify your presentation.

Communication

6. Look back at Figure 10.1 on page 333.
   a) Use the Internet to research the NAMES Project ("the largest community art project in the world"). Create a timeline to show the development of the AIDS Memorial Quilt from 1987 to the present. Briefly outline what you think the NAMES Project has achieved.
   b) Research Day With(out) Art, Postcards From the Edge, Dancers for Life, or another initiative by artists to combat HIV/AIDS. In a paragraph, describe the goals and activities of the group of your choice.

7. Research one of the following international organizations, and report to the class on its composition, mandate, and the ways in which Canada interacts with it:
   • the Organization of American States
   • the European Union
   • the African Union
   • the Asia–Pacific Cooperation
   • the League of Arab States
   • the G8
   • the Arctic Council

8. Use Internet, library, or other resources to learn what NGOs are doing to improve environmental conditions and address concerns. Prepare a report of your findings, or convert them into graphic form to post in the classroom and around your school to increase students' awareness.

9. Use the Internet and other references to research a non-governmental organization with an international presence not discussed in this chapter. Report to your class on any international impact that this NGO has had from its activities.

10. In groups of three or four, research one of the countries plagued by or responsible for landmines. (See www.emp.ca/cwp for details.) Some of these states are losing innocent people to landmines, while some states are producers of landmines. Familiarize yourself with your chosen country with background information on culture and religion, government, economy, geography, and current issues. Also examine who put landmines there, why they are still there, and what the global community is doing about this issue. Present your findings to the class, using visual aids and a creative performance.

Application

11. Would you rather buy a product you want that is "made in Canada" or one that is manufactured in another country where it can be produced cheaply and sold to you for less money? Discuss this question in small groups, allowing for debate and determining how much more you might be willing to pay to "buy Canadian." Look at the idea of outsourcing jobs and the effect on the economy, and brainstorm how trade issues affect everyone. Try to reach consensus. Then, write a letter to the editor of a newspaper or to your federal MP expressing your collective viewpoint.

12. Research and evaluate the effectiveness of Canada's role in one of the following international trends or events. Present your findings to the class in a role-play, news report, or debate:
    • apartheid in South Africa
    • the banning of landmines
    • performance-enhancing drugs in sports
    • genocide in Darfur, Sudan
    • generic drugs to treat HIV/AIDS
    • worldwide awareness and concern over global warming

13. "The quality and quantity of school physical and sports programs are suffering in Canadian schools. This . . . will have long-term effects on the number of elite athletes representing Canada in the future." (Canadian Association for Health, Physical Education, Recreation, and Dance)

    As a class, brainstorm this quotation, determining various viewpoints. Research physical education programs in other provinces, comparing them to those in Ontario schools. Try for consensus among the class. Draw up recommendations to send in a letter to the Minister of Education, advocating change to Ontario's current policy.

14. Practise responsible citizenship. Contact an organization such as Amnesty International, Greenpeace, Oxfam Canada, or the Sierra Club to find out what you can do locally to be a responsible global citizen.

The Global Community

Chapter 11
Conflict Resolution in
the Global Community

Chapter 12
Globalization

*"The human family now exists under the conditions of a global village. . . .
[W]e live in a single constructed space resonant with tribal drums."*
Marshall McLuhan, The Gutenberg Galaxy, *1962*

Conflict Resolution in the Global Community

Agenda

In this chapter, you will consider

- the causes of conflict
- diplomatic responses to conflict
- the need for security
- technologies and the changing nature of war
- the development, nature, and impact of terrorism
- the "war on terrorism" and the dangers it may pose to democracy
- the global quest for peace
- how a resolution is debated in the UN General Assembly

Figure 11.1 In *Grib* (2001), Russian artist Kirill Chelushkin reflects on the relationship between the threat of armed conflict and ordinary citizens. In Russian, the word *grib* means both "beach umbrella" and "mushroom."

Every day, threats to global security create headlines and lead the newscasts. Armed conflicts abound worldwide. Often, they take place in developing regions where social and economic conditions lead to hardship and struggle.

In this chapter, you will examine the causes of conflict and war. You will consider the reasons underlying terrorism, the newest threat to global security. You will look at how various countries are responding to this threat and question how these measures may affect you directly. For example, what civil and human rights would you be willing to sacrifice in exchange for national security? Finally, you will develop a greater understanding of the ways in which states, governments, groups, and individuals work together to resolve conflict, make peace, and ensure global security in the future.

Global Conflict and Security

During the English Civil War in the 1640s, philosopher Thomas **Hobbes** believed that, faced with a world in conflict, the greatest human desire was for security. This security, he believed, had to be provided, above all, by government. As you learned in Chapter 1, Hobbes wrote in his book *Leviathan*, in 1651, that "life in the state of nature is poor, solitary, nasty, brutish, and short."

The world has changed in the centuries since Hobbes expressed this belief, yet the idea is still true. The impact of age-old conflicts, such as war, and new global threats, such as terrorism, mean that the search for security continues to shape global politics and the role of governments.

The Causes of Conflict

Why do nations fight? Conflicts and wars have many causes. In the modern age, ethnic nationalism, **tribalism**, imperialism, and economic competition all create turmoil around the world.

Ethnic Nationalism and Tribalism

As you learned in Chapter 4, ethnic nationalism emerged as a powerful force in Europe in the 1800s. Italy, Germany, Russia, and the Austrian and Ottoman Empires all faced nationalist conflicts as various groups struggled to create their own nation-states. Since then, nationalist groups around the globe have fought for territory and political power.

Another source of conflict is tribalism. Ethnic differences within a state can produce instability and armed conflict. The effects can be devastating. In 1994, in the central African country of Rwanda, ethnic tensions between the minority Tutsi and the majority Hutu led to genocide. Hutu militia murdered 800,000 Tutsis and moderate Hutus. The genocide sparked both a civil war in Rwanda and instability and conflict in central Africa (see Taking a Stand, page 399).

In the early 1990s, Bosnia, in southeastern Europe, also experienced the effects of tribalism. As you learned in Chapter 4, Bosnia was part of the communist state of Yugoslavia during the Cold War. After the collapse of communism, Bosnia declared independence in 1992. This heightened ethnic and religious differences among Bosnian Muslims, Croats, and Serbs and led to a bloody civil war.

These cases of ethnic nationalism and tribalism are not unique. Throughout history, political leaders have exploited these forces in their pursuit of power, and in so doing have created widespread death and destruction. It is likely this pattern will continue in the future.

SOUND BITE "The world must deeply repent this failure. Rwanda's tragedy was the world's tragedy. . . . In their greatest hour of need, the world failed the people of Rwanda."

UN Secretary-General Kofi Annan, to the Rwandan Parliament, May 7, 1998

THE WEB

Learn more about the issues and conflicts in the Middle East today at www.emp.ca/cwp.

Imperialism and Economic Competition

Imperialism has also led to conflict and war as countries seek to expand their control in a quest for wealth, power, strategic advantage, and glory. The creation of the world's great empires involved wars of conquest to gain colonial territories. From the time of the Spanish–American War in 1898, in which the United States seized control of Spain's crumbling empire, to Italy's invasion of Abyssinia (Ethiopia) in 1935, states have used war to achieve their economic and colonial goals.

Economic competition for scarce resources, such as oil and fresh water, can also spark disputes and wars. Perhaps nowhere is this competition more evident than in the Middle East. This region has been embroiled in many conflicts as the United States and other powers seek to ensure continued access to vital oil supplies. Iraq's invasion of Kuwait in 1990, for example, was viewed by other Middle Eastern countries and the United States as an attempt to gain control over Kuwait's vast oil fields. The invasion led to the Gulf War, in which US and allied forces drove Iraq out of Kuwait in 1991.

The Quest for Security

In their quest to ensure their security and resolve disputes before they become armed conflicts, governments use a number of tactics. These range from military action (either alone or as members of an alliance) to diplomacy and negotiation.

Unilateral Action

One of the key responsibilities of any government is to ensure the security of its territory and the safety of its citizens. To that end, governments reserve the right to take **unilateral action**—that is, states can decide to act in their own defence, with or without the global community's approval or support.

Many countries have taken unilateral action in recent decades. In 1982, Argentina invaded the Falkland Islands, a British Crown Colony, in the South Atlantic Ocean. Britain rejected attempts by the international community to mediate a political solution to its dispute with Argentina over the sovereignty of the islands. Instead, it launched a military campaign that succeeded in recovering the territory. In 1981, Israel used a surprise air raid to destroy a nuclear reactor in Iraq. The Israeli government feared that Iraq would use the facility to develop nuclear weapons that it would then use against Israel. In 2003, the United States and Britain launched a war against Iraq without the approval of the United Nations. Many traditional allies of the United States and Britain, including Canada, refused to support the invasion.

Governments that resort to unilateral action find many ways to justify it. They may claim they are protecting their citizens from harm or looking after their economic interests. Not everyone agrees with unilateral action, however. Some people believe that it destabilizes the world order by challenging inter-

Figure 11.2 Bombs rain down on Baghdad during the second night of the US-led invasion of Iraq, March 2003.

national laws governing the legitimate use of force and by disregarding the authority of international organizations such as the United Nations.

Alliances and Collective Security

In their efforts to resolve or prevent conflict, governments often rely on one another. These military alliances have existed throughout history. Alliances provide their members with reassurances about security and help to deter potential enemies.

Canada is a member of many alliances. As you learned in Chapter 8, two of the most important are the North American Aerospace Defense Command (NORAD) and the North Atlantic Treaty Organization (NATO). Through NORAD, Canada and the United States share responsibility for the defence of North American airspace under a united military command. NATO is a military alliance among Canada, the United States, and 24 European countries (as of 2004). Like many alliances, NATO provides collective security for its members. An attack against any one NATO member is seen as an attack against all members. Therefore, all NATO members will come to its defence.

Diplomacy and Negotiation

Not all efforts to ensure a country's security involve the use of force. Usually, states first use diplomacy to try to resolve disputes (see Figure 8.2, page 263). If direct negotiations between diplomats fail, mediators may intervene. These are often regional organizations, such as the African Union (AU) or the Organization of American States (OAS). The United Nations also plays a vital role in the diplomatic process. It is a forum for negotiating and resolving disputes. UN diplomats may also intervene directly to resolve a conflict. Even the secretary-general may become involved.

Diplomatic Sanctions

Diplomatic sanctions are another way to pressure a country to respect international law. Sanctions may include embargoes and trade restrictions, which are meant to isolate a country and persuade it to change its policies. For example, the North African country of Libya was isolated by international sanctions. In the 1980s, Libya openly supported terrorist groups and was suspected of being involved in the 1988 bombing of a US airliner over Lockerbie, Scotland. In response, the United States and Britain launched a trade embargo. The United Nations endorsed the embargo in 1992. The sanctions eventually included restrictions on air travel and trade, and political isolation. As a result, in 1999 Libya turned over those people suspected of orchestrating the Lockerbie bombing to stand trial in the Netherlands. In 2003, after Libya finally acknowledged its involvement in the bombing and agreed to compensate the families of the victims, the UN Security Council lifted its sanctions. Thus, the international community had convinced Libya to end its support of terrorists without waging war.

THE WEB
Learn more about the Lockerbie bombing at www.emp.ca/cwp.

Check YOUR UNDERSTANDING

1. In what ways do nationalism and tribalism serve as sources of international conflict?
2. How do imperialism and economic competition lead to conflict and war?
3. Are there any circumstances under which the unilateral use of force can be justified in today's global community? Give reasons for your answer.
4. What diplomatic sanctions can be used to pressure a state to respect international law? Cite an example in which sanctions were successful.

War

Despite humanity's longing for peace—as expressed in art, religion, and philosophy—war has been a common element of the human experience. A glance at literature, from the ancient Greek epic poem the *Iliad* to Ernest Hemingway's novel *A Farewell to Arms*, confirms this. Across cultures, continents, and centuries, societies have exalted their warriors. This has been true from the Persians and Romans to the Aztecs and Mongols, from Napoleon's France and Hitler's Germany to Kosovo and Iraq.

There are many reasons why states wage war. Some countries go to war to conquer territories. Some go to war to gain greater economic power. Some want to spread ideologies. Still others fight to defend their land, their people, and their beliefs. Some political leaders launch wars to satisfy their person-

SOUND BITE "The importance of physical terror against the individual and the masses . . . became clear to me. . . . The great masses of the people . . . will more easily fall victim to a big lie than to a small one."

Adolf Hitler, Mein Kampf *(My Struggle), 1925, vol. 1, chap. 10*

al thirst for power. Others simply turn to war to distract their citizens from activities taking place at home.

Karl von Clausewitz was a Prussian (German) officer and military strategist. In 1833, he established a new foundation for the relationship between politics and war in his work *On War*. Clausewitz argued that war was a legitimate tool when other means, such as debate and negotiation, fail. Although *On War* was written in another era, many people believe that the ideas it contains still apply today.

Traditional War

From earliest times until the 19th century, infantry soldiers dominated traditional war. These were professional armies and they were small by modern standards—rarely more than 100,000 men. Infantry soldiers generally fought in close combat. Many soldiers were recruited from rulers' subjects. Some, however, were **mercenaries**—professional "men at arms" who fought for the side that offered the highest pay. Some army officers were trained military commanders. Most, however, were members of the nobility and aristocracy. Their positions were due to social rank rather than personal merit.

There were other notable characteristics of traditional war. Technology was limited and weaponry was unsophisticated. As a result, battle casualties (wounded) were fairly low. On the other hand, sanitation was poor and medical knowledge was limited. More soldiers died from disease than from combat. Traditional wars had little impact on wider society. People living near the battlefields faced destruction from marauding armies. People

> **SOUND BITE** "It is clear that war is not a mere act of policy but a true political instrument, a continuation of political activity by other means."
>
> *Karl von Clausewitz, from a 1976 translation of* On War

Figure 11.3 *The Battle of Waterloo, June 18, 1815* by Paul Artaria (1763–1841) gives a contemporary's view of traditional warfare.

removed from the fighting, however, were usually spared the physical effects of war.

Total War

During the late 1800s, the nature of war was transformed. Armies became larger. The new railways transported troops, supplies, and equipment quickly and easily.

New technologies led to deadlier weapons. These included rapid-fire machine guns and cylinders filled with chlorine gas. The Industrial Revolution enabled states to mobilize citizens to fight and to work in factories to mass-produce new weapons. Chemical warfare in particular changed the nature of war. No longer was war solely about combat. **Total war** was about extermination. Combined with these terrible new means of waging war was a new emphasis on nationalism as a cause for war.

World War I (1914–18) highlighted the consequences of these changes. Across Europe, nationalist fervour prompted masses of citizens to enlist when war broke out in August 1914. In Canada, more than 30,000 soldiers signed up to fight alongside Britain "for king and country" within the first two months. For the first time, governments mobilized and coordinated all their human, economic, and political resources to support a war effort. The eurocentric (Europe-centred) world had plunged into total war.

The enthusiasm of 1914 faded as the realities of total war became evident. The combination of mass armies and lethal technologies led to unprecedented casualties. Army ranks on both sides were devastated. Over time, hundreds of thousands of soldiers lost their lives in the quest to capture a single square kilometre of territory. In July 1916, the entire Royal Newfoundland Regiment—consisting of almost 1,000 men—was killed or wounded in a single day. Faced with carnage on the battlefields, Canada turned to conscription to ensure a continuous supply of troops. It proved to be a politically divisive issue, particularly in Quebec (see Chapter 4).

Demands on industry to ensure military victory were also great. During the Battle of Waterloo in 1815, for example, Napoleon's troops fired no more than 24,000 shots. In contrast, during the days leading up to the Battle of the Somme in July 1916, British forces fired more than 1,000,000 rounds of ammunition. With total war, increased industrial production was crucial. Failure to keep pace with the industrial production of the enemy would mean certain defeat. As a result, warring states

Figure 11.4 At the height of World War I, more than 35,000 women were working in factories in Toronto and Montreal. This represented a huge increase in the number of women in the work force. How would this fact affect the political aspirations of these and other women?

competed, and the production and technology of weaponry became more sophisticated as the war went on. By 1917, Canada alone had more than 600 weapons factories. They employed more than 150,000 workers, many of them women.

The need to maintain industrial production also expanded government involvement in the economy. Governments coordinated factory activity and output. They borrowed vast sums of money to finance the war. As the war raged on, they introduced new taxes, such as the income tax, to raise even more money.

The Realities of Total War

The horrors of World War I prompted political leaders to seek ways to prevent future conflicts (see the League of Nations in Chapters 4 and 8.) Yet these steps proved to be largely ineffective. During the 1930s, total war re-emerged, beginning with the Spanish Civil War (1936–39). In Spain, the widespread use of aerial bombardment to destroy cities (see Art and Politics, Chapter 2, page 53) was designed to strike fear among civilians and to disrupt war industries. This marked a new and terrible phase in the evolution of total war.

The full impact of technological changes became even clearer during World War II (1939–45). Both sides engaged in heavy aerial bombardment of enemy cities. The Germans bombarded Rotterdam and London during the early years of the war. Toward the end of the war, the British bombarded Dresden, Cologne, and other German cities. The bombing campaigns were intended to disrupt the enemy's industrial production and to kill and demoralize its citizens. Therefore, the impact of total war on civilians was far greater in World War II than in World War I.

Governments sought to bolster public morale. During the bombing of London in 1940 and 1941, for example, British Prime Minister Winston Churchill (1874–1965) regularly visited bombed-out neighbourhoods. He gave rousing speeches as he flashed his famous "V" for victory sign to cheering crowds. King George VI and Queen Elizabeth did their part, too. They refused to seek shelter outside war-torn London. Instead, they toured areas of London that had been flattened by German bombs.

The age of total war culminated in 1945 with the introduction of the atomic bomb. During the early 1940s, the United States became the first state to develop this weapon of unprecedented mass destruction. On August 6, 1945, a US bomber

SOUND BITE

"Endless money forms the sinews of war."

Marcus Tullius Cicero, Roman politician, 106–43 BCE

SOUND BITE   "We have but one aim and one single, irrevocable purpose. We are resolved to destroy Hitler and every vestige of his Nazi regime. From this nothing will turn us—nothing."

Winston Churchill, May 1941

Figure 11.5 Ruins of buildings in the city of Dresden after firebombing raids, 1945.

Casualties in the Two World Wars

World War I	Military Deaths	Civilian Deaths
Allies		
Russia	1,700,000	
France	1,345,000	
Britain	702,000	
Italy	460,000	
USA	115,000	
Canada	60,000	
Central Powers		
Germany	1,676,000	
Austria–Hungary	1,200,000	
Ottoman Empire	325,000	
TOTAL	8,500,000	10,000,000*
World War II	**Military Deaths**	**Civilian Deaths**
Allies		
USSR	13,600,000	7,700,000
China	3,500,000	10,000,000
Britain and Commonwealth	452,000	60,000
Canada (incl. in above)	45,000	minimal
Yugoslavia	300,000	1,300,000
USA	295,000	minimal
France	250,000	360,000
Poland	120,000	5,300,000
Czechoslovakia	20,000	330,000
Axis Powers		
Germany	3,250,000	3,810,000
Japan	1,700,000	360,000
Italy	330,000	85,000
Romania	200,000	465,000
Hungary	120,000	280,000
TOTAL	25,000,000*	30,000,000*

* Estimates.

Source: Adapted from http://www.historylearningsite.co.uk and N. Ferguson, *The Pity of War: Explaining World War I* (Penguin, 1999), pp. 295, 299.

Figure 11.6 These statistics show the devastating impact of total war on human life. Statistics for casualties—military and civilian—vary widely, depending on sources. Why do you think this is so?

SOUND BITE "The dropping of the atomic bombs was not so much the last military act of the Second World War as the first major operation of the cold diplomatic war with Russia."

British physicist P.M. Blackett, Fear, War, and the Bomb, 1949

dropped the first atomic bomb on the Japanese city of Hiroshima. Three days later, a second bomb hit Nagasaki. In total, more than 100,000 people died. Hundreds of thousands more were injured and maimed, many for life.

Using the A-bomb had the desired strategic effect. It convinced Japan to surrender, thus avoiding prolonging conventional war in the Pacific and

Figure 11.7 The atomic bombs dropped on Hiroshima (shown here) and Nagasaki created death and destruction on a scale the world had never known. How could the development and use of such a weapon be justified?

ending World War II. Yet the use of the atomic bomb had a broader impact. It signalled the beginning of an awesome new age of warfare: the Cold War.

The Cold War

As you learned in Chapter 8, the Cold War began after World War II. It was a period marked by military and ideological competition between two global superpowers, the United States and the Soviet Union (USSR). The US and its NATO allies squared off against the USSR and its satellite states in Eastern Europe (the Warsaw Pact).

At the heart of the Cold War was the arms race. Each side amassed a growing nuclear stockpile in an effort to maintain a balance of power. This strategy, known as **MAD**, for Mutually Assured Destruction, helped ensure that neither side launched a nuclear attack, since massive retaliation was almost certain. The consequences of these nuclear strikes would be devastating, not only for the superpowers themselves but for their allies and the world. Thus, the policy of **deterrence** prevented a nuclear conflict between the superpowers for more than 40 years.

Still, the Cold War created ongoing tensions. Occasionally, crises threatened the fragile peace. In Korea in the early 1950s, in Vietnam during the 1960s, and in Afghanistan, Africa, and South America during the 1970s and 1980s, the superpowers fought each other indirectly. At times, the United States and the Soviet Union became active participants in limited non-nuclear wars. They offered military advice and support for local armies and sometimes contributed their own troops to conflicts. The Cold War marked an ongoing battle for power and influence in regions around the world.

SOUND BITE

"In the 1950s and 1960s we put several thousand nuclear weapons into Europe. To be sure, we had no precise idea of what to do with them."

US Secretary of State Henry Kissinger, 1973

 PRESS PLAY

In *Dr. Strangelove: Or How I Learned to Stop Worrying and Love the Bomb* (1964), a dark satire about the Cold War directed by Stanley Kubrick and starring Peter Sellers, a deranged US Air Force colonel orders nuclear bombs to be dropped on the Soviet Union, which threatens to unleash a doomsday device in retaliation. (PG)

Law in Motion

Making War Illegal

Can laws prevent war? Legal theorists have long argued about the circumstances under which war is lawful. Some have even drafted rules for waging a "just" war. Following the destruction of World War I, many leaders wanted to prevent future armed conflicts. The growth of international law was one way to do that. To achieve their goal, leaders signed treaties to regulate war (see the *Geneva Conventions*, Chapter 8, page 285). Among them was the *Geneva Protocol*, created in 1925 in response to Germany's use of poison gas against Allied forces in 1915. Signed by 133 nations, the Protocol prohibited future use of chemical and biological weapons.

> Whereas the use in war of asphyxiating, poisonous or other gases, and of all analogous liquids, materials or devices, has been justly condemned by the general opinion of the civilized world; and
>
> Whereas the prohibition of such use has been declared in Treaties to which the majority of Powers of the world are Parties; and
>
> To the end that this prohibition shall be universally accepted as a part of International Law, binding alike the conscience and the practice of nations;
>
> DECLARE:
>
> That the High Contracting Parties, so far as they are not already Parties to Treaties prohibiting such use, accept this prohibition, agree to extend this prohibition to the use of bacteriological methods of warfare and agree to be bound as between themselves according to the terms of this declaration.
>
> **Source:** *Protocol for the Prohibition of the Use in War of Asphyxiating, Poisonous or other Gases, and of Bacteriological Methods of Warfare*, Geneva, June 17, 1925.

Other treaties were more ambitious. They sought not only to regulate war, but to prevent it altogether. The *Kellogg–Briand Pact* of 1928 was signed by 15 nations, including Canada. It condemned the use of war as a means of resolving disputes. In theory, states that signed the Pact were prohibited from participating in future wars.

> ARTICLE I
> The High Contracting Parties solemnly declare in the names of their respective peoples that they condemn recourse to war for the solution of international controversies, and renounce it, as an instrument of national policy in their relations with one another.
>
> ARTICLE II
> The High Contracting Parties agree that the settlement or solution of all disputes or conflicts of whatever nature or of whatever origin they may be, which may arise among them, shall never be sought except by pacific means.
>
> **Source:** *Treaty between the United States and Other Powers Providing for the Renunciation of War as an Instrument of National Policy*, Paris, August 27, 1928.

Despite the best intentions of these treaties, however, war did not disappear. Germany, Italy, and Japan all signed the *Kellogg–Briand Pact*. Yet this did not deter them from committing acts of aggression against their neighbours in the 1930s. Ultimately, these acts led to the outbreak of World War II in 1939.

Why did the *Kellogg–Briand Pact* fail? There were two main reasons. First, it depended on the goodwill of states to refrain from war. Second, the Pact lacked effective sanctions or punishments against signatories that later did not obey it. Despite the failure of the *Kellogg–Briand Pact*, the international community kept up efforts to use international law to prevent conflict. Following World War II, the *Charter of the United Nations* in 1945 made it clear that member states are legally obligated not to use war to resolve international disputes. Article 2 states:

1. The Organization is based on the principle of the sovereign equality of all its Members.
2. All Members, in order to ensure to all of them the rights and benefits resulting from membership, shall fulfill in good faith the obligations assumed by them in accordance with the present Charter.
3. All Members shall settle their international disputes by peaceful means in such a manner that international peace and security, and justice, are not endangered.
4. All Members shall refrain in their international relations from the threat or use of force against the territorial integrity or political independence of any state, or in any other manner inconsistent with the Purposes of the United Nations.

Source: *The Charter of the United Nations*, Article 2, 1945.

The UN Charter did not rid the world of war. However, it did establish the principle that an offensive war violates international law. Today, it remains the foundation of the world's efforts to preserve peace and control armed conflicts.

Questions

1. Create a table listing the treaties described above and how they attempted to (a) limit, (b) regulate, or (c) eliminate war.
2. Summarize the legal excerpts found above in your own words.
3. Can we rely upon international law to limit or even eliminate warfare? Why or why not? Discuss your views in small groups and present your findings to the class.

> **SOUND BITE** "There never was a good war, or a bad peace."
>
> *Benjamin Franklin, US political leader and signatory of the US* Declaration of Independence, *1783*

Figure 11.8 Political leaders sign the United Nations Charter on June 26, 1945.

Press Play

The Fog of War (2003) is a documentary about Robert McNamara, a former US Secretary of Defense (1961–68), and the various difficult lessons he learned about the nature and conduct of modern war. (PG-13).

Press Play

In *Thirteen Days*, Kevin Costner portrays an aide to US President John F. Kennedy during the "13 most dangerous days in world history"—the Cuban missile crisis of 1962. The film also recreates tense negotiations at the UN and between the US and the Soviet Union under President Nikita Khrushchev. (PG)

The Cuban Missile Crisis

Diplomacy succeeded in containing Cold War conflicts, for the most part. Yet some crises brought the superpowers to the brink of nuclear war. One of the gravest was the Cuban Missile Crisis. In 1962, the US government discovered that the Soviet Union was building nuclear missile bases in Cuba, a communist state that lies south of Florida (see Figure 11.9). Fearing the Soviets would use the sites to launch nuclear strikes against the United States, President John F. Kennedy (1917–63) warned the USSR to dismantle the bases. He sent the US Navy to stop Soviet ships carrying cargo from reaching Cuba. For six nerve-racking days in October, the world watched as the crisis mounted. The two sides finally reached a delicate diplomatic compromise in October. The Soviet Union agreed to dismantle its missile bases in Cuba. In return, the United States removed nuclear missiles from Turkey near the Soviet border.

The Cuban Missile Crisis represented the peak of Cold War tensions. Both sides realized how close they had come to a nuclear catastrophe. As a result, they began to make serious efforts to shrink their nuclear arsenals through a series of Strategic Arms Limitation Talks (SALT) beginning in 1969. They also opened the doors to greater diplomatic exchanges. This period of **détente** succeeded in keeping the Cold War in check during the 1970s and 1980s.

The End of the Cold War

By the late 1980s, the Soviet Union was no longer able to sustain the economic cost of military competition with the United States. The communist

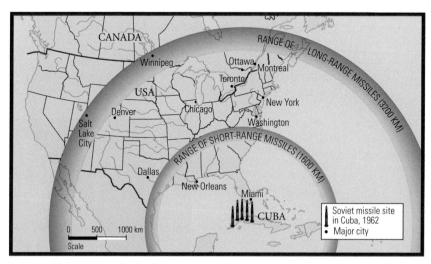

Source: BBC Schools GCSE Bitesize Revision, http://www.bbc.co.uk/schools/gcsebitesize/history/1945to89/5cubatest.shtml.

Figure 11.9 Missiles launched from Cuban sites could have hit a wide range of targets in the United States, Canada, Latin America, and the Caribbean.

world began to unravel. Soviet satellite states in Eastern Europe were demanding democratic reforms and independence from the USSR. As you learned in Chapter 4, the Soviet Union was dissolved in 1991. Now, the United States took centre stage as the world's sole superpower.

The end of the Cold War did not end the threat of nuclear war, however. At the beginning of the 21st century, seven countries—the United States, Britain, Russia, France, India, Pakistan, and China—are known to have nuclear arsenals. Several others, including Israel, Iran, North Korea, Ukraine, and Australia, are believed to have nuclear weapons, and this number may increase. There is also a concern that politically unstable states and terrorist groups may obtain materials to make nuclear weapons and so-called dirty bombs—ordinary explosives designed to spread radioactive material over a wide area. The consequences of either type of attack would be catastrophic.

Tracking and safeguarding nuclear materials has become a major security concern. The United Nations and its agency, the International Atomic Energy Agency (IAEA), devote a great deal of time, effort, and money to controlling the spread of nuclear technology and materials. They monitor and inspect nuclear reactors and research facilities to ensure that they are not developing or producing weapons of mass destruction.

THE WEB

Learn about the detective work of the International Atomic Energy Agency by visiting www.emp.ca/cwp.

Virtual War

The post–Cold War era introduced a new age of warfare—the age of "virtual war." Several factors make war fundamentally different today. As in the past, the most significant of these factors is technology. With its advanced technological ability and its economic dominance, the United States has developed the world's most sophisticated weapons. In 2003, total military spending in the world was estimated at $1 trillion. Of that total, the United States accounted for 47 percent—more than 10 times the amount spent by any other single country.

The impact of virtual war technology is remarkable. Today, the military uses "smart" weapons to pinpoint targets, with the aim of minimizing damage and casualties, both military and civilian. Often the military does not succeed in this aim, and it is difficult to get accurate figures on the numbers of civilians killed and injured. However, in the war in Kosovo in 1999, NATO forces used air strikes to inflict damage on the enemy, without experiencing a single casualty among NATO troops. Advanced communications technology also makes it possible for military leaders to conduct campaigns from their home bases. Many operations in the Iraq War, for example, were directed from command centres in the United States.

Virtual war has also limited the role of civilians living outside the combat zone. In the past, total war mobilized the entire population of a state, as either soldiers or workers. Today, professionals run war. The mass armies of the two world wars are no longer required. Civilians outside of the conflict

SOUND BITE   "War thus becomes virtual, not simply because it appears to take place on screen, but because it enlists societies only in virtual ways."

Michael Ignatieff,
Virtual War: Kosovo and Beyond, *2000*

Figure 11.10 People around the world watch wars unfold on their television sets. This boy in Iraq is watching Osama bin Laden on the Al-Jazeera television network, which broadcasts news from an Arab perspective. How might this perspective differ from a newscast from the CBC or CNN?

THE WEB

Learn more about war and virtual war at www.emp.ca/cwp.

are part of a passive audience who watch events unfold on television, thereby giving the term "theatre of war" new meaning.

This point leads to the third component of virtual war: the media. Conflicts like the Iraq War are packaged for television in much the same way that entertainment programs are packaged and promoted. Military leaders become media personalities. Language masks the reality of virtual war. People pick up new terms, such as "smart bombs" and "shock-and-awe" tactics. The deaths of civilians in enemy states become "collateral damage," while the accidental killing of soldiers by colleagues is masked as "friendly fire." For most civilians living outside the war zone, news networks such as CNN, CBC Newsworld, and Al-Jazeera mould their impressions of war. As a result, the networks become part of a passive audience. War is made to appear bloodless.

Finally, virtual wars are more limited in scope. Advanced weaponry destroys specific targets, such as command and communication networks. As a result, virtual wars do not usually result in the unconditional surrender of the enemy. Instead, the outcome may be inconclusive.

It is important to remember, however, that virtual war appears to be bloodless only to those people not directly involved in the conflict. For those living and fighting in the combat zone, virtual war remains traditional warfare. Advanced technologies such as "smart" weapons do not always succeed in pinpointing their targets. In the Iraq War in 2003, for example, misguided missiles often hit civilian sites, killing innocent people. Following the war, many foreign civilians working on reconstruction projects in Iraq also became victims of war when they were killed by Iraqi insurgents opposed to the US-led invasion. Whatever its nature, war remains an instrument of foreign policy—a tool for the "continuation of political activity by other means," just as Karl von Clausewitz described it almost two centuries ago.

Check YOUR UNDERSTANDING

1. What were the main characteristics of traditional war?
2. How did technology transform war in the 1800s?
3. Should states be able to impose conscription—mandatory military service—on citizens? Give reasons for your answer.
4. Why is it important for political leaders to bolster public morale when waging a total war?

5. How did the development of nuclear weapons alter the nature of war after 1945? How did MAD serve as a deterrent to nuclear war?
6. Evaluate the impact of the media on warfare in recent years.
7. If television can alter the perception of war, how do viewers know that they are not getting biased information?

Terrorism

Perhaps even more than conventional war, the threat of terrorism dominates today's news. Suicide bombs, hijacked aircraft, schools under siege, and political assassinations attract global attention. Terrorism preoccupies politicians and creates public fear and anxiety. This is especially true since the terrorist attacks against the United States on September 11, 2001. These events led the United States and its allies to embark upon a "war against terrorism."

The political preoccupation with terrorism, however, reflects catastrophic events such as the September 11 attacks rather than any profound change in the world of terrorism. Political terrorism has a long history in all corners of the world. Today, the causes and objectives of various terrorist groups remain unchanged. What has changed are the tactics they use.

Defining Terrorism

The first step in understanding **terrorism** is to define the term. A basic definition is "the use of violence to meet political objectives." For example, by assassinating a political leader, terrorists may attempt to destabilize or overthrow a government. Yet this definition does not distinguish between terrorist acts by groups such as al-Qaida and state acts of war, which also involve "the use of violence to meet political objectives."

The crucial component of terrorism is *terror*. Terrorists intend for their acts of violence to create fear among civilians and thus have a political impact. Although at times a state may use terror for its own purposes, terrorism in general is directed against the state by those who wish to change the political system. Therefore, a more accurate definition of terrorism may be "the unlawful use of force or violence against people or property to intimidate or coerce a government or population to further a political or social objective."

Who decides what is a terrorist act and who is a terrorist? It depends on the perspective. For example, the American media often described Iraqi citizens who shot at American troops occupying their country during and after the Iraq War as terrorists. Many Iraqis disagreed with this interpretation. They saw Iraqi citizens who used terrorist tactics not as terrorists but as **freedom fighters**. In such cases, violence is seen as a legitimate means of defending a people's rights and achieving its objectives. In fact, when acts of violence achieve the desired results, people who committed the acts often emerge as legitimate political leaders. For example, Menachem Begin was a leading figure in the militant Zionist movement that fought for the creation of an independent state of Israel; he later served as Israeli prime minister (1977–84). In 1978, he signed the first peace treaty with Israel's enemy, Egypt. As a result, he was awarded the Nobel Peace Prize that same year, together with the Egyptian leader, Anwar Sadat.

The Evolution of Terrorism

The modern use of terror for political purposes emerged during the French Revolution (1789–99). The widespread use of the guillotine (a frame containing a heavy blade used in beheadings) as an instrument of death created an atmosphere of fear throughout France. This era of radical political change was known as the *Reign of Terror*. The use of terror helped sustain the French Revolution and transform a country.

Political Assassinations

In the 19th century, political terrorism grew increasingly common in Europe. It led to the assassination of the Russian Czar, Alexander II, in 1881. His killers—who called themselves "the People's Will"—sought to strike fear into the ruling classes. Their goal was to destabilize the political system and incite political and social revolution. The murder of the czar was a political act designed to deal a fatal blow to the status quo in Russia. It marked the emergence of **revolutionary terrorism** as a political force.

This trend toward political assassinations culminated in the murder of the heir to the throne of Austria–Hungary, Franz Ferdinand, in Sarajevo in June 1914. Ferdinand's killer was a Serbian nationalist who hoped the assassination would facilitate the creation of an independent Serbian state outside of the Austro–Hungarian Empire. Instead, it ignited World War I.

In the 20th century, terrorist groups began using other methods to achieve their goals. In July 1946, for example, members of a radical **Zionist** group bombed the British military headquarters in Jerusalem. They were fighting for a Jewish state in Palestine, which was then under British control. Terrorist attacks have continued in the Middle East.

ASSASSINAT DE L'ARCHIDUC HÉRITIER D'AUTRICHE
ET DE LA DUCHESSE SA FEMME A SARAJEVO

Figure 11.11 This illustration from *Le Paris Journal* shows the assassination of Archduke Ferdinand and his wife in 1914.

Types of Terrorism

There are many ways to classify terrorists and their acts. Political scientists often distinguish them by the motivation for their actions. These fall into three broad categories: nationalist, revolutionary, and religious.

Nationalist Terrorism

Members of nationalist movements often turn to terrorism to advance their causes. Some ethnic minorities use bombings and assassinations to try to win their independence or achieve their nationalist goals. Because of their commitment to their cause, and at times because of the support they enjoy in the broader community, nationalist terrorists are difficult to contain. As a result, their terrorist campaigns often achieve some degree of success.

Nationalist terrorism has proliferated around the world. On the island state of Sri Lanka, south of the Indian subcontinent, civil war has raged for years. The revolutionary group known as the Tamil Tigers is fighting for independence for the Tamil people. In Spain, the Basque nationalist group known as ETA (in the Basque language, *Euzkadi Ta Askatasung*, meaning Basque Homeland and Freedom) commits acts of terror. The group wants to gain independence for the Basque-speaking community that straddles the border between northern Spain and southwestern France. In Russia, the government has tried to control the republic of Chechnya by force. In response, Chechen nationalists have resorted to terrorist tactics (see Chapter 4, pages 132–33).

Perhaps the best-known nationalist group is the **Palestine Liberation Organization** (PLO). Formed in 1964, the PLO now comprises many groups. Some of these have carried out high-profile terrorist attacks in the Middle East and elsewhere, including one at the 1972 Olympics in Munich, Germany. One objective was to draw international attention to the plight of Palestinian refugees in Israeli-occupied territories and to create an independent Palestinian state. Terrorist tactics, which included hijackings, bombings, and assassinations, created revulsion, but also motivated governments and political leaders to search for solutions. In 1988 talks, the PLO renounced terrorism. Later, the Palestinian Authority was created to administer security and civilian matters in the West Bank and Gaza Strip (see Chapter 3).

As you learned in Chapter 4, nationalist terrorism erupted in Quebec in the 1960s through the actions of the FLQ (Front de Libération du Québec). This culminated in the October Crisis of 1970, when the federal government sent the army into Montreal, Quebec City, and Ottawa to guard government buildings and political leaders. On October 16, the government invoked the *War Measures Act*. Civil liberties were suspended. Over 450 people suspected of being sympathetic to the FLQ were arrested and held without charge. Prime Minister Pierre Trudeau defended the government's actions. He argued that tough measures were needed to protect Canadians, even if

Figure 11.12 This recruitment poster in Sri Lanka encourages women to join the terrorist Tamil Tigers in their campaign for independence.

SOUND BITE

"The moment [the FLQ] resorted to using bombs . . . or assassination attempts, we were no longer dealing with democratic opposition, and it became our duty to hunt them down . . . so we could put an end to their criminal activities. . . . It is the duty of any democracy to protect itself against the forces of dissolution as soon as they raise their heads."

Pierre Trudeau,
Memoirs, 1993

Figure 11.13 Soldiers guard public buildings in Montreal during the October Crisis in 1970. Do you think Trudeau was justified in suspending civil liberties?

THE WEB

Learn more about Castro and communism in Cuba at www.emp.ca/cwp.

Press Play

Fidel: The Untold Story (2001), a documentary by Estella Bravo, uses interviews and archival footage to examine the personality and political philosophy of Cuba's revolutionary leader. (NR)

it meant suspending democratic rights in the short term. This is the same dilemma that democratic governments face today as they combat terrorism.

Revolutionary Terrorism

Revolutionary terrorists hope to incite a social and political uprising to overthrow the state and to create fear among its citizens that the state cannot protect them. Revolutionary terrorists, such as those who assassinated Czar Alexander II in Russia in 1881, believed their actions would weaken the state and the government's control over society and awaken the population to the need for revolution.

Other examples of revolutionary terrorist groups include the Red Brigades in Italy and the Red Army Faction in Germany. In the 1970s and early 1980s, these communist-inspired groups used guerrilla tactics to spread fear across Europe. Powerful figures—such as former Italian Prime Minister Aldo Moro and the German business executive Hanns-Martin Schleyer—were kidnapped and murdered. The terrorists' goals were ambitious: to overthrow the liberal democracies of Western Europe.

Revolutionary terrorists have also had an impact in Latin America. Perhaps the best-known example is the revolution in Cuba in 1959. Led by Fidel Castro, communist revolutionaries overthrew the country's corrupt regime. In Peru during the 1980s and early 1990s, the terrorist group Shining Path embraced Maoist ideology and tried to launch a peasants' revolution. Its members bombed power stations, attacked the army, and used terrorist acts in a failed attempt to overthrow the government.

Religious Terrorism

Since the mid-1980s, another form of terrorism has gained prominence and taken many forms: **religious terrorism**. While religious terrorism has a long history, it is receiving more attention than ever before.

The most active form of religious terrorism is militant Islam, which has emerged in the Middle East in recent decades. Militant Islam blends both religious and nationalist goals. Groups such as Hezbollah ("party of God") and the armed wing of Hamas ("fighting spirit") use terrorist tactics against Israel's military and civilians. Their goal is to establish the political and territorial rights of Palestinian Arabs displaced when the state of Israel was created in 1948. They also target Western interests in the Middle East that support Israel.

One tactic that often distinguishes religious terrorism is the use of suicide bombers. Under the leadership of radical clerics, Hamas has launched a series of suicide bombings against Israel. The goal is to promote the Palestinian cause and to punish or destroy Israel for its actions, which terrorists see as crimes against the Palestinian people. Suicide bombers hide explosives on their bodies and then detonate them in crowds of Israeli soldiers or civilians. Traditionally, most suicide bombers in the Middle East were young men. Increasingly, women, children, and older men have also become suicide bombers. Trapped in a life of poverty, they are willing to sacrifice themselves for their cause and their families, who often receive cash payments from organizations opposed to Israel. Their supporters hail suicide bombers as martyrs for Palestine and Islam.

Al-Qaida

In the 1990s, a new terrorist group emerged that would become synonymous with terrorism. **Al-Qaida** (commonly translated as "the base,") was founded by a wealthy Saudi named Osama bin Laden, who first opposed foreign intervention in the Middle East when he fought against the Soviet Union in Afghanistan during the early 1980s.

Al-Qaida is a loose association of groups whose ideology blends fundamentalist interpretations of Islam with modern revolutionary ideas. It focuses its terrorist activities on the perceived threat that Western culture presents to Islam. In particular, al-Qaida opposes American influences in the Muslim countries of the Middle East, especially bin Laden's native Saudi Arabia. In 1996, bin Laden declared a *jihad*—a holy war—against the United States.

Al-Qaida's attacks against the United States began in 1994, when it detonated a bomb at the World Trade Center in New York City. Then, in August 1998, it bombed American embassies in Nairobi, Kenya, and Dar es Salaam, Tanzania.

The most destructive act of terrorism, however, came on September 11, 2001, when al-Qaida terrorists hijacked four airplanes over the United States. Two planes were flown into the World Trade Center, destroying both towers. A third plane was flown into the Pentagon in Washington, DC, while the fourth plane (apparently intended to hit Washington's US Capitol building) crashed in a Pennsylvania field after passengers fought the hijackers. In total, almost 3,000 people were killed. It was the deadliest terrorist attack in history.

Despite efforts to eliminate al-Qaida and its leaders, its terrorism has continued. Al-Qaida operatives perpetrated bombings in Bali and Jakarta in Indonesia in October 2002 and in Madrid, Spain, in March 2004. Al-Qaida and Osama bin Laden became synonymous with modern terrorism, largely overshadowing other nationalist and revolutionary groups.

SOUND BITE "You cannot exercise your powers to the point of humiliation for the others. And that is what the Western world . . . has to realize. . . . There are long-term consequences if you don't look hard at the reality in 10 or 20 or 30 years from now. . . . I do think that the Western world is going to be too rich in relation to the poor world and necessarily, they look upon us as being arrogant, self-satisfying, greedy, and with no limits. And the 11th of September is an occasion for me to realize that even more."

Canadian Prime Minister Jean Chrétien, CBC News Online, September 16, 2002

Figure 11.14 In October 2002, a car bomb exploded outside a nightclub in Bali that was popular with Australian tourists, killing more than 180 people.

Language and Politics

Irshad Manji: "Muslim Refusenik"

Irshad Manji was a child in 1972 when her family came to Canada fleeing racial persecution in Uganda. Growing up in Vancouver, Manji struggled to reconcile her Muslim faith with life in a liberal democracy that embraced intellectual freedom and gender equality. As a television journalist, activist, and author, she has consistently tackled social injustices and promoted global diversity.

Manji does not fear controversy. She thrives on it. Despite popular portrayals of Islam as a repressive religion opposed to democracy, she passionately believes the two are compatible. She publicly challenges what she calls "Islamic totalitarianism": a perspective that rejects debate about Islam and nurtures supporters of Osama bin Laden and other radicals.

In *The Trouble with Islam: A Wake-up Call for Honesty and Change*, Manji argues that Muslims must take steps to renew their religion. She rejects radical Islamic teachings that support terrorism and oppress women and minorities. Manji's use of language—her attack on "Islamic totalitarianism," her call for "Islamic reformation"—are intentionally provocative.

Through . . . our conspicuous silences, we Muslims are conspiring against ourselves. We're in crisis, and we're dragging the rest of the world with us. If ever there was a moment for an Islamic reformation, it's now. For the love of God, what are we doing about it?

You may wonder who I am to talk to you this way. I am a Muslim **refusenik**. That doesn't mean I refuse to be a Muslim; it simply means I refuse to join an army of automatons in the name of Allah. I take this phrase from the original refuseniks —Soviet Jews who championed religious and personal freedom. Their communist masters refused to let them emigrate to Israel. For their attempts to leave the Soviet Union, many refuseniks paid with hard labour and, sometimes, with their lives. Over time, though, their persistent refusal to comply with the mechanisms of mind-control and soullessness helped end a totalitarian system.

Not solely because of September 11, but more urgently because of it, we've got to end Islam's totalitarianism, particularly the gross human rights violations against women and religious minorities. You'll want to assure me that what I'm

Figure 11.15 Irshad Manji has sparked debate and faced strong criticism from some Muslim groups, in Canada and abroad. In doing so, she has become a potent symbol of outspoken thought.

describing in this open letter to you isn't "true" Islam. Frankly, such a distinction wouldn't have impressed Prophet Muhammad, who said that religion is the way we conduct ourselves towards others—not theoretically, but actually. By that standard, how Muslims behave is Islam. To sweep that reality under the rug is to absolve ourselves of responsibility for our fellow human beings. See why I am struggling?

As I view it, the trouble with Islam is that lives are small and lies are big. Totalitarian impulses lurk in mainstream Islam. That's one hell of a charge, I know.

Source: Irshad Manji, *The Trouble with Islam: A Wake-up Call for Honesty and Change* (Toronto: Random House Canada, 2003), pp. 2–3.

Questions

1. The author refers to herself as a "Muslim refusenik." What does she mean? Why is this phrase powerful?
2. How does Manji define "Islamic totalitarianism"? What arguments does she use to support her calls for reform? Do you agree with her call for reforms? Explain.
3. Religions such as Christianity, Buddhism, Hinduism, Islam, and so on have many sects, some of them intolerant and militant. Using a technique similar to Manji's, create a "passionate wakeup call" or defence for a religion with which you are familiar.

THE WEB

Learn more about Irshad Manji and her ideas at www.emp.ca/cwp.

Press Play

Kandahar (2001), by Iranian director Mohsen Makhmalbaf, vividly captures the clash of cultures and the impact of war as it recounts the experience of Nelofer Pazira, an Afghani Canadian journalist who slips into Taliban-controlled Afghanistan in desperate search of her childhood friend. (PG)

Terrorism and Politics

The purpose of terrorist violence—whether nationalist, revolutionary, or religious—is to bring about political change. How successful are terrorists in achieving this goal? What impact does terrorism have on the political status quo? Governments are reluctant to acknowledge that terrorists have an impact. In part, they believe that to do so would encourage more terrorism. Usually, acts of terrorism also increase the public's determination not to give in to terrorist demands.

Terrorism, however, clearly does have political consequences. It may force governments to address at least some of the grievances that motivate terrorists in the first place. This was so, for example, in the al-Qaida train bombings in Madrid, Spain, on March 11, 2004. The Spanish government supported the US-led war against Iraq in 2003, even though public opposition was widespread. This made Spain a target for terrorists. Days before Spain's national elections in March 2004—an election the government was expected to win—al-Qaida detonated bombs on several trains in Madrid. Almost 200 people were killed and many hundreds more were injured.

Point:
Counterpoint → Debating Civil Liberties and the War on Terrorism

"Yes": The War on Terrorism Threatens Civil Liberties

by Michael Ignatieff

As the threat of terrorism targets our political identity as free peoples, our essential resource has to be that identity itself. We cannot fight and prevail against an enemy unless we know who we are and what we wish to defend at all costs. If the automatic response to mass casualty terrorism is to strengthen secret government, it is the wrong response. The right one is to strengthen open government. Democratic peoples will not lend assistance to authorities unless they believe in the system they are defending. No strategy against terror is sustainable without public assistance and cooperation, without eyes that detect risks, ears that hear threats, and the willingness to report them to authorities. As two world wars have shown, a democratic people mobilized by fear and led by hope can prove a formidable foe. Despite their checks and balances, democratic systems do not have to be less decisive than authoritarian ones, and democratic institutions have the advantage of marshaling the wisdom, experience, and talent of the citizens as a whole rather than relying on the shallow pool of a closed elite.

Faith in democracy need not make us blind to its faults. Indeed, our democracies are not doing as well as they could in dealing with conventional threats, and it is to be feared that they will do still worse with weapons of mass destruction. So far, information about risk has been doctored for public consumption. Media, with more concern for market share than for the public interest, have colluded in disinforming the public. Judges have accorded excessive deference to government actions. Legislatures have lacked the courage to subject the facts of risk to clear-eyed scrutiny. Government departments have abridged the liberties of aliens and minorities, safe in the knowledge that the victims lack the voice to make the injustice heard. The public has gone along, unable or unwilling to force their elected officials to serve them better. When democratic institutions malfunction in this way, bad public policy is the result. Legislatures have crafted legislation that provides the police with powers

they do not need; the public lends its support to measures that do not increase its security; the secret services, observing a deceived public and a deceiving leadership, may take the law into their own hands. A war on terror thus waged by secret and unaccountable agents, working on or beyond the margins of the law, on behalf of depoliticized and demobilized citizens who remain in the dark about what is being done in their name, may end up damaging democracy forever.

We do not want a war on terror fought on behalf of free peoples who are free only in name.

Source: Michael Ignatieff, *The Lesser Evil: Political Ethics in an Age of Terror* (Toronto: Penguin Canada, 2004), pp. 154–55.

"No": The War on Terrorism Does Not Threaten Civil Liberties

by David Frum and Richard Perle

The *Patriot Act* grants the [US Federal Bureau of Investigation] the ability to conduct twenty-first century surveillance of terrorist suspects. . . .

But it was not a general wariness of obsolescence that caused the *Patriot Act* to be made temporary, but a very specific fear that the passions of the moment might stampede us into doing something "hysterical." Two years on, however, it is those fears of hysteria that themselves look hysterical. Civil liberties in the United States continue robust. The privacy of the American home is many millions of times more likely to be invaded by an e-mail spammer or a telemarketer than a federal agent. The right to dissent flourishes unrestrained—indeed, to judge by the way some of [US] President Bush's wilder opponents carry on, it flourishes unrestrained even by common politeness or basic accuracy.

All of this is as it should be. Yet in our appropriate zeal to preserve and defend the right to speak freely and think differently, there is a real danger that Americans will make the opposite mistake. We may be so eager to protect the right to dissent that we lose sight of the difference between dissent and subversion; so determined to

The United States is proud to call itself a nation ruled by law. But even a nation of laws must understand the limits of legalism. Between 1861 and 1865, the government of the United States took tens of thousands of American citizens prisoner and detained them for years without letting any one of them see a lawyer. We targeted and shot down the plane of the Japanese admiral who had planned Pearl Harbor and felt not a twinge of remorse at his extrajudicial killing. War has its rules, of course—but by those very rules our enemies in this war on terror are outlaws.

Source: David Frum and Richard Perle, *An End to Evil: How to Win the War on Terror* (New York: Random House, 2003), pp. 74, 228–29.

Articulating a Personal Stand

1. List both Ignatieff's and Frum's arguments. With which do you agree and disagree? Explain.
2. Provide one more argument for each side of this debate.
3. Describe how the struggle against terrorism "damages democracy forever."
4. In small groups, discuss whether the "war on terrorism" poses a significant threat to democratic rights and civil liberties. Then, write a five-paragraph editorial on the issue. Include a response to the following question: *Which is the greater threat, a potential act of terrorism or restrictions on civil rights?* Alternatively, present your ideas orally to the class.

Figure 11.16 A young passenger hesitates before going through a metal detector gate at a security checkpoint at Denver International Airport, 2002.

defend the right of privacy that we refuse to acknowledge even the most blatant warnings of danger. . . .

In the little more than two years since 9/11—the same space of time in which our grandparents swept from disaster and humiliation at Pearl Harbor to triumph at Guadalcanal and in Sicily—many of our leaders have succumbed to a troubling weakening of the spirit, a disturbing lapse of grit and seriousness. In a speech at New York University in August 2003, former [US] vice president Gore made the stunning assertion that the United States government under George Bush has ceased to be one that "upholds the fundamental rights even of those it believes to be its captured enemies." Even in the midst of a global struggle, this prominent American apparently cannot free himself from the delusion that foreign terrorists are to be read their Miranda rights [the right to legal council and to remain silent upon arrest] before they are questioned.

At first, fearful of the political repercussions at the polls, the government immediately blamed Basque terrorists for the attack. It was soon evident, however, that the bombs were the work of al-Qaida. Spaniards were both horrified by the terrorists' actions and angry with their conservative government for what seemed to be **disinformation** about the attacks and for supporting the Iraq war. The socialist party promised to withdraw Spain's troops from Iraq if it won the election, and did just that once it was in office. Thus, in this case, terrorists' actions succeeded in influencing political policy.

Waging War against Terrorism

Since the September 11 attacks on New York and Washington, the United States, Canada, and many other liberal democracies have embarked on a "war against terrorism." Their goal is to hunt down terrorists and to implement security measures that will thwart future terrorist attacks. Many countries have restructured their federal bureaucracies and intelligence services. As part of its government's "war on terrorism," the US Department of Homeland Security was created. Canada created a Ministry of Public Safety.

In response to the threat of terrorism, governments and law enforcement agencies have taken a number of other steps. Immigration checks, border controls, and airport security have been tightened. Governments have also tried to disrupt the financial networks of terrorist organizations, which are often linked to organized crime. Intelligence agencies such as the US Central Intelligence Agency and the Canadian Security Intelligence Service work with police forces, including the RCMP and Interpol (the main international organization of police forces; see Chapter 12, page 423) to investigate terrorist organizations.

The war against terrorism is not without controversy. While citizens have long accepted the need for governments to exercise extraordinary powers during times of emergency, the government response to September 11, 2001 is different. In the past, governments imposed emergency powers for a limited time. Many of the new anti-terrorism laws seem more permanent in nature. Legislation such as the *USA PATRIOT Act* and Canada's *Anti-Terrorism Act*, which extend the power of authorities to investigate suspected terrorists, have sparked debate about civil and human rights—fundamental principles in liberal democracies. Some believe the new measures infringe on the due process of law and the right to privacy. They question how much power authorities should have to question and detain citizens.

There are also concerns about the rights of people who are arrested and detained as terrorist suspects. In many cases, these people do not receive the same legal rights as criminal suspects or prisoners of war. Some critics have charged that the United States is using torture and other illegal tactics at its military base at Guantanamo Bay, Cuba, where terrorist suspects are being held. Some people justify these actions. They argue that they are needed to defend democracy and the rule of law from terrorist threats. Others, how-

SOUND BITE "America has given the world a model of democracy which is founded on the rule of law, on fundamental human rights, including the right to fair trial, the right to silence. Guantanamo offers an alternative model to the world, a model where no rights are sustained."

Corin Redgrave, human rights activist, the Guantanamo Human Rights Commission, March 5, 2004

ever, fear that such actions destroy the very principles they are supposed to be defending.

Thus, the war against terrorism raises many pressing political questions. How far can, or should, a democratic government go to fight terrorism? Are governments justified in using whatever means necessary to fight terrorism, even if their actions violate the law? Is torture ever justified? Is it acceptable for the state to spy on its citizens? Should citizens sacrifice their political and legal rights to ensure national security?

THE WEB

Learn more about Canadian security measures at www.emp.ca/cwp.

Check YOUR UNDERSTANDING

1. What are the main motivations for terrorism? Give examples of each.
2. Why do nationalist terrorists often enjoy the greatest success?
3. What steps did the Canadian government take during the October Crisis of 1970 and why?
4. What is al-Qaida, and what are its objectives?
5. Reread the Sound Bite by former Prime Minister Jean Chrétien on page 389. What point is he making? Do you agree? Give reasons for your answer.
6. Why might some people argue that terrorism is an effective political tool?
7. In small groups, evaluate the impact terrorism has on democracy. Present your conclusions orally to the class.

The Quest for a Lasting Peace

Territorial disputes, ethnic and religious divisions, and ideological differences continue to cause conflicts and wars around the world. Therefore, the need for nations, political leaders, and individuals to work for peace is as urgent as ever. While the specific causes of conflict may change, the fundamental challenges of promoting peace remain the same.

Peacekeeping, Peacemaking, and Peace-Building

You learned about Canada's central role in United Nations peacekeeping in Chapters 8 and 9. It is worth recalling that preserving peace and preventing international conflicts remain fundamental objectives of the United Nations. Of course, the UN is not the only international organization that tries to prevent conflict. NATO and the European Union also use their military or diplomatic resources in peacekeeping and peacemaking missions, as they did in Kosovo in 1999 and Afghanistan in 2001.

The Human Security Agenda

Peacekeeping has changed radically since Lester Pearson put forward his proposal in 1956 (see Chapter 8). Traditional efforts to

Figure 11.17 Former Canadian Foreign Affairs Minister Lloyd Axworthy has been an important contributor to the Human Security Agenda.

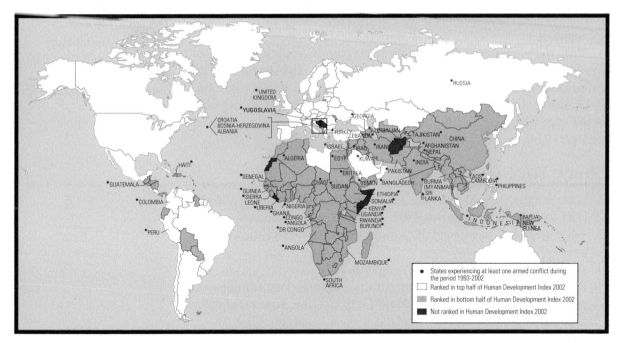

Source: UN Development Program, *Human Development Report 2002*; Project Ploughshares, *Armed Conflicts Report*. The Human Development Index is published annually by the United Nations Development Program. It ranked 173 states in its report for 2002 (based on 2000 data).

Figure 11.18 Only 12 percent of the countries ranked in the upper half of the UN Human Development Index, 2002 were involved in armed conflicts between 1993 and 2002. In contrast, 43 percent of the countries ranked in the lower half of the index were at war during the same period.

prevent conflict focused on the physical security of a state and its people. In the past decade, however, the understanding of security and the prevention of conflict has gained a new perspective. Governments, NGOs, and international organizations have come to understand that military intervention alone cannot ensure world security. It is also necessary to eliminate the many causes of conflict. These include poverty, HIV/AIDS, and human rights abuses. Known as the **Human Security Agenda**, this new approach looks beyond military action to the delivery of humanitarian aid and government services and the promotion of democratic principles and values.

Development specialists and police forces, such as the Royal Canadian Mounted Police stationed in Haiti in 2004, are often part of these new peace-

THE WEB

Learn more about the Human Security Agenda at www.emp.ca/cwp.

SOUND BITE "Peace is not just the opposite of war. The eloquently visual Mandarin language uses three symbols/words for peace. The first word for peace literally means rice in the mouth, or economic security. The second means a woman with a roof over her head, or social security. The third means two hearts beating together in understanding and friendship, or human security."

Lois Wilson, The Armed Conflict Report 2003, *Project Ploughshares*

SOUND BITE "If September 11 taught us that we have to fight and win the 'war on terrorism,' it should also have taught us that if we do not immediately address the underlying . . . causes of those young terrorists' rage, we will not win the war. For every al-Qaida bomber that we kill there will be a thousand more volunteers from all over the earth to take his place."

Lieutenant-General Roméo Dallaire, Shake Hands with the Devil: The Failure of Humanity in Rwanda, *2003*

keeping forces. They help to conduct democratic elections, set up medical facilities, and deliver aid to local people. Many international peace efforts today are in fact peace-building.

What brought about this change? Today, the global community realizes there is more to ensuring peace and security than simply ending conflicts. There is a need to rebuild societies, economies, governments, and institutions to eliminate the problems that lead to conflicts in the first place. As a result, peacekeeping missions have a broad mandate to create physical, political, and economic security in societies and states around the world.

Inevitably, this new role in the peacekeeping mandate has led to longer and more complex missions. It has increased costs for both the United Nations and participating countries. Yet pursuing this new path is essential if the international community is truly committed to building a peaceful world.

The United Nations does not work alone in this new approach. There are many non-governmental organizations (NGOs) dedicated to easing the hardships caused by conflict and war. A few of the NGOs involved include the International Committee of the Red Cross (ICRC) and Doctors Without Borders (see Chapters 8 and 10). Often, these groups are the first to arrive in a conflict zone and the last to leave. They have an important role to play in the new Human Security Agenda.

Personal Peace Initiatives

Individuals also play an active role in promoting peace through their involvement in social movements and peace organizations. Beginning in the 1950s, groups around the world campaigned to abolish nuclear weapons and end development of new weapons programs. Other groups have demanded both total and unilateral **disarmament**. The British Campaign for Nuclear Disarmament (CND), for example, condemns US and NATO military actions through public protests, marches, and civil disobedience. In Canada, organizations such as Project Ploughshares have urged Canada to become a nuclear-weapons–free zone. This would prevent, for example, American submarines armed with nuclear weapons from entering Canadian waters.

Many peace activists in Canada oppose some of the country's military activities. In 1999, activists opposed Canada's role in the NATO bombing of Yugoslavia. After 2001, many opposed Canada's participation in NATO oper-

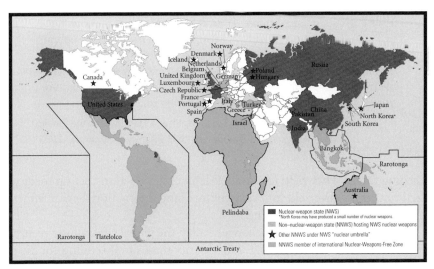

Source: Project Ploughshares, www.ploughshares.ca/imagesarticles/ACR02/
NW&NWFZ.02.pdf.

Figure 11.19 Nuclear-weapons countries and nuclear-weapons–free zones.

ations in Afghanistan as part of the war against terrorism. Others carry their peace commitment even further. Pacifists oppose all forms of war on religious or philosophical grounds. They refuse to serve in the military, even at the risk of facing punishment and imprisonment. Other activists travel to war zones to act as "human shields." Before the invasion of Iraq in 2003, for example, small groups from Canada, including politicians, went to that country and positioned themselves near potential targets such as mosques in the hope of discouraging an attack. It is dangerous work, and some activists have lost their lives. Their campaigns usually have little impact on political or military leaders. However, peace activists do focus public attention on the human cost of war. They remind people of the ever-present need to seek other, more peaceful, solutions to political conflicts.

Figure 11.20 Human shields demonstrate in Baghdad prior to the US-led invasion, March 2003.

Taking a Stand   Lieutenant-General Roméo Dallaire

"We watched as the devil took control of paradise on Earth and fed on the blood of the people we were supposed to protect."

With these words, the Canadian commander of the UN Assistance Mission for Rwanda (UNAMIR), Lieutenant-General Roméo Dallaire, summarized the greatest peacekeeping failure in the history of the United Nations. Dallaire's mission was to preserve peace and security in Rwanda, a small African state where simmering ethnic divisions threatened to turn violent. In April 1994, following the assassination of Rwanda's president, leaders of the majority Hutu launched a massacre against the minority Tutsi in Rwanda and moderate Hutus who refused to support them. Machete-wielding Hutu militias murdered over 800,000 men, women, and children. It was one of the worst acts of genocide since the Holocaust in World War II.

Dallaire struggled to do what he could with a limited number of troops, but he was powerless to stop the killing. His pleas for more troops and assistance went unheeded at the United Nations. The Security Council voted to cut the peacekeeping force from 2,500 troops to just 270. Three weeks later, the Council reversed its decision and agreed to send 5,500 troops to Rwanda. They were never deployed, however, as the major powers could not agree who would pay the cost. Why did the UN and the world's major powers turn their backs on Rwanda and its people?

In his gut-wrenching account of his experience, *Shake Hands with the Devil: The Failure of Humanity in Rwanda*, Dallaire tries to answer that question. He points to the world's developed countries, who he says were unwilling to risk soldiers in a country that was of no strategic importance to them. Simply put, Rwanda and its people did not matter:

> In the last decades of the twentieth century, self-interest, sovereignty and taking care of number one became the primary criteria for any serious provision of support or resources to the globe's trouble spots. If the country in question is of any possible strategic value to the world powers, then it seems that everything from covert operations to the outright use of overwhelming force is fair game. If it is not, indifference is the order of the day.

For Dallaire, the guilt he felt from UNAMIR's failure was almost too much to bear. Suffering from post-traumatic stress disorder, he attempted suicide. Eventually, Dallaire was released from the Canadian armed forces for medical reasons. A distinguished military career that had spanned more than 30 years was over.

Roméo Dallaire has not allowed the world to forget what happened. In 2004, he testified at the International Criminal Tribunal at the trials of those accused of plotting the genocide. He continues to take a personal stand by speaking out about his experiences. Dallaire wants Canadians to remember that their humanitarian concerns must be backed by the political will to take action. He wants to ensure that the global community never allows another tragedy to take place like the one that engulfed Rwanda.

Source: Roméo Dallaire, *Shake Hands with the Devil: The Failure of Humanity in Rwanda* (Toronto: Random House, 2003), pp. 519–20.

Questions

1. According to Dallaire, what lessons should be learned from Rwanda?
2. Why does Dallaire see the genocide in Rwanda as a failure for the United Nations?
3. Do you think Dallaire's verdict is justified? Give reasons for your answer.

Check YOUR UNDERSTANDING

1. What conclusions can you draw from the information on the map in Figure 11.18 on page 396?
2. Briefly explain the differences between peacekeeping and peacemaking.
3. Why has the traditional understanding of peacekeeping changed in recent years?
4. What is the Human Security Agenda? How does it differ from traditional approaches to world security?
5. In small groups, debate the effectiveness of acting as a human shield. Do you think this is an effective strategy for promoting peace? Why or why not?
6. How important do you think it is for people to take action to promote peace? What might you and other Canadians do to promote peace?
7. Reread the Sound Bite by Roméo Dallaire on page 397. Do you agree that poverty promotes religious extremism that leads to terrorism? Why or why not?

METHODS OF POLITICAL INQUIRY

Simulation: Debating a Resolution in the United Nations General Assembly

When you work with groups to make decisions about issues, you have to consider and respect the opinions and interests of all group members. This is especially true in the United Nations. In order to represent the interests of all people and countries, delegates to the UN must research, discuss, and debate an issue before passing a resolution to take action.

In Chapter 8, you created a list of resolutions for presentation at the United Nations. Now you have the opportunity to conduct a simplified simulation of a session of the UN General Assembly. You may choose one of the resolutions from Chapter 8 (page 295) or create a new resolution based on one of the issues in this chapter.

Simulating the General Assembly

Begin this simulation by selecting one student to assume the role of President of the General Assembly. The President must distribute the full draft of the resolution in writing before the session begins. He or she must also post a list of the speakers who intend to address the resolution.

Participants should be divided into delegations to represent actual member states of the United Nations. Have at least two delegates per member state. Delegates should be seated in alphabetical order, by country, and should have a placard identifying the country they represent.

To begin, have the President call upon the head of the delegation presenting the resolution to read the resolution aloud. Members of the delegation then have two minutes to speak about the issue. Speeches should demonstrate the quality of the delegates' research and reflect the policies of the states they represent.

When the sponsoring delegates have presented their resolution, delegates from other countries may ask up to four questions. The President must formally recognize a delegate before he or she can speak. In turn, a delegate must formally address the Assembly—that is, "Mr./Ms. President and Honoured Members of the General Assembly. . . ." Then the delegate has two minutes to express his or her point of view.

When speaking, delegates should present a brief introduction to the issue, their country's position on the issue, a justification for that position, appropriate references, and a closing summary. Comments may refer to previous actions taken to address the problem, future actions, or both.

Delegates may then propose amendments to delete, augment, or revise part of the resolution. (Note that amendments cannot be made to the preamble, or introduction, to the resolution.) Any proposed amendments must be in writing and must be seconded by another delegate. Delegates have two minutes to speak about their proposed amendment. Then two delegates who oppose the amendment have two minutes each to express their points of view.

Delegates may rise on a Point of Order if they believe there has been an irregularity in procedure, such as a misrepresentation of policy. It is the job of the President to rule on the Point of Order. Delegates may also rise on a Point of Information after a speech to question the speaker. The President decides whether to accept or refuse a request to rise on a Point of Information.

Once the resolution and the proposed amendments have been presented, the delegates must vote. Most resolutions in the General Assembly must pass by a majority vote. However, decisions on certain issues, such as international peace and security, the expulsion of member states, and amendments to the UN Charter, require a majority of two-thirds of the delegates.

The United Nations is not a world government. It cannot pass international laws that apply to all states. However, resolutions passed by the General Assembly carry the force of world opinion. They usually represent what the majority of the global community believes is right, and they may prompt action by the Security Council or a member organization of the United Nations.

Applying the Skill

1. Conduct research on the resolution to enable you to express your country's position. After researching the issue, prepare reference notes to help you present your position in the General Assembly. Write down key information in point form on index cards. Think of each point as the central idea of a paragraph. Use your notes to help keep your speech focused. Avoid reading the notes directly. Instead, maintain eye contact with your audience, glancing at your notes only as the need arises.

2. Once the resolution and amendments have been presented and debated, the President will conduct a vote. All delegates must vote by saying "Yes," "No," or "Abstention." Post the resolution, amendments, and the results of the vote in the classroom.

Study Hall

Thinking and Inquiry

1. Do you agree that nationalism remains the most important cause of war and armed conflict in the world today? Explain your answer.

2. In your opinion, why is terrorism used as a political tactic despite the risk that acts of violence may discredit the terrorists' cause?

3. Using the Internet and media sources, research Canada's current involvement in UN peacekeeping missions. How has Canada's participation in recent missions reflected the emphasis upon peacemaking?

4. Some commentators have argued that the Human Security Agenda promoted by Canada, with its emphasis on non-military solutions to conflicts, is simply an excuse for neglecting Canada's armed forces. Do you agree? Why or why not?

Communication

5. Look back at Figure 11.1 on page 370.
   a) What statement, if any, do you believe the artist wished to make? Explain your reasoning, referring to specific details of the drawing.
   b) Speculate why the artist might have chosen black and white for this work rather than colour.

6. Imagine that you are a foreign correspondent sent to report on a current armed conflict. Using the Internet, newspapers, and news magazines, research the impact of the conflict on the civilian population and write a brief news report outlining these effects.

7. Write a letter to the editor of a national newspaper expressing your support for or opposition to the imprisonment of terrorist suspects without charge and other restrictions placed on civil liberties in the war against terrorism.

8. Together with your classmates, prepare a debate on the following resolution: "Given the global military dominance of the United States and the technological sophistication of modern warfare, Canada no longer needs its armed forces."

Application

9. In order to counter a perceived terrorist threat, a state decides to take unilateral military action against the terrorists and a neighbouring state that is harbouring them. Assume the role of a political adviser to the head of the state that is being threatened. Prepare a brief outline of the pros and cons of taking military action.

10. Working in a group, identify an ongoing war or conflict in which you believe Canada and other states should take a more active role in peacemaking. Based on your research and discussion, prepare persuasive arguments for foreign intervention in this case and present them to the class. At the end of each group's presentation, put the motion to a class vote.

11. Many activists are motivated by the maxim "think globally, act locally." Wars and armed conflicts may seem far removed from daily life in Canada, but the basic principles of conflict resolution are universal. Working with a partner, formulate three principles of conflict resolution that could apply to your local community or to the global community.

Globalization

Figure 12.1 This satellite photograph appeared on a Web site devoted to "identity and globalization." Visitors were invited to download, alter, and upload the image. The map was captioned: "So as the light concentrates over the industrialized countries—leaving the rest of the planet in darkness—so are wealth, resources and services forbidden for the majority of the world population. *This is the light of hunger and death.*"

Agenda

In this chapter, you will consider

• differences between and within developed and developing countries
• debt crises in the developing world
• trends toward global decision making in economics and politics
• the impact of globalization on local cultures
• transnational corporations as world economic powers
• responses of government, groups, and individuals to economic and cultural globalization
• what it means to be a global citizen living in Canada
• how to write a review of a political book

Globalization has been hailed as the cure for economic inequalities and denounced as a new form of imperialism. While political and business leaders work to create a global trading system, opponents protest that globalization crushes local cultures and enslaves workers in low-wage sweatshops in developing countries. Where does the truth lie?

This concluding chapter probes transformations brought about by globalization. You will examine the impact of global trade and communications upon different economies and cultures. You will study the perils and promise of economic development for developing countries of the global South. You will consider difficult questions. What responsibilities do developed countries such as Canada have in the global economy? Are humankind's basic needs and rights being met and respected? You will reflect upon the economic development and political turmoil that have accompanied globalization. Does Canada have a unique place in this interconnected world, where trade, culture, and even organized crime and terrorism cross national borders with increasing ease?

Figure 12.2 Water-borne diseases spread sickness and death in developing countries. These children in Ghana, Africa, collect clean, safe water from a pump funded by the Canadian International Development Agency and built and maintained by their community.

SOUND BITE   "Today, a growing injustice confronts us. More than 90 percent of all death and suffering from infectious diseases occurs in the developing world."

Dr. James Orbinski, Nobel Peace Prize Lecture, 1999

A World of Inequalities

Most people in Canada live in comfort. Although there are wide differences in wealth and many Canadians live in poverty, the vast majority have access to electricity, fuel, clean water, adequate food, and medical care. For billions of our neighbours in Africa, Asia, and South America, daily life is very different. The majority of citizens of our global *polis* lack these basic necessities. Occasionally, Canadians experience a glimmer of that reality.

In August 2003, a power blackout struck large portions of Ontario and the eastern United States. It took several days to restore power reliably. The impact on the economy and on daily life was dramatic. National and local politicians rushed to deal with the emergency and to reassure people that it would not happen again. Looking back, it is worth remembering that almost a third of the people of our planet—almost 2 billion people—live with no access to electricity. For another third, the electricity supply is unreliable; blackouts such as Ontario experienced in the summer of 2003 happen almost daily. We live in a world of inequalities.

Developed and Developing Countries

As you learned in Chapter 8, countries can be classified in different ways. Canada is one of the privileged minority of countries known as the "developed world." What criteria define a developed county? Most people in developed countries enjoy a high standard of living. They have access to abundant food, safe drinking water, medicines, fuel, and power, and also to many services, products, and the latest technologies. These are benefits that result from industrial and technological development and stable political institutions.

Most countries in Europe, parts of Asia (such as Japan), Australia, and North America (Canada and the United States) are part of the developed world. Because most developed countries are in the northern hemisphere, this group is also known as the North. The remaining countries of the world —and most of its population—are grouped in the developing world (primarily South and Central America, Africa, and most of Asia). The developing world lies largely in the southern hemisphere and is often called the South.

One measure of the disparities (inequalities) between the countries of the world is the UN's annual **Human Development Index** (HDI), which ranks life expectancy, literacy, educational levels, and personal income. It also considers the range of difference in wealth within each country. Canada is regularly ranked at or near the top, together with countries such as Norway and the United States. At the bottom of the HDI are African countries such as Sierra Leone and Ethiopia.

Examining other economic benchmarks reveals similar differences. A brief comparison of **gross domestic product** (GDP) **per capita** (person) illustrates the gulf dividing the richest and poorest countries (see Figure 12.3). Other data further expose the stark differences between the highly developed North and the developing South. For example, the countries of the North account for 20 percent of the world's population but consume 80 percent of its resources. The countries of the South account for 80 percent of the world's people but use only 20 percent of its resources.

At the same time, classifying countries as developed/developing or North/South can result in oversimplification. For example, theories of economic development have long questioned the relationship between the accumulation of **capital** (wealth accumulated in the form of money or goods) and the rate of economic growth. In recent decades, many political scientists and economists have come to recognize that the elimination of poverty, unemployment, and economic inequalities *within* states is also a valid measure of development.

In addition to the disparities within each country, there are vast differences among countries in the developing world. Some, such as India and Brazil, are experiencing strong economic growth and technological diversification. They seem about to emerge as greater economic and political powers. Others, such as Nigeria and Venezuela, have economies that remain dependent upon a single resource—in both cases, oil. Still other developing countries, including many sub-Saharan states, lack exploitable natural resources and even a rudimentary industrial economy.

Models of Economic Development

Economists have developed different models to explain how countries develop. In most, capital is essential to investment and to produce economic growth. Non-industrial societies begin as largely agricultural economies and produce traditional political and social structures. Eventually, preconditions for industrial development emerge. In particular, banks are established to accumulate capital and provide loans as, simultaneously, new technologies are developed and used. Investment and technological innovation lead to improved productivity, which further accelerates development. Canada, for example, experienced its industrial transformation in the late 1800s; India did so in the 1950s.

Next, the economy matures. This stage is marked by diversification, as the economy moves from reliance upon a small number of key industries. Canada's economy, for example, went from relying on resource industries to include technologically advanced manufacturing and services. Today, member states of OPEC still remain heavily reliant on marketing crude oil.

Country	GDP per Capita
Norway	$36,600
United States	$35,750
Switzerland	$30,010
Canada	$29,480
Nigeria	$820
Ethiopia	$780
Sierra Leone	$520

Source: United Nations Development Programme, *UN Human Development Report 2004.*

Figure 12.3 Gross domestic product (in US$) for selected countries.

SOUND BITE "We [Canadians] use as much energy as the entire continent of Africa, home to 700 million people."

David Suzuki Foundation, CBC News Online, June 11, 2003

THE WEB

Link to two organizations that focus on consumerism at www.emp.ca/cwp.

The final stage of economic development is the creation of **mass consumption societies**, such as modern Canada. These societies are overwhelmingly urban and highly industrialized, and most citizens consume large amounts of consumer goods and services. Governments disperse some of the surplus wealth to fund programs that improve social conditions. According to this economic model, development depends on the accumulation of capital, access to new technology, and political institutions that encourage investment, social stability, and continuing economic growth.

Other development theories have emerged to deal with the glaring inability of many Asian and African countries to participate in the global economy. One theory from the 1970s—**dependency theory**—argues that developed countries effectively use their wealth and technological advantages to control economic development in the developing world and set the rules for the global economy. From this point of view, organizations such as the Inter-

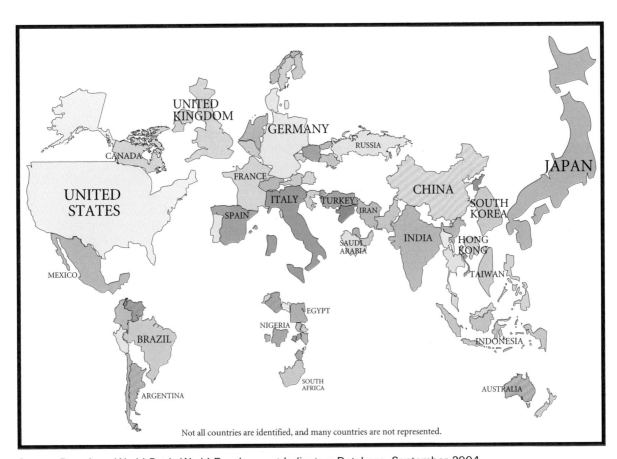

Not all countries are identified, and many countries are not represented.

Source: Data from World Bank, World Development Indicators Database, September 2004.

Figure 12.4 This map shows the size of national economies relative to total world GDP (based on 2003 World Bank rankings). How does the map compare to your usual view of the world?

national Monetary Fund (IMF) and the World Trade Organization (WTO) use loans and trade rules to maintain the dependency of developing countries upon the developed world for economic survival. Like Marxist theory, dependency theory sees capital as a tool of the rich to exploit the poor.

Causes and Consequences of Inequalities

Whatever theory of economic development is used, fundamental questions arise about disparities between developed and developing countries. Why do inequalities exist? How is it that people in developed countries such as Canada enjoy great wealth, while people in many developing countries languish in **mass poverty societies**? In part, the differences are the product of historical forces and economic systems: of technological breakthroughs, empire building, and the need for capital and the debt that results.

The Industrial Revolution and Imperialism

Countries of Europe and, later, North America were the first to undergo the Industrial Revolution in the 18th and 19th centuries. Financial revolution (which made capital available for investment) combined with technological innovations (such as steam technology) led to industrialization and then mass production. This gave states such as Britain, Germany, and the United States a tremendous economic advantage by the mid-19th century.

Economic advantage translated into military superiority, which enabled the first industrialized states to shape a world economic system to support their own needs. As described in Chapter 4, states competed to create global empires, colonizing most of Africa, Asia, and South America. From Cambodia to Cuba to the Congo, early industrialized states established and exploited colonies for raw materials and as markets for their manufactured goods. To preserve their economic preeminence, imperial powers often discouraged industrial development in their colonies. The process of empire building thus widened the economic gap between industrialized states and the rest of the world.

Development Loans and Plans

Many developing countries are rich in natural resources—for example, copper in Chile and petroleum in Nigeria. What they lack is the technology and capital needed to exploit resources, develop industry, and diversify their economies. Developed countries have long recognized this need for capital. Perhaps the oldest international economic development organization

Figure 12.5 A soldier stands guard in 2001 at one of two sites in China where CANDU nuclear power plants are being built. CANDU reactors are a cornerstone of Canada's atomic export industry. The Canadian government funded the Chinese purchases with a $1.5 billion loan in 1996.

was proposed by Canada in 1950 at a meeting of the Commonwealth in Colombo, Sri Lanka. The Colombo Plan for Co-operative Economic Development in South and Southeast Asia was founded in 1951 to provide development funds to Asian countries that had been British colonies. As the United States, Japan, and European countries became donor countries, the plan grew.

As you learned in Chapter 9, the federal Canadian International Development Agency (CIDA) was founded in 1968 to support development through small-scale loans and projects throughout the world. However, development programs often blended economic theory and good intentions with self-interest and geopolitical realities.

During the Cold War, the Colombo Plan was one way the West discouraged developing countries from turning to the Soviet Union for investment and technology. The banks and political leaders of the developed world encouraged developing countries to borrow to build massive **infrastructure** projects, such as hydro-electric dams (see Chapter 8, The Suez Crisis and the UN Emergency Force, pages 289–90), communications systems, transportation systems, and so on. Developing countries were also encouraged to increase military spending. Often the projects and loans were ill advised. Once the projects were started, many developing countries were unable to earn the foreign currency to repay the loans.

Debt Servicing and Protectionism

Why do developing countries have problems paying off their debts? Many developing countries use up their limited wealth simply servicing foreign debts. That is, they pay interest only, with little hope of ever repaying the principal. African states alone pay over $200 million every week in interest on their foreign debts. They have nothing left over to invest in development or in such services as clean drinking water and basic health care (see Drop the Debt, Chapter 1, page 31).

There are many other reasons for the ongoing debt crisis. War, natural disasters, and environmental degradation leave some of the poorest countries unable to feed their populations. They become dependent on foreign governments for assistance, including development loans. For many developing states, the chief exports are agricultural commodities such as sugar, coffee, or grains. Despite efforts of agencies such as the World Trade Organization to promote freer trade, developing countries remain at a disadvantage. In particular, the United States and the European Union have used subsidies to protect their agricultural industries. Leaders of developing countries that rely on agricultural exports have argued that the multilateral trade system has failed to remove trade barriers. Until the system gives them greater access to markets in developed countries, they say, they will be trapped in a spiral of foreign debt and economic crises. As you read in Chapter 10 (pages 362–63), WTO members have committed to reducing agricultural subsidies.

Canada has been a world leader in efforts to get developed countries to forgive the debts of developing nations. For example, in September 2004,

THE WEB

Learn more about debt at www.emp.ca/cwp.

SOUND BITE "Trade is key to development and development objectives are best served by a strong multilateral world trade system, [but] trade is not a direct cure for poverty."

Cham Prasidh, Cambodian commerce minister, addressing a UN Conference on Trade and Development, June 2002

the Canadian government forgave the $9 million in debts owed by Ethiopia, Ghana, and Senegal, which are among the most indebted countries in sub-Saharan Africa. Canada also announced plans to forgive a further $1.1 billion in debt from the world's poorest countries. The IMF and the World Bank also intend to pardon a portion of developing countries' debts. Still, developed countries have forgiven only a small portion of debt.

Consequences: The Asian Economic Crisis

The desperate need of developing countries for investment capital has had other consequences. The Asian economic crisis of the late 1990s is one example. Countries such as Thailand, Indonesia, South Korea, and the Philippines borrowed heavily so that they could develop economically. To attract foreign capital, they increased interest rates and "tied" their currencies to the US dollar. That is, the value of local currencies fluctuated with the value of the US dollar. Foreign investors were attracted by the possibilities of quick profits and invested heavily. Share prices on Asian stock markets reached dizzying heights.

The new communications and banking technologies that had made the boom (economic expansion) possible made the bust (economic contraction) just as dramatic when Thailand's currency, the *bhat*, ran into trouble. In the resulting crisis, fearful foreign investors quickly pulled out more than US$100 billion. The Asian governments then had to spend their foreign currency reserves to pay interest and support their own currencies. Unemployment soared as exports collapsed and factories closed. Foreign banks demanded payments and refused further credit, compounding the crisis.

The Asian crisis spread from emerging industrial economies such as Thailand and Indonesia to industrial powers such as South Korea and the massive developed economy of Japan. With a world economy based on global trade, the impact was soon felt globally. Countries such as Canada were affected, especially in British Columbia. A global response was required. The IMF extended emergency loans to the hardest-hit developing countries, with conditions, and those governments had to cut back on their already limited social programs. Industrial assets were often sold at discount prices, increasing foreign control.

1997 January–March Thai and South Korean currencies heavily traded

1997 July 1 China regains Hong Kong from Britain

1997 July 2 Thai currency falls 30% in value

1997 July–1998 November Asian currencies dive in value

1997 October 20–23 Hong Kong stock market suffers historic losses

1997 October 27 Global stock markets plunge to decade lows

1998 Hong Kong, South Korean, Thai, Indonesian economies decline; economic crises in Russia and Brazil; British Columbia enters recession

1999 Asian economies begin to grow again

Figure 12.6 Timeline: The Asian economic crisis.

Economic Disparities and Daily Life

Economic inequalities and debt burdens are more than theories. They have daily consequences for people living in many developing countries. You have already considered how most people in the world have no access to reliable electricity. More dramatically, almost 40 percent of humankind lacks basic sanitation. Approximately one billion people have no access to clean drinking water. The results: disease and death, particularly for infants and children.

Taking a Stand   Dr. James Orbinski

Confronted with global inequalities and human suffering, how can an individual or organization take action? There have been few clearer indications of how this question might be answered than the speech given by Dr. James Orbinski when he accepted the 1999 Nobel Peace Prize for Doctors Without Borders/Médecins Sans Frontières (MSF). Orbinski told his audience that for the developed world, as for MSF, humanitarian action must be taken, and it must be free—free of conditions and political interference: "humanitarian action that is not tied to state interests, that is not tied to conditional aid, that is not tied to military objectives, but . . . humanitarian assistance that is tied to the dignity of people."

James Orbinski and his MSF colleagues are dedicated to upholding human dignity by providing medical and humanitarian assistance to victims of natural disasters and human conflicts. In the process, they often put their lives on the line. They refuse to be political pawns (see Chapter 10, pages 340–41).

Born in 1960, James Orbinski arrived in Montreal from Britain as a young boy. At university, he studied both medicine and international relations because he wanted to make a difference in the world. After graduating, he worked with MSF missions in Africa and South America. He was one of the few foreign doctors working in Rwanda in 1994 (see Chapter 11, pages 371, 399). His work helping victims of the ethnic violence there deepened his commitment to MSF and his anger at international indifference. In 1999, he wrote that the failure of Western governments to take action in humanitarian crises was not only a moral failure, but the single greatest challenge facing global security:

> State humanitarianism is a smoke screen that hides a profound dereliction of political duty. More often than not, states have failed to uphold international humanitarian law, particularly in the face of genocide and crimes against humanity. In Rwanda, up to a million people died in the genocide as the UN Security Council and member states stood by and cut UN troops back from 2,000 to 400. After the worst of the killings were over, international troops were deployed in neighbouring Zaire to deliver aid and smile for the cameras.

Orbinski continues to devote his energies to humanitarian action. He helped to establish Dignitas International, an NGO dedicated to improving the quality of life of people affected by HIV/AIDS in the developing world, especially in sub-Saharan Africa, and especially children. He has spearheaded Canadian efforts to encourage multinational pharmaceutical companies to make drugs for HIV/AIDS available at low cost to developing countries. He has lobbied the same companies to develop drugs to combat neglected diseases, such as malaria, that are confined to the developing world—and which, therefore, do not promise enormous profits.

Orbinski's work raises economic and political questions. He insists that the solutions to health crises are chiefly political. In a recent speech, Orbinski was typically direct: "We need to change the global rules to prioritize people's health needs over profit." Because he is keen to involve young people, Orbinski has spoken at schools across Canada. He encourages and challenges students to inform themselves about the HIV/AIDS crisis and the issue of drug costs, and then to work to promote human dignity over profit and political expediency.

Questions

1. What types of work could be included under humanitarian action?
2. Explain why James Orbinski views the struggle over HIV/AIDS as a political battle.
3. In what ways can Orbinski and his colleagues be considered true global citizens?
4. Visit www.emp.ca/cwp to learn more about the NGOs MSF and Dignitas International. What are their objectives? How might you become involved with their work?

In earlier chapters, you considered the HIV/AIDS crisis in the developing world (see Chapter 9, Stephen Lewis, page 327). The United Nations estimated in 2004 that US$15 billion is required to deal with HIV/AIDS in Africa each year, at a time when African countries spend more than $13 billion annually servicing foreign debts. In the developed world, HIV/AIDS is increasingly treatable with drugs. The same drugs are simply too expensive for many developing countries and health care systems that are being overwhelmed by the HIV/AIDS pandemic. The result is a humanitarian catastrophe. In 2003 more than 5 million people worldwide became infected with HIV/AIDS. The disease is also spreading in Eastern Europe and South Asia. By 2020, it is estimated that more people will have died across the world from HIV/AIDS than were killed in the two world wars of the 20th century.

Check YOUR UNDERSTANDING

1. Create a flow chart or step diagram to show the main stages in the process of economic development.
2. Explain briefly why economies incur debt (as do businesses and individuals) in their efforts to develop and expand wealth.
3. In point form, list at least three causes and three effects of the Asian economic crisis.
4. Why do some leaders in developing countries argue that the global trading system is not truly free?
5. How does the AIDS pandemic reveal the inequalities between developed and developing countries?

Global Impact of Trade and Business

Economic disparities and the pace of change vary enormously among developing countries. There are extreme contrasts between rich and poor within each developing country, and between urban and rural life. Development sometimes makes these differences more pronounced. Even in the slums of cities such as Mumbai, India, or Mexico City, people have access to amenities such as electricity and clean drinking water, which are lacking in rural areas. Thus cities become magnets, and slums expand. Because the middle class, professionals, and political and business leaders concentrate in cities, rural areas become more isolated, lacking many services.

India provides an example of a developing country experiencing rapid change. Until the late 1980s, India was largely closed to foreign investment. Reforms were introduced to attract foreign investment to fuel economic growth. India's middle class and business elite grew, prospering in major cities such as Mumbai and New Delhi as new industries—particularly information technology—expanded. The majority of Indians, however, still live in poverty in rural villages, or in the slums of Kolkata, Mumbai, and other large cities. According to 2002 World Bank statistics, 35 percent of Indians live on less than US$1 a day.

Political debates within India about persistent economic inequalities and the consequences of development are intense. In the 2004 election, the Bharatiya Janata Party government boasted of its economic policies and of India's growing prosperity. The majority of Indians had not shared in this prosperity, however, and the disillusionment of many poorer Indians contributed to defeat the BJP at the polls (see Chapter 3, pages 78–79).

Figure 12.7 This cyber café in Bangalore, India, is always busy. Bangalore is a centre of India's burgeoning information technology industry.

Not just in India, but around the world, the gap between the poor and the prosperous is widening, despite efforts of the United Nations and other organizations. The scale is staggering. For example, the combined wealth of the world's richest 1 percent of people exceeds that of the poorest 60 percent. Some significant progress has been made among the poorest countries. Life expectancy has increased and infant mortality has decreased in most developing countries, except in sub-Saharan Africa. The basic fact of global economic disparity, however, remains.

> **SOUND BITE** "Is globalization about 'eradication of world poverty,' or is it a mutant variety of colonialism, remote controlled and digitally operated? . . . [A]nswers vary depending on whether they come from the villages and fields of rural India, from the slums and shantytowns of urban India, from the livingrooms of the burgeoning middle class, or from the boardrooms of the big business houses."
>
> *Arundhati Roy,* Power Politics, *2001*

World leaders have acknowledged that ignoring world inequalities could lead to environmental, economic, and political chaos. Many leaders also recognize that the dominant model of economic development—based on competition, constant economic growth, and mass consumption—has to change. Development must be sustainable. This recognition raises hard choices for both the developed countries of the North and the developing countries of the South. The situation demands new levels of global cooperation.

Chapter 9 described how the UN Millennium Development Goals were established to stimulate sustainable development in important areas. The targets, to be reached by 2015, are to cut extreme poverty in half, provide universal access to primary education, reduce infant mortality by two-thirds, and improve access to clean water and adequate sanitation. Progress, however, has been painfully slow: developed countries have not pledged the needed funds.

Global Financial Institutions

Earlier chapters have described international efforts after World War II to create organizations that would preserve peace, protect the environment, and respect human rights. Driving these efforts was a political realization that the world's financial and trading systems must be stable and open. In Chapter 10, you learned about global organizations such as the IMF, the World Bank, GATT, and the WTO. Perspectives differ on their success and fairness, but few would argue that these organizations were not integral and necessary to the international financial system.

> **SOUND BITE** "This is an impressive crowd: the haves and have-mores. Some people call you the elite; I call you my base."
>
> *George W. Bush, addressing a fundraising dinner for the Archdiocese of New York, October 2000*

> **SOUND BITE** "Countries have really got to be able to manage their economies much better or they are going to be hurt and won't get the benefits of globalization. . . . [B]eing bailed out by the IMF, even with rules and everything, is not the way to solve their problems."
>
> *Vernon Smith, 2002 Nobel Prize winner in economics*

Figure 12.8 How does this cartoon portray the relationship between global business and the world? Do you agree with this view? Explain.

The IMF and World Bank commonly place conditions on loans to developing countries. Governments are usually required to practise **fiscal austerity**. This means they cannot run deficits and must reduce spending. Often, social and education programs are the first to be cut. Thus it is usually the poorest citizens who suffer most from austerity measures. Developing countries may also be required to allow direct foreign investment. Naturally, many citizens resent these requirements as a form of **neocolonial** economic control.

As you read above, large debt led to political and economic instability in Asia in the late 1990s. In 2001–2, fiscal policies imposed to meet IMF loan conditions led to popular hostility and repeated collapses of Argentina's government. Obviously, debt can leave governments, particularly in Africa and South America, unable to meet the most basic needs of their citizens. Politics is about making choices. For many developing countries facing debt, financial institutions such as the IMF and World Bank have left little or no room in the most fundamental choice of all: how to use scarce resources.

Transnational Corporations

PRESS PLAY

The Take (2004), a documentary written by Naomi Klein and directed by Avi Lewis, explores a movement by unemployed Argentinian workers to take over factories that were abandoned in the wake of Argentina's financial collapse. (NR)

Shell, Sony, IBM, and Coca-Cola are household names around the world. For supporters and opponents of economic globalization alike, these and other **transnational corporations** (TNCs) are the symbols of the new global economic order. While businesses with operations in several countries are hardly new, TNCs are truly global, with operations and offices in dozens of countries. Their impact upon the global economy is enormous.

The world's 200 largest TNCs—including Exxon–Mobil, General Motors, and Mitsubishi—account for the majority of the world's industrial output. More significantly, their power is concentrated in only a few countries. In 1999, more than 140 of the largest 200 TNCs were headquartered in the United States, Germany, or Japan. None had headquarters outside Europe, North America, Japan, or South Korea. The concentration of economic power and influence is not being diluted.

One way to gauge the relative influence of TNCs is to compare them to national economies. To do this, economists compare GDPs of countries with the economic contribution (value added) of TNCs, which includes income, wages, and so on. This is a more accurate comparison than using sales figures alone. As Figure 12.9 shows, 29 of the largest 100 economic entities in the world in the year 2000 were TNCs, not states. In addition, both the number of TNCs on the list, and their share of the total, rose steadily between 1990 and 2000. The trend continues.

TNCs in the World Economy, 2000 (billions US$)

Rank	TNC/Country	Value added*	Rank	TNC/Country	Value added*	Rank	TNC/Country	Value added*
1	United States	9810	35	Israel	110	69	Wal-Mart Stores	30
2	Japan	4765	36	Portugal	106	70	IBM	27
3	Germany	1866	37	Iran	105	71	Volkswagen	24
4	United Kingdom	1427	38	Egypt	99	72	Cuba	24
5	France	1294	39	Ireland	95	73	Hitachi	24
6	China	1080	40	Singapore	92	74	TotalFinaElf	23
7	Italy	1074	41	Malaysia	90	75	Verizon Communications	23
8	Canada	701	42	Colombia	81	76	Matsushita Electric Industrial	22
9	Brazil	595	43	Philippines	75	77	Mitsui	20
10	Mexico	575	44	Chile	71	78	E.On	20
11	Spain	561	45	Exxon Mobil	63	79	Oman	20
12	South Korea	457	46	Pakistan	62	80	Sony	20
13	India	457	47	General Motors	56	81	Mitsubishi	20
14	Australia	388	48	Peru	53	82	Uruguay	20
15	Netherlands	370	49	Algeria	53	83	Dominican Republic	20
16	Taiwan	309	50	New Zealand	51	84	Tunisia	19
17	Argentina	285	51	Czech Republic	51	85	Phillip Morris	19
18	Russia	251	52	United Arab Emirates	48	86	Slovakia	19
19	Switzerland	239	53	Bangladesh	47	87	Croatia	19
20	Sweden	229	54	Hungary	46	88	Guatemala	19
21	Belgium	229	55	Ford Motor	44	89	Luxembourg	19
22	Turkey	200	56	Daimler-Chysler	42	90	SBC Communications	19
23	Austria	189	57	Nigeria	41	91	Itochi	18
24	Saudi Arabia	173	58	General Electric	39	92	Kazakhstan	18
25	Denmark	163	59	Toyota Motor	38	93	Slovenia	18
26	Hong Kong, China	163	60	Kuwait	38	94	Honda Motor	18
27	Norway	162	61	Romania	37	95	Eni Group	18
28	Poland	158	62	Royal Dutch/Shell	36	96	Nissan Motor	18
29	Indonesia	153	63	Morocco	33	97	Toshiba	17
30	South Africa	126	64	Ukraine	32	98	Syria	17
31	Thailand	122	65	Slemens	32	99	GlaxoSmithKline	17
32	Finland	121	66	Vietnam	31	100	BT	17
33	Venezuela	120	67	Libya	31			
34	Greece	113	68	BP	30			

* Value added is the sum of salaries, pretax profits, depreciation, and amortization.

Source: United Nations Conference on Trade and Development, August 12, 2002; http://r0.unctad.org/en/Press/pr0247en.htm.

Figure 12.9 Transnational corporations and countries: a comparison. This table shows the world's top 100 economies, based on value added.

Point:
Counterpoint → TNCs in the Developing World: Curse or Cure?

TNCs as Cure

by Gary M. Quinlivan

Let's address some of the myths that critics of multinational [transnational] corporations claim to be facts. This article does not . . . deny that there are specific cases that reflect badly on all multinational corporations. . . . Such cases, however, are rare, given that there are over 60,000 multinational corporations.

Competition is not destructive; . . . given free trade, [it] delivers mutually beneficial gains from exchange and sparks the collaborative effort of all nations to produce commodities efficiently. As a consequence, competition improves world welfare while dampening the spirit of nationalism and, thus, promoting world peace. . . .

[C]oordinated international manipulations of markets are rarely conducted by large multinational corporations but are almost always government supported and directed (for example, OPEC, the Association of Coffee Producing Countries, and the Cocoa Producers Alliance). Further, government-sponsored **cartels** are not concerned about the poor. In the 1970s, OPEC's price distortions were a major source not only of world recession but also of the increased external debt and poverty of developing countries. Free markets protect the poor from the prolonged abuses of cartels.

Concerns about multinational corporation infringements on national sovereignty lack substance. Multinational corporations . . . are heavily monitored. . . . From 1991 to 1998, according to the United Nations, there were 895 new foreign direct investment regulations enacted by more than 60 countries.

Further, multinationals are not siphoning jobs from high- to low-wage countries; in fact, they tend to preserve high-wage jobs in developed countries; in 1998, 75 percent of foreign direct investment went to developed countries. Besides, labor costs alone do not determine where multinational corporations base their affiliates; other variables—such as political stability, infrastructure, education levels, future market potential, taxes, and governmental regulations—are more decisive. In 1998, multinational corporations had eighty-six million employees—nineteen million in developing countries. . . .

Evidence supplied by the World Bank and United Nations strongly suggests that multinational corporations are a key factor in the large improvement in welfare that has occurred in developing countries over the last forty years. In sub-Saharan Africa and South Asia, where the presence of multinational corporations is negligible, severe poverty rates persist. . . .

[F]rom 1980 to 1998, world child labor rates (the percentage of children working between the ages of 10 and 14) tumbled from 20 to 13 percent. [They] dropped from 27 to 10 percent in East Asia and the Pacific, from 13 to 9 percent in Latin America and the Caribbean, and from 14 to 5 percent in the Middle East and North Africa. Interestingly, regions lacking multinational corporations had the worst child labor rates and the smallest reductions: sub-Saharan Africa's and South Asia's child labor rates dropped from 35 to 30 percent and from 23 to 16 percent, respectively. . . .

Moreover, multinational corporations are not committed to the destruction of the world's environment but instead have been the driving force in the spread of "green" technologies and in creating markets for "green products." Market incentives such as threat of liability, consumer boycotts, and the negative impact on reputation have forced firms to police their foreign affiliates and to maintain high environmental standards. . . .

When multinational corporations make profits, . . . [b]oth the multinational corporations and [the] domestic country are better off—the developing country receives jobs, an expanded tax base, and new technologies. . . .

Developing countries must be allowed to further themselves economically through free markets and the expansion of multinational corporations. . . .

Source: Excerpted from Gary M. Quinlivan, "Multinational Corporations: Myths and Facts." Acton Institute for the Study of Religion and Liberty, *Religion and Liberty* (November/December, 2000); http://www.acton.org/publicat/randl/article.php?id=364.

TNCs as Curse

by A.K.M. Enayet Kabir

[U]nplanned industrialization for manufactured goods has often meant the disruption of the agricultural cycle in many developing countries. The effect of a cash crop or wage economy on nutrition has been one of lowering the level of nutrition by disturbing the balance achieved under **subsistence economy** (producing enough goods to sustain life, with no surplus), introducing multinationals' processed foods as "prestige foods," limiting the amount and quality of subsistence crops in favor of cash crops. To introduce adequate nutrition, it is important to bring about changes that are in keeping with the established food habits of the people, and are acceptable within the framework of their value system.

The globalization of the world economy is stimulating massive investments by the transnational corporations, which are acting as dynamo to produce more jobs and higher profits worldwide. However, poverty and inequality are on the increase in the developing world. The absence of agreed rules on basic rights of workers . . . could threaten the whole elaborate edifice of the global market. Governments are trying to gain competitive advantage through the . . . exploitation of workers. The media image of the global economy is of a technology-driven, high production, free market gearing itself up for this 21st century. But how "free" is the market . . . without a workers' rights clause? The world cannot tolerate an economic system that depends on repression for profit, that exploits women, and that makes slavery a sound business option. The workers' rights clause will help protect workers from exploitation. Its aim is not to undermine economic competition, but to enhance it by removing unfair advantages. Unlike fly-by-night transnationals, who are interested only in making cheap goods for a quick profit, workers have a long-term interest in their countries' prosperity. A workers' rights clause will restore to people the basic human rights that globalization has stolen from them.

Unfortunately, the real beneficiaries of the current world trading system are not the developing countries, but the TNCs. . . . Unchecked and unregulated, the labor market in the global economy is becoming nothing more than a vast shopping mall for the TNCs. . . . [I]f there is a passionate agreement among the multinationals that they should cover copyright and the Protection of Intellectual Property, why should these rules not cover workers' rights? A workers' rights clause will help bring the TNCs under the rule of law, and would make it impossible for some irresponsible TNCs to leap from country to country in search of a government prepared to violate workers' rights. . . .

With their growing power, corporations are regulating themselves. Issues once considered a responsibility of the state or of religious institutions—such as social justice, environmental impact or human rights—are all affected by corporate decision-makers. Considering this fundamental shift of power—with the TNCs becoming a "law unto itself," who will bring the global corporations into account?

. . . [S]ociety may affirm the legitimacy of the profit motive, so long as business is also conscious of its contributions to the wider society. Corporate governance, therefore, must balance both the interests of the wider society and the interests of the corporations. Worldwide citizens, consumers, NGOs, etc. have the key role to play in linking corporate governance structures to societal stakeholders, and must find a mechanism to make corporations accountable. . . .

We need strategies to create a world with a human face. We need new economic systems that put people first—not profits. The law of profit alone . . . could not feed the downtrodden and starving millions in the developing world. Possibly realizing this, the 1998 Nobel Laureate for Economics, Amartya Sen, said that the validity of any economic policy should be based on whether it takes into account its impact on people who are on the "down side of the economy."

The rich and powerful—who are paradoxically as much at risk as the poor and the weak—must recognize that they cannot continue on the present course. . . .

Source: Excerpted from A.K.M. Enayet Kabir, "Transnational Corporations in the Age of Globalization." *The Independent* (Dhaka, Bangladesh, May 27, 2001); http://www.globalpolicy.org/socecon/tncs/2001/kabi0527.htm.

Articulating a Personal Stand

1. Rank both Quinlivan's arguments in favour of transnational corporations and Kabir's arguments against transnational corporations from most to least effective (see Chapter 6, Debating a Political Issue, page 227).

2. Research at least three specific examples that further support both arguments. The articles' source Web sites are useful starting points. Using the information you gather, hold a political debate on this topic.

PRESS PLAY

In *Roger & Me* (1989), popular American documentary filmmaker Michael Moore tries to get an interview with Roger Smith, chief executive officer of General Motors, after GM closes its plant in Flint, Michigan, Moore's hometown. (14A)

The impact of TNCs is undeniable, but the issue of who benefits from them is hotly debated (see Point Counterpoint, Chapter 10, pages 364–65). In developing countries, TNCs create employment and provide the foreign investment and advanced technologies needed for development and improved living conditions. Because TNCs control 70 percent of all world trade (as of 2004), they can also help developing countries integrate into the global economy and gain access to foreign markets. Most political leaders in developing countries, including China and India, now encourage TNC investment.

Economic power gives TNCs great political influence. The mere threat of withdrawing investment is often enough to convince politicians to meet their demands. Moreover, TNC practices in developing countries have raised labour and environmental issues. Many TNCs, for example, have used subcontractors who exploit workers. Clothing manufacturers such as Nike and The Gap, among others, were targeted by anti-globalization activists when it was revealed that some of their products were manufactured in low-wage **sweatshops**, where working conditions were dangerous and unhealthy. Despite international activism, child labour remains an issue. Well-intentioned efforts by TNCs to enforce better working standards often break down.

Check Your Understanding

1. What role do global financial institutions such as the World Bank and IMF play in promoting economic development?
2. Should global financial institutions have the right to impose conditions on the governments of developing countries? Why or why not?
3. Construct a graphic organizer summarizing the positive and negative impacts TNCs have on developing countries.
4. Explain how TNCs exert political control over developing countries.

Globalization and Globalism

Few words in contemporary politics have become more politically charged than "globalization." Further examination of this phenomenon and the conflicts it provokes requires a closer look at the concept. **Globalization** is a set of processes by which countries and people around the world become increasingly interdependent. Those processes encompass not only global trade and international finance, but technological and cultural exchange. In recent decades, globalization has been driven by mass media and digital technologies and characterized by rapid change and world economic integration (including the spread of global brands).

Globalization Through Time

The processes of globalization are as old as human society. Cultural and technological exchange between societies is not new. For example, when Venetian merchant Marco Polo travelled to the Mongol court in Beijing,

China, in the late 13th century, he was an agent of globalization. Marco Polo returned to Venice not only with goods, but also with insights about the advanced culture and technologies he had encountered. Trade with China and Japan came to dominate European economic activity. Two centuries later, Europeans went in search of a sea route to "the East" and instead encountered Aboriginal peoples of the Americas. Cultures clashed, and European diseases killed millions of Aboriginal people. As you read earlier, globalization changed and accelerated during the 19th century as European states built empires using advancements in communications, weapons, and transportation technology—including the steamship and the telegraph.

In recent decades, globalization has been transformed not only by powerful new technologies, but by a powerful new ideology: **globalism**. Globalism is not a single, fixed idea. It is a continuum, or spectrum, of beliefs. People may adhere passionately to all of these beliefs, accept many of them, a few, or none at all. Taken together, the fundamental ideas of globalism construct a coherent worldview. These include the beliefs that

- global markets must be integrated and free of trade barriers (such as tariffs or government regulations)
- national governments and international institutions (such as the World Trade Organization) must promote world trade
- globalization is inevitable and cannot be avoided or reversed
- powerful economies such as that of United States may be able to influence globalization, but no single state can control it
- impersonal market forces direct globalization
- globalization is beneficial, particularly for the poor, who need the prosperity it alone can offer
- globalization, particularly through the mass media, will spread democracy globally.

There is considerable evidence to support globalism. For example, most observers would agree that mass media and globalization are spreading democracy in the developing world. Still, globalism can also be used by political and business leaders to deflect criticism. For example, they might claim that globalization is inevitable and beyond their control. As you have seen, many critics say that the gap between the world's wealthy and impoverished countries is widening, despite increases in global trade. These critics insist that international institutions must change and adopt regulations to correct this.

Most analysts of globalization now believe that most nation-states are better able to resist the negative impacts

Figure 12.10 This relief sculpture in Merida, Mexico, shows a Spaniard with his feet planted on the heads of Mayans, the indigenous people of the area. What does this say about the impact of European contact?

of globalization than was previously thought. That is, developed countries can capture the benefits of global economic integration and also devise adjustment strategies to protect those adversely affected at home. International institutions, such as the WTO, have also proven to be much less of a threat to domestic policy autonomy than was initially feared (see Chapter 2, defeat of the MAI, page 65).

There are also cultural issues. Many of the familiar icons of globalization—Coca-Cola, McDonald's "golden arches," US movies and pop music—are specifically Western. Some politicians and activists in Africa and Asia denounce globalization as an encroachment of Western values upon their civilizations: a not-so-subtle form of cultural imperialism. Yet globalization is a long-term process going back millennia, involving the sharing and borrowing of ideas, cultures, and goods across continents. It has never been entirely one-way. In different eras it has travelled from East to West, and West to East. Amartya Sen of India, who won the 1998 Nobel Prize in economics, has written: "Globalization is not new nor is it just Westernization: over thousands of years, globalization has progressed through travel, trade, migration, spread of cultural influences and dissemination of knowledge and understanding (including science and technology)."

The Global Village

Globalization is about more than trade. It is about ideas—on politics, for example—and communications. Indeed, the main force driving recent globalization has been mass media and innovations in communications technology. As you read in Chapter 1, Marshall McLuhan, the Canadian "philosopher of communications," was one of the first to foresee how electronic mass media were transforming society. More than 40 years ago, he coined the term the "global village" to describe a world in which all humanity would be interconnected—or "wired." Today, e-mail and the Internet connect people and businesses globally and instantaneously, and television broadcasts events live around the globe.

Figure 12.11 Marshall McLuhan's communications theories became immensely popular in the 1960s and were then dismissed. With the advent of the Internet, they are influential once more.

What does it mean to live in a global village? In part, it means that we are instantly and constantly aware of events happening across the globe, and that no nation or state is entirely isolated from global issues. Communications technology draws all people closer together. Political leaders cannot ignore external influences or world events, even if they might wish to do so. More importantly, living in a global village means that we are neighbours, responsible for one another.

A Global Culture?

McDonald's restaurants spring up beside cafés on Paris boulevards, in Moscow, and in Jaipur. American and English top-10 hits blare from radios in southeast Asia. Familiar magazines crowd racks in airports from Toronto to Tokyo. US movies break attendance records around the world. According to some critics, popular products from corporations such as McDonald's, Starbucks, and Disney are not just convenient and enjoyable lifestyle choices; they may be displacing local cultures. Will we end up with a global culture that looks, sounds, and tastes American? Evidence that a single dominant global culture is emerging seems overwhelming.

Cultural industries—music, movies, and media—are dominated by a small number of corporations, chiefly American. Disney Corporation, for example, not only makes children's movies and runs theme parks, it owns television networks ABC and ESPN and a variety of print media and Internet sites. News Corporation, a massive media conglomerate headed by Australian Rupert Murdoch, controls television networks, film studios, newspapers, book and magazine publishers, and satellite and cable television services throughout the English-speaking world and in Asia and Latin America. The dominance and reach of these and other TNCs also seem to be contributing to a kind of linguistic globalization. Will the richness of traditional cultures and languages be lost?

Mandarin is still the most common native language, but English is well on its way to being the undisputed *lingua franca* (common language) of the global economy and culture. Most TNCs use English as their primary business language. Eighty percent of the documents posted on the Internet are in English. In fact, half the languages spoken today are expected to disappear by the end of the century.

There are other cultural—and environmental—consequences. Globally driven economic changes have had a huge impact upon indigenous peoples. In Tanzania, Africa, forests have been cleared to create large commercial farms to produce export crops. This has displaced the cattle-herding Masai people and their way of life. In the highlands of Vietnam, rapidly expanding coffee plantations—also serving the export market—have led to deforestation and the loss of indigenous lands. In British Columbia, the Haida are dealing with the impact of NAFTA and forest exports upon their traditional lifestyle as they fight to protect the ancient Pacific coastal forests from overexploitation.

THE WEB

Find out who owns what when it comes to media at www.emp.ca/cwp.

PRESS PLAY

In *Super Size Me* (2004), US documentary filmmaker Morgan Spurlock turns the camera on himself and his health when he forces himself to eat nothing but the fast food of a famous TNC for one whole month. (PG)

Figure 12.12 Quebec director Denys Arcand and his daughter Ming Xia pose in Hollywood in 2004. Arcand's film won the Oscar for best foreign language film. Quebec's film industry has thrived internationally, telling Québécois stories in French.

Cross-Cultural Enrichment and Glocalization

Globalization is not all doom and gloom. As cultures and cultural products become increasingly mobile and interconnected, most cultures are proving to be surprisingly robust. India's film industry, for example, continues to thrive. "Bollywood," as it is known, produces more movies than Hollywood, and they are not in English. Hindi films with local stars fill theatres across South Asia; video and DVD extend the industry's reach worldwide. Filmmakers in global cities like Hong Kong, Beijing, and Tokyo also influence Hollywood. The presence of foreign cultures can reinvigorate local cultures and traditions that might otherwise be lost.

Music, theatre, art, science, and cuisine in all cultures have developed through contacts with outside forces. The British taste for tea, for example, was acquired centuries ago through contact with India and Sri Lanka. The word "algebra" comes from Arabic. Cultural exchange and borrowing are not new; mass media and information technology have simply accelerated the processes of globalization.

As you learned earlier, urbanization is characteristic of globalization. Some commentators have identified a related economic process: **glocalization**. Professor Thomas Courchene of Queen's University in Kingston, Ontario, has coined the term to refer to the increasing importance of the local, or regional, unit of government in a global economy. The argument is that "global cities" are becoming increasingly important relative to nation-states in an era of global competitiveness. As a result, Canadian cities, such as Toronto, experience pressure to become both more autonomous and more directly integrated into the global economy. Thus, many Canadian cities are renegotiating their relationship with the provincial and federal levels of government.

> **SOUND BITE** "The tendency for economic power to shift both to the global and the local levels is captured by the term 'glocalization.'"
>
> *Thomas Courchene, 1999*

Global Crime

Globalization has also changed crime and policing. Powerful, sophisticated terrorist networks and criminal syndicates control the vast trade in drugs, for example. New technologies allow "dirty" money to flow between states and bank accounts, almost without trace. Sharing information between local and national police forces and investigative bodies—such as the RCMP and the FBI—has become vital. Police forces have had to adapt and use global strategies to track and combat international crime. **Interpol**—the world's largest police organization—acts as a global communication centre to help police forces in its 182 member states coordinate efforts and share data. When priceless works of art disappear from post-war Iraq, for example, or when human smugglers exploit the desperate desire of the poor to escape to a better life, global police efforts are essential.

At the same time, some individuals and groups are concerned that so much personal data in the hands of police and government could lead to abuses of the rule of law and invasions of privacy—a kind of police state. As you learned in Chapter 11, these concerns have become especially pronounced since the United States and its allies embarked upon a "war on terrorism" after the attacks of September 11, 2001. Security and police forces now have access to such data as international air traveller lists, for example, and states are often willing share this information in the quest for security.

THE WEB

Learn more about the workings of Interpol at www.emp.ca/cwp.

Check Your Understanding

1. Why is it said that globalization is not a new phenomenon?
2. List and briefly explain four key components of the ideology of globalism.
3. What does it mean to live in a global village?
4. What is glocalization?
5. How and why has the process of globalization changed the nature of crime and policing?

Globalization: Protest and Debate

Globalization has become a political flashpoint, provoking a wide variety of responses that range from discussion and debate to violence and protests. As involved citizens, many young people in developed countries such as Canada have become active in the anti-globalization movement. Sometimes the protests seem hypocritical: how can you protest globalization while you enjoy living standards that benefit from it, including the cheap and plentiful goods that you consume? For their part, many governments have responded to anti-globalization demands, not by making trade negotiations and summits more open to public input and scrutiny, but by increasing security to keep people out. Security is a legitimate concern, but how can governments and economic organizations expect protestors—and the public—to believe the process is open when G8 summits and WTO meetings are held behind barricades guarded by riot police?

Political Responses to Globalization

THE WEB

Learn more about globalization at www.emp.ca/cwp.

Many societies feel besieged by the social, cultural, and economic changes wrought by globalization. In communities across Canada and the United States, people feel threatened by global competition. As TNCs strive to increase profits, insecure workers fear jobs will be **outsourced** to developing countries to increase profits. Nor is it only lower-skill manufacturing jobs that are being outsourced. Developing countries with highly educated workforces, such as India, are attracting high-skill jobs such as computer programmers, engineers—perhaps even online medical diagnoses in the near future. Numerous North American computer firms have outsourced their networks to Indian companies, and the trend appears to be accelerating.

Some leaders in developed countries promise to use tariffs and trade barriers to insulate their communities from globalization and foreign competition. Protectionism is not new, but low-priced imported goods and lower labour costs in the developing world have made it popular again in many developed countries. In the 2004 US presidential election, for example, outsourcing was portrayed as the chief reason that the American economy had "exported" new jobs instead of creating them.

Fears of the cultural changes that come with globalization can also provoke racist reactions. As you learned in Chapter 4 (page 137), Jean-Marie Le Pen drew on racist ideas about immigration and won surprisingly widespread support in France. He blended those ideas with fears of economic and social changes and promised to keep French culture safe and "pure." Leaders in developing countries have also appealed to extreme nationalism, portraying globalization as the spread of "evil" Western values. Mohammad Mahatir, Malaysia's authoritarian prime minister for 22 years, often praised Asian and Islamic values and condemned "sinful" Western influences. Bowing to growing public pressure, he left office in 2003.

Labour Responses to Globalization

Some of the strongest voices questioning globalization come from labour groups, often in association with NGOs and other citizens' groups. Unions have long been involved in social justice issues, locally and globally. For example, the Canadian Auto Workers (CAW), Canada's largest private sector union, analyzes the potential environmental impact of global trade negotiations in developed and developing countries. In "solidarity," it supports the efforts of workers in the developing world to ensure safer workplaces and better living conditions. It works to safeguard the rights of national governments to continue programs—such as health care, workers' compensation, and employment insurance—free from constraints imposed by global trade rules.

At the same time, unions exist to advance the interests of their members. Outsourcing has made it much more difficult to negotiate higher wages and job security. How unions in Canada and the developed world have dealt with globalization points up a difficult contradiction in opposing globalization. No doubt unions are motivated by altruistic concerns about the impact of globalization on the developing world, but to survive, they must also protect the economic advantage of their members. Perhaps it is only fair that rich, developed countries share higher-paid, skilled jobs with the developing world. Can unions struggle effectively on behalf of women working in appalling sweatshop conditions in the developing world on the one hand, and on the other negotiate to keep and protect high-wage automobile assembly-line workers in Ontario?

Anti-Globalization Protests

Ranks of armed riot police advance, banging their shields. Clouds of tear gas billow through the streets. Thousands of young protestors shout and chant, waving placards denouncing corporate globalization, environmental degradation, and labour and human rights abuses. Images and sounds of confrontation, vandalism, and smashed storefronts are broadcast around the world. These images of anti-globalization protests are etched into the minds of people around the world. Even as political leaders argued the need for increased trade and the alleged inevitability of economic globalization, others rejected this notion as dogma. In Seattle, United States; Davos, Switzerland; Quebec City, Canada; and Genoa, Italy, demonstrators have sought to stop globalization plans that would remove environmental and other protections in the name of economic progress.

Figure 12.13 A protestor lies on the ground during a rally in front of the Italian consulate in Toronto in July 2001. A crowd of some 400 people packed the downtown street, beating drums, chanting, and carrying signs with the image of Carlo Giuliani, 23, a protestor shot and killed by police the previous day at the Genoa summit.

THE WEB

Learn more about the Seattle and Quebec City summits at www.emp.ca/cwp.

The first major anti-globalization protests to grab worldwide media attention erupted during WTO trade talks held in Seattle in late 1999. Using the Internet, activists built a worldwide coalition that saw approximately 50,000 people descend on the summit. During protests, organizers used the same technologies, including cell phones and webcams, to coordinate and broadcast information about the four days of demonstrations that became known as the "Battle of Seattle." Protestors demanded that the WTO and the elite leaders inside open up talks. As confrontations between demonstrators and police escalated into violence, a state of emergency was declared (see Figure 10.11, page 349). The WTO talks themselves collapsed when representatives of developed and developing countries could not reach consensus. It was a public relations disaster for the WTO, but many in the media also questioned the motives and methods of anti-globalization organizers.

After Seattle, anti-globalization protests greeted a series of trade gatherings of world leaders. In April 2001, more than 30,000 activists descended on the Summit of the Americas in Quebec City. Authorities seemed less open to dissent and more committed to security measures that would allow the talks on the Free Trade Area of the Americas (FTAA) to proceed. Chain-link fences and concrete barricades blocked demonstrators from the conference site in old Quebec. Eventually, police clashes resulted in more than 400 arrests. Many people supported the demonstrators' right to speak out and criticized official efforts to undermine protests. Others, including leaders attending the summit from developing countries in South America, criticized the protests. Some suggested demonstrators were arrogant middle-class youth who were indifferent to the desire of governments and citizens in the developing world to take part in trade talks so that they could attain comparable prosperity. From this viewpoint, anti-globalization protests would only delay or damage economic development for developing countries.

Targeting Transnational Corporations

While mass demonstrations attract media attention, other protests are quieter. Many citizens' groups and NGOs, for example, conduct public campaigns to shame TNCs into treating developing countries, their peoples, and the environment in a manner that these groups consider to be more just. Sometimes these campaigns achieve their goals. For example, in early 1995, Shell's plans to sink the *Brent Spar*—a disused oil platform—in the North Atlantic raised a storm of protest. Spearheaded by Greenpeace, public protests and boycotts spread. In Germany alone, Shell gasoline sales dropped by half. By June 1995, Shell reversed its decision and dismantled the *Brent Spar* on land. The incident showed that well-organized campaigns could affect the policies of TNCs.

In the 1990s, acclaimed Nigerian writer and human rights activist Ken Saro-Wiwa criticized Royal Dutch/Shell's oil and gas operations in the Niger Delta and its dealings with Nigeria's military government. Saro-Wiwa's campaign drew international attention to the environmental impact of the oil industry on the traditional way of life of the Ogoni people of the region and their struggle for autonomy. Greenpeace took up the case. Nigeria, however, relies on oil exports for 95 percent of its foreign revenue. The military government arrested Saro-Wiwa in 1992 for activities supporting the Ogoni. Amnesty International launched a letter-writing appeal, as did other NGOs. Saro-Wiwa was released in 1993 and continued his campaign. That year, Shell stopped its operations in the Ogoni region. Ken Saro-Wiwa continued his campaign supporting the Ogoni people and against the government and its dealings with oil and gas companies. In 1995, he was arrested on what appeared to be fabricated charges of murder. Despite worldwide protests, he was hanged. The same year, Nigeria was expelled from the Commonwealth.

The *Brent Spar* campaign and the fate of Ken Saro-Wiwa shone a spotlight on the TNCs and their relationships with governments. TNCs have become the highly visible symbols of economic globalization and lightning rods for opponents of capitalism. Many anti-globalization campaigns now use human rights as a universal standard to measure TNC business practices. Activists argue that TNCs should push for global workers' rights and human rights with the same enthusiasm with which they pursue global trade. They say TNCs often prefer to look the other way when it comes to how their operations are run in developing countries. TNCs sometimes do not ask such vital questions as: Are wages fair? Are workplaces safe? Are children or women exploited? Activists demand that trade talks put these questions centre stage. (See Point Counterpoint, page 416.)

Activists such as Canadian Naomi Klein have focused on this area, which has been called "employment globalization." As was the case with the *Brent Spar*, campaigners against sweatshops have media know-how. For example, before the Athens Olympics in 2004, several anti-sweatshop organizations launched "Play Fair at the Olympics," a campaign to publicize the plight of workers in developing countries who make the brand-name sportswear and equipment used by athletes and heavily promoted during the Olympic Games. Play Fair was intended to pressure the International Olympic Committee and major TNC sponsors to take action to ensure that workers' rights are respected in the developing world.

THE WEB
Learn why some experts say Shell's original plan for the *Brent Spar* was best at www.emp.ca/cwp.

Effective Global Citizenship

As this book has stressed, politics is about making choices. Political leaders and communities large and small must regularly decide which services to fund—health care, education, water, welfare, policing, and so on—and how to fund them. Globalization confronts all citizens, especially young people, with difficult challenges. Even the smallest community in Canada is part of the global village and its pressing needs—from war and terrorism to HIV/AIDS and Third World debt. These issues are complex and troubling, with no easy answers, and they demand our attention and action.

Global citizenship requires critical thinking, if you are to understand and act upon issues effectively. Critical thinking is not cynical thinking. You are

Grassroots Politics and Protest

Naomi Klein and the No Logo Campaign

With her 2000 bestseller *No Logo: Taking Aim at the Brand Bullies,* Toronto activist and journalist Naomi Klein dissected consumer culture to expose the injustices of global capitalism. In particular, she zeroed in on TNC sweatshops where many mass consumer goods are produced. She visited infamous **export processing zones** (areas in developing countries where TNCs set up manufacturing facilities) in the Philippines and elsewhere, where everything from running shoes to laptop computers are produced in often dangerous conditions for low pay. She documented the efforts of North American workers to improve their wages and organize unions. Klein also chronicled the dramatic rise of grassroots anti-globalization protest. The result was impressive. *No Logo* became—in the words of the *New York Times*—a "movement bible" around the world.

One of the most striking elements of anti-globalization grassroots organizing is a masterly use of information technology. Activists have used e-mail and the Internet to focus, publicize, and organize with imagination and skill. Protestors against Shell, Nike, McDonald's, and other TNCs quickly establish Web sites, databases, online petitions, and newsletters that detail upcoming campaigns. Other TNCs, such as Microsoft, have been targets of electronic attacks. According to Klein, these chaotic protests are "the Internet come to life." No Logo has a Web site, of course, which features activist advice and links to other organizations.

In addition to militant public demonstrations—such as the "Battle of Seattle" in 1999 and the Quebec Summit in 2001—grassroots anti-globalization protestors have developed other strategies to subvert (destabilize) corporate advertising (or propaganda, as activists often call it). Through "culture jamming," activists parody marketing campaigns, altering advertising imagery and messages. For example, a graffiti artist in Toronto spray-painted the faces of models on a Gap billboard, transforming them into skulls. Other activists, aware that a corporation's brand and reputation are among its most valuable assets, aim to shame TNCs into improving their employment and environmental practices in developing countries. Still others organize product boycotts to pressure TNCs to end their investments in and support of undemocratic regimes.

Students at Carleton University, for example, organized a boycott of Pepsi in the 1990s, pressuring it to have no dealings with the military dictatorship of Myanmar (Burma).

The No Logo campaign is about much more than selective shopping, however. As Naomi Klein makes clear, "This is not a consumer issue; it's a political issue." The aim of the anti-globalization grassroots protest is more ambitious: to empower citizens to inform themselves about the global economy, to act in their local communities, and to redress the apparent imbalance between global corporations and democratic institutions.

Questions

1. In formulating their tactics, the opponents of global capitalism have learned much from their corporate opponents. How is this so?
2. In what ways can the No Logo campaign be considered political? Explain.

Figure 12.14 The No Logo Web site (www.nologo .org) is constantly updated—offering visitors articles by Naomi Klein and links to anti-globalization organizations.

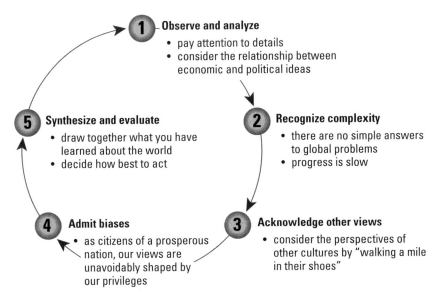

Figure 12.15 Critical thinking is essential for active local and global citizenship.

not tearing issues, institutions, or leaders apart (or down) to feel superior. Critical thinking requires detachment. It involves observing and analyzing, acknowledging and assessing evidence and multiple perspectives. At the same time, it requires that we recognize our biases—as citizens of a prosperous and highly industrialized mass consumption society. Only then can we effectively evaluate the challenges facing us as global citizens and make meaningful choices (see Figure 12.15).

What does global citizenship look like in action? How can the individual citizen respond effectively to global needs? A popular maxim urges you to "think globally and act locally." There are many examples, from Craig Kielburger, who took on the issue of global child labour and sweatshops at the age of 12, to Toronto teenager Nick Dodds, who campaigned against exclusive multimillion-dollar contracts between local school boards and TNCs Coca-Cola and Pepsi. Canadian engineering students helped organize Engineers Without Borders to undertake small-scale development projects (for example, to provide clean water to small communities in sub-Saharan Africa). All these examples share a common element: young people identify global issues about which they are passionate and take concrete steps to address them.

THE WEB

Learn more about Nick Dodds and commercialization of schools at www.emp.ca/cwp.

Check Your Understanding

1. Explain outsourcing.
2. How has outsourcing altered employment patterns in developed and developing countries?
3. Describe several ways in which politicians have responded to the challenges of globalization.

4. Why did the *Brent Spar* campaign mark a turning point in opposition to globalization?
5. How has communications technology such as the Internet affected anti-globalization protest?
6. What, in your view, does it mean to be a global citizen?

The Future of Globalization

As you have seen, opinions on globalization cover the political spectrum. Some leaders and observers say globalization is an inevitable and irreversible force that will bring democracy and better living standards to all humankind. Governments and critics, they say, should trust and facilitate the marketplace and capitalism. Others argue that globalization must be tightly regulated and undergo fundamental change if it is to work in the interests of the world's poor, preserve the environment, and create sustainable development. Is globalization indeed inevitable? Or is it in fact in retreat in the face of rising nationalism and organized protest?

Another Kind of World Summit

Parallel to the WTO meetings, G8 summits, and World Economic summits in Davos are the **World Social Forum** (WSF) summits. According to its charter, the World Social Forum was founded in 2001 to provide an open forum for

> reflective thinking, democratic debate of ideas, formulation of proposals, free exchange of experiences and inter-linking for effective action, by groups and movements of civil society that are opposed to . . . domination of the world by capital and any form of imperialism, and are committed to building a society centered on the human person.

Dubbed the "anti-globalization summits" by the media, the first summit of the World Social Forum, held in Brazil in 2001, attracted 20,000 participants. Instead of focusing on global trade and investment, however, delegates discussed how to establish global labour and environmental standards and a single global development agenda. They applied the logic of globalization (increasing interdependence) to social and environmental issues, rather than merely to questions about the flow of trade and investment capital. The result was globalization with a new direction and a broader base. The WSF summits have grown in size. In September 2004, 75,000 participants attended the World Social Forum in India.

THE WEB

To learn more about the World Social Forum, visit www.emp.ca/cwp.

Globalization and Nationalism

Many supporters claim that the trend to globalization marks an end to the age of nationalism and the nation-state. Some welcome this outcome as a positive consequence of globalization, given the wars and genocides that extreme nationalism has caused over the past century. Others, such as Canadian thinker and writer John Ralston Saul, disagree. Ralston Saul suggests that, on the contrary, nationalism has emerged anew in recent years, marking the end of globalization.

As evidence, Ralston Saul points to the resurgence of nationalist parties in Europe and elsewhere as political responses to increased immigration and economic uncertainties blamed upon outsourcing and globalization. He points to the global resurgence in ethnic and nationalist conflicts since the end of the Cold War, such as in the Balkans, Rwanda, and Sudan. The growing willingness of nation-states—particularly the United States—to act unilaterally in their own national interests, ignoring global institutions such as the United Nations, lends further weight to Ralston Saul's argument. Economic and financial scandals, such as that of Enron in the United States in 2002 and questionable accounting practices involving some of the largest TNCs, have also undermined confidence in the corporate world and in the willingness and ability of governments to regulate business.

Finally, Ralston Saul sees evidence that the globalization agenda directed by international financial institutions and TNCs is being replaced by one that stresses the primary role of countries and citizens in making decisions about global issues, such as the protection of human rights and the environment. Citizens' groups and NGOs have been most active in debating, creating, and supporting such major initiatives as the *Kyoto Protocol* and the International Criminal Court.

Globalism and nationalism: are they incompatible ideologies? Or are they constantly interacting and changing each other in the global village? There are no simple answers to these questions, but how national governments and individuals deal with them will have political consequences in the years ahead.

Canada and Globalization: What Kind of Destiny?

Throughout this course, you have explored Canada's place in the world and, in turn, the impact of global politics and issues upon Canada. It is therefore appropriate to consider a final question: What do the processes of globalization mean for Canada's future?

Canadian activists such as Naomi Klein have drawn attention to the abuses of globalization. Representatives of trade unions have expressed concerns about the loss of traditional manufacturing jobs from Canada to developing countries.

Others see a different future through globalization. Canadian journalist Gwynne Dyer suggests that globalization may in fact be good for the world and especially good for Canada. Canada's multicultural heritage and extensive immigration over the past 30 years have made it into what may be the most global country in the world. Because Canada has already experienced globalization at home, it may have a competitive advantage and

SOUND BITE "As with all successful religions, globalization lodged ultimate responsibility in invisible, untouchable hands."

John Ralston Saul, "The Collapse of Globalism," Harper's, *March 2004*

Architecture and Politics

Public Buildings and Their Political Messages

What messages were the Romans sending when they built the Coliseum? What did Louis XIV communicate when he built Versailles? When you visit Ottawa and see the Parliament buildings, what messages do they send to you? To visitors from all over the globe?

Sometimes politics and architecture get entangled. Consider this incident. Every three years, the International Union of Architects holds a World Convention of Architecture, where different countries present a variety of projects. Controversy erupted in 2002 when the Israeli Association of United Architects (IAUA) decided not to submit the work selected by its own steering committee. The work of architects Eyal Weizman and Rafi Sega (entitled "Civilian Occupation: The Politics of Israeli Architecture") focused on Jewish settlements in the occupied territories, and argued that architecture and planning were being used as "executive arms of the Israeli state." In defending the decision not to submit the work to the exhibition, IAUA head Uri Zerubavel claimed that the association is apolitical: "The architects' association and its cultural and material access have been used here to transmit messages that are blatantly political and not professional." The controversy raised many questions about the role architecture can play in politics. Do politicians erect buildings to symbolize and solidify their power?

Abbye A. Gorin of Tulane University has argued that "architecture in the service of politics is inscribed on the landscape." In her view, it is through public architecture that the ethics and morality of the political system in control are made clear. Inga Saffron, architecture critic for the *Philadelphia Inquirer*, believes that architecture is a political art

Figure 12.16 Left: Arthur Erickson was the architect of the Canadian Embassy in Washington, DC. It has been called "magic" by some critics and "one of the 10 ugliest buildings in the world" by others. Right: US President Bill Clinton dedicated the new US Embassy in Ottawa in 1999. It was the first time any American president had dedicated a US Embassy in person.

Figure 12.17 Representatives of the European Parliament are elected by all citizens of the European Union's member countries every five years. It has full legislative powers, just like a national parliament.

form. She states that "When you see Hitler's Foreign Ministry in Berlin, you understand exactly what the Nazi fascists were all about—control and power. When you look at the urban renewal buildings of the 1960s and 1970s in America, you see architecture that was an attempt to marginalize, control, or erase poor communities."

Architects *are* deeply conscious of political symbolism. In designing the new European Parliament buildings in Strasbourg, France, the architects aimed to represent the idea of "democracy in motion." In part, their plans were based upon the form of the *agora* (market), the central meeting place of the ancient Athenian democracy (see Chapter 1, page 3). The widespread use of clear glass was intended to convey the openness of the democratic political process within the European Union.

The next time you visit a government or public building, ask yourself: Is it simply a building? What political ideas does it convey?

Source: Simona Fuma Shapiro, "Debate Builds Over the Politics of Israeli Architecture," *Forward* (October 25, 2002), http://www.forward.com/issues/2002/02.10.25/news7.html; Abbey A. Gorin, "Architecture in the Service of Politics," Chapter 1 of *The Rivergate: Architecture and Politics No Strangers in Pair-a-Dice*, http://www.rivergate.tulane.edu/chapter1_text.html.

THE WEB

For more on architecture and politics, go to www.emp.ca/cwp.

Questions

1. Look at the photos of the US and Canadian embassies and the European Parliament. Describe the political messages you think the two countries and the EU are sending through these buildings.

2. The architects of the European Parliament describe their design as "democracy in motion." Suggest at least three concrete ways in which a government building might be designed to promote the values of democracy (openness, participation, active citizenship, rule of law, and so on).

3. Identify three other buildings that you believe make political statements. Describe what the architecture of each building says about political systems to you.

political flexibility. Through a history of immigration and political accommodations among its founding cultural groups—the Aboriginal peoples, the English, and the French—Canada has offered the world an example. It can continue to grow by responding to the tensions that result from interactions among societies and cultures: the very tensions that lie at the heart of globalization.

Politics is about balancing competing interests and making difficult choices. The processes of globalization present us with many options. What will be Canada's role in the world? How can we act to reduce global inequalities? How can we be responsible global citizens? These are questions that lie at the heart of Canadian and world politics today.

Check YOUR UNDERSTANDING

1. How are the world's poor attempting to reshape the globalization agenda to reflect their concerns?
2. Why does John Ralston Saul argue that globalism is declining?
3. Explain why Canada is in a position to benefit from globalization.

Methods of Political Inquiry

Writing a Political Book Review

Find a book with a political theme that interests you. You may select one dealing with contemporary issues, such as Naomi Klein's *No Logo*, Arundhati Roy's *Power Politics*, or Roméo Dallaire's *Shake Hands with the Devil*. You might wish to read a political biography, such as *Mrs. Thatcher's Revolution: The Ending of the Socialist Era*, by Peter Jenkins; *Iron Man: The Defiant Reign of Jean Chrétien*, by Lawrence Martin; or Ken Wiwa's biography of his father, *In the Shadow of a Saint*. Have your teacher approve your selection.

Take Notes

As you read your book, compose short notes about the subject, jotting down the page numbers where you find particularly relevant material. Reflect on what you have read. Make notes about the author's biases. For example, you might write that Naomi Klein expresses a bias against brand-based TNCs. Identify some of the techniques the author uses to lead you to a certain point of view. Refer to how the author uses statistics, personal vignettes, and language. For example, Klein notes that Indonesian workers are paid $2 a day making running shoes that sell for $120 in San Francisco, and that some Philippine seamstresses making clothes for Western chains are forbidden to take bathroom breaks and must urinate into plastic bags under their sewing machines. As a result, she concludes that production is "degraded" in the "age of the superbrand."

Create an Outline

After reading your chosen book, reflect on its content and use an outline to organize your notes into four or five significant themes or subtopics. In the case of *No Logo*, you might identify the following: globalization, brand advertising, modern manufacturing, and anti-corporate activism.

Write Your Review

Using specific examples taken from your notes, write at least one paragraph about each theme. Each time you use a statistic, a direct quotation, an author's opinion, or a controversial piece of information, cite the source by using a documentation style such as footnotes, endnotes, or parentheses (see Chapter 9, Methods of Political Inquiry, page 330). Check with your teacher about which style to use.

In your first paragraph, introduce the book, author, and the major topics you will discuss in your review. The concluding paragraph should summarize the book's major arguments and your opinions of the book.

Write a first draft of your review and check it for grammar, flow of argumentation, transitions between paragraphs, and proper page citations in your documentation. Take the approach that your review should be good enough to be published.

Applying the Skill

1. Compare your author's opinion about a political issue with a second author's view on the same issue. This will require you to investigate the work of another author. The authors' opinions may be similar, differ a great deal, or differ only slightly. Make specific reference to each author's approach by means of a partial quotation; mention the authors and their books or articles by name, and correctly document the opinions presented. Include this comparison of the authors' views in your review.
2. After following the directions above to write your first draft, produce a polished copy of your book review.

CAREERS

Dana L. Miller, Green Party Candidate

Dana L. Miller was the Green Party candidate for Delta–Richmond East (British Columbia) in the June 2004 federal election. The Green Party describes itself as a "global party" with representation in countries around the world. In the 2004 election, the party ran a candidate in every riding in Canada and received 4.3 percent of votes nationally, qualifying for $1 million in annual federal funding. Dana L. Miller is the party's "shadow cabinet minister" for human rights, which means that she monitors the human rights track record and policies of the current government for the purpose of commentary and critique.

Q: What life experiences helped shape your political views?

A: Travel has been a tremendous influence. Exploring other cultures has allowed me to gain a unique perspective on my own country. Without seeing how other people live, especially in less fortunate countries, it's difficult to appreciate the opportunities and advantages we have here.

There are also key lessons to be learned from other cultures. I'm concerned with some of the myths that we perpetuate in our society, for example, that the more you have, the more you become. I think we're irresponsible in how we allow the media and advertisers to influence our children, encouraging them to think about what they can consume, as opposed to what they can contribute. We don't give our youth enough opportunities to develop a sense of purpose.

Q: Did your views influence your decision to run for the Green Party? Where do you draw your motivation to work hard on behalf of a minority party?

A: The Green Party was the only party with a platform that was in line with my own values. I think that it's important to contribute to the democratic process. This takes bravery, because it means standing up for your beliefs and for humanity even when your views are in conflict with leadership, and when you're battling a media agenda that makes it difficult for some people (especially women and youth)

to be taken seriously based on what they think and say.

Q: What are your key political goals?

A: I'll be running for election provincially—that's a personal objective. With respect to the Green global movement, I will be working to publicize and promote the party's charter of principles in my community. I will also work locally to resolve some key environmental issues.

Q: What advice would you have for a young Canadian who wants to use the political process to make a difference?

A: First, for women, I'd strongly recommend attending the Canadian Women's Voters Congress School, which provides strong support for new female voices in the political process. I'd also share a quote from Gandhi that has been an inspiration to me: "Be the change you want to see in the world."

Questions

1. How has travel influenced Dana Miller politically?
2. What does Miller say about consumer society and personal responsibility? Turn her statements into punchy political slogans.
3. In what ways do you think the Gandhi quotation has inspired Miller? Does it inspire you? Explain.

Study Hall

Thinking/Inquiry

1. Activists meeting in Senegal, West Africa, in 2000 issued the *Dakar Declaration*, which states: "Countries of the North owe Third World countries, particularly Africa, a manifold debt: blood debt with slavery; economic debt with colonization, and the looting of human and mineral resources and unequal exchange; ecological debt with the destruction and the looting of its natural resources; social debt (unemployment, mass poverty) and cultural debt (debasing of African civilizations to justify colonization)." Should these debts be considered in evaluating the debts developing countries owe to the World Bank and wealthy countries of the North? Explain your view.

2. Many supporters of globalization claim that the processes of economic and cultural integration are irreversible. Do you agree? Why or why not?

3. Should investment by TNCs in developing countries be encouraged or restricted? Present your opinion in a brief paragraph.

4. Critics suggest that opposition to globalization in the developed world is actually harmful to the developing world because it denies citizens in the global South the advantages of economic progress already enjoyed by Northern protestors. Is this a fair complaint? Why or why not?

5. Identify and explain two lessons that Canada's political experience could offer to a world dealing with globalization.

Communication

6. Look back at Figure 12.1 on page 403. What does the author of the caption mean? Do you agree or disagree with the view expressed? Explain. Create an original piece of art (digital or otherwise) on the theme of globalization.

7. Debt burden remains an obstacle to better living standards and development for many developing countries. Write an editorial for a national newspaper advocating that Canada forgive all debts owing from developing countries and encouraging other states to do likewise.

8. Create a poster to promote and raise awareness in your school of the issue of sweatshops in developing countries. Your poster should illustrate working conditions and suggest practical steps that young people might take to tackle the problem.

9. Prepare a three-minute public speech on the subject: "Life in the Global Village."

10. Together with a partner, prepare a mock interview with the leader of a developing nation, discussing increased trade and globalization and their importance for development. The interview should consider both beneficial and harmful impacts of globalization. Perform your interview before the class.

Application

11. Imagine that you and a partner are leaders of a TNC preparing a proposal to invest in developing countries in South America. Together, consider some of the advantages and disadvantages of your strategy. How might you answer critics concerned about sweatshops and poor working conditions? What benefits could your investment offer the developing countries? What political issues might affect your decision? You can submit your proposal in writing or make an oral or audio-visual class presentation.

12. You and several classmates are appointed as advisers to the leader of a small and impoverished country in sub-Saharan Africa, struggling with the twin burdens of debt and the devastation caused by HIV/AIDS. What options might be available to improve living conditions? Why might turning to the international community—including NGOs and the IMF and World Bank—be difficult?

13. Many developing countries desire their own "industrial revolution," which could bring widespread environmental degradation. Is it fair for the developed world to impose restrictions on these countries in the name of environmentalism? Research how this question is being dealt with globally, and prepare a brief class presentation of your findings.

Glossary

Aboriginal peoples: The original or earliest-known people to live in a region; in Canada, this term includes Indian, Métis, and Inuit peoples (also called *indigenous peoples*)

Aboriginal title: Aboriginal legal rights beyond those provided by treaty or statute, rooted in Aboriginal peoples' historic "occupation, possession, and use" of traditional territories. As such, title existed at the time of first contact with Europeans, whether or not it was recognized by them

Aborigine: a member of the Aboriginal peoples of Australia. The term is used only in the singular, with "Aboriginal" preferred as the plural or as an adjective

absolute monarchy: a political system based on the belief that the monarch has absolute power and that the state should be centralized under this authority

advisory: an official statement issued by a body, such as the World Health Organization, warning of a potential danger

Age of Enlightenment: an intellectual movement in 18th century Europe that emphasized the predominance of reason and science over tradition and religion; the movement provided a framework for both the American and French revolutions and the rise of capitalism

alliance: a formal union or agreement among nations to cooperate for a specific goal

amending formula: a method for making changes to a country's constitution; in 1982, a Canadian amending formula was devised that would no longer involve the British Parliament

anarchism: a political ideology that holds all forms of enforced control and authority to be unnecessary and undesirable

The philosophy advocates a society based on voluntary cooperation in which government is unnecessary

apartheid: a policy of the South African government from 1948 to 1990 that enforced discrimination against non-whites, segregating the races

arbitration: the hearing and resolution of a dispute by a referee, usually chosen and agreed upon by the disputants, who has the power to impose a settlement

aristocracy: government by a small group of the nobility or the wealthy who hold and exercise power under law

Aristotle (384–322 BCE): Greek philosopher who wrote *Nicomachean Ethics* and *Politics*; he believed that individuals achieve their highest potential by interacting with others for the good of all

arms race: competition among states in the development and accumulation of weapons

authoritarian government: a government in which power is concentrated in the executive branch. The government's authority may or may not be based on electoral support

authoritarianism: a belief in the individual's duty to follow established rules. As a political ideology, authoritarianism entails strong government power and is found on both the left and right sides of the political spectrum

Auto Pact: a 1965 trade agreement between Canada and the United States, permitting vehicles and their parts to travel across the border duty-free, creating a continental market

backbencher: an elected member of a legislature on the government side who does not hold a position in the cabinet.

While cabinet ministers sit in the front benches, non-cabinet members sit in the "back benches"

Bentham, Jeremy (1748–1832): English thinker who first conceived of utilitarianism, a philosophy that promotes the greatest good for the greatest number of people

bilateral treaty: a treaty negotiated between a limited number of nations, often only two, establishing legal rights and obligations

biodiversity: the degree to which species are varied, in number and in genetic structure

bourgeoisie: a Marxist term referring to the class that owns capital and property, such as landlords, factory owners, and store proprietors

bureaucracy: non-elected public servants who administer government in departments, such as transportation, foreign relations, and finance

cabinet solidarity: a principle that members of the cabinet do not disagree publicly with government policy

capital: wealth in the form of money or property, used or accumulated in a business by a person, partnership, or corporation

capitalism: an economic theory that supports free trade, private property, individual profit making, private ownership of capital, and minimum government intervention in the economic system

cartel: a group of producers or suppliers formed to set or fix prices, control production, and limit supply and competition

centrist: a person whose beliefs lie in the middle of the political spectrum

civic nationalism: nationalism based on a belief that the state is home to all people who subscribe to its political values and ideals; an outgrowth of the European Age of Enlightenment

civic religion: patriotism and nationalism that has assumed a religious character; often used as a tool to help spread state ideology

civil disobedience: peaceful protest by which a person or group refuses to obey a particular law as a matter of conscience

civil society: non-governmental institutions, such as human rights and environmental groups, labour unions, and charitable and religious organizations, which form the bedrock of a functioning democracy

client state: a country dependent upon one of the two superpowers of the late 20th century (the US and the Soviet Union) in matters of trade and defence

closure: a measure introduced by the government to cut off further debate on an individual clause of a bill

cloture: a measure invoked in the US Senate to end a filibuster

Cold War (1945–91): a rivalry and arms race between the United States and the USSR that began at the end of World War II and ended with the dissolution of the USSR in 1991

collective rights: rights acquired as a result of membership in a group; all members of the group share the same rights

collective security: the mutual protection of a group of nations against a common opponent (e.g., through the North Atlantic Treaty Organization)

collectivism: the theory and practice of common ownership of land and the means of production

collectivist: marked by central state control

collectivized: organized on the basis of common ownership

colonialism: a policy by which one power acquires or appropriates the land and resources of a weaker power

command economy: an economic system in which a central authority makes decisions about what to produce and how to produce it

communalism: the belief in, or practice of, common ownership of goods and property; also, strong devotion to the interests of one's own minority or ethnic group rather than those of society as a whole

communism: a political ideology that seeks to bring about economic equality in society by seizing power from the bourgeoisie and giving it to the proletariat (the workers who do not own property). In practice, communism is characterized by public ownership and central planning of the economy

community-based organizations (CBOs): local grassroots non-governmental organizations

community living: the concept that individuals with physical or other challenges develop their capacity to live, learn, work, and participate in all aspects of the community. At the same time, the community develops its capacity to welcome and support people with various challenges

concordat: a treaty between a state and the Roman Catholic Church that outlines the powers of the state and the legal rights of the Church and its personnel in that state

Congress: the body comprising both branches of the US federal legislature (the House of Representatives and the Senate)

conquest, discovery, and settlement: the theory that the sovereignty or power of a state may be obtained through conquest by force of arms, or by the discovery of an unknown land and its subsequent settlement. This theory is no longer accepted under international law

conscientious objector: someone who refuses to serve in the military for religious or moral reasons (e.g., a belief that fighting or killing is wrong under any circumstances)

conservatism: a political and social ideology that advocates limited government intervention and the preservation or restoration of traditions

constitutional monarchy: a political system in which the power of the monarch is limited by a constitution

constitutionalism: the view that the government will obey the rules and principles written in the constitution and will uphold the rule of law

convention: a way of doing something that has been accepted for so long that it amounts to an unwritten rule; also, a formal agreement between two or more nations (often called a *covenant*, *protocol*, or *treaty*)

cooperative federalism: cooperation between the federal and provincial levels of government in policy making

corporatism: a system under which citizens are organized into supposedly representative organizations, based on profession or vocation, that are closely controlled by government

cosmopolitanism: the understanding and acceptance of diverse cultures that are different from one's own

countries in transition: former republics of the Soviet Union that received autonomy in 1991 and are moving from socialism to capitalism

coup d'état: a sudden and quick political or military action that results in the overthrow of an existing government (also called a *coup*)

Cuban Missile Crisis: the 13-day confrontation, in October 1962, between the United States and the USSR over the presence of Soviet missile bases in Cuba, during which the world came close to nuclear war

cultural genocide: deliberate and systematic destruction of the culture, traditions, language, and customs of a specific group

debt: money owed. A government's debt is the total of all previous deficits

decolonization: the withdrawal of a state from its colonies, leaving them independent

deficit: the amount by which a government's expenditures exceed revenues in a given year

democracy: a system of government in early Greece in which the majority ruled without legal restraint; today, a government in which laws are made by elected representatives of the people

democratic socialism: a political movement that seeks to lessen the gap between the wealthy and the poor within a democracy (e.g., through a minimum wage, universal health care, old age pensions, unemployment insurance, parenting benefits, housing subsidies)

demographics: characteristics of a population as revealed though statistics (e.g., age, sex, marital status, socio-economic factors)

dependency theory: a view of economic development in which developing countries are seen to face significant challenges because of their colonial past. The global system is seen to serve the interests of industrialized nations, which dominate the world economy

détente: a policy toward a rival country or bloc characterized by increased diplomatic, commercial, and cultural contact and a desire to reduce tensions, as through negotiation or talks

deterrence: a policy under which the possession of nuclear weapons is seen to discourage or prevent opponents from attacking

developed countries: countries that have a well-developed industrial base and a strong service sector, and where citizens enjoy high standards of literacy, health services, and food supplies

developing countries: countries that are shifting from a traditional economy to more mechanized production methods and services, in which citizens may have limited access to education, health care, clean water, food, and fuel

devolution: the process by which a unitary state creates regional parliaments that are not mandated in its constitution

diaspora: the dispersion of the Jews after the Babylonian and Roman conquests of Palestine (from the Greek word *diaspeirein*, to scatter); also, any group of people similarly dispersed

Diderot, Denis (1713–84): French philosopher and editor of the first modern encyclopedia. He stated that a belief in God is "not necessary"

direct democracy: a form of democracy in which all citizens can directly participate in decision making. Typically, the state limits the process either to many decisions by a small population or to few decisions by a large population (e.g., a referendum)

disarmament: the decision by a state to destroy weapons and not build or acquire others

disinformation: deliberately misleading information announced publicly or leaked by a government, or especially by an intelligence agency, in order to influence public opinion or the government of another state

divine right of kings: the belief that the monarch's source of royal power comes from God and not from the governed

dogma: a set of doctrines proclaimed to be absolutely true by the representatives of a religious faith

Earth Summit: an international meeting held in Stockholm, Sweden, in 1972 to discuss the responsibilities of countries and citizens in protecting the world's environment. Later Earth Summits were held in Nairobi, Kenya (1982) and Rio de Janeiro, Brazil (1992)

ecology: a science that examines the interactions between living things and the environment

egalitarianism: the belief in, or promotion of, equal political, economic, social, and civil rights for all people

emerging democracy: a partial democracy that is attempting to become a full democracy

environmental movement: any social or political movement that has as its goal the preservation, restoration, or enhancement of the natural environment

environmentalism: a movement or trend aimed at protecting and preserving the environment by modifying human behaviour

equality of opportunity: a condition in which all people have fair and equal access in education and employment

equality of result: a condition in which all citizens can achieve similar economic and social success

equality of rights: a condition in which everyone is entitled to the same rights

ethnic cleansing: the expulsion of an "undesirable" population from a given territory because of religious or ethnic discrimination, political, strategic, or ideological considerations, or a combination of these

ethnic nationalism: idea put forth by German philosopher Johann Gottfried von Herder in the late 18th century; he theorized that language was the primary source of culture. To be legitimate, the state must be built around a culturally distinct *Volk* (folk), or people

ethnocentric: regarding one's own group and culture as superior to all others

European Union (EU): a regional organization and trading bloc based on the European continent and containing 25 member countries in 2004. Most member states use a common currency called the euro

executive branch: the branch of government that makes decisions and enforces rules

executive privilege: the discretionary right claimed by some US presidents to withhold information from Congress or the judicial branch of government

export processing zones: areas in developing countries where transnational corporations are offered favourable terms and taxation to set up factories and produce goods solely for export. Many include sweatshop factories with poor working conditions

fascism: a political ideology of the extreme right that blends authoritarianism, paternalism, and capitalism; it supports a hierarchical view of society, and builds its appeal on nationalism, opposition to communism, and the use of force

federal system: a political system in which constitutional powers and decision making are shared between a national government and local or regional governments (e.g., Canada)

feminism: a philosophy that advocates social, political, legal, and economic equality for women; since the early 19th century the philosophy has evolved principally in Western societies

fifth estate: a term used in the late 20th century to describe television news

filibuster: the use of irregular or obstructive tactics by members of a legislature, especially the US Senate, to prevent the passage of a bill (e.g., "talking a bill to death" by continuing debate indefinitely)

First Nations: Indian bands or communities that originally settled a region; term does not include Métis or Inuit peoples

fiscal austerity: policies designed to reduce debt and inflation rates through cuts in government spending; often imposed on developing countries by institutions such as the IMF as a condition for further loans and assistance

fourth estate: a term used since the 19th century to describe newspaper journalism

franchise: the right to vote

Francophonie, La: an international organization of francophone and observer governments that provides a forum for discussions of worldwide cultural and linguistic diversity

free trade: international trade free from protective duties and quotas

freedom fighters: a term applied by their supporters to groups that use terrorism as a political tactic; "one person's terrorist is another person's freedom fighter"

full democracy: a political system based on (1) a constitution that guarantees rights and freedoms, (2) election of rulers and representatives who agree to govern according to the constitution, (3) majority rule, (4) protection of minority rights, (5) voter choice among political parties, (6) recognition of free and fair elections, and (7) an independent judiciary

fundamentalism: any religious movement that seeks to return to the founding principles of a faith in the belief that holy texts are the literal and authentic word of God

***Geneva Conventions*:** internationally accepted rules of conflict adopted in 1864, 1906, 1929, and 1949 to protect armed forces, prisoners of war, and civilians

geopolitics: the interplay among political, economic, and geographical factors (at a national or international level) that affects government decision making and relationships among countries

gerrymandering: the manipulation of constituency boundaries to maximize popular support for one party

globalism: an ideology in which the world is viewed as the appropriate sphere for a state's influence, and globalization is seen as a natural and irresistible economic and political force

globalization: the trend toward greater interconnectedness of the world's economic, technological, political, cultural, and environmental systems

glocalization: the process of adapting global trends and products to local cultures

government: institution that makes and enforces collective decisions for a society

graduated taxation: a system of taxation in which higher-income earners pay higher taxes

grassroots: political actions undertaken by ordinary individuals and groups, as opposed to large organizations or powerful individuals

gross domestic product (GDP): the total value of all goods and services produced in a country in a single year, often used as a measure of the size of the national economy

guerrilla: a person engaged in unconventional, low-tech fighting, such as raids and sabotage; a method of warfare, often revolutionary, used against occupation by superior military powers

hegemony: the predominant influence of a state, region, or group over another or others

***Helsinki Accords*:** agreements signed in 1975 by the United States, Canada, the Soviet Union, and 35 European states outlining a broad basis for peaceful relations in Europe, including recognition of post–World War II borders and respect for human rights

hereditary monarchy: a system of government in which the ruler's authority derives from power inherited from a parent or other relative

Hobbes, Thomas (1588–1679): English political philosopher who wrote *Leviathan*, which advocated rule by a powerful authority to prevent constant warfare

Holocaust: word introduced after World War II that refers to Nazi Germany's mass extermination of 6 million European Jews from 1941 to 1945; also refers to the Nazi state's killing of groups classified as "undesirable" in the same period. Based on the Greek word *holokauston*, "a completely (*holos*) burnt (*kaustos*) sacrificial offering"

Holy Roman Empire: created by Charlemagne (742–814 CE) when, as King of the Franks, he used Christianity to convert "pagans" and to unify what is now France and part of Germany. The Empire endured until 1806, when Napoleon, as Emperor of the French, refused to recognize it

Human Development Index (HDI): a comparative measure of national development prepared annually by the United Nations. It combines three significant elements: gross domestic product (GDP), literacy rates and schooling, and life expectancy

Human Security Agenda: a foreign policy program developed during the 1990s and adopted by Canada (led by then Minister of Foreign Affairs Lloyd Axworthy). It stressed the need to relieve social and economic injustices in order to remove the causes of armed conflict

human societies: groups whose members observe common rules

impeach: to charge a high official, including a head of state, with misconduct. In the US, impeachment is a constitutional power given to Congress (the House of Representatives has exclusive power to begin impeachment proceedings and the Senate to conduct the trial and convict the accused)

imperialism: the political, economic, and military control of one country over another country or countries

inalienable: unable to be surrendered or transferred

Indian Act, 1876: an act of the Parliament of Canada that amended and consolidated previous laws concerning the rights of indigenous peoples. The legislation dealt with reserve lands, "Indian status," and enforcement powers of the federal government over Aboriginal people

indigenous peoples: the original inhabitants of a region (also called *Aboriginal peoples*)

inflation: a general increase in prices

infrastructure: basic facilities needed for the functioning of a community or society, such as transportation and communications systems, water and power lines, and public institutions, including schools and prisons

initiative: a petition submitted by citizens to force a vote on a particular issue

intellectual property: non-tangible property that is the result of creative activity, such as patents and copyrights

intelligence: information of military or political value

interest group: an organization that seeks to influence legislators on behalf of a particular cause or interest; it may have a local, national, or international base

intergovernmental organization (IGO): a group of sovereign states working cooperatively toward a shared purpose (e.g., the UN, the WTO, the EU)

intergovernmentalism: a political philosophy, followed by some members of the European Union, holding that members maintain their separate or sovereign powers and that decisions are made by unanimous agreement

internationalism: a belief in friendly cooperation among nations for mutual benefit

Interpol: an international mutual-assistance organization of police forces to share intelligence and counter international crime, based in Lyons, France

Iron Curtain: the guarded boundary to the passage of people and information that existed between the West and the countries of the former Soviet bloc until the decline of Communism

jihad: in Islam, a holy war or spiritual struggle against non-believers; also, an individual Muslim's struggle for spiritual perfection (from Arabic, "to strive")

Jim Crow laws: a system of racial segregation instituted in the southern US states during the late 19th century; laws required blacks and whites to be segregated in all venues of daily life

judicial activism: the tendency of some judges to take a flexible view of their powers; a willingness to interpret the law in such a way that it can be adapted to changing circumstances

judicial branch: the legal branch of government, composed of the courts, that resolves legal conflicts among citizens, between citizens and government, and among levels of government

judicial restraint: the low-key approach of some judges to their powers; a tendency to interpret law literally and a hesitancy to apply new interpretations

judicial review: the power of the courts to overturn legislation that contravenes the constitution

junta: a coalition, usually of military officers, that forms a government, especially after a revolution or coup d'état (from Spanish, "group")

jurisdiction: the recognized right of a state to exercise control over people, property, territory, and events within a given geographical area

laissez-faire: the theory or practice of government abstention from interference in the economy (from French, "leave it alone"). Used by 18th century French economist Anne-Robert-Jacques Turgot when advising the government on the workings of the market

League of Nations: an intergovernmental organization dedicated to preventing armed conflict, spearheaded by US President Woodrow Wilson in 1919, in the wake of World War I and the *Treaty of Versailles*. Based in Geneva, Switzerland, it grew to 63 member states and was dissolved in 1946 after the founding of the UN

legislative branch: the branch of government that makes laws

legislature: the body of government, such as a parliament or national assembly, that makes laws

legitimacy: the right of a government or ruler to make binding rules that are accepted by the *polis*

liberalism: a political and social ideology that advocates government activism, civil liberties, and social reform

libertarianism: a belief in total personal freedom without the constraints of imposed rules; as a political ideology, advocates maximum individual freedom and an absence of government intervention

lobby group: an interest group that seeks to influence legislators on behalf of a particular cause; may have a local, national, or international base

Locke, John (1632–1704): English political philosopher who believed that humans have natural rights such as life, liberty, and property, which they protect by entering into a social contract with government

MAD (Mutually Assured Destruction): a military strategy premised on the ability of both the Soviet Union and the United States to survive a first nuclear strike and then inflict catastrophic damage upon the other. Thus, neither side was prepared to provoke a nuclear confrontation

Magna Carta: document in which English nobles forced King John in 1215 to acknowledge that the king is subject to law

majority rule: the principle that the greater number of a population should exercise greater decision-making power within the *polis*

mandate: a government's or agency's scope of authority, as defined by law or democratic process

mandate of heaven: belief in China from the Zhou dynasty (1027–256 BCE) onward that a monarch's power was not absolute; a ruler who behaved poorly could be dethroned, and successors did not have to come from the nobility

Marx, Karl (1818–83): German political and social theorist whose writings, including *Das Kapital*, analyzed the history of capitalism and the means of production, and became the basis of later socialist and communist movements

mass consumption society: an urban, industrialized economy in which citizens consume large amounts of consumer goods and services

mass poverty society: an economy in which citizens have limited access to consumer goods and services, including education and health care

means of production: a Marxist term referring to the physical, non-human inputs used in production such as factories, machines, and tools

mercantilism: a philosophy that advocated strict government control over trade and commerce; dominant in Western Europe in the 17th and 18th centuries

mercenaries: professional soldiers paid for service in a foreign army

middle power: a moderately powerful nation, like Canada or Australia, that can act as a negotiator between more powerful nations and have some influence internationally

militant nationalism: aggressive enthusiasm and support for one's own nation

Mill, John Stuart (1806–73): English economist, philosopher, and influential liberal thinker; author of *On Liberty* and *Utilitarianism*

minority rights: the right of minority populations to freedom from discrimination based on race, ethnicity, language, sexual orientation, or disability.

mixed economy: an economy based on both private and public (government-controlled) businesses

Montesquieu, Baron de (1689–1755): French political thinker whose theory of the separation and balance of powers in government has been adopted by many countries, including the United States

moral suasion: a formal term for persuasion (as opposed to force)

most-favoured nation: a trade category by which one state extends preferred trading policies and protection to another

multilateral: pertaining to an agreement, treaty, or organization in which three or more parties participate

multilateral treaty: a treaty negotiated among many states, establishing shared legal rights and obligations

nation: a political community, or a people, that shares a collective identity based on ethnicity (race, language, culture, history, and possibly religion)

nation-state: a country that is viewed as something more than an organized system of government over a certain territory; usually built on ethnic foundations and often seen as a homeland

nationalism: a feeling of attachment and loyalty to a particular nation, society, or territory and strong support for its interests

nationalist terrorism: the use of terror by groups determined to secure independence or national liberation (e.g., the Tamil Tigers, the FLQ)

neocolonialism: a policy by which a major power uses economic and political means to perpetuate or extend its influence over less developed countries or regions

neoconservatism: a political ideology that advocates an end to governmental growth and a reduced role for government in the economy, achieved through downsizing, privatization, and deregulation

New Deal: program initiated by US President Franklin D. Roosevelt during the Great Depression; it represented a major shift away from a free-market economy to one that relied on government intervention to create wealth and employment more equitably

non-aligned country: a country that was not associated militarily or politically with the West or the Soviet Union during the Cold War

non-aligned movement: countries not allied with either the West or the Soviet Union during the Cold War; also called the Third World

non-governmental organizations (NGOs): agencies that work independent of any government to develop interest and involvement in world affairs. NGOs create a flow of ideas, materials, and people across international boundaries (e.g., International Red Cross, International Olympic Committee)

non-intervention: the policy that one state does not involve itself in the affairs of other states

non-sectarian: not limited to, or associated with, a particular religious denomination or belief

North Atlantic Treaty Organization (NATO): a multilateral defence organization based on the *North Atlantic Treaty* (1949) to promote military, political, and economic cooperation among signatory states. An armed attack on one member is considered an attack on all

oligarchy: a form of government in which power rests in the hands of a small group of people; in the view of Plato and Aristotle, the members of an oligarchy rule for their own interests outside the law

ombudsman: an official appointed to receive and investigate citizens' grievances against the government

outsourcing: the procuring of services or products, such as the parts used in manufacturing a motor vehicle, from an outside supplier or manufacturer in order to cut costs

pacifist: a person who believes that war is never justifiable and that all disputes between nations should be settled peacefully

Palestine Liberation Organization (PLO): an umbrella group dedicated to the creation of an independent Palestinian state. Mahmoud Abbas was elected leader in December 2004 after the death of Yasser Arafat (1929–2004)

partial democracy: a democracy that has some of the characteristics of full democracies

patriarchy: a form of social organization in which community authority is based on male domination (e.g., males are the heads of families)

patriate: to transfer control over a constitution from a ruling country to its former dependent. This happened in 1982 when Canada's constitution was brought under Canadian control

patronage: the granting of political favours; the practice of appointing political supporters to public office or to desirable positions on public boards, commissions, or committees

pay equity: equal pay for work of equal value

peace-building: actions taken on the root causes of conflict between warring parties to create the conditions for long-term peace; includes efforts in the political, developmental, humanitarian, and human rights spheres

peacekeeping: keeping warring parties or states from attacking one another by placing a barrier between them, such as a multilateral force of peacekeeping soldiers

peacemaking: the processes involved in negotiating a peaceful settlement between disputing parties, often with a third-party mediator; military force may be used to enforce peace and prevent human suffering or human rights abuses

per capita: for each person

Plato (427–347 BCE): Greek philosopher and author of *The Republic*, in which he argued that humans could not achieve happiness or fulfillment outside the community (*polis*). With Aristotle, Plato developed a classification and description of types of governments

pogrom: an organized massacre of one identifiable group by another (originally, of Jews in Russia)

polis: a term used during the time of Plato and Aristotle to describe the community of the Greek city-state; today the term is used to describe political communities at the local and global levels

political ideology: an organized collection of ideas and values that describes a political system, movement, or way of thinking

political influence: the power to sway opinion by use of the media, public opinion polls, rewards, and promises

political party: an organized group that shares a common set of values and goals

political power: the ability of those in authority to induce members of the community to do what they want them to do

political science: the systematic study of government and politics

political spectrum: a means of comparing political ideologies; an imaginary left–right line with communism and liberalism on the left and fascism and conservatism on the right

politics: connections among human beings; also, the science and art of government (from Greek *polis*, "community")

polity: in the definition of Plato and Aristotle, a system of government in which the majority rules within a constitutional framework that prevents the oppression of minorities

potlatch: ceremony celebrated by Aboriginal peoples of the Northwest Pacific Coast; a means of distributing wealth among groups and of acquiring status through gift giving

preferential ballot: an electoral system in which voters rank candidates on the ballot from preferred to least preferred. If the leading candidate fails to gain a clear majority, the second and third preferences come into play until one candidate has a majority

pressure group: an interest group that seeks to influence legislators on behalf of a particular cause or interest; may have a local, national, or international base (also called *lobby group*)

private member's bill: a bill introduced in the legislature by an elected member who is not in the cabinet

privatization: the process of changing an industry or business from government ownership or control to private enterprise

proletariat: a Marxist term referring to the working class, who sell their labour to the bourgeoisie

proportional representation: an electoral system in which each qualified party wins seats in the legislature in proportion to its total popular vote

protectionism: the economic policy of imposing high tariffs or custom duties to protect domestic producers from foreign competition

Protestant Reformation: 16th century movement protesting abuses of the Roman Catholic Church and advocating reforms, ending in the establishment of Protestant churches

public-interest group: a pressure group that focuses on issues for all members of society (e.g., Greenpeace lobbies to save the environment for everyone)

al-Qaida: terrorist network founded by Saudi dissident Osama bin Laden in 1988. The group has claimed responsibility for attacks worldwide, including those of September 11, 2001

Quiet Revolution: a period of major social, political, and educational change in Quebec (1960–66) associated with the government of the provincial Liberal Party under Jean Lesage

radicalism: a political ideology advocating drastic reforms by direct and often uncompromising methods (from the Latin word meaning "root," as in "getting to the root" of a matter)

ratification: formal acceptance or confirmation of a treaty; occurs after the agreement has been signed and before it is implemented

realism: a perspective that sees international politics as largely an anarchic (without rules or regulation) arena in which each state pursues its self-interest regardless of the interests of others

realpolitik: the "politics of reality" in which ethics is less important than pragmatism (e.g., the actions of Otto von Bismarck in Germany and Camillo di Cavour in Italy in the 19th century to unite their respective countries)

recall: a voting mechanism that allows citizens to recall from office a politician who has been unresponsive to the needs of constituents

recession: a temporary downturn in economic activity; less serious than a depression

referendum: a direct yes–no vote by the electorate on a policy proposal

refuseniks: individuals who oppose an authoritarian government; originally, citizens of the Soviet Union (many Jewish) who were denied the right to emigrate, and campaigned for human rights

religious terrorism: the use of terror by groups motivated by religious radicalism (e.g., al-Qaida, Hamas)

representative democracy: a system of government in which decisions affecting the community are made by elected representatives; allows large numbers of people to participate in the political process without having to be physically present (e.g., constitutional monarchies, republics)

republic: a government in which supreme power rests with voters, who elect the head of state; in the US the head of state and the head of government are the same, while in France they are two separate persons

responsible government: government in which the executive branch keeps the confidence of a majority of the members of the legislature; if it is defeated in a vote of non-confidence, the government must resign or call an election

revolutionary terrorism: the use of organized terror to create fear among citizens and incite social and political upheaval

Rousseau, Jean Jacques (1712–78): Swiss-born French philosopher and political theorist who believed in a social contract to protect rights such as liberty and equality

royal assent: approval by the monarch or the monarch's representative (in Canada, the governor general or the lieutenant governor) that turns a bill passed by a legislature into law

rule of law: the fundamental principle that society is governed by laws applying equally to all persons and that neither any one person nor the government is above the law

sanctions: penalties or actions imposed as a means of influencing behaviour

satellite state: a state that is dominated by another, usually larger, country (e.g., the Eastern European states that were satellites of the USSR could not pursue economic, social, or foreign policies that ran counter to Soviet policy)

secular humanism: a philosophy that affirms the ability of people to lead an ethical life without reference to the supernatural and which seeks to separate religion from politics; based on the works of the philosophers, scientists, and poets of Classical Greece and Rome

secular state: a state that is governed without reference to religious doctrine

self-determination: the right of a people to decide its own form of government or political status

self-government: administering one's own government without interference from any other state

separation of church and state: a legal principle by which the functions of the state are kept separate from those of religion (e.g., as provided in the First Amendment of the US constitution)

shaming tactics: strategies devised by a pressure group to embarrass their targets into changing their actions and policies (e.g., Amnesty International mounts publicity campaigns against countries that abuse human rights)

sharia: the Islamic code of religious law based on the Qur'an

signatories: the parties or nations that sign a document and have both moral and legal obligations to respect its terms

single-issue interest group: a pressure group that focuses exclusively on one matter, such as peace or abortion

single-member constituency: an electoral district whose voters elect a single member to represent them in the legislature. By contrast, in some jurisdictions, two members or more are elected from a single district

single-member plurality: an electoral system in which the winning candidate is the one who receives the most votes (a plurality), even if the winning total is not a majority (over 50 percent) of the votes cast

Smith, Adam (1723–90): Scottish economist and philosopher who wrote *The Wealth of Nations*; spokesperson for capitalism and advocate of the philosophy that the best government is the least government

social Darwinism: the application of the evolutionary theories of Charles Darwin (1809–82) to human society (e.g., the phrases "survival of the fittest" and "natural selection" were used to justify imperialism in the 19th century)

social justice: the philosophy that advocates upholding human rights and, often, a more equitable distribution of wealth and resources in society

social movement: an informal network of individuals and groups whose shared values and identity lead them to undertake collective action to expand the boundaries of the political system (e.g., anti-slavery, women's rights, gay rights movements)

social spectrum: a continuum in which a belief in personal freedom is at one extreme and a belief in authority is at the other

socialism: a political and economic system in which the means of production and distribution of goods are owned collectively and political power is exercised by the whole community

sovereignty: the exclusive right to the exercise of force within a given territory and the sole right to raise taxes, pass laws, and represent that territory internationally

sovereignty-association: concept put forth by the Parti Québécois government of René Lévesque, whereby Quebec would become a sovereign jurisdiction in all areas of law making, but would maintain economic association with the rest of Canada

state: a geographical territory containing a population that is ruled by a sovereign government

state church: a church officially supported by the state that receives special status from the government, possibly including financial backing and official political functions

state religion: a religious body or belief officially supported by the state

status Indian: in Canada, Aboriginal people who have rights and benefits not granted to unregistered Indians, Inuit, or Métis; chief benefits include the granting of reserves and of the rights associated with them, such as exemption from federal and provincial taxes. In 1985, the *Indian Act* was amended to restore Indian status to those who had lost it through the Act's discriminatory provisions (e.g., losing one's status by marrying a man who was not a status Indian)

strike down: to rule that a piece of legislation is inconsistent with the *Canadian Charter of Rights and Freedoms* and is no longer valid

subsistence economy: an economy in which the vast majority of people barely earn or grow enough to survive (subsist)

suffrage: the right to vote in political elections

superpower: status attributed to countries as a result of their size, population, industrial–technical abilities, and military strength that allows them to exercise world influence

supranationalism: a political philosophy followed by some members of the European Union that considers power to be held by independently appointed officials or by representatives elected by the legislatures or peoples of member states

sustainable development: development that meets the needs of the present without compromising the ability of future generations to meet their own needs; balancing today's social, economic, and environmental needs to meet the needs of future generations

sweatshop: a shop or factory in which employees work long hours at low wages under poor conditions

Taliban: an Islamic fundamentalist movement that came to power in Afghanistan during the 1990s and was ousted by a US-led invasion in 2001 in retaliation for the terrorist attacks of September 11 (from Arabic, "students" or "scholars")

tariff: a customs duty or tax placed on imported or exported goods to protect domestic industries

terrorism: the use of violence and terror to achieve political ends, particularly when directed by individuals against a state or society

theocracy: a form of government in which religious law is dominant over civil law (e.g., the Puritan Massachusetts Bay Colony in the 17th century)

think tank: a research organization that analyzes problems and proposes solutions, which often affect government public policy

third parties: political parties organized as opposition to the existing parties in a two-party system (e.g., the former Reform Party; the New Democratic Party)

tied aid: assistance given by one country to another that requires the receiving country to buy goods and services from the donor country

total war: the expansion of war to include attacks on civilians, in an effort to weaken the enemy's society and economy

totalitarianism: a form of government in which the state assumes total control of all aspects of society and individual life

trade union: an organization formed by a group of workers to bargain collectively with employers to improve working conditions, benefits, and wages

transnational corporations (TNCs): companies that do business in many countries; also called *multinational corporations* (MNCs)

treaty: a formal agreement between two or more sovereign states; sometimes called a *convention, covenant,* or *protocol*

tribalism: a strong feeling of identity with and loyalty to one's tribe or group

typology: a classification scheme for government systems

ultramontanism: the Roman Catholic policy that the absolute authority of the Church should be vested in the pope. This ideology was favoured by 19th century Roman Catholic Church leaders in Quebec who upheld the supremacy of religion over civil society and insisted on loyalty to the Church in Rome

unilateral action: action taken by a state without consideration of views or interests other than its own

unitary system: a democratic system in which one central authority makes decisions for all regions of the country (e.g., Britain)

utilitarianism: the theory, originally put forward by Jeremy Bentham, that the law should achieve the greatest good for the greatest number of people

Velvet Revolution: the relatively bloodless revolution in Czechoslovakia from November 16 to December 29, 1989, which overthrew the communist government

veto: the power to reject something, usually a law or a political resolution

Voltaire, François-Marie Arouet (1694–1778): French author and philosopher who wrote *Philosophical Letters, The Age of Louis XIV,* and *Candide*; attacked existing institutions and often focused on the Roman Catholic Church, which he viewed as corrupt and intolerant

Warsaw Pact: military alliance established in 1955 to protect European Communist countries from aggressive acts by rival NATO countries. The Pact was dissolved in 1991

weapons of mass destruction: weapons designed to kill large numbers of people, including civilians. They include nuclear, biological, and chemical weapons

welfare state: a political and social system in which the state assumes primary responsibility for the welfare of its citizens (e.g., in health care, education, employment, and social security)

women's liberation: second-wave feminism, sometimes called the "women's movement"; began in 1963 with the publication of *The Feminine Mystique* by Betty Friedan, who argued that women must be free to realize their full potential in both private and public spheres

World Social Forum: an international forum for free exchange of ideas and proposals by groups and movements within civil society that are opposed to neoconservativism and are committed to building a society based on humanistic principles

Zionism: a movement that considers the Jewish people a nation and thus entitled to a homeland

Index

Abbas, Ferhat, 163
Aberhart, William, 61
Aboriginal peoples
    internationalism, 138–140
    nationalism, 140–142
    rights movement
        Australia, 247–248
        Canada, 244–246
        United States, 246–247
    sovereignty, 118–119, 141
    worldviews, 11
Aboriginal title, 245
absolute monarchy, 157
Act of Supremacy (Britain), 88
*Act Respecting Certain Aspects of Legal
    Capacity for Marriage* (Can.), 159
Adams, Michael, 145–146
advisories, 343
Afghanistan, 300, 306
African Council of Churches, 94
African National Congress, 187–188
African nationalism, 131
African Union, 30, 354, 373
Afrikaner, 186
age of democracy, 156
Age of Enlightenment, 90, 161
Agenda 21, 319
agricultural subsidies, 262–263, 408
ahimsa, 78, 80, 95
ahl ul-kitab, 81
AIDS epidemic, 252, 327–328, 350–351,
    410–412
Airborne Regiment, 300
Al-Jazeera, 236
al-Qaida, 133, 161, 306, 341, 389
Alexander II, 386, 388
Alfonsin, Raul, 181
Algeria, decolonization, 163–165
Ali, Syed Mumtaz, 87
Allah, 86
Allende, Salvador, 21
alliance, 278, 373
amending formula, 144, 195
American Indian Movement, 246–247
Americans United for Separation of
    Church and State, 111
Amnesty International, 136, 335–337
Amnesty International Canada, 272
Analects, 79

anarchism, 43–45
Anarchist Prince, The, 45
Anglicanism, 89
Annan, Kofi, 267, 268, 293, 325, 327, 371,
    420
anti-Semitism, 82, 100
"anti-terror fence," 177
Anti-Terrorism Act (Can.), 160, 394
apartheid, 94, 187
"apartheid wall," 177
Arar, Maher, 161
Arbenz, Jacobo, 189
arbitration, 362
Arbour, Louise, 328–329
Arctic Council, 356–357
Arendt, Hannah, 42, 92
Argentina, 180–182
Aristotle, 4, 31, 185, 186
arms race, 278–283
Arone, Shidane, 300
Articles of Confederation (US), 162
Aryan race, 52
Ashoka, 80, 239
Asia–Pacific Economic Cooperation
    (APEC), 355
Asian Economic Crisis, 409
Asper, Israel, 237
assassination, 33–34, 386
Assemblée Nationale, 126
Aswan High Dam, 289
atheism, 90
Atlas Shrugged, 45
Attlee, Clement, 208
Aung San, 32
Australia
    Aboriginal rights movement, 247–248
    legislature, 206
    nationalism, 136
Austria, nationalism, 137–138
Austro-Hungarian Empire, 130, 135
authoritarian government, 6, 41
authoritarianism, 38, 41–43
authority, types of, 12–13, 17
Auto Pact, 358
Axworthy, Lloyd, 299, 339

Babri Mosque, 99
Babur, 86
backbencher, 200

Baez, Joan, 284
Balkans, 133–135
Bangladesh, 98–99
Baraheni, Reza, 238
Barlow, Maud, 64
Bartholomew I, 85
Battle of the Plains of Abraham, 148
Begin, Menachem, 385
Bellamy, Carol, 276
Benchicou, Mohamed, 165
Benenson, Peter, 335
Benflis, Ali, 165
Benin, decolonization, 165–166
Bennett, R.B., 68, 146
Bentham, Jeremy, 40
Berger, Oscar, 190
Berlin Wall, 157, 176
Bernstein, Carl, 236
Beshai, Mary, 355
Bethune, Norman, 54
Bharatiya Janata Party, 78, 412
Bible, 239
bilateral trade agreements, 362
bilateral treaty, 146
Bill of Rights (Can.), 58
bin Laden, Osama, 133, 389
biodiversity, 320
Bismarck, Otto von, 127–128
Black Power, 241
Black Shirts, 52
Blackett, P.M., 378
Blair, Tony, 56, 203
Bloc Québécois, 62, 151, 222
Blood and Belonging, 116
B'nai Brith, 232
Body Politic, The, 252
Boer War, 143, 186
Bojaxhiu, Agnes Bonxha, *see* Mother Teresa
Bonhoeffer, Dietrich, 92–93
Bono, 31
Borden, Robert, 143
Bosnia, 133–135
Bouchard, Lucien, 62, 151
Bourassa, Henri, 143
Bourassa, Kevin, 253
Bourgault, Pierre, 149
bourgeoisie, 11, 47
Bouteflika, Abdelaziz, 165
Boutros-Ghali, Boutros, 293

brahman, 78
branches of government
    executive, 5, 198–205
    judicial, 6, 212–217
    legislative, 6, 206–211
Brent Spar, 426
Britain
    Canadian nationalism, and, 143–145
    influence on Canadian politics, 66–68
    judiciary, 217
    parliamentary executive, operation of,
        203–204
British Empire, 123, 309
British North America Act (Can.), 144, 195
Brook Farm, 48
Brown Shirts, 52
Brundtland, Gro Harlem, 318
Brundtland Report, 318
Buddha of Compassion, 95
Buddhism, 80–81
Buissonnire, Marine, 341
bureaucracy
    composition, 6
    defined, 5
Burke, Edmund, 39, 226
Burns, E.L.M., 291
Bush, George, Sr., 359
Bush, George W., 104, 105, 160, 203, 267,
    322, 413
bushido, 239
butterfly 208, 308
Byng, Viscount, 199
Byzantine Empire, 85

cabinet, Canada, 199–200
cabinet shuffle, 200
cabinet solidarity, 199
caliph, 7, 120
Calvin, John, 89
Calvinism, 89
Cambodia, 178–179
Campion-Smith, Bruce, 224
Canada
    Aboriginal rights movement, 244–246
    electoral system, 221–222
    executive branch, government
        advisers to, 202
        formal executive, 198–199
        political executive, 199–200
    federal–provincial/territorial
        relations, 219–221
    foreign policy
        Foreign Affairs, Department of,
          298
        International Development
          Agency, 303–307
        International Trade Canada,
          298–299

        National Defence, Department
          of, 299–303
    global environmental initiatives,
        317–319
        Johannesburg Earth Summit,
          320
        Kyoto Protocol, 321–323
        Rio Earth Summit, 319–320
    global influence, individual
        Canadians and
        Arbour, Louise, 328–329
        Coon Come, Matthew, 324–325
        Fréchette, Louise, 326
        Lewis, Stephen, 327
        Strong, Maurice, 325
        Suzuki, David, 325–326
    globalization, and, 431, 434
    international partners
        Commonwealth, the, 309–312
        Francophonie, La, 313, 316–317
    international trade
        dispute resolution, 362–363
        free-trade agreements, 358–362
    internationalism, 146–147
    judicial branch, government, 213–214
    legislative branch, government
        bill, passage of, 208
        composition, 206
        House of Commons, 207
        Senate, 208–209
    nationalism
        British influence on, 143–145
        Quebec, 148–151
        United States, effect on, 145–146
        wars, effect on, 143
    women's rights movement, 249–251
Canada–Chile Free Trade Agreement, 362
Canada–Costa Rica Free Trade Agreement,
    362
Canada Elections Act, 233
Canada–Israel Free Trade Agreement, 362
Canada–US Automotive Agreement, 358
Canada–US Free Trade Agreement, 232
Canadian Alliance Party, 62
Canadian Auto Workers, 424
Canadian Broadcasting Corporation, 237
Canadian Charter of Rights and Freedoms,
    13, 16, 59, 87, 112, 144, 158, 195, 213,
    245, 250, 253, 272, 277
Canadian Citizenship Act, 1947, 145
Canadian Civil Liberties Association, 329
Canadian Coalition for Responsible
    Environmental Solutions, 323
Canadian Forces
    defence spending debate, 302–303
    peacekeeping, 1990s, 300–301
    politics, role of, 301–302
Canadian Human Rights Foundation, 272

"Canadian initiative," 289
Canadian International Development
    Agency
        Afghanistan, commitment to, 306–307
        human rights, and, 305–306
        role of, 303–305
Canadian Labour Congress, 350, 360
Canadian Medical Association, 343
Canadian Red Cross Society Act, 342
Canadian Security Intelligence Service, 394
Canadian Supreme Court, 213–214
Canadian Women's Suffrage Movement, 69
CanWest Global Communications, 237
capital, investment, 405
capitalism, 50
Cardinal, Harold, 245
Carmichael, Stokely, 241
cartel, 416
Carter, Jimmy, 202, 412
Cartier, Jacques, 148
Cashore, Harvey, 257
Cassin, René, 271
Castro, Fidel, 388
Catholic Church, *see* Roman Catholic
    Church
Catholicism, 83–85
Cavour, Camillo, 127
Central Intelligence Agency (US), 21, 189,
    394
centrist, political spectrum, and, 38
chador, 103
Cham Prasidh, 408
Chanak Crisis, 144
charisma, 18
Charlemagne, 120
Charter of the United Nations, 263
Chechnya, 132–133
Chiang Kai-Shek, 172
Chicoutimi, 302
children's rights movement, 255–256
China, *see* People's Republic of China
Chirac, Jacques, 107, 108, 137, 205
Chomsky, Noam, 364
Chrétien, Jean, 27, 68, 112, 196–197, 200,
    261, 298, 299, 301, 309, 311, 350, 356,
    359, 389
Christendom, 125
Christian fundamentalism, 104, 111
Churchill, Winston, 18, 377
civic nationalism, 116–117
civic religion, 79
Civil Constitution Law (France), 107
civil disobedience, 78
Civil Rights Act (US), 158, 242
civil rights movement (US), 240–243
civil society, 170
Civil War (US), 231
Clarity Act (Can.), 196–197

Clark, Joe, 56, 207
Clarkson, Adrienne, 198
Classical Period, 3
Clausewitz, Karl von, 375
client state, 135
Clinton, Bill, 210, 253, 322
Clinton, Hillary Rodham, 274
closure, 208
cloture, 209
Cohen, Raymond, 234
Cold War, 279–283, 379, 382–383
"collateral damage," 384
collective rights, 245
collective security, 279, 373
collectivization, 172, 257
colonialism, 354
command economy, 168
Commonwealth Heads of Government
    Meeting, 310
Commonwealth of Independent States,
    132, 167
Commonwealth Plan of Action on
    Terrorism, 312
Commonwealth, the, 30, 309–312, 314–315
communalism, 131
communism, 22
Communist Party (China), 80, 172, 173
Communist Party (Russia), 168, 170
Communist Party (USSR), 167
"communist threat," 279, 289
community-based organization, 334
community living, 233
Comprehensive Test Ban Treaty, 278, 287
concordat, 107
Confessing Church, 92
conflict, see global conflict
Confucianism, 79–80, 102
Confucius, 88, 79
Congress (US), 195, 209
Congress of Vienna, 123
conscientious objector, 44
conservatism
    ideology, 39–40
    political spectrum, and, 38
"cradle to grave" protection, 49
Conservative Party of Canada, 58
Constantine, 76, 85
Constitution Act, 1867 (Can.), 111, 195
Constitution Act, 1982 (Can.), 13, 112, 142,
    144, 195, 213, 220, 245
constitution, importance of, 195
Constitution of the Republic of South Africa,
    1996, 272
constitutional monarchy, 14–15, 158
constitutionalism, 9
Consumers' Association of Canada, 232
Convention for a Democratic South Africa,
    188

Convention for the Preservation of the
    Halibut Fishery of the Northern Pacific
    Ocean, 146
Convention on the Elimination of All
    Forms of Discrimination Against
    Women, 276
Convention on the International Trade in
    Endangered Species, 345
Convention on the Rights of the Child, 273,
    276
Cook, James, 152
Coon Come, Matthew, 324–325
Co-operative Commonwealth Federation
    (CCF), 48, 59–60
cooperative federalism, 220
Copps, Sheila, 200
corporatism, 52
Corrigan Maguire, Mairead, 31
cosmopolitanism, 117
Council of Canadians, 64–65
countries in transition, 305
coups d'état, 21
Courchene, Thomas, 422
Crawley, Brenda, 87
Cray, Ed, 216
Crerar, Thomas, 59
Croatia, 133–135
Cross, James, 149
cross-cultural enrichment, 422
Crusades, 85, 88, 120
Cuban Missile Crisis, 283, 288, 353, 382
cultural genocide, 96
Czechoslovakia, 135–136

Dalai Lama, 56, 81, 95–96
Dallaire, Roméo, 28, 397, 399–400
d'Aquino, Thomas, 323
Darwin, Charles, 128
Das Kapital, 11
Davis, Gray, 223
Day, Stockwell, 28, 62
de Gaulle, Charles, 117, 204–205
de Klerk, F.W., 188
de Mello, Gergio Vieira, 328
debate, 227
debt, government, 50
Declaration of Helsinki, 343
Declaration of Independence (US), 11, 126,
    162, 240
Declaration of the Rights of Man and the
    Citizen (France), 240
Declaration on the Rights of the Child (UN),
    273
decolonization, 131, 156, 161–166
deficit, 50
Demilitarized Zone, 176
Democratic Kampuchea, see Cambodia
democratic socialism, 48–49, 50

democracy
    constitution, importance of, 195–196
    decision making, 194–227
    decolonization, and, 161–166
    emerging democracies, 166–171
    full democracy
        indicators of, 158–160
        limitations of, 160–161
    Greek typology, 4
    individual rights and responsibilities,
        230
    interest groups
        role of, 231
        types of, 232–233
    media
        government, and, 235–237
        ownership of, 237–238
        role of, 234
    social movements
        human rights, and, 239–240
        role of, 238–239
        US civil rights, and, 240–244
demographics, 98
Deng Xiaoping, 173
denominational schools, 111
dependency theory, 406
Desbarats, Peter, 300
détente, 382
deterrence, 379
developed countries, 334
    see also economic development
developing countries, 334
    see also economic development
devolution, 218
Dewey, Thomas, 216
diaspora, 81, 82
Dickens, Charles, 51, 52
dictatorship
    Argentina, 180–182
    assessment of, 185
    Cambodia, 178–179
    left-wing, 171
    North Korea, 184–185
    People's Republic of China, 172–173
    Republic of Korea, 182–183
    right-wing, 171
Diderot, 107
Diefenbaker, John, 58, 282–283, 290, 311
diplomacy, 373
diplomatic sanctions, 374
"Dirty War," 181
Disabilities Act (US), 252
disarmament, 397
Disclosure, 236, 257
Dishonoured Legacy, 300
Dispute Settlement Body, 362
distinct society, 150, 220
divine right of kings, 76

Doctors Without Borders, 272, 350, 397, 410
Dodds, Nick, 429
dogma, 90
"Don't Ask, Don't Tell" policy, 253
Doukhobors, The, 45
draft dodger, 284
Drop the Debt, 31, 408
Duma, 168, 169–170
Dunant, Jean Henri, 341
Duplessis, Maurice, 77
Durham Catholic District School Board, 16
Durham, Earl of, 66
Dutch Reformed Church, 89, 188
Dyer, Gwynne, 431
Dylan, Bob, 284

Earth Summit
    criticism of, 320–321
    first, 317–318
    Johannesburg, 320
    Rio, 319–320
Ebadi, Shirin, 70, 105
ecology, 72
Economic and Social Council, 264, 268
economic competition, global conflict, and, 372
economic development
    inequalities, causes of
        debt servicing, 408
        development loans and plans, 407–408
        Industrial Revolution and imperialism, 407
    models, 405–407
economic spectrum, 54
economic theory
    capitalism, 50–52
    communism, 46–47
    democratic socialism, 48–49
    fascism, 52–54
    socialism, 47–48
Eden, Anthony, 289
Edict of Nantes, 84
Edward VIII, 20
egalitarianism, 40
Egypt, Old Kingdom of, 7
Eisenhower, Dwight D., 19, 211, 216, 251
electoral systems
    preferential ballot system, 222
    proportional representation, 222–225
    single-member plurality system, 221–222
Elizabeth II, 20, 203
embedded journalist, 236
emerging democracies, 158, 166–171
Emerson, Ralph Waldo, 51
Endersby, Alastair, 315
Engels, Friedrich, 46
Engineers Without Borders, 429

environmental movement, 71
environmentalism, 71–72, 95
equality of opportunity, 11
equality of result, 11
equality of rights, 11
Estates Général, 126
ethnic nationalism, 117
ethnocentric, 118
European Economic Community, 123, 352
European Enlightenment, 163
European Union, 30, 123, 352–353
executive branch
    advisers, role of, 202–203
    composition, 5
    parliamentary system
        Britain, 203–204
        formal executive, 198–199
        political executive, 199–200
        presidential system, 200–202
        France, 204–205
executive privilege, 215

Fabian Society, 48
Falun Gong, 103
Family Law Act (Ontario), 253
Farewell to Arms, A, 374
Farrugia, Alastair, 155, 158
fascism, 22, 52–54
Fatah, Tarek, 87
fatwa, 104
Federal Bureau of Investigation (US), 246
federal–provincial powers, 219–221
federal system, 218–219
Feminine Mystique, The, 69
feminism, 69–71
Ferdinand, Franz, 386
Ferron, Jacques, 63
Fetherling, Doug, 45
fifth estate, 234
fifth estate, the, 236, 257
filibuster, 209
Filo, John, 73
Fire and Ice, 145–146
First Nations, 11
first-wave feminism, 69
fiscal austerity, 414
"five days that shook the world," 28
Flanagan, Thomas, 119
Fletcher, Stephen, 233
Foreign Affairs, Department of, 298
foreign aid program, 303–307
fortress mentality, 176
Fountainhead, The, 45
Fourier, Charles, 48
fourth estate, 234
France, 137
    semi-presidential system of government, 204–205
    separation of church and state, 107

franchise, 206
Franco, Francisco, 52, 53
Francophonie, La, 30, 313, 316–317
Franklin, Benjamin, 381
Fraser Institute, 65
Fraser, Sheila, 33
Fréchette, Louise, 326
Frederick III of Saxony, 88, 125
Free Trade Agreement, 30, 64, 358–359
Free Trade Area of the Americas, 426
freedom fighter, 385
Freedom Party (Austria), 137–138
French Revolution, 9, 107, 126, 206
Friedan, Betty, 69–70
"friendly fire," 384
Front de Liberation du Québec, 149
Frost, Robert, 176
Frum, David, 264, 392–393
full democracies, 158–161
Fulton, Jim, 321
fundamentalism, 96

G7/G8, 355
Galtieri, Leopoldo, 181
Gandhi, Indira, 34
Gandhi, Mahatma, 33, 56, 78, 91–92, 96, 98, 117
Gandhi, Rajiv, 34
"Gathering Strength" policy, 246
Gaullist, 205
gay and lesbian rights movement, 251–254
gay marriage, legalization of, 253–254
Geldof, Bob, 31
gender-inclusive language, 70
General Agreement on Tariffs and Trade, 348
General Assembly, 264, 266
generic drugs, 350–351
Geneva Conventions, 124, 285–286, 342
Geneva Protocol, 286, 380
geopolitics, 117
George VI, 20, 377
George, David Lloyd, 144
George, Dudley, 141, 159, 336
gerrymandering, 222
Gestapo, 92
"giant to the south," 145
Gillese, Eileen, 253
Gin Lane, 26
glasnost, 167
Glassman, James K., 364
global citizenship, 427, 429
global conflict
    causes
        ethnic nationalism and tribalism, 371
        imperialism and economic competition, 372

global conflict (cont.)
  terrorism
    definition, 385–386
    evolution of, 386
    politics, and, 391, 394
    types of, 386–389
    waging war against, 394–395
  war
    cold war, 279–283, 379, 382–383
    reasons for, 374–375
    total war, 376–379
    traditional war, 375–376
    virtual war, 383–384
global crime, 422–423
global culture, 421–422
Global Monitoring Report, 348
global village, the, 29, 420–421
globalism, 419
globalization, 30, 347
  anti-globalization protests, 425–427
  Canada, and, 431, 434
  definition, 418
  future of, 430–431, 434
  globalism, and, 419
  history of, 418–420
  labour responses to, 424–425
  nationalism, and, 430–431
  political responses to, 424
glocalization, 422
"god-king," 76
Godwin, William, 43, 45
"going to Canossa," 84, 121
Gorbachev, Mikhail, 132, 167
Gorin, Abbye A., 432
government
  branches of, 5–6
    executive, 198–205
    legislative, 206–211
    judicial, 212–218
  classical Greek classification, 4
  defined, 5
  democracy
    constitutional monarchy, 158
    decolonization, and, 161–166
    direct democracy, 158
    emerging, 158, 166–171
    full, 158–161
    partial, 158
    representative democracy, 158
    republic, 158
  divisions of, 5–6
  internal and external influences on, 157
  legitimacy, 5
governor general, 198–199
graduated taxation, 46
Graham, Bill, 287
Grand Council, 139, 140
grassroots, 61

Gray, Fred, 243
Great Law of Peace, 239
Great Proletarian Cultural Revolution, 172
Great Schism, 83, 85
Great Wall of China, 176
Green Party, 71–72, 222, 436
Greenpeace, 71, 232, 344–345
Grey Nuns, 77
gross domestic product, 323, 405
Guatemala, as oligarchy, 188–191
Guernica, 53
guerrilla, 129
Gupta Dynasty, 5, 6
Gush Emunim, 101
Gyatso, Tenzin, *see* Dalai Lama

Hadrian's Wall, 176
Haider, Joerg, 137–138
Hall, Marc, 16
Hamas, 388
Hamilton, John, 253
Hammarskjold, Dag, 291
Hanisch, Carol, 5
Hanseatic League, 123
Harper, Elijah, 151, 220
Harper, Stephen, 62
Harris, Jim, 223
Haudenosaunee, 139
Havel, Vaclav, 135
Heaps, Abraham Albert, 66
Hearst, William Randolph, 235
"heavenly emperor," 76
hegemony, 136
Helsinki Accords, 337
Hemingway, Ernest, 374
Henry, Fred, 112
Henry VIII, 88, 125
"Hermit Kingdom," 184
Herder, Johann Gottfried von, 117
hereditary monarchy, 12–13, 20
Hezbollah, 388
hijab, 10, 103, 107, 108–109
Hinayana Buddism, 80, 81
Hinduism, 78–79
Hiroshima, 378
Hitler, Adolf, 42, 52, 83, 92, 116, 135, 146, 374
Ho Chi Minh, 129
Hobbes, Thomas, 8–9, 371
Hogarth, William, 26
Holocaust, 83, 342
Holy Roman Empire, 120, 125
Holy Wars, 88
homeland, 116
House of Commons, 199, 207–208
House of Representatives, 201
Howard, John, 136
Hua Guofeng, 174
Hughes, Sam, 143
Huguenots, 84

Human Development Index, 404
human rights
  foreign aid linked to, 305–306
  non-governmental organizations, 335–338
  origins of, 239–240
  social movements, and, 239
  Universal Declaration of Human Rights (UN), 103, 240, 249, 271–273
Human Rights and the United Nations, 27
Human Rights Watch, 272, 337–338
Human Security Agenda, 395–397
"human shields," 398
human societies, 3
Humphrey, Hubert, 203
Humphrey, John Peters, 271–272
Hungarian Revolution, 282, 288
Hussein, Saddam, 27, 104
Huxley, Aldous, 45
Hyde Park Declaration, 147

I, Rigoberta Menchu, 190
Ignatieff, Michael, 116, 298, 383, 392
Iliad, 374
impeach, 210
Imperial Order of the Daughters of the Empire, 66, 143
imperialism
  global conflict, and, 372
  internationalism, and, 122–123
  nationalism, and, 128
India, 98–99, 412
Indian Act (Can.), 141, 245
Indian National Congress Party, 79, 92
indigenous peoples, 122
Indochinese Communist Party, 129
inflation, 168
infrastructure, 408
initiative, 223
intellectual property, 348
intelligence, 281
interest groups, 159, 231–233
intergovernmental organizations, 334
intergovernmentalism, 30
international agreements, 123–124
International Atomic Energy Agency, 287, 383
International Bill of Human Rights, 276–277
International Campaign to Ban Landmines, 339–340
International Committee of the Red Cross/ Red Crescent, 285, 286, 341–342, 397
International Court of Justice, 101, 264, 269
International Covenant on Civil and Political Rights, 277
International Covenant on Economic, Social, and Cultural Rights, 277
International Criminal Court, 29, 286, 298, 328

International Criminal Tribunal, 328–329
International Monetary Fund, 30, 160, 347–348, 407, 413–414
International Olympic Committee, 345–346, 427
international organizations
    economic organizations
        International Monetary Fund, 347–348
        World Bank, 347
        World Trade Organization, 348–350
    non-governmental organizations
        Amnesty International, 335–337
        Doctors Without Borders, 340–341
        Greenpeace, 344–345
        Human Rights Watch, 337–338
        International Committee of the Red Cross, 341–342
        International Olympic Committee, 345
        Physicians for Human Rights, 338
        World Health Organization, and, 343
        World Medical Association, 342–343
    regional and specialized organizations
        African Union, 354
        Arctic Council, 356–357
        Asia–Pacific Economic Cooperation, 355
        European Union, 352–353
        G7/G8, 355–356
        League of Arab States, 355
        Organization of American States, 353–354
International Trade Canada, 298–299
International Union of Architects, 432
internationalism
    Aboriginal peoples, 138–140
    by means of agreement, 123–124
    Canadian, 146–147
    imperialism, and, 122–123
    realpolitik, 117
    religion, and, 120–121
    trade, and, 123
Interpol, 423
interview, conducting, 113
Iran, 103–104
Ireland, Republic of, 97
Irish War of Independence, 97
Iron Curtain, 274
Iroquois Confederacy, 139–140, 239
Islam, 86–88
Islamic Salvation Front (Algeria), 164
Israel, 100–102, 222
Israeli Association of United Architects, 432

James II, 9
Jefferson, Thomas, 24, 110, 163, 234, 235
Jiang Qing, 173
jihad, 88, 389
Jim Crow laws, 240
Johannesburg Earth Summit, 320
John Paul II, 85
Johnson, Andrew, 210
Johnson, Lyndon, 202, 203
juche, 184, 185
Judaism, 81–83
judicial activism, 213
judicial branch
    American judiciary, 214–217
    British judiciary, 217
    Canadian judiciary, 213–214
    role of, 6, 213
Judicial Committee of the Privy Council, 213
judicial restraint, 213
judicial review, 213
Julius Caesar, 171
junta, 32, 180
jurisdiction, 118
"Just Society," 19

Kabir, A.K.M. Enayet, 416–417
Kadyrov, Akhmad, 34
Kampuchean Revolutionary Army, 179
Kellogg–Briand Pact, 380–381
Kennedy, John F., 19, 25, 33, 11, 203, 283, 284, 382
Kennedy, Robert, 33, 284
Kerekou, Mathieu, 165
Keynes, John Maynard, 67
Keynesian economics, 67–68
Khakamada, Irina, 170
Khan, Sheema, 109
Khatami, Muhammad, 104
Khmer Rouge, 178–179
Khodorkovsky, Mikhail, 169
Khomeini, Ruhollah, 10, 17, 18, 103–104
Khrushchev, Nikita, 21, 281
Kielburger, Craig, 429
Kim Dae Jung, 184
Kim Il-Sung, 20, 184, 185
Kim Jong-Il, 20, 184
Kim Young Sam, 183
King–Byng affair, 199
King, Martin Luther, Jr., 33, 241, 243, 258–259, 284
King, William Lyon Mackenzie, 18, 60, 144, 146, 199, 357
Kirchner, Nestor, 182
Kissinger, Henry, 21, 179, 202, 379
Klein, Naomi, 337, 427, 428, 431
Knesset, 102
Knox, John, 89
Korean Central Intelligence Agency, 182

Kosovo, 133–134
Kropotkin, Peter, 43
Kurdistan, 130
Kyoto Protocol, 65, 72, 232, 325
    Canada's implementation plan, 322–323
    goals of, 321
    implementation, 321
    opposition to, 322

Labour Party (Britain), 67
laissez-faire, 50
LaMarsh, Judy, 250
Lapham, Lewis H., 56
Laporte, Pierre, 149
Lasswell, Harold, 5
Laurier, Wilfrid, 59, 111, 143, 219
Law of Hospitality, 139
Layton, Jack, 224
Le Pen, Jean-Marie, 137, 424
League for the Independence of Vietnam, 129
League of Arab States, 30
League of Nations, 124, 144, 146, 202, 263, 355
legal authority, 13
legislative branch
    bicameral composition, 206
    Canada
        bill, passage of, 208
        House of Commons, 207
        Senate, 208–209
    origin, 206
    role of, 6
    United States
        bill, passage of, 211
        House of Representatives, 209
        Senate, 209
        standing committees, 210–211
legislature, 5
legitimacy, 5
Lenin, Vladimir, 17, 20, 46
Leo XIII, 85
Leong, Pandora L., 70
Leopold II, 122
Lesage, Jean, 77, 148
lesbian separatists, 70
Leshner, Michael, 253
Lévesque, René, 149, 150, 220
Leviathan, 8, 371
Lewinsky, Monica, 210
Lewis, David, 67
Lewis, Stephen, 327–328
libertarianism, 38, 45–46
Liberal Party, 56, 59
liberalism
    ideology, 40–41
    political spectrum, and, 38

Libya, political isolation of, 374
"life, liberty, and pursuit of happiness," 66
Lightfoot, Gordon, 284
Lindh, Anna, 34
lingua franca, 421
"little red book," 172, 185
Live Aid, 31
lobby groups, *see* interest groups
Locke, John, 8, 9, 162
Lockerbie bombing, 374
Lon Nol, 178
Lopinski, Bob, 153
Lord's Day Act (Can.), 112
Loyalists, 126
Luther, Martin, 26, 88, 89, 125
Lutheranism, 89

Ma Yinchu, 174
MacArthur, Douglas, 159
Macdonald, John A., 27, 57, 219, 357
Machiavelli, Niccolo, 8
MacKenzie, Lewis, 300, 303
Mackenzie, William Lyon, 68
MacKinnon, Robert, 16
Macmillan, Harold, 203, 311
MacPherson, James, 253
MAD, 379
Madison, James, 110
Magna Carta, 13, 163, 195
Mahatir, Mohammad, 424
Mahayana Buddhism, 80, 81
Major, John, 204
majority rule, 158
Malcolm X, 33, 241, 284
Malone, David, 266
managed democracy, 169
mandate, 100
mandate of heaven, 76
Mandela, Nelson, 187–188, 239, 310, 311, 336
Manji, Irshad, 390
Manley, John, 14, 200
Manning, Preston, 62
Mao Zedong, 46, 80, 102, 172–173, 185
Maoism, 102
map interpretation, **152**
Marco Polo, 419
Marsden, Rachel, 314
Marseillaise, La, 126
Marshall, John, 195, 214
Martin, Paul, 56, 112, 200, 302
Marx, Karl, 11, 46–47
mass consumption societies, 406
mass poverty societies, 407
Massachusetts Bay Colony, 89
Massey, Vincent, 145
media
     government, and, 235–237
     ownership of, 237–238
     role of, 234

McCarthy, Joseph, 44, 210
McClung, Nellie, 69, 144
McCrae, John, 376
McDermott, Galt, 284
McGraw, Desiree, 320
McGuire, Barry, 284
McLuhan, Marshall, 29, 420
McMurtry, Roy, 253
means of production, 47
Médecins Sans Frontières, 340–341
media convergence, 237
Meech Lake Accord, 150–151, 220
Meighen, Arthur, 144, 199
Menchu, Rigoberta, 190–191
Menem, Carlos, 181
mercantilism, 50
mercenaries, 375
Mercer, Rick, 28
Métis Nation, 142
middle power, 147, 279
Milewski, Terry, 237
militant nationalism, 128
Mill, John Stuart, 40, 41, 69
Millennium Development Goals, 306, 348, 413
Millennium Summit, 306
Miller, Dana, 436
Milner, Henry, 224
Milosevic, Slobodan, 22, 134, 329
Ming Dynasty, 176
Ministry of the Attorney General (Ontario), 87
minority rule, 158
Mock Parliament, 69
Monarchist League of Canada, 66
Montesquieu, Baron de, 9–10, 107, 162, 194, 212
Moore, Michael, 19
Moore, Roy, 111
moral suasion, 263
More, Thomas, 48, 125
Moro, Aldo, 388
Mosher, Steven, 176
most-favoured-nation status, 357
Mother Teresa, 93
Mothers Against Drunk Driving, 232
Mugabe, Robert, 19, 43, 311
Mughal Empire, 86
Muhammad, 86, 120
Mulroney, Brian, 68, 150, 209, 220, 299, 301, 358
Multilateral Agreement on Investment, 65
multilateral treaty, 144
Murdoch, Rupert, 421
Murphy, Emily, 69, 144
Musharraf, Pervez, 311
Muskie, Edmund, 203
Muslim Canadian Congress, 87
Muslim Empire, 86, 120

Mussolini, Benito, 52, 146
Mutually Assured Destruction, 379
Mwalimu, 131

Napoleon, 20, 76, 107, 126
Napoleon II, 20
Nasser, Gamal Abdel, 288–289
nation, defined, 116
nation-state, 116
National Action Committee on the Status of Women, 250
National Association for the Advancement of Colored People, 240–241
National Citizens' Coalition, 231
National Defence, Department of
     Canadian Forces as peacekeepers, 300–301
     defence spending debate, 302–303
     objectives, 299
National Front party (France), 137
National Indian Brotherhood, 244
National Liberation Front (Algeria), 163
National Organization for Women, 249
National Religious Party (Israel), 102
national security
     alliances, use of, 373
     diplomacy, use of, 373–374
     diplomatic sanctions, use of, 374
     unilateral action, use of, 372–373
nationalism
     Aboriginal peoples, 140–142
     Canada
          British influence on, 143–145
          Quebec, 148–151
          United States, effect on, 145–146
          wars, effect on, 143
     Chechnya, 132–133
     civic, 116–117
     Czechoslovakia, 135–136
     defined, 72
     democratic revolutions, and, 126–127
     dissolution of empires, and, 128, 130
     ethnic, 117
          global conflict, and, 371
     globalization, and, 430–431
     immigration, and, 136–138
     imperialism, and, 128
     political science, and, 7
     Quebec
          mainstream separatism, 150–151
          roots of, 148
          separatism, 149
     realpolitik, 117, 127–128
     World War I, 376
     Yugoslavia, 133
nationalist terrorism, 387–388
Nature of Things, The, 326

Nazi regime, 83, 92, 116, 137, 252, 270
Nehru, Jawaharlal, 286
neocolonial, 414
neoconservatism, 68
New Deal, 68
New Democratic Party, 48, 61
"New Frontier," 19
New Plan for African Development, 356
Nicholas II, 22–23
Niemöller, Martin, 270
Nixon, Richard, 21, 202, 210, 215, 236
No Logo, 428
No Logo campaign, 428
Nobel Peace Prize, 93, 94, 105, 167, 190, 271, 290, 336, 339, 386, 410
non-aligned country, 131
non-aligned movement, 289
non-governmental organizations, 29, 71, 334
    Greenpeace, 71, 232, 344–345
    health and humanitarian aid
        Doctors Without Borders, 272, 340–341
        International Committee of the Red Cross/Red Crescent, 285, 286, 341–342
        World Health Organization, and, 343
        World Medical Association, 342–343
    human rights
        Amnesty International, 136, 272, 335–337
        Human Rights Watch, 337–338
        Physicians for Human Rights, 338
    International Olympic Committee, 345–346
non-intervention, 353
Non-Proliferation of Nuclear Weapons Treaty, 185, 278, 286
non-sectarian, 112
North American Aerospace Defense Command, 282–283, 373
North American Air Defense Agreement (NORAD), 278, 282–283
North American Free Trade Agreement (NAFTA), 30, 65, 359–361, 364–365
North Atlantic Treaty Organization (NATO), 147, 278, 279–281, 373
North Korea, 184–185
Northern Ireland, 97–98
NOW, 44
nuclear-weapons control initiatives, 286–287
Nyerere, Julius, 131

October Crisis, 149, 387
Office of the High Commissioner for Human Rights, 298
Official Languages Act, 149

Ogdensburg Agreement, 147
Oka Crisis, 342
Old Age Pension Act, 60
oligarchy
    classical Greece, 4, 186
    Guatemala, 188–191
    South Africa, 186–188
"oligarchy of the wealthy," 161
Olthuis, John A., 118
Olympic Movement, 345
ombudsman, 237
On War, 375
one-child policy, 173, 174–175
One Nation party (Australia), 136
"one person, one vote," 19
"open society," 22
Open Society Institute, 22
Orbinski, James, 341, 404, 410–411
Organisation for Economic Co-operation and Development (OECD), 349
Organization for African Unity, 354
Organization of American States, 326, 353–354, 373
Organization of Petroleum Exporting Countries (OPEC), 349
Origins of Species, 128
Orwell, George, 45, 47, 54, 171
Osgoode Hall Law School, 329
Ottawa Declaration, 339
Ottoman Empire, 85, 100, 120, 127, 163, 371
Our Common Future, 318
outsourced jobs, 424
Oxfam, 350

pacifism, 44
Pahlavi, Reza, 18, 103
Paine, Thomas, 126
Pakistan, 98–99
Palestine, 100–101
Palestine Liberation Organization, 387
Palme, Olof, 34
Pankhurst, Emmeline, 69
papal authority, 83
Paris Peace Conference, 100, 129, 144
Parizeau, Jacques, 151
Park Chung Hee, 182
Parks, Rosa, 243–244
Parti Québécois, 149, 150
Partial-Birth Abortion Ban Act (US), 159
partial democracy, 158
Partial Test Ban Treaty, 286
Passional Christi und Antichristi, 26
patriarchy, 70
patriation, 13
patronage, 208
Patton, Gwendolyn, 244
pay equity, 70
peace-building, 292, 293, 294, 395–397
peace initiatives, 397–398

"peace, order, and good government," 66
Peace People Organization, 31
peacekeeping
    after Cold War, 292–294
    Canadian Forces, 1990s, 300–301
    Cyprus, 290
    Human Security Agenda, 395–397
    Suez Crisis, 288–290
peacemaking, 292, 293, 395–397
Pearson, Lester, 145, 249, 263, 283, 290, 291–292, 395
Peltier, Leonard, 246
people power, 22–23
People's Republic of China
    government structure, 172–173
    one-child policy, 174–175
    religion, and, 102
perestroika, 167
Perle, Richard, 264, 392–393
Peron, Eva (Evita), 18, 180, 185
Peron, Juan, 18, 180–181
Persons Case, 144
photojournalism, 73
Physicians for Human Rights, 338
Picasso, Pablo, 53
Pinochet, Augusto, 21, 42, 56
Pius VII, 107
Planet for the Taking, A, 326
Plato, 3–4, 24, 186, 258
Play Fair at the Olympics, 427
plebiscite, 226
pogroms, 82, 272
Pol Pot, 178–179, 185
polis, 3, 4, 5, 12, 18, 19, 25, 28, 31, 33, 34, 75, 125, 185, 404
political assassination, 33–34, 386
political cartoons, 26
political change
    coup d'état, 21
    elections, 19
    hereditary and designated succession, 20–21
political ideology
    blended, 54–57
    Canadian political parties
        Bloc Québécois, 62
        Canadian Alliance Party, 62
        Co-operative Commonwealth Federation (CCF), 59–60
        Liberal Party, 59
        New Democratic Party, 61
        Progressive Conservative Party, 57–59
        Progressive Party, 59
        Reform Party, 62
        Rhinoceros Party, 63
        Social Credit Party, 61
    defined, 38
    economic theory, and, 46

political influence
  defined, 12
  interest groups, and, 22
  lobby groups, and, 22
political inquiry method
  debate, 227
  documentation of sources, 330
  Internet research, 191–192
  interviews, 113
  map interpretation, 152
  photojournalism, 73
  political book review, writing, 435
  UN resolution, writing, 295
political leadership, charisma, and, 18–19
political parties, 6
  authoritarian governments, and, 41
  Canadian
    Bloc Québécois, 62
    Canadian Alliance Party, 62
    Conservative Party, 57–59
    Co-operative Commonwealth
      Federation (CCF), 59–60
    Liberal Party, 59
    New Democratic Party, 61
    Progressive Party, 59
    Reform Party, 62
    Rhinoceros Party, 63
    Social Credit Party, 61
  Russia, 169–171
political power, defined, 12
political science
  17th and 18th century thought, 8–10
  20th century influences, 10–11
  defined, 7
political spectrum, 38
politics
  architecture, and, 176–177, 432–433
  art, and, 26–27, 53, 308
  Canadian, influences on
    American influence, 68–69
    British influence, 66–68
    environmental influence, 71–72
    feminist influence, 69–71
    nationalist influence, 72
  Classical Greek thought, 3–4
  daily life, and, 24
  defined, 3
  etymology, 3
  formal and informal, 4–5, 24
  language, and, 55, 390–391
  music, and, 284
  religion, and
    contemporary issues, 96–106
    eastern religions, 78–81
    history of, 76–77
    individuals, 91–96
    separation of church and state,
      106–112
    western religions, 81–90

technology, and, 25, 28
terrorism, and, 391, 394
worldwide, individuals, and, 31
polity, 4, see also democracy
Popper, Karl, 22
Popular Socialist Party (Cambodia), 178
potlatch, 139
Pound, Dick, 346
Powell, Colin, 203
Prague Spring, 135
preferential ballot, 222
pressure groups, see interest groups
Prince, The, 8
private member's bill, 208
privatization, 68
Progressive Conservative Party, 56, 57–59
Progressive Party, 59
Project Ploughshares, 397
proletariat, 46
proportional representation, 101, 222–223,
  224–225
protectionism, 357
Protestant Reformation, 26, 88, **121**, **123**, **125**
Protestantism, 88–89
Proudhon, Pierre-Joseph, 43, 45
public-interest group, 232
Public Safety Act (Can.), 160
Pulitzer, Joseph, 235
Puritanism, 89
Putin, Vladimir, 133, 168, 169

Quakers, 89
Quebec Act, 148
Quebec nationalism
  mainstream separatism, 150–151
  roots of, 148
  separatism, 149, 196–197, 387
Quiet Revolution, 77, 148, 149
Quiet Strength, 243
Quinlivan, Gary M., 416
Qur'an, 7, 81, 86, 88, 120, 239

Rabin, Yitzhak, 34, 101
radical feminism, 70
"Radical Jack," see Durham, Earl of
radicalism, 44
Radwanski, George, 33
Rafiqui, Asim, 73
Ralston Saul, John, 431
Rand, Ayn, 45
Rasi, Marjatta, 268
read into, 250
realism, 117
realpolitik, 117, 127–128
recall, 68, 223
recession, 67
Red Crescent, 341–342
Red Cross, 285, 286, 341–342
"red scare," 44, 160

"red Tories," 56
Redgrave, Corin, 394
Reed, Christopher A., 174
referendum, 28, 68, 97, 226
Reform Party, 62, 68
refusenik, 390
Regina Manifesto, 48, 49, 60
Reichstag, 121
Reid, Escott, 279
religion
  contemporary case studies
    China, 102–103
    India, Pakistan, and Bangladesh,
      98–99
    Iran, 103–104, 105
    Israel, 100–102
    Northern Ireland, 97–98
    Republic of Ireland, 97
    United States, 104
  eastern religions
    Buddhism, 80–81
    Confucianism, 79–80
    Hinduism, 78–79
  history, in, 76–77
  internationalism, and, 120–121
  political individuals
    Dalai Lama, 95–96
    Desmond Tutu, 94
    Dietrich Bonhoeffer, 92–93
    Mahatma Gandhi, 91
    Mother Teresa, 93
  separation of church and state,
    Canada, 111–112
    France, 107–109
    United States, 110–111
  social stabilization, and, 76–77
  terrorism, and, 388–389
  validation of rule, and, 76
  western religions
    Catholicism, 83–85
    Islam, 86–88
    Judaism, 81–83
    Protestantism, 88–89
    secular humanism, 90
religious fundamentalism, 96
religious terrorism, 388–389
ren, 79
Renaissance, 122
representative democracy, 68
republic, 158
Republic, The, 3
Republic of Korea, 182–183
Republican Party (US), 104
responsible government, 66
"revenge of the cradle," 148
revolutionary terrorism, 386, 388
Rhee, Syngman, 182
Rhinoceros Party, 63
Rich, Adrienne, 46

Richards, Dennis, 225
Richards, Noel, 152
Riddell, Walter, 146–147
Riel, Louis, 58
right to bear arms, 161
Rigveda, 78
Rio Convention, 321
Rio Earth Summit, 319–320
"Rio Plus 10," 320
Rock, Allan, 200, 267
Roman Catholic Church, 77, 82, 83–85, 88, 97, 107, 148
Roman Empire, 122
Roosevelt, Eleanor, 272
Roosevelt, Franklin D., 68, 357
Rousseau, Jean-Jacques, 8, 9, 162
Roy, Arundhati, 413
royal assent, 198
Royal Commission on the Economic Union and Development Prospects for Canada, 358
Royal Commission on the Status of Women, 249, 272
rule of law, 158
Rushdie, Salman, 104
Russia, 167–171
Rwanda genocide, 371, 399–400
Ryan White CARE Act (US), 252
Ryo Moo Hyun, 183

Sadat, Anwar, 34
Saffron, Inga, 432
Sainte-Marie, Buffy, 284, 407
"salt march," 92
same-sex marriage, legalization of, 253–254
sanctions, 263
Sangha Supreme Council, 81
Saro-Wiwa, Ken, 426–427
Satanic Verses, The, 104
satellite states, 135
Saunders, Chris, 302
Schmitz, Peter, 336
Schroeder, Gerhard, 56
scorched earth policy, 189
second-wave feminism, 69
Secretariat, 264, 267
secular humanism, 90
secular state, 76
security, *see* national security
Security Council, 264, 266–267
Seeger, Pete, 284
Sega, Rafi, 432
self-determination, 130
self-government, 116
Sen, Amartya, 420
Senate
    Canada, 208–209
    United States, 201, 209
"separate but equal" doctrine, 214–215, 240

separation of church and state, 66, 90, 106–112
separatism, Quebec, 149–150
Sexual Offences Act (Britain), 251
Shah of Iran, *see* Pahlavi, Reza
Shake Hands with the Devil, 399
shaming tactics, 336
sharia, 87, 103
Shevardnadze, Eduard, 22
Shiite, 104
"shock-and-awe" tactics, 384
Siddhartha, 80
Sierra Club, 231, 323
Sihanouk, Norodom, 178
Simpson, Wallis, 20
single-issue interest group, 232
single-member constituencies, 206
single-member plurality, 221
Six-Day War, 101, 290
Six Nations Confederacy, 139
Sloane, P.F., 284
Slovakia, 136
"smart bombs," 384
Smith, Adam, 9, 10, 50–51
Smith, J.W., 419
Smith, Stan, 246
Smith, Vernon, 413
social activist, 69
Social Credit Party, 61
social Darwinism, 128
social democracy, 48–49
social ideology, 38
social justice, 72
social movement
        first-wave feminism as, 69
        human rights, and, 239–240
        US civil rights, and, 240–243
social spectrum, 38
socialism, 47–48
socialist market economy, 173
Society of Friends, 89
"soft separatists," 150
Softwood Lumber Agreement, 278
Soglo, Nicephore, 165–166
Solidarity for Palestinian Human Rights, 232
Solidarity movement, 85
Sopinka, John, 213
Soros, George, 22
sources, documentation of, 330
South Africa, oligarchy, as, 186–188
South Korea, *see* Republic of Korea
sovereignty
        Aboriginal peoples, 116, 141
        Quebec, 149
        Tibetan, 95
sovereignty-association, 150
Spanish Inquisition, 84, 125
Speech from the Throne, 198
Spirit of Laws, The, 10

Sputnik, 29, 47
St. Laurent, Louis, 19, 59
Stalin, Joseph, 20, 21, 42, 56
Stanfield, Robert, 11
Stark, Michael, 253
state, defined, 116
state church, 88
status Indian, 119
Statute of Westminster, 144, 357
Steinem, Gloria, 43
Stevenson, Adlai, 264
Stoll, David, 190
Stowe, Emily, 69
Strategic Arms Limitation Talks (SALT), 382
strike down, 213
Strong, Maurice, 325, 326
Student Nonviolent Coordinating Committee, 241
subsistence economy, 417
Suez Crisis, 288–290
suffrage, 89
Sun Yat-Sen, 172
Sunni, 104
"sunshine policy," 184
super-power, 132
supranationalism, 30
sustainable development, 303, 318–319
Suu Kyi, Daw Aung San, 31, 32
Suzuki, David, 325–326
sweatshop, 418, 428

Taiping Rebellion, 102
Taliban, 306, 341
Tampa, 136–137
Tang Dynasty, 8
Tang Taizong, 8, 79
tariffs, 348
taxation without representation, 162
Temple of Jerusalem, 82
terra nullius, 152
terrorism
        definition of, 385–386
        evolution of, 386
        types of
                al-Qaida, 389
                nationalist terrorism, 387–388
                politics, and, 391, 394
                religious terrorism, 388–389
                revolutionary terrorism, 388
        waging war on, 394–395
Thatcher, Margaret, 68, 203–204
theocracy, 89
think tank, 65
third parties, 59–63
third-wave feminism, 70
This Hour Has 22 Minutes, 28
This Hour Has Seven Days, 236
Thurow, Lester C., 19
Tiananmen Square, 25

Tibetan Buddhism, 81, 95
Tibetan National Uprising, 95
tied aid, 304
Torah, 82, 101
total war, 376–379
totalitarianism, 22, 42
Townshend, Roger, 118
trade
    dispute resolution, 362–363
    international trading blocs, 361–362
    internationalism, and, 123
trade union, 47
traditional authority, 12–13
traditional war, 375–376
transnational corporations, 21, 414–418, 424, 426, 428
treaty, 118
Treaty of Paris, 162
Treaty of Rome, 352
Treaty of Versailles, 124, 144, 146
Treaty of Westphalia, 125
Treaty on Extradition, 278
tribalism, 371
"Triple-E" Senate, 209
Trotsky, Leon, 21
Trouble with Islam, The, 390
Trudeau, Pierre, 11, 18, 19, 25, 59, 61, 149, 150, 220, 245, 250, 251, 283, 301, 387
"Trudeaumania," 18
Truman, Harry, 159
Trusteeship Council, 264, 268
Truth and Reconciliation Commission, 188
Tudjman, Franjo, 22, 134
Turgot, Anne-Robert-Jacques, 50
Tutu, Desmond, 1, 2, 94, 188
typology, 4

Ugresic, Dubravka, 134
ujamaa, 131
ultramontanism, 77
UN Convention Relating to the Status of Refugees, 136–137
UN Emergency Force, 289
UN resolution, drafting, 296
unilateral action, 372
union republics, 133
unitary system, 218
United Nations
    birth of, 263–264
    children's rights, and, 273, 276–277
    diplomacy, use of, 374
    human rights, and, 270–277
    humanitarian law, 285–286
    nuclear-weapon control, 286–287
    peacekeeping, 288–294
    structure
        Economic and Social Council, 268
        General Assembly, 266

        International Court of Justice, 269
        Secretariat, 267
        Security Council, 266–267
        Trusteeship Council, 268
United Nations Children's Fund, 256, 268, 327
United Nations Convention on the Rights of the Child, 255
United Nations Educational, Scientific, and Cultural Organization, 268
United Nations International Criminal Tribunal for Rwanda, 28
United Torah Judaism Party, 102
United States
    Canadian nationalism, and, 145–146
    Christian fundamentalism, 104
    civil rights movement, 240–243
    constitution, importance of, 195
    decolonization, 161–163
    electoral college system, 201
    executive branch of government, 200–202
    influence on Canadian politics, 68–69
    legislative branch of government, 209–211
    separation of church and state, 110–111
Universal Declaration of Human Rights (UN), 103, 240, 249, 271–273, 277
US Supreme Court, 214–215
utilitarianism, 40
Utopia, 48

Vaid, Urvashi, 239
Vajrayana Buddhism, 80
Vallières, Pierre, 149
Varnell, Joe, 253
Vautour, Anne, 253
Vautour, Elaine, 253
Velvet Revolution, 135
veto, 266
Vietnam independence, 129
Vike-Freiberga, Vaira, 150
Vimy Ridge, 143
Vindication of the Rights of Woman, A, 69
virtual war, 383–384
Volk, 117
Voltaire, 107
voter apathy, 33
Voting Rights Act (US), 158, 242

W5, 236
Wallace, George, 217
war
    Cold War, 279–283, 379, 382–383
    total war, 376–379
    traditional war, 375
    virtual war, 383–384
War Agriculture Committee, 44

War Measures Act, 149, 325, 387
"war on terror," 105, 133, 161, 385, 392–395, 423
Warren, Earl, 216–217
Warsaw Pact, 281–282
Warsaw Treaty of Friendship, Cooperation, and Mutual Assistance, 281
Watergate affair, 215, 236
Wealth of Nations, The, 9, 10, 50
weapons of mass destruction, 267
Weber, Max, 89
Weinberg, Scott, 174
Weizman, Eyal, 432
welfare state, 50
Western Labour News, 60
Williams, Betty, 31
Williams, Jody, 339–340
Wilson, Lois, 396
Wilson, Woodrow, 124, 130, 202, 263
Winnipeg General Strike, 67
Woiceshyn, Glenn, 275
Wolfenden Report (Britain), 251
Wollstonecraft, Mary, 69
Women's Franchise League, 69
Women's Human Rights Network, 249
women's liberation, 69
women's movement, 69, 248–251
Women's Remembrance Day, 252
Woodcock, George, 43, 44
Woodsworth, James Shaver, 60
Woodward, Bob, 236
Woolf, Virginia, 90
World Anti-Doping Agency, 346
World Bank, 21, 30, 303, 347, 413–414
World Convention of Architecture, 432
World Health Organization, 29, 268, 343
World Social Forum, 430
World Trade Organization, 28, 30, 160, 173, 322, 348–350, 355, 362–363, 407, 426
World Wildlife Fund, 323

Xtra!, 252

yarmulke, 10, 107
Yavlinsky, Grigory, 168
yellow journalism, 235
Yeltsin, Boris, 167, 168
Young, Neil, 284
Ypres, 143
Yugoslavia, 133

Zerubavel, Uri, 432
Zhou Dynasty, 172
Zimbabwe, 311
Zionism, 100
Zionist fundamentalism, 101, 386
Zollverein, 123
Zhu Rongji, 175

Credits

Images

Page 1, Clockwise: Antoine Gyori/France Reportage/Corbis/Magma, Lawrence Manning/Corbis/Magma, Owen Franken/Corbis/Magma, Nathan Benn/Corbis/Magma; Page 2: Jerilea Zempel, *Guns and Rosettes*, 1998, Poznan, Poland; Page 3: Mary Evans Picture Library; Page 5: Ryan Remiorz/CP Photo Archive; Page 7: Bibliothèque Nationale de France; Page 8: Massimo Listri/Corbis/Magma; Page 9: © National Gallery Collection; By kind permission of the Trustees of the National Gallery, London/Corbis/Magma; Page 11: © Corbis/Magma; Page 13 Left to right: Mary Evans Picture Library, Archivo Iconografico, SA/Corbis/Magma; Page 14: Kirsty Wigglesworth/CP Photo Archive; Page 16: Kevin Frayer/CP Photo Archive; Page 17: Bettmann/Corbis/Magma; Page 18 Left to right: Peter Bregg/CP Photo Archive, National Archives of Canada, C-123991; Page 19: Themba Hadebe/CP Photo Archive; Page 20 Top to bottom: © Corbis Sygma/Magma, Courtesy Fr. Richard R. Rolfs, S.J., Loyola Marymount University; Page 21: Roberto Candia/CP Photo Archive; Page 23: Antoine Gyori/France Reportage/Corbis/Magma; Page 24: © Frederic Neema/Gamma/PONOPRESSE; Page 25 Top to bottom: Bettmann/Corbis/Magma, CP/AP/CNN; Page 26 Left to right: Courtesy of American Studies at the University of Virginia, Barney Burstein/Corbis/Magma; Page 27 Clockwise: Reprinted with permission—Torstar Syndication Services, Reprinted with permission from *The Globe and Mail*, National Archives of Canada, C-078864; Page 29: Courtesy of NASA; Page 31: Michelle Pelletier/Corbis/Magma; Page 32: Alison Wright/Corbis/Magma; Page 33: Bettmann/Corbis/Magma; Page 37: © 1992 Newsweek, Inc. All Rights Reserved. Reprinted by permission; Page 39: Rick Eglinton/CP Photo Archive; Page 40: Lawrence Manning/Corbis/Magma; Page 42: Bettmann/Corbis/Magma; Page 44: Queen's University Archive, George Woodcock fonds, Locator #2095, Box 39, file 12; Page 48: Mary Evans Picture Library; Page 49: Jacques Boissinot/CP Photo Archive; Page 51: Michael McQueen/Stone/Getty Images; Page 53: Archivo Fotografico, Museo Nacional Centro de Arte Reina Sofia, Madrid; Page 55: Peter Steiner, The Cartoon Bank, 29056; Page 56 Left to right: Jim Phillips/Artizans, Michael De Adder/Artizans; Page 58: National Archives of Canada, C-095470; Page 60: National Archives of Canada, C-055451; Page 61: CP Photo Archive; Page 62: Malcolm Mayes/Artizans; Page 64: Fred Chartrand/CP Photo Archive; Page 65: Jeff McIntosh/CP Photo Archive; Page 67: Provincial Archives of Manitoba, N#2757; Page 71 Top to bottom: Courtesy of Sarinder Dhaliwal, Fred Chartrand/CP Photo Archive; Page 75: Reprinted by permission of Joanne Tod; Page 77: Art Gallery of Ontario, no. 2574; Page 78: Gurinder Osan/CP Photo Archive; Page 79: Nathan Benn/Corbis/Magma; Page 83: Pascal Le Segretain/Corbis Sygma/Magma; Page 84: Fabian Cevallos/Corbis Sygma/Magma; Page 86: Archivo Iconografico, SA/Corbis/Magma; Page 89: Bettmann/Corbis/Magma; Page 91: Hulton-Deutsch Collection/Corbis/Magma; Page 92: Mary Evans Picture Library; Page 93: J.P. LaFon/Corbis Sygma/Magma; Page 94: Richard Lam/CP Photo Archive; Page 95: Jonathan Hayward/CP Photo Archive; Page 98: Cedric Arnold/Corbis/Magma; Page 99: Arif Ali/AFP/Getty Images; Page 100: Jeffrey L. Rotman/Corbis/Magma; Page 102: Anet Giron/CP Photo Archive; Page 104: Jean Chung/Corbis/Magma; Page 105: Reuters/Landov; Page 107: Gianni Dagll Ortl/Corbis/Magma; Page 108: Pascal Le Segretain/Getty Images; Page 110: Corbis/Magma; Page 115: National Gallery of Canada, Ottawa, Purchased 1968; Page 116: Kitchener-Waterloo Record/CP Photo Archive; Page 118: Tom Hanson/CP Photo Archive; Page 121: Historical Picture Archive/Corbis/Magma; Page 124: Christel Gerstenberg/Corbis/Magma; Page 126: Leonard de Selva/Corbis/Magma; Page 129: Hulton-Deutsch Collection/Corbis/Magma; Page 130: Ali Haider/EPA/Landov; Page 131: Bettmann/Corbis/Magma; Page 137: Owen Franken/Corbis/Magma; Page 140: © Bibliothèque publique et universitaire-Geneva; Page 144: Mary Evans Picture Library; Page 145: CP Photo Archive; Page 147: Adrian Wyld/CP Photo Archive; Page 149: Karl Tremblay/CP Photo Archive; Page 151: Ryan Remiorz/CP Photo Archive; Page 153: Nora Rock. Page 155, Clockwise: Thierry Orban/Corbis/Magma, Catherine Karnow/Corbis/Magma, Joe Marquette/Corbis/Magma, Thomas Kienz/CP Photo Archive; Page 156: Esclarecimiento © 1998 Daniel Hernandez-Salazar, from his series Eros & Thanatos, http://www.geocities.com/daaniieel/; Page 157: Thomas Kienzle/CP Photo Archive; Page 159: Paul Henry/CP Photo Archive; Page 161: Tom Hanson/CP Photo Archive; Page 162: Bettmann/Corbis/Magma; Page 164: Antoine Gyori/Corbis Sygma/Magma; Page 166: Thierry Orban/Corbis Sygma/Magma; Page 169: Misha Japaridze/CP Photo Archive; Page 173: IISH Stefan R. Landsberger Collection, http://www.iisg.nl/~landsberger; Page 177: Lefteris Pitarakis/CP Photo Archive; Page 179: Andy Eames/CP Photo Archive; Page 181: Horatio Villalobos/Corbis/Magma; Page 184: Tom Wagner/SABA/Corbis/Magma; Page 187: Mike Hutchings/CP Photo Archive; Page 189: Jaime Puebla/CP Photo Archive; Page 190: CP Photo Archive; Page 194: Ian Wallace, Vancouver Art Gallery, VAG 99.15.9; Page 196: Jacques Boissinot/CP Photo Archive; Page 198: Jonathan Hayward/CP Photo Archive; Page 199: National Archives of Canada, C-024725; Page 200: Tom Hanson/CP Photo Archive; Page 201: Joe Marquette/Corbis/Magma; Page 202: Sr. Airman Rodney Kerns/Corbis/Magma; Page 203: Eva-Lotta Jansson/Corbis/Magma; Page 204: Howard Davies/Corbis/Magma; Page 206: Bass Museum of Art/Corbis/Magma; Page 207: Jonathan Hayward/CP Photo Archive; Page 209: Bettmann/Corbis/Magma; Page 211: Wally McNamee/Corbis/Magma; Page 121: Vincent Yu/CP Photo Archive; Page 215: Bettmann/Corbis/Magma; Page 216: Bettmann/Corbis/Magma; Page 224: Reprinted by permission of Theo Moudakis; Page 229: National Gallery of Canada, 18624; Page 231: Albert Olive/EPA/Landov; Page 232: Catherine Karnow/Corbis/Magma; Page 233: Mike Aporius/CP Photo Archive; Page 235: Bettmann/Corbis/Magma; Page 236: Mark Lennihan/CP Photo Archive; Page 239: Brian A. Vikander/Corbis/Magma; Page 241: Terry McEvoy/CP Photo Archive; Page 243: Bettmann/Corbis/Magma; Page 245: CP Photo Archive; Page 246: Bettmann/Corbis/Magma; Page 247: Mike McKee/Eye Ubiquitous/

Text